Marketing Management: Strategies and Cases

M. Wayne DeLozier and Arch Woodside

University of South Carolina

Charles E. Merrill Publishing Company
A Bell & Howell Company
Columbus   Toronto   London   Sydney

Published by
Charles E. Merrill Publishing Company
A Bell and Howell Company
Columbus, Ohio 43216

This book was set in Harry family, Optima, and Times Roman.
The production editor was Rosemary Barnett.
The cover was prepared by Larry Hamill.

Library of Congress Catalog Card Number: **77-85593**
International Standard Book Number: **0-675-08417-2**

Printed in the United States of America

1 2 3 4 5 6 7 8 9 10/ 85 84 83 82 81 80 79 78

To our children who also bear the burden of our work

Jil and Mitchell (MWD)
Chris and Judy (AGW)

PREFACE

Marketing Management: Strategies and Cases is the product of the contributions of many outstanding marketing scholars. All cases are based upon the contributors' research and consulting experiences with a variety of businesses and organizations. Thus, students are exposed to authentic and realistic marketing problems and situations. Although some cases are disguised, all are based on actual situations. Some noteworthy features are:

1. Ten strategy chapters, each of which introduces the student to marketing strategies and concepts useful in analyzing that sections' cases.

2. Variety in case length and complexity to allow instructors to tailor their courses to the level and needs of their students.

3. A discussion of the case method of learning and how students should analyze and present a marketing case.

4. A list and description of major sources of marketing information at the end of relevant chapters.

5. Cases which describe contemporary and nontraditional marketing problems and applications.

Although the cases focus on particular marketing areas such as product, pricing, and advertising, students should understand that marketing decisions regarding one marketing mix variable cannot be made in isolation, rather they must be made in light of the organization's total marketing program, goals, and environment. Therefore, a case which focuses directly on a channel issue will, in all likelihood, require students to consider market segments, pricing, product characteristics, promotion decisions, and other marketing-related topics.

This book is designed to be self-contained. However, some instructors might wish to use either a supplementary book of readings, another text, or outside assignments. *Marketing Management: Strategies and Cases* can be used in both undergraduate "capstone" marketing courses and in MBA courses in marketing management.

The authors/editors are indebted to the many outstanding marketing scholars who contributed their time, energy, and expertise in developing cases for this book. Thanks go to editors, Bill Lochner and Rosemary Barnett, at Charles E. Merrill Publishing Company for their patience and hard work in making this book a reality. Special appreciation is given to James F. Kane, dean, College of Business Administration, University of South Carolina, for providing support and encouragement, and the working environment that made this endeavor possible.

Columbia, South Carolina   M. Wayne DeLozier
January 1978   Arch G. Woodside

CONTENTS

Chapter 6

Advertising Strategies   419

Chapter 7

Strategies in Sales Management and Buyer-Seller Interactions   499

Chapter 8

International Marketing Strategies   581

Chapter 1

The Marketing Process

Marketing involves a series of exchanges between two or more parties. Such exchanges include physical objects, information, opinions, and activities. Marketing exchanges are often viewed as limited to utilitarian exchanges: an interaction between two or more parties whereby goods are given in return for money or other goods, the motivation behind the actions lying in the anticipated use or tangible characteristics commonly associated with the objects in the exchange.[1] However, marketing exchanges are often symbolic. *Symbolic* exchanges are the mutual transfer of psychological, social, or other intangible entities between two or more parties.[2] They are likely to involve both utilitarian and symbolic interactions. The study of one type of exchange separate from the other provides a limited and possibly invalid interpretation of the reasons for the exchanges. Selling and buying a hot dog at a baseball game, a Thanksgiving turkey, a new car, a disc refiner in a paper mill, and computer software equipment involve a number of utilitarian and symbolic exchanges.

Four conditions are required for exchanges to occur:

1. Interaction of two or more persons.

2. Each person's possession of something of value to the other.

3. Each person's ability to communicate and deliver.

4. Each person's freedom to accept or reject the offer.[3]

Whether an exchange takes place depends upon the persons agreeing to terms

---

[1] Richard P. Bagozzi, "Marketing as Exchange," *Journal of Marketing,* **39** (October 1975), pp. 32–39. Published by the American Marketing Association.

[2] *Ibid*

[3] Adapted from Philip Kotler, *Marketing Management: Analysis, Planning, and Control,* Third Edition, (Prentice-Hall: Englewood Cliffs, N.J., 1976), p. 6.

beneficial (or at least not harmful) to all persons in the exchange. Thus, exchanges create value and satisfy needs between two or more parties.

Marketing as exchange is a broader view of marketing compared with the more limited definition popular in the 1960s and early 1970s. The most well-known limited definition of marketing is "the performance of business activities that direct the flow of goods and services from producer to consumer user." [4] This definition has been criticized for several reasons: (1) the definition implies that marketing begins only after goods have been produced, (2) it limits marketing only to business activities, and (3) it describes only one direction (from producers to consumers or users).

The concept of marketing has broadened since the late 1960s and early 1970s to include utilitarian and symbolic exchanges in business and nonbusiness settings. Since then, marketing has been applied explicitly to enhance exchanges related to hospitals, churches, zoos, and civic and government organizations, for example, the United States Army. Also, a buyer's perspective rather than (or in addition to) a seller's perspective has been advocated for marketing. Specifically:

> Buyers benefit from consumer studies which lead to greater customer satisfaction and marketing efficiency. However, marketing scholars rarely study how buyers can personally improve their effectiveness vis-à-vis sellers. In the last few years, consumers' welfare has reentered marketing discussions through the growing interest in consumerism. The consumer viewpoint still forms a relatively small part of most marketing teaching and research. Little consideration is given in the literature to the question of how buyers can perform better in the marketplace.[5]

Thus, there are substantial changes in philosophies related to marketing. Most business and nonbusiness organizations can be placed primarily in one of three locations on a continuum of marketing philosophies. The continuum is shown in Figure C—1–1.

Marketing Philosophies

The Product Concept

Many managers and top executives focus their organizations efforts on either the product or service which they offer to customers. The managers stress the physical features and the quality of the product. The sales department and salespersons are likely to report to the production manager in this situation. The credit manager, product research director, and service manager are managed separately. No person below the chief executive office (CEO) has responsibility for all contacts made with customers of the organization under the product concept.

The late Robert J. Keith, CEO of the Pillsbury Company, describes his firm as production oriented from its start in 1869 until into the 1930s:

---

[4] Committee on Definitions, *Marketing Definitions: A Glossary of Marketing Terms* (Chicago: American Marketing Association, 1960), p. 15.

[5] Philip Kotler and Sidney J. Levy, "Buying is Marketing Too!" *Journal of Marketing,* **37** (January 1973), pp. 54–59. Published by the American Marketing Association.

Figure   C—1–1
A Continuum of Marketing Philosophies

	Product Concept	Marketing Concept	Societal Marketing Concept
Focus:	Products sold	Customer needs	Customer needs and long-run customer interests
Organization:	Sales Department and Advertising Department	Integrated Marketing	Customer Department
Goal:	Maximize profits through sales volume	Maximize profits through customer satisfaction	Satisfactory profits and long-run customer welfare

Our company philosophy in this era might have been stated this way: "We are professional flour millers. Blessed with a supply of the finest North American wheat, plenty of water power, and excellent milling machinery, we produce flour of the highest quality. Our basic function is to mill high quality flour, and of course (and almost incidentally) we must hire salesmen to sell it, just as we hire accountants to keep our books."[6]

Executives operating under the product concept have been accused of marketing *myopia,* or tunnel vision. "The railroads did not stop growing because the need for passenger and freight transportation declined. They grew. The railroads are in trouble today not because the need was filled by others (cars, trucks, airplanes, even telephones), but because it was *not* filled by the railroads themselves. They let others take customers away from them because they assumed themselves to be in the railroad business rather than in the transportation business. The reason they defined their industry wrong was because they were railroad-oriented instead of transportation-oriented; they were product-oriented instead of customer-oriented."[7] In banking, if a marketing department exists, the department is likely to be assigned as a staff function and is not assigned responsibility for actions related to direct contacts with customers. A bank can easily spend $100,000 or $10,000,000 in advertising, but it is unlikely to spend any money studying the effectiveness of its advertising. The vice-president of marketing reports to another vice-president in most banks.[8] In general, banks are product oriented with executives who usually "pay lip service" to the marketing concept.

---

[6] Robert J. Keith, "The Marketing Revolution," *Journal of Marketing,* **24** (January 1960), pp. 35–38. Published by the American Marketing Association.

[7] Theodore Levitt, "Marketing Myopia," *Harvard Business Review,* **38** (July-August, 1960), pp. 45–56. Copyright © 1960 by the President and Fellows of Harvard College; all rights reserved.

[8] S. Douglas White and Arch G. Woodside, "Marketing Philosophies in Banking," *Journal of Banking Research,* 1973.

The Marketing Concept

The marketing concept was introduced in a few firms in the 1950s to correct for the marketing myopia of the product concept. The need to change the organization to increase marketing efficiency to match product efficiency was recognized. In 1962 General Electric Company's annual report heralded this new marketing philosophy:

> The marketing concept introduces the marketing man at the beginning rather than at the end of the production cycle and integrates marketing into each phase of the business. Thus, marketing, through its studies and research, will establish for the engineer, the design and manufacturing man, what the customer wants in a given product, what price he is willing to pay, and where and when it will be wanted. Marketing will have authority in product planning, production scheduling, and inventory control, as well as in sales distributions and servicing the product.[9]

The *marketing concept* can be defined as the philosophy of focusing all the activities of the organization on satisfying *customer needs* through the use of *integrated marketing* to achieve maximum profits through customer satisfaction. The adoption of the marketing concept usually involves the adoption of a new structure for operating the organization. An example of this structural change is shown in Figure C—1–2.

Notice in Figure C—1–2 that all activities in the firm related to direct contacts with customers become the responsibility of a line office (marketing management) after the adoption of the marketing concept. Before the marketing concept was introduced, research and development was a part of engineering and product planning in production. Research and product planning become part of marketing service management after the introduction of the marketing concept.

Conflicts still occur between departments after the adoption of the marketing concept. However, the conflicts are more likely to concern how best to serve the customer profitably rather than how to divide responsibility and authority for action along departmental lines.

F. J. Borch reports what happened in the vacuum cleaner division a few years (by 1957) after the introduction of the marketing concept at General Electric. In 1951, General Electric's vacuum cleaner division was "practically unrecognized in the industry, with only a minor percent share of the market. We had no unique product identification to form the basis of our advertising and selling appeals. In fact, we had no national advertising." The vacuum cleaners were priced high relative to other appliances throughout the industry. Distribution was inadequate, with only 30 percent of vacuum cleaners being sold through retailers and the rest door-to-door. A large number of models was offered by each manufacturer.[10]

After the introduction of the marketing concept, the following actions and results occurred in the vacuum cleaner division:

> Through product improvements and the decision to concentrate on a single model, rather than the 15 we were previously offering, our prices were lowered.

---

[9] *1952 Annual Report* (New York: General Electric Company, 1952), p. 21.

[10] F. J. Borch, "The Marketing Philosophy as a Way of Business Life," address to the American Management Association, February 4, 1957.

Figure   C—1–2
One Company's Organization Chart Before and
After Acceptance of the Marketing Concept

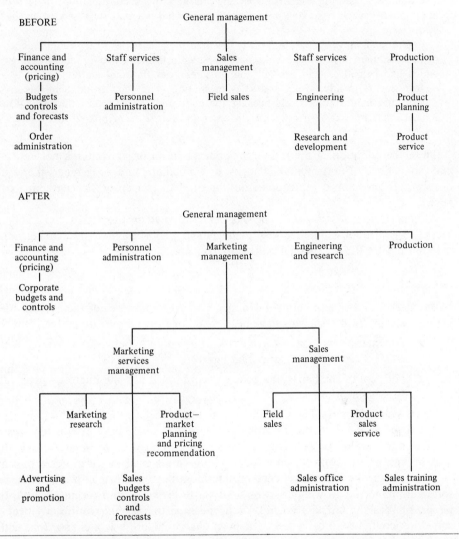

Source: Eugene B. Mapel, "What Is the 'Marketing Concept'?" Barrington Associates, New York; reprinted from *Sales Management*, July 5, 1957.

Surveys have shown that even today most housewives do not yet realize that they can buy a good vacuum for under $100. Consequently, we feel that we made a contribution to the consumer in widely advertising our best selling model last year at $49.95.

Cleaners are now available in practically every retail outlet normally handling home appliances, and product repair service is improved.

Cleaners are now better-designed, performing household tasks more efficiently under the concept of cleaning the entire home rather than merely the rug.

The isolation and assigning of the product planning and market research responsibilities has built leadership in the market, the subsequent decisions are being made on the basis of a sound analysis of what we *knew* was needed by the customer.

Engineering and production quickly oriented their activities to the requirements of the customer, with some revolutionary results in terms of new product offerings which had helped expand not only our business, but the total market.

Investments in advertising and sales promotion (and they are high in this industry) are made more wisely because the copy and scripts reflect the real sales appeals that market research and customer awareness have proved to be effective.[11]

Thus, the adoption of the marketing concept in an organization is not "all talk and no action." Fundamental changes in immediate and long-range plans are necessary to move an organization from the product concept to the marketing concept.

Although the marketing concept was being adopted in the 1950s and 1960s in several organizations, another new management philosophy was also being advocated in the 1970s, the societal marketing concept.

Societal Marketing Concept

Is the marketing concept enough? No, according to advocates of the societal marketing concept. Two criticisms have been made of the marketing concept:

1. The marketing concept overlooks the conflict between individual want satisfaction and long-run public interest.

2. The goal of the marketing concept represents only one interest—profits for the organization.

Consumer satisfaction may conflict with long-run citizen satisfaction. For example, as consumers, we don't particularly care if our cars have exhaust devices or whether our gasoline is lead-free. As citizens, we don't want to breathe in air that makes living in Los Angeles equivalent to smoking a pack of cigarettes a day. As consumers, we like the convenience of aluminum beer cans. As citizens, we search for solutions to the growing crisis of solid waste disposal. In a recent election, the people of Washington state voted on a proposition that would require any beer or soft drink container to carry a $.05 deposit charge. "Here was a chance for people to choose between their convenience as a consumer and their concern for the environment as a citizen. Results: consumers, 52 percent; citizens, 48 percent. This example of people groping for a solution to the dilemma is typical of the ambivalence we face as we work toward a compromise; a similar dilemma confronts marketing strategists." [12]

Adoption of a *stakeholder* rather than a *stockholder* view of the organization has

---

[11] *Ibid.*

[12] Peter D. Bennett and Harold H. Kassarjian, *Consumer Behavior* (Englewood Cliffs, New Jersey: Prentice-Hall, 1972), p. 3.

been advocated to solve abuses created by the organization's profit goal. The stockholder view is that the sole purpose of the organization is to provide profits for its owners—the stockholders. The stakeholder view is that all parties who have "a stake" in the organization's decisions should be represented and have a voice in those decisions; such parties would include representatives from customers, employees, and the community. Also, the stakeholder view is that the multiple goals of all parties should be considered in decision making, and profit maximization for the organization will likely unfairly hurt the goals of the other parties concerned with the organization's decisions.

Thus, a societal marketing concept has been developed.

> The societal marketing concept is a management orientation aimed at generating customer satisfaction and long-run consumer and public welfare as the key to satisfying organizational goals and responsibilities.[13]

The need to measure the costs and profits to *all parties affected by the organization's decisions* has been suggested as part of the societal marketing concept. This measurement process is the definition of *social accounting*. An example of social accounting has been provided by Armstrong for a drug product, Panalba.[14]

Panalba was marketed in the United States by Upjohn Corporation until banned by the Food and Drug Administration in 1972. Panalba was one of the most profitable products in Upjohn's product line. However, the product had serious shortcomings: death was a possible side effect from taking the drug and competitors offered substitute drugs at least as effective as Panalba.

The profits and costs to different parties from continuing to market Panalba or discarding the product are shown in Table C—1–1. The calculations are based on

Table   C—1–1
Costs of Alternative Decisions
on Panalba to Different Stakeholders

	Estimated Losses (in millions $)			1 + 2 + 3
	1 Stockholders	2 Customers	3 Employees	Total Losses
A "Recall immediately"	20.0	0.0	2.0	22.0
B "Stop production"	13.0	13.6	1.8	28.4
C "Stop promotion"	12.0	16.8	1.2	30.0
D "Continue until banned"	11.0	19.6	1.0	31.6
E "Take action to prevent ban"	4.0	33.8	0.2	38.0

Source: J. Scott Armstrong, "Social Irresponsibility in Business," *Journal of Business Research,* **5** (September 1977).

[13] Philip Kotler, *Marketing Management: Analysis, Planning, and Controls, op. cit.,* p. 18.
[14] J. Scott Armstrong, "Social Irresponsibility in Business," *Journal of Business Research,* **5** (September 1977).

the assumption that each consumer's death costs $1 million to consumers. The social accounting suggests that the best decision would be to abandon the product after considering the costs and profits of all major parties.

Few firms should be expected to adopt the societal marketing concept unilaterally. Industry wide adoption may be required because of the likely competitive disadvantage of not acting in a socially responsible manner compared to actions of other firms. Thus, federal regulations were required to introduce automobile emission standards and to reduce the size of automobiles to increase miles per gallon; federal laws and regulations will likely be set to reduce the amount of sugar in presweetened cereals and the availability of handguns in the United States.

Introduction to the Marketing Decision Process

Even though organizations may adopt different marketing philosophies, all organizations have the same types of marketing decisions to make. Marketing decisions can be classified as having two major elements:

1. Market segmentation decisions
2. Marketing mix decisions
   - product decisions
   - channel and distribution decisions
   - promotion decisions
   - pricing decisions

A marketing decision process should begin with the selection of customer segments to develop a marketing mix. A *marketing mix* is a blend of decisions to provide a marketing offer to the selected market segment. The concept of the marketing mix includes recognition that certain blends of product and service attributes, product prices, channels of distribution, and advertising and personal selling choices will produce greater customer satisfaction than other blends. For example, a high-priced vacuum cleaner made available via door-to-door salepersons with limited advertising support may produce less satisfaction for full-time homemakers living in the suburbs compared with a different marketing mix.

The first question of marketing management is: Who are our organization's present and potential customers? Defining the organization's customers usually leads to rejecting several tentative marketing mixes and suggesting the comparison and possible use of a few candidate mixes.

How large is the organization's share of the market? How many potential customers are part of the organization's market segment? Are there other market segments that would be more profitable for the organization to satisfy with marketing mixes different from the mix presently used? These are marketing segmentation questions.

What are the demographic characteristics of our customers? Where and how do they purchase our products? Who and what influence their purchase decisions? These also are market segmentation questions.

Market segmentation decisions lead to marketing mix decisions. For example, the selection of the market target of low income families, with two or more children, who buy automobiles every three to five years would likely lead to the development of a marketing mix represented by the Volkswagen Rabbit while a different market segment is intended to buy the Mercedes Benz 300D.

Compare the marketing mix strategies for the Volkswagen Rabbit and a Mercedes Benz. The product, price, channel, and promotional strategies are different for each automobile. This reflects the manufacturers' selection of different market segments to satisfy their market offerings.

The reasons for segmenting markets and how to segment effectively are reviewed in Chapter 2 with examples presented for consumer and industrial organizations. Most of the other chapters in this book concern the elements of the marketing mix, a list of which is presented in Table C—1–2. Other lists could have been used to describe the marketing mix. Table C—1–2 is not intended to be a standard for comparison but to indicate the breadth of marketing management.

The *product mix* includes product planning, branding, packaging, and servicing decisions. These decisions are also listed in Table C—1–2.

The *channel mix* includes channels of distribution and physical handling decisions. Personal selling, advertising, promotions, and display decisions are part of the *promotion mix*. Pricing decisions usually are considered as one of the marketing mixes.

Assume that an organization is attempting to evaluate the payoffs for planning and implementing a marketing mix for one of two market segments. Assume two levels or choices exist for each of the four major marketing mixes. For example:

> Price: low versus high
> Product: low quality versus high quality
> Promotion: personal selling mainly versus advertising mainly
> Channel: direct versus distributors

Many different payoff evaluations must be made for this simple situation. A total of 16 payoff evaluations would be necessary for each market segment for a total of 32 evaluations. The 16 payoff evaluation cells for one market segment are shown in Figure C—1–3. Cell 1 in the figure represents the following marketing mix:

> Channel: direct
> Promotion: personal selling mainly
> Price: low
> Product quality: low

Several payoffs could be listed in each cell such as Figure C—1–3. Payoffs could include (1) sales volume, (2) profits, (3) market share, and (4) consumer welfare (e.g., percent of deaths not associated with the product's use).

Marketing management would likely dismiss several alternative marketing mixes with limited evaluations. For example, cells 1, 7, 13, 15, and 16 in Figure C—1–3 might be described as unrealistic for market segment 1 and different cells might be discarded for market segment 2. Payoffs of the marketing mixes in the remaining cells might be established using marketing research; for example, each marketing mix might be field tested using three cities (test markets) for each mix. Comparisons of the payoffs for each marketing mix could then be examined.

Table   C—1–2
Elements of the Marketing Mix of Manufacturers

Product planning. Policies and procedures relating to:
        Product lines to be offered—qualities, design, etc.
        The markets to sell—whom, where, when, and in what quantity.
        New Product policy—research and development program.
Pricing. Policies and procedures relating to:
        The level of prices to adopt.
        The specific prices to adopt (odd-even, etc.).
        Price policy—one price or varying price, price maintenance, use of list prices, etc.
        The margins to adopt—for company; for the trade.
Branding. Policies and procedures relating to:
        Selection of trade marks.
        Brand policy—individualized or family brand.
        Sales under private brand or unbranded.
Channels of Distribution. Policies and procedures relating to:
        The channels to use between plant and consumer.
        The degree of selectivity among wholesalers and retailers.
        Efforts to gain cooperation of the trade.
Personal Selling. Policies and procedures relating to:
        The burden to be placed on personal selling and the methods to be employed in
            (1) the manufacturer's organization, (2) the wholesale segment of the trade, and (3) the retail segment of the trade.
Advertising. Policies and procedures relating to:
        The amount to spend—i.e., the burden to be placed on advertising.
        The copy platform to adopt (1) product image desired, (2) corporate image desired.
        Advertising mix—to the trade; through the trade—to consumers.
Promotions. Policies and procedures relating to:
        The burden to place on special selling plans or devices directed at or through the trade.
        The form of these devices for consumer promotions, for trade promotions.
Packaging. Policies and procedures relating to:
        Formulation of package and label.
Display. Policies and procedures relating to:
        The burden to be put on display to help effect sales.
        The methods to adopt to secure display.
Servicing. Policies and procedures relating to:
        Providing service needed.
Physical Handling. Policies and procedures relating to:
        Warehousing
        Transportation
        Inventories
Fact Finding and Analysis. Policies and procedures relating to:
        The securing, analysis, and use of facts in marketing operations.

Source: Neil H. Borden, "The Concept of the Marketing Mix," in George Schwarts, ed., *Science in Marketing* (New York: John Wiley & Sons, Inc., 1965), pp. 389–390.

Figure   C—1–3
Evaluating Alternative Marketing Mixes

Product Quality	Promotion	Channel Mix			
		Direct		Distributors	
		Price		Price	
		Low	High	Low	High
Low	Personal Selling	1	2	3	4
	Advertising	5	6	7	8
High	Personal Selling	9	10	11	12
	Advertising	13	14	15	16

Thus, the number of marketing mixes to be evaluated is determined by multiplying the number of promotion, price, product, and channel levels being considered. Multiple payoffs may be used to evaluate each marketing mix. Payoffs are likely to change depending upon the market segments selected.

The Marketing Environment

Several environmental forces affect an organization's choice of markets and marketing mixes. Four such forces include (1) customers' buying behavior, (2) the trade's behavior, (3) competitors' positions and behaviors, and (4) governmental behavior. Several of these forces are listed in Table C—1–3. Such forces can affect marketing strategies and payoffs quickly and substantially.

Several questions and answers should provide some indications of the importance of environmental forces in managing the marketing process.

- Will consumers be willing to purchase stockings in supermarkets? Yes, based on the success of L'eggs hosiery displays.
- Will retailers attempt to buy direct from manufacturers (a trade behavior questions)? Yes, in the United States, but no in Japan.
- Do competitors attempt to market chickens by brand name? Yes, but not until Frank Perdue started his campaign, "It takes a tough man to make a tender chicken," with fresh, high-priced chickens and selective distribution.[15]
- Will governments ban cigarette advertising? Yes in Canada, and partially in the United States.

Several relationships among environmental forces, marketing mixes, and payoffs are shown in Figure C—1–4.

The marketing system shown in Figure C—1–4 was developed for the candy bar

---

[15] Bill Paul, "It Isn't Chicken Feed to Put Your Brand on 78 Million Birds," *The Wall Street Journal* (May 13, 1974).

Table   C—1–3
Market Forces Bearing on the Marketing Mix

1. *Consumers' Buying Behavior,* as determined by their:

    a. Their motivations.
    b. Buying habits.
    c. Living habits.
    d. Environment (present and future, as revealed by trends, for environment influences consumers' attitudes toward products and their use of them).
    e. Buying power.
    f. Number (i.e., how many).

2. *The Trade's Behavior*—wholesalers' and retailers' behavior, as influenced by:

    a. Their motivations.
    b. Their structure, practices, and attitudes.
    c. Trends in structure and procedures that portend change.

3. *Competitors' Position and Behavior,* as influenced by:

    a. Industry structure and the firm's relation thereto.
        (1) Size and strength of competitors.
        (2) Number of competitors and degree of industry concentration.
        (3) Indirect competition—i.e., from other products.
    b. Relation of supply to demand—oversupply or undersupply.
    c. Product choices offered consumers by the industry—i.e., quality, price, service.
    d. Degree to which competitors compete on price vs. nonprice bases.
    e. Competitors' motivations and attitudes—their likely response to the actions of other firms.
    f. Trends technological and social, portending change in supply and demand.

4. *Governmental Behavior—Controls over Marketing:*

    a. Regulations over products.
    b. Regulations over pricing.
    c. Regulations over competitive practices.
    d. Regulations over advertising and promotion.

Source: Neil H. Borden, "The Concept of the Marketing Mix," *Journal of Advertising Research,* **4,** June 1964, pp. 2–7.

market but the figure may be modified for all industries. The lines and arrows indicate the need for comparison or evaluation between elements in the system. Such basic diagrams of relationships are often used as a basis for developing marketing information systems (MIS). Each of the parts and the relationships shown in Figure C—1–4 should be reviewed when evaluating the marketing problems of a specific organization.

The Marketing Information System

An MIS is a formal method of gathering, processing, and reporting marketing information to increase the payoffs from marketing decisions. Internal accounting

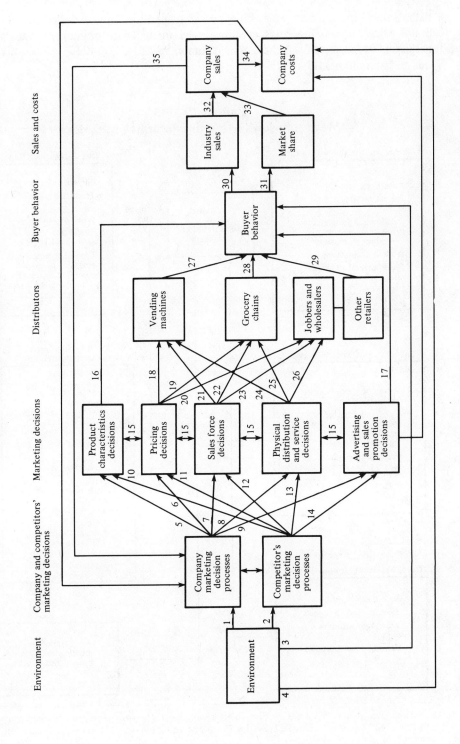

Figure C—1—4
Comprehensive Marketing System

13

data, sales reports, and marketing research findings are included in an MIS. Standardized processing rules are developed in an MIS to interpret information gathered. Reports are usually issued daily, weekly, monthly, bimonthly, and quarterly from an MIS.

Figure   C—1–5
Mead Johnson's Marketing Information System

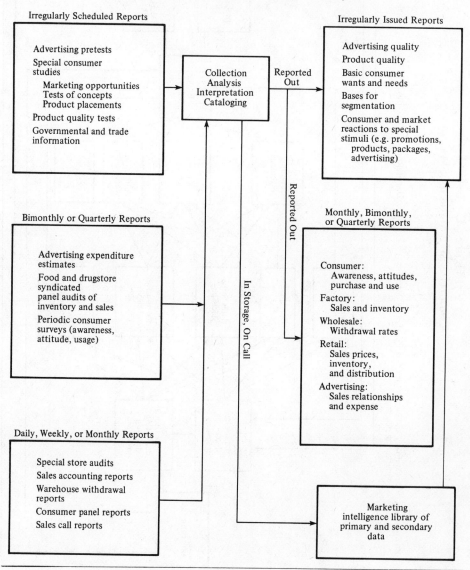

MISs were first developed by a number of large manufacturers of packaged goods during the 1960s. The information collected and processed and reports issued for Mead Johnson's MIS is shown in Figure C—1–5. The reports issued from the MIS provide management with information to examine many of the relationships shown in Figure C—1–4.

Before the late 1960s, few organizations had MISs to help them learn the causes of changes in market share, industry sales, or company costs. Today, MISs are being developed for several nonprofit organizations, such as hospitals and health organizations.

Summary

Marketing is a series of exchanges between two or more parties. Both buying and selling are part of marketing and viewpoints of both parties should be considered for a broad focus on marketing decisions.

Organizations can be identified usually as having one of three marketing philosophies: production orientation, market concept orientation, or societal marketing orientation. Marketing myopia is a symptom of the production-oriented firm. Reorganization of the firm is likely to occur with a change to a marketing concept orientation. Consumer goals as well as profit and sales goals are recognized as legitimate concerns among firms with a societal marketing orientation.

The two major marketing decisions include (1) market segmentation decisions and (2) marketing mix decisions. Environmental forces affect both marketing decisions. Marketing information systems were first developed in the 1960s to learn about the relationships of environmental forces, marketing decisions, and marketing payoffs.

Discussion Questions

1. List the four conditions required for marketing exchanges to occur.

2. Complete the following diagram and explain each concept:

```
●————————————————●————————————————●
   product
   concept
```

3. What are the two major decision elements in marketing?

4. Given 3 levels of product quality, 2 marketing channel alternatives, 4 types of sales forces, and 3 price levels, how many alternative marketing mixes could be evaluated?

5. Label all boxes in Figure C—1–4 as environmental force, marketing mix element, or output of the marketing system. Explain the reason for your choice of labels.

The Case Method

The *case method* is a learning approach in which the student studies a description of facts, problems, and opinions of a specific organization such as a business firm. A *case* is the term used for such description.

Usually, students are requested to read a case, to prepare either an oral or written analysis of the problems and key facts, and to recommend solutions. *Key facts* are the pieces of information in the case which you, the student, select to support your recommendations. You should identify and describe several key facts in support of each *major* recommendation you offer.

Each case is different. The problems you identify in one case are unlikely to be found in another. Rarely should the same recommendations be used for two different cases. This may seem obvious, but it is not; many students follow a pattern of identifying the *same* problems in a number of cases. For example, the need for a different advertising program often appears as the first recommendation in written analyses prepared by students, even when the major problem concerns the selection of market segments and marketing channels.

The case approach to learning helps you improve your skills in oral and written communications, and this experience provides you the practice needed to increase your ability to write effective reports.

Because many cases are developed from actual organizational settings, you are likely to recognize several of the business firms described in the cases in this book. The cases describe current marketing management practices in these organizations; thus, you can learn when studying a case how firms apply concepts and marketing methods.

Final decisions chosen by the organization to solve the problems usually are omitted. You should recommend decisions and support these recommendations with key facts you have found in the case. Following class discussion of the pros and cons of different decision choices, the instructor might inform the class of the decisions and actions actually taken by the organization. (This is not intended to mean that the actual actions taken were correct; sometimes decisions recommended by students may be better solutions.)

The case method departs from on-the-job learning in that written descriptions of facts, opinions, and problems usually are unavailable in organizations. Written communications relevant to several problems usually are scattered in different parts of the organization, and opinions and problems rarely occur in written form. Here, however, problem solving essentially is completed in the cases in this book. You may use outside materials from libraries, company records, and personal interviews to augment the case materials. Reference sources and brief descriptions of each can be found at the end of several of the chapters. You should become familiar with these important sources of information.

Do's and Don'ts for Case Analysis

A list of suggestions might be helpful at the start of case analysis. The following list, however, is neither intended to be complete nor absolute but it might serve as a useful guide to better communications and problem solving. Read over the list of suggestions after reading each case to be discussed in class or before writing a case report.

1. *You find the problem.* You are being asked to look into a situation in order to come up with solutions to particular problems. Some of the time someone in the company tells the reader what the problem is. This person usually is wrong. If you hear from the production manager, "We need more sales," this may mean "We need a better product, oriented to customer needs."

Finding the problem is the most difficult job in report writing. A company faces many difficulties, but there usually are one or two causing nearly all the headaches. Solve these and the rest fade away.

Solving the problem is less than half as difficult as finding it. Finding it requires a background in marketing, production, finance, and management along with the creative ability of Sherlock Holmes. However, detailed knowledge in these fields is not needed and the ability improves with practice.

If the situation is involved, that is, problems are present in all fields, and you don't know where to begin, start your analysis with the company's customers and their needs. Is the company meeting the needs of its customers at a profit? More basic: Who are the firm's customers? Is the firm maximizing opportunities of its market? This is the proper starting place for most reports.

2. *Write to a specific person or group.* Think of yourself as a business consultant hired at $1,000 per week by your particular firm to solve its problems. What you write is worth something. Address your case analysis to the person requesting the report: "To: Mr. Smith; Subject: Solutions to the Smith Corporation's Problems."

3. *Do give and emphasize recommendations.* Your written analysis should begin with your recommendations to future company action *such as,* the new product now under consideration should be nationally distributed.

There is always fear in making recommendations (decisions). Try to control this fear by doing a thorough analysis and by backing up your decision with supporting facts. Remember, you are going to have to stick your neck out somewhere.

In making your recommendations, list and number them according to their importance. Discuss each in turn on the following pages of your report.

Everyone likes to call for more information before recommending that any action be taken. Sometimes this is the right solution, but usually it is the easy way out. Problems usually need to be solved yesterday. You call for more information and more research, then recommend courses of action based on the possible outcomes of this new information. Also assume that this information you requested will not be obtained—there is no time—and make recommendations accordingly.

Emphasize your recommendations by presenting them twice: at the beginning and the end of your analysis. After giving facts supporting your recommendations, make a statement such as: "Therefore, the South Corporation should . . ." This looks impressive, as if nothing but your recommendation could possibly be considered.

4. *Do give detailed recommendations.* If you call for national distribution of a new product, tell how it should be distributed. What channels should be used? What price should the company set? Who is responsible for the product's success?

5. *Be positive.* Don't mention company or people's faults unless they are needed to support your recommendations. Tell where the company is going wrong and why but don't run it into the ground. It's always easy to criticize. Stick to what you think needs to be done.

6. *Support your recommendations.* Why should your recommendations be adopted? Are there better ones? List at least one alternative for each recommendation you make and explain why your recommendations should be adopted.

Support your recommendations in detail. You have to convince your reader that your approach will solve the organization's problems. This is a critical point in case analysis. Gather and present all the material you can in support of the recommendations.

7. *Summarize.* Don't state a fact just to state a fact. Tell the reader what it means when you say return on investment will be 15 percent. Is this adequate, substantial? Summarize through the analysis. Don't assume the reader will see the way back to your recommendations based on the facts you discuss.

8. *Think of your reader.* Assume the reader to be intelligent. Even though he's your boss, assume that he's knowledgeable but inexperienced. This does not mean writing down to him, but it does mean he may not be familiar with the latest operations research technique. If you use such a technique, present your methodology in a technical appendix. Even if you give only a financial ratio, show what the ratio consists of and tell what its outcome means.

9. *Use outside material.* Gather more facts from published sources or your own research. Don't feel limited to the information given by one or two people in the case. Go to other sources and study related material. Ask experts for their opinions.

Don't forget to quote and footnote any additional information or ideas you find. This gives authority to your recommendations; experts seem to concur with your opinions.

10. *Don't present a history of the organization.* Many business writers feel a need to begin at the beginning; "The company was founded in 1892 by John A. Smith and makes widgets." Your boss either knows this or does not care. The

founding of the company and other descriptive material need not be discussed. Stick with the problem and its solution.

Be relevant. Don't ramble on the history or on minor problems. Your reader doesn't have much time. He is bored easily; and you may weaken the case for the recommendations.

11. *Use financial data.* If given figures, analyze them. They usually are very useful. If you don't use the figures provided, tell why they aren't relevant. Some people feel figures never lie. They lend support to your solutions. Know how to compute a few financial ratios such as guides to profitability, liquidity, and protective margins. Also, know what it means when one of these ratios is 10 percent instead of 5 percent. Such ratios are helpful in pointing the way toward finding the problems.

12. *Use subheadings* (such as this one). Subheadings are useful for telling what you plan to say, for emphasizing your ideas, and for easier reading.

13. *Use graphs and tables.* These are good summary tools. They also hold the reader's interest. Graphs are especially imposing (see figure 1). Besides using a graph or a table, explain what it means. For example, Figure 1 means that it may be hard to say anything worthwhile in less than five typed pages, but you have lost the reader's interest after 15 pages.

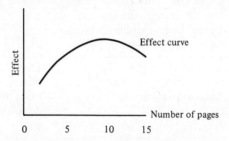

14. *Be brief.* Long reports have a way of never being read. Effective analyses usually are less than 15 pages long. (See Figure 1.) Effectiveness is having your recommendation adopted and/or receiving a promotion.

15. *Never use the word "I."* You are not the highlight or the star of your case analysis. There is no need to call attention to yourself. There is always a different word order you can use to get all expressions such as "I feel" or "I believe" out of your report.

Table 1 is a checklist of the ideas in good case analysis. Give these ideas some thought before you write your next case.

Summary

The previous discussion gives some "rules of thumb" for effective report analysis. Business writing is an art and like most arts requires practice. Exceptions can be found to any rule or suggestion. This list of do's and don'ts is intended as a guide, not a substitute to your own analysis of cases.

Table 1
Checklist of Do's and Don'ts in Case Analysis

Concept	Do	Don't
Finding the problems	Start with the firm's customers and their needs if you don't know where to begin.	Don't assume the problem is given. No problem is self-evident.
Problem reporting	List the two or three major problems in the company.	Don't mix minor and major problems together. Solving small problems usually is not enough.
Report direction	Provide direction to your written analysis. Address your report to a specific person or group.	Don't write without a particular person in mind. You have an audience to whom you are selling your ideas.
Report content	Cover the following areas: statement of the problem, proof you've found the problem. Recommendations. Prove your recommendations are worthwhile.	Don't cover the following areas: the firm's history or minor personality problems.
Financial data	Use the data given. Know how to compute basic financial ratios.	Don't skip over tables and charts. You should spend more time on these than you do with text space of similar size.
Recommendations	Make specific recommendations and prove why they should be adopted.	Don't be vague or call for a "reevaluation." You have to be meaningful when offering improvements.
Plans	Offer the steps (method) that should be used to carry out your recommendations.	Don't assume a good recommendation is enough. The method of implementing your recommendation should be given in detail.
Organization	Use a format that has subheadings to ensure good organization of thoughts and a reader.	Don't write without breaks between major sections in your paper.
Imagination	Use outside material. Experts on the subject can be interviewed. You could even do your own market survey.	Don't begin writing without gathering all relevant data.

Cycle Enterprises

Charles Comegys, Merrimack College

In mid-summer 1977, Jack Fenway, owner and manager of Cycle Enterprises, was faced with a large number of dirt-bikes in inventory. This situation was particularly distressing to Jack since the typical peak season for motorcycles and accessories runs through September. Also, because of recent environmentalists' pressures on off-street motorcyclists, sales have been much lower than usual with no apparent upturn in sight.

Company History

Fred Miller of Englewood, California was a sheetmetal worker by profession. In 1969, he purchased a small trail bike and began riding the off-street paths and fields in his leisure time. Under the strain of this rough terrain, Fred noticed that the front fork of his motorcycle was rather weak and would bend somewhat when exposed to certain stress conditions.

Because of Fred's knowledge and ability to work with metal material, this situation presented no real problem for him. He merely designed and made a simple but sturdy fork brace which he installed on his cycle in his home workshop. The fork brace solved the problem.

While cycling with friends, Fred was asked about the additional apparatus he had attached to his machine. His explanation created interest in the apparatus among his friends, and as a result, Fred began manufacturing the fork braces for his friends. Needless to say, friends have friends and the next thing Fred Miller knew his side-line business had grown significantly.

Operating out of a double-car garage located behind his home, Fred's business, now named Cycle Enterprises, continued to increase. Over the next few years, Fred added several additional items to his line and also took in a part-time associate to help him handle the increasing demand. As the trend persisted, Fred invested in

21

some metal presses, cutters, and other equipment which allowed his operation to run more efficiently by mass-producing certain items. The additional equipment also provided the opportunity to produce a wider variety of parts and accessories.

By 1975, the garage had been expanded to 1200 square feet, compared to the original 400 square feet. Several part-time employees, a manager and four welders, were also added to the payroll. Fred's policy was to hire only part-time workers who could legally be paid underscale hourly rates and thus keep overhead as low as possible.

All the items Cycle Enterprises manufactured were accessories for the dirt-bike (off-street) market segment. Distribution was mostly dealer-oriented with 75 percent dealers and 25 percent distributors. Fred felt that because his production facility capacity was limited, selling directly to motorcycle dealers and keeping overhead as low as possible was his most profitable method of operation. This strategy meant low volume, but a high margin on each unit sale, an advantage he would not have if he channeled mainly through distributors.

Fred Miller did not advertise. He contacted dealers himself and relied on the unique nature of his product line and word-of-mouth to sell it. Consequently, the Enterprises' geographic distribution was somewhat limited. Sales volume in 1976 was $100,000.

Reorganization of Cycle Enterprises

In early 1977, Jack Fenway purchased Cycle Enterprises from Fred Miller for $45,000. Jack immediately relocated the business in a facility 3 times the size of the old garage complex. The location of the new building was in the West Long Beach industrial area. Advantages to this move were that the new manufacturing plant had room to expand and that all the support industries (tool grinder, machine shop, steel supplier, carton supplier, and chrome plater) were located within a half mile. Also, this location was very close to the main freeway system, an advantage the old location did not possess.

Next, Jack Fenway shifted Cycle Enterprises from a part-time operation to a full-time one. Two full-time employees were hired in addition to the 6 part-time employees who all now had agreed to work 40 hours a week at the new location.

The product line also underwent changes. In 1976, Cycle Enterprises' product line was 100 percent dirt-bike accessories. In 1977, this proportion was altered to 85 percent dirt-bike and 15 percent street-bike accessories. Several dirt-bike items, such as the filter line, were slow movers and were gradually discontinued as their inventory became depleted. Some street-bike accessories were added, such as solo rests and back rests. See Exhibit 1–1.

Jack personally designed most of the product-line additions except for items such as the carburetor accessories manufactured elsewhere but sold by Cycle Enterprises to complete their accessory line.

An example of Fenway's designing ability is the solo rest. While cycling with his wife, she often complained that the standard "sissy bar" was uncomfortable. The sissy bar, which sells from $45 to $50, is attached to the rear of the bike and parallel to the front fork. Thus, the passenger is placed in a reclining position over the back

Exhibit 1-1

CYCLE ENTERPRISES
1977 *CATALOG*

manufacturers: motorcycle parts and accessories

SOLO RESTS

SOLO BACK REST. Tuck and roll black expanded naugahyde; bright chrome; large cushion area provides greater comfort and security; mounts directly on motorcycle; includes mounting instructions.

MAKE	MODEL	c.c.	MODEL YEAR	PART NO.	WEST RETAIL	EAST RETAIL
Honda	CB	750	1975-1978	CB-1000-1	19.95	20.95
	CL,CB	350,450	1974-1978	CB-1100-1	19.95	20.95
	CL,CB	175	1975-1978	CB-1200-1	19.95	20.95
Kawasaki	Mach 3	500	1975-1978	CB-2000-1	19.95	20.95
Yamaha	XS-1	650	1976-1978	CB-3000-1	19.95	20.95
	R-5	350	1976-1978	CB-3100-1	19.95	20.95

Exhibit 1-1 (con't)

LUGGAGE RACKS

LUGGAGE RACKS. Strong tubular steel and precision weld construction; installs easily with hand tools; stylized design and bright chrome enhances the appearance of your motorcycle; functional design for greater strength and larger luggage area; square tubing provides flat surface over entire luggage area for easier storage of large or small articles; enclosed front mounting slot for greater safety; ready to install; includes mounting instructions.

MAKE	MODEL	c.c.	MODEL YEAR	PART NO.	WEST RETAIL	EAST RETAIL
Honda	CB	750	1975-1978	R-100	24.95	26.50
	CL,CB	350,450	1974-1978	R-120	22.95	23.95
	CL,CB	175	1975-1978	R-130	22.95	23.95
Kawasaki	Mach 3	500	1975-1978	R-200	22.95	23.95
Yamaha	XS-1	650	1976-1978	R-300	22.95	23.95
	R-5	350	1976-1978	R-320	22.95	23.95

BACK RESTS

BACK REST FOR LUGGAGE RACK (LOW STYLING). Expanded black naugahyde; bright chrome; wide, stable cushion area provides comfort and security; easily attaches to luggage rack; includes mounting hardware and mounting instructions.

MAKE	MODEL	c.c.	FITS LUGGAGE RACK NO.	BACK REST PART NO.	WEST RETAIL	EAST RETAIL
Honda	CB	750	R-100	BR-100-2	13.95	14.95
	CL,CB	350,450	R-120	BR-120-2	13.95	14.95
	CL,CB	175	R-130	BR-130-2	13.95	14.95
Kawasaki	Mach 3	500	R-200	BR-200-2	13.95	14.95
Yamaha	XS-1	650	R-300	BR-300-2	13.95	14.95
	R-5	350	R-320	BR-320-2	13.95	14.95

Exhibit 1-2
A Comparison of the Sissy Bar and the Solo Rest

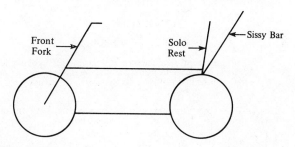

wheel. Using this knowledge, Jack developed the solo rest, which allows the passenger to ride in a more comfortable vertical position. (See Exhibit 1–2.) Jack began to produce the solo rest which sold at between $20 and $21 per unit. There was no product research or testing conducted prior to manufacturing this innovative item. Jack claims he "rolled the dice." This method has proven extremely successful thus far.

Distribution Channels

Distribution channels also were altered after the takeover. Cycle Enterprises shifted to a distributor-oriented operation with only 20 percent of their sales through dealers. Jack hoped that by working the operation on a full-time basis he could achieve the high-volume turnover he needed to make a profit at the lower margin that resulted from using distributors. This channeling approach also would give Cycle Enterprise products a complete market penetration in the southern California area. Additionally, there was a cost savings associated with the new distribution system; whereas in 1976 Cycle Enterprises was burdened with billing 80 accounts each month, in 1977 only 25 monthly invoices had to be processed.

Jack's promotional effort involves sending dealers and distributors a copy of his catalog which lists his product line of motorcycle parts and accessories. A 40 percent discount on the suggested retail price is provided to dealers. Distributors are given an additional 5 percent discount for volume orders. No advertising is initiated by Cycle Enterprises. See Exhibit 1–3 for dealers' price schedules.

By the end of the first 6 months of 1977, Cycle Enterprises had surpassed its 1976 dollar sales volume figures, with a profit margin of 20 percent.

The Market Situation in the U.S.

Motorcycles were a $500 million business in the United States in 1969 and, recession or not, this industry grew 17 percent in 1970. The motorcycle industry, which seemed in 1967 to be washed out, made a dramatic comeback.

Exhibit 1-3

CYCLE ENTERPRISES

1977 CATALOG

DEALER'S PRICE SCHEDULE

A 40% discount, from the suggested retail price, is given to all
dealers. The schedule below converts the suggested retail price
to the dealer discount price for all items in the catalog.

Suggested Retail Price	Discount Price	Suggested Retail Price	Discount Price
$ 1.25	$ .75	$11.50	$ 6.90
1.35	.81	11.95	7.17
1.49	.89	12.95	7.77
1.59	.95	13.50	8.10
1.65	.99	13.95	8.37
1.75	1.05	14.95	8.97
2.25	1.35	15.50	9.30
2.35	1.41	15.95	9.57
2.50	1.50	16.50	9.90
2.60	1.56	18.95	11.37
2.65	1.59	19.95	11.97
2.75	1.65	20.95	12.57
2.95	1.77	22.95	13.77
3.25	1.95	23.95	14.37
3.95	2.37	24.95	14.97
4.25	2.55	25.95	15.57
4.50	2.70	26.95	16.17
5.95	3.57	29.95	17.97
6.25	3.75	30.95	18.57
6.95	4.17	34.95	20.97
7.45	4.47	35.95	21.57
7.50	4.50	37.95	22.77
8.95	5.37	38.95	23.37
9.50	5.70	39.95	23.67
9.95	5.97	40.95	24.57
10.50	6.30	41.50	24.90
10.95	6.57	42.95	25.77
		49.95	29.97
		51.50	30.90

All prices subject to change without notice.

"Cycle sales were almost too good," claimed Cook Neilson, the editor of *Cycle*
magazine. "Some distributors were backed up on orders 6 or 7 months. We couldn't
even get some new models to test."

The unexpected demand started in the fall of 1969. A total of 641,000 cycles
was imported in the United States in 1969, an increase from 375,000 imported in
1968.

Caught somewhat unaware by the boom and afraid of piling up inventories in a
time of tight money, foreign factories were pushing to fill the growing orders. But
most of the 30 manufacturers of cycles knew they would not be able to meet the
demand. Many experts predicted that motorcycle sales would climb dramatically to

a record 750,000 units in 1970. "We did 80 percent better that year," said Alan Masek, general manager of Kawasaki Motors Corporation, United States, now a hot competitor in the import-dominated market. "If the factories could have been ready, the industry would have probably doubled its volume." That was a year when auto sales were off and the slowdown in the economy was cutting into sales of expensive leisure-time goods.

Motorcycle people have not forgotten the early 1960s when Honda Motor Company flooded the U.S. market with its lightweight 50-cc models. Motorcycle producers believed they were changing the ways of basic transportation in the nation. Sales rose to 725,000 cycles in 1966. But within a year, the market was saturated and sales slumped nearly 50 percent. The 50-cc bikes began to gather dust in warehouses around the country and gloom descended upon the industry.

Unit sales of motorcycles in 1976 recovered 16 percent to about 1.1 million units, following declines of 24 percent in both 1974 and 1975, and are expected to gain 10 percent in 1977 to 1.2 million units. However, these figures are below the peak 1.6 million units sold in 1973.

The motorcycle market has matured. It is much more sophisticated now. Customers apparently are more sure of themselves. They have a clear idea that they want motorcycles for pleasure rather than for basic transportation. Previously, the excuse often given for buying a lightweight cycle was commuting utility. But now customers desire all styles and models, from putt-putting Honda minibikes or Mo-Peds at $350 each to imposing 1200-cc Harley-Davidson Electra Glides at $2,700. Some 5.5 million cycles show up on government registration books, and there probably are 1.1 million trail and minibikes that operate off the main roads without licenses.

The lightweight sector of the market is dominated by Japanese concerns, accounting for 94 percent of the total motorcycle market. Here, Honda is the largest (48 percent market share), followed by Yamaha (19 percent), Kawasaki (12 percent), and Suzuki (10 percent); other imports account for 5 percent of the market. Harley-Davidson (a division of AMF) has concentrated on heavyweight bikes and has an estimated 6 percent of the market.

About half of all motorcycle owners are under age 24; 27 percent are between 25 and 34; and close to 20 percent are over 35. The average owner of a Triumph cycle is 27 years old and makes $14,000. Exhibits 1–4 through 1–7 provide additional industry trend information.

In spite of the fact that movies such as "Easy Rider" continue the connotation of motorcycles as black leather jacket gangs or hopped-up hippies, Americans generally accept motorcycles. They often feel closed in by city life, auto congestion, and social and personal problems and desire to roam, to go where fancy takes them. Thus, the industry is concentrating on this pleasure principle to serve customers who have plenty of leisure time.

Thoughtful motorcycle businesses see some potential problems ahead. For example, although further moderate growth is expected in the market, it is reasonable to assume that the 1973 peak level of sales will not be duplicated during this decade. The economic and technical burdens on manufacturers to comply with the future exhaust emission, noise, and vehicle equipment regulations will restrain the growth of the industry during the next 2 to 3 years. Furthermore, prospective buyers are likely to react negatively to subsequent market changes, specifically retail price increases, performance degradation, and a diminished product selection.

There may well be, too, a clash with the environmentalists. Too many bird-watchers, hikers, and equestrians, seeking peace and quiet, have been annoyed by the roar of trailbikes. The Motorcycle Industry Council has moved to Washington where it can more efficiently work against anti-motorcycle legislation. Moreover, many parents, recalling stories of fatal accidents, are horrified when a child desires a motorcycle. The industry tends to downplay the fact that, without the protection of a steel body, the motorcyclist is much more vulnerable in an accident than the driver of an automobile.

In spite of the above, motorcycling now seems firmly established as a major branch of the leisure-time industry. Exhibit 1–8 presents a 1977 Standard & Poor's basic analysis of the leisure-time industry.

The Market Situation in Southern California

Exhibit 1–9 illustrates that California has more than twice as many registered motor-cycles as any other state. The American Motorcycle Association estimated that in 1976 there were 50,000 motorcycles registered in Orange County and probably another 50,000 unregistered ones used only for dirt riding. They expect that there will be more than 90,000 by the end of 1977 and 200,000 very shortly thereafter.

A representative of the Motorcycle Owners, Riders, and Enthusiasts recently stated that in Long Beach alone there were 8,600 youngsters, too young to hold valid operator's licenses, who ride their bikes off the streets in fields and/or the desert.

Exhibit 1-4
Motor Vehicle Travel in the United States
1975

Item	Passenger Cars*	Motorcycles*
Total motor-vehicle travel (in million miles)	1,028,121	23,351
Number of vehicles registered (in thousands)	106,712.6	4,966.8
Average miles traveled per vehicle	9,634	4,500
Fuel consumed (million gallons)	76,010	447
Average fuel consumption per vehicle (gallons)	712	90
Average miles traveled per gallon	13.53	50

* Separate estimates of passenger car and motorcycle travel are not available by highway category.
Source: U. S. Office of Highway Planning, Tables VM–1 and VM–2.

Exhibit 1-5
Vehicle Miles of Travel and Fuel Consumption

Year		Vehicle Miles of Travel (in billions)	Average Annual Miles Traveled Per Vehicle	Fuel Consumed (millions of gallons)	Average Fuel Consumption Per Vehicle (gallons)
1975:	Passenger Cars	1,028.1	9,634	76,010	712
	Motorcycles	22.4	4,500	447	90
1974:	Passenger Cars [1]	990.7	9,448	73,770	704
	Motorcycles [1]	22.3	4,500	447	90
1973:	Passenger Cars	1,016.9	9,992	77,619	763
	Motorcycles	19.6	4,498	392	90
1970:	Passenger Cars	890.8	9,978	65,649	735
	Motorcycles	10.1	3,605	135	48
1965:	Passenger Cars	706.4	9,387	50,206	667
	Motorcycles	5.2	3,770	69	50
1960:	Passenger Cars [2]	588.1	9,446	41,169	661
	Motorcycles [3]				
1955:	Passenger Cars	492.6	9,359	33,548	644
1950:	Passenger Cars	363.6	9,020	24,305	603
1940:	Passenger Cars	249.6	9,080	16,323	594

[1] Revised.
[2] Alaska and Hawaii included since 1959.
[3] Motorcycles are included in passenger cars.
Source: U. S. Federal Highway Administration, *Highway Statistics*, annual.

Exhibit 1-6
Motor Vehicle Registrations: 1940 to 1975[1]

Year	Total Cars, Trucks, Buses	Passenger Cars and Taxis	Trucks and Buses	Motorcycles
1940	32,525 [2]	27,466	4,987	136
1950	49,300[2]	40,339	8,823	454
1955	62,689	52,145	10,544	412
1960	73,858	61,671	12,187	574
1965	90,358	75,258	15,100	1,382
1966	93,950	78,128	15,822	1,753
1967	96,905	80,407	16,499	1,953
1968	100,898	83,618	17,280	2,089
1969	105,093	86,872	18,221	2,316
1970	108,404	89,259	19,145	2,824
1971	112,987	92,742	20,245	3,344
1972	118,782	97,096	21,686	3,760
1973	125,671	101,986	23,685	4,357
1974	129,893	104,857	25,036	4,966
1975	133,727 [3]	107,371 [3]	26,356 [3]	5,494 [3]

[1] Includes publicly owned vehicles. Excludes vehicles owned by military services.
[2] Total includes, components exclude, Hawaii.
[3] Estimate.
Source: U. S. Federal Highway Administration, *Highway Statistics,* annual.

According to a *Cycle* magazine study, 20 percent of the dollar sales for accessories are for dirt-bike items. The Southern California area is responsible for 45 percent of the total U.S. dirt-bike accessory sales.

Due to numerous dust and noise complaints from the residents of Los Angeles, Orange, and San Diego Counties, ordinances were passed in the summer of 1977 banning motorcycles from private property in county areas, unless the bike riders had the permission of the property owner. Many southern California cities, including Huntington Beach, Anaheim, Los Angeles, and San Diego, also passed similar ordinances. This legislation virtually closed these areas to the dirt riders. It prohibited them from vacant lots, parking lots, and all other vacant acreage.

Generally, recreation officials were unresponsive in providing alternative public riding areas for the growing number of off-road enthusiasts. The only place a rider could take his bike in dirt was for a fee at several private areas including Saddleback Motorcycle Park (Orange), Claude Osteen's Motorbike Park (Pomona), and Indian Dunes (Castaic Junction).

Exhibit 1-7

U.S. DRIVERS BY AGE, SEX AND MILES DRIVEN

NUMBER OF DRIVERS, 1976*

Age	Male (000)	Female (000)	Total (000)
Under 16	76	58	134
16	1,039	835	1,874
17	1,624	1,321	2,945
18	1,902	1,579	3,481
19	1,953	1,662	3,615
Under 20	6,594	5,455	12,049
20-24	9,654	8,553	18,207
25-29	9,215	8,323	17,538
30-34	7,343	6,580	13,923
35-39	6,061	5,452	11,513
40-44	5,468	4,840	10,308
45-49	5,591	4,851	10,442
50-54	5,561	4,747	10,308
55-59	4,993	4,111	9,104
60-64	4,285	3,346	7,631
65-69	3,396	2,494	5,890
70 and over	4,376	2,585	6,961
Total	72,537	61,337	133,874

*Estimated
SOURCE: U.S. Federal Highway Administration

AVERAGE ANNUAL MILES DRIVEN

Age	Male	Female	All
16-19	5,461	3,586	4,633
20-24	11,425	5,322	8,260
25-29	13,931	5,539	9,814
30-34	14,496	5,752	10,274
35-39	13,035	6,232	9,878
40-44	13,133	5,950	9,833
45-49	12,818	6,271	9,875
50-54	12,345	5,454	9,447
55-59	11,495	5,439	9,009
60-64	9,710	5,291	8,112
65-69	6,915	4,173	5,850
70 and over	5,302	3,183	4,644
All ages	11,352	5,411	8,685

SOURCE: Based on unpublished data from National Personal Transportation Survey conducted by Bureau of the Census for the Federal Highway Administration 1969-70.

PERCENTAGE OF DRIVERS BY AGE AND SEX, 1976

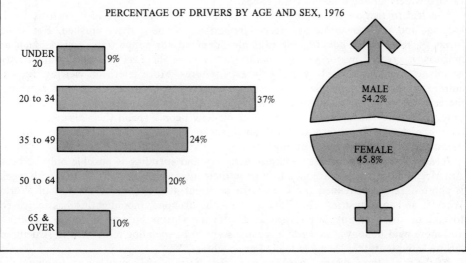

UNDER 20   9%

20 to 34   37%

35 to 49   24%

50 to 64   20%

65 & OVER   10%

MALE 54.2%

FEMALE 45.8%

Exhibit 1-8
Leisure-Time Industry Analysis

The leisure-time industry is truly an amalgam of widely diversified businesses, including the manufacture of sporting goods and recreational vehicles, photography, movies, recorded music, and the operation of amusement parks. Depending on definition, the size of the industry could range anywhere from $50 billion to $200 billion. The one common feature shared by many of the products and services in this wide array of markets is that they are used by the consumer during spare time. According to one estimate, more than one-third of the lifetime of most Americans is free, unoccupied time. And the ways in which they use it are almost endless.

The leisure market grew rapidly in the 1960s and early 1970s when real disposable income rose substantially. After a pause during the sluggish years of the mid-1970s, income picked up once again. An advance of about 10 percent in personal recreation expenditures is shaping up for 1977, not far out of line with the projected growth in personal income. That would put personal recreation expenditures at close to $80 billion. A rise of about 8 percent is possible in 1978. This spending increased 9.7 percent to $72.6 billion in 1976, from $66.2 billion in 1975, according to the Commerce Department.

Although the industry is expected to grow at an above-average rate, the gains probably will not match those of the 1960s and early 1970s. In effect, it has been demonstrated in the last few years that demand for certain leisure goods and services can be quite sensitive to levels of consumer spending and can be adversely affected by high inflation and by recession. These characteristics are expected to persist, with the impact varying widely among different leisure subgroups.

The leisure market is very complex. Certain leisure-related services, such as food, lodging, and transportation, are needed regardless of the activity pursued. For some forms of recreation—boating, for example—demand for supporting services, such as marinas, is created by the sale of goods. However, an increase in a particular activity is not necessarily followed by a rise in expenditures. More television viewing, for example, will not necessarily lead to greater sales of television receivers. It can, however, increase the need for maintenance and repairs. Another complication is that, although time and money have an important effect on how people spend their leisure, the ultimate choice may be determined by habits, social customs, or fads that have little or nothing to do with either time or money.

In any case, the sharp rise in leisure activities and spending is possible only because Americans have time and money to pursue their interests. It is not that the work week is shorter. It has remained fairly constant at about 40 hours since the end of World War II; and in industries where the average has dropped, moonlighting has increased to take up the gap. But the average work year has shrunk because of longer vacations and more paid holidays. As a result, people seem to be spending more time in structured leisure activities rather than just loafing or watching TV.

At the same time, discretionary income—that portion of income over and above the amount needed for the essentials of everyday life—has resumed its gradual upward climb, following a brief dip during the 1974–75 recession. And the demographic situation also is favorable. People who were born during the postwar baby boom are getting older and, thus, the age group that is inclined to spend more money on leisure activities —young adults—will expand.

But perhaps most important of all is a discernible change in basic attitudes toward leisure. In preceding generations, leisure was associated with the idle rich. The only way to get ahead was to work. People still believe in the work ethic, but the quality of life has changed. People are more inclined now to regard recreation as a necessity, not just something to do with surplus income. A young married couple will eat hot dogs, skimp on clothes, live in a 4-room instead of a 5-room apartment, just to make sure they have ample funds for their vacation.

All indications are that the overall leisure market will continue to grow at a rate at least as rapid as that for real GNP. Not all segments, however, will expand equally as fast. That most Americans will have the time and money to pursue whatever activity or activities they choose seems almost certain. The choice, however, will be determined partly by the age distribution of the population, by its educational background and social values, and by the goods and services offered in the market place.

Source: "Leisure-Time Basic Analysis," *Standard & Poor's Industry Surveys* (New York: Standard & Poor's Corporation, September 1977, Section 2), pp. L9–L10.

U.S. Population Projections*

Age Group	1977 Number (000s)	1977 % of Total	1980 Number (000s)	1980 % of Total	1985 Number (000s)	1985 % of Total
Under 5 yrs.	15,174	7.0	16,020	7.2	18,803	8.1
5 to 14 yrs.	36,371	16.8	33,896	15.3	32,826	14.1
15 to 19 yrs.	21,181	9.8	20,609	9.3	18,007	7.7
20 to 24 yrs.	20,089	9.3	20,918	9.4	20,510	8.8
25 to 29 yrs.	17,745	8.2	18,930	8.5	20,581	8.8
30 to 34 yrs.	15,416	7.1	17,242	7.8	19,278	8.3
35 to 39 yrs.	12,339	5.7	14,033	6.3	17,274	7.4
40 to 54 yrs.	34,592	16.0	34,386	15.5	36,559	15.7
55 to 64 yrs.	20,406	9.4	21,188	9.5	21,737	9.3
65 yrs. & over	23,430	10.7	24,927	11.2	27,305	11.8
All Ages	216,745	100.0	222,159	100.0	232,880	100.0

* Includes Armed Forces abroad.
Source: Department of Commerce, Population Series P–25, as of July 1, 1977.

Recently, Congress was told: "Motorcycle bums, vandals, and litterbugs are turning the wide open spaces of the West into vast outdoor slums." That was the situation described by a spokesperson for conservationist organizations, who joined the Assistant Interior Secretary in urging legislation to give the Bureau of Land

Exhibit 1-9
Motorcycle Registrations
By State
(1975 estimate in thousands)

Alabama	85	Montana	42
Alaska	12	Nebraska	55
Arizona	73	Nevada	18
Arkansas	50	New Hampshire	32
California	699	New Jersey	93
Colorado	101	New Mexico	36
Connecticut	73	New York	117
Delaware	8	North Carolina	135
D.C.	4	North Dakota	25
Florida	212	Ohio	260
Georgia	117	Oklahoma	111
Hawaii	10	Oregon	83
Idaho	49	Pennsylvania	335
Illinois	234	Rhode Island	22
Indiana	157	South Carolina	69
Iowa	154	South Dakota	25
Kansas	102	Tennessee	112
Kentucky	63	Texas	309
Louisiana	67	Utah	55
Maine	28	Vermont	15
Maryland	75	Virginia	105
Massachusetts	95	Washington	124
Michigan	327	West Virginia	66
Minnesota	156	Wisconsin	123
Mississippi	38	Wyoming	17
Missouri	121	Total U.S.	5,494

Source: U.S. Federal Highway Administration, *Highway Statistics,* annual.

Management greater authority over recreational uses of public lands. The Bureau is a federal agency that looks after more than 450 million acres of public land.

There were several citizens' committees in Sacramento trying to force legislation to restrict dune buggies and motorcycles from California's 16 million acres of federal land. More than 80 percent of the land under the Bureau of Land Management in California is in Southern California's deserts which are popular among motorcyclists.

Victorville property owners said, "Cyclists are replacing desert peace, plants, and wildlife with dust, noise, rubble, and impromptu racetracks." The City Council ordered a fine of up to $500 and a 6-month jail term for motorized trespassers.

Complaints forced closure of the Bixby Slough area near Anaheim and Gaffey Streets to motorcyclists according to a planning officer for the Los Angeles City Department of Recreation and Parks, the agency responsible for this regional park.

The Folson, California office of the Bureau of Land Management stated that motorcycles have proven "completely incompatible with livestock and wildlife. The machines panic the animals until they do not feed or adequately care for their young." Their representative further told a session of the annual meeting of the Society for Range Management that "Mexican steers were reported to flee for 15 miles over rugged terrain through barbed wire fences."

The Bureau of Land Management had tried to reserve certain areas in California for use by cyclists, but the cyclists refused to stay within those areas, and the areas were eventually closed altogether.

Because of this situation, Cycle Enterprises' season dropped off sharply in mid-summer, 1977. The season usually does not begin to taper off until the end of September.

The 3-month premature season's end left Jack Fenway with vast amounts of dirt-bike inventory on hand and not enough demand for his street-bike items to carry the business at a break-even point. Bankruptcy seemed imminent since money was scarce, his orders low; and thus, his credit would not carry much weight.

Discussion Questions

1. What internal and external events caused Cycle Enterprises to find itself in its current position?

2. How should the management of small businesses like Cycle Enterprises develop and maintain an awareness of the environment within which they operate? Who should have the responsibility in a small business for monitoring the business environment? Explain. What are the stumbling blocks to your recommendation and how might they be overcome?

3. What should Cycle Enterprises do with its excess inventory?

4. What short-run marketing strategy should Cycle Enterprises adopt? Why?

5. What long-range marketing strategies should they consider? Why?

Sebring-Vanguard, Inc.: The CitiCar

James E. Williams and Frederick E. Webster, Jr.*
Dartmouth College

In February 1976, a variety of problems faced Mr. Robert Stone, marketing manager of Sebring-Vanguard, Inc. (SV). SV manufactured the first mass-produced electric car in the United States, the SV-48 CitiCar shown in Exhibit 2-1. The first CitiCars experienced both engineering and production problems, but by 1976 these problems had been largely eliminated. Unfortunately, Consumers Union had purchased one of the early substandard cars and had issued a damaging evaluation of the CitiCar in the October 1975 issue of *Consumer Reports*. Mr. Stone believed that this was having far-reaching demoralizing effects on the entire SV dealer organization. In addition, retail sales had slowed. Mr. Stone suspected that many dealers were not pushing the CitiCar, and that it was being used primarily as a traffic builder by some dealers for the "big-four" automobile companies. Mr. Stone was therefore considering either expanding his field force to allow better supervision of CitiCar dealers, or changing his dealer organization drastically. Continued product improvements also were planned. Sebring-Vanguard's president, Mr. Robert Beaumont, had set two goals for 1976: cost reduction throughout all phases of the operation and a sales volume sufficient to give SV its first profitable year of operations.

Company Background

Mr. Robert Beaumont, the president of Sebring-Vanguard, Inc., had been involved in electric vehicle development since the late 1960s, and had been instrumental in the development of the Vanguard Coupe, the predecessor of the

---

* This case was prepared as the basis for classroom discussion. It is not intended to illustrate either correct or incorrect handling of a management problem. Copyright © 1976 by the Trustees of Dartmouth College.

Exhibit 2-1

CitiCar. He eventually attracted the financial backing of wealthy individual in-vestors living in Florida. Sebring-Vanguard, Inc. was formed on May 14, 1973, to manufacture, assemble, and sell electric vehicle (EVs), with its headquarters and only manufacturing facility at Sebring.

On August 9, 1973, the company entered into an agreement with Vanguard Vehicles, Inc. (Mr. Beaumont also was the president and a stockholder of Van-guard Vehicles, Inc.) to acquire inventories and rights, and to pay royalties for the use of technology and trade names relating to the design, engineering, manu-facture, and sale of the Vanguard Coupe. Beginning in August 1973, SV began recruiting people to develop systems, procedures, and an understanding of the EV industry. Key production and operation positions were soon under the control of competent personnel. The first CitiCar prototype was produced in February 1974.

In August 1974, SV was producing 28 CitiCars per week; a year later produc-tion had risen to 40 cars per week. The current physical plant was deemed suitable for production of 240 cars per month. Other facilities capable of handling 800 cars per month were available near the present production location. In August 1975, SV was recognized by *Automotive News* as the sixth largest manufacturer of cars in the United States. By January 1976, SV employed a total of 100 people, with 15 to 20 involved in management or supervision.

Mr. Robert Stone was a 1970 graduate of Dartmouth College. He had been a school teacher for a few years until he became totally absorbed in the electric car concept. He then worked for a Boston insurance company while searching for the right opportunity in the EV industry. He had met Mr. Beaumont in May 1973 and immediately joined SV as marketing manager.

Net sales for the first complete year of operations ending June 30, 1975 amounted to $2.37 million with a net loss from operations of $488,000 or $.86 per share. These results are compared with net sales of $185,000 and net loss of

$651,000 ($1.85 per share) during the startup period from May 1973 through June 30, 1974. Financial statements are shown in Exhibits 2–2 through 2–4. Due to the high element of risk perceived in the SV venture by lending institutions, SV had not been able to borrow money and establish strong banking relationships. All of the stock was privately held by individuals until mid-1975 when International Nickel Company (INCO) purchased 100,000 shares at $3.00 per share and also acquired warrants to purchase an additional 60,000 shares at an average price of $5.00 by April 30, 1978. As a result of this investment, ESB, Inc., a wholly-owned subsidiary of INCO that manufactured batteries, contributed technical assistance to SV. As of January 1976, SV's management believed that there was virtually no chance of raising additional capital by a new equity issue. Debt financing consisted of notes from individual stockholders, notes from banks secured by essentially all SV's equipment and inventory, and long-term financing leaseholds.

During the year ending June 30, 1975, SV had sold an average of 83 vehicles per month. Sales in the last two months of that year had averaged 99 vehicles, and during September and October of 1975, SV showed a monthly profit for the first time. It was estimated by management that monthly sales of roughly 150 CitiCars were necessary for profitable operations.

The most difficult task facing SV, commented Mr. Beaumont, was "determining our costs of doing business and our break-even level of operations. Due to the rapid fluctuation in the costs of materials and components in an inflationary

Exhibit 2-2
Sebring-Vanguard, Inc.
Statement of Operations and Accumulated Deficit

	For the Year Ended June 30, 1975	From Inception (May 14, 1973) to June 30, 1974
Net Sales	$2,369,683	$185,364
Costs and Expenses:		
Cost of products sold	2,319,761	181,624
General and administrative expenses	252,267	129,097
Selling expenses	259,581	44,422
Research and development	25,915	375,197
Preoperating Expenses	—	107,272
Net Loss	$ 487,841	$652,248
Accumulated Deficit:		
Beginning of period	652,248	—
End of period	$1,140,089	$652,248
Number of Weighted Average Shares Outstanding	564,251	351,661
Net Loss Per Share	$.86	$1.85

climate, it is difficult to determine month to month just what our costs were. A number of cost and engineering studies currently are being undertaken to reduce vehicle costs and to increase production efficiency and output."

The CitiCar

The top speed of the car (38 mph) and the acceleration capacity (0–25 mph in 6.3 sec)
The CitiCar was designed to fulfill the needs of the average urban and suburban

Exhibit 2-3
Sebring-Vanguard, Inc.
Balance Sheet

Assets	June 30 1975	1974
Current Assets:		
Cash (including $35,094 held in escrow at June 30, 1974)	$　84,362	$ 48,178
Accounts receivable	135,140	36,639
Inventories	789,761	534,778
Prepaid expenses	81,774	17,096
Total Current Assets	$1,091,037	$636,691
Fixed assets at cost, less accumulated depreciation	188,103	194,212
Organization expenses	15,095	19,407
Total Assets	$1,294,235	$850,310
Liabilities and Stockholders' Equity		
Current Liabilities:		
Notes payable	$　91,786	$112,355
Accounts payable	442,423	371,355
Accrued expenses	97,681	84,838
Customer deposits	20,467	25,094
Total Current Liabilities	$　652,357	$593,642
Notes payable, due after one year	371,966	8,915
Stockholders' equity:		
Common stock, $.10 par value—1,000,000 shares authorized, 659,667 and 489,667 issued	65,967	48,967
Capital in excess of par value	1,443,034	950,034
Accumulated deficit	(1,140,089)	(652,284)
	386,912	346,753
Less: Notes receivable from stockholder	(　99,000)	(99,000)
Total Stockholders' Equity	$　269,912	$247,753
Commitments	—	—
Total Liabilities and Stockholders' equity	$1,294,235	$850,310

Exhibit 2-4
Sebring-Vanguard, Inc.
Statement of Changes in Financial Position

	For the Year Ended June 30, 1975	From Inception (May 14, 1973) to June 30, 1974
Financial resources were provided by:		
Issuance of common stock	$510,000	$999,001
Less: Notes receivable from stockholder	—	(99,000)
	$510,000	$900,001
Proceeds from borrowings	405,003	14,860
Total sources	$915,003	$914,861
Financial resources were used for:		
Operations:		
Net Loss	$487,841	$652,248
Charges not affecting working capital:		
Depreciation	55,215	25,248
Amortization	4,312	2,156
Working capital used in operations	$428,314	$624,673
Purchase of fixed assets	49,106	219,631
Increase in organization expenses	—	21,563
Reduction in notes payable due after one year	41,952	5,945
Total uses	$519,372	$871,812
Increase in working capital	$395,631	$ 43,049
Working capital at beginning of period	43,049	—
Working capital at end of period	$438,680	$ 43,049

Analysis of Changes in Working Capital

Increase in current assets:		
Cash	$ 36,184	$ 48,178
Accounts receivable	98,501	36,639
Inventories	254,983	534,778
Prepaid expenses	64,678	17,096
Total	$454,346	$636,691
Decrease (increase) in current liabilities:		
Notes payable	$ 20,569	($112,355)
Accounts payable	(71,068)	(371,355)
Accrued expenses	(12,843)	(84,838)
Customer deposits	4,627	(25,094)
Total	($ 58,715)	($593,642)
Increase in working capital	$395,631	$ 43,049

driver, with a range of up to 50 miles on one electrical charge for the batteries. 6.2 seconds) were believed to be more than adequate for stop-and-go city driving. Furthermore, the size and maneuverability were considered ideal for parking ease. The 95-inch length and 22-feet turning circle allowed the driver to pull into and out of a standard parking space without using reverse. It could be parked in places where even subcompacts would not fit. The low center of gravity and wide track (63-inch wheelbase) allowed easy handling and safe performance, even on ice and snow. A description of the car is given in Exhibit 2–5 and a price list, including a list of available options, is shown in Exhibit 2–6.

Economy of operation and maintenance were the major reasons for buying a CitiCar, according to a survey of new owners. Whereas city or in-town driving was harsh on more expensive, conventional "family cars," SV emphasized the

Exhibit 2-5

STANDARD EQUIPMENT: 110 volt on-board built-in charger - high impact urethane bumpers - laminated safety glass windshield - shoulder harness seat belts - head rests - dual speed windshield wiper - windshield washer - emergency flashers - back up light - license plate light - signal lights - sideview mirror - rearview mirror - courtesy light - horn - speedometer/odometer - voltmeter - 4 ply rated tires - wheel covers - vinyl top - custom side windows - side moldings - shock absorbers - custom woodgrain dashboard, inner door straps, 25' HD extension cord, drip rail moldings, rear carpeting.

BODY COLORS: Red   -   Yellow   -   Orange

Blue   -   Green   -   White

Custom Colors (to order) Available

OPTIONAL EQUIPMENT: radio and antenna - cigar lighter - heater - right side view mirror - single car trailer (to tow CitiCar) - spare tire and wheel - hydrometer - CitiCar jack - car cover (Custom) - flat tire inflator - defroster - fully automatic custom charger - door locks - custom paint (to order).   Radial tires - Sebring - Vanguard battery saver caps - white wall tires - tinted glass.

NOTE: The CitiCar is best suited on roads where the posted speed limit does not exceed 50 MPH. The CitiCar should not be used on interstate highways.

LIMITED WARRANTY. Under normal use, the CitiCar is warranted by Sebring-Vanguard, Inc. for a period of ▒▒▒▒6months after purchase by the customer. This warranty applies to all parts of the vehicle found defective in material or workmanship; except for tires and batteries, which are warranted separately by their respective manufacturers.
    This is a summary of the entire warranty, which is available at your authorized Sebring-Vanguard, Inc. dealership.

SEBRING VANGUARD, INC

P. O. Box 1963, Sebring, Florida 33870

CitiCar®

*Specifications
&
Answers
to
Questions*

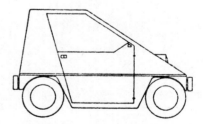

AUTHORIZED   DEALER

SEBRING VANGUARD, INC

Q: How fast does the CitiCar by Sebring-Vanguard go?
A: The current version, CitiCar/SV-48 cruises at up to 38 miles per hour.

Q: Can the CitiCar be licensed for on-the-road use?
A: The CitiCar complies with most Federal Motor Vehicle Standards applicable to that vehicle. Therefore, it should be licensable in all states.

Q: What is the CitiCar designed for?
A: The CitiCar is designed for low speed, short distance driving by housewives, commuters, students, retired persons, etc. Because it has been constructed on a truck chasis, the CitiCar is also ideal for such off-road users as security patrol, in-plant transportation, etc. The CitiCar has been sold as a messenger and delivery vehicle and is useful for city meter maids and utility companies.

Q: How far will the CitiCar go before recharging?
A: The range is up to 50 miles, depending on temperature, terrain, and traffic conditions. Thirty-five to forty miles is a typical range in city driving conditions. Fortunately, the CitiCar does not use energy when stopped at a light or coasting to a stop.

Q: Will the CitiCar fulfill my driving needs?
A: Chances are it will. The average urban and suburban automobile in the United States is driven only 22.6 miles per day. This makes the CitiCar a very practical second or third car for many families.

Q: How does the top speed hold up as the CitiCar is driven during the day?
A: A top speed of 35-38 miles per hour should be attainable during all but the last few miles of the charge.

Q: How will the CitiCar handle in snow?
A: Exceptionally well; its low center of gravity plus the rear-mounted motor and transaxle provide excellent traction.

Q: What affect do the lights and wiper have on the range of the CitiCar?
A: Owners experience has shown that there is a decrease of approximately 10% in the CitiCar's range during night operation.

Q: Can the CitiCar be towed?
A: Only for short distances at low speed. We recommend using a trailer when taking the CitiCar on vacation.

Q: How will the CitiCar handle on hills?
A: Very well. A warning lamp is provided which will alert the driver that the CitiCar motor might be overheating while ascending an unusually long, steep hill.

Q: Is the CitiCar really pollution free?
A: Electric vehicles are classified as inherently non-polluting vehicles by the U.S. Environmental Protection Agency. The relatively little pollution that is emitted from the power plant is usually far from populated areas and is easier to control than automobile pollution. Of course, many power plants do not burn fossil fuels, and in these cases the CitiCar is virtually pollution-free.

Q: Do electric vehicles indirectly burn just as much fuel as conventional cars via the electric power plant?
A: No, because fuel-burning power plants which generate electricity for the CitiCar can operate more efficiently than small internal combustion engines, the CitiCar's actual fuel usage is only a fraction of that of an average sub-compact.

Q: If millions of electric vehicles were used around the country, wouldn't this cause black outs and brown outs?
A: Surprisingly enough, no. Electric vehicles would most likely be recharged at night during off peak periods, when utility companies have sufficient capacity to recharge many millions of electric vehicles. In this way, power plants will operate more efficiently and electricity rates may stabilize.

Q: Could the CitiCar be powered by solar energy?
A: Once the people of this country develop the technology to economically convert solar energy into electricity the CitiCar batteries could then be recharged by a solar charging station.

Q: Can electric vehicles be made to go faster and further?
A: Yes, but at a much greater cost. We have designed the CitiCar based on a comprehensive survey that urban traffic moves at an average of 28 miles per hour, and that most 'second cars' are driven only 5-40 miles per day.

Q: Is the CitiCar as safe as the average small car?
A: The CitiCar is equipped with seat and shoulder belts and most other safety equipment required by law. It is constructed on a rugged aluminum chasis and has a tubular aluminum body support structure surrounding the passenger compartment. Because the CitiCar will not be used on intersate highways, the possibility of a high speed collision is eliminated. We feel that these features and the fact that the CitiCar will be used only in low speed areas make it one of the safest small cars on the road today.

Q: What about insurance?
A: Insurance should be no different from any other compact motor vehicle. In fact, because the CitiCar will be used only at low speeds and for short-distance driving around town, we think rates for this vehicle will someday be less than for cars driven at highway speeds and for possible hundreds of miles per day.

Q: What makes the CitiCar a good investment?
A: The CitiCar is a good investment because of its low operating costs, low maintenance costs, and anticipated low depreciation.

Q: Will the CitiCar depreciate as fast or as much as a conventional car does?
A: We think not. The CitiCar's frame is constructed of corrosion-resistant aluminum. The body is of rust-proof cycolac ABS, with the color impregnated throughout the material. Also there is no internal combustion engine with its associated support systems to require repair or replacement. For these reasons, the CitiCar should retain more of its value over a longer period than a conventional car.

Q: How much maintenance does the CitiCar require?
A: Much less than for a conventional car. The CitiCar has no spark plugs, points, mufflers, radiator, valves, rings, carburetor, anti-pollution controls, or transmission. The batteries are the most important part of the CitiCar and should be checked weekly. (Consult your owner's manual for correct procedures.)

Q: How much battery maintenance does the CitiCar require?
A: Approximately 15 minutes per week to refill the batteries with distilled water.

Q: How long will the batteries last?
A: With proper care in accordance with the owner's manual, the batteries should last from 12,000 to 18,000 miles, under normal use.

Q: How much does replacing batteries add to the cost of operating CitiCar?
A: On the average about 2 to 3 cents per mile.

Q: How do the CitiCar batteries differ from regular car batteries?
A: These heavy-duty 6-volt batteries are designed for hundreds of recharging cycles, which electric vehicles require.

Q: How will I know when my batteries need recharging?
A: The CitiCar's voltmeter will indicate approximately when a recharge is necessary.

Q: How do I recharge the batteries?
A: The CitiCar is equipped with a built-in on-board charger. The batteries may be recharged by simply plugging the charger cord into any standard 110 volt household outlet.

Q: How long does it take to recharge the batteries?
A: Usually overnight, depending on the state of battery discharge, in turn, depending on daily mileage.

Q: How does the cold weather affect the CitiCar?
A: The efficiency of the batteries decreases proportionately to the temperature drop. If the batteries are kept in a state of charge during non-use, loss of battery efficiency can be minimized.

Q: How much does an average battery recharge cost?
A: About 25 cents, depending on local rates. The CitiCar SV-48 will go about three city miles on one KWH of electricity. Consult your local utility company to compute the per mile cost of operating a CitiCar in your area. Also, ask if your utility company sells off-peak electricity at a cheaper rate.

Q: Why not attach a generator or alternator to the CitiCar in such a way that the batteries can be recharged during operation?
A: This had not been shown to be an effective way of increasing range because more energy is required to turn the generator than is won back.

Q: Is there a chance that my CitiCar could run out of charge while on the road?
A: Not very much, unless you have forgotten to recharge the CitiCar the night before. However, if the CitiCar does run out of charge before you return home, (perhaps you had to run an unexpected errand at the end of the day,) by simply resting for 15 or 20 minutes, the batteries should recharge themselves enough to get you a mile or so further.

Q: Is air-conditioning available?
A: No, this would cause too much of a drain on the batteries. However, because the CitiCar has large side windows and because there is no engine heat to leak into the passenger compartment, air-conditioning should not be needed.

Q: Suppose I drive my CitiCar for 20 or 30 miles in the morning; can I charge up the batteries for an hour or so during lunch before going out again in the afternoon?
A: Yes, indeed. Every little bit helps. Some customers report driving as far as 70 miles a day by recharging the batteries whenever the CitiCar is not in use.

Q: I have to drive thirty miles to work every morning. Could the CitiCar meet my commuting needs?
A: If your employer will find you a place to charge up the CitiCar during the day, you should have enough charge for the return trip in the evening.

Q: Why should I buy a CitiCar instead of a small similarly-priced sub-compact?
A: In addition to the fact that the CitiCar is a good investment, an electric vehicle is inherently pollution-free and it can be operated independent of the available supplies of gasoline. Energy independence is one of our country's greatest goals and everyone must do his part to help.

Q: Who can service my CitiCar?
A: Any authorized Sebring-Vanguard, Inc. dealer. The CitiCar is designed so simply that many owners will find that they can perform most service tasks themselves. Technical assistance is always available through the Customer Service department of Sebring-Vanguard, Inc.

Q: Are replacement parts available?
A: Yes, at any authorized Sebring-Vanguard dealer, or at the Sebring-Vanguard National Service Department, Sebring, Fla. 33870.

Q: What about the motor?
A: The electric motor is a heavy-duty 3.5 HP series wound G. E. motor, designed to last for many years. Very little maintenance is required.

Q: Where can I buy a CitiCar?
A: At any authorized Sebring-Vanguard, Inc. Sales and Service dealership. Contact the National Sales Office of Sebring-Vanguard for the name of the dealer nearest you.

CitiCar tomorrow's transportation here today!

SV FORM M-1   11/75,

Exhibit 2-6
Price List for CitiCar and Optional Equipment
February 18, 1976

Code	Body Style	Sugg. Retail	Dealer
111-DW	CitiCar (Dana Differential)—Convenience & trim pkg., solid state automatic charger, separate accessory battery, vinyl roof, new silent ride drivetrain, eight 6-volt 106 min. batteries, 6HP motor, fuelless heater & defroster system, full doors with locks & sliding windows, carpeting throughout.	$2,988.00	$2,480.04
111-D	Same as 111-DW, except for full doors & sliding windows. Has removable flexible plastic side curtains with locks.	$2,888.00	$2,425.92
111-T	CitiCar (Terrell Differential)—Serial #2780 & prior. Includes convenience & trim pkg., door/window locks, Lester charger with timer, 3½ HP motor, vinyl roof, 8 6-volt, 106 minute batteries, carpeting.	$2,738,00	$2,299.92
	Colors 201—Red; 202—Orange; 203—Yellow 204—Blue; 206—White; 207—Green		
299	Custom Paint with added charge of:	57.00	38.00
	Upholstery/Vinyl Roof 301—White; 302—Black		
	Optional Equipment		
426	Hatchback, including tinted rear glass	57.00	38.00
401	Radio/Antenna	57.00	38.00
424	Tinted glass (windshield)	27.00	18.00
427	Tinted glass (front and rear)	33.00	22.00
411	Right side-view mirror	9.00	6.00
407	Hydrometer	6.00	4.00
405	Spare tire and wheel	36.00	24.00
419	Seal n Drive tire repair	4.98	4.00
423	Radial ply tires (Michelin)	72.00	48.00
412	CitiCar jack (custom)	18.00	12.00
416	Cigar lighter	7.50	5.00
418	Battery saver caps	58.50	39.00
413	All weather car cover (custom)	48.00	32.00
428	Custom rally stripes	27.00	18.00
408	Single car tilt trailer fully-equipped		

Prices subject to change without notice. All prices are FOB Sebring, FL. Dealer preparation: $35.00 (on retail only). We also have available several demonstrator Citicars especially discounted at various prices for those interested in requesting a list.

use of the CitiCar as an economical second family car, saving the "gas-powered rig" for longer trips.

The CitiCar was able to travel about three miles on each kwh of electricity, about $.01 per mile (depending on local rates), or roughly $6.00 per month. Maintenance requirements were minimal because no tune-ups or periodic parts replacements were required as for vehicles with internal combustion engines. Typical maintenance needs involved checking electrical connections to see if they were tight, tire air pressure, and maintaining batteries (charge and water levels). Exhibit 2–7 shows the recommended maintenance schedule necessary for optimal battery life and CitiCar performance. A new set of batteries was required after

Exhibit 2-7
Maintenance

For your convenience, your vehicle has been designed to give long, reliable service with the simplest and least costly maintenance requirements possible.

You play an important part in maintenance—only you can make sure that your vehicle regularly receives the care it needs.

Scheduled Maintenance Services

The following schedule of periodic servicing of your CitiCar should be adhered to closely. Daily, weekly, and monthly maintenance can usually be performed by you, the owner. We strongly recommend that more detailed servicing, at six-month intervals, be performed by an authorized Sebring-Vanguard dealer. Also, please make every effort to return your CitiCar to the selling dealer after sixty days for various required maintenance checks, as your CitiCar's warranty should be protected. If you are located so far from a Vanguard dealer as to make service visits impractical, be sure to make arrangements for equivalent servicing. The last pages of your manual are set aside to maintain a record of all scheduled servicing.

As the following services are not covered by the warranty, you will be charged for the labor, parts, and lubricants used.

Daily

Keep batteries in a constant state of charge.

Weekly or Biweekly

Check the water level of each battery. Refill as needed.

Monthly

Clear dirt, if any, from batteries. If pad protectors should deteriorate, or if new batteries are required, pads should be replaced. Tighten all terminal connections. (DO NOT OVERTIGHTEN.)
Hydrometer reading of batteries.
Check tire pressure and look for excessive wear, cuts, or other damage. Tighten wheel nuts.

Two Months After Purchase

Thorough vehicle check-up.
Change the transaxle fluid—use SAE 90-EP Nondetergent Mineral Base Oil—11 ounces.

Every Two Months

Check fluid level in rear axle.

Six Months After Purchase and Every Six Months Thereafter

Lubricate chassis—two grease fittings in front suspension. Also lubricate door hinges, parking brakes, cable guides, and linkage.
Check level of brake fluid in master cylinder. If brake fluid must be added, use Type-3 Heavy Duty. Check the brake system for possible leakage or worn out pads. Also, check brake lines and hoses for cracks, chafing, deterioration and proper attachment. Replace or repair any defective parts immediately.
Battery voltage check and battery rotation.
Check suspension and steering for damaged, loose or missing parts or parts showing visible signs of excessive wear or lack of lubrication. Defective parts should be replaced by a qualified mechanic without delay.
Check the motor brushes. Replacement of the motor brushes and the K-1 solenoid (in the controller) may be necessary when the batteries are replaced.
Check the manual steering gear for seal leakage around the pitman shaft and housing. If leakage is evident (heavy oil oozing out—not just oily film), it should be corrected immediately.
Clean underbody of road accumulation.
Clean front wheel bearings and make necessary adjustment.
Check controller points.

Every Twelve Months

Rotate tires.
Change rear axle lubricant.
Repack front wheel bearings.

Equipment Safety Checks

As an on-going check on the proper working order of the safety related features of your CitiCar, the following areas should be periodically looked at during normal use of the CitiCar. All appropriate replacements, repairs, adjustments, and cleaning of these features should be performed as soon as possible after problems are detected.

A. Safety belts	H. Horn
B. Windshield Wiper & Washer	I. Parking Brake
C. Steeering	J. Brakes
D. Tires	K. Headlights & Taillights
E. Glass Areas	L. All Running Lights
F. Mirrors	M. Underbody
G. Fluid Leaks	N. Shock Absorbers

Source: CitiCar SV-48 1975 Owner's Manual.

400 to 600 complete recharges, or every 15,000 to 20,000 miles, at a cost of approximately $300.

In December 1975, SV made available a variety of kits to dealers to enhance and update their stock of 1975 CitiCars, to make them equivalent to the newer 1976 models. The list of kits available is shown in Exhibit 2–8.

A research and development program had been established to implement design and engineering improvements. For example, the CitiCar would soon have sliding windows rather than sideflaps and a hatchback window. Other recent modifications included a fully automatic battery charger and side rocker panels.

Exhibit 2-8

Memorandum to	All Sebring-Vanguard Dealers
From	Terry R. Keller, National Parts Manager
Subject	CitiCar update
Date	December 4, 1975

Kits now are available for many of the improvements incorporated in the CitiCar since the beginning of production. We are sending this bulletin to you so you can select the items you want to update your stock to make it more appealing to prospective customers. You can choose any or all of these kits. Full instructions will accompany all items you order.

Intem Description	Part No.	Dealer Cost	Labor
1. Drip moldings 2 @ 3.95	6170–1 & 2	$ 7.90	.4
2. Rocker panels 2 @ 12.00	6827 & 8	24.00	.6
3. Disc to drum brakes	909	120.00	3.0
4. Defroster	941	14.00	1.0
5. Heater—Terrell adaption	942	69.50	2.0
6. New Pitman arm	999	15.75	.2
7. Michelin radial tires—4	10161	187.70	.8
8. Automatic charger*	10004	259.17	.7
9. Circuit breaker**	10420–1	1.50	.1
10. Carpeting for rear floor	6550	5.76	.1
11. Door locks	908	8.00	.6
12. Window locks	1011–2	7.20	.4
13. Battery saver caps	987	39.00	.4
14. Thicker seat	66616–10	48.60	—
15. Heavier cables—3	6062–7	15.57	.6
16. Door pull straps—2	6604	2.70	.4
17. External charging plug	6151–6172	9.12	.5
18. White upholstery	10023–11–12	115.74	.8
19. New style parking lights—2	6838	25.44	.2

* allowance for old charger, $70.00
** replace 40A fuse

Longer-lived batteries to extend the range of the CitiCar also were being developed by suppliers and were expected to be commercially available by 1979. Plans also were being made to introduce a CitiVan and CitiTruck on a chassis common to the CitiCar.

Mr. Stone believed that the resale value of a used CitiCar should be high due to very little depreciation. "Calculated obsolescence is not our philosophy," he said. "Since nominal maintenance is required, and very few moving parts are present, there is no reason to expect increased maintenance for older cars, as is the case with all contemporary gasoline-powered vehicles. In addition, the body of the car is made of high-impact shatter-resistant ABS Cycolac® plastic, the same material used in football helmets, which will not rust, peel, or corrode with age."

The CitiCar complied with practically all federal safety standards. An integral roll-cage-type construction surrounded the passenger compartment. Polyurethane bumpers reinforced with a steel beam protected the front and back of the car. A variety of interlock systems also were included as safety features: a shift interlock prevented the driver from inadvertently shifting into the wrong gear; the parking brake stopped the car and simultaneously shut off the power; and a charger interlock prevented the car from being driven away while still plugged in.

In October 1975 Consumers Union published their evaluation of the CitiCar in *Consumer Reports* (appendix a). The CitiCar was rated "not acceptable."

Concerning this report, Mr. Stone commented:

> *Consumer Reports* really hurt us. Unfortunately they tested an *early* model which did have substantial problems and was defective in some respects. They wouldn't let us correct the defects under the service and parts warranty. We have a superior product now. The car is much better built and more reliable, especially the controller and the new brakes, and a variety of options are now available that were not earlier.
>
> The (CU) article implied that safety problems existed because the car had been exempted from federal safety rules which require other cars to withstand low-speed crashes. The CitiCar has been exempted until June 1, 1978, only from those standards covering defrosting systems, antitheft devices, and side door strength. It meets all remaining standards that apply to every passenger car. The above exemptions were allowed by the government to facilitate development of electric vehicles (EVs). The 'lifesaving protection' for frontal and side impacts, and rollovers are not yet requirements for any vehicle, but are only proposed amendments to existing legislation.
>
> We've had difficulty combatting the inaccuracies of this report, mainly because nationwide news release of the 'findings' by many news services accompanied the issuance of the report. We can effectively fight this deleterious effect only if the local news media around each of our dealerships carry the SV news release "A Report on the Level of Safety Incorporated in the Sebring-Vanguard CitiCar" (appendix b). We are confident that once the media in a dealer's area are aware of the truth concerning safety, they will allow equal time to the dealer to report the truth about the CitiCar. Mr. Beaumont has written strong letters of encouragement to each dealer to try and keep morale and dealer support high. Many satisfied owners have written Consumers Union in protest, which is encouraging to us.
>
> The CitiCar is so unique that it's difficult to make comparisons with cars of

today, as CU has done. Society has been spoiled to expect high performance, speed, size and plush comfort. We believe that our society needs the CitiCar to help alleviate ecology, energy, and urban problems facing us today.

We are unique in another sense. We are the world's foremost producer of electric vehicles for personal transportation. There is no serious competition. The Elcar, which was also rated by *Consumer Reports,* is an Italian import, and does not have the high quality of workmanship or design that CitiCar does. There is no roll-cage construction for safety; the batteries are automotive which may have only one-fourth the life that CitiCar batteries have; shifting speeds is required while driving; Elcar does not have roll-up windows contrary to the article's claim; and their estimate of .005¢ per mile operating cost is based on electricity rates of two years ago. A more current figure is about 1¢ per mile. Finally, the cost of an Elcar is higher—$3,395 for the 35 mph (top speed) version. We expect no serious competition from the major automotive manufacturers. It would take them 10 to 12 years to make an engineering change and to undertake conceptual re-education of this magnitude.

Mr. Beaumont also added his comments concerning the viability of the CitiCar:

The most economical, abundant source of energy today for motor-powered personal transportation available is the lead-acid battery. The EV concept is very consistent with our nation's energy goals. EVs are not dependent on any one (original) source of energy. All they require is to convert that energy—coal, nuclear, geothermal, solar, etc.—to electricity to recharge the lead-acid batteries. We at SV have undertaken a giant educational process. EVs like the CitiCar now can provide a substantial portion of personal transportation almost anywhere in the world.

Pricing

One of the most appealing characteristics of the CitiCar, according to a survey of purchasers, was its price. The CitiCar was originally priced at $2,269, and the "unimproved" 1976 models still in dealer inventories were currently selling for $2,738 plus taxes, freight and dealer preparation. A price of $2,888 recently had been announced for a new model with a less noisy differential, and a price of $2,988 was to be announced on February 18, for a model with several new features, including heater and defroster, carpeting, separate accessory battery, new door and latch design, and sliding windows as shown in Exhibit 2-5. (SV management originally felt that a heater was "not essential" for small errands, etc.) Mr. Stone believed that many people felt that electric cars were much more expensive than they actually were.

Dealers were allowed a 16 percent discount from list price on the car and 33⅓ percent on all optional accessories. These trade discounts were comparable to those allowed for conventional compact and subcompact cars. For example, American Motors allowed dealers a 12 percent discount on its Gremlin. Some companies also gave the dealer no more margin on options than they received on the car. However, it should be noted that dealers were allowed higher margins, up to 20 percent and more, on bigger and more expensive conventional automobiles.

Electric Car Market

It had been estimated by a variety of trade sources and consumer surveys that over 80 percent of all motor vehicles were operated in urban areas, with average daily usage of under 22 miles at an average speed of 29 mph. Furthermore, SV estimated that the total cost to the consuming public of the gasoline-powered automobile over the last three years had been $410 billion. These costs covered the initial expense of new and used cars, gasoline, interest and insurance, depreciation, maintenance, and costs of scrapping and discarding.

"There is hardly a foreign country that has not requested (unsolicited) information in connection with manufacturing and marketing this vehicle," Mr. Beaumont had said in his testimony before a Congressional subcommittee studying energy research. "What this means is that the world is eagerly awaiting a new form of transportation. If the world can be transformed in a few short years to computer programming of all facets of business, it would seem logical that it shouldn't be difficult to teach the mass market to drive electrically. This market is simply awaiting a product."

Mr. Beaumont estimated that the U.S. government represented a large potential market for electric cars. He had learned that the U.S. General Services Administration Interagency Motor Pool had 70,574 vehicles in use as of September 30, 1975 of which 36,591 were sedans. Agency officials estimated that 10 to 15 percent of these vehicles traveled less than 30 miles per day. Military vehicles were another major potential market. Mr. Beaumont had testified before several subcommittees in the U.S. Senate and House of Representatives considering programs encouraging electric vehicle research and development.

The only available data concerning attitudes and socioeconomic backgrounds of consumers in the electric car market had been obtained from a survey of a small number of current CitiCar owners. The results of this survey are presented below. Selected comments from this survey are contained in appendix c.

CitiCar Owner Survey

Region		*Sex*	
South	48.2%	Male	60.7%
East	25.9	Female	39.3
Midwest	14.8		
Other	11.1		

Age		*Family Income*	
20–30	23.1%	Less than $10,000	10%
30–40	23.1	$10–$20,000	55
40–50	11.5	$20–$50,000	20
Over 50	42.3	Over $50,000	15

Occupation		*Reasons for Purchase*	
		(more than one could be given)	
White collar and		Economy	88.0%
professional	54.5%	Energy	40.0
Blue collar	22.8	Environment	36.0
Retired	22.7		

Use	
In town	46.0%
Commute	46.0
Other	8.0

Note: 75 percent of CitiCar owners surveyed were not in the market for a car when they purchased CitiCars.

Dealer Organization

At the beginning of 1976, CitiCar was available to the public from 200 dealers: 84 dealers in the South, 58 in the Midwest, 52 along the East coast (excluding Florida and Georgia), and 6 in the far West. The type of dealer outlet varied considerably. Of the 200 dealers, 110 to 120 were established automobile agencies franchised for one or more brands of domestic and imported cars. Ten CitiCar dealers were used-car dealers. The remaining CitiCar dealers covered a broad spectrum of retail outlets; 10 to 20 golf cart or equipment houses; 2 bicycle dealers; 2 or 3 electric motor repair dealers; 2 boat dealers; 6 recreational vehicle and/or mobile home dealers; 6 battery dealers, selling to golf courses and to industries; and one lawnmower dealer. A few of these dealers had gone into business solely for the purpose of selling CitiCars. CitiCar was available to 85 to 90 percent of the U.S. population within a 50-mile radius of one of these dealerships.

SV recommended that a dealer keep 4 to 12 CitiCars in stock (minimum requirement was 4 cars) depending on the size of the dealer's market. Unless the dealer was an already established automobile dealer, SV recommended that dealers have at least one salesperson, an office worker, and a factory-trained mechanic to handle the CitiCar. They estimated that total initial investment should be within the $10,000 to $35,000 range. No separate franchise fee was required. The only additional requirement was that the dealer send a maintenance person to Sebring for in-plant training to become expert in servicing cars. Room and board during training was provided by SV. SV used technical literature and newsletters to dealers to keep them abreast of new developments. No SV technical representatives were as yet available for back-up field support.

Although most dealerships conducted business directly with the factory, a distributor in New Jersey had been given the East coast (north of Georgia) as his exclusive territory. He developed new and existing dealerships who were required to order all their CitiCars from the distributor's inventory. The distributorship was allowed a margin of $200 for each car sold. The distributor also became a SV stockholder as part of the agreement with the company. All other new CitiCar dealers were solicited by the national sales manager, Robert Balfour, and their orders were processed and shipped from Sebring.

Approximately 1,600 CitiCars had been manufactured by the end of 1975, although half of these were still in the dealers' inventories. Retail sales (and subsequent reorders from the factory) had slowed tremendously in the past few months. The apparent lack of enthusiasm shown by the dealers was attributed in part to the effect of the *Consumer Reports* article.

Mr. Stone also feared that established automotive dealers were using CitiCar as a "traffic builder"—to lure curious potential customers into the showroom and then sell them conventional gasoline-powered cars.

Interviews were conducted by the casewriter with 2 car dealers in the Northeast who had CitiCar franchises (see appendix d). Both dealers were located near metropolitan areas. Dealer X had sold no CitiCars since he had obtained them in August, 1975. Dealer Y, a much larger dealership, had sold 16 of the 24 ordered since the spring of 1975.

In order to achieve the sales goal of 150 to 200 cars per month, Mr. Stone was considering moving away from established car dealerships as a distribution channel for CitiCar, and using other outlets, such as appliance stores and catalog stores (for example, Montgomery Ward). Other possibilities included establishment of a direct sales/service force to handle large national or industrial accounts, or to solicit and service local, state, and federal government agencies. Mr. Beaumont, however, was of the opinion that the best approach was to establish as many retail dealers as possible, with a minimum inventory of cars, but to expect that 20 percent of the dealers would account for 80 percent of sales. He argued that local availability was the key to sales.

Promotion

SV emphasized the newsworthiness of CitiCar to its dealers and relied heavily on the free publicity gained from automotive magazines, electric industry trade journals, quasi-technical lay periodicals, such as *Popular Mechanics* and *Popular Science* and magazines, such as *U. S. News and World Report, Reader's Digest, Wall Street Journal,* and *Family Circle.* In addition, heavy local news media coverage had always been generated in an area when a new CitiCar dealership had opened or following such events as the purchase of CitiCars by police forces, car-rental agencies, universities and local industries. Editorial columns had discussed CitiCar in the context of public concern for environmental, energy, and transportation problems. Further exposure had been obtained by featuring the CitiCar on national television shows, such as "The Mike Douglas Show," "The Price is Right," and "NBC Network News." The CitiCar also had been displayed in automobile shows, parades, and a variety of other public gatherings.

As Mr. Beaumont pointed out in SV's annual report for 1974–75, ". . . the free ride cannot last forever." Therefore, in December 1975, SV produced a TV commercial for $500 that it hoped to sell to dealers for $20 to $25. The 30-second commercial showed the CitiCar on a revolving pedestal and the voiceover commented on the negative features of a conventional car which the CitiCar did not have. In addition, a cooperative advertising program had been established to help dealers finance the costs of television air time and other advertising expenses. SV planned to allow dealers $25 per car ordered as reimbursement for up to 50 percent of their media costs. However, no plans for a nationwide mass media campaign had been considered. A variety of promotional aids and point of purchase displays also were available to dealerships. A listing of these materials and their cost to the dealer is shown in Exhibit 2-9.

The national sales force consisted of Mr. Balfour (the sales manager) and Mr. William Beaumont, brother of SV's president, both of whom had joined the company in late 1974. Mr. Balfour spent most of his time on the road developing new dealers, whereas Mr. William Beaumont was concerned primarily with dealer follow-up via telephone. Until very recently, Mr. Balfour had been the sole sales representative for SV and was responsible for the establishment of many new dealerships. Mr. Balfour had been involved with EVs since 1966. He was the author of numerous papers and pamphlets on lightweight vehicles and had been vice-president and sales manager of the major golf cart manufacturer that had produced the Vanguard Sport Coupe.

Mr. Balfour's major responsibility was to solicit new accounts. He traveled nationwide, with CitiCar in tow on a trailer behind his Ford LTD sedan, giving demonstration rides to prospective dealers and displaying the vehicle at car shows across the country. Mr. Stone described Mr. Balfour as ". . . the last of the great American salesmen, with the bearing and dignity of a senator. He is totally positive and is entirely committed to the EV concept. His enthusiasm is unquenchable. As a

Exhibit 2-9
Sales Materials

Order	Description	Price*
_____	Single Car Trailer (shipped via common carrier)	$332.00
_____	Exterior 4′ x 8′ Double Face Illuminated Sign	$439.00
_____	Exterior 4′ x 8′ Single Face Illuminated Sign (flush mounting)	$429.00
_____	Special Construction for Centerpost Mounting	$ 33.00 additional
_____	CitiCar Illuminated Clock/Indoor Sign 20″ x 49″ single face	$ 98.00

Dealer Name: _____

Order Date: _____

* Signs are shipped freight collect to dealers; prices are subject to change without notice.

Sales Material

The following is a list of all currently available sales aids. There is a space available for your name and address on the printed materials. Please feel free to contact me if you have any further suggestions for various marketing materials. There is a space available below for you to place an order for any sales materials you may need. Mark and return to my attention. An invoice will be sent to you when we mail the materials out.

Order	Description	Price Per Minimum Order Quantity*
_____	Answers to Questions and Specifications (revised 2/75)	$25.00 per 1000
_____	8½ x 10 Color Brochure	$ 6.00 per 100
_____	"ELECTRIC" License Plates	$ 1.50 each
_____	Electric Vehicle News Subscription	$10.00 per year
_____	Customer Order Form—2 page	$ 5.00 per 50
_____	T-Shirt ("Give Mother Nature a Break— Buy an Electric CitiCar)	$ 3.50 each (in quantities of 6 doz.—$3.25 each)

Dealer Name: _____

Order Date: _____

* Price does not include postage and handling; prices are subject to change without notice.

result, his credibility level is very high. He has been an inspiration to many of us." The absence of technical representatives and an adequate field sales force made follow-through and support of a fledgling dealership difficult. Some people did feel that Mr. Balfour was too enthusiastic initially and had a tendency to oversell the CitiCar.

In addition to Mr. Balfour's efforts, the New Jersey distributor had one sales representative to solicit new accounts. The distributor also helped new dealerships with promotional campaigns.

Promotional efforts of a different nature were being undertaken as well. The environmental and energy problems of the 1970s prompted the U.S. government to investigate and fund proposed alternatives to existing energy and transportation technologies.

In the autumn of 1975, the "Electric Vehicle Research, Development and Demonstration Act of 1975" was passed by the House of Representatives (HR 5470) establishing a $160 million project over a 3-year period whereby "production and use within one year of several thousand electric vehicles designed about *existing* vehicle chassis ('as yet unnamed) and then within three years several thousand vehicles would be introduced . . . to insure . . . widespread use." This would allow performance and maintenance standards to be established and an adequate evaluation program of the "electrical concept" to be initiated. Other R&D work would be authorized for control systems, overall optimal design, and environmental and urban impact. Passage of this bill was believed by SV executives to be partly due to the testimony of Mr. Beaumont, as an expert on electrical vehicle technology.

Mr. Beaumont commented:

> If our government will encourage the use of electric vehicles by funding a program, let the funds be made available only to companies with experience and background in small vehicle manufacturing (preferably electric) and/or those companies willing to participate as peripheral component suppliers. We definitely must not squander taxpayers' money on banal and redundant study papers that gather dust in the archives. The net effect of any funding program must be based on providing value for monies expended. What is needed is one company to thrive; then others will most certainly follow.

Mr. Beaumont and SV were planning continued major lobbying efforts to ensure complete passage of the bill and hopefully to ensure favorable dispensation for SV or its suppliers for government contracts. In February of 1976, this legislation was in the Senate Commerce Committee.

Consumer Reports Evaluation of the CitiCar*

Two Electric Cars

Electric cars have been marketed without much success since before the turn of the century. In recent years, concern over air pollution caused by the internal combustion engine and the rising cost of gasoline have revived interest in electric cars. CU therefore decided to test the only two electric cars being sold in any volume in this country: the *CitiCar SV-48* and the *Elcar 2000*. We found major safety and operating problems.

The *CitiCar*, made by Sebring-Vanguard, Inc., of Sebring, Fla., cost $2946 delivered to our Auto Test Center in Connecticut. The *Elcar*, an Italian import distributed in the U.S. by Elcar Corp., Elkart, Ind., cost $3475 delivered.

Conventional passenger cars must conform to certain Federal safety standards. But to spur the development of low-emission vehicles, the Government has granted temporary exemptions from some of those standards to manufacturers of electric cars—with unfortunate results.

Conventional cars must provide life-saving protection to occupants in a 30-mph barrier crash, a 30-mph rollover, and a 20-mph side impact from another car. We believe any such crash would imperil the lives of persons inside these tiny, fragile, plastic-bodied vehicles. A rollover or a severe crash holds the further threat of sulfuric acid pouring from ruptured batteries. (The batteries are under the padded-plywood seat cushion in the *CitiCar* and under the plywood floor in the *Elcar*—both within the passenger compartments.)

There are other obvious hazards no longer tolerated in conventional automobiles. Adjusting the safety belts is discouragingly complicated. Yet the windshield frame in the *Citi-Car* is just a few inches in front of the forehead of tall occupants, making the use of shoulder belts especially important. The *Elcar's* safety belts are not much better.

CITICAR SV-48

The *CitiCar* has no steering-wheel lock, and the doors cannot be locked. The hinges and latches looked so flimsy that we tied the doors shut before performing any emergency-handling tests. (The *Elcar's* door hardware also looked flimsy, but at least the doors and steering column had locks.)

In both cars, very wide front and rear roof pillars interfere with the driver's view, as do single wipers in the center of the windshields. The spare tires are free to roll around behind the seats and could cause injury in an accident.

The *CitiCar* has a welded-aluminum "roll cage" intended to keep the plastic body from collapsing during a collision; we doubt that it provides as much protection as a well-designed steel body. But steel is heavy, of course, and would make the car even slower than it already is.

The *Elcar* has yet another mark against it: Its suspension is too flimsy to cope with even the low level of performance of which the vehicle is capable. During hard braking tests from 30 mph, the front suspension collapsed, putting an emphatic end to our testing of the *Elcar*.

The manufacturer of the *CitiCar* specifically warns owners that the vehicle should be used only on roads where the speed limit does not exceed 50 mph. The *Elcar* is promoted simply as "perfect on-street transportation for in-town use." But we believe it would be foolhardy to drive either car on any public road. Neither provides anything close to adequate crash protection; and neither handles or accelerates well enough to give us confidence that they're capable of getting out of a tight spot.

CU hopes experiments with electric cars continue. A practical, safe, economical electric car might be just right as a second car limited to short commutes and shopping trips. But neither the *CitiCar* nor the *Elcar* is practical, safe, or economical. We rate both of them Not Acceptable.

On the two pages that follow we report on our tests of these two cars in more detail. However, the results are presented primarily to satisfy the understandable curiosity about electric cars, not as the basis for a rational purchase.

ELCAR 2000

The *CitiCar* is a two-seater, 95 inches long and 55 inches wide. Ours weighs 1303 pounds, including a propane heater ($90) for the occupants and a spare tire and wheel ($36). The *Elcar* also is a two-seater, but it is only 84 inches long and 53 inches wide. Ours weighs 1145 pounds.

The *CitiCar's* 3.5-horsepower motor is powered by eight six-volt batteries similar to those used in golf carts. The accelerator pedal actuates a three-way speed control. Step down one notch and a resistor allows a smooth take-off by limiting the amount of voltage to the motor. Depressing the accelerator pedal further feeds 24 volts to the motor. Stepping down on the accelerator pedal all the way supplies 48 volts to the motor for maximum speed. A built-in charger (photo, below left) plugs into a household outlet to recharge the batteries.

The *Elcar* has a smaller motor rated at 2.7 hp and powered by eight 12-volt batteries. Its electrical controls are more complicated than the *CitiCar's*. A rotary actuator on a column (much like those in old-time trolley cars—see photo, below right) provides three positions: 24 volts, 36 volts, and 48 volts. There's also an accelerator pedal that provides two speeds in each selector position, for a total of six forward speeds. For maximum cruising speed, one flicks a "booster power" toggle switch when in the third selector position. A charger is included in the price of the *Elcar*, but it is not mounted on board. We mounted ours in the rear compartment.

IS ELECTRICITY A CHEAP FUEL?

To test the batteries' endurance, we ran each car repeatedly around a substantially level one-mile course, permitting the car to rest for one minute after each mile and for 15 minutes every half hour. That cycle

was designed to simulate an urban drive with several shopping stops.

With the temperature at about 80°F., the *CitiCar* was able to run 33.6 miles on that cycle and then required 14 kilowatt hours (kwh) to recharge fully. In the New York City area, where a kwh costs about nine cents, the energy cost per mile would be 3.7 cents; in some areas, it might be as low as 1.2 cents. By comparison, if the *Honda Civic CVCC* (see page 625) delivered its city mileage of 21 mpg in that same cycle, fuel cost per mile would be about three cents, assuming gasoline at 60 cents a gallon.

The *CitiCar* does not need the oil changes and tune-ups that the *Honda* and other gasoline-burning cars require. However, the *CitiCar* will require a new set of batteries after 400 to 600 recharges, or about 11,000 to 16,000 miles. The batteries would cost about $320, plus labor.

In the same urban shopping cycle, the *Elcar* was able to run 33.2 miles and required 12.8 kwh to recharge the batteries. That figures out to 3.5 cents per mile where electricity costs nine cents per kwh. The *Elcar* would also need new batteries every 11,000 to 16,000 miles. Cost: $250 to $300, plus labor.

Thus, where electricity is relatively expensive, neither electric car would be cheaper to run than the most economical of standard subcompacts.

A BATTERY OF WOES

How well (or, more precisely, how poorly) these cars perform depends a great deal on the outside temperature. For example, during the summer, our *CitiCar's* useful range without rest periods was about 20 miles; but when the temperature fell to 40°F., the batteries needed to be

recharged after less than 10 miles. A full charge usually took more than eight hours.

Other factors affect range. Running at top speed (32.5 mph for the *CitiCar*, 30 mph for the *Elcar*) drains batteries relatively quickly. So does driving in hilly country. Because the headlights of both the *CitiCar* and the *Elcar* dimmed to virtual uselessness by the time half the charge had been consumed, you couldn't (or shouldn't) drive these cars more than about 15 miles after dark.

Acceleration was slow. The *CitiCar* required 17.7 seconds to reach 30 mph. The *Elcar* couldn't quite get up to 30 mph on our test track; it took an excruciating 27.5 seconds to reach 29.5 mph, dangerously slow acceleration even for city streets. Hill-climbing ability of both cars was poor.

The handling of these vehicles hardly inspired driver confidence. During sharp steering maneuvers, the *CitiCar* at first plowed straight ahead; then it would suddenly swing its rear end rapidly to and fro. Bumps caused the car to hop sideways, off course; that characteristic was aggravated by the *CitiCar's* violent ride motions, which caused the driver to turn the steering wheel unintentionally.

The breakdown of the *Elcar's* front suspension prevented us from performing formal handling tests on that vehicle. But the *Elcar* felt tippy and directionally unstable during normal driving. As in the *CitiCar*, the steering was very quick and unpredictable.

Our braking tests went no better. The *CitiCar's* nonpower brakes (discs in front, drums in rear) required high pedal effort —about 120 pounds to lock the wheels. From 30 mph, the *CitiCar* stopped in 51 feet with no wheels locked and in 43 feet with all wheels locked and the tires sliding. Directional stability was not good; the car swerved and pulled, generally coming to a stop at about a 45-degree angle from the direction of travel.

The *Elcar*, with its nonpower all-drum brakes, weaved and leaned sharply when braking from 30 mph. During one hard stop, it almost rolled over. When we tried to stop shorter than about 70 feet, the rear axle hopped. Our shortest stop, 47 feet, involved a sharp veer to the left.

INCONVENIENCE, DISCOMFORT

One would imagine that small electric cars would be most useful for short shopping trips in urban and suburban areas. But

Built-in charger and an optional propane heater take up foot space in the *CitiCar*.

***Elcar's* speed is controlled by rotary actuator (in the hand of the driver above).**

even here, the *CitiCar* and the *Elcar* fell down. Neither vehicle has a rear opening, so one must fold the seatback forward and load shopping bags through the narrow door openings. In the *CitiCar*, a horizontal bar that supports the seatback obstructs

access to the cargo area. And in the *Elcar*, the seatback doesn't stay folded without a prop. Neither car can hold more than a few small packages.

The seats in both cars were too firm and gave inadequate support. In the *Elcar*, the seat cushions can be adjusted both forward and backward. When tall drivers adjusted the *Elcar's* seat all the way back, they found the leg room adequate—but then the steering wheel was too far away. The small brake pedal was too far to the right. Protruding wheel housings limited foot room for the driver and passenger. Entry and exit were difficult.

The seat in the *CitiCar* allows no adjustment. You either fit comfortably or you don't (most CU drivers didn't). Leg room was very tight. The optional propane heater encroached on the passenger's foot room, the steering wheel was too far to the right, and the brake and accelerator pedals were awkwardly high and close. Entry and exit were difficult. The inside mirror not only threatened one's head during entry, but it was distractingly close to the driver's eye.

The *Elcar's* door windows slide horizontally rather than rolling down. They gave adequate protection from the elements. The *CitiCar*, however, has only drafty, flimsy side curtains like those of many early British sports cars.

One might expect an electric car to be quiet. The *CitiCar* and the *Elcar* are quiet only when stopped. At 30 mph on a coarse road, our sound measurements showed the *CitiCar* to be the noisiest vehicle we have tested this year—about as noisy as the *Honda Civic CVCC* was at 60 mph.

The failure of the *Elcar's* front suspension prevented us from recording that vehicle's noise levels, but the *Elcar* seemed to us at least as noisy inside as the *CitiCar*.

The *CitiCar* felt as if it had no springs at all. The car rode uncomfortably on every type of road surface. The *Elcar's*

independent suspension gave a somewhat less painful ride. Even so, the car bobbed busily on all but the smoothest roads.

MISCELLANEOUS COMPLAINTS

The *Elcar* has no fresh-air ventilation system. Even with the windows open, the car was hot and stuffy in the summer. The *Elcar* also lacks a heater or defroster, perhaps a concession to the fact that cold weather makes the car's range impractically short anyway. In its petition for exemption from Federal safety standards, the manufacturer of the *Elcar* claimed that the sliding windows would alleviate fogging—but that proved true only when the car was moving.

What fresh air entered the *CitiCar* came in mainly past the ill-fitting side curtains. In cold weather, the constant draft was unpleasant. A switch labeled "defroster" is a dummy. According to the owner's manual, it's "not functional on most models." The optional propane heater was hard to light and modulate. And it quickly fogged all the windows (one of the products of the heater's combustion is water vapor).

In our opinion, most of the many serious breakdowns that afflicted our *Elcar* were design flaws. Our *Elcar* sat in the shop awaiting parts or undergoing repair for a total of 74 days—more than half the time we owned it—until its virtual demise. The main power fuses for the high speed ranges blew repeatedly for no apparent reason during the 370 miles we drove the car. We had to order replacement fuses from the distributor. Each time a fuse blew, we limped home in low speed range and waited for a new fuse to arrive. Recently, the distributor shipped us a circuit breaker to replace the fuse box—a much-needed improvement scheduled for future production.

At just over 100 miles, a short circuit produced a brilliant flash of light from the headlights, and the wiper went berserk, wiping at a frantic pace. According to the distributor, such short circuits occur occasionally, because of inadequate accessory wiring design. We received a wiring kit to correct the defect.

Loose connections at the main power fuse box resulted in a loud clicking noise from the turn-signal flasher when we tried to charge the batteries. That flasher, incidentally, was another weak component; it had to be replaced twice.

At 210 miles, the differential gears disintegrated during normal driving and the car ground to a halt. The replacement gears lasted another 160 miles before crumbling during our braking tests.

The horn failed when grease from the steering column fouled the switch contacts. A moderate tug on the parking-brake handle caused the parking-brake assembly to break in two. The wiper arm, retained only by a set screw, slipped on its drive shaft. The final blow was the suspension failure mentioned earlier.

Our *CitiCar* never left us completely stranded during the time we owned it, although it gave us some anxious moments, as the diary on the facing page indicates. The *CitiCar* suffered from fewer defects than the *Elcar*, and most of those were caused by sloppy manufacture rather than by design flaws. However, four defects were serious. After about 125 miles, the warning light for motor overheating went on even though the motor was only normally warm. At 370 miles, a loose wiring connection caused the voltmeter to flicker and the horn to fail. Most serious, the steering wheel retaining nut was very loose, and all the spring fasteners in the front and rear suspension were loose; had those items gone unnoticed, they could have caused an accident.

THE FUTURE OF ELECTRIC CARS

These two electric cars are clearly unsuitable for any normal transportation function. But the main safety and design problems are solvable, either in these cars or in future competitors.

Whether there is any future for the concept of electric cars probably depends on how well they compete in fuel economy and cleanliness with vehicles powered by internal combustion engines. At this point, electric cars are no cheaper to run than such economical subcompacts as the *Honda Civic CVCC* and the *Volkswagen Rabbit*—at least not where electricity is costly. And, of course, those two subcompacts and others like them are not limited to trips of under 30 miles at speeds of less than 30 mph.

The cleanliness of electric cars is another open question. Electric cars themselves produce no air-fouling emissions. But most of the generating plants that produce the electricity needed to recharge the cars' batteries do produce emissions. Advocates of the electric car maintain that generating plants are more efficient than the internal-combustion engine, and that generating plants can disperse emissions high into the atmosphere, rather than concentrating them in city streets. Others, however, point out that wide use of electric cars might require double or triple the present electrical generating capacity of the country. At this writing, Congress is considering initiating a program, under the authority of the Energy Research and Development Administration, to explore further the feasibility of electric vehicles. Such exploration is obviously required.

Notes from an Auto Tester's Diary

Notes from an Auto Tester's Diary

CU's auto testers customarily familiarize themselves with vehicles by driving them to and from work and on errands before and during the formal testing program. Here is how it went with one of CU's testers during a day of driving the CitiCar:

8:00 A.M.: Went out to car, unplugged battery charger, and coiled up the extension cord. Wiped dew off glass with hand-

kerchief. Got in, buckled up with some difficulty. Glass fogged again from my breath. Wiped glass again. Switched on power and stepped gingerly on accelerator. Powertrain screams. Fluttering along at top speed, about 30 mph, with unsteady siren emanating from somewhere below the seat. More window wiping to keep pace with breathing. Fairly smooth road tosses the little plastic box so violently that steering a steady course is difficult.

The scream from the powertrain drops in pitch, and the speedometer needle plummets. Momentary panic--then realize the car is negotiating a slight grade, one I hardly ever noticed in other cars. Car climbs slowly but steadily. Incredulous glances from other motorists. Otherwise, the remainder of the trip to work is uneventful.

5:00 P.M.: Returning from work. Confidence builds. Ignore catcalls. Pleased about all the gasoline I'm saving.

8:05 P.M.: After dinner, daughter asks for a ride to friend's house, three miles away. So far, car has gone just 10 miles to and from work. Should be no problem; manufacturer claims at least 25 miles on full charge. On return trip, decide to detour to cigar store in next town, another five miles, for a total of 21 miles. On the way, car lacks zip. But battery indicator shows plenty of charge left.

8:20 P.M.: Getting dark. Coasting down hill to cigar store, turn on headlights. Buy a magazine, start for home.

8:25 P.M.: With the lights of town behind me, notice only faint orange glow on pavement from headlights. Can hardly see road ahead. Let up on throttle, lights brighten appreciably. Feeling uneasy. Switch off headlights and drive along on parking lights.

8:30 P.M.: Instrument-panel light now dull orange. Car really slowing down. Pull to right as far as possible to let line of cars behind pass.

8:35 P.M.: The car with the red blinker doesn't pass. Police. Park and explain to officer that stopping 10 minutes or so would allow batteries to recover. Officer mumbles to himself, drives off. All power off, waiting.

8:47 P.M.: Apply power. Car leaps forward as if fully rejuvenated. Proceed without headlights, just to be sure.

8:50 P.M.: Spurt of energy lasts only about one mile. Back at the side of the road. Watch mirror

for approaching cars; when one comes along, on with emergency flasher for just a few blinks.

9:05 P.M.: Start out again. Progress obviously labored. Creep to a halt after another quarter-mile, at the foot of a small rise.

9:20 P.M. Patience near end. Only quarter-mile more to go. Two more rest stops needed.

9:45 P.M.: Finally roll down driveway. Driver and batteries both drained.

Safety Level Incorporated in the Sebring-Vanguard Electric CitiCar

Energy, air pollution, gas prices—major topics of today—are making millions of people around the country look at the newly discovered advantages of electric cars. In response to the growing needs of the American people, Sebring-Vanguard, Inc. of Sebring, Florida, has developed CitiCar, perhaps the most advanced car on the road today.

CitiCar was designed with more than energy-efficiency, economy, and pollution control in mind. CitiCar may soon be regarded as one of the safest motor vehicles in automotive history.

High vehicle performance is an important factor in the overall safety of the electric CitiCar. CitiCar was designed to become integrated into city and town traffic patterns. The characteristics of electric propulsion are such that acceleration capabilities far exceed average traffic requirements. From 0 to 25 mph takes 6.2 seconds. The CitiCar's top speed is 38 mph which is consistent with speed limit laws in urban and suburban areas. Maneuverability of the CitiCar is exceptional permitting the CitiCar's operator to respond to tight traffic situations. CitiCar has been designed with a high profile and bright body colors to be seen easily. Four-wheel brakes are on all CitiCars, the 1976 version incorporating a newly designed 4-wheel Bendix drum brake system. Because of its light weight, the CitiCar's stopping distances meet or exceed those of most other conventional car models available today.

Maximizing crashworthiness in a small lightweight electric car was no easy task for Sebring-Vanguard designers and yet the results may put CitiCar on the top of the list of safety vehicles. To maximize passenger safety without adding excessive weight, Sebring-Vanguard departed from conventional auto design and adapted aircraft technology to this new 4-wheel form of personal transportation. CitiCar's frame includes an aircraft aluminum alloy roll-cage body-support structure which totally surrounds the passenger compartment. The CitiCar body is made of high-impact space age plastic called Cycolac ABS, the same material from which football helmets are made. Any Sebring-Vanguard dealer would be happy to demonstrate how tough and resilient this material is.

In testing and in real life accidents where front-end, rear, and even broadside collisions occurred, the CitiCar and its pasengers have held up admirably. The record should speak for itself: CitiCars have been on the road now for over one year. There are more than 800 in daily use around the country and, having clocked an estimated total of three million vehicle miles to date, there have been no fatalities nor injuries more serious than a broken leg. Hit from any conceivable angle, a CitiCar is likely to remain upright due to the strategic placement of 500 lbs. of lead-acid batteries located along the lower center of the car. The CitiCar's widetrack makes for great stability in normal driving conditions and in emergency situations.

Although all of the above-mentioned safety features represent a new and effective approach to motor vehicle safety, the superior long-range safety record of the CitiCar probably will be more closely linked to a more important safety feature than those. The National Safety Council reports that most auto fatalities occur at high speeds. Sebring-Vanguard is the first modern auto manufacturer to develop a passenger car with a top speed of under 40 mph, designed for in-town driving in low-speed areas. While all other conventional auto manufacturers, both domestic and imported, are building large and small fragile passenger cars with speed capabilities of 30, 40, and even 50 miles greater than federal speed limit laws permit, Sebring-Vanguard believes that a responsible car manufacturer should design a car to travel only as fast as that at which the car's occupants can be protected in the event of a collision at top speed. For, if a driver is intoxicated or in any other way loses control of his conventional 2500 lb. car, and inadvertently depresses the accelerator pedal, the lives of pedestrians and other motorists are threatened.

With a top speed of only 38 mph the likelihood of such massive death and destruction from a CitiCar is largely eliminated. Therefore, CitiCar represents the first serious attempt of a manufacturer to develop a totally safe passenger car no matter at what speed the car is being driven. The success of Sebring-Vanguard's CitiCar demonstrates that passenger protection can be maximized without turning the vehicle into a veritable weapon.

Owner confidence in the high level of safety became evident in the spring of 1975 when Sebring-Vanguard petitioned the United States Department of Transportation for an exemption from certain safety standards. (It should be noted that all standards in effect were developed based on the design configuration of the conventional automobile.) A total of 45 letters were received by the Department of Transportation unanimously supporting our petition. Most of the letters were from CitiCar customers who indicated that the level of safety in the CitiCar was more than adequate for the type of use that the CitiCar was designed for. Customer letters received at Sebring-Vanguard regularly, overwhelmingly corroborate this opinion.

Sebring-Vanguard wishes not only to improve public safety from the standpoint of CitiCar passengers, pedestrians, and other motor vehicle operators, but also to improve the quality of life and public safety in our total environment. The National Academy of Sciences recently reported that as many as four thousand people a year die from air pollution directly attributed to the conventional gasoline-operated automobile. In spite of federally-mandated pollution control devices, there is good reason to believe that these devices are either disconnected, removed, or do not operate properly on millions of cars around the country, thus eliminating the benefit from these controls. In contrast, air pollution from power plants generating electricity to recharge CitiCar batteries is significantly less than the air pollution coming from a conventional car on a per mile basis, and it is much easier to further curtail pollution from one power plant than from thousands of individually owned conventional cars. Although figures are not yet available, it is now known that the CitiCar's electric motor produces a small amount of ozone which, if reaching the upper atmosphere, may help shield the earth against harmful cancer-causing radiation. Therefore, the widespread use of electric vehicles would not only reduce conventional forms of pollution, but may also add to the earth's shield against radiation.

In conclusion, the electric CitiCar represents a lot more than a significant means of reducing America's dependence on foreign oil. CitiCar represents the form personal transportation will take in the future. Someday most commuters, housewives, students, businesses, and government will use this type of vehicle for the "around town" driving which makes up as much as 75 percent of the driving done in America. The development of Sebring-Vanguard's CitiCar is an important step in that direction and, as this transition in personal transportation occurs, we should witness a gradual improvement in America's traffic safety record and in environmental quality.

appendix c

Owners' Comments on the CitiCar

We find the speed and range of the CitiCar adequate to handle most errands.

Am satisfied so far but time will be necessary for the car to prove itself.

So ugly it is beautiful.

I love the car, and have done a considerable amount of advertising for your company. Thank you very much.

You have a good thing going and so do we.

Other than a few other (quality) things, I think it is a pretty nice little car.

After sale the dealer seemed indignant because he sold me a car which did not perform. I requested service to repair the car and it has been sitting there for four days without full service performed.

Fun and economical, too.

The heater is a $90 ripoff—it's worth about $15 and doesn't turn on the way the instructions say.

Is the CitiCar made to climb hills? I have burned out two fuses already. Our town is all hills.

Car is too expensive for what is offered. Engineering is not the best. Great fun to drive, though—provides great conversational item.

We have heard a great deal about warranty service problems. Mechanics don't want to do warranty repairs because, they say, the factory is too slow in paying them for their work—like five or six months. I might be the one needing warranty service (at some future time).

We wish the range and speed were extended, but we know the cost would be out of our range if you did this.

Salesman was very accommodating. However, seems very unenthusiastic about the CitiCar. A very negative attitude.

We like it when it is running, but we've had a lot of trouble with it. The dealer has been very nice about it, though—and more cooperative than Sebring-Vanguard. I hope we have the bugs worked out by now.

(Source: 1975 Survey of Owners Conducted by Sebring-Vanguard, Inc.)

appendix d

Interview Summary with Two CitiCar Dealers

Dealer X

This dealership was located in a somewhat economically depressed suburb of a metropolitan area. The dealer carried a major domestic automobile franchise as well as several foreign import lines. When the interviewer entered the dealership, no CitiCar or SV advertisements were visible. The CitiCar was in the back of the showroom, relatively obscure in its niche behind a large pillar.

Dealer X commented:

I think the concept is great—the electric car is here to stay. I don't mind pioneering, but remember, I'm not the average consumer either. *This* electric car as it is now will never make it without modifications, a lot of the right kind of advertising, and changes in dealer relationships with the factory.

To sum up the product, the CitiCar needs to be made more utilitarian or more sexy, for example, a hatchback for shoppers' convenience; quality locks and lockable windows are needed on the doors. Can you expect shoppers to carry all of their bundles with them while they complete their errands because they can't lock their car? Some customers comment that the interior looks 'cheap'—the switches, instruments, etc.—and the seats are really uncomfortable. There's no heater in the models I have. (Note: They were all 1975 models.) I don't mind sideflaps, even in a snowstorm, but again, I'm not the average, middle-income suburbanite, either. Most of these changes will come with time, and the adventuresome early owners of CitiCar will put up with the inconvenience.

The car will never be a second family car, but rather a third car. It's too small for a family with school-age children. What about taking the kids and their friends to and from Girl Scouts or Little League practice? The only way that the CitiCar will become a second car for families is if mass transportation to and from the inner city becomes more prevalent. The breadwinner drives the CitiCar to and from the mass transit terminal, thus freeing the bigger car for family use.

The CU report hit hard. It's unfortunate that they compared EVs with standard cars, because they *are* different. However, that's exactly what the consuming public will do. Contrary to the implications in the report, the car is very durable. It withstood a 20-mph crash one of my salesmen had with a steel post. We were all impressed.

The best advertising I know of is to get the cars on the road. All of the free press and radio coverage I received when we got the CitiCar in netted me very few inquiries. Most inquiries have come from either passers-by who saw it in the showroom window, or who saw me driving it. Even then, most people are just curious. I've had very few spinoff sales of my regular line because of the CitiCar. Maybe I'm just in a bad marketing area. . . . As to TV advertising, you're selling a concept, not just another car. It would take a lot of money and a variety of approaches for television to be effective.

The margins are satisfactory. There are ways to control your actual margin. It's similar to other cars of the same price range. However, the older salesman scarcely try to push them, apparently because they have been selling conventional cars for so long that they don't want to relearn their trade. The younger people seem to take a greater interest in trying to sell the CitiCar.

My big complaint is with the quality of factory support. Don't forget, we sell service as much as we sell cars—50 percent of my revenue is from service. I've been five months waiting for replacement parts from the factory for the car that was damaged. How can my sales force stay motivated and sell a product in good faith when the necessary factory follow-through is not forthcoming? And another thing, it's aggravating to put in an order for $600 worth of parts and get a shipment billed for $900, after they throw in 'extras' I didn't want or need.

The way the procedures are set up now, as they iron out problems at the factory, I'm stuck with obsolete cars, updated eventually by us with those 'kits.' They need to work out a trade-in allowance system to replace obsolete cars with the improved versions, rather than requiring dealer on-site modification. They could do the modifications a lot better at the factory. That certainly would boost our morale, and should help guarantee customer service.

How can I do a good job selling these (pointing to a luxurious 'Detroit special')

The interviewer then chatted with one of the "older salesmen." He said,

if I try to push those CitiCars? It's like slitting my own throat. I'm here to sell cars, not to convince people of their duty to confront the problems facing us today. I could really lose customers fast. Anyway, it's tough to sell them (the CitiCar) when they're 'tied' to a plug. Sure, gasoline cars are 'tied' to gas pumps, but there are a lot of gas stations conveniently located, aren't there? The range isn't nearly as good as for a gasoline car either—that will bug people. No, electrics will never have a chance against regular cars . . .

Dealer Y

This dealership also was located near a metropolitan area. It was a large agency carrying two major makes of U.S. cars. When the interviewer entered the showroom, the CitiCar was prominently displayed, as were other SV signs and displays. The general manager for the dealership commented,

We like these little cars, and have been moderately successful in merchandising them. We've sold two-thirds of our inventory since we've had them. In addition, it has been an effective traffic builder for the agency. At first, the novelty appeal to the buyer was overwhelming, and the free advertising brought about by the news releases was heartening, but all that wears off fast. We've had to advertise and promote the CitiCar on its merits. It will never replace the gasoline-powered car, but will complement it nicely for city and town use.

We think it's a good buy for the money. The consumer is getting exactly what's advertised, even for the outdated 1975 models—a safe, economical, clean car for city use *only*. Any car travelling at 35 mph on an interstate highway is unsafe.

The car is very well built. We've had two occasions to observe CitiCars in collisions, resulting only in superficial damage to it, but with expensive repair work required for the other (standard) car involved. The illusion of flimsiness due to the great flexibility of the plastic used in the body was dispelled by these incidents.

We felt that CU was unfair in many aspects in its report. It's my understanding that they tested a defective, early model, rather than one of the new models. The 1976 Cars are much improved, and the kits now are available to update the earlier cars as well. Soon, we even expect to see glass windows and other more standard and useful features as CitiCar evolves and becomes more generally accepted. The transportation industry always has been evolutionary, but changes take time.

Margins are never as high as we want them. However, the margins offered by SV are comparable to other cars in the same price range, presenting no real problems. I don't think we have a problem with the older salesmen. They sell CitiCars just as other salesmen working for us do.* Obviously, though, we have

---

* Note: Excerpt from a customer who purchased a CitiCar from this dealership and responded to the "CitiCar Survey:"

Question: Were you treated courteously at the dealership?

Answer: Yes—exceptionally accommodating—However, seems very unenthusiastic about the CitiCar. A very negative attitude.

to make comparisons with standard cars concerning economy, comfort, and so forth.

Yes, the CitiCar will require a little more fussiness by the owner—checking cables and adding distilled water periodically and so forth. However, these services can be performed at any garage at a small charge to the owner, and labor costs will be minimal compared to standard maintenance required for gasoline engines.

Although the CitiCar is not particularly lucrative now, we think that electric cars are the car of the future for urban use. We firmly believe that the majority of Americans will want to own one, but they don't necessarily want to be the 'first ones on the block.'

McDonald's Corporation

Larry J. Rosenberg, New York University

Corporate Background: Big Mac Gets Bigger

McDonald's Corporation is one of the best known companies in America and is increasingly becoming one of the best known in the world. It qualifies as a legend in the history of modern marketing success stories. In 1955, McDonald's opened its first fast-food outlet in Des Plaines, Illinois, not too far from its current head-quarters on McDonald's Plaza, Oak Brook, Illinois. The current chain of 4,000 restaurants is in all 50 states and 21 countries. Seventy percent of these outlets are licensed to independent firms, called "franchisees," and 30 percent of the outlets are directly owned by McDonald's. Hardly any of these restaurants has failed.

The 1976 sales volume was $2.7 billion, making it the largest food service in the world—with a 19.6 percent share of market. By September 1976, the sign posted near the "golden arches" outside each McDonald's outlet boasted 20 billion hamburgers sold. Although it took eight years for the company to sell its first billion burgers, it now takes only four months for the sign to be revised another billion. In 1976, McDonald's spent $100 million on advertising. Profit has steadily increased with an average annual rise of 40 percent.

Growth has clearly been the driving force of McDonald's 2-decade history. Coinciding with increasing population and the great expansion of the suburbs, McDonald's has added more restaurants and significantly raised the sales volume per restaurant. The modern building, "golden arches," and parking lot have become familiar fixtures on the American suburban landscape.

In pursuing its growth objectives in the mid-1970s, McDonald's has vigorously placed outlets within cities—including downtown areas and shopping avenues adjacent to residential neighborhoods as small as 25,000 population. These restaurants usually have no parking lots and the architecture is adapted to the tighter space requirements of city properties.

McDonald's management has been surprised by the increasing eruption of community groups protesting building local McDonald's restaurants. These reactions have occurred mainly in urban neighborhoods, but also in some suburban communities as well.

What Shall We Do About West 86th Street?*

The place is the McDonald's Eastern Regional Office, in Bloomfield, New Jersey, a suburb of New York City. The date is March 15, 1975. A meeting of 3 executives is about to begin in preparation for tomorrow's confrontation with a neighborhood group opposing the location of a McDonald's restaurant in its community at 168 West 86th Street, Manhattan, the major borough of New York City. The protest leaders claim to have a petition with 3,000 signatures against the proposed outlet at a major intersection of the Upper West Side. This area is populated by diverse ethnic groups, artists, professionals, and the elderly, and most are living in fairly old, once elegant, high-rise apartment buildings and 3-story townhouses.

Today's meeting is chaired by Henry Pace, assistant regional manager—a hardliner regarding expansion in Manhattan. In the last 2 years, he supervised opening 13 restaurants (there is a total of 40 in New York City). Also at the meeting is Mary Lambert, director of public information, who advocates image building and careful compromise. The third participant is Kenneth Roman, senior market analyst, who has considered the community point of view to which he has recently been personally exposed and about which he feels there may be some merit.

Growth Is Great

Henry Pace, at 45 years of age, is an assistant regional manager with responsibility for directing the expansion of the McDonald's chain in New York City. Although he did not graduate from college, he has advanced as the McDonald's organization grew. Next month he will be considered for promotion to vice-president, which would give him prestige and a host of excellent fringe benefits. He has worked hard to attain this goal, and he dreams of little else.

Success at McDonald's has meant expansion in a number of outlets and sales. His record in Manhattan has been excellent; however, top management has expressed displeasure at his cancellation of plans for 2 other Manhattan outlets in the face of community protests.

Pace feels McDonald's has been a national, indeed an American cultural, success. Virtually every new outlet does well, demonstrating that McDonald's is meeting consumer demand for, as he puts it, "good, cheap food." Location decisions are based on solid marketing research. First, the company studies demographic data (which neighborhoods have the population to support a new McDonald's and how intense the competition is). Second, it pursues the goal of providing convenient locations in already commercially-zoned areas. Pace knows that McDonald's has an economic right to try to satisfy existing consumer demand and a legal right to

---

* The meeting and characters described in this case are fictional. But the account of the McDonald's general situation in Manhattan and the West 86th Street protest in 1975 are based largely on facts.

own property to do it. On the other hand, he regards a neighborhood group of 20 members or so, springing up to claim that *their* rights are being violated, as elitist, radical, and illegitimate. He suspects that this group is comprised mainly of local food store and restaurant owners who fear competition from a new McDonald's. He cannot quite understand why some businesspeople—such as clothing, antique, and other nonfood store owners—are among the protest supporters. He feels that they all will benefit from the added flow of people who will end up around West 86th Street to eat at the new McDonald's. He is unimpressed with the 3,000-signature petition, even assuming all the names are of real people. With all "those liberals" in Manhattan on a sunny February day, it would be relatively easy to get that many passersby to sign practically anything. This would hold true, especially if the protest is against an "establishment" corporation like McDonald's.

As a future strategy, Pace is thinking about a plan to avoid, or at least minimize, protests against a new McDonald's by some fringe community members and outside radicals. After the former building is demolished, no announcement should be made nor sign erected (stating "on this site will be built . . .") regarding the coming McDonald's. Not until the new McDonald's building is nearly completed should the Golden Arches and name sign be installed. If the protestors don't know what is coming, he reasons, then how can they either object to it or seek support against it?

Another Side of the Story

Mary Lambert, now 35 years old, came to McDonald's after a brilliant period with J. Walter Thompson, the New York advertising agency. There she did public relations for the L&M cigarette account, advising them on responding to anti-smoking attacks. As director of public information, she believes that image building for McDonald's is its best long-term defense.

Lambert has skillfully created a case based upon the facts and assumptions, as she sees them, regarding the McDonald's story. This case states that a new McDonald's would upgrade the neighborhood; store personnel would keep the premises clean and well policed; the store would serve a family clientele; added street lighting and pedestrian traffic would reduce crime; the franchisee would be a new small business person who would be "Mr. or Ms. McDonald" in the neighborhood; and the franchisee would hire local people to work in the restaurant, especially teenagers who have difficulty finding decent part-time jobs. She is encouraged by reinforcement of the notion that McDonald's contributes to the social and economic life of a community in the form of two recent "average citizens' " letters in the *New York Times* (see Exhibits 3-1 and 3-2).

To defuse the West 86th Street protestors' demands at tomorrow's meeting, Lambert wants to suggest a "compromise." She personally would admit that it is more real in appearance than in substance. She will propose that McDonald's try to sell the West 86th Street property before building the restaurant. Should it not be possible to find a customer, however, McDonald's then would be able to go ahead and build. Given the slow real estate market on the Upper West Side, she estimates that there is less than a 50-percent chance that a buyer will be found.

Time for a Change

Ken Roman, at the age of 55, has long been a specialist in restaurant site selection before joining McDonald's as a senior research analyst 5 years ago. He was transferred last month from McDonald's Oak Brook headquarters to help with further

Exhibit 3-1
5,347,890,386,903,274,711,310 Sold

By David S. Sampson

The old woman crossed herself, pushed aside her tattered coat and knelt down by the table to pray. Her lips moved, her head nodded up and down. Nobody paid much attention, even though she was nowhere near a church.

This happened at a restaurant. Not just any restaurant, because even though this is New York, the old woman would probably have been tossed out, along with the rest of the somewhat ragged crew that shared the same eating quarters.

The restaurant was McDonald's. I like McDonald's.

The McDonald's restaurants are, of course, an eyesore to behold. The little golden arches seem to pop up in the least likely and most unpopular spots; property values are lowered; "undesirables" flock in.

But the "undesirables" are all around us anyway. McDonald's simply gives them a place to go. Anyone with a little change in the pocket can come up with a pretty full meal. Instead of shuddering on an outside corner, there is warmth. There are other people. There is the assurance that no one will come up and ask you to leave because you happen to be a little crazy.

Gormets shudder at the mere mention of McDonald's. Property owners and nearby residents cringe; hungry people don't.

McDonald's, on the West Side, at least, are perhaps the only restaurants around that come equipped with full-time security men, all decked out in policeman-blue and a billy club.

They are places filled with lonely people who have no place else to go. Residents of the welfare hotels don't exactly hit your finest restaurants. But they can go to McDonald's and, for a brief time maybe, not feel like they're on welfare.

And the chain seems to encourage it. Little tickets are passed out offering free meals for $5 in pennies.

Stop and think about that for a while and it's actually a pretty nice thing to do. Stop and think a little longer and realize that no one else is doing it. Unemployment is up, prices are up. McDonald's still says come on in and have a cheap meal, we don't care who you are.

I like McDonald's. I don't like the food. I don't like to eat there. I feel uncomfortable when I go in. But I like McDonald's because they seem to care a little. Maybe it's all business and they really don't. But they seem to, and even that's rare enough these days.

David S. Sampson, a lawyer who is studying natural resources for the Commission on Critical Choices for Americans, says he has "absolutely no connection" with McDonald's.

The New York Times, March 2, 1975.

Exhibit 3-2
In Defense of McDonald's

To the Editor:

I am appalled at the concerted action that is being taken against McDonald's. I fail to see anything reprehensible about the operation of an inexpensive, wholesome establishment like McDonald's—at least nothing more reprehensible than could be said against Burger King, Kentucky Fried Chicken, Papaya, Orange Julius or any of many other fast-food places that have been allowed to flourish without a voice being raised.

The argument of undesirables gathering at McDonald's is ridiculously unfair. All my children and their friends go to McDonald's and I'd rather have them eat there than consort with the motley crew that is to be bound in, for example, the Blimpie Base at 86th Street and Broadway.

As for cars double-parking, could that be any more extreme than what I've seen outside Zabar's and Murray's Sturgeon Shop—rows of Rolls-Royces and Cadillacs and assorted other metal monsters, exuding fumes while their engines idle?

Are intelligent New Yorkers going to listen to remarks such as that of Dr. Gabriel Roz—a "social psychiatrist"—that "the hamburger stand" (at 86th and Amsterdam) "would lower the quality of mental health in the area?" Please, something's gone awry when neighborhoods with real problems choose to waste their energies fighting against an innocuous fast-food chain.

Miranda Knickerbocker
New York, Feb. 4, 1975

Letters to the Editor, *New York Times,* February 22, 1975 p. 26. Published by permission of the author.

---

expansion in the New York metropolitan area. He found an apartment in Manhattan at 125 W. 86th Street because he wanted one of those grand old, roomy, high-ceiling Upper West Side apartments he had seen in movies. At the time he signed the lease, he was unaware his apartment was near an intended location for a McDonald's outlet. He recently discussed the neighborhood protest with some of its leaders, not identifying himself as a McDonald's employee in order to hear their full story.

Roman learned the community group's feelings about the new outlet harming the tenuous balance in the present character of the community, resulting from its blend of population, distinctive store types, and dwelling units. It is believed that consequences of building a McDonald's at this location would be to seriously accelerate the decline of this community's uniqueness. The quality of life in the community would be subverted without its being consulted. Specific fears centered on McDonald's producing more street noise, litter, automobile traffic, congestion and pollution; teenagers hanging out and drug-dealers being attracted; additional fast-food chains opening and pushing rents up to the detriment of the long-time small independent stores in the area. He visited other Manhattan sites and found that each neighborhood is struggling in one way or another to maintain its quality of life. It was surprising for him to see two major newspaper editorials, in the *New York Times* and *Wall Street Journal*, discuss this issue in such strong terms (see Exhibits 3-3 and 3-4).

Roman is reasonably certain about the ignore-the-protestors position Pace will take. He also senses that someone like Lambert will advocate a public relations offensive. However, Roman is not as sure about either strategy's success given this new kind of community issue. He begins to question what McDonald's has learned from the three community protests so far, and he believes that others will occur unless the company does something. He seriously doubts whether McDonald's can win on this issue. He is leaning toward a new location policy that focuses on community criteria developed in a dialogue with community representatives. But he is quick to ponder: What are these criteria? Who should these representatives be? The question troubling him most is: should his corporation

Exhibit 3-3
Battle of the Burger

The battle of the burger continues in New York, generating heat and litter. Community protest increases as the number of fast-food places grows. "Protest is a fact of life which we accept," says one McDonald's spokesman. "We must be doing something right," says another, referring to an apparently insatiable demand for Big Macs.

Undimmed opposition from almost every neighborhood threatened with the blessings of Burger King and its brothers suggests more clearly that they must be doing something wrong. The message just doesn't seem to be getting through their demographic data.

City neighborhoods are more than population figures indicating potential markets. The impact of fast-food chains in an urban setting is completely unlike the effect on suburbia or the open road, because the environmental patterns are different. It has taken planners decades to find out what makes a successful city neighborhood tick. It works because it is a strongly individualized collection of close-knit, small-scaled, personalized, related living, service and amenity facilities stacked together in tight pedestrian proximity. The balance shifts constantly and precariously, but these are the stable constants. It can be ruptured easily, and physical damage can lead to social dislocation.

Therefore it is not a question of esthetics, or decorum, or the good will of the franchisee. The promise of voluntary policing, or cleanup, or changes in design to make fast-food outlets more acceptable neighbors are beside the point. What is fatal to city residential neighborhood character is the mass market formula itself, with its high volume turnover and mass-produced plastic image that sabotages individuality and a sense of place.

Fast-food places are neighborhood-busters before one burger is bitten or one redundant wrapper dropped. It is a matter of scale, style and standards that are destructively incompatible with the urban fabric and functions. They simply do not cut the mustard in New York.

The New York Times, February 20, 1975, p. 32.

Exhibit 3-4
Trouble in River City

Those New Yorkers who are ever alert to signs that their city is threatened from within are now up in arms, waving petitions and promising lawsuits, because McDonald Hamburger, Burger King and their like are making inroads in New York City. The watchdogs of public taste are alarmed at the "apparently insatiable demand for Big Macs," in the words of The New York Times.

According to the Times, "The impact of fast-food chains in an urban setting is completely unlike the effect on suburbia or the open road, because the environmental patterns are different. It has taken planners decades to find out what makes a successful city neighborhood tick. . . . What is fatal to city residential neighborhood character is the mass market formula itself, with its high volume turnover and mass-produced plastic image that sabotages individuality and a sense of place."

Besides, it is simply not necessary that the style, the grace, the ambience of lovely New York be spoiled just because the great unwashed mob has a craving for double cheesers and whoppers. If a New Yorker wants to take his wife and kiddies out for hamburgers and fries, he can always hail a cab and hop down to P. J. Clarke's. Or, if he's a poor person, an outing via subway to Coney and Nathan's Famous is always a lot of fun. As for the watchdogs of public taste, they can pile the family in the old bus and take to the open road for a visit to suburbia. This activity is only recommended for those New Yorkers whose will is strong enough to resist the plastic and dehumanizing influence of those golden arches.

The Wall Street Journal, March 5, 1975, p. 14.

somehow give a community a "veto" over whether a McDonald's can be built there? In his 30-year career in marketing research and site selection, he has never had to deal with questions like these.

Discussion Questions

1. What are the social responsibility aspects to this marketing situation?

2. Given the nature of Manhattan neighborhoods like West 86th Street, can McDonald's growth policy be justified today?

3. What good can a public relations response do? What harm? In the short run? In the long run?

4. What are the rights of a community? Who should determine them?

5. Do you feel there should be any new marketing strategy similar to what Ken Roman is suggesting? What kind?

6. What recommendations would you make to McDonald's?

Hasbro Industries, Inc.*

David Loudon and Albert Della Bitta
University of Rhode Island

Hasbro Industries, Inc. is a consumer products manufacturer and one of the ten largest toy manufacturers in the United States. In the fall of 1972 it faced certain consumer pressures, many of which have been strongly felt by Hasbro and other toy companies. The Federal Trade Commission, Food and Drug Administration, Federal Communications Commission, Consumers Union, and parents groups were continuing to pose challenges to the toy industry, particularly in the area of product safety and promotional techniques.

Company Background

Hasbro Industries, Inc. began in Rhode Island in 1926. Originally, the firm was engaged in the textile business and in the 1940s, the company entered the toy-making industry.

Hasbro has grown substantially over the years. The company now employs a permanent labor force in its toy operations of approximately 2,750 persons. The tremendous growth of Hasbro is largely a result of changes in the company's management and marketing approaches. These include assigning responsibility for all day-to-day operations to Stephen Hassenfeld—Hasbro's 30-year-old executive vice-president and the third generation of the founding family—and his introduction into the company of a new, young group of executives. Most of the new executives were drawn from outside the toy industry and outside Rhode Island.

According to Steve Hassenfeld, who recruited the new management team, "Five years ago we were what Wall Street would call a small family business. We've

---

* This case was prepared as a basis for classroom discussion rather than to illustrate effective or ineffective solutions to problems. All rights are reserved to the contributors.

worked hardest lately in getting the kind of management team a small family business doesn't have."

Major Product Lines

Toys

The company designs, manufactures, and markets a broad line of toys, dolls, games and accessories designed for children of different age groups. Over 90 percent of the company's toy sales result from items which retail at prices from $1 to $10. The company's toy line now consists of approximately 450 items, the principal categories of which are preschool toys, action toys, dolls, craft sets and staple items.

In 1969, Hasbro effected a "repositioning" of "G. I. Joe", a toy which accounts for a significant share of the company's volume. The toy became more adventure-oriented and less a military figure. The reason for the image change was the apparent waning interest in military toys. At the peak of its popularity in 1965, "G. I. Joe" had sales of $23 million, but by 1968 the category was producing only $4.8 million in sales. After the repositioning in 1969, the "G. I. Joe Adventure Team" and related accessories reassumed their position of importance within the industry, and in 1971 accounted for approximately $12.5 million in sales.

In 1970, Hasbro introduced the "Romper Room" preschool line in an attempt, as Steve Hassenfeld put it, "to upgrade the quality level of the products that we were then manufacturing." This line, which presently consists of over 65 items, accounted for approximately $11.8 million or 22 percent of net toy sales in 1971.

Television Programming

The company, through its recently acquired and wholly-owned subsidiary, Romper Room Enterprises, Inc., is involved in the production of television programs. The principal program is the Romper Room television nursery school, a 20-year-old internationally syndicated program—the oldest in the business—currently shown on approximately 85 television stations in the United States and on 55 stations in foreign countries. The show has received commendations from parents and the President's Council on Youth Fitness for its exercise routines that encourage children to use their muscles while they play.

Hasbro has financed several projects to improve the show. The company works with the child development staff of Hood College, Frederick, Maryland, and the Hood staff approves the entire show content. Also with the Kennedy Institute of Johns Hopkins University, Romper Room has developed 90 new visual perception games of value to children who will be learning to read.

Sales and Profits

Table 4-1 shows, for each of the company's 5 fiscal years ended December 31, 1971, the amounts and percentages of net sales and of earnings before taxes attributable to the company's toy lines. Table 4-2 shows toy industry and selected toy manufacturers' sales for the period 1965–1971.

Table 4–1
Hasbro's Toy Sales and Earnings
(in thousands of dollars)

Year	Net Toy Sales	Percent of Total Net Sales	Earnings before Income Taxes	Percent of Total Earnings
1967	$27,156	73	$ 504	74
1968	30,234	74	1,483	99
1969	32,252	72	(2,012)	(105)
1970	32,053	71	878	133
1971	53,570	79	2,925	123

Table 4–2
Total Industry and Selected Toy
Manufacturers' Sales
(in millions of dollars)

Company	1967	1968	1969	1970	1971
Mattel	154.3	210.9	288.6	357.0	272.2
General Mills	na	na	91.7	104.1	148.7
Milton Bradley	43.0	69.4	72.9	90.1	109.7
Quaker Oats	na	na	na	34.7	69.0
Aurora	na	na	na	na	30–40
Kenner	na	na	na	na	18–20
Ideal	49.3	52.2	61.7	75.1	70.9
Total Toy Industry Sales	1,560	1,824	2,041	2,259	2,351

Source: Toy Manufacturers of America, Inc., *Moody's Handbook* and *Standard and Poor*.

Industry Background and Competitive Situation

U. S. toy manufacturers' sales increased to over $2.3 billion in 1971 from about
$800 million in 1960. Shipments rose only 4.7 percent in 1971, however, compared
to almost 10 percent in the late 1960s.

Success in the toy industry largely depends upon a particular company's ability to respond to changing shifts in buying preferences through development of new products. The toy industry is rather volatile because most manufacturers change a large segment of their product lines each year in an attempt to find a big selling item. Moreover, the sales pattern is highly seasonal, with the Christmas selling season accounting for over 50 percent of the retail toy volume.

An important structural transformation has taken place within the industry in the past few years. There has been a trend toward larger companies. About 40 percent of industry sales are accounted for by the 10 largest manufacturers. Also, large food companies have diversified into the toy market. Thus, the toy industry probably will remain a highly competitive field. The large publicly-held companies which are financially strong should continue to secure an increasing share of the consumer dollar spent for toys. These firms have the capital and management expertise necessary to develop, and then aggressively advertise, a broad and constantly changing product line.

However, the changing social-economic patterns in the United States, particularly consumer demands for safer toys and a low-key approach to television advertising, are presenting major challenges to the industry. Thus, an uninterrupted growth rate for toy manufacturers may be difficult to sustain, particularly for promotional toy producers. The future merchandising outlook for promotional toys in the United States is clouded by consumer pressure to tone down television advertising and to ban unsafe toys. In addition, a decline is projected in the television-oriented 5 to 14 age group. (The approximately 40.21 million in 1975 is projected by the Department of Commerce to decrease to 36.48 million in 1980.) However, with the number of children under 5 years of age expected to rise from 17.30 million in 1971 to approximately 18.85 million in 1975 and 20.51 million in 1980, the pre-school market should continue to be one of the fastest growing segments over the remainder of the 1970s.

The trend toward smaller families, along with the projected rise in upper-income families, is expected to produce steady increases in the average yearly expenditure for toys per child. In 1971, the average annual expenditure on toys for children under 15 years of age was $62.50, in contrast to $60.55 in 1970, $55.00 in 1969, and $49.50 in 1968.

Consumerism

Various facets of toy marketing have come under increasing criticism over the past few years. The areas of major concern to toy producers are those relating to product safety and advertising.

Product Safety

The U. S. Public Health Service has estimated that there are about 700,000 injuries involving toys every year. Because of congressional reaction to dangerous toys, toy products now are subject to the provisions of the Federal Child Protection and Toy Safety Act of 1969. Under this legislation, the Secretary of Health, Education and

Welfare can prohibit marketing items intended for use by children which, after appropriate proceedings, have been determined to be hazardous. In addition, marketing items deemed imminently hazardous to the public health and safety can be barred for limited periods without a hearing. Furthermore, manufacturers may be required to repurchase hazardous items and reimburse certain expenses, even if such items were manufactured and sold prior to the adoption of the act. From time to time, the government has issued regulations affecting toy manufacturers, specifically with respect to the lead content of paint and classification of electrically operated toys. Regulations have been proposed affecting other aspects of toy manufacture. However, Hasbro is uncertain as to what effect such regulations, if finally adopted, will have on its business or on the entire toy industry.

Hasbro did not anticipate that some of its products would draw government and consumer criticism. For example, the company's "Javelin Darts" (one of a number of lawn dart games then on the market) came under government fire as a hazardous toy. Another product, "Super-Dough," drew a warning to toy buyers from *Consumer Reports*. The product contained an elaborate instruction sheet along with warnings that the product was not for internal consumption and that children with allergies could experience serious reactions. Hasbro removed both of these toys from the market.

In responding to the issue of dangerous products, Toy Manufacturers of America, the industry association, has officially approved a set of safety guidelines. However, because of the huge number of products involved, the organization will not undertake the testing of each separate product in order to issue a seal of compliance.

In order to maintain and improve the safety of its toy products, Hasbro has instituted more extensive screening and quality control procedures. Product quality and "playability" are important concerns for Hasbro. The company uses laboratory tests of its products and also observes children playing with the item—the latter serves as much to determine how well the children like a certain toy as it does to test the product quality and durability. The company also interviews parents to obtain their viewpoints.

One problem for the toy industry has been the conflict between the desire to maintain competitive secrecy and the need for test marketing new products. Hasbro began several years ago to test market its new products. At that time Steve Hassenfeld stated, "We're tired of having made mistakes because of not going into test markets."

Violent Toys

Marketing war toys has elicited opposition from some consumer groups. The American Toy Fair has been picketed by various anti-war toy groups concerned about the psychological development of children. The toy industry's position has been that war toys do not cause war, they only reflect it. In other words, the industry association feels that violence is learned from human example, not from things. Nevertheless, in deference to anti-war sentiment, Hasbro's "G.I. Joe," which used to be outfitted in military dress, has taken on an adventure theme. However, the company does maintain in its G.I. Joe line a replica of an Army jeep with a recoilless rifle mounted on it.

Although not classified as a violent toy, a water gun which Hasbro marketed—"Hypo Squirt"—was fashioned like a giant hypodermic needle. Even though the product had been on the market for 7 years before the drug issue developed, the toy was suddenly dubbed "play junior junkie" in the press and drew considerable criticism from the public. Hasbro withdrew the toy from the market.

Packaging

The Federal Trade Commission has spot checked packaging of Hasbro's products as part of an apparent investigation of "slack-filled" packaging practices within the toy industry. Although no action was taken by the FTC against Hasbro, the company has no assurance that the packaging of some of its products does not violate FTC regulations.

Advertising

Hasbro extensively advertises its toy products on children's network television programs and uses commercials on local television stations in the more important consumer market areas. In 1971, Hasbro spent approximately $5,700,000 in its toy promotion program, nearly all of which was used for television advertising. This amount was expected to increase significantly in 1972. Hasbro has advertised in the past on such varied shows as the "Tonight Show" and "H. R. Puf'nstuf."

Children's television advertising has come under increasing scrutiny by the government and mounting criticism from retailers, parents, and consumer groups. The focal point for such concern centers around the use (or as consumer groups term it—the misuse) of advertising on television shows aimed at children, particularly within Saturday and Sunday morning programming. In 1970, marketers spent $75 million on network television programs. Eight companies—primarily cereal and toy manufacturers—accounted for about half of this total.

Even toy retailers have criticized the magnitude of such advertising. According to a survey conducted among 5,200 toy and hobby retailers by Pepperdine College of Los Angeles and directed by Consultants to Management, Inc., toy store operators dislike national television advertising despite the fact that such advertising has increased the retailers' business. According to the report, the prime reason for the toy retailers' concern is their suspicion that the cost of television advertising increases the retail price of toys and draws the resentment of parents.

Protests have been made by parents and consumer groups concerning the nature of advertising on children's shows as well as the extent of such promotion. One rather vocal organization, in the forefront of the criticism, is ACT (Action for Children's Television), a Boston-based citizens' group that claims 2,500 members and supporters. ACT is fundamentally opposed to commercialization of children's television and has argued for the elimination of advertising during such programming. The Federal Communications Commission (FCC) has instituted an inquiry and proposed rule-making procedure in response to a petition from ACT, which requested that the FCC prohibit sponsorship and commercials on children's programs and prohibit the inclusion, use, or mention of products, services, or stores during such programs.

The ACT petition cited the Romper Room television program produced by Hasbro's subsidiary, among other programs, as being commercially oriented. They argued that children were being unfairly influenced through the program's use of Romper Room teachers doing commercials. In addition, the group criticized the fact that toys used on the program were those advertised on Romper Room.

Slightly before the ACT charges surfaced, Hasbro was taking steps to counter such criticism. The company decided that no Romper Room teacher could do a commercial for any toy product. In addition, the company stopped advertising any Romper Room toy used on the program. At the time this action was taken, however, it did not appear to satisfy ACT. For example, early in 1971 one of ACT's directors and the mother of 2 children stated, "I don't think Hasbro has reached the heart of the problem which is selling to unsophisticated preschool children." By using Hasbro products on the program, she added, "They still have their commercial by having the children play with the toys on the program."

The ACT group has criticized not only Hasbro's advertising, but also that of many other companies which heavily promote their products to children. Particularly distressing to such critics is the number of advertisements typically run within children's programs shown between 7:00 am and 2:00 pm on Saturdays and Sundays. Commercials and nonprogram material may amount to no more than 12 minutes per hour (down from 16 minutes) according to the Television Code Review Board of the National Association of Broadcasters. Critics also have advocated that commercials during the children's programs be clustered.

The FTC has brought action against several toy manufacturers (although not against Hasbro) for deceptive advertising practices. Hasbro attempts to comply with the principles established in these actions, as well as with the rules promulgated by the FTC, and with the regulations prescribed by the National Association of Broadcasters. The NAB standards for toy commercials are quite specific. Before a toy commercial can be shown on television, it must be approved by the NAB.

The FTC is expected to hold public hearings to study the impact of advertising on children and consumers. Rules or regulations, if any, which may result from the FCC or FTC investigations, are likely to affect the advertising practices of Hasbro and the rest of the toy industry.

Some firms within the industry have made moves to reduce criticism of advertising practices affecting children. For example, Ideal Toy Company, which advertised directly to children via network television, has dropped sponsorship of Saturday morning television—where the major controversy is—and now buys early weekday evening prime time.

Nielson data indicate that 2 to 5-year-olds watch an average of 3.2 hours of television on fall Saturdty mornings (8:00 am to 1:00 pm) and 6 to 11-year-olds watch 2.6 hours. However, both groups watch approximately 3.5 hours per week between 5:00 and 7:30 pm on weekdays.

Other toy marketers, such as Fisher-Price, have for some time been pursuing a strategy of targeting their message almost exclusively at parents, particularly mothers. Hasbro had decided to continue its present policy of weekend television advertising.

Although a leader sometimes can turn into a follower in a season, Steve Hassenfeld declares with regard to Hasbro, "We believe we have the momentum that will carry us to leadership in the industry." As far as the consumer movement and its effects upon the toy industry and Hasbro are concerned, Hassenfeld remarked that, "The worst seems to be over."

Western Denim, Inc.

Bartow Hodge, University of South Carolina

The Role of a Marketing Information
System in the Management of a Sales Force

In July 1975, Mr. Art Millman of Western Denim, Inc., which manufactures women's coordinated dresswear, was considering a proposal from Mr. Gene Mills, the Spartanburg office manager. This proposal advocated expansion of a recently installed marketing information system to encompass several new types of sales reports. According to Mr. Mills, the new reports would permit more effective management of the sales force and would more than justify the time and expense of the field and home office personnel in gathering the required information and preparing the reports for the Western Denim sales force and its management. Mr. Mills envisioned further expansion of the marketing management information system so that it would be a total "Sales Information System" (SIS).

Mr. Mills is a 1973 MBA graduate from a southeastern graduate school of business. He is responsible for budgeting and marketing company reports. In developing these reports, Mr. Mills uses an IBM 370/135 computer system which Western Denim began renting in September 1974. This system has made it possible to carry out new kinds of analyses and to report more kinds of information, more accurately and frequently, than had been practical previous to its installation.

Apparel Industry Background

The apparel industry is comprised of about 25,000 firms which manufacture clothing and related products from textile fabrics (knit and woven), and other materials, including leather, rubberized fabric, plastic, and fur.

Industry firms are characterized by small profits, little capital investment in equipment, and few employees. In fact, the apparel industry has one of the lowest

81

profit/sales ratios of all manufacturing categories. During the 1960s, each company averaged about $4,500 as the annual investment in new capital equipment. This figure compares with about $45,000 investment in new capital equipment for other manufacturing firms. About 70 percent of the clothing industry firms had fewer than 50 employees. Companies employing fewer than 100 workers make up more than 90 percent of the firms in the industry.

Trade association officials have predicted that the $30 billion retail sales of women's wear would increase at a rate of 5 to 8 percent annually between 1975 and 1980. This growth rate was attributed to the growing number of women entering the work force who would need office clothes. Also, there has been an increase in the number of women moving from blue-collar to white-collar positions because of a higher level of education among women. This change in job status has created a desire among women, in general, to dress to match their improved job position. Fashion magazines reach about 10 million readers monthly with the latest styles and have created the impetus for women to spend their more readily available money on apparel purchases. During the 1970s the women's wear publications publicized several trends in the apparel business. Larger firms grew by acquisitions and diversification from single product to full line firms. The full lines include products for both men and women, lessening the traditional dependence on having a "hot number." Companies began to expand through vertical integration and building textile plants. Many large firms were going public in the 1960s.

Part of the explanation for the growth of larger concerns is attributed to the attitude of store buyers. More buyers prefer to concentrate their purchases among fewer, larger manufacturers than buying individual products from smaller manufacturers. The reasons for this preference are ease of viewing new fashions, better quality control in larger firms, competitive pricing, faster filling of orders, and fewer communications problems. The buyers also claim that brand preferences among teenagers and young adults were developed in the 1960s and early 1970s because of the full lines available and because advertising created brand awareness. The larger firms have earned a place of respect in the industry.

In the 1960s, the apparel industry increased their expenditures for advertising on an annual basis by about 35 percent. This increase was less than other manufacturing industries, but significant in the apparel industry. The increase was credited to the larger number of medium and large-sized firms in the industry.

During early 1975, retailers found themselves saddled with uncomfortably high inventory levels, but without sufficient demand to warrant them. Their task was to align inventory levels with the current 1975 pace of business. By the closing months of 1975, apparel outlets found themselves looking into a hefty influx of demand, but in many cases not having a sufficient range of goods to satisfy all consumer needs. With consumers apparently more willing to spend and having an increased supply of discretionary funds (because of tax cuts), prospects for apparel sales were much better. Retailers began to place substantial orders with apparel companies—first to bring their inventories to normal levels, and second to keep up with the acceleration in current business.

With retailers no longer operating on a hand-to-mouth basis, they began to take a broader view by giving the manufacturers longer lead times. The longer lead times allowed manufacturers to plan more efficiently and to have more profitable production runs.

The Coordinated Dresswear Business

Although there are many small firms in the coordinated dresswear market, there are only 11 firms that compete directly with Western Denim. Among these Aileen, Inc.; Blue Bell; Bobbie Brooks; Jonathan Logan; Levi Strauss; Koracorp; Manhattan Industries; Munsingwear; Oxford Industries; Russ Togs; and V. F. Corp.

The phrase, "coordinated dresswear," means that items within each group are compatible in terms of matching colors, styles, and fabrics. The consumer is offered different sizes (a size 8 top and 10 bottom), different silhouettes (a jacket with a slim pleated or an A-line skirt), and a selection of colors (a brown/blue skirt with either a brown or blue shirt).

Western Denim management believes that coordinated dresswear will do better than the other categories of women's wear because they feel "coordinates" offer the chance to "mix and match," and thus create a variety of outfits appealing to young women, especially those under 30. (In the 1960s, women between the ages of 15 and 24 purchased over 30 percent of all female clothes. In the early 1970s, women under 30 purchased over 50 percent of all female clothes.)

The Retail Trade

Retail outlets for women's coordinated dresswear include 43,000 women's clothing specialty stores, 27,000 women's ready-to-wear stores, 14,000 family clothing stores, and 3,000 department stores. Other outlets include mail order houses, discount department stores, general merchandise stores, and military stores.

The vice-president of Western Denim described the method by which the typical women's wear buyer for either a department store or chain store purchases clothes, and the manner in which the function is being affected by the computer. A buyer "shops the market" before placing initial orders. The buyer examines the trade publications' articles and advertisements, discusses with other buyers the new styles, views visiting sales representatives' lines, visits companies' showrooms in New York and other leading market cities, and reviews last year's sales to determine which companies' merchandise had and had not sold well.

When items that the buyer likes are found, initial orders are placed. A large proportion of the buyer's budget is set aside for later in the season, so that money is left for adding to the lines and reordering out-of-stock items. The buyer typically purchases coordinated dresswear from more than one manufacturer to give a "total look" to the department.

Buyers traditionally also play the role of operating management. In this role, they are responsible for obtaining and reviewing information on what is and is not selling in their departments as well as reviewing expenses and profits for particular lines. Previously, sales information has been obtained by standing on the sales floor to watch what is being sold from manually-maintained, perpetual inventory records, and by physical stock counts of the merchandise after a selling period.

With the advent of the Kimball ticket and computerized processing of sales slips and inventory data, the buyer has less need to be on the selling floor. In addition, the increase in branch store operations of many large retailers makes it difficult for the buyer to spend much time on the sales floor of each store. These 2 factors have resulted in the buyer being increasingly separated from the selling function and more restricted to the purchasing function.

The computer system makes it possible for buyers to determine sales and inventory in each price range by style, color, and size, and the manner in which sales of each of the categories vary by branch. Since additions to the line and reorders depend on quick, accurate determination of trends, the computer lessens the element of chance and permits the buyer to reorder more quickly in more economical quantities than was possible previously. In addition, electronic data processing permits the buyer to identify slow moving items and make markdowns quickly.

The Company

Western Denim was formed in 1946, but the family's experience in the clothing industry predated the Civil War. It started with the great grandfather of the present family. Currently, Richard Millman is president and directs designing: Steven Millman is a vice-president; and Arthur Millman is treasurer and responsible for financial control and sales management. Art Millman is also the chief executive officer of the firm as chairman of the board. The 3 brothers joined the firm after completion of college and military service. The firm went public in 1964 to allow for mobility of the company stock. Exhibit 5–1 shows an organization chart of Western Denim, Inc., and Exhibit 5–2 presents the company's financial condition.

Western Denim produces misses' sizes for the average woman compared with juniors' for the short and petite girl or woman, and women's sizes for the larger, heavier woman. Prices are "upper-medium" for the coordinated dresswear market. For example, in the coordinated dresswear business, the low-price range for skirts at retail are around $10, the medium-price range for skirts at retail are about $20, and the higher-price range starts at about $28. Western Denim skirts sell for about $23 retail.

Over a 12-month period, Western Denim manufactures 27 groups comprising 6 seasonal lines. A line is a collection of groups designed to be sold during a specific time of the year or for a specific purpose. The lines are called: Early Spring, Late Spring, Summer, Transitional, Fall, and Mid-Winter. A group consists of a number of items, such as jackets, skirts, blouses, and shifts color coordinated and made of similar or coordinated fabrics in a series of styles. This coordination allows the retailer to choose desired items and still present a full range of clothes to the consumer. The total items in a group can run into the hundreds because

Exhibit 5-1
Organization Chart

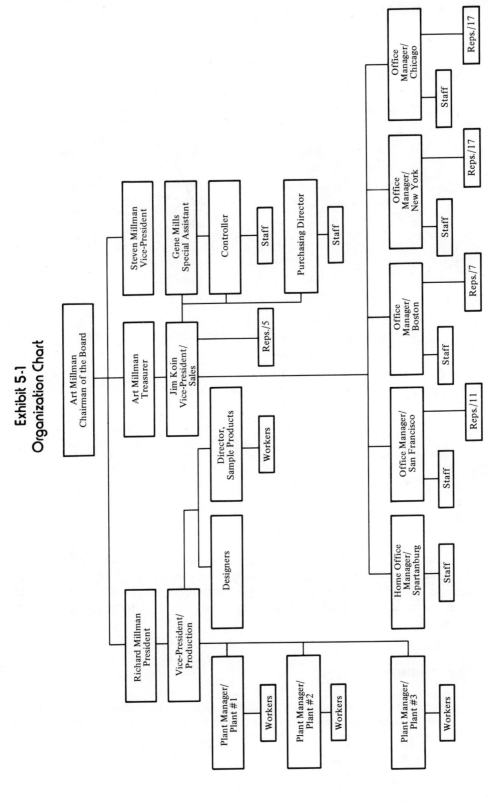

Exhibit 5-2
Financial Condition[a]

	1974	1975
Sales Per Share	38.15	40.30
"Cash Flow" Per Share	(1.85)	.50
Earnings Per Share	(2.25)	.10
Dividend Declared	— [b]	— [b]
Tangible Book Value	7.85	7.95
Sales ($ millions)	53.00	56.00
Operating Margin	NMF [c]	3.5%
Depreciation ($ millions)	.60	.60
Net Income ($ millions)	(3.10)	0.20
Income Tax Rate	NMF [c]	45.0%
Net Income Margin	NMF [c]	.3%
Working Capital ($ millions)	17.00	17.50
Long-Term Debt ($ millions)	11.00	10.50
Net Worth ($ millions)	11.50	12.00
Percentage Earned Total Capital	NMF [c]	3.0%
Percentage Earned Net Worth	NMF [c]	1.5%
Earnings Plowback Ratio	NMF [c]	1.5%

[a] Has about 2,300 employees and 2,400 stockholders. The Millman family controls about 42 percent of the common stock.
[b] Negligible.
[c] Not a measurable factor.

there are 9 to 100 styles, 1 to 5 colors, and 5 to 8 sizes. Some groups are: tweed, boating, shift, and pants and tops groups.

Western Denim has 2,000 active accounts. The company has sold its lines to 8,000 firms during its history. The vice-president of sales says that if the company sells to 7,500 accounts actively, it would have essentially complete coverage of its potential market. The company sells 65 percent of its lines to traditional department stores, 30 percent to specialty shops, and 5 percent to chain discount department stores.

The Production Cycle

Western Denim's design department consists of 5 designers for style and one designer for color and fabric. They produce sketches of successful items from the past year, use fashion magazines for other sketches, and create sketches of some of the more expensive styles of clothing, in addition to using their own talent and experience. The company's designers said they did not originate fashion, but translated it into upper-medium price garments after the fashion had been established by the trendsetters.

Samples from the sketches are made by the sample department. These garment samples are then modeled for top management, and the ones judged to have the best possibility of selling are then sent to the cutting floor where the cutting department uses the samples to cut patterns. Information on the patterns to be used for the coming year is given to the sales department to generate a master control and status report on promised dates of delivery, by units of sales and by color and size. From the early orders, decisions are reached to produce quantities of some items in excess of orders on hand, to discontinue others, and to await specific orders on other line items. Completed orders are either shipped immediately to customers or hung on racks in inventory to await the completion of some of the other garments included in an order. It takes from one to six weeks to produce product line items. Over 5 million garments are produced every year, with average wholesale prices of $9 for cotton garments and $11 for wool garments.

Organizational Structure of the Selling Effort

Western Denim employs 57 field sales representatives. The field reps report to the branch office managers who report to the vice-president of sales. The vice-president of sales reports to the treasurer and chairman of the board, Mr. Art Millman. The Spartanburg office manager has no field sales representatives reporting directly to him. His main function is to direct the staff personnel. The vice-president of sales directs the activity of the field sales force out of the home office in Spartanburg, South Carolina. Mr. Mills reports directly to the treasurer for special assignments as called upon.

The president, Mr. Richard Millman, is responsible for overall direction of advertising and coordinates this activity with the treasurer. The president serves as a major contact with many of the more important customers. The New York office manager maintains showrooms at the merchandise marts for the convenience of out-of-town buyers on their periodic trips to New York City. The field sales force spends most of its time on the road, but frequently accompanies its buyers to New York, especially during the heavy buying seasons of spring and fall. The other offices have showrooms for buyer use.

Fifty-four of the sales representatives are paid a commission of 6 percent of net sales. They are responsible for their own sales expenses. This figure amounts to about 3 percent of net sales. The other 3 representatives are on salary, plus commission for exceeding their sales quotas. Three means of controlling sales representatives' effectiveness are (1) adjusting the size of the territory, (2) adjusting the amount of cooperation from the home office concerning mailings and publicity, and (3) controlling the amount of service the company extends to customers of particular representatives (which is the most effective method). It is within the company's discretion to determine which sales representative's accounts receive rapid delivery of reorders for fast-selling merchandise. The company has found that the third method of control is easier than the first two.

Western Denim management feels that the control problem is minimized when sales representatives are confident that the firm has their best interests at heart. Once their confidence is gained, the company is in a position to influence the working habits of its representatives. Management hopes that an improved sales information system will be instrumental in gaining greater confidence from its field sales force. Mr. Art Millman described the salary plus commission for exceeding sales quotas for 3 of his representatives as an experiment. Its purpose is to ascertain if more control could be exercised over the sales force if its income depends not only on booking orders, but also on cooperation with the home office plans. The idea is to relate the base salary partly to cooperation with home office plans. To date, success of the experiment has been hard to determine.

Management communicates with its sales representatives through a weekly memo. This memo reviews current magazine articles about the trade and about selling techniques and provides notices concerning the addition or the discontinuance of specific items in a clothing group. Regional sales meetings are held before each major selling season (spring and fall) providing an additional opportunity for management to communicate with its sales force. Also, a national sales meeting is held annually, primarily for social and morale purposes. In addition, the president and vice-president travel around the country before the beginning of each major selling season to visit their sales representatives and their larger customers. The sales representatives file activity reports on their visits to each account. See Exhibit 5–3 for a typical activity report. These reports are intended to keep management up to date on the activities of its sales force. Currently, only 14 sales representatives regularly file the reports. Of this number, two are currently on salary plus commision.

Sales Forecasting

A sales forecast is used by management both for production planning and evaluation of sales force members. The forecast is developed by first deciding upon either an expected or desired percent increase over the previous year. The individual lines and groups are apportioned a dollar amount in order to reach a total budget. Each sales representative is then given a percent of each group based upon success or failure with each corresponding group the previous year. If a new group is introduced, a comparable group is used as a basis for the previous year. The forecasts, according to management, frequently have been inaccurate and usually are revised several times each season. For example, the forecast for a partcular group might be changed to make it more compatible with initial reactions from major retailers or with the actions of competitors. The forecast might be modified also for a specific sales representative if management becomes aware of changes that have taken place in the sales rep's territory. There are no separate forecasts, however, for specific accounts.

Exhibit 5-3
Sample of a Sales Representative's Activity Report

Account Activity Report

Date: __4-1-75__   Salesman: __JACK FRILLS 0211__

Account
Name: __RICHWAY__   Buyer: __MRS. ELSIE MYERS__

                                     Mdse. Mfr.: _____

Street
Address: __305 STATE__   Adv. Mgr.: _____

City and
State: __ATLANTA, GA.__   Total Units
                                     Ordered: _____ $_____

Order   Transi-   Mid-   Early   Late
Recvd. ____Summer ____tional ____Fall ____Winter ____Spring ____Spring ____

Where Showed Line		Status of Order		Type of Store		Classification	
In Store	√	Mailing Order		Department		Exclusive	
Sample Room		Promised Later		Specialty		Medium	
New York Show Room		Won't Buy Now	√	Chain or Branch	√	Popular	
Market Show		No Interest		Other (specify)		Advertising	
Phone		Buyer Out				No Advertising	

Mailing List Information

Prospect _____   New Account _____   Old Account ——

Correct List _____   Remove From List _____   No Mail _____

Customer Reactions and Comments

THE SALESMAN WHO LEFT US TO GO TO LOGAN HAS

BEEN SUCCESSFUL IN SELLING COMPLETE LINES AND

RAPID DELIVERY. NEED LETTER AND VISIT BY MR. MILLMAN.

The Need for a Sales Information System

In late spring of 1975, Mr. Mills proposed systematic collection of sales information which, when processed on the S/370 acquired during the previous year, would provide management with a better basis for controlling the sales force and for making other marketing decisions. Mr. Mills explained why improved control of the sales force was important to firms in the apparel field, including Western Denim.

Sales representatives in the apparel industry traditionally have acted essentially as "agents," rather than as employees of the manufacturers. Since the majority of firms have not been able to generate sufficient volume to support their own sales force, sales representatives generally have been encouraged to represent more than one manufacturer. The time savings involved in showing more than one line in a store also contributes to the representative's handling of several manufacturers.

Feelings of independence also are fostered by the commission compensation system since the representatives' incomes have been directly dependent upon their own efforts. The retail buyer who has had success in purchasing from a specific sales representative often develops trust in that representative's judgment and ability. These factors, coupled with the lack of consumer brand preference, enable many sales representatives to retain their accounts despite occasional changes in the manufacturers they represent.

As apparel firms become larger, they tend to employ sales representatives on an exclusive basis in those territories where they potentially can support themselves on the offerings of one manufacturer. Many of these representatives view themselves as relatively independent agents and tend to resent bookkeeping chores imposed by the manufacturer, since it obviously does not benefit the representative. Indeed, manufacturers have sometimes been at the mercy of their exclusive sales representatives. Many representatives take great care to reveal as little information as possible about their customers and their relationships with them. Thus, if a good sales representative decides to move to another manufacturer, that representative frequently takes the customers' loyalty also and the manufacturer is unable to retain many of that representative's accounts.

Until Western Denim acquired the computer, they were not able to compile enough information about a specific representative to know in what direction they should try to move him. If they could get the sales information system working, they believed they could quickly obtain a reading of how well a representative was doing relative to the potential of his territory. With this information, they could either make changes in territory size or take other steps to bring the representative into line.

Mr. Mills also noted that up until Western Denim acquired the S/370, management had little information with which to evaluate each sales representative. At that time, each of three reports were prepared on a seasonal basis (twice a year), and one on a weekly basis. One of these reports showed sales for each representative, listed by account. The second report showed sales of individual items within each group for each representative. The third report showed total bookings per week for each representative. Management believed that the latter report was the most important of the 3. These reports required the services of 6 clerks per year on a half-time basis. The clerks were among 28 who manually posted orders received from representatives to various billing and production forms. Clerks earned from $100 to $135 per week.

The SIS Proposal

Mr. Mills proposed that a file be constructed for each member of the sales force from which management could evaluate representatives and decide what changes should be made. From a summary "recap" sheet prepared weekly for each representative, management would be able, according to Mr. Mills, to "evaluate each representative without becoming burdened with excessive details. Each recap sheet would be derived from several more detailed reports which management could use to evaluate any particular representative in depth." He proposed that the following procedure be used:

(1) A file would be made for each sales representative.
(2) The file would contain the most recent copy of each report.
(3) The file would be prefaced with a weekly recap analysis of that representative's productivity on a standardized form.
(4) All decisions regarding each representative and his territory could be made on the basis of the information in that representative's file.

Exhibit 5–4 shows the contents of a recap analysis.

Exhibit 5-4
Recap Analysis

A. From the Weekly Booking Report
1. Compare net dollar sales this year with last year and list percentage differences.
2. Compare origin of sales—road vs. branch office in percentage.
3. Compare actual sales this year with budget and list percentage differences.
4. Analyze which groups are strong or weak for that particular sales representative.
5. Compare 1, 2, 3, and 4 against last week.
6. Comment on above, for example:
   a. Does sales representative know how to sell all groups?
   b. Is there a territory problem with specific groups?
   c. Is too much business written in the branch office?
   d. How does representative compare with company averages?
   e. Are next two weeks sales last year reasonable for this year?
B. From the Sales Distribution Report (by trading areas)
1. Compare net sales against "Area Potential Guide."
   a. Is representative obtaining volume where potential exists?
   b. Is he travelling correct areas (analyze field activity reports)?
   c. Comment further.

    2. Check into specific trading areas.
      a. Compare this year with last year by account.
      b. Where does problem lie?
      c. Is executive help needed for specific accounts?
      d. Comment further.

C. From Field Activity Reports (filled out by representative after each call).
    1. Total number of accounts called on.
      a. Current accounts (bought within the last year from Western Denim).
      b. Inactive accounts (formerly bought from Western Denim).
      c. Prospects (never bought from Western Denim).
    2. Number of times line shown.
    3. Number of accounts sold.
      a. Number mailing in orders.
      b. Number which took order forms.
    4. Number of groups sold to all accounts. Analysis on above, for example:
      a. Is sales representative covering enough accounts? If not, why? Poor planning? Lack of appointments?
      b. Is representative adequately servicing current and inactive accounts? Is he making sufficient number of calls on prospects?
      c. How effective is he in showing the line? (number of times shown divided by number of calls made)
      d. How effective is he in closing the sale? (number of accounts sold divided by number of times line shown)
      e. When a sales representative leaves, what proportion of his accounts does he take with him?
      f. Is the representative placing enough groups with Western Denim accounts? (number of groups sold divided by number of accounts sold)

D. From Volume Distribution Report
    1. What volume categories are his accounts in?
    2. Is there a trend in moving his accounts up into the next higher volume category?
    3. How many accounts from last year are unsold this year?
    4. How many new accounts has the representative opened?
    5. How many accounts has he maintained from last year to this year?

E. From the Weekly Shipping Report by Sales Representatives
    1. Percentage of unjustified cancellations to gross bookings.
    2. Percentage shipped to gross bookings, less unit cancellations.
    3. Backlog this year.

F. From Linear Programming Study of Territories
    1. Optimum route sheet for each territory.
    2. Compare sales with optimum.

The SIS

The reports needed for parts A, B, and C of the recap report would be programmed for the IBM System 370 and would be available to management on a weekly basis. The first of these reports would be a representative's weekly booking report with a tabulation of bookings (orders) by each representative for each merchandise group presented on a "this year" versus "last year" basis. The second report would be a weekly sales distribution report by city, to represent a tabulation of sales to individual stores with a specific city (area) for each representative. It would show sales for each merchandise group for the year-to-date, last year's sales of the comparable group, and last year's sales for the period corresponding to the forthcoming two weeks. The third report, the sales representative's credit limit report, would show a listing of current credit limits for each store in a representative's sales territory.

Each representative would be given access to each of these reports for his territory. The reports would also be distributed to the president, treasurer, sales vice-president, and particular office managers for the branch officers.

Much of the additional information needed for the sales information system proposal would be obtained from an analysis of the activity reports requested from each sales representative after he called on an account. In addition, staff personnel in each branch office would develop territory potentials using statistical sources and lists of stores in each area covered by the branch office.

Mr. Mills indicated that if management accepted the proposal, complete implementation of the system could take effect in 12 to 15 months. He indicated that even if the complete system was not adopted, the present sales information reports still would be quite useful in making sales force decisions.

Cost of the Proposed SIS

The 3 reports currently prepared required intracompany charges of $18,000 in computer time each year, including the charge for the services of the computer center personnel. This figure excluded the time needed to prepare the necessary input data. Mr. Mills thought these input charges were not appropriately chargeable to the sales information reports since the same data also were used for other purposes.

The programs used to prepare the 3 existing reports were constantly being modified to make them more efficient. Mr. Mills believed that to date such increases in efficiency were offset by the charges allocated to the project for the company programmer's time in making the programs more efficient. The programmer was paid $12,500 per year. Mr. Mills estimated that 40 percent of the programmer's time for one year would be required to complete programming of the as yet unprogrammed portions of the current proposal. Mr. Mills also estimated that routine processing of additional portions of the sales information system proposal would involve intracompany charges of $4,700 per year in computer and personnel costs in the computer center.

Even with these additional reports, total computer usage would still remain below 176 hours per month which Western Denim was obligated to pay the computer vendor. Within the next 2, or possibly 3, years the use of the computer would exceed 176 hours use per month. At that time, additional expense would be incurred for extra machine time and computer personnel.

Mr. Mills believed that the value of the additional information developed by the computer would more than offset the costs involved in processing the sales reports. He argued that the sales information reports could and should be used for many purposes beyond evaluation and control of the field sales force.

In evaluating the proposal, Mr. Millman was concerned about the positive and negative effects the system would have on the sales force; whether management could make effective use of the information; and whether the system adequately prepared the company for future changes in the apparel field. Specifically, he wondered if all of the reports were necessary or if perhaps some other reports might be more useful to management.

Mr. Millman completed his initial reading of the proposal for the sales information system just prior to conducting the following sales meeting.

The Sales Meeting

In preparation for the winter selling season in July, several members of the sales force came to New York early to confer with company executives. At this meeting, the participants included Mr. Art Millman; Mr. Gene Mills; Jerry Matz, the New York sales office manager; Jack Gamet, a New England sales representative from the Boston office; and Thomas Wildcat, the Chicago office manager, with 2 of his sales representatives.

After discussing the best way to sell the new groups, the conversation drifted to filing reports by sales representatives and the amount of time taken without monetary return for the effort they would need to expend. The following comments were made at the meeting:

Tom Wildcat: Gene, I keep receiving your requests for all different types of forms to be filled out by my sales representatives. I'm a busy man. I give my representatives a large territory to cover. We don't need the additional paperwork you are asking. Between the records and the order blanks, we do enough pencil pushing. If I could see some constructive use for the reports, maybe I might feel differently; but I just don't have the time.

Gene Mills: Tom, I know you're busy. But a couple of minutes after each account is all that is needed to fill in an activity report. It provides different information than the order blank. Under the present system, our information is about the successful order, not the reasons for firms not buying.

Tom Wildcat: I have all the useful information in my notebooks. As long as I know who to see and who not to see, the company has nothing to worry about. Instead of worrying about my reports, why don't you help me get some additions to the line that would really sell in my territory?

Jerry Matz: Tom, your problems are no different from mine or anybody else's. If we listened to every one of the sales representatives, we would be carrying twice the number of items and still have

	the same sales. Production costs would eat us up. It's like the budget, accept it—don't question it.
Tom Wildcat:	The worst thing is those damn budgets. Art, Jim Koin keeps sending me your figures on what *you think* I should sell. You sit back in your easy chairs never having traveled hundreds of miles a week and never having been on commission, and tell me that I'm not booking enough business. I get these figures with no explanation and every time I try to pin you down, Gene, you hem and haw.
Jerry Matz:	You can always protest if you think the home office is unfair. I noticed that you and Jack haven't picked up your weekly reports.
Tom Wildcat:	Save the company the money. My office and my sales representatives' records are in shape. I don't know why we need a computer to tell us what we sold this year or last.
Jack Gamet:	I have been with the firm for 8 months. The report isn't worth anything to me. The comparable figures are set by the sales representatives that went to Logan. I keep all my records on cards in black books. I follow these for my route.
Gere Mills:	Jack, how long do you spend each night bringing these cards up to date?
Jack Gamet:	To tell the truth, I have been getting a little lax. With my four kids running around, nothing gets done. I have been thinking about getting a small tape recorder to use going from customer to customer. Usually after the kids are asleep, I do the reports in front of the TV with my wife. That takes a long time.
Jerry Matz:	I can sympathize with you, Jack. I spend anywhere from 2 to 3 hours daily reviewing all the figures by territory and by line. In that way, I can spot trends to keep you men informed and tell you where to place your emphasis in selling. These reports may be an adjunct to the operations, but they're the Bible as far as I'm concerned.
Tom Wildcat:	If you didn't review each individual sales representative, it wouldn't take that long. Why do you keep up with all of the statistics? That's the representative's responsibility. Their personal records, like Jack's, have all the information on one sheet that we need. There's no need to wade through the reports each week; instead you should allow the computer to do something more useful like bookkeeping.
Gene Mills:	The computer was purchased for both bookkeeping and marketing statistics. The computer and the reports are here to stay!

Two more sales representatives joined the conversation which turned back to the best way to sell the winter line.

Discussion Questions

1. Evaluate the current proposal. What are the strengths and weaknesses?

2. What courses of action should Mr. Art Millman consider? Which course of action would you recommend to Mr. Millman and why?

3. If the proposed sales information system is put into effect, what information would you want to collect and why? How would this information be useful to Western Denim, Inc?

4. Develop a diagram of the inputs and outputs you would propose for the SIS. Explain. How would you collect and use this data? Explain.

5. How would you handle potential sales representatives' morale in being requested to fill out the additional forms? Explain.

Market Analysis, Ltd.
Peter Doyle, University of Bradford, England*

Market Analysis, Ltd. is a British marketing research and consulting firm specializing in assisting manufacturers in analyzing and interpreting market data and providing consulting advice for business decision making. The firm consists of 3 psychologists, 14 statisticians, 17 account executives, and 23 staff and support personnel. Recently, Marketing Analysis, Ltd. acquired two new accounts—Bradford Engineering Company, Ltd. and Causeway Engineering, Ltd. These two companies represent typical problem situations with which Market Analysis deals. Charles Healy acquired the Bradford account and Robert Brewster acquired the Causeway account. Both men were new with the company and quite proud of their new accounts.

Healy and Brewster reviewed the Bradford and Causeway situations with company analysts. After a thorough investigation of company records, market data pertaining to their industries, and considerable discussion, several relevant sets of data and questions were generated. The following is a brief synopsis for each of the two companies.

Bradford Engineering Company, Ltd.

Bradford Engineering Company, Ltd. manufactures brake drums for trucks and buses. BEC drums are considered superior in quality to most others, lasting over 200,000 miles as opposed to 150,000 miles for ordinary drums. The drums retail at about 35 percent above competitive prices.

Brake drum purchasers include bus and truck manufacturers, garages and

---

* © Copyright 1977 by Peter Doyle, University of Bradford Management Centre. Permission granted by author.

Exhibit 6-1
BEC Balance Sheet
(£ 000)

Current Assets				**Current Liabilities**		
Inventory	£1,500			Accounts Payable	£ 700	
Accounts Receivable	800			Notes Payable	500	
Other	700			Other	800	
		£3,000				£2,000
Fixed Assets				**Long-term Liabilities**		£2,000
Buildings	£2,000			**Net worth:**		
Equipment	2,000			Common Stock (50,000 shares)	£1,000	
		£4,000		Retained earnings	2,000	
						£3,000
Total		£7,000		**Total**		£7,000

Exhibit 6-2
BEC Income Statement
(£000)

Net Sales (1m units @ £ 10)		£10,000
Cost of Goods Sold		
Direct Materials	£4,000	
Direct Labour	2,000	
Manufacturing Overhead	1,100	7,100
Gross Profit Margin		£ 2,900
Less: Operating Expenses		
Selling Expenses	£1,700	
General and Administrative	800	2,500
Net Profit Before Taxes		£ 400

Exhibit 6-3
Bradford Engineering Company
Variable Budget

Sales (1m. units at £ 10)		£10,000,000	100%
Variable costs:			
Trade discounts	300,000		
Materials	4,000,000		
Labor	2,000,000		
Commissions	700,000		
Manufacturing O/H	100,000		
Commercial O/H	100,000		
Total		7,200,000	
Profit Contribution		2,800,000	28%
Specific Product Expenses			
Program costs:			
Advertising	200,000		
Promotion	200,000		
Selling	150,000		
Product development	70,000		
Standby:			
Product management	80,000		
Fixed mfg.	500,000		
Total specific expenses		1,200,000	
Product Earnings		1,600,000	16%

General Expenses

Program	200,000	
Standby	1,000,000	
Total specific expenses		1,200,000
Net Profit		400,000	4%

Exhibit 6-4
Break-Even Formulas

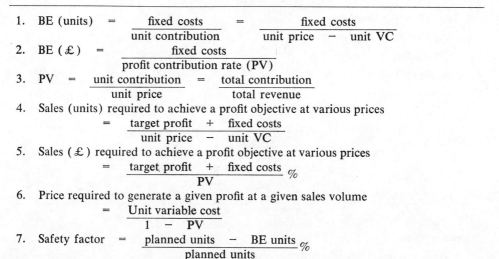

1. BE (units) $= \dfrac{\text{fixed costs}}{\text{unit contribution}} = \dfrac{\text{fixed costs}}{\text{unit price} - \text{unit VC}}$

2. BE (£) $= \dfrac{\text{fixed costs}}{\text{profit contribution rate (PV)}}$

3. PV $= \dfrac{\text{unit contribution}}{\text{unit price}} = \dfrac{\text{total contribution}}{\text{total revenue}}$

4. Sales (units) required to achieve a profit objective at various prices
$$= \dfrac{\text{target profit} + \text{fixed costs}}{\text{unit price} - \text{unit VC}}$$

5. Sales (£) required to achieve a profit objective at various prices
$$= \dfrac{\text{target profit} + \text{fixed costs}}{\text{PV}} \%$$

6. Price required to generate a given profit at a given sales volume
$$= \dfrac{\text{Unit variable cost}}{1 - \text{PV}}$$

7. Safety factor $= \dfrac{\text{planned units} - \text{BE units}}{\text{planned units}} \%$

Table 6–1
Bradford Engineering Company
Break Even Table of Unit Sales
Current Contribution %

% Change in Price	10%	15%	20%	25%	30%	35%	40%	45%	50%
+ 25	28.6	37.5	44.5	50.0	54.6	58.3	61.5	64.3	66.7
+ 20	33.3	42.8	50.0	55.6	60.0	63.7	66.7	69.2	71.4
+ 15	40.0	50.0	57.2	62.5	66.7	70.0	72.7	75.0	76.9
+ 10	50.0	60.0	66.7	71.5	75.0	77.8	80.0	81.8	83.3
+ 5	66.7	75.0	80.0	83.3	85.7	87.5	88.9	90.0	90.9
0	100.0	100.0	100.0	100.0	100.0	100.0	100.0	100.0	100.0
− 5	200.0	150.0	133.3	125.0	120.0	116.7	114.3	112.5	111.1
− 10		300.0	200.0	166.7	150.0	140.0	133.3	128.6	125.0
− 15			400.0	250.0	200.0	175.0	160.0	150.0	142.9
− 20				500.0	300.0	233.3	200.0	180.0	166.7
− 25					600.0	350.0	266.7	225.0	200.0

Percentage of new unit sales to old unit sales required to break even on a price change for products with various current gross margin percentages.

Table 6–2
Bradford Engineering Company
Break Even Table of Dollar Sales
Current Contribution %

% Change in Price	10%	15%	20%	25%	30%	35%	40%	45%	50%
+ 25	28.6	37.5	44.5	50.0	54.6	58.3	61.5	64.3	66.7
+ 20	40.0	51.4	60.0	66.7	72.0	76.4	80.0	83.1	85.7
+ 15	46.0	57.5	65.7	71.9	76.7	80.5	83.6	86.3	88.5
+ 10	55.0	66.0	73.3	78.6	82.5	85.6	88.0	90.0	91.7
+ 5	70.0	78.8	84.0	87.5	90.0	91.9	93.3	94.5	95.5
0	100.0	100.0	100.0	100.0	100.0	100.0	100.0	100.0	100.0
– 5	190.0	142.5	126.7	118.8	114.0	110.8	108.6	106.9	105.6
– 10		270.0	180.0	150.0	135.0	126.0	120.0	115.7	112.5
– 15			340.0	212.5	170.0	148.8	136.0	127.5	121.4
– 20				400.0	240.0	186.7	160.0	144.0	133.3
– 25					450.0	262.5	200.0	168.8	150.0

Percentage of new dollar sales to old dollar sales required to break even on a price change for products with various gross margin percentages.

repair shops, and large fleet operators. Currently, BEC sells one million units, largely through distributors. Its ex-factory price averages £ 10 per unit.

Healy wanted to evaluate management's new strategy to improve profitability. This strategy involved a major expansion to take up spare capacity and to increase market share from its current 20 percent level. The company's Balance Sheet (Exhibit 6–1) and Income Statement (Exhibit 6–2) are shown above. To develop better financial information Healy worked with his accountants to develop a variable budget (Exhibit 6–3). This gave a useful breakdown of costs and facilitated the use of break even analysis (Exhibit 6–4 and Tables 6–1 and 6–2).

Discussion Questions

1. How many units does BEC have to sell to break even?

2. How much (£ sales) does it have to sell to break even?

3. What is the safety factor?

4. Next year inflation is expected to push up variable labour and material costs by 15 percent. What impact will this have on the safety factor?

5. What is break even in units and sales at a price of £ 8? At £ 12?

6. How many units does it have to sell at £ 12 to make it the same budgeted profits?

7. How much sales (£) does it have to make at £ 8 to make the same profit as budget?

8. What is sales break even if a 10 percent return on sales is set as the minimum acceptable profit level?

9. If sales increase by 10 percent, by what percentage will profits increase? What happens if sales decline by 10 percent?

10. a. Adding a top sales representative to the salesforce would cost £15,000. You estimate he would increase sales by £40,000. Should you hire him?
b. If you trim advertising and promotion by £300,000, how much could sales fall before profits are hit?

11. Suppose you decide to invest £800,000 to reduce material costs by 10 percent. By how much would sales have to increase to recover this investment in the first year and to maintain current profits?

12. If the following changes are introduced simultaneously—(a) advertising and promotion cut back by £300,000, (b) a reduction of material costs by 10 percent for an investment of £800,000, and (c) a new sales representative hired at a cost of £15,000—then (1) what is the new break even volume and safety factor, and (2) what sales are needed to maintain budgeted profits?

13. What market segments offer the most potential for BEC?

14. Next year you have the potential of many more orders than you have capacity to fill. Scarce facilities in the finishing shop limit output to 14,000 facilities hours. You have the possibility of 8 major orders which generate the following revenue and contributions and require the numbers of facility hours shown. Which of these orders should you take?

Order	Revenue (£ 000)	Contributions (£ 000)	PV	Facilities Hours
E	350	90	.26	2,400
H	640	160	.25	5,000
I	480	60	.12	1,200
L	920	140	.15	2,700
K	760	130	.17	2,400
J	620	120	.19	2,000
F	470	110	.23	3,000
G	520	110	.23	3,600

15. Will a significant price cut be profitable? If so, how much of a price cut?

16. What is your advice to BEC? Explain.

Causeway Engineering, Ltd.

Causeway Engineering has an annual turnover of £38 million generated from four product lines. Each line contains a number of closely related products.

Line A is the company's original product line. This line is a group of standard, nondifferentiated electric components. Over the years, the market for this type of component has been declining as technologically more advanced systems have been introduced.

Line B, a specialist line of cable fittings, is the next oldest group of products. Although growth in this market also is now negligible, Causeway holds a leading position with most of the larger buyers in this field.

Line C is an advanced engineering device developed by Causeway six years ago. Sales have built up rapidly, and though there is increasing competition, a volume expansion of 15 percent is anticipated over the coming year.

Line D is the most recent introduction. A high-value product developed by the company's own research staff, it is regarded as a potential "real winner" for the

Table 6–3
Causeway Engineering Ltd.
Summary of Product Profitability (£000)

Product	Sales	Cost of Goods Sold	Gross Profit	Selling Expenses	Net Profit
A1	2,200	2,000	200	220	−20
A2	2,000	1,820	180	200	−60
A3	500	530	−30	50	−80
A4	200	200	0	20	−20
A5	100	100	0	10	−10
Total A	5,000	4,650	350	500	−150
B1	6,500	5,050	1,450	650	800
B2	6,000	4,880	1,120	600	520
B3	1,300	1,330	−30	130	−160
B4	200	140	60	20	40
Total B	14,000	11,400	2,600	1,400	1,200
					80
C1	8,000	6,200	1,800	800	
C2	2,000	1,720	280	200	1,000
C3	1,500	1,510	−10	150	80
C4	500	370	130	50	−160
Total C	12,000	9,800	2,200	1,200	1,000
D1	4,000	3,480	520	400	120
D2	2,000	1,840	160	200	−40
D3	1,000	800	200	100	100
Total D	7,000	6,120	880	700	180
Total	38,000	31,970	6,030	3,800	2,230

company. The market is expected to be large, perhaps £60 million per annum, and Causeway is encouraged by early buying interest.

Management keeps the profitability of all products under review. Table 6–3 shows the data presented to management by the chief accountant. Here, the cost of goods sold includes manufacturing overhead allocated in proportion to direct labour costs. Selling expenses are allocated at 10 percent of sales. Tables 6–4 and 6–5 show the profitability of the product mix using a variable budget system.

The question of most concern to Market Analysis, Ltd. relate to the Causeway's control system and marketing mix. In particular, the marketing analysts are concerned about limitations of and possible improvements in Causeway's control system, as presented in Table 6–3. Also, they feel the company's marketing mix must be thoroughly evaluated.

Table 6–4
Causeway Engineering Ltd.
Variable Line Budget (£000)

Product	A	B	C	D	Total
Sales	5,000	14,000	12,000	7,000	38,000
Variable costs:					
Labour	2,000	3,600	4,200	900	10,700
Materials	1,400	3,800	2,000	1,900	9,100
Manuf. & comm. OH	1,200	3,400	2,410	1,700	8,700
Total	4,600	10,800	8,610	4,500	28,500
Profit Contribution	400	3,200	3,400	2,500	9,500
% of Sales (PV)	8%	23%	28%	36%	25%
Specific programme costs:					
Advertising	200	560	480	400	1,640
Selling	280	380	400	300	1,360
Line management	50	60	60	30	200
Depreciation	20	500	610	670	1,800
Total	550	1,500	1,500	1,400	5,000
Product Earnings	−150	1,700	1,850	1,100	4,500
% of Sales	−3%	12%	15%	16%	12%
General program costs					960
Fixed costs					1,310
Total prog. & fixed costs					7,270
Net Profit					2,230
					6%
Specific investment	4,000	12,000	9,000	11,000	36,000
Earnings on investment	−3.8%	14%	20%	10%	12%
					(ROI=6%)

Table 6–5
Causeway Engineering Ltd.
Summary of Product Contributions (£000)

Product	Sales	Variable Costs	Contribution	PV	CFH* (£)
A1	2,200	1,920	280	12.7	280
A2	2,000	1,870	130	6.5	130
A3	500	510	−10	−2.0	−12
A4	200	190	10	5.0	14
A5	100	110	−10	−10.0	−20
Total A	5,000	4,600	400	8.0	100
B1	6,500	4,810	1,690	26.0	845
B2	6,000	4,820	1,180	19.7	590
B3	1,300	1,000	300	23.1	200
B4	200	170	30	15.0	20
Total B	14,000	10,800	3,200	22.9	457
C1	8,000	5,690	2,310	28.9	2,310
C2	2,000	1,500	410	25.0	273
C3	1,500	1,060	440	29.3	293
C4	500	360	140	28.0	70
Total C	12,000	8,610	3,400	28.3	567
D1	4,000	2,550	1,450	36.3	1,450
D2	2,000	1,350	650	32.5	650
D3	1,000	600	400	40.0	400
Total D	7,000	4,500	2,500	35.7	833
Total	38,000	28,510	9,500	25.0	475

* Contribution per hour of scarce facility.

Chapter 2

Identifying Market Segments

Market segmentation is a management strategy in which one or more groups of potential customers having similar within group characteristics is selected and separate marketing mixes *are developed* for each group. Thus, the strategy of market segmentation recognizes that capturing bigger pieces of a few markets may be better than gaining a share of all available markets.

There are three notable features in the above definition:

1. *Groups of potential customers.* Market segmentation is concerned with the behavior of groups of potential customers not individual behavior.

2. *Similar characteristics.* There are substantial differences in consumer behavior characteristics among groups of customers (e.g., differences in demographics, psychographics, and patterns of product usage among heavy versus light product users).

3. *Separate marketing mixes.* A basic proposition of market segmentation is that different groups of customers respond differently to different combinations of price, product attribute, market channel, and promotional levels (marketing mixes). Thus, separate marketing mixes need to be developed for each population segment the organization tries to reach.

These tenets were proposed by Wendell Smith in 1956. "Market segmentation consists of viewing a heterogeneous market as a number of small homogeneous markets in response to differing product preferences among important market segments. It is attributable to the desires of consumers or users for more precise satisfaction of their varying wants. Segmentation often involves the use of advertising and promotion. It is a merchandising strategy." [1]

---

[1] Wendell Smith, "Product Differentiation and Market Segmentation as Alternative Marketing Strategies." *Journal of Marketing,* **21** (July 1956), pp. 3–8. Published by the American Marketing Association.

Table   C—2-1
Toothpaste Market Segment Description
Benefit segmentation of the toothpaste market

	Sensory segment	Sociables segment	Worrier segment	Independent segment
Principal benefits sought	Product appearance, flavor	Brightness of teeth	Decay prevention	Price
Demographic strength	Children	Teens, young people	Large families	Men
Special behavioural characteristics	Users of spearmint flavor	Smokers	Heavy users	Heavy users
Brands highly flavoured	Colgate Stripe	Macleans Plus white	Crest	Any
Life style	Hedonistic	Active	Conservative	Value oriented

Source: Russell I. Haley, "Benefit Segmentation: A Decision-Oriented Research Tool," *Journal of Marketing,* **32** (July 1968), pp. 30–35. Published by the American Marketing Association.

Market segmentation as a strategy is likely to include some consumer research to relate or match product features preferred by particular groups of consumers with demographics, psychographics, product use behavior, and response rates to different marketing mixes.

Examples of Market Segmentation

Toothpaste. Four market segments have been identified as seeking different benefits from toothpaste. Each segment has a unique demographic, psychographic (lifestyle), and personality profile.[2] These four segments are summarized in Table C—2-1.

Notice in Table C—2-1 that worriers seek decay prevention as a principal benefit. This group contains a disproportionately large number of families with children. The worriers are seriously concerned about the possibility of cavities and show a definite preference for flouride toothpaste. This is reinforced by their personalities —worriers tend to be a little hypochondriacal and are less socially-oriented than some of the other groups.

Based on their different market profiles, each of the four market segments is likely to have different purchase responses to different marketing mixes. The sensory segments' search for flavors and product appearance may produce high purchase responses to multiple product flavors, while worriers may be affected more by

---

[2] Russell I. Haley, "Benefit Segmentation: A Decision Oriented Research Tool," *Journal of Marketing,* **32** (July, 1968), pp. 30–35. Published by the American Marketing Association.

Table   C—2–2
Marketing Mixes
For Toothpaste Market Segments

		Market Segment		
Marketing Mix	The Sensory Segment	Sociables	Worriers	Independent Segment
Product	Variety Multiple Flavors	Mouthwash and/or whitening additives	Flouride Additives	Economy Size
Price	Medium	Medium	High	Low
Channel	Selective	Selective	Selective	Intensive
Advertising				
Media	Television	Television	Magazines	Point-of-purchase displays
Appeal	Excitement, Oral Gratification	Social acceptance, Sex	Health	Value Economy,

medical endorsements for a specific brand of toothpaste. The marketing mixes likely to produce high purchase responses are shown in Table C—2–2 for the four toothpaste market segments. Differences in product, price, channel, and promotional programs are shown in Table C—2–2.

The marketing manager might use market tests of alternative marketing mixes to measure the purchase response rates from selected segments. Such market tests provide sales information on (1) the effects on sales of different combinations of levels of marketing variables *within a given segment* (response to low price and intensive distribution versus high price and selective distribution from the independent toothpaste segment), and (2) the effects of different combinations of levels of marketing variables *across segments* (response to low price and television advertising versus high price and magazine advertising for the worriers versus the sensory segment.)

New Banking Service. Assume that a bank wants to identify the market segment that will generate the greatest revenue for a new service enabling users of regular checking acounts to use their accounts as a bookkeeping system (thereby facilitating family budgeting and completion of tax forms). "Two major segments are identified, personal and small business checking account customers. The personal account customers are segmented further into two additional segments. An examination of the profiles of each suggests that the first may be called the *anxious* segment and the second may be labeled the *affluent* segment." [3]

The behavioral characteristics of the three segments are shown in Table C—2–3.

---

[3] G. David Hughes, *Demand Analysis for Marketing Decisions* (Homewood, Ill.: Richard D. Irwin, 1973), pp. 19–22. Reprinted by permission of the publisher.

Table C—2—3
Market segments for a new banking service

Behavioral characteristics	Segments		
	Personal accounts		Business accounts
	Anxious	Affluent	<5 employees
Demographic			
Age	42	42	39
Education	High school	Two or more years of college	Heterogeneous
Residence	Urban and suburban	Suburban	Suburban
Occupation	Blue collar and clerks	Executive, salesmen, and engineers	Lawyers, small retailers, and craftsmen
Economic			
Income	$10,000	$21,000	$18,000
Acceptable monthly charge	$0.10	$0.50	$1.00
Social			
Dominant beliefs about banks	Safe, stable	Facilitate transactions	Basic to financial management
Life style	Worrier	Outgoing optimist	Very mixed
Reference groups	Relatives and friends	Professional and business	Professional and business
Sources of information about innovations	TV, relatives, and friends	Business associates and trade papers	TV, friends, business, trade papers, and journals
Life cycle	Youngest child <15	Youngest child 10–15	Youngest child 10–15
Social class	Upper lower	Upper middle	Mixed
Psychological			
Criteria of good money management	Security	Growth and to avoid inflation	Profit and keep capital working

Attitudes toward	Friendly, convenient locations	Working-class bank, not convenient	Old-fashioned convenient locations
Bank A			
Bank B	For rich people, not convenient	Modern, most convenient	Modern, business oriented
Bank C	Vague image, little known	New bank, aggressive	Out for new business, innovative
Attitudes toward new service	For those who need a budget	Income tax aid, help plan family finances	Supplement to present accounting
Subjective probabilities of using service by			
Present depositors	0.20	0.15	0.10
Depositors switching from other banks	0.05	0.01	0.01
Noncustomers opening an account	0.07	0.00	0.00
Market characteristics			
Bank A market share	30%	20%	20%
Number of accounts (all banks)	40,000	10,000	1,200
Prospects with no checking account	30,000	0	0

Source: G. David Hughes, *Demand Analysis for Marketing Decisions*, (Homewood, Ill.: Richard D. Irwin, 1973). Reprinted by permission of the publisher.

comparison of the anxious and affluent personal accounts columns reveals substantial demographic, economic, social, psychological and market characteristic differences. The average income of the affluent ($21,000) is more than twice that of the anxious segment, and the affluent segment is more "upscale" (executives, sales representatives, and engineers) compared with the anxious segment.

The importance of the new service to the affluent is reflected in their willingness to pay more for the service ($.50 versus $.10 payment monthly by the anxious segment).

> Sociological and psychological variables reveal sharper distinctions between the first two segments. Worriers view banks as institutions for security while the affluent see banks in a facilitating role. Differences are revealed in sources of information, life-cycle stage, class, attitudes toward three commercial banks serving the community, salient attitude toward the new service, and the subjective probability of using the service.[4]

Notice in Table C—2–3 that the subjective probability of using the new service by present customers in the anxious segment is .20 and the bank (Bank A) has 30 percent of the market share of anxious customers (40,000 accounts). This information produces a monthly projected expected revenue from present customers in the anxious segment of $240.

Monthly expected	=	Number of	Market	Probability	Monthly	
Revenue		Accounts	Share	of Use	Charge	(11–1)
$240	=	40,000	.30	.20	.10	

Monthly expected revenues for other types of prospective customers (those who switch and new depositors) are shown in Table C—2–4. The data in Table C—2–4 suggests attracting members of the anxious segment to use the new banking service, if the goal is to maximize expected revenue.

Assuming a strategy to maximize expected revenue, the best marketing strategy may be to reinforce beliefs and attitudes presently held by the anxious segment. Promotional messages should be developed to present the service as a new convenience that reduces worry and entrances the security of sound money management. "The influence of friends could be incorporated by using testimonial ads. Later promotion might emphasize the need for good money management by children."[5]

These two examples (toothpaste and new banking service) illustrate the interactive effects of demographic, psychographic, and market behavior variables to influence and define market segments. The importance of the interaction of size of market (number of accounts, market share, probability of use, and net revenue per transaction [monthly charge]) should be noted. In the banking service example, the relatively high acceptable monthly service charge ($.50) among the affluent is counteracted by the relatively small size of the market (10,000 acounts), smaller market share (20%), and lower subjective probability of using the new service (.15) compared with the anxious segment.

---

[4] Ibid.
[5] Ibid.

Table   C—2–4
Expected revenue generated by a new bank service; bank A

Type of prospect	Monthly expected revenue generated by segments		
	Personal accounts		Business accounts
	Anxious	Affluent	<5 employees
Present customers (accounts × share × probability of use × monthly charge)	$ 240	$150	$24.00
Customers who switch			
New service (accounts × (1 − share) × probability of using × monthly charge)	140	40	9.60
Other service*	1,400	160	50.00
New depositors			
New service	210	—	—
Other services	2,100	—	—
Total expected revenue	$4,090	$350	$81.60

 * Estimated monthly revenue per customer is as follows: anxious, $1; affluent, $2; small business, $5.
   Source: G. David Hughes, *Demand Analysis for Marketing Decisions* (Homewood, IL: Richard D. Irwin, 1973). Reprinted by permission of the publisher.

Conditions for Effective Segmentation

Kotler identified three conditions necessary to measure the usefulness of particular characteristics for segmentation purposes: (1) measurability, (2) accessibility, and (3) substantiality.[6]

Measurability is the degree to which information exists or is obtainable for a particular buyer characteristic. Many characteristics that suggest the need for management action may not be easy to measure. The likelihood of using a new banking service among members of different market segments would be one example.

Accessibility is the degree to which a firm can effectively focus its marketing efforts on chosen segments. Identifying opinion leaders as a target segment may be ill-advised. If opinion leaders' media habits are not always distinct from opinion followers, focusing on the leaders will be misleading.[7] Competition may prevent accessibility to certain markets segmented by benefits sought, for example, the Crest brand of toothpaste may be found to have too high a loyalty among the worriers to change effectively.

Substantiality is the degree to which the segments are large and/or profitable enough to be worth considering for separate marketing programs. Remember in the new banking service example, the small relative size of the affluent segment

---

[6] Philip Kotler, *Marketing Management* (Englewood Cliffs, New Jersey: 1975).
[7] Ibid.

(10,000 accounts) counteracted the high acceptable monthly charge. The market segment willing to purchase prestuffed turkeys may be one example of a segment too small for developing a separate marketing mix or offering such a product (yet the product continues to be available for purchase every fall in the United States).

Reasons for Market Segmentation

"We market to everyone" is a phrase often heard from some managers. "Marketing to everyone is marketing to no one" is a response to this phrase likely to be given after analyzing market segments for different products and services. Most business firms and nonprofit organizations do not have the financial and marketing resources to develop and market products to all groups of consumers. American Motors and Rolls-Royce automobiles are examples of specializing marketing efforts on two different market segments based, in part, on *limited resources* of the industrial firms.

The majority of the consumers for most products can be meaningfully grouped into a limited number of groups (2 to 5) based upon usage behavior and demographic, psychographic, and marketing response characteristics. Consumers are identified as members of particular segments based on their segmentation profile (for example, the heavy fast-food franchise user, who is a woman working full-time, married with children, pro credit, risk taker, relatively price insensitive, and influenced by convenient locations). Not all consumers who are heavy product users or women with young children would be placed in the same market segment, but a substantial proportion (5%–30%) of consumers for a product category may have a similar segment profile. Thus, a second reason for market segmentation is that there are *market segments* and the responses of different segments to a marketing mix will likely be different.

This should not be meant to imply that there is no purchase variability of consumers *within* segments. Bass, Tigert, and Lonsdale have shown that product usage rates are likely to vary for segments of consumers defined by demographic characteristics. However, average usage is likely to be substantially different *between* market segments, and *most* consumers within a particular demographic and psychographic segment of heavy users will have higher usage rates than consumers within another demographic and psychographic segment of light users.[8] Table C—2–5 emphasizes these points by studying household beer purchases (bottles per month), shown cross-classified by family income and years of education of the head of household. For example, the average beer purchase in households with income under $3,000 where the head of the household had 6 years of education was 10.01 bottles per month with a standard deviation (standard error) of 1.64.

Notice in Table C—2–5 that consumption varies widely by demographic segments. Households with 12 years of education and $8,000–$9,999 annual family income have an average consumption of 32.14, about 5 times the consumption rate of households with 12 years of education and under $3,000 income. (The sample size n's, in Table C—2–5 provide some estimate of the relative size of the segments. For example, households with low educational levels of household heads

---

[8] Frank M. Bass, Douglas J. Tigert, and Ronald T. Lonsdale, "Market Segmentation: Group Versus Individual Behavior," *Journal of Marketing Research,* **5** (August 1968). Published by the American Marketing Association.

Table   C—2–5
Cross-Classification Analysis of
Beer Purchase of 1,400 Households,
Education by Income

Annual Family Income		Years of Education				
		6	10	12	14	16
Under $3,000	$\overline{X}$	10.01	6.53	6.18	12.27	15.21
	$s\overline{x}$	1.64	2.38	1.74	7.78	13.17
	n	1.24	36	38	7	4
$3,000–	$\overline{X}$	27.74	20.27	11.70	17.40	1.79
4,999	$s\overline{x}$	3.93	4.03	2.98	9.51	1.65
	n	48	38	45	14	7
$5,000–	$\overline{X}$	25.23	26.03	22.63	24.23	16.80
7,999	$s\overline{x}$	2.62	2.45	1.85	3.48	3.85
	n	115	122	196	57	35
$8,000–	$\overline{X}$	27.72	24.21	32.14	21.78	23.23
9,999	$s\overline{x}$	4.62	3.38	2.13	4.41	4.93
	n	30	56	88	32	30
$10,000–	$\overline{X}$	34.24	24.05	21.54	20.63	24.18
14,999	$s\overline{x}$	6.47	4.51	3.07	3.92	3.78
	n	15	37	61	45	50
$15,000	$\overline{X}_a$	36.58	12.50	28.49	34.17	17.86
and Over	$s\overline{x}$	10.68	0.00	6.93	8.52	3.80
	n	7	1	15	10	37

Source: Frank M. Bass, Douglas J. Tigert, and Ronald T. Lonsdale, "Market Segmentation: Group Versus Individual Behavior," *Journal of Marketing Research,* 5 (August 1968). Published by the American Marketing Association.

tend to have low annual family incomes and vice versa. Households with six years of education and $15,000 and over family incomes averaged 36.58; only 7 of 1,400 households entered this demographic segment.)

Market segment characteristics *provide implications for adjusting the mixes* to affect changes in consumer beliefs, attitudes, intentions, and behaviors. This is a third reason for segmenting markets. Consumers grouped (segmented) by consumption rates, demographics, and psychographics are likely to have different demand elasticities for changes in prices, advertising expenditures, sales messages, and types of retail outlets. The market segments for toothpaste and the suggested alternative marketing mixes are examples of adjusting marketing mixes to increase demand and profits from specific groups of consumers. There are similar examples for industrial market segmentation.[9]

[9] For examples, see Yoram Wind and Richard Cardozo, "Industrial Market Segmentation," *Industrial Marketing Segmentation,* 3 (1974), pp. 153–166, and Frederick E. Webster, Jr. and Yoram Wind, *Organizational Buying Behavior* (Englewood Cliffs, N.J.: Prentice–Hall, 1972).

Bases for Segmentation

By examining the segmentation examples for toothpaste brands and for the new banking service in Tables C—2–1 and C—2–3, you can see a substantial number of possible bases for market segmentation. The most frequently used bases are occupation, life-cycle, social class, geographic location, psychographics, brand loyalty, usage rate, sensitivity to changes in marketing variables (demand elasticity to price changes), and benefits sought.

Frank, Massy, and Wind have grouped (segmented) the bases for market segmentation in a 2 x 2 classification as shown in Table C—2–6. There are two levels of customer characteristics: general and situation (product) specific. Consumption patterns and demographic factors are objective measures, whereas psychographics (life-style), personality traits, attitudes, perceptions, and benefits sought are inferred.

Sometimes the effects of changes of marketing variables on market segments (price changes, changes in types of advertising themes) are inferred by asking consumers for their preference or likely purchase response. Or, the effects of alternative levels of marketing variables may be measured objectively in market experiments using combinations of prices, product types, promotion themes, and channel arrangements.

Buyer demographics, psychographics, and personality variables are represented in cells 1 and 2 of Table C—2–6.

Usage level (a situation specific and objective measure shown in cell 3) is often a dependent variable in market segmentation. Usage level is affected differently by different levels and combinations of independent variables. Variables in cells 1 and 2 in Table C—2–6 often are called independent variables.

Table   C—2–6

A Classification Sceme of Alternative Bases for Market Segmentation

		Customer Characteristics	
		General	Situation Specific
M e a s u r e s	Objective	Demographic Factors (Age, Stage in Life Cycle, Sex, Place of Living, Etc.) Socioeconomic Factors	Consumption Patterns (Heavy, Medium, Light) Brand Loyalty Patterns (Brands, Stores) Buying Situations
	Inferred	Personality Traits Life Style	Attitudes Perceptions and Preferences

Source: Ronald E. Franks, William F. Massy, and Yoram Wind, *Market Segmentation* (Englewood Cliffs, N.J.: Prentice–Hall, 1972), p. 27.

Figure   C—2–1
Income and Education Effects on Usage Rate

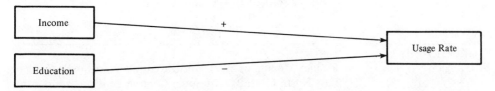

Table C—2–5 shows the individual (main) and combined (interactive) effects of two market segmenting variables (income and education) on another market segmenting variable (usage rate). This structure may be represented in a very generalized form as shown in Figure C—2–1.

Notice in Figure C—2–1, a positive income effect is hypothesized, for example, as income increases usage rate increases. A negative education and usage rate (for beer) is hypothesized, for example, as education increases, usage rate decreases. Do the findings shown in Table C—2–5 support these hypotheses? What marketing implications (recommendations for price, promotion, product and channel levels) could you suggest if the hypotheses were supported by data analysis?

Findings in Table C—2–5 support the two hypothesized main effects (if you compute the average beer consumption for each row and each column and observe the increases in usage as income increases, and the decreases in usage as education increases). Table C—2–5 also shows an interaction effect between income and education on usage level. An increase in usage level for *increases* in education is observed for the household with under $3,000 income, and conversely, for the $15,000 and over income group.

Similar analyses may be done using other bases of market segmentation. Five levels of education and six levels of family income were used in Table C—2–5 to produce 30 combinations or cells. If three usage levels (heavy, light, and none) were used in the table instead of average consumption levels, a total of 90 cells would be needed (5 x 6 x 3). Thus, when multiple bases with multiple levels of market segmentation are used, cross-classification analysis, such as in Table C—2–5, becomes unmanageable.

Typical levels for different market segmentation variables are shown in Table C—2–7. Usually, a number of demographic, geographic, psychographic, and buyer-behavior variables need to be used to develop different marketing mixes for market segments.

Since over 1,000,000 cells would be needed if all the levels of all the market segmentation variables were used in Table C—2–7, more powerful multivariate procedures are often used instead of cross-classification analysis when we examine 5 or more bases for segmentation. Multiple regression analysis, factor analysis, automatic interaction detection (AID), and multidimensional scaling are mulivariate procedures which have been used in segmenting markets.[10] One example of a

---

[10] For examples see Peter T. Fitz Roy, *Analytical Methods for Marketing Management* (New York: McGraw–Hill, 1976).

Table   C—2–7
Major segmentation variables and
their typical breakdowns

Variables	Typical Breakdowns
GEOGRAPHIC	
Region	Pacific; Mountain; West North Central; West South Central; East North Central; East South Central; South Atlantic; Middle Atlantic; New England
County size	A; B; C; D
City or SMSA size	Under 5,000; 5,000–19,999; 20,000–49,999; 50,000–99,999; 100,000–249,999; 250,000–499,999; 500,000–999,999; 1,000,000–3,999,999; 4,000,000 or over
Density	Urban; suburban; rural
Climate	Northern; southern
DEMOGRAPHIC	
Age	Under 6; 6–11; 12–17; 18–34; 35–49; 50–64; 65+
Sex	Male; female
Family size	1–2; 3–4; 5+
Family life cycle	Young, single; young, married, no children; young, married, youngest child under six; young, married, youngest child six or over; older, married, with children; older, married, no children under 18; older, single; other
Income	Under $5,000; $5,000–$7,999; $8,000–$9,999; over $10,000
Occupation	Professional and technical; managers, officials and proprietors; clerical, sales; craftsmen, foremen; operatives; farmers; retired; students, housewives; unemployed
Education	Grade school or less; some high school; graduated high school; some college; graduated college
Religion	Catholic; Protestant; Jewish; other
Race	White; Negro; Oriental
Nationality	American; British; French; German; Eastern European; Scandinavian; Italian; Spanish; Latin American; Middle Eastern; Japanese; and so on.
Social class	Lower-lower; upper-lower; lower-middle; middle-middle; upper-middle; lower-upper; upper-upper
PSYCHOGRAPHIC	
Compulsiveness	Compulsive; noncompulsive
Gregariousness	Extrovert; introvert
Autonomy	Dependent; independent
Conservatism	Conservative; liberal; radical
Authoritarianism	Authoritarian; democratic
Leadership	Leader; follower
Ambitiousness	High achiever; low achiever
BUYER BEHAVIOR	
Usage rate	Nonuser; light user; medium user; heavy user
Readiness stage	Unaware; aware; interested; intending to try; trier; regular buyer

Benefits sought	Economy; status; dependability
End use	(Varies with the product)
Brand loyalty	None; light; strong
Marketing-factor sensitivity	Quality; price; service; advertising; sales promotion

Source: Philip Kotler, *Marketing Management: Analysis, Planning, and Control,* 3rd ed. (Englewood Cliffs, N.J.: Prentice–Hall, 1976), p. 146.

Figure   C—2–2
Multiple discriminant analysis of eight beer brands

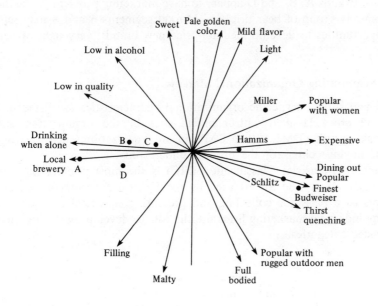

Johnson, R. M. "Market segmentation: a strategic management tool," reprinted from the *Journal of Marketing Research,* **8, 1,** February 1971, pp. 13–18. Published by the American Marketing Association.

multivariate procedure applied to market segmentation is provided by Johnson for the Chicago beer market.[11] He used 35 bases for segmenting approximately 500 males for eight brands of beer. The 35 bases were all consumer perceptions (beliefs) for 35 product attributes for each brand. Using multiple discriminate analysis,[12]

[11] Richard M. Johnson, "Market Segmentation: A Strategic Management Tool," *Journal of Marketing Research,* **8** (February 1971), pp. 13–18. Published by the American Marketing Association.

[12] Multiple discriminate analysis is a multivariate procedure that finds the linear combination of variables (for example, product attribute perceptions) which maximizes the discrimination between groups.

Johnson found two product dimensions that adequately discriminated between the brands, as shown in Figure C—2–2. Notice that the vertical axis reflects relative lightness and the horizontal axis contrasts premium quality on the right with popular price on the left.

The different brands of beer are perceived to be in different regions of the two dimensional space. According to Figure C—2–2, Schlitz and Budweiser are perceived as somewhat heavy, premium beers while brand A (not identified) is perceived as a popular priced beer, medium in body.

Beer drinkers were asked to rate their ideal brand of beer according to each of the 35 attributes. The beer drinkers were grouped (using another multivariate procedure called cluster analysis) into 9 segments according to their ideal points. These segments are shown in Figure C—2–3. Figure C—2–3 suggests several marketing implications. Brands A, B, and D appear to have marketing problems since they are distant from any group of beer drinkers. Market segments 6 and 8 may represent market opportunities to develop medium-price new brands, very light or heavy in body.

Bases for Segmenting Organizational Markets

General and situation specific organizational characteristics are listed in Table C—2–8 and cross-classified with characteristics of the organization and the decision-making unit (DMU). The DMU in an organization, such as a business firm, is the buying center for the product under study.

The Standard Industrial Classification (SIC) is the most popular basis for industrial segmentation. The SIC is used by the Federal government and all state governments as a basis for collecting and presenting statistical data on business firms. Many industrial marketing firms use the SIC to develop marketing mixes for different coded categories.

Figure   C—2–3
Distribution of ideal points in product space

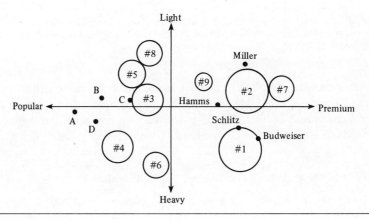

Source: Johnson (1971).

Table   C—2–8

A Classification Scheme of Bases for Organizational Segmentation

Type of Measure by (Object)		Nature of Characteristics	
		General Characteristics	Situation Specific Characteristics
Organiza-tional Character-istics	Objective Measures	Organization Demographics; SIC category, geographic location. Organization Structure & Technology	Product Usage Loyalty Pattern The Buying Center Buying Situation
	Inferred Measures	Buying tasks and Pur-chasing Decision Rules	Attitudes, Perception and Preference The Determinants of the Purchase Decision and Their Relative Im-portance
DMU Character-istics*	Objective Measures	Demographic Characteris-tics; Age, Sex, Education	Loyalty Pattern
	Inferred Measures	Personality and Life Style	Attitudes, Perception and Preference

* Decision-Making Unit.

Source: Ronald E. Frank, William F. Massy, and Yoram Wind, *Market Segmentation* (Englewood Cliffs, N.J.: Prentice–Hall, 1971), p. 95.

Notice the similarity between Tables C—2–6 and C—2–8 for the situation specific characteristics. In both cases, the objective measures of situation specific characteristics, for example, product usage, are used most often as the dependent variable in segmentation analysis.

The bottom portion of Table C—2–8 lists the variables used to classify a specific organization by the behavior of its buying center. Organizations may have similar characteristics but different DMU characteristics. (For example, purchasing actions of the buying center for MacDonald's and the U.S. Army may be similar even though the two organizations have different characteristics.)

Wind and Cardozo offer a six step sequence for segmenting industrial markets.[13] This sequence is shown in Figure C—2–4.

The sequence starts with identifying macro-segments based on *objective measures* of *general and situation specific* characteristics, for example, firm size, usage rate, SIC category, location. Next, the marketing firm selects a set (usually 1 to 4) of "acceptable macro-segments" based on corporate objectives and resources for fur-ther analysis. Third, each selected segment is evaluated in terms of whether it exhibits distinct responses to the firm's marketing stimuli (a set of *alternative mar-keting* mixes).

---

[13] Yoram Wind and Richard Cardozo, "Industrial Market Segmentation," *Industrial Market-ing Management,* **3** (1974), pp. 153–166.

Figure   C—2–4
An Approach to Segmentation of Organizational Markets.

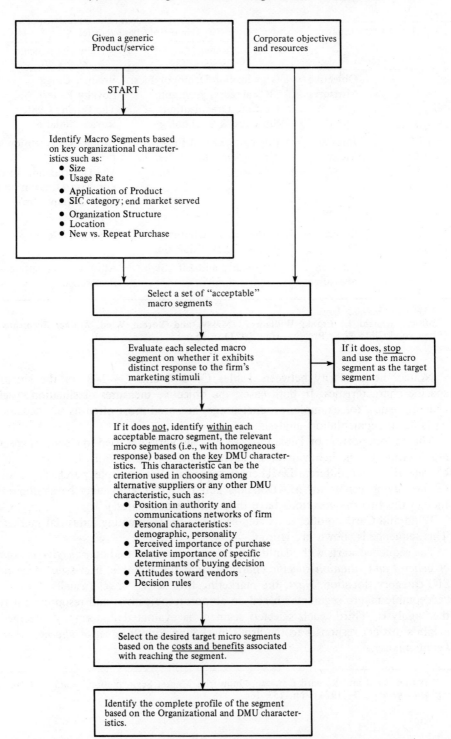

Source: Yoram Wind and Richard Cardozo, "Industrial Market Segmentation," *Industrial Marketing Management,* **3** (1974) pp. 153–166.

If the segment responds favorably, it is selected as a target. If the segment does not respond favorably, then the relevant micro-segments based on key DMU characteristics are selected and marketing mixes are developed for selected DMU segments.

Four types of organizational segments are shown in Table C—2–9 as an example of the possible combinations of market segments and marketing mixes. The example is for a lumber manufacturer with four broadly defined market segments: (1) wholesalers, (2) retailers and chains, (3) industrial accounts, and (4) contractors. Four types of promotion and four types of product-service are shown in the table for a total of 64 possible combinations.

Following the analysis of the likely response of each of the four segments to each of the possible product-service and promotion mix combinations, the firm would select the segments most likely to provide the best return on dollars invested and/or the highest profits. Market segment responses for alternative channels and price mixes would be similarly evaluated.

Summary

The purpose of this chapter has been to introduce the reasons and bases for market segmentation. Market segmentation is a management strategy used to locate groups of customers most likely to respond to specific marketing mixes.

Table   C—2–9
Customer-Prospect Mix

Customer-Prospect Mix

Product Service Mix	(1) Wholesalers — Promotional Mix					(2) Retailers and Chains Promotional Mix	(3) Industrial Accounts Promotional Mix	(4) Contractors Promotional Mix
	Advertising	Personal Selling	Merchandising	Sales Promotion	Field Service			
(1) Lumber								
(2) Plywood								
(3) Shingles and Siding								
(4) Pre-cut Components								

Source: William J. E. Crissy and Robert M. Kaplan: "Matrix Models for Marketing Planning," *MSU Business Topics* (Summer 1963), pp. 48–67. Reprinted by permission of the publisher, Division of Research, Graduate School of Business Administration, Michigan State University.

Measurability, accessibility, and substantiality are three conditions necessary for segmenting a market.

Most firms do not have the resources to market to all potential customers. Therefore, they market to segments grouping consumers according to consumer attitudes, usage rates, psychographic and demographic characteristics. Different market segments respond in varying degrees to alternative marketing mixes. Both objective and inferred bases for measuring general and situation specific characteristics may be used to segment consumer and industrial markets. A sequence of six stages may be used to segment organizational customers.

Discussion Questions

1. Define market segmentation. Give an example of market segmentation for a consumer product.

2. What are the conditions necessary for effective market segmentation? Briefly explain each.

33. Which cell in Table C—2–5 represents the highest total purchases of beer? (Hint: compute average sales times the number of respondents for each cell.) Offer two conclusions to your analysis.

4. Complete the following diagram and explain its meaning.

		Customer Characteristics	
		General	
M E A S U R E S		(1)	(3)
	Inferred	(2) Personality Traits, Life Style	(4)

5. List several types of general and situation specific characteristics of firms for organizational segmentation. Provide an example of organizational market segmentation based on these characteristics.

Some Major Marketing Information Sources

American Statistics Index—Congressional Information Service. A comprehensive guide and index to the statistical publications of the U.S. government. (monthly)

A Basic Bibliography on Marketing Research—compiled by Robert Ferber et al; 3rd ed., American Marketing Association. The basic divisions of this bibliography are background materials, techniques of marketing research, areas of applications, and miscellaneous topics such as research communication and administration.

Business Periodicals Index—a cumulative subject index to English language periodicals in the fields of accounting, advertising and public relations, automation, banking, communications, economics, finance and investment, insurance, labor, management, marketing, taxation, and specific businesses, industries and trades.

County and City Data Book—contains a wide variety of economic and social facts on local areas, such as counties, cities, metropolitan areas, urbanized areas, and unincorporated places of 25,000 inhabitants or more in the United States. Subjects covered include bank deposits, birth and death rates, business firms, education, employment, income of families, manufacturers, population, retail trade, savings, and wholesale trade.

Current Sources of Marketing Information: A Bibliography of Primary Marketing Data—compiled and edited by Edgar Gunther and Frederick A. Goldstein; American Marketing Association, 1960. Although this book was published in 1960, the sources listed are still appropriate for finding sources of statistical information. The aim of the authors was to list the principal statistical sources most used by market researchers.

Data Sources for Business and Market Analysis—by Nathalie D. Frank; 2nd ed., Scarecrow Press, 1969. Arranged by type of source, for example, census, abstracts and indexes, and directories; this annotated bibliography lists references selected on the basis of their general usefulness in researching economic conditions, business trends, and consumer and industrial markets.

Editor and Publisher Market Guide—current data on newspaper markets in cities and towns in the United States and Canada. Provides information on transportation facilities, population, housing facilities, banks, types of industry and other similar data. (annual)

Guide to Consumer Markets—Conference Board. Provides statistical information concerning the consumer including demographic, social, and economic data. (annual)

Guide to U.S. Government Statistics—by John L. Andriot; 4th ed., Documents Index, 1973. A list designed to help the user thread his way through the voluminous statistical contents of federal publications. The entries are arranged alphabetically by government agency and summarize their purpose, content, frequency, and availability.

Market Guide—issues offer individual market surveys of approximately 1,500 United States and Canadian cities where a daily newspaper is published. Data are presented by state and city; data give for each city such information as population, location, trade area, banks, principal industries, colleges and universities, largest department stores, chain stores, retail outlets and sales, and newspapers.

Predicasts—quarterly with annual cumulations. Contains abstracts of published forecasts with historical data for the United States. Coverage includes general economics, all industries, detailed products and end-use data. Arranged by SIC number.

Predicasts Basebook—Predicast, Inc. Contains annual data from 1960 to the current year for over 18,000 statistical series. Subject coverage of the U.S. economy ranges from population and gross national product to specific products and services. Series are coded and sequenced by Standard Industrial Classifications. (annual)

Sales Management—offers information on all phases of the marketing process. This book concentrates on the strategies and the tactics of marketing, including the research and evaluation of markets for products and services, the operations involved in bringing them to the consumer, and the building of effective sales teams. Most of the articles are short reports of developments in business and selling, or descriptions of individual campaigns, selling techniques, and the use of media. Of particular note is the annual service issue, *Survey of Buying Power,* which factually and statistically reports the current estimated figures in buying power, showing population, sales, and income changes. Definitions, descriptions, sources, methods, and application of the data also are supplied. This enables readers to use the facts for specific needs.

Social Indicators—U.S. Office of Management and Budget. Selected statistics on social conditions and trends in the United States including health, public safety, education, employment, income, housing, leisure and recreation, and population.

Statistical Abstract of the United States—a single-volume work presenting quantitative summary statistics on the political, social, and economic organization of the United States. It serves not only as a first source for statistics of national importance but also as a guide to further information, as references are given for sources to all tables. Statistics cover a period of several years, usually about 15 or 20; some tables run back to 1789 or 1800. A statistical abstract supplement, issued for 1972, presents the latest available census figures for each county, and for the larger cities in the U.S. (The 1972 volume includes data for cities having 25,000 inhabitants or more in 1970.) Also has summary figures for states, geographical regions, urbanized areas, standard metropolitan areas, and unincorporated places.

Statistics Sources—edited by Paul Wasserman, 4th ed., Gale Research Co. A subject guide to data on industrial, business, social, educational, financial, and other topics for the United States and internationally.

Survey of Current Business—U.S. Department of Commerce. Analysis of current business trends is followed by statistical series on national income, gross national product, personal and farm income; expenditures for new plant and equipment, retail and wholesale sales, and other basic series. Important issues are February which reviews the previous years, and July, on national income. (monthly)

United States Census of Manufacturers—contents of volumes vary, but cover general statistics, statistics by industry, area statistics, and products.

State Power Company

William O. Bearden, Richard M. Durand, Jesse E. Teel, Jr.
The University of Alabama

State Power Company is the only electric utility company currently operating within a large southern state. Recent economic and environmental changes have caused the management of State Power to realize a need for reevaluating its interface with the public and to plan for the development of future power sources. Before actual changes in operating and marketing policies were to be implemented, management felt the need to enlist the assistance of an independent marketing research firm to gather information relating to the provision and consumption of electric energy.

Current Situation

Consumer dissatisfaction with electric utility companies recently has been intensifying. Management of State Power believes this discontent is due largely to the following phenomena:

(1) declining service as perceived by consumers

(2) increasing utility bills (faster than inflation)

(3) reports of high profits made by utility companies which are state-regulated monopolies

(4) increasing consumer activism.

Electric utility personnel need a better understanding of the nature of this dissatisfaction so that more effective communications for reaching the public can be developed.

Furthermore, due to declining oil supplies and rising demand for energy, management feels that it must begin to develop new sources of energy. Currently under consideration are the construction of a coal-powered and a nuclear-powered plant as supplemental means of providing electric power for future needs. State

Power management believed it was necessary for them to know public opinion concerning these two pending energy-related issues to aid in their decision making. To that end, State Power conducted a survey among consumers in their service area.

Data Collected

A total of 754 randomly selected residents provided demographic, life-style, media consumption, and public policy issue-related data for use by the company. The demographic characteristics assessed were: age, residence, education, family income, sex, and race. Summary statistics describing the entire sample are provided in Exhibit 7–1.

Sample members also provided information on 29 life-style variables. On the basis of factor analysis, five composite psychographic dimensions were formed from the original 29 variables. Sample statements and reliability coefficients for the composite psychographic characteristics are presented in Exhibit 7–2. These dimensions reflect the following general behavioral characteristics: traditionalist, outgoing/individualist, concerned with quality/service, socially conscious, and

Exhibit 7-1
Summary of Selected Demographic
Characteristics of the Data

A. Race and Sex:

    White males—41.0%   Black males—9.3%

    White females—40.3%   Black females—9.4%

B. Age:

    Range = 17 to over 65 with approximately 50% of sample under 35

C. Annual income:

    1. Respondent's income:

        Range = less than $3,000 to more than $50,000 with approximately 50% of sample under $5,000

    2. Respondent family's income:

        Range = less than $3,000 to more than $50,000 with approximately 50% of sample under $10,000

D. Education:

    Over 50% of sample graduated from high school, and

    Over 12% of sample graduated from college

Exhibit 7-2
Sample Statements and Reliability Coefficients
For Psychographic Dimensions

Dimension	Sample Statement [1]	No. of Items	Alpha Coefficient
Traditionalist	I have some old-fashioned tastes and habits.	11	.66
Outgoing/ Individualist	I would rather fix something myself than take it to an expert.	5	.57
Quality/ Service	I will go out of my way to find a bank with good service.	5	.68
Socially/ Conscious	If my clothes are not in fashion, it really bothers me.	5	.69
Other- Directed	I usually ask for help from other people in making decision.	3	.56

[1] All AIO statements were operationalized as five-place scales ranging from strongly disagree to strongly agree.

other-directed. Media consumption information was obtained from respondents for local television stations, local radio stations, three weekly news magazines, and three daily newspapers. Radio and TV use were operationalized as the total number of occasions a respondent was exposed to either a radio or TV station for at least 15 minutes during the previous 5-day period. Newspaper use was operationally defined as the total number of daily newspapers each respondent read for at least 10 minutes over a 5-day period. Magazine use was measured as the number of weekly news magazines the respondent reported as having read for at least 10 minutes per week over a 4-week period.

In addition to psychographic and demographic information, questions also were included to provide more complete profiles of satisfied and dissatisfied electric utility consumers. These questions dealt with energy problems, related cost issues, and the political orientation of each respondent (see Exhibit 7–5).

Specifically, all respondents were asked the following three questions concerning energy problems and related cost increases:

1. There has been a lot of discussion recently about energy. Do you think that energy problems in this area are: very serious, somewhat serious, or not serious at all?

2. Do you feel that our energy problems are temporary or do you think the problems we face are something we will have to deal with for a long time? (Temporary or enduring?)

3. Given the present economic situation, do you think that there will be additional increases in your electric rates in the next 12 months?

A second set of issues were included as surrogate measures of political aliena-

Exhibit 7-3
Individual Characteristic Mean Scores for
Committed and Uncommitted Consumers

Characteristics	Nuclear Plant		Coal Plant	
	Committed n = 553	Uncommitted n = 201	Committed n = 524	Uncommitted n = 230
Demographics				
Age (Yrs.)	39.01	40.02	39.15	40.85
Residence: Urban [1]	69.00	79.70*	69.16	78.20*
Rural	31.00	20.30	30.90	21.80
Education (Yrs.)	12.06	11.60*	12.06	11.66*
Income	9,280	8,100**	9,385	8,065**
Sex: Male [1]	55.50	35.80**	56.70	35.70**
Female	44.50	64.20	43.30	64.30
Race: White [1]	84.30	73.10**	84.50	73.90**
Black	15.70	26.90	15.50	26.10
Life Style Characteristics				
Traditionalist	39.34	39.54	39.17	39.90
Outgoing/Individualist	16.80	15.04**	16.91	15.00**
Quality/Service Concern	18.09	16.30**	18.11	16.48**
Other-Directed	9.35	9.23	9.41	9.09
Socially-Conscious	16.27	15.21**	16.42	15.01**
Media Consumption				
Newspapers	4.62	3.92**	4.63	4.00*
News Magazines	1.69	1.01**	1.72	1.02**
Television	3.16	2.77*	3.13	2.89
Radio	.74	.66	.75	.64
Voting Orientation				
Voter: Registered [1]	74.9	58.2 **	75.4	59.6 **
Nonregistered	25.1	41.8	24.8	40.4
Liberal-Conservative [2]	3.29	3.53*	3.26	3.56

* p < .05
** p < .01
[1] Distribution of each category are presented as percentages. Significance levels refer to Chi-square statistic.
[2] Lower score reflects a more liberal orientation.

tion. Respondents were asked whether they agreed or disagreed with the following statements:

1. There doesn't seem to be anything that people like me can do to get our voice heard in government and politics.

2. Most politicians can be trusted to do what they think is best for the country.

In addition to these questions, respondents also were asked whether they were

Exhibit 7-4
Distributions of Committed and Uncommitted Consumer Opinions Regarding Personal Involvement in Public Policy-Making

	Nuclear Plant		Coal Plant	
Public-Policy Dimensions	Committed n = 553	Uncommitted n = 201	Committed n = 524	Uncommitted n = 230
Voice in Politics: [1]				
Heard	51.2	42.1*	51.6	42.2**
Unheard	48.8	57.9	48.4	57.8
Voice Makes A Difference:				
Agree	56.5	43.3**	55.5	46.6**
Disagree	43.5	56.7	44.5	53.4
Politicians Can Be Trusted:				
Agree	42.7	41.7	41.9	43.9**
Disagree	57.3	58.3	58.1	56.1
Frequently Fail to Vote:				
Agree	38.8	53.5**	38.5	53.2**
Disagree	61.2	46.5	61.5	47.8
Overall Community Change:				
Better	28.0	20.4*	27.3	23.0*
Worse	38.2	35.3	39.7	32.2
Same	33.8	44.3	33.0	44.8
Service in Political Campaign:				
Willing	30.5	13.1**	30.3	24.5
Unwilling	69.5	76.9	69.7	75.5
Contributions to Campaigns:				
Willing	27.8	16.3**	27.4	18.9**
Unwilling	72.2	83.7	72.6	81.1

* $p < .05$
** $p < .01$
[1] Proportions in each category are reported as percentages. Significance levels refer to Chi-square statistic for each policy concern.

registered to vote and to rate their political philosophy (very liberal—very conservative) along five point scales.

General Data Analysis

State Power research analysts decided to use factor analysis on the data. Factor analysis is a multivariate technique useful in reducing the number of variables in a data set into a more manageable subset of composite dimensions which maintains most of the original information. The 29 life-style (psychographic) dimensions originally collected were factor analyzed. Five factors accounted for 87 percent of the variation in the data (see Exhibit 7–2). Composite variables were constructed to represent the five dimensions which emerged. Sample statements and the coefficient alphas as indicators of internal reliability are depicted in Exhibit 7–2.

Commitment groups were determined by whether respondents favored, opposed, or responded "don't know" to a series of questions intended to measure community opinion toward construction of both nuclear and coal-fired energy plants. Individuals with either positive or negative attitudes toward each energy plant were combined to form the committed group for that issue. Differences in mean scores between the two groups on the demographic, psychographic, and media use variable were evaluated by t-tests. Chi-square analysis also was used to examine the distributions of committed and uncommitted consumers across those dimensions dealing with respondent attitudes toward their personal involvement with public decision making.

A separate analysis of relationships between respondents' satisfaction with the utility company and their demographic, political, psychographic, and media use characteristics was conducted for each of three dimensions, reflecting respondent beliefs concerning the following aspects of State Power:

1. the firm's ability to provide good customer service and further the development of local communities

2. the firm's ability to control costs

3. the firm's ability to provide and maintain electricity.

Approximately 58 percent of the sample consumers were satisfied with the company in terms of "service-to-community" and 61.5 percent were satisfied with the firm's ability to provide electricity. However, only 10.3 percent were satisfied with the firm's ability to control costs. The latter probably is due to rapidly rising utility bills and the general saliency of this issue to most consumers. Differences between satisfied and dissatisfied respondents on the various characteristics were evaluated by Chi-square analysis and t-tests of mean differences.

Summary

State Power Company is faced with rising consumer dissatisfaction in an uncertain environment. Regulation increases significantly the importance of community relations as an element of the marketing mix. To management's credit, an extensive research project attempted to probe two primary and essential areas of concern:

1. the nature of the dissatisfied consumer segment concerning current operations

2. the nature of the uncommitted consumer segment regarding future power sources.

Exhibit 7-5
Differences Between Satisfied and Dissatisfied Utility Customers

| | | Belief Dimensions | | | | | |
| | | Service to Community | | Control of Costs | | Ability to Provide Electricity | |
Variables	df	X^2	t-value[1]	X^2	t-value	X^2	t-value
Energy and Political Issues							
Seriousness of Energy Problems	3	10.22**		2.15		29.95***	
Time Span of Energy Crises	2	24.85***		2.19		31.47***	
Possibility of Rate Increase	2	11.55***		6.06**		18.19***	
Voice Heard	1	3.95**		6.96***		4.10**	
Trust in Politicians	1	13.18***		3.02*		4.51**	
Registered to Vote	1	6.81***		3.79*		3.10*	
Political Philosophy			-.14		.55		-.99
Demographics							
Race	1	.77		1.84		6.11**	
Sex	1	4.62**		4.42**		10.69***	
Residence	3	16.34***		6.87*		11.55***	
Age	752		1.48		-.09		.25
Income	752		.64		.54		-1.06
Education	752		.44		.32		1.94*

134

Psychographics				
Traditionalist	752	-1.65*	.40	-2.35**
Outgoing/Individualist	752	-2.68***	-2.67***	-3.73***
Quality/Service	752	-4.60***	-2.11**	-3.92***
Socially Conscious	752	-1.23	.99	-3.46***
Other-Directed	752	-1.15	.91	-1.55
Media Usage				
Magazine Usage	752	-3.98***	-.81	-1.36
Newspaper Usage	752	-1.34	-.85	-1.23
Radio Usage		-1.19	-.98	-.49
TV Usage		-1.00	-.15	-.24

[1] A negative sign indicates that the mean value for that variable was less for dissatisfied than for satisfied respondents.

*** p < .01
** p < .05
* p < .10

Data has been depicted in summary forms and requires interpretation for subsequent use in planning marketing strategy.

Management realizes that implementation of new policies and operating procedures affecting the general public is becoming increasingly difficult due to vociferous opposition from special-interest groups. These individuals may have strongly held attitudes not easily changed by promotional efforts. State Power management appears to understand the importance of the uncommitted consumer segment as a major target audience for creating favorable attitudes. Furthermore, the alternative to understanding and communicating with dissatisfied consumers may be more frequent denial of rate increases and further erosion of the utility company's capacity to meet rising service demands.

Discussion Questions

1. How might the demographic information be used in the development of promotional strategies for State Power Company? Psychographics? Reported media consumption?

2. What implications for management does the "uncommitted" segment suggest in gaining acceptance of the proposed energy plants?

3. What promotional messages would be most appropriate for communicating with satisfied consumers? Dissatisfied consumers?

4. Develop a promotional program for gaining public acceptance regarding the construction of both a nuclear and a coal-fired power plant.

5. How does government regulation affect the nature of public utility marketing?

6. How might the operational measures described be improved upon? What additional data might also have been gathered to assist management in its planning for the future?

Suggested References

1. Dyer, Robert F. and Terrence A. Shimp, "Enhancing the Role of Marketing Research in Public Policy Decision Making," *Journal of Marketing,* **41** No. 1 (January 1977), pp. 63–67.

2. Francis, Joe D. and Lawrence Busch, "What We Don't Know About 'I Don't Knows'," *Public Opinion Quarterly* **39** No 2 (Summer 1975), pp. 207–218.

3. Gergen, Kenneth J. and Kurt W. Back, "Communication in the Interview and the Disengaged Respondent," *Public Opinion Quarterly,* **30** (1966), pp. 358–398.

4. Lambert, Zarrel V. and Fred W. Kniffin, "Consumer Discontent: A Social Perspective," *California Management Review,* **18** (Fall 1975), pp. 36–44.

5. Wells, W. D., "Psychographics: A Critical Review," *Journal of Marketing Research,* **12** (May 1975), pp. 196–213.

6. Wilkie, William L. and David M. Gardner, "The Role of Marketing Research in Public Policy Decision Making," *Journal of Marketing,* **38** No. 1, (Jan. 1974), pp. 38–47.

Pleasure Shelter: Identifying Market Segments for a New Product

M. Wayne DeLozier, University of South Carolina

In 1971 Jack and Henry Jacobs hit upon an idea they felt would bring them a lot of money—a recreational shelter made out of grain bin tops, supported by metal posts (or legs). Most recreational shelters were made of wood and subject to rot, and were easily damaged in high winds and severe weather

Jack and Henry had been distributors of grain bins for 18 years, having built a substantial business in the southeastern part of the United States. Operating out of their home on 20 acres of farmland in Springly, Georgia, Jack and Henry were making a good living from grain bin sales and other farm-related items.

Jack Jacobs got the idea of a recreational shelter made from grain bin tops after observing his two children playing under a grain bin top supported by several stacks of bricks. The kids were having a picnic in the shade of the grain bin top during a summer day which reached a high of 102 degrees.

Jack discussed his new idea with his brother, Henry, and both contacted a draftsman, Mike Connally, the next day. After obtaining several designs from Mike, they presented their idea to Chuck Mills, president of Bowman-Austin who was their supplier of grain bins. Within several weeks, Chuck was sold on the recreational shelter and negotiated a deal with the Jacobs brothers, agreeing to pay them 10 percent of all net profits on the sale of the recreational shelter they had designed. Chuck saw many advantages to this new product design over conventional recreational shelters and was very excited about getting started.

The Bowman-Austin Company

Bowman-Austin (B-A) is a manufacturer of grain bins, fans and heaters for grain drying, perforated grain bin floors, harrows and draw bars, bulk tanks, hog shelters, and other farm equipment. They have sales in all 50 states, U.S. territories, and neighboring countries, such as Mexico and Canada. The company has been in business since 1923 and operates out of Amosville, Ohio. Although B-A is a

137

conservatively run company, Chuck Hills was open to new ventures that used his company's existing facilities and resources. The pleasure shelter, he felt, was such an idea.

B-A is a financially successful company. They had sales of nearly $8 million in 1976, and net profits of $1.5 million. Table 8–1 presents sales by product for the years ending November 30, 1975 and 1976.

The Product Design and Mix

The Pleasure Shelter is an open recreational shelter designed for protection from sun and rain. The shelter uses several upright posts anchored in the ground to support a cononical roof (a grain bin top) which has a 2-foot overhang extending downward from the roof. The roof has a ventilation opening at the top center portion of the cone roof. The ventilator is available either with or without a roto fan exhaust.

This product relates generally to buildings, and more particularly to open shelters designed for recreational use. In the construction of outdoor shelters, many factors must be considered, such as economy, durability, and stability. Most of the shelters known have anchoring floors, walls, and shingled roofs. Although these shelters provide stability in high winds, the advantage generally is lost in construction costs and repair or general upkeep. The shelters that are relatively economical to purchase and erect generally are incapable of withstanding the high winds and inclement weather common to most of the United States. The Pleasure Shelter, however, has been tested in winds up to 80 miles per hour and has withstood the test.

Pleasure Shelter has the advantage of economy in purchasing and erection durability by requiring little if any upkeep, and *stability* to endure all common weather elements—in addition to providing a pleasant appearance. In 1974, the Jacobs brothers received a design patent on their new product. See Figure 8–1.

Table 8–1
Sales by Product for Bowman-Austin, 1975–1976

Product	Year Ended November 30	
	1975	1976
Grain bins	$3,927,761.00	$4,122,096.90
Items purchased for resale	888,289.44	597,850.99
Fans and heaters for grain drying	763,757.74	977,488.06
Perforated grain bin floors	838,655.63	932,079.70
Harrows and draw bars	348,976.05	432,026.67
Bulk tanks	353,012.30	458,974.02
Hog shelters	—	123,043.89
Other products	127,260.46	336,816.74
Total sales	$7,247,712.40	$7,980,376.00

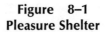

Figure 8–1
Pleasure Shelter

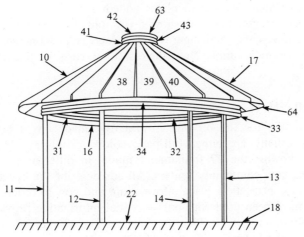

Table 8–2
Production Costs Per Unit
for Pleasure Shelter, 1972–1976*

Size	1972	1973	1974	1975	1976
15 ft.	$322.53	$272.35	$261.26	$276.14	$367.21
21 ft.	414.67	403.39	401.58	438.32	585.25
27 ft.	587.96	570.67	540.21	575.29	772.30

* Includes materials and labor only. Add $12.00 to each unit for roto fan.

The Pleasure Shelter is constructed of heavy, galvanized steel, and either a U-channel or structured angle support the shelter. It is relatively simple to construct; the 15 ft size can be erected by 2 people in 4 hours.

The 15 ft shelter is supported by 4 metal legs, whereas the 21 ft and 27 ft diameter shelters are supported by 6 and 8 legs, respectively. The legs require 2 ft holes which either may or may not require concrete depending upon soil and other conditions.

The production of Pleasure Shelter is relatively simple. A standard grain bin top is produced with 3 color combinations and a "skirt" or 2 ft overhang. Four, six, or eight metal legs are packaged with the cononical top and other materials, such as bolts, and nuts, for construction. Costs of producing the shelters are shown in Table 8–2.

The Price Mix

Prices on each unit vary according to size and whether a plain top or roto ventilator (fan) top is purchased. List prices to consumers from 1972 through 1976 are shown in Table 8–3. Price increases reflect 2 things: first, management recognized that its first-year prices were set too low. Secondly, inflation caused by higher labor costs and higher steel prices added to per unit costs of production. Although the figures in Table 8–2 show a per unit decrease in production costs during the first few years, these figures reflect increasing economies of scale with the production of more units. Nevertheless, total costs of materials and labor increased.

The Promotion Mix

The promotion mix for the product is primarily made up of advertising. The advertisements usually are either full-page color or full-page black and white magazine ads showing the 27 ft diameter model in different settings, including parks, backyard, and community centers. All ads describe the benefits of Pleasure Shelter—ease of construction, price information, and how to order. Some quarter-page ads also have been used with only essential information provided and small, artwork representations of the Pleasure Shelter. The smaller ads usually include a small space at the bottom asking readers to mail in their names and addresses requesting a free color brochure on Pleasure Shelters. Several thousand requests have been received by B-A to date. Advertising expenditures for the B-A shelter from 1972 to 1976 are shown in Table 8–4. The magazines which B-A has used to advertise Pleasure Shelter are wide and varied. These magazines and dates of insertion are shown in Figure 8–2.

In addition to magazine advertising, B-A once used a blitz direct mail campaign. Over 6,000 direct mail brochures were sent to potential consumers in 1975. Approximately 2,300 returns requested further information on the Pleasure Shelter. However, no follow-up was made beyond mailing out the requested brochures.

B-A management believe that their greatest selling effort comes from their

Table 8–3
List Prices for Pleasure Shelter

Size	1972	1973	1974	1975	1976
15 ft. diameter:					
Plain top	$ 410	$ 455	$ 470	$ 505	$ 530
Roto ventilator top	435	480	495	530	555
21 ft. diameter:					
Plain top	725	795	830	865	925
Roto ventilator top	755	825	860	895	955
27 ft. diameter:					
Plain top	1,145	1,245	1,325	1,365	1,425
Roto ventilator top	1,175	1,275	1,355	1,395	1,455

Table   8–4
Advertising Expenditures for Pleasure Shelter
1972–1976

Year	Advertising Expenditures
1972	$ 4,265
1973	6,335
1974	6,475
1975	14,870
1976	15,525

Figure   8–2
Magazines in Which Pleasure Shelter Appeared

Date	Magazine
1972: June 30	Campground and RV Park Management
June 30	Recreation Magazine
1973: February 21	Campground and RV Park Management
April 21	Tourist Attractions
May 31	Tourist Attractions
June 26	Campground Merchandising Buyer
November 30	Campground Marketing
1974: February 28	The Rotarian
March 31	Tourist Attractions and Park Annual
March 31	Campground and RV Park Management
April 18	Better Homes and Gardens: Hundreds of Ideas Annual
April 18	The Kiwanis Magazine
April 24	Better Homes and Gardens: Ideas and Outdoor Living
1975: January 1	The Kiwanis Magazine
January 1	The Rotarian
January 1	National Hog Farmer
February 26	The Lion Magazine
March 8	Park Maintenance
April 3	Farm Building News
April 27	The Rotarian
1976: February 3	Park Maintenance
February 21	The Kiwanis Magazine
March 5	Tennis
March 24	National Hog Farmer
April 18	RX Medical and Vet Future
April 29	The Lion Magazine
May 3	Park Maintenance
May 10	Farm Building News
May 17	The Rotarian
May 21	The Kiwanis Magazine

distributors. Advertising and direct mail are used only as entre for their distributors who actually make the sale. B-A has sold very few units directly to consumers.

The Channel/Distribution Mix

B-A has established over the years a strong relationship with grain bin and farm equipment distributors throughout the United States and its possessions, and Canada and Mexico. B-A provides a range of discounts on products they sell. For the Pleasure Shelter, B-A gives a 40 percent discount to its distributors. A list of B-A distributors is shown in Figure 8–3.

Sales/Cost Performance of Pleasure Shelters

Pleasure Shelter sales were less than satisfactory during the first 5 years. The sales record for unit and dollar sales by year (1972–1976) is shown in Table 8–5. A partial list of the customers who have bought Pleasure Shelters is shown in Table 8–6. Profits on Pleasure Shelter for the years 1972 through 1976 are shown in Table 8–7.

Figure 8–3
Bowman-Austin Distributors, 1976

Baker Building Systems, 7933 Lake Drive, Mino Lakes, MN

Five Liners, Box 405, 121 Southeast, Bellview, OH

Jim Williams, Box 1970, Tulsa, OK

Vernon Taylor, 501 Garfield, Holdridge, NE

Tunball Recreation Company, 713 Campbell Street, West Haven, CT

Ralph J. White Associates, 475 Chestnut Street, Southfield, IL

Baird Implement Company, Aaronsville, IL

Jose Luis Conception, Delgado Street, Villa Navarra Rios, Piedras, Puerto Rico

Speedo Sales, 804 S.W. Third Avenue, Portland, OR

Hansel H. Hulart and Associates, 309 Genoa Street, Coral Gables, FL

Hal Haines, Jr., P. O. Box 683, Alexandria, VA

The Horning Company, Box 886, Latimer, IA

R. L. Huffman, 1413 Sarah Drive, Lake Charles, LA

McAffe and Company, 345 W. Broadway, Alton, IL

Jason Marchant, 15547 Rutland Avenue, Detroit, MI

American Capital Flag Company, 5623 Calvin Street, Alexandria, VA

Supreme's Sportland, 6532 Merrimac Road, Bellmore, NY

Charles H. Corolle, P. O. Box 622, Grand Island, NY

Henry Cappelo, 15116 Mason Blvd., Pico Rivera, CA

Picado Estates, 6 Chocolate Avenue, Hershey, PA

Inn Keepers Supply Company, Box 37318, Memphis, TN

John R. Kennedy, 6215 S. Concho Drive, San Angelo, TX

Agri Products, Inc., Box 471, Janesville, WI

Burnett Refrigeration Company, 1800 Valleyview, El Paso, TX

Center Building Store, Harbor Loop, Gloucester, MA

John Geller, Farm RR #4, Anna, IL

Southeast Grain Storage, P. O. Box 26, Turpin, GA

Recreation Equipment, Unlimited, P. O. Box 7460, Philadelphia, PA

Bobby L. Sisco, P. O. Box 17, Livingston, NJ

Puerto Rico Playground Equipment, 226 Villa Navarra, Rio Piedras, Puerto Rico

Table   8–5
Sales For Pleasure Shelter
1972–1976

Year	# Unit Sales	$ Sales
1972	7	$ 3,031.50
1973	18	9,044.25
1974	26	18,692.90
1975	80	46,636.88
1976	64	52,292.30

Table   8–6
Sales of Pleasure Shelters

Year	Customer	Quantity	Size
1972	Mr. Frank McGee 5600 Little Creek Godfrey, IL	15′	1
	Jones & Baker 333 Cedar Street Batavia, NY	15′	1
	City of Baytown P. O. Box 947 Baytown, TX	21′	1
	England Development P. O. Box 762 Murray, KY	21′	1
	Foruff Fertilizer Service Kilbourne, IL	21′	1
	Mike Mills Bins Weldon, IL	15′	1

Year	Customer	Quantity	Size
	Taylorville "J.C." Taylorville, IL	27'	1
1973	Fiver Limers, Inc. P. O. Box 603 Bellevue, OH	15'	2
	Southeastern Grain Storage P. O. Box 36 Ruffin, SC	27'	1
	City of Towana Parks & Recreation Garage Robinson & Bryant Street Towana, NY	21'	1
	Department of Parks & Recreation City of Utica, NY	21'	1
	City of Connecticut Municipal Building Middleton, CT	15'	1
	Perry Fertilizer R. R. 1 Canton, IL	21'	1
	The Henley Company Latimer, IA	15'	1
	City of Pawtucket Park Department Pawtucket, RI	21'	1
	Richard Johnson Box 25 Springfield, NH	21'	1
	Stuckey's P. O. Box 7 Colorado Springs, CO	21'	1
	Southern Farm Supply Aberdeen, SD	15'	1
	The Henley Company Latimer, IA	15'	2
	Kiwanis Club of Middletown Middletown, NY	27'	1
	Lake Bren K.O.A. P. O. Box 258 St. Joseph, LA	21'	1
	Studkey's P. O. Box 707 Eastman, GA	15'	2

Year	Customer	Quantity	Size
1974	County of Henrico Division of Recreation and Parks P. O. Box 72320, R.R. 3 Richmond, VA	21'	1
	American Capital Flag Company 5632 Calvin Street Alexandria, VA	15'	1
	Hubert Hunt 309 Genoa Coral Gables, FL	27'	1
	Inn Keepers Supply Col 9737 Laman Avenue Holiday City Station Memphis, TN	27'	2
	T. B. Patrick & Sons San Diego, CA	27'	1
	Fiver Limers, Inc. P. O. Box 603 Bellevue, OH	27'	1
	Inn Keepers Supply Co. Memphis, TN	21'	1
	Seabreeze Family Campground Sanford, NC	27'	1
	Baird Implement Col Arenzville, IL	27'	1
	P. M. McKaine & Sons 25 Marshall Street Nashua, NH	21'	4
	Sun Valley Beach Club Stafford Springs, CT	21 & 15'	3
	Southern Farm Supply Aberdein, SD	15'	1
	Million Acre Campground Franklin, NH	27'	1
	Crest Building Supply El Dorado, KS	27'	1
	Park Hills Estates Baron, CA	27'	1
	Peeler Farm Supply Anna, IL	15'	1
	Mansville Park Route 7 Oceanview, NJ	27'	2

Year	Customer	Quantity	Size
	Holly Hills Conc. Rio Piedias, Puerto Rico	15'	1
	Southeastern Grain Storage Ruffin, SC	27'	1
1975	Milbury Manor Bristolm, NH	15'	1
	Forest Hills Golf Club Forest Lake, MN	15'	1
	American Lumber Wanona, MN	15'	1
	Gilford-Tigert Mfg. Co. Clay Center, KS	15'	2
	Donald R. Spedel Memorial Des Moines, IA	15'	1
	Fred S. Johnson San Angelo, TX	15'	1
	Scott Jefferson Realty Co. Pittsburg, PA	15'	1
	City of Wood River Woodriver, IL	15'	5
	Naval Air Facility El Centro, CA	15'	1
	Suffolk Music Institute Bayport, NY	15'	2
	T & G Sales Janesville, WI	15'	1
	Brockman Feed Breda, IA	15'	2
	Colchester Lions Colchester, IL	15'	4
	Bill Calis Downers Grove, IL	15'	1
	G & T Sales Janesville, WI	15'	1
	Space Metal Buildings East Tauton, MA	15'	3
	J. T. Ward Company Wilmington, DE	15'	1
	Sal's Kiddieland Inc. (cash sale)	21'	1
	Village of Marysville Marysville, OH	21'	1
	Manchester Park Board Manchester, IA	21'	1

Year	Customer	Quantity	Size
	Percy Estates Hershey, PA	21'	2
	Percy Estates Hershey, PA	21'	1
	Winfield State Hospital Winfield, KS	21'	1
	Gardner Lions Club Gardner, IL	21'	1
	City of Baltimore Baltimore, MD	21'	1
	T & G Sales Janesville, WI	21'	1
	City of Cole Camp Cole Camp, MO	21'	1
	Chase Memorial Nursing New Berlin, NY	21'	1
	T & G Sales Janesville, WI	21'	1
	Space Metal Buildings East Tauton, MA	21'	1
	Sal's Kiddieland Inc. (cash sale)	27'	3
	City of Haverhill Haverhill, MA	27'	1
	John Carlton Construction Rio Piedras, Puerto Rico	27'	6
	City of Evansville Evansville, IN	27'	1
	Village of Lyons Lyons, IL	27'	1
	Variety Club Philadelphia, PA	27'	1
	City of Sweeney Sweeney, TX	27'	1
	T & G Sales Janesville, WI	27'	3
	Richmond Lions Club Bangor, PA	27'	1
	Gilmore-Tatge Manufacturing Co. Clay Center, KA	27'	1
	Mountain Grove Rotary Club Mountain Grove, MO	27'	1
	Space Metal Buildings East Tauton, MA	27'	1

Year	Customer	Quantity	Size
	Mt. Carmel Rotary Club Mt. Carmel, IL	15'	1
	John Newman Construction Nashville, GA	15'	1
	City of Chula Vista Chula Vista, CA	15'	1
	Winfield State Hospital Winfield, KA	15'	1
	T & G Sales Janesville, WI	21'	1
	Gradie Patterson City Coll. Savannah Beach, GA	27'	1
	Peoples Bank Crescent City, FL	15'	1
	New Orleans City Park New Orleans, LA	27'	1
	Fred C. Smith San Angelo, TX	15'	1
	Boy Scouts of America Nashville, TN	27'	1
	Building Center Store Glouschester, MA	21'	1
1976	Bob Williams Tulsa, OK	15'	1
	John Labisba Rio Piedias, Puerto Rico	15'	1
	Keller Farm Supply Marion, IL	15'	1
	Pots Potpourri McAllen, TX	15'	1
	Tayco Inc. Taylorville, IL	21'	1
	John Labisba Rio Piedias, Puerto Rico	21'	1
	City of Chulsa Vista Chula Vista, CA	21'	2
	Carl Hadley Strathroy, Ontario, Canada	21'	1
	City of Winnipeg Manotoba, Canada	21'	2
	Mary Aston Taylorville, IL	21'	1
	Max Jones Dale, IN	21'	1

Year	Customer	Quantity	Size
	Keeley Farm Supply Anna, IL	21'	1
	Keeley Farm Supply Anna, IL	21'	1
	Allied Farm Supply Anna, IL	21'	1
	Allied Farm Supply Anna, IL	21'	1
	Allied Farm Supply Anna, IL	21'	1
	R & F Insulation Owensboro, KY	21'	2
	William J. Saltie Grover Hill, OH	21'	1
	City of Pico Rivera Paco Rivers, CA	21'	1
	Jane Cooley Borden, IN	21'	3
	Allied Farm Supply Anna, IL	21'	1
	Allied Farm Supply Anna, IL	21'	1
	Allied Farm Supply Anna, IL	21'	1
	J. T. Ward Co. Wilmington, DE	21'	1
	Salem-Hammer Salem, VA	21'	1
	Richard J. Marshall Grand Island, NY	21'	7
	Spahn Mizerski Dyersville, IA	21'	1
	Jones & Smith Waco, TX	21'	2
	West Point West Point, GA	21'	1
	Tower Hill Park Tower Hill, IL	21'	1
	Allied Farm Supply Anna, IL	27'	1
	Allied Farm Supply Anna, IL	27'	1
	Allied Farm Supply Anna, IL	27'	1

Year	Customer	Quantity	Size
	Allied Farm Supply Anna, IL	27'	1
	Allied Farm Supply Anna, IL	27'	1
	Allied Farm Supply Anna, IL	27'	1
	Allied Farm Supply Anna, IL	27'	3
	Allied Farm Supply Anna, IL	27'	3
	Allied Farm Supply Anna, IL	27'	1
	Allied Farm Supply Anna, IL	27'	1
	Bob Williams Tulsa, OK	27'	2
	L & L Insulation Owwnaboro, KY	27'	1
	Veterans Administration Austin, TX	27'	1
	Veterans Administration Austin, TX	27'	1
	Jaws Construction San Truce, Puerto Rico	27'	3

Table   8–7
Profits (Losses) on Pleasure Shelter 1972–1976

Year	Profits
1972	($8,042)
1973	($6,074)
1974	($1,147)
1975	$6,096
1976	$9,016

Problems With Pleasure Shelter

Pleasure Shelter has had problems from the start. One problem was that many customers got angry over shipping. Greg State Hospital in New York, for example, sent an order for 3 shelters in April of 1972, but the order was not shipped until December 1972. This, of course, created ill will among many B-A customers. Several orders were never processed and sales were lost. Somehow the orders got lost among other orders for grain bins and other farm-related products. Some customers simply cancelled their orders after waiting 6 months or more.

Also, some B-A customers complained that they could not erect the shelter according to the instructions provided. B-A learned from these complaints that their instructions were incorrect, and changes were made in the instructions in 1973.

B-A management was very concerned by the sales performance of the Pleasure Shelter for which they had great hopes. In the spring of 1976, Sally Robins, special projects director, was asked to examine the company's problems with Pleasure Shelter and make recommendations regarding its future at B-A. Sally felt that the shelter had not been marketed properly. In particular, she felt that the company had not done a thorough market analysis for recreational shelters prior to her employment by B-A in June 1975. She felt that the first step in any marketing program was an analysis of market segments and their needs for a product. Once that was determined, she felt a sound marketing strategy for each segment could be developed.

Discussion Questions

1. Evaluate the current Bowman-Austin marketing program for Pleasure Shelter. What mistakes have they made? How would you correct them?

2. What are the potential market segments for the Pleasure Shelter? Provide data from library sources to substantiate your analysis.

3. How would your marketing approach to each of the market segments you identified above differ?

4. What level of expenditures in advertising do you feel are necessary to support an adequate program to market Pleasure Shelter? How would you evaluate B-A's advertising effort in terms of expenditures and media used over the past 5 years?

5. Evaluate the current distributor system for Pleasure Shelter. What changes would you make?

Segmenting the Ridesharing Market*

Abraham D. Horowitz, General Motors Research Laboratories
Jagdish N. Sheth, University of Illinois

Background

The literature on ridesharing, a phenomenon which developed mainly as a consequence of the energy shortage of 1973–74, is concerned with the travel characteristics of carpoolers, ridesharing matching, the study of incentives for inducing people to share a ride, and with the clinical-social aspects of ridesharing.

Studies on matching and ridesharing incentives are based on the presumption that solo drivers can be induced to carpool by offering them direct positive incentives (for example, parking and traffic priorities) or by negative incentives for driving alone such as raising the cost of gasoline. Effective promotion of ridesharing requires a direct knowledge of how commuters who drive alone and those who share a ride to work view ridesharing.

Attitudes toward ridesharing have been investigated by Alan M. Voorhees and Associates, by Carnegie-Mellon University, and by Dueker and Lewin. The Alan M. Voorhees and Carnegie-Mellon studies showed that there are profound differences in attitudes toward ridesharing between solo drivers and carpoolers. However, they did not study the structure of attitudes in depth, nor did they attempt to identify homogeneous subgroups that differ in their attitudes. Dueker and Lewin examined how the desirability of ridesharing varies as a function of the sex of a rider and whether the rider is a prior acquaintance.

Horowitz developed a theoretical framework for the measurement of attitudes toward ridesharing and driving alone and presented mathematical models relating mode choice to the perceived advantages and disadvantages of ridesharing and to other attitudinal and socioeconomic characteristics. The model is an adaptation of the Howard-Sheth model of buyer behavior to the area of ridesharing behavior. For the purpose of testing this framework and achieving the aims of this research,

---

* This case is based on "Riresharing to Work: An Attitudinal Analysis" in "Predicting Carpool Demand," Transportation Research Board, National Research Council.

General Motors Research Laboratories contracted with a marketing research firm to collect the required data.

Data

A survey was conducted among residents of the Chicago metropolitan area contacted through their employers. The main reason for choosing Chicago was its wide variety of businesses, types and sizes in the city and its suburbs, and its variety of public transit services.

Personnel departments of 43 firms, chosen randomly from a large list of companies that employ at least 100 people, were first contacted. Table 10–1 summarizes the distribution by size and location of employers who expressed their willingness to participate. About 60 percent of these firms are manufacturing companies; the others are distributors, insurance companies, and other types of organizations. Personnel departments were asked to contact roughly equal numbers of carpoolers, solo drivers, and public transit users to answer a self-administered mail-back questionnaire that was hand delivered. During the fall and winter of 1975 2,000 questionnaires were distributed of which 1,020 questionnaires were returned. After eliminating questionnaires with a large amount of missing data, 822 remained for analysis: 323 carpoolers, 382 solo drivers, and 117 public transit commuters.

Since virtually all carpoolers in this sample owned at least one car and 75 percent of transit users did not own cars, it was assumed that car ownership is a necessary condition for sharing a ride to work. It was decided, then, to analyze data relating to carpoolers and solo drivers only.

The method of contacting commuters through their employers, seldom used in transportation research, proved to have certain advantages over traditional methods of data collection. First, the rate of return was relatively high (about 50 percent) compared to mail surveys. Second, the cost for data collection was smaller than that required for home interviews.

Table 9–1
Employers Distribution by
Size and Location

Number of Employees Per Firm	Chicago	Suburbs	Total
100– 300	2	9	11
301–1,500	6	6	12
1,501–8,000	7	4	11
	15	19	34

Nomenclature

Throughout this study the underlying modes of travel will be "drive alone" and "ridesharing," and the types of commuters "solo drivers" and "carpoolers," respectively. The concept of ridesharing is restricted in the present study to the use of privately-owned cars.

Questionnaire

Three types of information were collected through the questionnaire: the first 2 are socioeconomic and travel characteristics. The third type is attitudinal data with respect to both ridesharing and driving alone.

A few words are in order to describe the theoretical approach that guided the formulation of the attitudinal questions. There is a concensus among attitude researchers that attitudes consist of one or more of 3 elements: (1) cognitive evaluations or beliefs, (2) affect (like-dislike emotional tendency), and (3) behavioral intention.

Cognitive Evaluations. It is hypothesized that an individual has a set of evaluative beliefs about ridesharing and drive-alone modes of travel to work with respect to cost, time saving, and convenience. Ten such attributes presented in the upper part of Figure 9–1 were elicited from informal interviews conducted individually with a few carpoolers and solo drivers. The cognitive evaluations are measured on a 7-point scale from "very low" to "very high."

Affect. Affect is the positive or negative emotional predispositions toward an object and is presumed to be unidimensional, although it is possible that there is a complex cognitive structure underlying it. A measure of the affect toward ridesharing was obtained by the use of the rating scale shown in Figure 9–1.

Intention. Ridesharing intention refers to the stated plan of an individual to carpool and was measured by the last question that appears in Figure 9–1. Intention is hypothesized also to be related to the cognitive profile of evaluations. Intention is a qualified expression of behavior: given a span of time when behavior is likely to be manifested, the individual estimates at the beginning of the period of time whether he or she would or would not behave in a certain manner. The time span was limited to 2 to 3 months because a shorter time period between intention and behavior yields a more valid intention.

Results

Demographic and Travel Characteristics

Table 9–2 summarizes the socioeconomic characteristics of the solo driver and the carpooler groups. A MANOVA (multivariate analysis of variance) test using Wilks-Lambda criteria performed on 13 variables showed that solo drivers differ significantly from carpoolers ($F = 5.8$, $p \leq 0.001$). The column "Prob. $\leq$" indicates the probability at and under which the difference between the means of the 2 groups is due to chance.

Figure   9–1
Evaluations (cognitive profile) Scales

	Driving Alone							Carpooling						
	Very Low						Very High	Very Low						Very High
	1	2	3	4	5	6	7	1	2	3	4	5	6	7
Expensive	[]	[]	[]	[]	[]	[]	[]	[]	[]	[]	[]	[]	[]	[]
Comfortable	[]	[]	[]	[]	[]	[]	[]	[]	[]	[]	[]	[]	[]	[]
Pleasant	[]	[]	[]	[]	[]	[]	[]	[]	[]	[]	[]	[]	[]	[]
Reliable	[]	[]	[]	[]	[]	[]	[]	[]	[]	[]	[]	[]	[]	[]
Saves time	[]	[]	[]	[]	[]	[]	[]	[]	[]	[]	[]	[]	[]	[]
Convenient	[]	[]	[]	[]	[]	[]	[]	[]	[]	[]	[]	[]	[]	[]
Safe from crime	[]	[]	[]	[]	[]	[]	[]	[]	[]	[]	[]	[]	[]	[]
Energy consuming	[]	[]	[]	[]	[]	[]	[]	[]	[]	[]	[]	[]	[]	[]
Traffic problems	[]	[]	[]	[]	[]	[]	[]	[]	[]	[]	[]	[]	[]	[]
Pollution	[]	[]	[]	[]	[]	[]	[]	[]	[]	[]	[]	[]	[]	[]

Affect Scale

All things considered, which statement best describes how you
like the idea of <u>YOU</u> being a member of a carpool?

LIKE EXTREMELY	[]	DISLIKE SLIGHTLY	[]
LIKE MODERATELY	[]	DISLIKE MODERATELY	[]
LIKE SLIGHTLY	[]	DISLIKE EXTREMELY	[]
	NEITHER LIKE NOR DISLIKE	[]	

Intention Scale

How likely are you to join a carpool within the next two
or three months?

DEFINITELY WILL	[]	SOMEWHAT UNLIKELY	[]
VERY LIKELY	[]	VERY UNLIKELY	[]
SOMEWHAT LIKELY	[]	DEFINITELY WILL NOT	[]
	CANNOT SAY	[]	

The variables presented in Table 9–2 are self-explanatory and are ordered according to their power to discriminate between the 2 groups. For descriptive purposes a univariate t-test was performed on each variable. The column "F-ratio" displays the value of t^2. The column "Explained Variance" for the multivariate test is the square of the canonical correlation between the vector of variables and the artificial MANOVA variables (a vector of 0s and 1s according to that group to which an observation belongs) expressed in percentages. For a univariate test the explained variance is the percentage of the sum of squares between groups of the total sum of squares. This measure equals, for large samples, the ω^2 measure developed by Hays, increasingly used in psychology and consumer research. The column "Prob. $\leq$" indicates the level of significance between the means, as it

Table 9–2
Socioeconomic Comparisons among Solo Drivers and Carpoolers

	Solo Drivers			Carpoolers			F-Ratio**	Prob. $\leq$	Explained Variance (%)
	Mean$_1$	N$_1$*	SD$_1$	Mean$_2$	N$_2$	SD$_2$			
Multivariate Statistics									
MANOVA	—	382	—	—	323	—	5.8	0.001	9.8
Univariate Statistics									
CAR SIZE (1 = subcompact, 2 = compact, 3 = intermediate, 4 = full size)	2.5	328	2.5	2.9	259	1.0	25.5	0.001	4.1
Years at Present Employer	8.3	374	9.0	11.2	318	9.5	17.2	0.001	2.4
Marital Status (1 = single, 2 = married)	1.67	381	0.5	1.75	323	0.4	7.2	0.007	1.0
Years at Present Residence	7.1	375	6.9	8.6	317	9.0	6.2	0.013	0.6
Age (1 = under 25, 2 = 25–34, 3 = 35–44, 4 = 45–54, 5 = 55–64, 6 = 65 or over)	2.74	380	1.3	2.93	322	1.2	4.1	0.044	0.6
Household Size	3.0	366	1.4	3.3	316	1.6	3.8	0.05	0.5

Number of Licensed Drivers in Household	2.2	378	1.0	2.2	315	0.9	0.0	N.S.	—
Household Auto Ownership	1.9	379	0.9	1.8	311	0.8	1.3	N.S.	—
Car Age (years)	3.6	342	2.8	3.7	260	2.3	0.4	N.S.	—
Sex (1 = male, 2 = female)	1.45	381	0.5	1.50	323	0.5	1.8	N.S.	—
Household Annual Income (2 = $3,001–5,000, 3 = $5,001–7,000, etc., 9 = $17,001–19,000, . . . , 13 = $25,001–27,000, 14 = $27,001 and more)	8.9	331	2.8	9.1	278	2.8	1.0	N.S.	—
Occupation (1 = professional, 2 = manager, 3 = clerical worker, 4 = craftsman, 5 = operator, 6 = service worker)	2.46	377	1.1	2.38	319	1.1	0.9	N.S.	—
Education (3 = attended high school, 4 = graduated high school, 5 = attended college, 6 = finished college)	5.0	377	1.1	5.0	321	1.2	0.0	N.S.	—

*N–Number of Individuals
SD–Standard Deviation
N.S.–Not Significant
** Degrees of Freedom: 13 and 691 for the Multivariate Test
1 and $N_1 + N_2 - 2$ for each Univariate Test

may be between the groups. The ω^2 measure indicates the discriminability between the groups; that is, the degree of nonoverlapping of the 2 distributions.

The socioeconomic variable that discriminates most between the 2 groups is size of the car owned: carpoolers own larger cars than solo drivers. Note that in spite of the significant difference ($p \leq 0.001$), the explained variance for this variable is only 4.1 percent. A better and direct description is provided in Figure 9–2 that shows that differences in car size ownership are mainly for the full-size and subcompact categories.

Other discriminant variables, though weaker than the previous ones, indicate that carpoolers have worked longer at their present places of employment, are married rather than single, and have lived longer at their last residence. They are somewhat older and have larger families. The following variables do not discriminate between the two groups: (1) number of persons in household with driver's license, (2) number of autos owned, (3) age of the car used for the work trip, (4) sex, (5) income, (6) professional status, and (7) education.

Thus, the emerging picture of the typical carpooler in the Chicago area, in comparison with those who drive alone in their private automobile, is that the carpooler has a larger family, a larger car, has lived a longer time at his or her last residence, and has been working longer at the same place of employment. In short, the carpooler may be somewhat older than the solo driver.

Figure   9–2
Car Size Distribution

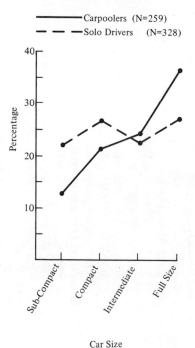

Car Size

Table 9–2 also shows that auto ownership is not related to ridesharing practice. Although carpoolers own on the average 1.8 cars per household, solo drivers own 1.9 cars per household, a slight and statistically insignificant difference. The average number of licensed persons per household is 2.2 in both groups.

Travel characteristics of solo drivers and carpoolers are summarized in Table 9–3. Cost and time are subjective measures as reported by respondents in the survey. A multivariate test using Wilks-Lambda criteria performed on 7 variables showed that solo drivers differ significantly from carpoolers ($F = 22.2$, $p \leq 0.001$). The multivariate explained variance is larger than that of the socioeconomic characteristics (13.5 percent vs. 9.8 percent). The variables are ordered according to their discriminant power where the first variable, the total reported cost including gasoline and depreciation, explains 8.7 percent of the variance. As expected, if carpoolers would drive alone they would be expected to have a higher travel cost than solo drivers since carpoolers live farther from work. Note that carpoolers on the average spend 2.1 minutes more in ridesharing than if they would drive alone. The last two variables listed in Table 9–3 show that walk time from car to work and also the distance from home to the nearest public transportation station do not significantly differentiate the two groups.

Because the cost, time, and distance measures are highly correlated, the multivariate explained variance does not equal the sum of the individual measures.

Figure 9–3 provides more detail on how carpoolers differ from solo drivers with respect to the distance to work. Although the percentage of commuters in the range of 11 to 20 miles is rather similar for the 2 groups, this percentage differs somewhat in the less-than-10-mile range and the more-than-20-miles work trips.

A few comments are in order. First, a discriminant analysis (appendix a) performed on both the demographic and travel characteristics showed that only 61.7 percent of the 705 commuters were correctly classified by the discriminant function. Since by pure chance the expected correctly classified proportion is 50 percent, it follows that demographic and travel characteristics add in only 11.7 percent of the cases, a small and negligible proportion. In summary, the percentage of explained variance presented in Tables 9–2 and 9–3 and the results of the discriminant analysis indicate the demographic and travel characteristics are poor indicators of whether a commuter to work is driving alone or sharing a ride.

Second, a comparison of the "explained variance" column of Tables 9–2 and 9–3 shows that the solo drivers and carpooling groups are better distinguished from each other by travel characteristics than by socioeconomic characteristics. Note also that the socioeconomic variable that best distinguishes between the groups is car size. This result is consistent with the declining role of socioeconomic variables in the explanation and prediction of consumer choice among the relatively affluent middle class population.

Finally, the results are partially inconsistent with Alan M. Voorhees and Associates' study of commuters on the Hollywood Freeway in the Los Angeles area. The only statistically significant discriminant variables in common with the present study and the Alan M. Voorhees study are distance to work and travel time. The earlier study, in contrast to the present one, found that carpoolers tend to be somewhat younger than solo drivers. This discrepancy may be attributed to

Table 9–3
Travel Characteristics Comparison Among Solo Drivers and Carpoolers

	Solo Drivers			Carpoolers			F-Ratio**	Prob. ≤	Explained Variance (%)
	Mean₁	N₁*	SD₁	Mean₂	N₂	SD₂			
Multivariate Statistics									
MANOVA	—	382	—	—	323	—	22.2	0.001	13.5
Univariate Statistics									
TOTAL COST, including gasoline and depreciation, driving alone one-way ($)	1.27	337	0.94	1.75	271	1.71	58.0	0.001	8.7
Gasoline Cost, one way ($)	0.54	347	0.42	0.84	285	0.60	54.4	0.001	7.9
Travel Time One-Way (minutes)	26.5	380	14.8	34.3	321	16.8	40.8	0.001	5.5
Travel Time Driving Alone (minutes)	26.5	380	14.8	32.2	318	15.9	31.1	0.001	4.3
Distance Home-Work (miles)	11.2	376	9.1	16.3	319	12.9	37.1	0.001	5.0
Distance to Nearest Public Transp. Sta. (miles)	3.7	263	6.6	3.7	215	7.5	0.0	N.S.	—
Walk From Car to Work (minutes)	2.8	342	2.3	3.1	294	2.0	3.1	N.S.	—

*N–Number of Observations
SD–Standard Deviation
N.S.–Not Significant
** Degrees of Freedom: 7 and 697 for the Multivariate Test
  1 and N₁+N₂−2 for each Univariate Test

Figure   9–3
Distance to Work Distribution

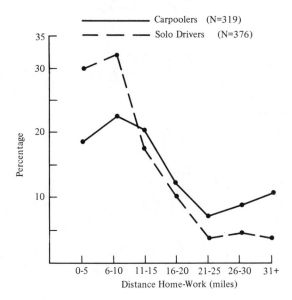

Distance Home-Work (miles)

the small number of carpoolers, 108, in the Alan M. Voorhees study and also to the different locations of the studies. Attitudinal differences between carpoolers and solo drivers were found to be similar and perhaps are more universal than the demographics and travel characteristics.

Ridesharing Cognitive Profile

Of the 10 attributes of the cognitive profiles (Figure 9–1), only the attribute "Safe From Crime" was found not to differentiate the 2 groups or to correlate with any of the attributes. Table 9–4 presents the means and standard deviations of the ridesharing cognitive profile of the 9 remaining attributes for solo drivers and carpoolers. Each attribute has been rated on a semantic scale from "1" to "7": "1" means very low, "7" very high, and "4" is the neutral ground. A multivariate test showed that the groups of respondents differ significantly ($F = 30.6, p \leq 0.001$).

The univariate tests and the means, displayed for convenience in Figure 9–4, lead to the following observations. First, solo drivers differ highly from carpoolers in the evaluation of ridesharing with respect to convenience, reliability, pleasure, comfort, and time (in this order), but do not differ in their evaluation of ridesharing with respect to cost, energy, traffic problems, and air quality. Note that the F-ratios and the explained variances are large when compared with the respective measures for travel and socioeconomic characteristics.

Second, solo drivers tend to evaluate carpooling on all 9 attributes on the average at or near the middle ground "4" on the low side of the scale between "3" and "4." This result implies that solo drivers hold a neutral position toward ridesharing with a slight tendency to perceive it inconvenient and not reliable. If solo drivers would have a clearly negative attribute profile toward ridesharing one

Table   9–4

Differences in Ridesharing Evaluations among Carpoolers and Solo Drivers
(1 = very low; 7 = very high)

	Means				Explained Variance (%)
	Solo Drivers (N = 382)	Carpoolers (N = 323)	F-Ratio**	Prob. ≤	
Multivariate Statistics					
MANOVA			30.6	0.001	28.4
Univariate Statistics					
Convenient	3.3 (1.7)*	5.1 (1.6)	197.6	0.001	22.0
Reliable	3.7 (1.6)	5.3 (1.5)	195.7	0.001	21.8
Pleasant	3.9 (1.5)	5.3 (1.4)	162.7	0.001	18.8
Comfortable	3.6 (1.6)	5.1 (1.5)	144.5	0.001	17.1
Saves Time	3.5 (1.6)	4.6 (1.7)	80.5	0.001	10.3
Expensive	3.1 (1.4)	3.1 (1.4)	0.3	N.S.	—
Energy Consuming	3.7 (1.7)	3.9 (1.9)	1.9	N.S.	—
Traffic Problems	3.7 (1.5)	3.5 (1.7)	2.9	N.S.	—
Pollution	3.8 (1.5)	3.7 (1.6)	0.6	N.S.	—

*–Standard Deviations Are Given in Parenthesis
**–Degrees of Freedom: 9 and 695 for Multivariate Test
                         1 and 703 for Each Univariate Test

Figure   9–4
Evaluation of Ridesharing Profile

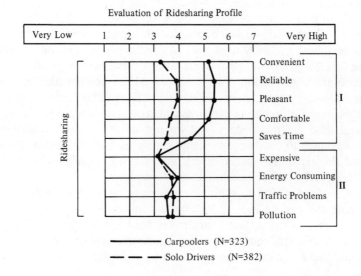

could not easily change their position; but it is suggested that given a general neutral position, a change in attitude might be achieved by advertisement and promotional means.

Third, on the average carpoolers evaluate ridesharing as being clearly convenient, reliable, pleasant, comfortable, and economical. To a lesser extent they perceive ridesharing as time saving and low in creating traffic problems and pollution. Ridesharing cognitions of carpoolers and solo drivers measured by Alan M. Voorhees and Associates were compatible with those obtained herein in spite of the differences among the scales used in the studies. The largest differences between carpoolers and solo drivers were found by Alan M. Voorhees in the following 2 bipolar semantic reliability scales:

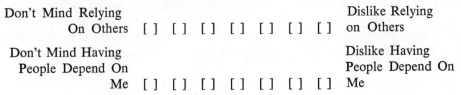

Don't Mind Relying
      On Others [ ] [ ] [ ] [ ] [ ] [ ] [ ] on Others
                         Dislike Relying

Don't Mind Having   Dislike Having
  People Depend On   People Depend On
         Me [ ] [ ] [ ] [ ] [ ] [ ] [ ] Me

Figure 9–5 details differences between carpoolers and solo drivers in the evaluation of ridesharing with respect to convenience. The 2 distributions are distinctly different, particularly at the extreme points of the scale, that is, at 1, 2, 6, and 7. Note that 22 percent of the variance is explained by classifying respondents into 2 groups (Table 9–4).

An additional measure of attitudinal differences between the 2 groups of respondents based on the carpooling attributes has been obtained through a discriminant analysis presented in appendix b. The discriminant function was able to correctly classify 73.6 percent of the respondents, that is, 23.6 percent in

Figure 9–5
Distribution of Ridesharing Convenience

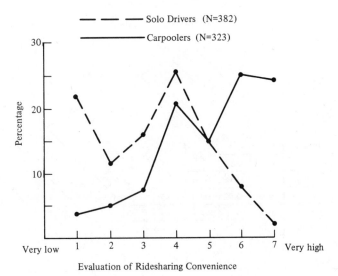

Evaluation of Ridesharing Convenience

addition to the 50 percent that are expected to be classified correctly by random assignments to groups, or about twice the discrimination beyond random that could be achieved by socioeconomic and travel characteristics.

Structuring Cognition

Insight into the latent psychological dimensions by which respondents evaluate ridesharing can be achieved by inspecting the correlations among the 9 evaluated attributes. There is no reason to expect independence among the 9 attributes. The attributes were chosen for inclusion in this survey on the basis of their potential importance for discovering the latent psychological dimensions. Table 9–5 presents the correlations among the ridesharing attributes as evaluated by carpoolers. Note that 2 clear subsets of attributes are formed. It is interesting that those first 5 attributes that best discriminate between the two groups (convenience, reliability, etc.) are interrelated but not related to the other attributes which are, however, themselves interrelated.

Principal component analysis with varimax rotation was applied to the correlation matrix. The number of factors retained was determined by a comparison of the set of eigenvalues obtained from analysis of random data matrices of the same order as the actual data matrix. Eigenvalues greater than one were retained. Either of these criteria resulted in the selection of 2 factors. The largest 3 eigenvalues, in decreasing order, were 3.3, 2.2, and 0.8.

Table 9–6 shows the 2 factors comprising the 9 ridesharing attributes. The "Factor" column gives the subjective label for each factor. Factor loadings are those significantly different from zero. The "Explained Variance" column lists the percent variance of each attribute accounted for by the factor in question (the square of the respective loading), and the percent accounted for by the other factor. This information (which sums to the total percent of the attributes variance ac-

Table 9–5
Carpoolers: Raw Correlations among
Ridesharing Evaluations

	Convenient	Reliable	Pleasant	Comfortable	Saves time	Expensive	Energy Consuming	Traffic Problems
Reliable	0.66							
Pleasant	0.58	0.63						
Comfortable	0.55	0.56	0.70					
Saves time	0.68	0.52	0.50	0.45				
Expensive	0.00	−0.05	−0.02	0.04	0.05			
Energy consuming	0.04	0.00	0.03	0.00	0.09	0.34		
Traffic problems	0.03	0.07	−0.04	0.02	0.16	0.28	0.39	
Pollution	0.04	0.04	0.01	0.00	0.13	0.29	0.42	0.69

Table   9–6
Carpoolers: Factor Structure of Ridesharing Evaluations

Factors (% variance explained)	Attribute	Factor Loading	Explained Variance (%)	
			in factor	in the other factor
I Time-Convenience (37.2)	Convenient	0.85	72.2	0.1
	Reliable	0.83	68.9	0.1
	Pleasant	0.84	70.3	0.2
	Comfortable	0.80	63.8	0.0
	Saves Time	0.76	57.5	2.7
II Private and Public Cost (24.8)	Expensive	0.58	33.2	0.0
	Energy Consuming	0.70	49.4	0.1
	Traffic Problems	0.83	68.9	0.1
	Pollution	0.84	70.3	0.1

counted for by both factors, or the commonality) indicate the strength and uniqueness of the attribute factor relationship, respectively. "Factor" includes the percentage of the variance in the corresponding attribute set accounted for by this factor and equals the average in factor variance (over all 9 attributes).

The very low figures in the "Other Factor" column and the relative high figures in the "In Factor" column show that each of the 2 factors is strong and unique.

Two revealing observations result from the factor analysis. First, grouping time with such qualitative attributes as convenience and comfort was unexpected. Indeed, the traditional approach in transportation research is to separate between time and cost on one hand and qualitative aspects on the other. However, the characteristics of ridesharing and, by comparison, also of solo driving, are related to a variety of time aspects such as fixed or flexible schedules, spending time to pick up other riders, spending time to wait for other riders, relying on others to be on time, and additional time required for errands.

The second insight into the latent psychological dimensions is the inclusion of personal cost ("expensive") in the same factor with the public cost attributes of energy, traffic, and pollution. The term "Private" in the label of Factor II is preferred over "Individual" because the cost typically involves the household rather than only the individual.

A factor analysis of ridesharing evaluations by *solo drivers* is presented in Table 9–7. The factor structure is similar to that obtained for carpoolers, but a comparison with Table 9–6 shows, however, that the percentage of variance explained by each factor is lower than for the carpoolers sample. Note also that the factor loadings and the "In Factor" explained variance for 8 of the 9 attributes are lower than for the carpoolers sample. These results suggest first that familiarity with an object of attitude (in this case, carpoolers with ridesharing) is enhancing their significance; second, that lack of familiarity with an object (solo drivers with ridesharing) is increasing noise (error) in the data.

An addition, but not independent, interpretation of the factor structure, is that Factor I captures the perceived disadvantages of ridesharing, while Factor II is associated with the perceived advantages in comparison to the drive-alone mode. This interpretation is substantiated by the following drive-alone evaluations.

Drive-Alone Cognitive Profile

These same 9 attributes were also rated in the context of the drive-alone mode as illustrated in Figure 9–1. The raw means, standard deviations, and the statistical tests performed on the drive-alone means are displayed in Figure 9–6 and the evaluations are presented in Table 9–8. A multivariate test performed on the vector of 9 attributes showed that the 2 groups differ significantly but to a lesser degree than in the case of the ridesharing evaluation ($F = 10.4$, $p \leq 0.001$).

Inspection of the individual means and the univariate tests leads to 2 observations. First, both groups of commuters perceive the drive-alone to work mode high on the qualitative attributes of convenience, reliability, comfort, and also on saving time. Second, solo drivers are somewhat more positive toward their own mode of transportation than carpoolers are toward driving alone. This difference is statistically significant for all attributes with the exception of the public cost attributes of energy, traffic, and pollution. It should be noted that the explained variance is small in spite of the statistically significant results.

Of special interest is the interrelation of the attributes; that is, the latent psychological dimensions by which respondents evaluate the drive-alone mode. It is

Table 9–7
Solo Drivers: Factor Structure of Ridesharing Evaluations

Factors (% variance explained)	Attribute	Factor Loading	Explained Variance (%)	
			in factor	in the other factor
I Time-Convenience (35.3)	Convenient	0.79	63.2	2.0
	Reliable	0.79	61.9	0.0
	Pleasant	0.80	63.4	0.4
	Comfortable	0.79	62.1	0.0
	Saves Time	0.77	58.8	2.8
II Private and Public Cost (21.0)	Expensive	−0.45	20.6	0.2
	Energy Consuming	−0.69	47.0	0.3
	Traffic Problems	−0.80	64.5	0.0
	Pollution	−0.77	59.9	0.3

Figure   9–6
Evaluations of Drive-Alone Profile

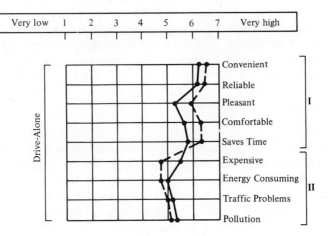

Table   9–8
Differences in Drive-Alone Evaluations among Carpoolers and Solo Drivers
(1 = very low; 7 = very high)

	Means				Explained Variance (%)
	Solo Drivers (N = 382)	Carpoolers (N = 323)	F-Ratio**	Prob. ≤	
Multivariate Statistics					
MANOVA			10.4	0.001	11.8
Univariate Statistics					
Convenient	6.6 (1.2)*	6.2 (1.5)	15.0	0.001	2.1
Reliable	6.5 (1.2)	6.2 (1.4)	8.7	0.003	1.2
Pleasant	5.9 (1.5)	5.3 (1.8)	23.9	0.001	3.3
Comfortable	6.3 (1.4)	5.7 (1.6)	26.0	0.001	3.6
Saves Time	6.4 (1.3)	5.9 (1.6)	26.7	0.001	3.7
Expensive	4.7 (1.8)	5.6 (1.7)	46.7	0.001	6.2
Energy Consuming	4.8 (2.2)	5.0 (2.2)	1.8	N.S.	—
Traffic Problems	5.1 (1.9)	5.2 (2.0)	0.8	N.S.	—
Pollution	5.1 (1.9)	5.3 (1.9)	1.1	N.S.	—

*–Standard Deviations Are Given in Parenthesis
**–Degrees of Freedom: 9 and 695 for the Multivariate Test
                         1 and 703 for Each Univariate Test

remarkable that in spite of the pronounced differences between the evaluations of the 2 modes of travel as seen by a comparison of Figures 9–3 and 9–5, the drive alone evaluation factors (Tables 9–9 and 9–10) are virtually identical to the previously described ridesharing factors. A comparison between Tables 9–9 and 9–10 suggests that the time-convenience factor explains more variance for solo drivers than for carpoolers (41.5 percent vs. 38.0 percent, respectively). On the other hand, the cost factor explains more variance for carpoolers than for solo drivers (26.2 percent vs. 24.8 percent, respectively). These results illustrate the high weight of the psychological time-convenience factor in the solo drivers cognition of driving alone.

Differences Among Ridesharing and Drive-Alone Cognitive Profiles

The attribute evaluations presented above were measured with respect to ridesharing and separately for the drive-alone mode. To get a more comprehensive grasp of the ridesharing cognition and to relate it to both the affective and the intentional components when the drive-alone mode serves as a baseline, consideration is given to the difference between the drive-alone and ridesharing evaluations as a measure of evaluation on each attribute. This difference is computed by subtracting the individual measures summarized in Table 9–4 from those in Table 9–8, and will be denoted by δ_i, $i = 1, \ldots, 9$, where

$$\delta_i = x_{i \text{ drive-alone}} - x_{i, \text{ ridesharing}}$$

and $x_{i, \text{ mode}}$ is the evaluation of the attribute i on the corresponding mode. The δ_i measures and the respective standard deviations are presented in Tables 9–11

Table 9–9
Carpoolers: Factor Structure of Drive-Alone Evaluations

Factors (% variance explained)	Attribute	Factor Loading	Explained Variance (%) in factor	in the other factor
I Time-Convenience (38.0)	Convenient	0.85	72.8	1.6
	Reliable	0.78	60.1	0.6
	Pleasant	0.76	57.7	0.2
	Comfortable	0.82	67.7	0.0
	Saves Time	0.85	71.8	0.3
II Private and Public Cost (26.2)	Expensive	−0.58	33.5	3.2
	Energy Consuming	−0.72	51.8	0.2
	Traffic Problems	−0.89	79.2	0.0
	Pollution	−0.87	76.5	0.0

Table   9–10
Solo Drivers: Factor Structure of Drive-Alone Evaluations

Factors (% variance explained)	Attribute	Factor Loading	Explained Variance (%) in factor	in the other factor
I Time-Convenience (41.5)	Convenient	0.90	81.2	0.0
	Reliable	0.90	80.6	0.2
	Pleasant	0.76	57.3	2.2
	Comfortable	0.87	75.9	0.6
	Saves Time	0.86	74.7	0.1
II Private and Public Costs (24.8)	Expensive	−0.54	29.1	1.8
	Energy Consuming	−0.70	49.4	1.2
	Traffic Problems	−0.85	71.5	0.8
	Pollution	−0.84	69.7	0.2

and 9–12 for solo drivers and carpoolers, respectively. The hypothesis that the δ_i measures are not different from zero has been rejected for both solo drivers and carpoolers for all attributes with the exception of "pleasant" in the carpoolers group. F-ratios and the percentage of explained variance for solo drivers show that the perceived differences between ridesharing and driving alone are very pronounced (compare also Figures 9–4 and 9–6) especially for the time-convenience factor, reinforcing those results obtained from the drive-alone cognitive profile.

Factor analysis applied to the δ_i measures yielded factors similar to those obtained by the individual measures and are presented in appendices c and d.

Affect Toward Ridesharing and the Intention to Share a Ride

Figure 9–7 presents the affect distribution toward ridesharing for the solo drivers and the carpoolers groups. The affect was measured by the answer to the question "All things considered, which statement best describes how you like the idea of your being a member of a carpool?" (See Figure 9–1.)

There is little need for a statistical test to determine that the 2 groups are highly differentiated by the affect measure. Solo drivers are split along the continuum from "Like Extremely" to "Dislike Extremely," with about 20 percent of the solo drivers being neutral, although almost all carpoolers are positive toward ridesharing.

Figure 9–8 displays the carpooling intention distribution for solo drivers. The intention was measured by the answer to the question "How likely are you to join a carpool within the next two or three months?" Less than 10 percent of the 376 solo drivers who answered the question stated a positive intention.

The intention measure is most appropriate for the prediction of behavior. The results suggest that under present conditions only a small percentage of solo drivers intend to carpool regularly in the immediate future. However, the overall prediction of future trends in ridesharing is quite complex because some of the present carpoolers are likely to switch back to the drive-alone mode. This statement is based on the fact that about 40 percent of the present solo drivers surveyed in this study reported that they had carpooled in the past on a regular basis for an average period of 2 years, but discontinued carpooling.

Models Relating Cognition Factors To Affect and Intention

Thus, 2 latent factors underly the cognition of ridesharing, drive-alone, or the difference between them. The time-convenience factor was interpreted as the perceived negative evaluation of ridesharing although the cost (private and public) factor is the perceived positive evaluation.

Researchers in both social psychology and consumer psychology have theorized that there is a linear additive relationship between evaluations (cognition) and between affect and intention. A linear additive relation implies that positive and

Table 9-11
Differences among Drive-Alone and Ridesharing Evaluations for Solo Drivers (δ Measures)

Factor		Mean Difference	F-Ratio**	Prob. $\leq$	Explained Variance (%)
	Multivariate Statistics MANOVA	—	144.2	0.001	77.6
I	Univariate Statistics Convenient	3.3 (2.2)*	873.6	0.001	57.6
	Reliable	2.8 (2.0)	763.9	0.001	52.1
	Pleasant	2.0 (2.2)	297.3	0.001	29.7
	Comfortable	2.7 (2.2)	570.8	0.001	44.8
	Saves Time	2.9 (2.2)	717.2	0.001	50.5
II	Expensive	1.6 (2.3)	167.6	0.001	19.3
	Energy Consuming	1.1 (2.9)	53.4	0.001	7.1
	Traffic Problems	1.4 (2.3)	136.3	0.001	16.2
	Pollution	1.3 (2.1)	166.4	0.001	19.1

*–Standard Deviations Are Given in Parenthesis
**–Degrees of Freedom: 9 and 373 for the Multivariate Test
                         1 and 381 for Each Univariate Test (N=382)

Table 9–12
Differences among Drive-Alone and Ridesharing Evaluations for Carpoolers (δ Measures)

Factor		Mean Difference	F-Ratio**	Prob. ≤	Explained Variance (%)
	Multivariate Statistics				
	MANOVA	—	64.8	0.001	65.0
	Univariate Statistics				
	Convenient	1.1 (2.2)*	81.5	0.001	10.4
	Reliable	0.9 (2.0)	67.2	0.001	8.7
I	Pleasant	0.0 (2.2)	0.2	N.S.	—
	Comfortable	0.6 (2.1)	26.3	0.001	3.6
	Saves Time	1.3 (2.1)	117.8	0.001	14.4
	Expensive	2.5 (2.3)	397.6	0.001	36.1
	Energy Consuming	1.1 (3.2)	40.1	0.001	5.4
II	Traffic Problems	1.7 (2.5)	157.6	0.001	18.3
	Pollution	1.6 (2.3)	160.4	0.001	18.6

*–Standard Deviations Are Given in Parenthesis
**–Degrees of Freedom: 9 and 314 for the Multivariate Test
                         1 and 322 for each Univariate Test (N=323)

Figure 9–7
Affect Toward Ridesharing

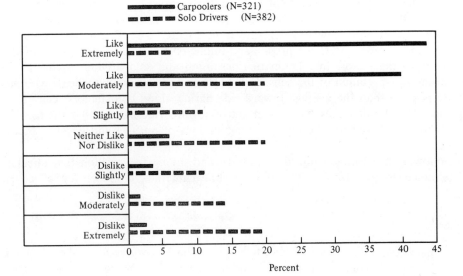

Percent

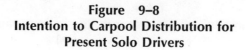

Figure   9–8
Intention to Carpool Distribution for
Present Solo Drivers

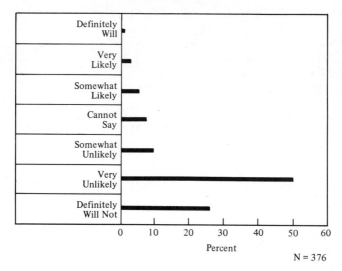

negative evaluations compensate for one another. However, an attitudinal ride-sharing model may be designed to allow noncompensatory relation to answer the following: Is it possible that evaluations *interact* among themselves so that a negative evaluation can reduce the intention to carpool regardless of the magnitude of the positive evaluation?

Assume that each individual is rated as either "High" or "Low" on each of the 2 factors according to whether the respective factor scores are higher or lower than the average score. (One could divide the continuum into more than 2 parts but for model testing it is sufficient to have 2 categories.) Then, each group (carpoolers and solo drivers) will be segmented into 4 subgroups according to the combination of the 2 factors, as shown in Figure 9–9. T denotes the time-convenience factor, and C the private-and-public-cost factor. Consideration of the meaning of the factors in relation to ridesharing and solo driving results in the following interpretation of the cells. Cell {1,2} includes those individuals who are more positive than the average toward ridesharing along both factors; cell {2,1} includes those individuals who are negative toward ridesharing on both factors; the other 2 cells include the obvious combinations of positive and negative factor scores.

Following the notation introduced above and taking the position that affect is determined by the factors T and C, a linear-interactive model for affect is:

$$A_{ijk} \;=\; \mu + T_k + C_j + \gamma_{ij} + \varepsilon_{ijk}$$

where

A_{ijk} =   individual k's affect toward ridesharing, where his or her T-factor score is i (low, high) and his or her C-factor score is j (low, high)

Figure 9–9
A Segmentation Based on the Cognitive Profile

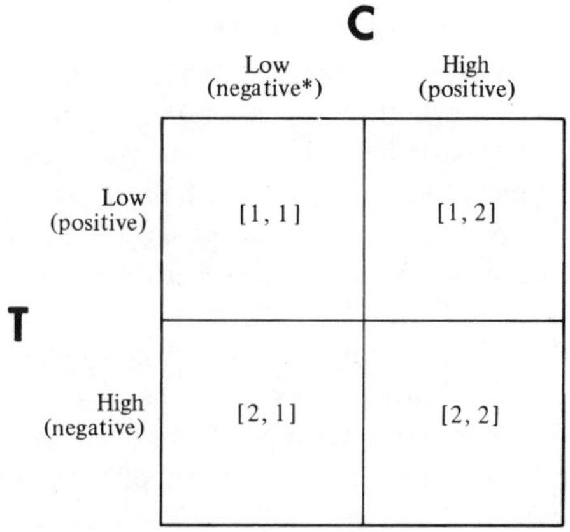

*"Negative" and "Positive" Toward
Ridesharing

μ	=	mean affect over all four cells
T_i	=	the contribution of factor T to affect at level i
C_j	=	the contribution of factor C to affect at level j
γ_{ij}	=	interaction between the T_i and C_j levels
ε_{ijk}	=	individual k's error in cell $\{i,j\}$

An ordinary 2x2 analysis of variance (ANOVA) can be used to test the model. The use of ANOVA depends on the statistical assumption that ε_{ijk} are independent random variables normally distributed with constant variance. In the present application of ANOVA these statistical assumptions pose no problem because the number of observations is relatively large. Use of ANOVA requires independence between observations. Hence, it is necessary that different individuals belong in different cells. This assumption is clearly satisfied in the present design. The ANOVA allows simple, powerful tests for each of the T_i, C_j, and γ_{ij} terms separately.

A similar model can be written for intention; that is

$$I_{ijk} = \mu + T_i + C_j + \gamma_{ij} + \varepsilon_{ijk}$$

where I_{ijk} denotes individual's k intention to share a ride and all other terms are similar to those in the affect model but refer to intention.

Test of the Affect Model

Based on the segmentation discussed, each respondent has been assigned to one of the four cells according to his or her factor scores, T and C. Note that "Low" and "High" are relative to the weighted (by factor loadings) average difference between the ridesharing and drive-alone evaluations.

Figure 9–10 presents the affect means for each cell for solo drivers and carpoolers separately. The corresponding standard deviations and cell sizes are included in appendix e. Two results emerge from Figure 9–10. First, the time-convenience factor (that is, whether a respondent is categorized into "low" or "high" on T) is related to his or her affect to a larger extent than is the factor C. This is seen from a comparison of the slopes of the lines to the distance between the lines for the carpoolers and solo drivers groups, separately. Second, that the lines are nonparallel suggests an interaction between the factors, especially for solo drivers.

Table 9–13 summarizes the test of the ANOVA model. The contributions of T and C are significant for both groups, but the F-ratios for T are markedly higher than for C. The interaction term TxC for the solo drivers group is significant but not so for carpoolers. Interpretation of the significant interaction is that those solo drivers who are "High" on T (a relatively large perceived difference in the time-convenience attributes between the two modes) have average affect toward ridesharing of "3" (dislike slightly) regardless of their perception of the private-and-public-cost of the two modes. An interaction suggests a noncompensatory model.

Figure   9–10
**The Relation between the Affect Toward Ridesharing
And the Cognitive Factors**

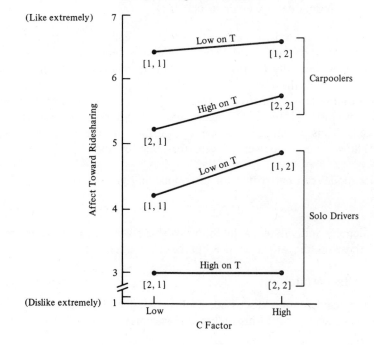

Table 9–13
ANOVA Test Results

		Sum of Squares	d.f.	Mean Square	F-Ratio	Prob $\leq$	Variance Explained (%)
	T	224.3	1	224.3	72.3	0.001	15.8
Affect Model	C	12.3	1	12.3	3.9	0.05	0.8
(Solo Drivers)	TxC	12.1	1	12.1	3.9	0.05	0.8
	Error	1171.8	378	3.1			
	Total	1420.5	381				
	T	40.8	1	40.8	26.9	0.001	6.5
Intention Model	C	10.2	1	10.2	6.7	0.01	1.6
(Solo Drivers)	TxC	0.1	1	0.1	0.0	n.s.	—
	Error	574.6	378	1.5			
	Total	625.7	381				
	T	78.7	1	78.7	56.8	0.001	14.8
Affect Model	C	8.3	1	8.3	6.0	0.015	1.6
(Carpoolers)	TxC	2.2	1	2.2	1.6	n.s.	—
	Error	442.0	319	1.4			
	Total	531.2	322				

The parameters of the affect model for solo drivers are obtained directly from the cell means and are:

$$\mu = 3.8, \ T_1 = 0.8, \ T_2 = -0.8, \ C_1 = -0.2, \ C_2 = 0.2, \ \gamma_{11} = \gamma_{12} = -0.2,$$

$$\gamma_{12} = \gamma_{21} = 0.2$$

and for carpoolers:

$$\mu = 6.0, \ T_1 = 0.5, \ T_2 = -0.5, \ C_1 = -0.2, \ C_2 = 0.2, \ \gamma_{11} = \gamma_{12} = 0.1,$$

$$\gamma_{12} = \gamma_{21} = -0.1$$

Note that the ratios between the absolute values of T and C are 4.0 and 2.5 for solo drivers and carpoolers, respectively, a finding consistent with the comparison of the F-values.

The lack of significant interaction term for carpoolers suggests that unlike solo drivers the perceived advantages of ridesharing due to private-and-public-cost, and the disadvantages due to time-convenience attributes, determine their general liking of the idea of being in a carpool in a noninteractive compensatory way.

Test of the Intention Model

In spite of the very skewed distribution of the Intention to Carpool variable toward "Very Unlikely," as previously shown in Figure 9–8, an additive compensatory model (Table 9–13 and Figure 9–11) was developed.

The two lines of Figure 9–11 are parallel suggesting that there is no interaction. The factors T and C, however, significantly determine the intention, factor T having a larger influence than C.

The values of the parameters of the intention model were obtained as:

$$\mu = 2.3, T_1 = 0.3, T_2 = -0.3, C_1 = -0.2, C_2 = 0.2, \gamma_{11} = \gamma_{12} = \gamma_{21} = \gamma_{22} = 0.$$

A Market Segmentation Technique

An aspect of enormous interest in the promotion of ridesharing is the identification of homogeneous market segments among solo drivers for whom different promotional methods will be required. Specifically, what socioeconomic variables are characteristic of solo drivers whose cognitive perceptions of ridesharing are maximum along its advantages (factor C) and minimum with respect to its disadvantages (factor T); that is, those who are assigned to cell {1,2} of the cognitive factorial design? Recall that among the four cells of the design, cell {1,2} includes those respondents with the highest positive attitudes toward ridesharing with respect to affect and intention.

To provide an answer to this question the univariate version of the MANOVA

Figure   9–11
The Relation between the Intention to Carpool
And the Cognitive Factors

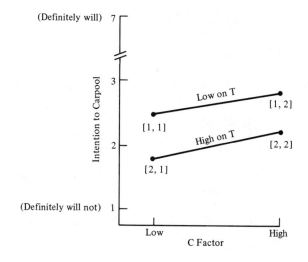

Table 9–14
The Distribution of the Solo-Drivers Socioeconomic Variables in the Cognitive Factorial Design

Cell	[1,1]			[1,2]			[2,1]			[2,2]		
Variable	Mean	N	SD	Mean	N	SD	Mean	N	SD	Mean	N	SD
Years at Present Employer	7.6	94	7.8	6.7	87	8.2	8.3	104	9.5	10.5	89	10.3
Years at Present Residence	6.7	95	5.9	5.8	87	6.1	7.2	105	7.3	8.8	88	8.1
Household Size	3.3	92	1.6	3.3	84	1.4	2.7	104	1.3	3.0	86	1.5
Number of Licensed Drivers in Household	2.2	95	1.1	2.3	87	1.1	2.0	106	0.9	2.4	90	1.1
Household Annual Income*	8.7	83	3.0	9.0	76	3.3	8.3	89	3.2	9.8	83	2.4
Occupation*	2.5	96	1.2	2.2	85	1.2	2.6	106	1.1	2.4	90	1.1
Education*	4.9	95	1.1	5.4	85	1.1	4.7	106	1.3	5.2	91	1.0
Sex (1 = male, 2 = female)	1.5	95	0.5	1.3	87	0.5	1.6	108	0.5	1.4	91	0.5
Distance Home-Work (miles)	10.3	95	7.7	13.4	84	9.9	10.0	107	9.3	11.7	90	9.1

*For Units, See Table 9–1.

Table   9–15
ANOVA Analyses* on Socioeconomic and Distance
Variables—Solo Drivers

Variables	Factor T		Factor C		Degrees of Freedom
	F-Ratio	Prob.	F-Ratio	Prob.	
Years at Present Employer	5.2	0.023	—	—	1;370
Years at Present Residence	5.1	0.024	—	—	1;371
Household Size	7.4	0.007	—	—	1;362
Number of Licensed Drivers in Household	—	—	5.7	0.018	1;374
Household Annual Income	—	—	8.2	0.005	1;327
Occupation	—	—	5.5	0.020	1;373
Education	—	—	20.6	0.001	1;373
Sex	—	—	11.6	0.001	1;377
Distance, Home-Work	—	—	6.4	0.012	1;372

* No interaction TxC was found significant

program was used with the same 2x2 factorial design as above, and the socio-economic variables (including the distance to work) serving as dependent variables, one for each analysis. All socioeconomic variables (Table 9–2) and the "distance" variable have been tested. Tables 9–14 and 9–15 enumerate only those variables for which at least one main contribution, T or C, was found to be significant at the level $p \leq 0.05$.

Discussion Questions

1. What market segments do you recommend for directing marketing programs to enhance ridesharing behavior? Provide numerical data in your analysis to support your position.

2. Develop two alternative marketing programs aimed at increasing ridesharing to 30 percent among Chicago commuters.

3. Develop research designs to test market your proposed marketing programs to enhance ridesharing behavior among commuters.

References

Anderson, N. H. "Scales and Statistics: Parametric and Nonparametric." *Psychological Bulletin,* **58** 1961, 305–316.

Barkow, B. "Carpooling: The Worm's Eye View." Paper presented at the American Psychological Association Annual Convention, Washington, D.C., 1976.

Ben-Akiva, M. E. and Atherton, T. J. "Choice Model Predictions of Carpool Demand: Methods and Results." Paper presented at the American Psychological Association Annual Convention, Washington, D.C., 1976.

Berry, W. L. *On the Economic Incentives for Commuter Carpooling.* Ph.D. Thesis, Graduate School of Business Administration, Harvard University, Cambridge, Massachusetts, 1975.

Bettman, J. R.; Capon, N.; and Lutz, R. J. "Cognitive Algebra in Multi-Attribute Attitude Models," *Journal of Marketing Research,* **12** 1975, 151–164.

Blankenship, D. P. *Utilizing Focus Group Dynamics to Ascertain Rules for Social Interaction for Carpoolers,* Orange County Transit District, Santa Ana, California, 1975.

Bunkrant, R. E. and Cousineau, A. "Informational and Normative Social Influence in Buyer Behavior," *Journal of Consumer Research,* **2** 1975, 206–215.

Carnegie-Mellon University, School of Urban and Public Affairs. *An Evaluation of the SPRPC Carpool Public Transit Program.* Report prepared for the Southwestern Pennsylvania Regional Planning Commission, Pittsburgh, Pennsylvania, 1975.

Davis, F. W. et al. *Ridesharing and the Knoxville Commuter,* Report No. TCUT–1–75. Prepared for the Office of Environmental Affairs, U.S. Department of Transportation.

Day, G. S. "Evaluating Models of Attitude Structures," *Journal of Marketing Research,* **9** 1972, 279–286.

Dueker, K. J. and Levin, I. P. "Carpooling: Attitudes and Participation." Paper presented at the American Psychological Association Annual Convention, Washington, D.C., 1976.

Festinger, L. *A Theory of Cognitive Dissonance.* Stanford: Stanford University Press, 1957.

FHWA, Department of Transportation, Federal Highway Administration News Letter 49–75, May 22, 1975.

Fishbein, M. "Attitude and the Prediction of Behavior," in Fishbein, (ed) *Readings in Attitude Theory Measurement.* New York: Wiley, 1967.

Harman, H. H. *Modern Factor Analysis.* Chicago: University of Chicago Press, 1967.

Hays, W. L. *Statistics.* New York: Holt, Rinehart, and Winston, 1963.

Herman, R. and Lam, T. "Carpools at Large Suburban Technical Center," *Transportation Engineering Journal,* **101** 1975, 311–319.

Horn, J. L. "A Rationale and Test for the Number of Factors in Factor Analysis," *Psychometrika,* **30** 1965, 179–185.

Horowitz, A. D. *An Attitudinal Model of Carpooling Behavior.* Research Laboratories, General Motors Corporation, Research Publication GMR–1969, August, 1975.

Howard, J. A. and Sheth, J. N. *The Theory of Buyer Behavior.* New York: Wiley, 1969.

Katona, G. *Psychological Economics.* New York: Elsevier, 1975.

Kendall, D. C. *Carpooling: Status and Potential.* Final Report No. DOT–TSC–OST–75–23, Transportation Systems Center, U.S. Department of Transportation, Cambridge, Massachusetts, June 1975.

Krishnan, K. S. and Clelland, R. C. "Selection of Undergraduate Freshmen Using Discriminant Analysis," *The Journal of Experimental Education,* **41** 1973, 28–36.

Margolin, J. B. and Misch, M. R. "Incentives and Disincentives to Ridesharing." Paper presented at the American Psychological Annual Convention, Washington, D.C., 1976.

Morrison, D. F. *Multivariate Statistical Analysis.* New York: McGraw-Hill, 1967. Raju, P. S. and Sheth, J. N. "Nonlinear, Noncompensatory Relationships in Attitude Research." Working Paper No. 176, College of Commerce and Business Administration, University of Illinois, April 1974.

Rosenberg, M. J. "A Structural Theory of Attitude Dynamics," *Public Opinion Quarterly* **24** 1960, 319–340.

Rosenbloom, S. and Shelton, N. J. "Carpool and Bus Matching Program for the University of Texas at Austin." Research Report No. 11, The Graduate Program in Community and Regional Planning, University of Texas at Austin, September 1974.

Sheth, J. N. "A Field Study of Attitude Structure and the Attitude-Behavior Relationship," in J. N. Sheth (ed.) *Models of Buyer Behavior.* New York: Harper and Row, 1974.

United States Congress, *Emergency Highway Energy Conservation Act,* Public Law 93–239, January 1974.

(Alan M.) Voorhees and Associates, Inc. *A Study of Techniques to Increase Commuter Vehicle Occupancy on the Hollywood Freeway,* November 1973.

Yankelovich, D. "New Criteria for Market Segmentation," *Harvard Business Review,* **42** 1964, 83–90.

Zerega, A. M. and Ross, R. B. "Application of Conjoint Measurement Techniques in Evaluating Carpooling Policies." Paper presented at the American Psychological Association Annual Convention, Washington, D.C., 1976.

**Discriminant Analysis between Solo Drivers
And Carpoolers—Socioeconomic and Travel Characteristics**

i	Variable	F-Value	d.f.	α_i^{Solo}	α_i^{CP}
1	Distance, Home–Work	37.1**	1;703	0.10	0.15
2	Car Size	22.2**	1;702	2.90	3.26
3	Sex	9.0**	1;701	14.18	15.12
4	Years at Present Employer	12.3**	1;700	0.16	0.19
5	Occupation	5.8*	1;699	4.59	4.42
6	Household size	5.8*	1;698	1.21	1.37
7	Marital Status	5.2*	1;697	9.50	10.03
0	(Constant)	—	—	−52.28	−62.71
	F Between Groups	14.2**	7;697		

** : $p \leq 0.01$
 * : $p \leq 0.05$

Classification into Groups

Actual	Classified as Solo Carpooler		
Solo	245	137	382
Carpooler	123	190	323
Total			705

Correctly Classified : 61.7%
Colo : 64.1%
Carpoolers : 58.8%

181

**Discriminant Analysis between Solo Drivers
And Carpoolers—Attitude Toward Ridesharing**

i	Variable	F Value	d.f.	α_i^{Solo}	α_i^{CP}
1	Convenient	197.6**	1;703	0.12	0.52
2	Reliable	38.9**	1;702	0.33	0.68
3	Pleasant	10.8**	1;701	1.43	1.64
4	Saves Time	4.1*	1;700	0.11	−0.04
0	(Constant)	—	—	−13.60	−17.50
	F Between Groups	66.6**	4;700	—	—

** : $p \leq 0.001$
  * : $p \leq 0.05$

Classification into Groups

Actual	Classified as Solo Carpooler		
Solo	280	102	382
Carpooler	84	239	323
Total			705

Correctly Classified : 73.6%
Solo : 73.3%
Carpoolers : 74.0%

Solo Drivers: Factor Structure of the δ; Measures

Factor (% Variance Explained)	Attribute	Factor Loading	Explained Variance (%)	
			In Factor	In the Other Factor
I Time– Convenience (38.3)	Convenient	0.86	73.6	0.5
	Reliable	0.84	69.8	0.0
	Pleasant	0.78	61.0	0.7
	Comfortable	0.82	67.2	0.3
	Saves Time	0.84	71.4	0.7
II Private and Public Cost (23.8)	Expensive	0.55	30.7	0.0
	Energy Consuming	0.70	49.5	0.4
	Traffic Problems	0.83	68.5	0.7
	Pollution	0.80	63.6	0.2

Carpoolers: Factor Structure of the δ Measures

Factor (% Variance Explained)	Attribute	Factor Loading	Explained Variance (%)	
			In Factor	In the Other Factor
I Time– Convenience (36.8)	Convenient	0.86	73.8	0.4
	Reliable	0.80	64.1	0.0
	Pleasant	0.79	63.0	0.5
	Comfortable	0.80	64.1	0.2
	Saves Time	0.81	64.9	0.5
II Private and Public Costs (26.6)	Expensive	0.57	32.8	0.3
	Energy Consuming	0.73	53.0	0.0
	Traffic Problems	0.88	76.8	0.0
	Pollution	0.87	75.3	0.4

Affect and Intention Distributions in the Cognitive Factorial Design*

Affect

T \ C	(1) low	(2) high
(1) low	mean = 4.2 SD = 1.8 N = 96	mean = 4.9 SD = 1.7 N = 87
(2) high	mean = 3.0 SD = 1.8 N = 108	mean = 3.0 SD = 1.7 N = 91

Intention

T \ C	(1) low	(2) high
(1) low	mean = 2.5 SD = 1.4 N = 96	mean = 2.8 SD = 1.4 N = 87
(2) high	mean = 1.8 SD = 0.9 N = 108	mean = 2.2 SD = 1.2 N = 91

*N : Number of Individuals
SD : Standard Deviation

Woodsmith, Inc.

Herbert E. Brown, Wright State University

In 1947 at the age of 35, John Durworth, a machinist by trade and an avid woodworking hobbyist in his spare time, combined his interests and invented an extraordinary power woodworking tool. Durworth coined the name Woodsmith for the tool and registered the name under the registration procedure of the Lanham Act. Soon after, he obtained a patent on his woodworking machine as well.

Having little capital himself Durworth convinced several investors to buy an interest in the product and soon was president of Woodsmith Woodworking Tool, Inc. His little company grew rapidly and by 1953 Durworth looked forward to ever-expanding wealth and early retirement. Unfortunately, disaster struck. While using a Woodsmith woodworking tool, a man was severely injured and left handicapped. Liability suits followed with the result that the entire company was wiped out in order to pay enormous court-awarded product liability damages.

A heartbroken John Durworth entered bankruptcy proceedings and lost his company to his creditors. The company was put in the hands of trustees who eventually sold it to a group of investors headed by an aggressive man, Elwood Burns. For some reason, perhaps Burns' lack of knowledge or perhaps lack of a market, within a year this company went bankrupt as well. After that, the Woodsmith name went into disuse and eventually lost its protection under the Lanham Act. Also, since nothing was done to protect the patent rights to the product, these too expired after the required 17 years.

Ironically, woodworking craftsmen and hobbyists who owned the Woodsmith woodworking tool were so enamored with it that a cult of sorts grew up around it. The tool was unusual only in that five basic woodworking tools (lathe, disc sander, table saw, vertical drill press, and horizontal drill press) were combined into one machine and driven by a central power source. With just a little practice, the typical

---

user could shift the tool's orientation from one woodworking operation to another in a matter of seconds, for example, from sawing to lathe work, and so forth. In addition, woodworking accuracy using Woodsmith was truly excellent. Furthermore, the tool was extremely durable, so durable in fact that by 1970, 23 years after the first Woodsmith was produced, not a single machine—so far as anyone could determine—had been retired. People who owned Woodsmiths bragged on them constantly and just as constantly kept on the lookout for other owners. When owners did find each other, lasting friendships often were formed and, sometimes even, groups with memberships spread across a hundred miles or so were organized to socialize and discuss any and all aspects of Woodsmith—its inventor, his success, his failure, and so forth.

One of these groups had three young business executives in it who were itching to strike out on their own. Their knowledge of the Woodsmith woodworking tool and of its owners led them to believe they could revive the product and market it. Finding the name and patents up for grabs, they quickly took steps to get control of both—which they did. A new company was formed with one of the three, Eric Tyler, as president; another, Larry Trenton, as sales and marketing manager and the third, Grant Gaston, in charge of manufacturing. About 40 employees, half of them sales representatives, were hired; and, on July 1, 1973, their first Woodsmith woodworking tool rolled off a very makeshift assembly line.

Enough orders were obtained to sustain the new company, but at the end of one full year of operation, Eric Tyler told Trenton and Gaston, "We're just about belly up."

Up to that time, sales had been made largely to individuals and to selected hardware and similar stores here, there, or anywhere, just to get volume—any volume. But in the late summer of 1974, Larry Trenton tried a new marketing approach. He convinced the management of a local enclosed-mall shopping center to let Woodsmith, Inc. set up a demonstration area in a high traffic zone within their mall. He then worked up a combined sales and demonstration talk, and trained three sales demonstrators to make the demonstration in the mall. The program was an instant success. Thirty-five Woodsmiths were sold on the spot in two days and another 20 were sold in a matter of days from leads obtained at the demonstration site. This success led to other demonstrations with overall excellent results.

Woodsmith, Inc. made this program the heart of their overall marketing strategy. Buoyed, and more liquid from the success of the mall marketing program, Trenton worked to refine it, eventually hitting on two devices to make it easier to "set up shop" in shopping centers. One of these was a trailer that could be opened on site to provide an instant stage, curtains for background, and the like. The other was a portable storefront for use in shopping centers where an empty store provided an apparently excellent display location. These efforts, combined with major refinements in the "canned" sales/demonstration talk, were marked with continuing success.

By 1976, Trenton's staff had grown to include a sales manager, a mail marketing manager, and an advertising manager. Trenton carefully monitored his new staff's efforts, but turned his attention more and more toward finding new ways for Woodsmith to grow.

He moved initially to energize the company's direct mail program. He first developed a quarterly newsletter called *Woodsmith Carvings* designed to permit Woodsmith owners to tell others of unique things they were doing, as well as how they did them, stories and information about woodworking, and Woodsmith's continuing success. Each issue spotlighted a specially priced add-on tool that could be ordered directly from the factory. Sales from this effort, combined with other periodic direct mailings, soon became almost as profitable as selling the basic machine. The machine itself cost about $500, but the complete assortment of add-on tools totaled slightly over $1,000.

Trenton next went to direct mail marketing the machine itself. Through the use of carefully selected lists and sophisticated direct mail pieces, this approach moved into the black quickly and soon was made an integral part of the overall marketing strategy. Woodsmith's growing direct sales force was now supplied with even larger lists of potential prospects who had responded to the direct mail program. In addition, to the surprise of everyone, a significant percentage of buyers were sending in orders for the Woodsmith woodworking tool without benefit of a sales call. A few even ordered all the basic add-on tools as well. Included among these were a band saw, a jointer, a belt sander, and a jig saw.

Trenton's creative mind soon produced still another strategy. This plan involved "contractors." High school industrial arts teachers and other woodworking craftspeople were recruited to set up display and demonstration sites in either their own shops or in rented space in their areas. To become a contractor, the Woodsmith woodworking tool had to be purchased unless the contractor already owned the latest model. The contractor was then trained in the Woodsmith demonstration/ sales technique, and was paid a sizeable commission for any order generated. Orders were shipped directly from the factory to customers sold by a contractor. This effort proved sound in a very short time and it was added to Woodsmith's structure of marketing strategies.

In late 1976, a little over three years after its revival, the overall success of the company was truly astonishing. Sales were so good, in fact, that new, modern manufacturing facilities and offices were built to house an organization grown to well over 200 people. The organization was so successful that it was beginning to run into the "problems of success." Specialization of and growth in functions, such as purchasing, finance, labor negotiations, advertising, pricing, sales management, mall marketing, and the like were producing communications and other problems new to the management. To deal with these problems, Tyler, Trenton, and Gaston began attending any and all executive development seminars which promised information that would augment their skills. By their own admission, all three men were "achievement oriented." In addition, all were intelligent enough to know that managing a large and growing organization in the 1970s was a much tougher job than in years past. To their surprise, they found that many of the skills they needed would be impossible for them to obtain and still have time to manage. They often were impressed, however, with the apparent depth of seminar leaders, and increasingly began to hire them for specialized projects, and sometimes just to talk over a particular problem.

Problems in the marketing area began to crop up, too. Although Trenton could define them, he neither had the skill nor the time to solve them. His mall marketing strategy, for example, still was working well, but he knew a lot of marketing money was being wasted there. Shopping malls welcomed and often recruited Woodsmith demonstrations. The problem, then, was not finding demonstration sites but selecting the best ones. This problem become obvious after one weekend in Tennessee. Demonstrations were simultaneously made in a Nashville regional mall and in a small and somewhat isolated Tennessee town over 100 miles away. The Nashville program produced a total of 8 units in sales, barely enough to meet expenses; the other produced 37 units in sales. Many other similar experiences across the country proved conclusively that some malls were good ones, some were poor ones, and some were absolutely awful. But the question was, which ones and why? Trenton's in-house discussion produced a variety of potential explanations. One, for example, was that the presence of a lot of men's shoe stores in a mall explained the problem. Another was that sales seemed to depend on whether the demonstration corresponded with crop harvests in the local area. Trenton concluded from this discussion that no one really knew and decided to call in a consultant to diagnose the problem and to make recommendations.

As it turned out, Trenton knew a marketing professor at a local university who already was consulting with another local firm who, in turn, recommended him as being competent and thorough. He was called in. The professor, Alfred Soloman, insisted on getting a full understanding of the entire Woodsmith operation by discussing virtually all aspects of it with Trenton and other key people. This annoyed Trenton at first, but he got the consent of others and agreed to allow Soloman to proceed anyway. The value of this soon became apparent as marketing issue after marketing issue surfaced that had previously gone unnoticed.

It became obvious, for example, that still another Trenton marketing idea—developing a retail store merchandising concept—would need careful consideration before implementation. Trenton already had set up a model store at the factory and planned to use it to work the bugs out of his merchandising plan before offering it to potential franchises. As planned, the franchised stores would sell not only Woodsmith and its add-on tools, but also a variety of related tools.

Obviously, some problems were going to occur if these stores were successful. In fact, some indication of their type was already evident. Contractors were protesting that the mail order program was taking business right out from "under their noses." Shopping mall demonstrations in contractor territories were receiving criticism for the same reason. Mail order prices, contractor sale prices, and demonstration sale prices all differed; and any special deal offered by the company that took business away from these contractors was an apparent source of potential conflict.

The net outcome of these discussions and resultant problems was that Soloman was asked to work with Woodsmith on three projects: a marketing study, a search for a model that would permit advance predictions of good versus poor shopping center demonstration locations, and the development of a pricing structure and set of channel relationships to maintain the momentum of all four marketing methods, yet reduce channel conflict to a minimum.

Discussion Questions

1. Evaluate Woodsmith's overall marketing strategy.
2. Advise Professor Soloman as to what to do and how to proceed on all three projects.

Chapter 3

Product Strategies

Organizations have to make several decisions concerning their product mix. These decisions can be grouped into six categories:

1. New product decisions
2. Product and service attribute decisions
3. Product-life-cycle and expansion decisions
4. Product-positioning decisions
5. Product-related-to-other-marketing-mix-decisions
6. Product-deletions decisions

Similarly, consumers have to decide several issues concerning product offerings. These issues include product adoption, consumption system, disposal, and product deletion decisions.

Governments and independent consumer testing services also are concerned with several product decisions. Product selection for evaluation, methods of evaluation, and product regulations and laws are some of the categories of decisions faced by governments.

The product decisions for organizations, consumers, and governments are analyzed in this chapter. The decisions of these groups interact and often produce several modifications in the product through time. However, the discussion should begin with the most basic question: What is a product?

Product Defined

A broad view of product should be assumed since product and marketing strategy can be applied to many problem settings, both in profit and nonprofit situations. A *product* is anything offered for exchange to another person including physical objects, services, places (such as retail stores, planned communities), organizations (Heart Association), and ideas (the need for a law requiring a $.05 deposit on all beverage containers).

Products may have both symbolic and physical characteristics. *Symbolic characteristics* are the beliefs consumers perceive about the product (for example, some consumers may perceive beer as a lower class drink and wine as an upper class drink); symbolic characteristics also include benefits consumers perceive in the product (for example, beer drinking may be perceived as an activity expressing friendship to others and wine drinking as an expression of status).

Consumers may recognize a product as a physical object having up to five characteristics: *quality level, features, styling,* a *brand name,* and *packaging.* If the product is a service, it may have some or all of these characteristics.

> We can say that the U. S. Income Tax Advisory Service exhibits a certain quality level in that government tax advisors have a certain degree of competence. The service has certain features, such as being offered at no charge and usually requiring some waiting time. The service has a certain styling, such as being brief, cursory, and impersonal. The service has a certain formal name, that of "Federal Income Tax Advisory Service." Finally, the service is packaged within branch offices located in various cities.[1]

Two or more levels or choices often must be evaluated for each of these five product characteristics. If three quality levels (Q), two feature groupings (F), three styles (S), four brand names (B), and three package designs (P) are being evaluated, a total of 216 combinations of these product characteristics could be evaluated.

$$PM = (Q) \quad (F) \quad (S) \quad (B) \quad (P)$$
$$PM = (3) \quad (2) \quad (3) \quad (4) \quad (3)$$
$$PM = 216$$

where PM = product mix combinations.

Management would likely evaluate a limited number (6 to 20) of product mix combinations in such a situation. Some initial choices would have to be made to reduce the possible 216 mixes to a limited number of candidates that could be market tested.

New Product Decisions

Over 50 new ideas may be needed before one commercially successful new product is marketed. Research by Booz, Allen, and Hamilton, management consultants, suggests that product development is a sequential decision process based on limited information and limited evaluation of alternative mixes. The product mix ultimately selected for commercialization is chosen based on hunch as well as skill.[2]

Five stages in the new product decision process are described in Figure C—3–1.

---

[1] Philip Kotler, *Marketing Management: Analysis, Planning, and Control* (Englewood Cliffs, NJ: Prentice-Hall, 1976), p. 184.

[2] *Management of New Products* (Chicago: Booz, Allen, and Hamilton, Management Consultants, 1968), p. 9.

The data in the figure are based on the average experience of 51 companies in six consumer and industrial manufacturing firms. For every 58 ideas, about 12 receive intensive profitability evaluation during the business analysis phase as shown in Figure C—3–1. The six ideas that survived the business analysis entered the development stage. The laboratory design and testing phase eliminated three more leaving only three products for testing. Commercialization was selecting the two products that succeeded in the test markets and launching the two through the regular distribution system. The final result of the decision process was the conversion of 58 new product ideas into one commercially successful product.

Some of the detailed activities likely to occur in the product development process for a successful new product are described in Figure C—3–2. The successful product development process should start with a *planned search* for new product ideas before screening. Salespersons, dealers in the channel, and customers often are sources of new product ideas.

Notice in Figure C—3–2 that the market potential should be evaluated early (in the screening stage) in the product development process. The test market stage includes testing the sales effectiveness of different combinations of promotion methods, prices, and distribution channels with one or two versions of the product.

As shown in Figure C—3–2, introduction of a new product may result in phasing out weak products in the evaluation stage. Some adjustments in the allocation of the sales force and advertising program usually are necessary given a successful introduction of a new product. Products producing lower sales or profits eventually are deleted after comparisons are made with the returns from successfully introduced new products.

Figure   C—3–1
Stages in the Product Development Cycle

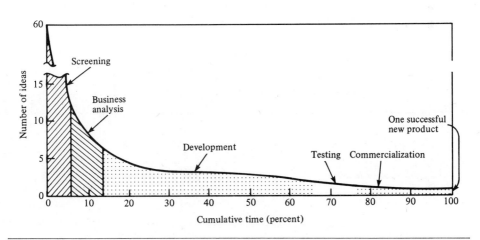

Source: Average experience of 51 companies as reported in *Management of New Products* (Chicago: Booz, Allen & Hamilton, Management Consultants, 1968), p. 9.

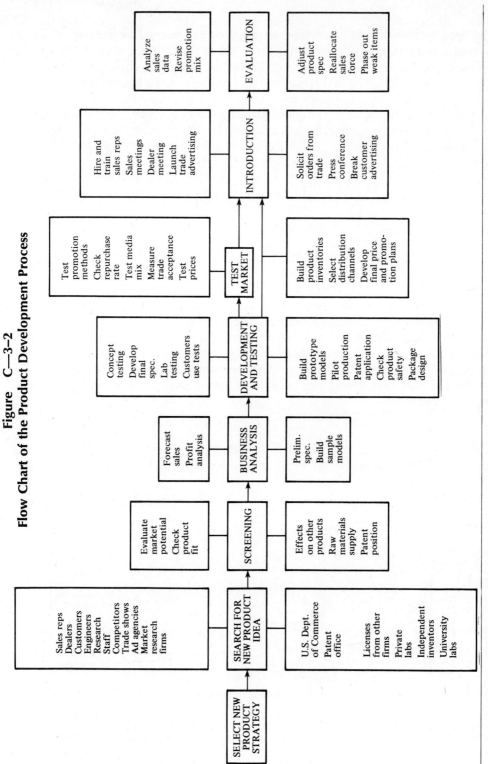

Figure C—3–2
Flow Chart of the Product Development Process

SELECT NEW PRODUCT STRATEGY → SEARCH FOR NEW PRODUCT IDEA → SCREENING → BUSINESS ANALYSIS → DEVELOPMENT AND TESTING → TEST MARKET → INTRODUCTION → EVALUATION

SEARCH FOR NEW PRODUCT IDEA

Sales reps
Dealers
Customers
Engineers
Research
Staff
Competitors
Trade shows
Ad agencies
Market research firms

U.S. Dept. of Commerce
Patent office
Licenses from other firms
Private labs
Independent inventors
University labs

SCREENING

Evaluate market potential
Check product fit

Effects on other products
Raw materials supply
Patent position

BUSINESS ANALYSIS

Forecast sales
Profit analysis

Prelim. spec.
Build sample models

DEVELOPMENT AND TESTING

Concept testing
Develop final spec.
Lab testing
Customers use tests

Build prototype models
Pilot production
Patent application
Check product safety
Package design

TEST MARKET

Test promotion methods
Check repurchase rate
Test media mix
Measure trade acceptance
Test prices

Build product inventories
Select distribution channels
Develop final price and promotion plans

INTRODUCTION

Hire and train sales reps
Sales meetings
Dealer meeting
Launch trade advertising

Solicit orders from trade
Press conference
Break customer advertising

EVALUATION

Analyze sales data
Revise promotion mix

Adjust product spec
Reallocate sales force
Phase out weak items

Source: Douglas J. Dalrymple and Leonard J. Parsons, *Marketing Management: Text and Cases* (New York: John Wiley & Sons, Inc., 1976), p. 240.

194

Managing the Product Development Process: The Venture Team

Some large manufacturing firms recognized both the need for a formal process of product development and its inherent complexity. Venture teams of different specialists have been created in such firms to manage the product development process. Characteristics of such venture teams can be described briefly.

1. *Organizationally separate*—the most successful product development units are separated from other plants and offices in the companies.
2. *Multidisciplinary*—the interaction of technical experts from design engineering, production, market research, finance, and other functional specialists is an essential ingredient of creativity.
3. *Diffusion of responsibility*—less structure of lines of authority are present in venture teams compared to the permanent organization.
4. *Environment of entrepreneurship*—a free-wheeling atmosphere is likely to be found among venture teams.
5. *Top management linkage*—venture team managers usually report to the division head or chief administrator of the firm.
6. *Broad mission*—the venture team's mission generally is defined in a manner which permits considerable discretion in its pursuit.
7. *Flexible life span*—virtually all teams are free of pressures imposed by strict deadlines.[3]

The need for venture teams must be balanced by the size of the organization. A venture team may be limited to one full-time, new product manager and several specialists working part-time in small firms. Because of the complexity of the product development process, the *venture team concept* is the recognition of the need for organization change to enhance the successful introduction of new products.

Product and Service Attribute Decisions

Organizations have a need to blend alternative types or levels of product attributes to satisfy both manufacturing and distribution cost constraints and consumer demand constraints. Demand constraints usually need to have precedence over cost constraints given the competitive environment of marketing-oriented economics.

Figure C—3–3 is an example of three package designs for a carpet cleaner being evaluated with different types or levels of brand names, prices, and other product characteristics. The last column in Figure C—3–3 is one consumer's ranked preference among 18 combinations of product attributes. The combinations were developed from the following product attributes, types or levels:

1. Package design: 3 types

---

[3] Richard M. Hill and James D. Hlavacek, "The Venture Team: A New Concept in Marketing Organization," *Journal of Marketing,* **36** (July 1972), pp. 44–50. Published by the American Marketing Association.

2. Brand names: 3 names

3. Price: 3 levels

4. Good Housekeeping Seal: 2 levels

5. Money-back guarantee: 2 levels

A total of 108 product concepts are possible (3x3x3x2x2) but the 18 combinations shown in Figure C—3–3 permit testing the relative importance of each product attribute to the consumer.

The two or three products concepts most preferred by the consumer might be examined with market tests and costs analyses. Market tests permit comparison of the likely payoffs in sales and profits of alternative product concepts as well as test the relationship between consumers' reported preferences and actual demand for different product concepts.

Notice in Figure C—3–3 that the particular consumer comparing the 18 alternatives prefers design C, Bissell, $1.19, the Good Housekeeping Seal, and the money-back guarantee. The product concept listed as tenth is preferred the least by this consumer.

Comparing consumer preference, demand, costs, and profits of alternative product concepts is an integral step in the product development process. Such comparisons also are useful in product modification decisions. Unfortunately, many product modification decisions usually do not include the careful planning described by the product development process. Product changes often are based strictly on cost comparisons which may result in a rapid decline in brand preference and demand for the product, thus reducing the initial benefits perceived in the cost reductions. In 1977, the shift in product ingredients, increase in advertising expenditures, and label change for Lowenbräu beer may prove to be an example of this situation.

Product Life Cycle and Expansion Decisions

The product life cycle (PLC) is the series of stages in sales volume, and percent of customers using the product likely to be observed for most products over time. Five stages and their distinguishing characteristics are noted.

1. Introduction: product is unknown; demand increases slowly; few competitors exist; one channel of distribution used.

2. Growth: rapid sales increase; there are substantial profits to the firm; several competitors enter the market; multiple channels used.

3. Maturity: sales plateau reached; profits decline because of lower prices and intensified brand competition.

4. Decline: demand declines for industry; price increases; the number of competitors decline.

5. Termination: few customers exist; there are substantial losses to the firm; there is overcapacity to produce the product.

Figure C—3–4 is an example of the stages of the PLC. Different products are shown at different stages in the PLC according to their level of potential saturation

Figure   C—3–3
Experimental Design for Evaluation of a Carpet Cleaner

Package designs

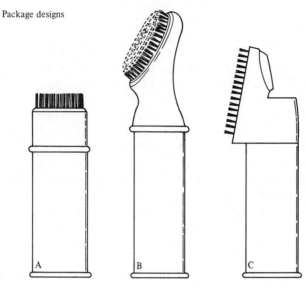

Orthogonal array

Package design	Brand name	Price	Good Housekeeping seal?	Money-back guarantee?	Respondent's evaluation (rank number)
1 A	K2R	$1.19	No	No	13
2 A	Glory	1.39	No	Yes	11
3 A	Bissell	1.59	Yes	No	17
4 B	K2R	1.39	Yes	Yes	2
5 B	Glory	1.59	No	No	14
6 B	Bissell	1.19	No	No	3
7 C	K2R	1.59	No	Yes	12
8 C	Glory	1.19	Yes	No	7
9 C	Bissell	1.39	No	No	9
10 A	K2R	1.59	Yes	No	18
11 A	Glory	1.19	No	Yes	8
12 A	Bissell	1.39	No	No	15
13 B	K2R	1.19	No	No	4
14 B	Glory	1.39	Yes	No	6
15 B	Bissell	1.59	No	Yes	5
16 C	K2R	1.39	No	No	10
17 C	Glory	1.59	No	No	16
18 C	Bissell	1.19	Yes	Yes	1*

*Highest ranked

Source: P. E. Green and Y. Wind, "New Way to Measure Consumers' Judgments," *Harvard Business Review,* **53**:108, July–August, 1975. Copyright © 1975 by the President and Fellows of Harvard College; all rights reserved.

for U.S. households. Freezers are at the top of the saturation curve in Figure C—3–4 (maturity stage) along with refrigerators. Both products have obtained over 90 percent of their potential market. Color television is more likely in the growth stage, although black and white television is classified best as in the decline stage.

The existence of the PLC should suggest the need to adjust the product mix and the entire marketing mix to changes that occur from one stage in the PLC to the next stage. For example, management may want to introduce model changes, reduce prices, develop new marketing channels to reach new customers, and increase promotion expenditures to change the shape of sales or potential saturation curves in the PLC.

Likely changes in environmental characteristics and marketing decisions in the different stages of the PLC are described in Table C—3–1. However, not all products fit the pattern shown in Table C—3–1 and described by Figure C—3–4. Management may introduce decisions designed to (1) increase the frequency of use by present customers of the existing product, (2) add new uses, (3) find new uses for the product, and (4) change package sizes, labels, or product quality. The sales data and product developments for nylon shown in Figure C—3–5 are examples of such decisions.

Nylon was used originally in parachutes, rope, and women's stockings. Demand peaked at about 50 million pounds per year in 1962 as shown in Figure C—3–5. However, demand actually approached 500 million pounds in 1962 because of the development of new uses in tires, carpet, gears, sweaters, and other products. Thus, decisions to modify the marketing mix of existing products might be planned

Figure   C—3–4
Life Cycle Stages of Various Products

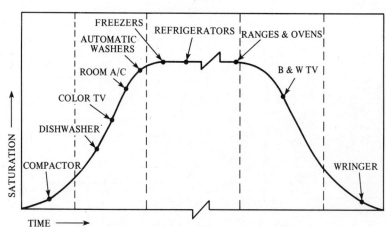

Source: John E. Smallwood, "The Product Life-Cycle A Key to Strategic Marketing Planning," *MSU Business Topics,* Winter, 1973, pp. 29–35. Reprinted by permission of the publisher, Division of Research, Graduate School of Business Administration, Michigan State University.

Table C—3—1
Product Life Cycle

	Introduction	Growth	Maturity	Decline	Termination
Marketing					
CUSTOMERS	Innovative/ High Income	High Income/ Mass Market	Mass Market	Laggards/ Special	Few
CHANNELS	Few	Many	Many	Few	Few
APPROACH	Product	Label	Label	Specialized	Availability
ADVERTISING	Awareness	Label Superiority	Lowest Price	Psychographic	Sparse
COMPETITORS	Few	Many	Many	Few	Few
Pricing					
PRICE	High	Lower	Lowest	Rising	High
GROSS MARGINS	High	Lower	Lowest	Low	Rising
COST REDUCTIONS	Few	Many	Slower	None	None
INCENTIVES	Channel	Channel/ Consumer	Consumer/ Channel	Channel	Channel
Product					
CONFIGURATION	Basic	Second Generation	Segmented/ Sophisticated	Basic	Stripped
QUALITY	Poor	Good	Superior	Spotty	Minimal
CAPACITY	Over	Under	Optimum	Over	Over

Source: John E. Smallwood, "The Product Life-Cycle A Key to Strategic Marketing Planning," *MSU Business Topics*, Winter 1973, pp. 29–35. Reprinted by permission of the publisher, Division of Research, Graduate School of Business Administration, Michigan State University.

Figure   C—3–5
New Uses Extend Nylon Life Cycle

Source: Jordan P. Yale, "The Strategy of Nylon's Growth: Create New Markets," *Modern Textiles Magazine* (February 1964), p. 33. Copyright © 1962 by Jordan P. Yale. Reproduced by permission.

through the PLC; such planning will likely have substantial sales and profit payoffs for the organization.

In fact, the opportunities to change the shape of sales volume during the PLC has lead to the suggestion to "forget the product life cycle!" [4] Instead, the effects of marketing mix variables on consumer attitudes, intentions, and brand share should be measured in different time periods. Then, adjustments should be made as indicated to several marketing mix variables. The important point to note is that the PLC is not necessarily a prediction of what has to occur. The life of a product can be extended and expanded using creative marketing strategy.

Product Positioning

Product positioning refers to a product's subjective attributes in relation to competing products. Product positioning is the perceived image of the brand held by

---

[4] Noriman K. Dhalla and Sonia Yuspeh, "Forget the Product Life Cycle," *Harvard Business Review,* **54** (January–February, 1976). Copyright © 1976 by the President and Fellows of Harvard College; all rights reserved.

consumers and the positioning may differ widely from the brand's true physical characteristics.

Positioning should not be confused with the product position of the brand. Position refers to the product's physical form, package size, and price. Positioning refers to a perceptual location of the brand in the consumer's mind compared with the mental location of competing brands.

Management may decide to introduce a repositioning strategy in order to increase sales, profits, and brand share payoffs. The shift of 7-Up from its image as a mixer near soda water and fruit mixers to the "Uncola" and near Coke and Pepsi is one example.

The case of L&M is another example of repositioning. In February 1974, Liggett & Myers announced that L&M brand of cigarettes was "not properly positioned as a brand." It was further stated that "L&M must be repositioned in the full-flavor category." To accomplish this repositioning, Liggett and Myers began by changing L&M's product position. This took the form of a new blend of tobacco and a new cork filter. The mainstay of the repositioning effort, however, was a massive advertising campaign (and a newly designed package). However, one limited research report available indicates that L&M was not moved into the intended location nearer to Winston and Marlboro cigarettes. The positioning location of brands shown in Figure C—3–6 for smokers among undergraduate students at the University of Arizona did not change substantially after the repositioning marketing attempt.

Product positioning points to the need to measure consumers' perceptions of brand images for competing brands. Development of perceptual maps, such as Figure C—3–5, may suggest product development opportunities to reach consumers with preferences unmet by present brand offerings.

Figure   C—3–6
Experimental Group—Before

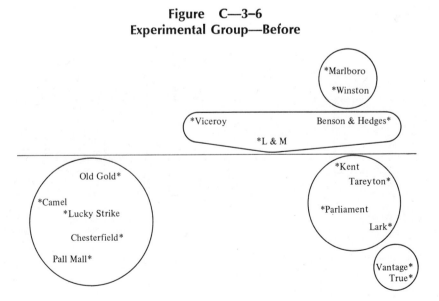

Consumer Adoption Decisions

Consumers go through a series of stages in the decision to adopt new products, similar in several characteristics to the product development process in organizations. A paradigm of the "innovation-decision process" consumers are likely to experience with new products has been proposed and tested. The paradigm includes four stages:

1. *Knowledge.*   The individual is aware of the innovation and has acquired some information about it.
2. *Persuasion.*   The individual forms an attitude, pro or con, toward the innovation.
3. *Decisions.*   The individual performs activities which lead to an adopt-reject decision about the innovation.
4. *Confirmation.*   The individual looks for reinforcement regarding his or her decision and may change an earlier decision if exposed to counter-reinforcing messages.[5]

---

[5] Everett M. Rogers and F. Floyd Shoemaker, *Communication of Innovation* (New York: The Free Press, 1971).

Figure   C—3–7
Paradigm of the Innovation-Decision Process

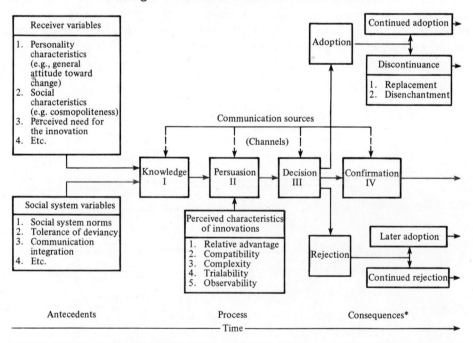

Source: Everett M. Rogers and F. Floyd Shoemaker, *Communications of Innovation,* 2nd ed. (New York: The Free Press, 1971), p. 102.

These four stages are shown in the center of Figure C—3–7. Notice in the figure that the adoption-rejection decision choices are alternatives of the third stage in the process. Variables shown to affect the innovation-decision process include receiver variables, social system variables, and perceived characteristics of innovations.

Research evidence indicates that consumers adopting an innovation earlier than most other consumers have higher levels of formal education, high social status, greater exposure to mass media, more contact with salespersons regarding the innovations and other change agents, have greater social participation, and are more cosmopolitan. Thus, receiver and social system variables affect the innovation-adoption process.

Consumers can be placed into adopter categories on the basis of relative time taken to adopt the innovations. The adoption process is shown in Figure C—3–8 to follow a normal distribution. That is, an increasing number of people adopt the innovation after a slow start, an adoption peak is reached; and then the number of adopters declines.

Adopters are in five categories in Figure C—3–8. Although the classification is somewhat arbitrary, the personal and social system characteristics of innovators (the first 2.5 percent of adopters) tend to be distinct from the adopters in other categories. (Innovators tend to be youngest in age and highest in social status. They are generally wealthier and better educated than other groups.) Each of the other adopter categories can be noted for different characteristics:

- Early adopters–integrated into the community with high status
- Early majority–deliberate, cautious and above average status
- Late majority–skeptical and below average in education and income
- Laggards–bound in tradition and lowest in social status and income

The innovation-adoption process is also influenced by the five characteristics of the innovation.

Relative advantage is the degree to which the innovation appears superior to

Figure   C—3–8
Adopted Groups Based on Innovativeness

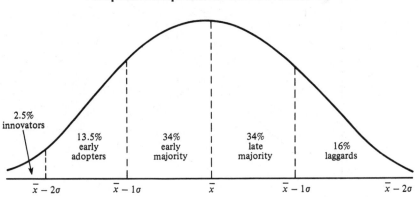

previous ideas. The greater the relative advantage, the faster the adoption rate. For example, the combination of physical ease-of-use, nonleak improvements, and low price of ball-point pens offered in the 1950s increased the speed of their adoption.

Compatibility is the degree to which an innovation is perceived to fit a consumer's way of doing things. A direct relationship has been found between compatibility and the speed of adoption.

An inverse relationship has been found between the perceived *complexity* of the innovation and the speed of adoption. That is, the more difficult it is to understand or use the new product, the longer will be the time period necessary for adoption.

Divisibility or trialability is the degree to which the innovation may be used on a limited basis. The opportunity to experience the product on a limited basis is likely to increase the adoption rate. Test driving automobiles, the free sample, and free weekend vacation in a summer home resort area are examples of attempts to increase trialability to produce increases in the rate of adoption.

The degree to which the results of an innovation are visible to others is *observability*. Innovations high in visibility are likely to be adopted rapidly.

The relationships of these five perceived characteristics of adoption and the rate of adoption are summarized in Figure C—3–9. Knowledge of the relationships between characteristics of innovations and the rate of adoption should be useful in developing marketing strategies with respect to innovations. Strategies can be designed to enhance the positive relationships and decrease the perceived complexity of the innovation.

Consumption System Decisions

Products fit or do not fit into a buyer's consumption system—"the way a purchaser

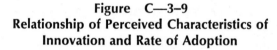

Figure   C—3–9
Relationship of Perceived Characteristics of
Innovation and Rate of Adoption

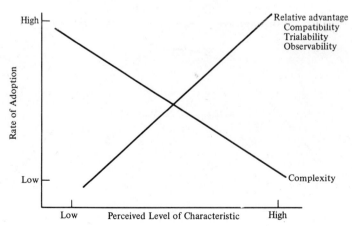

of a product performs the total task of whatever it is that he or she is trying to accomplish when using the product." [6]

A Thanksgiving turkey fits into a different consumption system than a Sunday evening chicken dinner. IBM is marketing information processing systems and not just computers. An automobile is purchased for part of a family's life style and another brand and style of car may be purchased for another part of the family's life style.

Changes in the consumption system may affect the purchase behavior of consumers. For example, in the 1960s, the decrease in eating breakfast in the United States was recognized as a serious problem for sales of Kellogg's cereals, and the need for breakfast was promoted to counteract this trend. (Per capita cereal consumption increased in the 1970s due in part to consumers' recognition of the health benefits of bulk in their diets.)

Organizations need to recognize and respond to the situations and how consumers will use products. Products are used in consumption systems and such systems influence brand decisions and frequency of use decisions.

Disposal Decisions

How consumers dispose of products has been infrequently studied but recognized as important for the future. How consumers use gasoline discard, beverage containers, and discard food scraps are now being studied.

For example, several research studies conducted in Arizona by examining the consumer garbage behavior indicated low brand loyalty behavior. "The most striking aspect of the data is the variety of brands, of any given commodity, used in a single household. In a 5-week period, the average household that discarded more than one example of a product type threw out two or more different brands of detergent, hand soap, and toothpaste, and three or more brands of bread, chips, and beer. Even so, it was clear that for many products, the lower-income household demonstrated the greatest brand 'loyalty.' " [7]

Some of the methods consumers use to dispose of products are shown in Figure C—3–10. Consumers have been found to use different disposition strategies for different product categories. For example, in one study toothbrushes are found to be the most likely converted product (to cleaning tools) among a study of eight products. Phonograph records were most likely to be stored even though the owner very often claimed that he or she would probably never play the records again. [8] Such information should prove useful in product modification decisions to satisfy new uses as well as suggesting changes to other marketing mix variables.

---

[6] Harper W. Boyd, Jr., and Sidney J. Levy, "New Dimensions in Consumer Analysis," *Harvard Business Review,* **41** (November–December 1963), pp. 129–140. Copyright © 1963 by the President and Fellows of Harvard College; all rights reserved.

[7] William L. Rathje, Wilson W. Hughes, and Sherry L. Jernigan, "The Science of Garbage: Following the Consumer through his Garbage Can," *Proceedings of the International Conference* (Chicago: American Marketing Association, 1977), p. 62. Published by the American Marketing Association.

[8] Jacob Jacoby, Carol K. Berning and Thomas F. Dietvorst, "What About Disposition?" *Journal of Marketing,* **41** (April 1977), pp. 22–28. Published by the American Marketing Association.

Figure   C—3–10
Disposition Decision Taxonomy

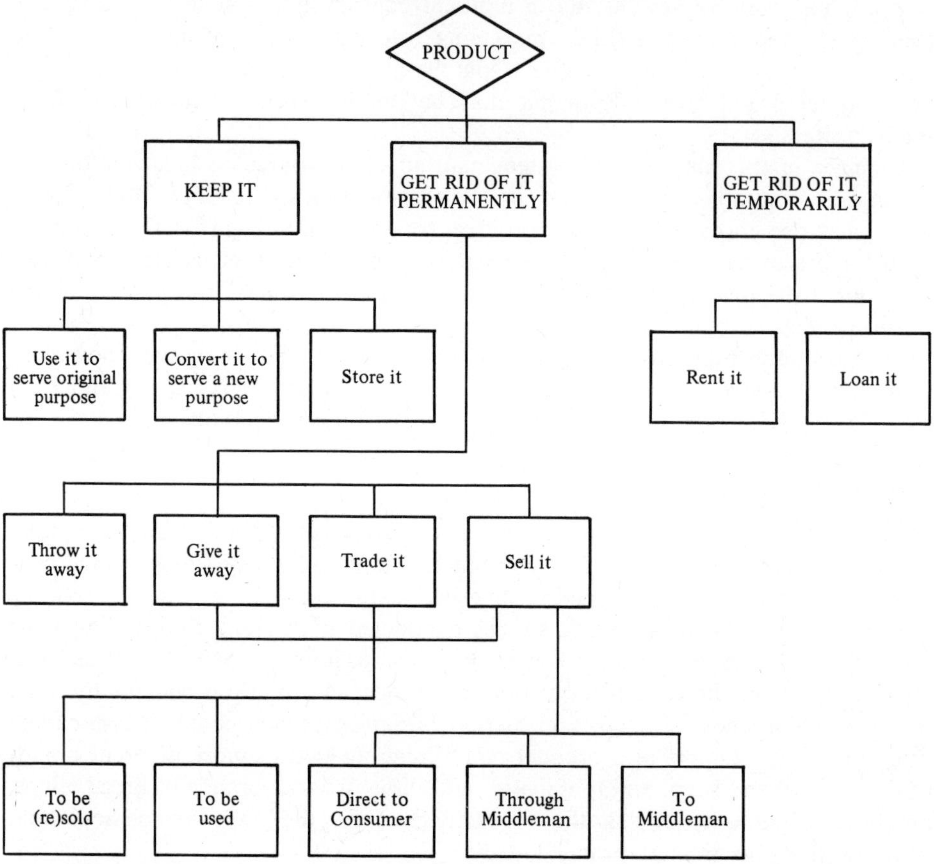

Source: Jacob Jacoby, Carol K. Berning and Thomas F. Dietvorst, "What About Disposition?" *Journal of Marketing,* **41** (April 1977), pp. 22–28. Published by the American Marketing Association.

Government Decisions with Respect to Products

In the United States, governments make decisions with respect to products to enhance competition, provide performance standards, enhance the dissemination of information, and protect consumers against physical and economic harm. Governments usually develop product decision processes at the request of special interest groups or consumers.

The creation and actions of the Consumer Product Safety Commission (CPSC) is a significant example of government action with respect to products. The CPSC was created in 1972 as a result of congressional findings that unsafe consumer products are distributed in unacceptable numbers; hence, consumers are frequently unable to anticipate and guard against the risks of unsafe products. More than 20 million Americans are injured in their homes each year as a result of accidents associated with unsafe consumer products. Of this total, 110,000 persons are permanently disabled and 30,000 others have lost their lives. The annual cost of product-related injuries exceeds $5.5 billion. It has been estimated that 20 percent of these injuries could have been prevented if manufacturers had produced safe, well-designed products.[9]

The CPSC has identified the 20 most dangerous products and the relative likelihood of danger of each as shown in Table C—3–2. Safety standards and design requirements have been introduced by the CPSC for some of them.

The CPSC operates on the premise that consumer product safety and injury are a function of the interaction involving the consumer, the product, and the environment. The basic idea is to attempt to modify the product to increase safety since modifying the consumer and environment are often more difficult tasks.

For example, before the creation of the CPSC, aspirin bottle tops were made child proof and this safety feature reduced by two-thirds the number of children under 5 years of age swallowing accidental doses of aspirin. Unfortunately, sys-

---

[9] Walter Jensen, Jr., Edward M. Mazze, and Duke Nordlinger Stern, "The Consumer Product Safety Act: A Special Case in Consumerism," *Journal of Marketing,* **37** (October 1973), pp. 68–78. Published by the American Marketing Association.

Table C—3–2
The Twenty Most Dangerous

Rank	Item	Frequency-Severity Index
1	Bicycles and bicycle equipment	863,490
2	Stairs, ramps, and landings	833,120
3	Nonglass doors	389,950
4	Cleaning, caustic compounds	386,310
5	Nonglass tables	369,990
6	Beds	304,890
7	Football	296,700
8	Playground apparatus	287,260
9	Liquid fuels	267,150
10	Architectural glass	267,100
11	Power lawn mowers	264,410
12	Baseball	262,310
13	Nails, tacks, and screws	267,650
14	Bathtubs and showers	187,800
15	Space heaters and heating stoves	182,720
16	Swimming pools	178,770
17	Cooking ranges and ovens	161,180
18	Basketball	158,770
19	Nonupholstered chairs	151,380
20	Storage furniture	143,610

Source: Consumer Product Safety Council.

tematic study of consumers' actual use of products and tests of methods to reduce accidents is just now underway.

Summary

A product is anything offered for exchange to another person. Organizations, consumers, and governments are involved in several related product decisions. Product development decisions are likely to include a complex sequence of steps and a team of specialists from different functional areas of the organization.

Different marketing strategies are likely to be observed for different stages in a product's life cycle. However, strategies may be changed in an attempt to change the shape of a product's life cycle. Reaching new markets, stimulating new uses, and increasing frequency of use among current users are three strategies to increase the PLC.

Positioning refers to a perceptual location of one brand in the consumer's mind compared with the mental location of competing brands. A brand's share of the market may change rapidly after repositioning, such as 7-Up from a mixer to the "Uncola."

The consumer's adoption decision is influenced by receiver variables, social system variables, and perceived characteristics of the innovation. Research evidence on consumer adoption decisions suggests useful insights for marketing strategy.

Consumers buy products to fit into their consumption system. Changes in a consumption system will affect the frequency of product use, and new consumption systems may represent product development opportunities. Consumer disposal decisions are being studied in the 1970s. Research results for methods of disposal and brand behavior now exist.

The Consumer Product Safety Act is a recent example of a government law affecting the product decisions of both organizations and households. The CPSC has far reaching powers to regulate the product decisions affecting the behavior of both groups.

Discussion Questions

1. Define product.

2. What are the five characteristics of products? Contrast these levels for a Volkswagen Rabbit and a Rolls Royce.

3. Draw the product life cycle for a product now in the decline stage. Label each axis. Discuss each stage in the product's life cycle.

4. What is a venture team?

5. Provide information and a drawing on each of 18, 3″ x 5″ blank note cards to represent the 18 combinations in Figure C—3–3. Show the cards to 10 persons and ask each to order the cards from most to least preferred. Do your findings parallel the findings shown for the consumer in Figure C—3–3?

6. What is a positioning of Budweiser, Schlitz, Old Milwaukee, and Miller's beers? Draw your own map.

7. Discuss an adoption decision process you have experienced recently.

8. List five characteristics of innovations affecting the adoption process. Explain each.

9. Collect the garbage of a family and analyze its contents. Prepare a written report of the contents.

10. Telephone 10 households and ask each if members of the households have had any accidents within the last seven days. Probe for possible accidents. Ask about the perceived causes of the accidents. Prepare a written report of your findings.

The Brace Company

John A. Howard, Columbia University

The Truth-in-Packaging Legislation

By the summer of 1966, it had become evident to people in the package-goods industry that a real problem was growing out of some legislation being considered in congress. This legislation had to do with government regulation of labeling, packaging, and, to a lesser degree, advertising. No one was exactly certain what had brought about the government action, but a few reasons had been hypothesized. Some thought it could be attributed to the Supreme Court decision on reapportionment which concentrated more power in urban areas, where there were more vocal and more highly educated people. Others claimed that the legislation was the product of a more highly educated group of consumers in the entire country. A third suggestion was that the problem arose from consumer frustration over the plethora of new products. Also, many conceded that business had not done an adequate job of transmitting information, either through packaging and labeling or through advertising.

At this time the management of the Brace Company, a large manufacturer of breakfast foods whose business was centered around the sale of various kinds of dry, ready-to-eat cereals,[1] became very concerned about the implications of the pending legislation. W. V. Brace, president, and P. Burns, executive vice-president, marketing, believed that if the strongest possible legislation were passed, the Brace Company would have to completely revamp its packaging lines and drastically alter its promotional plans and present advertising campaigns. This would cost the company a tremendous amount of money, easily in the multimillion-dollar range.

---

[1] The Brace Company is a fictitious entity whose problems and markets resemble those of large package-goods producers generally.

Since business interests had been rather ineffective up to the summer of 1966 in combating the governmental action, Brace had requested the opportunity to testify before a congressional subcommittee conducting hearings on the advisability of the proposed legislation to regulate packaging and labeling. Two weeks before Mr. Brace was to testify, J. Blackwell, the newly appointed assistant to the vice-president, marketing, was called in and asked to research the problem and to clarify the basic issues so that Mr. Brace could speak knowledgeably at the hearings. Several other men in the company brought in what they thought were pertinent data and gave it to Blackwell to analyze. Since actual data concerning the Brace Company had not been gathered, Blackwell was encouraged to use figures on other cereal manufacturers.

The Consumers' Environment—Proliferation

While doing his research, it became evident to Blackwell that the environment in which the consumer lived in 1966 was much different from that of 20 years before. The major change the consumer faced was that of product proliferation. With the emergence of the modern supermarket and advanced technology, price was being subordinated to innovation of products and packages as major promotional tools. These factors worked to put approximately 4,000 new products on supermarket shelves each year. In 1965, 40 percent of all manufacturing sales were from products not produced in 1950. It was estimated that in 1969, 15 percent of manufacturing sales would come from products not produced in 1965. Research and development, the source of innovation, increased 60 percent as a percentage of sales from 1954 to 1964 in 18 large food processors (see Exhibit 11–1).

Although innovation may have led to the expansion of consumer satisfaction and economic growth, it may also have engendered confusion in the marketplace. Not only did the consumer of 1966 face more variety than her 1946 counterpart, but she was confronted with an increasing inability to differentiate between products due to their increased complexity and subtleties of change. Blackwell found that there were approximately 8,000 different items in the average supermarket. It could be said that by 1966, product differentiation was a leading means of gaining and holding a preferred market position and that advertising and sales promotion are the most common way to gain access to customers.

The Cereal Industry

As far as the cereal business was concerned, Blackwell uncovered the following data: In 1964 there were 48,500,000 cereal-using households in which children between the ages of 3 and 12 influenced 70 percent of the sales of the ready-to-eat variety of cereal.

One of the reasons for the proliferation of cereals was a lack of brand loyalty and the introduction of new brands. The National Commission on Food Marketing

Exhibit 11-1

A. Expenditures for R&D by 18 large food processors

Year	Aggregate Sales (millions)	R & D Expenditures	
		Millions	Percent of Sales
1954	$4,974	$ 18.3	37%
1960	5,636	30.3	54
1964	6,579	39.6	60
Percent change:			
1954–64	+32.3	+116.7	
1960–64	+16.7	+ 30.6	

B. Proliferation of cereals, 1954–64

New cereals captured 23 percent of market.

Regular brands decreased share of market from 70 percent to 55 percent.

Number of cold cereals increased from 36 to 79 stocked in grocery chains.

C. Average number of items offered for sale per manufacturer and average share of manufacturer's cereal sales accounted for by manufacturer's 5 and 10 largest selling items, 1964

Size of Manufacturer	Items for Company (number)	Share of Company Sales	
		For 5 items (percent)	For 10 Items (percent)
Largest 4 companies	58	35.4	56.9
Next 4 companies	16	52.6	68.2
All other companies	6	86.6	—
All companies (24)	16	39.2	not available

Source: Part A—Robert P. Buzzell and Robert E. M. Nourse, *Product Innovations in Food Processing,* 1954–1964 (Boston, MA: Harvard University School of Business Administration, 1967), p. 95; Part B—A. C. Nielsen Company; Part C—National Committee on Food Marketing.

stated that 3 out of 5 consumers buy most popular brands 4 out of 10 times. However, the commission stated, company loyalty is higher than brand loyalty, and company market share is correlated to the degree of introduction of new cereals also (see Exhibit 11–2). A study by the Marketing Research Company of America put the repurchase rate for cereals at 50 percent.

Cereal companies also attempted to achieve their share of market goals via market segmentation. Arthur D. Little, Inc., stated that "one of the major determinants of a company's market position is not only the number of brands that it has, but also the number of brands that it has in each market segment." Thus, it appeared that innovation and segmentation were major product policies for cereal manufacturers and that both of these strategies required a high level of

Exhibit 11-2

A. Brand Loyalty

Product	Strong (chief brand bought 75% of time or more)	Moderate (chief brand bought 40–75% of time)	Weak (chief brand bought less than 40% of time)
Coffee	70%	25%	5%
Laundry detergent	88	9	3
Cold cereal	6	34	60

B. Cold Cereal Brand Loyalty

	Product Class					
	I	II	III	IV	V	VI
Percent of families	52%	10%	10%	10%	9%	9%
Percent of pound volume	14	8	10	14	19	35
Number of brands chosen per year	4	8	9	11	12	15
Number of packages purchased per year	8	21	27	37	52	96

Source: Part A—Benton & Bowles, Inc., 1962.

advertising and promotion to be effective. In 1964, $1.5 billion was spent by food processors on advertising, a 4 percent increase over 1963 expenditures (partially reflecting higher media costs). The president of Canadian Kellogg stated that $.17 of every cereal dollar went to promotion, advertising, discounts, and incentives, and the Arthur D. Little Company claimed that:

> 15.2 percent of sales went toward advertising in the cereal business. From 1958 to 1965 advertising expenditures increased 65 percent in the cereal industry. The medium for advertising also changed during the same period of time: television increased from 72.6 percent to 86.3 percent of cereal advertising dollars while newspaper decreased from 15.0 percent to 5.3 percent.[2]

For a more detailed picture of the cereal industry, see Exhibit 11–3.

The Role of Government

Blackwell realized that the problem of government action which Brace must recognize was not restricted to cereal manufacturers and the food industry. Rather, it appeared that the federal government had the ability to exercise control over certain aspects of all consumer goods. Theodore Levitt, of Harvard University, was of the opinion that the government was "moving implacably toward the

---

[2] Report of Arthur D. Little to Grocery Manufacturers Association, 1965.

Exhibit 11-3

A. The Cereal Industry, Profit Data and Revenue sources (in thousands).

		Largest Four Companies	Next Four Companies	All Other Companies	All Companies
A.	Profit data				
	1964 profit				
	Before tax	$ 77,330	$ 6,007	$ 540 [a]	$ 83,877
	After tax	38,727	3,037	281 [a]	42,045
	Return on sales				
	Before tax	15.6%	8.2%	5.0%	14.5%
	After tax	7.8%	4.2%	2.6% [a]	7.3%
	Stockholders' equity	$200,051	$26,893	$ 4,895 [b]	$231,906
	Return on stockholders' equity				
	Before tax	38.6%	22.3%	3.0% [b]	36.0%
	After tax	19.4%	11.3%	1.6% [b]	18.0%
	Total assets	$263,051	$33,091	$ 6,077 [b]	$302,219
	After tax return on assets	14.7%	9.2%	4.6%	13.9%
B.	Revenue sources, 1964				
	Ready-to-serve cereals	64.0%	43.4%	86.0%	90.8%
	To-be-cooked cereals	36.0%	56.6%	14.0%	9.2%
	Total sales	$491,973	$68,960	$19,368	$580,301

[a] Five companies.
[b] Three companies.
Source: National Committee on Food Marketing.

B. The Cereal Industry, Output by Product Category, U.S. 1963.

	Ready-to-Serve Cereals	To-be-Cooked Cereals	Total Cereals
Quantity (thousands of lbs.)	1,293,203	812,400	2,105,603
Share of total	61.4%	38.6%	100%
Value (thousands)	461,530	99,919	561,450
Share of total	82.2%	17.8%	100%

Source: Bureau of the Census.

possible destruction of brand-name marketing." Not only did it appear that the government visualized itself as having an obligation to protect the public from big business, but Congress was urged to take action by various committees. In June of 1966 the Consumer Advisory Council decided that mandatory standards should be established to control packaging and labeling. The decision was based on the premise that "the lack of familiarity with many new products, and the varying quality of some, especially when still in the developmental stage, has made shopping and selecting more worrisome not only for consumers but even for retailers.[3]

The shopping environment had changed, as Blackwell learned, and the consumer was faced with product and brand proliferation as well as changes in the dominant distribution outlets for food. The flux in the environment had produced, in the opinion of some, an information gap. Five basic arguments supporting this tenet are as follows:

1. The number of goods and services are increasing.

2. Goods and services are becoming increasingly complex.

3. The growth of self-service forces consumers to rely more and more on information on labels.

4. Technological change is so rapid that knowledge becomes obsolete overnight.

5. Many improvements in the quality and performance of consumer goods are below the threshold of perception.[4]

History of Government Action

Blackwell knew that the government's effort to control facets of marketing were not the first endeavors in the realm of consumer protection. In 1784, in Massachusetts, a general food law was passed to afford the public a modicum of protection concerning consumption. The real basis for consumer legislation in the United States came during an 8-year period, when, in 1906, the Federal Food and Drug Act was enacted, followed by the Federal Trade Commission Act in 1914. By 1961 it became evident that a new wave of congressional activity was starting to form. Senator Philip Hart (D-Michigan) first introduced legislation on packaging and labeling that year, but the proposed bill did not pass Congress. From that time through 1966, Senator Hart, believing that the business community had made little effort to police its own affairs voluntarily, promised that if industry would not take steps to protect the consumer, the government would. His promise came to life in 1966 with the "Fair Packaging and Labeling Act" (S 985 and H.R. 15440): "A bill to regulate interstate and foreign commerce by preventing the use of unfair or deceptive methods of packaging or labeling of certain consumer commodities distributed in such commerce, and for other purposes." The

---

[3] Majority Report on the Fair Packaging and Labeling Act of the Senate Committee on Commerce (89th Congress).
[4] Ibid.

bill basically empowered the government to standardize labeling the contents of the packages of consumer goods and gave it the necessary flexibility to also standardize the dimensions of packages as well as the weight of the contents within. For the basic aspects of the legislation under consideration, see Exhibit 11–4.

Exhibit 11-4
Extract from Fair Packaging and Labeling Act

H.R. 15440, June 2, 1966. Mr. Staggers introduced the bill.
Referred to Committee on Interstate and Foreign Commerce.

A bill to regulate interstate and foreign commerce by preventing the use of unfair or deceptive methods of packaging or labeling of certain consumer commodities distributed in such commerce, and for other purposes.

Shall be called "Fair Packaging and Labeling Act."

Section 2

Informed consumers are essential to the fair and efficient functioning of a free market economy. Packages and their labels should enable consumers to obtain accurate information as to quantity of the contents and should facilitate price comparisons. Therefore, it is hereby declared to be the policy of Congress to assist consumers and manufacturers in reaching these goals in the marketing of consumer goods.

Section 4

Labels must conform to the following provisions of the bill:

1. List the identity of commodity, name, and place of business of manufacturer, packer, or distributor.
2. The net quantity of contents (in terms of weight, measure, or numerical count) shall be separately and accurately stated in a uniform location upon the principal display panel of that label if that consumer commodity is enclosed in a package.
3. The separate label statement of net quantity of contents appearing upon or affixed to any package:
   a. If in weight or fluid volume (less than 4 pounds or 1 gallon), shall be expressed in ounces or in whole units of pounds, pints, or quarts.
   b. Shall be legible and conspicuous.
   c. Shall contain letters or numerals in type size which shall be in relationship to the area of the principal display panel of package and uniform for all packages of same size.
   d. Shall be placed parallel to base of box as displayed.
   e. No qualifying words *in label panel.*
   f. Other statements on package about quantity may not be exaggerating or deceptive terms.

Section 5

1. Authority to promulgate will be in the Secretary of Health, Education, and Welfare (for food, drugs, devices, or cosmetics) and the Federal Trade Commission with respect to other commodities.

2. Promulgating authority can exempt certain commodities where regulations are unnecessary for *adequate protection* of consumers.

3. If promulgating authority thinks that more regulations are needed to *prevent deception of consumers or to facilitate price comparisons,* it can:

   a. Establish and define standards for characterizing size of package which may be used to supplement label statement (may not authorize limit, size, shape, weight, dimensions of packages).
   b. Define net quantity of product which constitutes a serving if necessary.
   c. Regulate discount labels.
   d. Require information and ingredients and composition be placed on package of commodity.
   e. Prevent distribution of packages of size, shapes, and dimensional proportions which are likely to deceive purchasers in any material respect as to net quantity of contents.

4. If authority determines after a hearing that weights or quantity in a package are likely to impair the ability of consumers to make price-per-unit comparisons, the authority must:

   a. Publish determination in Federal Register.
   b. Establish reasonable weights or quantities, or fractions or multiples thereof, in which any such consumer commodity shall be distributed for retail sale.

General Discussion on the Bill

During the summer before Brace's president was to testify, many members of government and industry expressed their opinions on the legislation. Blackwell had obtained the statements and testimonies of these people so that he could arrive at an intelligent judgment for the company's position.

While Congress was deciding the fate of the consumer legislation, much was being said in Washington to urge the passage of the bill. President Lyndon B. Johnson said that:

> the shopper ought to be able to tell at a glance what is in the package, how much of it there is, and how much it costs . . . and the housewife should not need a scale, a yardstick, or a slide-rule when she shops. The housewife should not worry which is bigger: the "full jumbo quart" or the "giant economy quart." The law will free her from that uncertainty.

Paul Rand Dixon, chairman of the Federal Trade Commission (FTC), said, "The goal . . . is primarily to enable the supermarket shopper to make an intelligent choice of products from a cost savings and a quality standpoint." For additional comments on the desirability of consumer protection legislation, see Exhibit 11–5.

Blackwell believes that members of the administration were in favor of the bill for what it controlled and what it would enable the government to do in the future. Mrs. Esther Peterson, consumer advisor to the president, believed the bill would give the government the power necessary to curb proliferation of packaging, since under the bill standard-size packages could be forced upon companies. William W. Goodrich, assistant general counsel, Department of Health, Education,

Exhibit 11-5
Statements for Consumer Protection Legislation

Congressman Edward J. Patten:

> I do hope, too, we can protect our consumers against what I think are outright frauds in some of the packaging and labeling that I see.

Senator Philip Hart:

> [The bill is] aimed at bringing order out of the chaos of the modern marketplace as it pertains to consumer items.

Paul Dixon, Chairman FTC:

> Highest priorities will be given to correcting false or misleading advertising . . . and to deception in sale of . . . food, household equipment, home improvements, and other products of special significance to low-income families and to the elderly.

Consumer Advisory Council:

> In the marketplace, consumer ignorance and misinformation enable inferior workmanship and poor service to flourish. . . .

and Welfare, was in favor of the bill because it would authorize specification of serving sizes, control cents-off promotions, and generally "bring some order out of the chaos of proliferating packages sizes." Winton B. Rankin, of the Food and Drug Administration, was enthusiastic about the bill because he felt it gave authority to standardize the size of certain containers. Dixon, after being aggravated by 2 similar packages, one labeled 20 ounces and one labeled one and one-fourth pints, was happy to see control over weights and quantities in the bill. He felt that "the subject bills are aimed at preventing such confusion [about weights and quantities]."

Of course, industry was not overly enthusiastic about the legislation. A spokesperson for the National Canners Association warned that the bill "must have sufficient flexibility to enable packers to develop and try out new container sizes that meet shifting consumer tastes and demands." The worry of many businesspeople could be seen in a statement by Mr. Minter of the National Confectioners Association: "The bill gives authority to not only standardize weights but to interpret package sizes too." It was the interpretative aspect that had far-reaching consequences.

Sources of Controversy

Blackwell was also well aware of the lively debate on the legislation carried on during the summer prior to his assignment concerning the bill. The discussions were centered around a few major points. One of these was that the bill made shopping more enjoyable and less time consuming and facilitated price comparisons. (See Exhibit 11–6.) This argument had 2 sides to it. First, Mrs. Peterson cited a test by Monroe P. Friedman of Eastern Michigan University [5] which indicated that shoppers were confused by many different alternatives and unable to make intelligent choices (price comparisons). (See appendices a and b.) The advocates of the bill implied that if packages were labeled properly and in standard sizes, consumers would have little difficulty making rapid and accurate price comparisons between products. Industry partially refuted this argument when Edward J. Heckman, president of the Keebler Company, said: "The consumer is interested in more than price. Flavor and personal taste also are taken into consideration by the consumer. Price, obviously, is just one factor in the consumer's total concept of value." Similarly, Lee S. Bickmore, of the National Biscuit Company, said, "Especially for our wives' sake, let's not take the fun out of shopping. . . . Women love to shop and express their taste often in a nonmathematical and intuitive way."

The second side to the facility-of-price-comparison argument concerned the measurement of quality. Mr. Cohen, under-secretary of the Department of Health, Education, and Welfare, said that confusion could not be completely eliminated unless there were price regulations per ounce or per unit and unless there were quality determination (neither were provided for by the bill). Some said that even if price comparisons were easy for the consumer, quality comparisons might be very difficult. Speaking on the quality determination of detergents and soaps, Richard C. Beeson, president of Colgate-Palmolive Ltd. (Canada), said that there was no sure way of telling the cleaning power of various soaps and detergents because of variance in domestic laundry conditions and differences in the amount of soil in clothes.

---

[5] Monroe P. Friedman, "Consumer Confusion in the Selection of Supermarket Products," *Journal of Applied Psychology,* **50** (1966), pp. 529–34.

Exhibit 11-6
The Value of Legislation to Consumers

Mrs. Esther Peterson, Consumer Advisor to the President:

. . . this legislation would help the consumer to buy more wisely and more economically and, may I add, with less frustration than at present.

A poor label with inadequate information can prevent price comparisons and economical shopping, whether or not the intent is to deceive.

John Connor, Secretary of Commerce:

When the American housewife goes to the marketplace, she should be able to quickly and easily determine the measure or amount in the container and to compare its price with the prices of competitive products.

[The bill is] intended to enable the public to obtain more complete and meaningful information from labels and packages of consumer commodities.

The Deception Issue

Blackwell uncovered a great amount of controversy on the deception issue. The bill would allow the government to seize a product from the market or bar its introduction if the promulgating authority judged that the product was deceptive in either its package form or labeling. Although Dixon of the FTC thought that this would protect the consumer from deceptive marketing practices, William B. Murphy, president of Campbell's Soup Company, said that the promulgating authority could call a new package form deceptive simply because it was different (referring in case point to a new triple-condensed soup). A representative of the dairy industry said that the bill would stifle ingenuity and creativity because its deception clauses would lead to standardization.

Mrs. Peterson had said that there was a great cost to the consumer resulting from the confusion created by package proliferation and that the bill would help bring the proliferation to an end via the deception clauses. There were some who denied that package proliferation was deleterious to the consumer. They claimed that the consumer reaped benefits from innovation and a wide latitude of choice. (See Exhibit 11–7.) Another argument against the deception measures was posed by the minority opinion of the National Committee on Food Marketing. This group felt that consumers were not entirely at the mercy of food processors and had considerable market power in that "consumers are not misled for long or often on food or household items that are small-unit-cost, daily or weekly purchase, where the seller lives only by his success in attracting repeat business."

Blackwell had also come across the results of a marketing research study on consumer buying habits, which can be found in appendix c.

Exhibit 11-7
Statements Against Proposed Legislation

National Committee on Food Marketing (minority opinion):

> We assert that these developments, which have emerged in a freely competitive economic framework, have contributed to rising vigor in the food industry and have yielded substantial value to our competitive economy and to consumers.

Grocery Manufacturers Association:

> Successful differentiation eases the necessity of competing strictly on a price and quality basis with competitors of approximately equal production efficiency. . . . packaging has also provided a wider variety of sizes to meet the increasing variety of sizes to meet the increasing variety of household needs within the constraints of low-cost self-service retailing.

National Confectioners Association:

> We have to come up with ideas [new packages]; we can't compete on a brand-name basis.

Innovation Risks

One of the arguments against the bill emerged from the deception clauses. It was mentioned that the legislation would stifle innovation and creativity in packaging. Blackwell discovered that this argument was taken one step further by opponents of the bill who said that it would also stifle new-product development, increasing the risk of a new product's success by making it necessary for the product to pass the standards of the legislation.

Introducing a new product prior to any legislation on packaging was tenuous, but the proposed legislation could make it suicidal. (See Exhibit 11–8.) The difficulty arises from a loss in competitive timing which would occur if a company had to go to the government in order to get permission to bring out a new form of package necessitated by the new product. (See Exhibit 11–9.) A representative of the National Canners Association testified that "to get an amendment to a standard sometimes today requires years of time [at least a one-year time lag]." William B. Murphy of Campbell Soup Company mentioned that to package new products that are substantially different from present products would doom the new products, since they might not be compatible with the size of the container. (See Exhibit 11–10.)

A member of the Brace Company supplied Blackwell with estimates on the time necessary to bring out new products, as follows:

Cold breakfast cereal	55 months
Cake mixes	29 months
Frozen dinners	41 months

Also, research and development expenditures cost $122,000 per product for 6 companies producing 21 new cold cereals.

Exhibit 11-8
Innovation Risk

A. For the Food Industry

A total of:

40% of new products fail after introduction to market.

22% of new products fail after test marketing.

8% of new products fail after limited distribution.

9% of new products fail after full distribution.

B. For 127 New Products (1947–1964)

22% were dropped after test market.

17% were dropped after regular introduction.

30% broke even by end of 1st year.

44% broke even by end of 2nd year.

61% broke even by end of 3rd year.

73% broke even by end of 4th year.

Exhibit 11-9

	Breakfast Cereal (cold)	Cake Mixes	Pet Foods	Frozen Dinners	Margarine
A. Average number of months in each stage of development:					
R & D	32	15	11	18	15
Product testing	14	9	9	13	9
Test market	6	6	14	12	10
Limited distribution	5	11	9	12	8
Total months to full distribution	55	29	40	41	33
B. Profiles of typical distinctly new food products:					
Preinduction					
Total months to full distribution	55	29	40	41	33
Cost of R & D [1]	$ 122	$ 27	$ 91	$ 15	$ 65
Cost of marketing research [1]	$ 60	$ 13	$ 37	$ 8	$ 17
First year of regular distribution					
Sales [1]	$6,605	$938	$3,943	$416	$6,684
Marketing expenditures as share of sales	51%	61%	49%	20%	30%
Cumulative contributions as share of cumulative sales	−14%	−25%	−29%	−18%	+ 6%

[1] In thousands.

Source: Robert D. Buzzell and Robert E. M. Nourse, *Product Innovations in Food Processing, 1954–1964* (Boston, MA: Harvard University Graduate School of Business Administration, 1967), Table A—p. 107; Table B—pp. 107, 111, and 132.

Cost of Legislation

The final point of contention, Blackwell found, was concerned with the cost of the new legislation. The government did not have any figures to offer on the effects on price levels that the bill would have, but Connor, secretary of commerce, said, "Experience has shown that standardization can actually reduce costs and result in savings. Examples are savings in ice cream cartons and molds, can sizes, and paper bags." Mrs. Peterson maintained that the cost of the bill to the

Exhibit 11-10
Loss of Timing

William B. Murphy, Campbell Soup Company:

> Mr. Murphy said that if the bill had been in effect when Swanson brought out frozen food dinners, there would have been a severe loss of competitive timing.

> "By the time the problem had been discussed with a number of administration officials and a new or amended regulation had been published in the 'Federal Register' and made the subject of hearings, potential competitors all would have had full opportunity to get on the bandwagon."

> Therefore, Swanson might not have risked the investment in frozen food dinners, because "eight ounces of poultry would have been too much for an individual dinner, so the only alternative would be . . . to go to Washington for administration approval."

Exhibit 11-11
Cost Estimates

Lyle E. Roll, Kellogg Company:

> If breakfast cereals were standardized in 8 oz. and 16 oz. packages, Kellogg's capital costs would increase by $8 million and operating costs would increase $3 million.

> The bill would require 29 different sizes instead of the 11 sizes now existent (slack fill considerations). This would increase manufacturing costs by 4.2 percent which would be reflected by a 5.7 percent increase in the retail prices of cereals.

Proctor & Gamble:

> Estimated that changing package sizes for four brands would cost intially $8 million, with a $2 million annual increase.

consumer would be small compared to the price the consumer is paying for proliferation and the ensuing confusion.

On the other hand, it was estimated that the bill would require Campbell Soup Company to spend $35 million dollars over a total of 70 lines. When asked if he was going to absorb this cost, Murphy, Campbell's president, replied, "Well, I don't think you can. I think you have to pass it on."

See Exhibits 11–11 and 11–12 for information on costs.

Blackwell's Dilemma

After analyzing the information he had gathered, Blackwell was still not sure of the arguments the Brace Company should make for or against the Fair Packaging

Exhibit 11-12

A.   Machinery Costs in Breakfast Cereal Production

Equipment	Estimated Cost	Rating
Flaking mill	$ 28,000	20 pounds/minute
Toasting oven	50,000	—
Extruder	30,000	30 pounds/minute
Dryer	100,000	50 feet long
Packaging	150,000	70 family-size packages/minute

B.   Packaging Costs by Size of Firm, Breakfast Cereal Industry

Packaging Cost	All Companies	Largest 4 Companies	Next 4 Companies	All Other Companies
As percent of sales	17.4%	17.6%	15.1%	20.3%
Labor and supervision allocable to packaging	17.0	16.0	20.7	27.9
Packages, containers, case cartons	80.5	82.1	72.6	67.8
Other packaging costs	2.5	1.9	6.7	4.3

Source: National Committee on Food Marketing.

and Labeling Act. He thought that some provisions of the bill might be helpful to the consumer while not overly burdening the industry. However, certain aspects of the bill were quite indigestible to business. He thought that not only would the legislation greatly change the marketing strategy of the food industry but also, by containing "elastic clauses" allowing the government to judge what was deceptive and what was not, the bill gave the government a great deal of power that could be expanded to control almost all products in the future.

Despite the arguments proposed by industry against the legislation, Blackwell felt that perhaps even more powerful arguments against the bill could be formed. In any event, Brace was to testify shortly, and Burns wanted the information and cogent arguments outlined for him.

Truth in Packaging in an American Supermarket*

Purpose

The study attempts to objectively define the issues on the truth-in-packaging controversy by treating consumer confusion as a psychological variable capable of measurement.

Method

Thirty-three young married women at Eastern Michigan University served as subjects, and they were tested in a familiar local supermarket. The women were instructed to select the most economical (largest quantity for the price) package for each of 20 products on sale at the selected supermarket. The women were allowed a maximum of 10 seconds per package to reach their decisions unless there were less than 6 package types to a product class, in which they were limited to one minute. If there were more than 24 package types to a product class, the women were allowed four minutes to decide. In addition to stating what she believed to be the most economical package in each category, each woman reported to the experimenter accompanying her what information she used in making her decision.

Measures

Three behaviorly based, quantitative measures of confusion in unit-price information were used in the analysis of the data.

Confusion Measure 1: Indicates the number of women who made incorrect choices for each of the 20 products.

Confusion Measure 2: Calculates for each product the mean percentage increase in unit price for the women's selected packages compared with the most economical package.

Confusion Measure 3: Estimates the increase in price which an economy-minded household unit with a specified budget would pay over a

---

* By Monroe Peter Friedman, Eastern Michigan University.

constant time period if its purchases reflected the values found for Confusion Measure 2.

Results of Study

Product	Confusion Measure 1[1] (total errors)	Confusion Measure 2 (percentage errors)	Confusion Measure 3[2] (weighted errors in dollars)	Estimated Annual Consumer Expenditures[2] (dollars)
Canned peaches	8	2	.00	3.10
Canned peas	5	5	.20	4.10
Catsup	23	13	.28	2.40
Evaporated milk	2	0	0.0	6.60
Family flour	6	2	.13	6.70
Frozen orange juice	6	6	.36	6.40
Granulated sugar	0	0	0.0	10.70
Instant coffee	11	10	.92	10.10
Liquid bleach	32	32	11.70	2.90
Liquid detergent	8	4	.24	6.20
Liquid shampoo	14	63	1.01	2.70
Mayonnaise	8	16	.46	3.30
Paper towels	30	12	.48	4.50
Peanut butter	7	2	.06	3.20
Potato chips	22	1	.05	5.30
Powdered detergent	33	24	2.13	11.00
Soft drinks (cola)	27.0	17.0	2.01	13.80
Solid shortening	0.0	0.0	0.0	5.50
Toilet tissue	22.0	5.0	.37	7.70
Toothpaste	22.0	16.0	.69	5.00
Sum			10.15	121.20
Mean	14.3	11.5	.507	6.06

[1] $n = 33$.
[2] Based on a total annual supermarket expenditure of $1,000.

Package Confusion

Brand	Name	Dimensions	Weight
Tide and Bold	King	13 5/16 x 9 1/16 x 3 11/16	5 lb., 4 oz.
	Giant	11 1/6 x 8 3/16 x 3 1/16	3 lb., 1 oz.
	Regular	8 8/16 x 6 x 2 4/16	1 lb., 4 oz.
Rinso	King	13 5/16 x 9 12/16 x 3 8/16	5 lb., 4 oz.
	Giant	11 1/16 x 3 3/16 x 3 1/16	3 lb., 2 oz.
	Regular	8 8/16 x 6 x 2 4/16	1 lb., 4 oz.
Cheer	King	13 5/16 x 9 1/16 x 3 11/16	5 lb., 12 oz.
	Giant	11 1/16 x 8 3/16 x 3 1/16	3 lb., 6 oz.
	Regular	8 8/16 x 6 x 2 4/16	1 lb., 6 oz.
Ivory Snow	King	13 3/16 x 9 1/16 x 3 11/16	3 lb., 6 oz.
	Giant	11 1/16 x 8 3/16 x 3 1/16	2 lb., 13 oz.
	Regular	8 8/16 x 6 x 2 4/16	13 oz.
Condensed All	Jumbo	12 2/16 x 8 7/16 x 4 4/16	9 lb., 13 oz.
	Giant	9 14/16 x 6 13/16 x 2	3 lb., 1 oz.
	Regular	7 3/16 x 4 13/16 x 1 13/16	1 lb., 8 oz.
Salvo (tablets)	Giant	8 3/16 x 6 15/16 x 2 6/16	2 lb., 14 oz.

Brand	Type	Dimensions	Weight
Kellogg's	Cornflakes	12 1/16 x 8 2/16 x 3 5/16	1 lb., 2 oz.
		11 x 7 10/16 x 2 11/16	12 oz.
		9 5/16 x 6 13/16 x 2 7/16	8 oz.
	Special K	10 9/16 x 7 8/16 x 2 10/16	10.5 oz.
		8 14/16 x 6 5/16 x 2 4/16	6.5 oz.
	Rice Krispies	11 x 7 10/16 x 2 11/16	13 oz.
		9 14/16 x 7 x 2 10/16	10 oz.
		8 10/16 x 6 5/16 x 2	6 oz.
General Mills	Wheaties	12 x 8 5/16 x 2 12/16	1 lb., 2 oz.
		10 11/16 x 7 8/16 x 2 7/16	12 oz.
		9 7/16 x 6 12/16 x 2	8 oz.
	Cheerios	12 x 8 5/16 x 2 12/16	15 oz.
		10 11/16 x 7 8/16 x 2 7/16	10.5 oz.
		9 7/16 x 6 12/16 x 2	7 oz.

Behavior and Motivation Survey*

2,431 interviews were conducted concerning food products:
- 84% of women and 74% of men said people buy well-known brands because of confidence in quality.
- 54% of men and women said people buy less known brands because of inexpensiveness.
- 26% of men and 33% of women said people buy less known brands for variety and experimentation.
- 34% of women had strong preference for well-known brands.
- 14% of women had strong preference for less known brands.
- 50% of women had no strong brand preference.

Of those women who decide on a product because of price, 47% preferred private brands and 29% preferred nationally advertised brands.

Of those women who decide on a product because of quality, 69% favored nationally advertised brands and 33% favored private brands.
- 50% of women look for the lowest price brand.
- 55% of women look for what they consider most popular brand.
- 40% of women have no concern for brand popularity.

---

* By Arthur D. Little Co. and Opinion Research Center.

Diepole Electronics*

David J. Fritzsche, Illinois State University

Introduction

Diepole Electronics is a major producer of electronic products and components serving primarily the industrial market. Product lines manufactured by Diepole include motors, generators, transformers, switch gear, and industrial controls. Production facilities are located throughout the United States and in Germany and Spain.

Competition for electric motor sales has been keen within the industry. In the United States alone, there are over 400 manufacturers of motors. Many of these firms are small, employing less than 20 people. The *1972 Census of Manufacturers* lists 258 establishments which produce electric motors that employ 20 or more people. Diepole is one of six major motor manufacturers capable of producing volume orders. A number of motor manufacturers are actually in-house assemblers or affiliated with appliance manufacturers.

Electric motor manufacturers are heavily concentrated in the northern part of the country. Exhibit 12–1 shows that 119 of the 258 manufacturers employing 20 or more employees in 1972 were located in the North Central region. It is interesting to note that the regions of the country currently accounting for the greatest population growth, the West and the South, contain the smallest number of manufacturers among the four census regions.

Electric motors are classified as either fractional horsepower or integral horsepower motors. Diepole has concentrated primarily upon integral horsepower motors. Dollar volume of sales of such motors amounted to $567.7 million in 1972. As shown in Exhibit 12–2, that figure includes both alternating and direct current motors. Motor sales were somewhat depressed during the period from late 1974 to

* The author appreciates the assistance provided by Lloyd W. Jones, District Sales Manager, Gould Inc., Electric Motor Division and Robert M. Geist, New Products Manager, Pfaudler Company.

Exhibit 12-1
Electric Motor Manufacturers
Employing 20 or More People By Census Region

Region	Number of Manufacturers
Northeast	61
North Central	119
South	49
West	29

mid-1976 due to the lackluster performance of the economy. However, projections indicate the growth trend which began in 1977 will continue through 1981.

Diepole

Diepole Electronics began producing electric motors in 1947. They have established a reputation for high quality products which command a premium price justified by low maintenance requirements and long service life. Diepole offers a full line of three-phase AC motors in horsepower ratings from 1 to 600. In terms of both volume and dollar profit, their line of 1 to 25 horsepower motors is the backbone of their motor business. This segment of their motor operation is currently under review by management. The firm's sales records provide the information shown in Exhibit 12–3. Unit sales by horsepower of motor are shown for the past five years of operation.

Although profit margins on electric motors still are adequate, due to mounting competition and inflation, they are not nearly as strong as in the early 1970s. Currently, Diepole's prices yield a 12 percent ROI. This is down 15 percent from 1970. Future prospects for profit improvement do not look promising. There are indications that Japanese firms may be planning to enter the U.S. market with electric motors in a manner similar to that used to enter other electronic goods markets in the 1960s. These motors are likely to be high quality and compete directly with Diepole.

Diepole employs 52 sales representatives in the continental United States to handle their electric motors. In addition, these sales representatives are charged with selling generators, switch gear, transformers, and industrial controls manufactured by the firm. Last year it cost Diepole $32,500/sales representative to support its sales force. Some thought has been given to reorganizing and expanding the sales force. One of the latest proposals calls for fielding one force to sell motors and generators and fielding another force to sell switch gear, transformers, and industrial controls. However, this and other proposals still are being evaluated by management. There is some concern that such a split could further reduce profit margins to an unacceptable range.

Exhibit 12-2

Products and Product Classes

Quantity and Value of Shipments by All Producers: 1972 and 1967

36A-28   ELECTRICAL MEASUREMENT AND DISTRIBUTION EQUIPMENT

Products and Product Classes—Quantity and Value of Shipments by All Producers: 1972 and 1967

1972 product code	Product	Unit of measure	Total product shipments including interplant transfers			
			1972		1967	
			Quantity	Value (million dollars)	Quantity	Value (million dollars)
	MOTORS AND GENERATORS—Continued					
	Integral horsepower Motors and Generators, Except for Land Transportation Equipment:					
36212 00	As reported in the census of manufactures.........................	....	(X)	567.7	(X)	569.5
	As reported in Current Industrial Reports series MA-36H........	....	(X)	548.0	(X)	584.0
	Integral horsepower motors (excluding cranking motors for internal combustion engines, propulsion motors for land transportation, motors mounted on the same shaft as arc welding generators, and hermetics):					
36212 01	Aircraft and space motors (including a.c. and d.c. but excluding generators), all integral hp. ratings.............	1,000.........	(¹) (²)	(¹) (²)	2.5	.5
	Alternating current:					
	Motors classified by case diameter:					
36212 03	5-3/8" diameter and over but less than 6" diameter (1 hp. and over)...	...do.........	}	}	134.7	3.5
36212 05	6" diameter and over but less than 7-1/8" diameter (1 hp. and over)..	...do.........	995.1	32.6	421.0	12.6
36212 07	7-1/8" diameter and over but less than 9" diameter (1 hp. and over)..	...do.........	29.0	2.2	84.9	4.7
36212 11	Single phase, all hp. ratings............................	...do.........	231.7	20.6	261.9	19.0
	Polyphase-induction:					
36212 21	1 to 5 hp...	...do.........	1,115.6	89.1	1,177.1	91.1
36212 22	5.1 to 20 hp..	...do.........	382.6	61.2	457.8	72.7
36212 23	21 to 50 hp...	...do.........	123.6	46.5	122.0	49.3
36212 26	51 to 125 hp..	...do.........	46.4	41.0	54.5	48.6
36212 27	126 to 200 hp...	...do.........	15.0	34.5	13.6	26.8
36212 28	201 to 500 hp...	...do.........	7.1	34.7	6.9	31.1
36212 29	Over 500 hp...	...do.........	2.3	57.2	2.4	44.2
	Synchronous motors:					
36212 31	450 r.p.m. or below (all hp. ratings).................	...do.........	.1	6.7	.3	8.6
36212 32	Above 450 r.p.m. (all hp. ratings)....................	...do.........	.8	5.8	2.3	14.5
	Direct current motors and generators, excluding all arc welding generators, battery charging generators for internal combustion engines, and generators used as an integral part of land transportation equipment:					
36212 41	1 to 5 hp. (3/4-4 kw.)................................	1,000.........	16.0	6.7	17.7	9.6
36212 42	5.1 to 20 hp. (4.1-15 kw.)............................	...do.........	20.0	18.6	13.9	15.2
36212 43	21 to 50 hp. (16-40 kw.)..............................	...do.........	5.3	10.4	8.2	16.2
36212 46	51 to 200 hp. (41-150 kw.)............................	...do.........	3.7	14.2	8.1	26.1
36212 47	201 to 500 hp. (151-400 kw.)..........................	...do.........	1.1	8.4	1.2	12.7
36212 48	Over 500 hp. (over 400 kw.)...........................	...do.........	¹5.2	¹25.1	.5	27.8
	Alternating current generators, excluding all arc welding generators, generators used as an integral part of land transportation equipment, steam, gas, and hydraulic turbine driven generators, and aircraft and space generators:					
36212 51	450 r.p.m. and slower speeds (all kw. ratings)............	...do.........	(Z)	1.2	.1	2.9
	Over 450 r.p.m.:					
36212 53	3/4 to 5 kw...	...do.........	7.2	1.5	15.0	2.4
36212 54	5.1 to 15 kw..	...do.........	3.8	2.2	11.7	3.4
36212 55	15.1 to 50 kw...	...do.........	3.6	3.3	6.5	7.9
36212 56	50.1 to 150 kw..	...do.........	2.3	4.0	5.5	9.8
36212 57	150.1 to 400 kw.......................................	...do.........	1.4	4.5	1.0	4.3
36212 59	Over 400 kw...	...do.........	1.0	15.6	.8	15.2
	Land Transportation Motors, Generators, Control Equipment and Parts:					
36213 00	As reported in the census of manufactures....................	....	(X)	106.3	(X)	133.4
	As reported in Current Industrial Reports series MA-36H........	....	(X)	112.8	(X)	127.9
36213 11	Railway motors and generators, including those used for control purposes (for trolley cars, trolley coaches, rapid transit cars, trolley locomotives, third-rail locomotives, multiple unit cars for railway service, and mining locomotives), and parts and supplies.....................	....	(X)	18.7	(X)	22.7
36213 31	Motors and generators, including those used for control purposes, for gasoline-electric and diesel-electric buses, trucks, locomotives, railcars, and parts and supplies........	....	}	}	(X)	46.3
36213 51	All other land transportation motors, including those used for control purposes, for storage-battery powered transportation equipment (for industrial trucks, mining locomotives, and other transportation equipment) and parts and supplies.......	....	(X)	51.6	(X)	15.2
36213 98	Other electrical apparatus for land transportation equipment..	....	(X)	42.5	(X)	43.5

(x) not applicable (z) less than .01 when rounded.
(1) Figures for product codes 36212 01 + 32212 48 are combined.
* Source: 1972 Census of Manufacturers.

Exhibit 12-3
Unit Sales of Motors by Horsepower
1972-1976

Horsepower	1976	1975	1974	1973	1972
1	7452	6407	6968	6939	5685
1½	3435	2955	3215	3204	2845
2	5649	4819	5197	5130	4511
3	3752	3159	3359	3266	3104
5	3164	2731	2981	2981	2657
7½	2753	2292	2408	2309	1967
10	2365	2022	2186	2164	1908
15	2214	1872	1999	1953	1698
20	2201	1865	1996	1955	1704
25	2629	2247	2427	2401	2116

The motor lines at Diepole's production facilities are located in their Chicago and Bayonne, New Jersey plants. The finished units are inventoried at warehouses adjacent to their two manufacturing facilities and in Atlanta, Dallas, Los Angeles, and Denver. Management had planned to start an electric motor line in Los Angeles early in 1975, but those plans were tabled due to economic conditions at the time. A new target date still has to be set.

Diepole had given serious thought to acquiring a microcomputer manufacturer in order to further diversify their operation. This acquisition would provide an entry into the home computer market that many people believe to be the next electronics boom market. This would be a move out of Diepole's traditional industrial market which could benefit the firm by incorporating products with sales cycles that differ from industrial market cycles. Such a move, at this time, might also be a good decision from the standpoint of getting into the market early before consumer brand recognition and preference has been established. The consumer market for computers may take off in the next few years in a manner emulating the growth of the pocket calculator market.

Diepole management has made overtures to several small microcomputer manufacturers; however, no firm commitment has been made yet. Management currently is involved in studying the complexities of the consumer market as well as the similarities and differences between Diepole's present industrial market and the potential consumer market for microcomputers.

Electric Motors

There have been several significant changes in motor designs over the past 25 years. In 1952, there was a big push for manufacturers to convert their motor lines to U-frame motors. These new products required less material to manufacture and could be sold for less money due to lower production costs. In 1964, conversion was made to the T-frame motor which was even lighter and less expensive to produce than the U-frame. The T-frame motor has been the standard configuration to date. It is economical to operate and possesses a satisfactory service life. Recent energy developments may lead to a new round of design changes.

In 1976, Arthur D. Little, Inc. submitted a report to the Federal Energy Administration entitled "Energy Efficiency and Electric Motors." This report states that most of the energy consumed by electric motors in the United States goes for driving industrial pumps, compressors, blowers, and other production equipment. Motors used for these purposes are the 1 to 125 horsepower polyphase type which account for the bulk of Diepole's electric motor sales. Some other interesting statistics indicate that these motors account for 26 percent of all the electricity consumed in the United States, and that 1 to 25 horsepower motors account for 60 percent of all motors used in industry.

The two developments in motor design previously discussed came at a time when energy consumption was not an important criterion in the design of a motor. Thus, it is not surprising to find that the T-frame motor is less energy efficient than the U-frame motor which in turn is less efficient than its predecessor. The Arthur D. Little study found that if all 1 to 125 horsepower industrial motors were replaced with high efficiency models by 1990, the electrical consumption of the United States could be reduced 5 percent. This would be a reduction equivalent to 60 million barrels of oil per year which would not have to be imported. Thus, it is not surprising that the Little report has caused a great deal of discussion in Congress and in numerous statehouses. Proposals by public policy makers include offering tax inducements for conversion to energy-efficient motors, imposing tax penalties for the continuing use of inefficient motors, and possibly banning the use and/or sale of inefficient motors. The Little report argued against such extreme measures and called for the government to inform and educate electric motor users in an effort to move users toward more efficient motors on a voluntary basis.

Potential demand for more efficient motors is being fueled by economic considerations. The price of electricity has risen dramatically over the past several years with no end in sight. Electric rates for investor-owned utilities increased an average of 61 percent over the period from June 1973 to December 1974. Rates have been forecast to continue to increase 12 to 15 percent per year over each of the next five years. Thus, the cost of operating an electric motor may, in the future, become a much more important criterion in the industrial purchase decision.

Certainly with the OPEC oil boycott of 1973 and the natural gas shortage of the winter of 1976–77, industry has become more conscious of its energy consumption. President Carter helped develop energy consciousness among consumers with his energy program introduced in April, 1977. The advent of a developing energy awareness had caused Diepole management to seriously consider the development of a line of energy efficient motors.

Management's Concern

In a recent meeting, Mr. Geist, new product manager, was discussing this possibility with Mr. Smith, research manager, and Mr. Lustik, product manager for

Exhibit 12-4
Mr. Geist's Comparison of Diepole's
Current Electric Motor Line With a Redesigned Line

HP	Efficiency		Power Factor		Kilowatts
	redesign	current	redesign	current	saved/hr.
1	.816	.760	.841	.712	.067
1½	.830	.778	.850	.735	.090
2	.840	.791	.854	.750	.110
3	.854	.809	.856	.770	.145
5	.870	.831	.860	.791	.201
7½	.883	.848	.862	.804	.261
10	.888	.859	.862	.812	2.83
15	.898	.874	.864	.821	.342
20	.902	.884	.864	.827	.336
25	.908	.891	.865	.831	.391

$$\text{Efficiency} = \text{Eff} = \frac{746 \times \text{Hp output}}{\text{Watts input}}$$

$$\text{Power Factor} = \text{Pf} = \frac{\text{Watts input}}{\text{Volts} \times \text{Amps} \times 1.73}$$

$$\text{Kw saved} = 746 \times \text{Hp} \times 10^{-3} \times \frac{1}{\text{Eff motor X}} = \frac{1}{\text{Eff. motor Y}}$$

Exhibit 12-5
Direct Costs and Suggested List Prices
For the Current and NRG Line of Motors

HP	Current		NRG	
	Cost	List	Proj. Cost	List
1	$ 76	$127	$ 86	$143
1½	83	139	94	156
2	92	154	104	173
3	96	160	117	195
5	107	179	132	220
7½	157	262	192	320
10	190	317	233	388
15	254	424	310	518
20	334	556	390	650
25	389	649	482	770

electric motors. Mr. Geist had developed a set of data indicating the potential energy savings that could be realized by redesigning Diepole's existing line of motors for purposes of reducing energy consumption (see Exhibit 12–4). The design changes included lengthening the stator and rotor cores to reduce magnetic density, reducing the air gap to lower current requirements, reducing resistance by adding copper or aluminum to stator and rotor conductors, and adding a special low-loss steel to the core. The new design, which Mr. Geist designated the NRG, should be cooler, quieter, and longer-running according to Mr. Geist's calculations. However, it would be more expensive to produce due to the increased material requirements and the closer control required in the manufacturing process. Exhibit 12–5 contains both the cost and suggested price information assembled by Mr. Geist. It should be noted that Diepole price increases have matched the inflation rate over the past five years.

After examining the data, Mr. Lustik commented that the cost difference between the NRG and the standard line of motors certainly would place the NRG line at a cost disadvantage. Energy consumption would have to be an important consideration in order to offset those cost differentials. The marketing effort would have to focus heavily upon the payback period for the additional investment. The payback period would be based upon several factors. First, the hours of running time anticipated per day would have to be considered. Also, the firm's current electrical rates would have to be obtained. A more sophisticated approach would use the current rate then adjust it upward to reflect increasing rate costs over the time period required to recover the increased purchase cost. In the Northeast where electrical rates are high, the payback period would be much shorter than in the Pacific Northwest where rates are low. The payback period for a motor used 8 hours a day would be longer than for a motor used 16 hours a day. Of course, a motor used intermittently would have a much longer payback period.

Mr. Geist had projected that it would take a year and a half to bring the NRG motor on stream. This would include tooling up, material procurement, training, and initial pipeline filling. He estimates this would require an investment of from $5 to $7 million depending upon the production location and the nature of the line. These requirements reopen the question of whether Diepole should open a line in its Los Angeles plant, as previously planned, if the NRG motor is introduced.

The power factor shown in Exhibit 12–5 may be defined as follows:

> . . . the ratio of the power-producing current in a circuit to the total current in that circuit (so that) power factor equals kw/kva (kilowatts/kilovolt-amperes). In order to compensate for the extra investment required to serve low power-factor loads, utilities introduced the power-factor clauses in power bills. These clauses offer a reduction in power billing for high-load power factor or impose penalties for low power factor. The net result is extra money on the power bill if the power factor is below 85 percent in most cases. Some utilities base their rates on 100 percent power factor.[1]

---

[1] *Maintenance Engineering Handbook,* 2nd ed., L. C. Morrow, Ed., (New York: McGraw-Hill, 1966), pp. 7–132–137.

Industrial electric bills are based upon four variables: the actual electricity used in kilowatt hours, demand charges based upon the maximum amount of electricity used, a fuel adjustment charge based upon fuel costs, and a power factor penalty based upon reactive losses in the plant. The power factor is closely related to motor load. A motor that under full load may have a high power factor may experience a dramatic drop in power factor under a partially loaded condition.

In their discussion, Mr. Lustik brought up several points which he felt must be considered carefully before a decision is made on the NRG proposal. First, by bringing out the NRG line, Diepole would be opening up a new front for industry competition. This would provide customers with one more means of playing one manufacturer against another. Current points of competition already offer the buyer more than adequate opportunity to play this game. Second, by splitting the electric motor line into the standard and NRG lines, inventory costs would increase substantially. The stocking plan at each of the regional warehouses would have to be almost doubled. To make matters worse, buyers might limit their NRG purchases to continuous-duty applications, given the premium price of the NRG line. That could result in certain sizes within each line obtaining a very low sales volume in the market.

Third, in many cases it may not be appropriate for the customer to simply examine the motor when making a purchase. The user's whole operating system should be examined. The motor may account for a very small portion of the energy requirements of the system, and thus, motor energy requirements may not be an important criterion when building and operating the system.

Fourth, is there any demand for the NRG motor? Historically, as Mr. Smith pointed out, industrial purchasing decisions were made based upon purchase price of the motor. For all practical purposes, energy costs have been ignored. Diepole may bring out the NRG line only to find that there is no market for the motor. The market may develop in 7 to 10 years, but there is a real question as to whether it is here today.

Mr. Smith stated that the upward movement of electrical rates may tend to have some effect upon purchase decisions in the near future. The question is when, and what the magnitude of the effect is likely to be. It may be possible to speed up the market development through educational promotion. There also is the question of governmental action. Certain public policy decisions could create a market almost overnight. If Diepole were to bring out the NRG motor just as demand began to develop, it could cash in on having the first energy efficient electric motor line on the market. This could result in high sales volume and a progressive, socially positive image. However, if the market is not there, such dreams could end up simply as red ink.

Mr. Lustik also brought up the question of the sales force. Would the present sales force handle the NRG line or should a new force be developed specifically for this purpose? Possibly, reorganization of the sales force as had been proposed earlier could coincide with the introduction of the NRG line. How would the NRG line affect the quality image of the Diepole line of standard motors? What would be the sales force's reaction?

The meeting ended with the three men agreeing to meet in one week after further investigating the ramifications of introducing the NRG line. Mr. Geist agreed to determine the payback periods required by customers to cover the additional cost of the NRG motors. He also would attempt to get a feel for market acceptance of the new product and to assess the likelihood of governmental regulation and the nature of such regulation if it is likely to occur. Mr. Lustik would look into the pros and cons of the three production locations discussed, come up with a recommendation as to sales force requirements, and examine the distribution problems likely to be faced by the NRG line. Mr. Smith said he would develop a sales forecast for the line and determine the payback period required for the firm to recover its investment. With this additional information, the three would make a decision as to whether Diepole would commit itself to produce the NRG line at this time.

Note to students: Additional data which may be used to analyze this case can be found in the library. Data pertaining to the market and industry conditions may be found in census publications, business papers, and business magazines.

The Greensburg Alert: To Be or Not To Be

Gordon L. Wise, Wright State University

The Landmark Publishing Company is located in Paintsville, a city of 28,000 in the Midwest. Landmark owns controlling interest in 4 local newspapers located within a 30-mile radius of Columbia City. Although none of the newspapers have any appreciable circulation in Columbia City (population 300,000), they do lie in a configuration that approximately circles the city with those areas in which the Landmark papers are the dominant newspaper.

In addition to the *Paintsville Pioneer,* Landmark controls the *Greyston Press* in Greyston (population 18,000), the *Crafton Crayon* in Crafton (population 46,000), and the *Daily Gazette* in Greensburg (population 21,000).

During the past decade, a series of unique publications have appeared in the areas surrounding Columbia City. These publications—produced and distributed by a number of independent publishers—are "free" newspapers distributed in limited geographic areas and containing news, feature stories, recipes, and comics, as well as substantial amounts of local advertising. Throughout the Columbia City SMSA there are presently 9 such publications distributed in 2 distinct patterns. In some instances the "free" paper is delivered to all households in an individual area (a small town, a combination of several small towns, a county or portions thereof, etc.). In other instances the "free" paper may be delivered in an area only to those households that do not already subscribe to a newspaper produced by the publisher of the "free" paper. In the latter instance, the publisher thus is able to achieve near-saturation distribution without such massive duplication as might occur with the blind distribution achieved in the former distribution pattern. Each of the "free" papers is distributed on a weekly basis.

Prior to 1975, none of the Landmark newspapers produced or distributed "free" papers. However, in the spring of that year, the *Paintsville Pioneer* began such production. The rapid acceptance of the weekly *Pioneer-Partner* (the name chosen for the publication) soon led Landmark to introduce the *Weekly News-Record*

238

in Greyston (November 1975) and the *Chronicle* in Crafton (June 1976). Each of these "free" publications seemed to be accepted by readers in their respective areas. But this optimistic appraisal was informal at best, for nothing had been done to measure specifically reactions, attitudes toward usage, or perception of these publications. The Landmark publishers with "free" papers noted (after one to two years' experience with the auxillary publications) that the "free" papers did not appear to have any impact on the circulation of their regular publications. They also noted that they had no trouble selling sufficient advertising space to surpass break-even points. They did, however, encounter difficulties achieving advertising revenues as high as they had targeted in their more optimistic pre-entry forecasts. Thus, it appeared that there would be a strong chance of profitable operation for the "free" papers, but that earlier views of the "free" paper as a "gold mine" were too optimistic.

In early June 1977, Landmark Publishing Company faced a decision regarding the introduction of a "free" paper in the Greensburg market area. Such a move had been contemplated for some time; and, given the relative success of "free" papers in the other Landmark areas, it seemed that a companion publication to the Greensburg *Daily Gazette* would be appropriate.

On the positive side, by introducing such a publication, Landmark would be able to encircle the Columbia City market with both regular newspapers and "free" papers under Landmark control and management. Some members of Landmark management felt that there was great potential value in such a position since it would permit Landmark to sell advertisers a "package" of areas surrounding Columbia City which might well be used to supplement the Columbia City advertisers' coverage of their market. Additional advantages would be the experience gained by Landmark in successfully introducing the 3 present "free" papers, expertise gained in distribution, and contacts gained with sources of features which might be included in this latest "free" publication.

On the negative side, is the existence of the oldest and most widely distributed "free" paper either in the Columbia City area or in the entire area in which the Landmark newspapers are distributed. This "free" paper, *The Tornado,* is published in Trenton, a city of 25,000 located just 10 miles from Greensburg. *The Tornado* was introduced 10 years earlier and has a saturation-level circulation in several areas adjacent to Trenton (including the Greensburg area!). *The Tornado* is an auxillary publication of the *Trenton Terrier,* a regular daily newspaper with virtual saturation of the Trenton area and with a small but significant circulation in the Greensburg area.

The Tornado is an outstanding example of a success story for "free" papers. It has become an effective profit center for Trenton Newspapers, Inc., publishers of both the *Terrier* and *The Tornado*. It has much support from advertisers in the Trenton area and considerable support from those in the Greensburg area. In fact, one of the objectives of any Landmark "free" paper introduced in the Greensburg area would likely be to capture some share of the advertising dollars presently being taken from Greensburg by the Trenton *Tornado*. Indeed, it is contemplated by some members of Landmark management that the proposed "free" paper to be

Table 13–1
Overall Usage of a Free Newspaper
As a Source of Advertising Information
For Particular Types of Retail Establishments
Proportion of Respondents Who:

Type of Establishment:	Don't Use The Paper	Use Paper Only a Little	Use Paper Some Of the Time	Use Paper Most Of the Time	Use Paper All Of the Time
Grocery	33.5	8.5	14.2	13.8	30.0
Men's Clothing	68.3	13.9	10.5	2.6	4.8
Women's Clothing	65.1	13.5	11.3	4.8	5.4
Shoe Stores	73.8	13.4	8.9	3.0	1.0
Services (dry cleaning, beauty salon, etc.)	80.9	9.3	7.1	1.4	1.4
Auto Dealers	77.9	10.3	7.9	3.0	1.0
Drug Stores	71.6	11.2	9.1	2.8	5.4
Furniture/Appliances	70.0	16.2	9.7	3.0	1.2
Entertainment (theater, restaurant)	63.5	9.7	12.2	7.7	6.9
Financial (bank, savings and loan)	87.2	6.1	4.7	1.2	0.8

Table 13–2

Crafton Area Usage of a Free Newspaper
As a Source of Advertising Information
For Particular Types of Retail Establishments
Proportion of Respondents Who:

Type of Establishment:	Don't Use The Paper	Use Paper Only a Little	Use Paper Some Of the Time	Use Paper Most Of the Time	Use Paper All Of the Time
Grocery	47.0	8.4	13.3	13.3	18.1
Men's Clothing	78.0	8.5	11.0	2.4	0.0
Women's Clothing	73.5	7.2	12.0	3.6	3.6
Shoe Stores	79.5	4.8	12.0	2.4	1.2
Services (dry cleaning, beauty salon, etc.)	83.1	6.0	8.4	2.4	0.0
Auto Dealers	81.9	7.2	8.4	2.4	0.0
Drug Stores	72.3	6.0	12.0	3.6	6.0
Furniture/Appliances	73.5	10.8	10.8	3.6	1.2
Entertainment (theater, restaurant)	69.9	7.2	9.6	10.8	2.4
Financial (bank, savings, and loan)	89.3	4.8	4.8	1.2	0.0

Table 13–3
Greyston Area Usage of a Free Newspaper As a Source of Advertising Information For Particular Types of Retail Establishments Proportion of Respondents Who:

Type of Establishment:	Don't Use The Paper	Use Paper Only a Little	Use Paper Some Of the Time	Use Paper Most Of the Time	Use Paper All Of the Time
Grocery	32.0	4.0	16.0	14.7	33.3
Men's Clothing	68.0	9.3	10.7	9.3	2.7
Women's Clothing	57.3	9.3	18.7	12.0	2.7
Shoe Stores	73.3	10.7	9.3	5.3	1.3
Services (dry cleaning, beauty salon, etc.)	76.0	4.0	13.3	2.7	4.0
Auto Dealers	80.0	4.0	10.7	4.0	1.3
Drug Stores	61.3	5.3	22.7	6.7	4.0
Furniture/Appliances	73.3	9.3	9.3	5.3	2.7
Entertainment (theater, restaurant)	54.7	8.0	16.0	13.3	8.0
Financial (bank, savings, and loan)	86.7	2.7	5.3	1.3	4.0

Table 13-4

**Paintsville Area Usage of a Free Newspaper
As a Source of Advertising Information
For Particular Types of Retail Establishments
Proportion of Respondents Who:**

Type of Establishment:	Don't Use The Paper	Use Paper Only a Little	Use Paper Some Of the Time	Use Paper Most Of the Time	Use Paper All Of the Time
Grocery	28.5	14.0	16.9	16.3	24.4
Men's Clothing	55.6	28.7	13.5	1.2	1.2
Women's Clothing	56.1	26.3	12.3	3.5	1.8
Shoe Stores	63.4	25.0	8.7	1.7	1.2
Services (dry cleaning, beauty salon, etc.)	70.9	19.8	7.0	0.6	1.7
Auto Dealers	73.8	14.0	6.4	4.7	1.2
Drug Stores	70.3	20.9	5.8	1.7	1.2
Furniture/Appliances	61.6	26.7	9.3	1.2	1.2
Entertainment (theater, restaurant)	58.7	15.7	14.5	7.6	3.5
Financial (bank, savings, and loan)	80.8	12.8	5.2	0.6	0.6

Table 13–5
Greensburg Area Usage of a Free Newspaper
As a Source of Advertising Information
For Particular Types of Retail Establishments
Proportion of Respondents Who:

Type of Establishment:	Don't Use The Paper	Use Paper Only a Little	Use Paper Some Of the Time	Use Paper Most Of the Time	Use Paper All Of the Time
Grocery	31.8	4.0	10.2	11.4	42.7
Men's Clothing	75.5	2.8	6.2	1.1	14.3
Women's Clothing	72.6	4.6	5.7	3.4	13.7
Shoe Stores	81.8	7.4	7.4	3.4	0.0
Services (dry cleaning, beauty salon, etc.)	92.0	2.8	3.4	1.1	0.6
Auto Dealers	79.5	10.2	8.0	1.1	
Drug Stores	76.1	5.7	4.0	1.7	12.6
Furniture/Appliances	75.6	10.8	9.7	3.4	0.6
Entertainment (theater, restaurant)	75.6	4.5	8.5	4.0	14.8
Financial (bank, savings, and loan)	93.2	1.7	3.4	1.7	0.0

Table   13–6
Overall Relative Importance of
Features Which Could Be
Included in a Free Newspaper

Feature:	Proportion Who Indicated This Feature to Be:		
	Very Important	Somewhat Important	Not Important
Summary of local news	50.4%	28.1%	21.5%
Grocery shopping list	45.2	21.8	33.0
Coverage of local government activities	35.5	27.5	36.9
Television schedules and program details	27.6	22.6	49.8
Summary of upcoming events and activities	44.7	28.6	26.7
Feature stories on local people or places	45.5	33.4	21.0
Comic strips	17.5	20.0	62.5
Classified ads	43.8	29.4	26.8
Directory of business services available in the community	33.4	30.3	36.3
Advertising by local merchants	46.6	32.6	20.8
Advertising by Columbia city stores	22.0	28.9	49.2
Recipes	24.5	28.7	46.8
News from surrounding communities	27.4	36.7	35.7
Church directory/church news	24.2	26.9	48.9
Energy-saving tips	37.9	37.2	24.9
Crossword puzzles	16.1	21.3	62.6
Farm news	10.2	22.0	67.7
Gardening tips	32.9	31.2	35.7

published in Greensburg be circulated in the Trenton area to compete directly for advertising revenue with the long-established *Tornado,* not only in and around Greensburg but also in the areas surrounding Trenton.

In an effort to determine, among other things, the feasibility of entry of the *Alert* (the name chosen for the new "free" paper), the Landmark Publishing Company undertook extensive research in each of the 4 market areas in which the firm controlled publications. The topics researched, were the extent to which the "free" newspaper was used as an advertising information source for consumer selection of a retail establishment and the relative importance to the consumer of a number of features included in "free" publications. This study was conducted via personal interviews with 300 persons in each of the 4 Landmark areas (Paintsville, Greyston, Crafton, and Greensburg). In all cases only persons who acknowledged receipt of one or more "free" weekly papers were interviewed. The results of the study are shown in Tables 13–1 through 13–7.

In July 1977, just as the research effort was being initiated, Landmark learned

Table   13–7
Relative Importance in the Greensburg Area
Of Features Which Could Be
Included in a Free Newspaper

Feature:	Proportion Who Indicated This Feature to Be:		
	Very Important	Somewhat Important	Not Important
Summary of local news	41.8%	33.0%	25.3%
Grocery shopping list	44.6	20.2	35.2
Coverage of local government activities	37.6	16.5	45.9
Television schedules and program details	26.8	14.4	58.8
Summary of upcoming events and activities	45.4	24.2	30.4
Feature stories on local people or places	46.4	34.0	19.6
Comic strips	19.6	13.9	66.5
Classified ads	47.9	28.4	23.7
Directory of business services available in the community	33.0	25.3	41.8
Advertising by local merchants	47.9	30.9	21.1
Advertising by Columbia City stores	17.6	22.8	59.6
Recipes	39.8	19.4	40.8
News from surrounding communities	29.8	36.1	33.5
Church directory/church news	23.6	21.5	55.0
Energy-saving tips	47.4	29.7	22.9
Crossword puzzles	20.3	15.6	64.6
Farm news	17.7	17.7	64.6
Gardening tips	46.1	23.6	30.4

that Trenton Newspapers, Inc. was soon to introduce into the Trenton-Greensburg market a new Sunday newspaper. The new paper would have a name and distribution pattern designed to position it as a weekend paper for all of Mentor County in which both Trenton and Greensburg are located. This paper would be the first locally-published Sunday newspaper in the county. Columbia City has 2 daily newspapers, one of which has a Sunday edition which, heretofore, had had no meaningful competition in Mentor County.

After the results of the research were presented by the consulting firm, the management group of Landmark Publishing Company met in Paintsville to wrestle with the issue.

Discussion Questions

1. Should the *Alert* be introduced by Landmark? If it is introduced, should it be distributed in the Trenton area as well as in the Greensburg area?

2. What effect would the introduction of the new Sunday newspaper have on this decision?

3. How could introduction of the *Alert* be advantageous to Landmark? To the Greensburg *Daily Gazette?* Does it pose any significant disadvantages?

4. Is it realistic for Landmark management to foresee significant promotional advantages and advertising revenues from the encirclement of the Columbia City area which they would have with both regular daily and "free" weekly publications? How might they be advised to exploit such advantages?

5. How could the *Alert* be differentiated from *The Tornado?* What features might be included which would give the *Alert* a differential advantage?

6. How would you evaluate the effectiveness of the other Landmark "free" papers in their market areas? What recommendations might you make to them?

7. Would you use the results of the market study in dealing with present and prospective advertisers in the other Landmark market areas? How?

The Foreign Agricultural Service: Budgeting for Market Development

Theodore F. Smith, Indiana University[1]

The Foreign Agricultural Service (FAS) is a United States Department of Agriculture agency with the responsibility of promoting the export sales of U. S. agricultural commodities, including both feed and foodstuffs. With a network of agricultural attachés and assistants, in over 60 foreign service posts around the world—in addition to the support and administrative staff in Washington— FAS cooperates with major U. S. trade and commodity organizations to develop these export markets.[2]

In the fall of 1974, during a staff meeting of the Planning and Evaluation Division, a brainstorming session was held to generate ideas for different ways to allocate foreign market development joint-funding among the different trade and commodity programs employed in overseas markets. In the past, budget allocations had been made by starting with the previous year's budget then adjusting the allocations up or down. Adjustments depended upon the addition or deletion of programs, and on the market development tasks expected during the forecast year, subject to expected financial constraints. Although the Planning and Evaluation Division had been concerned for some time with improving the budget allocation process for foreign market development programs, increased impetus for this refinement was provided by the growing emphasis in the White House Office of Management and the Budget (OMB) on "zero-based budgeting." In addition, the Appropriations Committee of the House of Representatives had just cut the budget for foreign market development programs from $13 to $11 million for fiscal year 1975 (FY '75). The staff of the Planning and Evaluation Division was concerned about how to absorb such a funding cutback with minimal damage to the overall program.

---

[1] The writer appreciates the suggestions made by Professor Donald Granbois in the revision of this case. Any errors and ambiguities that remain are, however, the sole responsibility of the writer.

[2] *"What is the Foreign Agricultural Service?"* Foreign Agricultural Service, United States Department of Agriculture, July 1970, p. 2.

Background

USDA interest in overseas agricultural commodity sources and markets can be traced back to the establishment of the Department of Agriculture in 1862.[3] It was not until several years after World War II, however, that major emphasis was placed on foreign market development. Once domestic farm surpluses and overseas buying power had built up, Congress became concerned with various ways of disposing of the surpluses, without disrupting world markets. Public Law 480 (PL 480) was the result in 1954.[4] This act authorized the sale of U.S. farm surpluses to friendly countries for their currencies and also provided for barter and donation programs. The foreign currencies generated by such sales have provided some additional financial resources for foreign market development programs.

These programs are funded jointly by the Foreign Agricultural Service and various producer, trade, and commodity organizations, such as the American Soybean Association, the Cotton Council, Great Plains Wheat, the U. S. Feed Grains Council, and Western Wheat Associates. FAS works with over 60 such organizations (which represent commodities and not specific sellers), co-sponsoring programs in over 70 countries. Among the types of activities in the program are the following:

- Seminars and technical assistance to expand use of U. S. feed and foodstuffs.
- Exhibits and demonstrations.
- Tours by overseas processors, govermental officials, and educators to U. S. agricultural industry facilities.
- Publicity, advertising, and literature programs—both consumer and trade.
- In-store promotions.
- Exhibits at international trade fairs and U.S. Trade Centers.
- Product testing and research.
- Merchandising incentives.

The importance of agriculture exports is indicated by the increase of agricultural exports from $3 billion FY '55, when the foreign market development program began, to $21.3 billion in FY '74, enabling a favorable U.S. trade balance of $2.8 billion (net of the deficit in the commercial sector)—the first time the U.S. balance of payments was in the black since 1970.[5]

Proposed Conceptual Framework

During the brainstorming session in the Planning and Evaluation Division, one idea advanced was that the product life cycle be adapted to a market life cycle approach. Developmental stages then could be delineated and appropriate activi-

---

[3] *The Agricultural Attache: His History & His Work,* Foreign Agricultural Service, United States Department of Agriculture, No. FASM-91 revised, September 1972, p. 1.

[4] Ibid., p. 3.

[5] *Market Development Fact Sheet,* Foreign Agricultural Service, United States Department of Agriculture, November 22, 1974.

ties and funding for each stage be specified. For example, with a life cycle framework of 4 stages (introduction, growth, maturity, and decline) which activities (if any) discussed above should FAS encourage by approving joint funding? By answering this question, budget allocations or reductions then could be effected by denying FAS joint-funding for some types of activities during particular market development phases. Such specification of activities appropriate for joint-funding would not mean that particular activities should not be conducted at particular stages, but rather that FAS joint funds would not be approved for some types of activities at some stages.

Discussion Questions

1. Based on your knowledge of the product life cycle, how can this paradigm be adapted into a market life cycle approach as indicated in the case?

2. What would be the advantages of this approach? Disadvantages?

3. To what extent can market development activities be turned on or off depending on the extent of surplus agricultural production in a particular crop year?

4. How can you reconcile any advantages of this approach with the thesis advanced in the article titled, "Forget the Product Life Cycle Concept!" by Nariman K. Dhallia and Sonia Yuspeh, *Harvard Business Review,* January-February, 1976, pp. 102–112?

A Miniwarehouse for Mesa City

Kenneth E. Runyon, Northern Arizona University

In the spring of 1978, Mr. Robert Kile, an attorney, was looking for possible business ventures. Several years before, he and two associates had invested in a fast-food franchise that had been quite successful. A subsequent investment in a greeting card shop had produced a marginal operation that he recently had disposed of at a substantial loss. In analyzing this latter investment, which he privately admitted was a fiasco, Mr. Kile concluded that: (1) he had underestimated the length of time and the financial resources required to develop the business; (2) he had not anticipated the difficulties he had encountered in finding a manager with the requisite skills and temperament to deal with customers; and (3) he had failed to ascertain that there was a sufficient market in the vicinity to support a "specialty" shop such as he had originally contemplated. Although he was disappointed in the outcome, he was not wholly discouraged since he felt he could avoid similar mistakes in the future.

The Miniwarehouse

Mr. Kile had heard of miniwarehouses from a brother in Texas. They were extolled as being one of the most successful real estate developments to surface in several years. Although relatively new—the first such warehouses were built about ten years ago—they were demonstrating a vitality that made them appear to be a highly profitable investment opportunity. The bulk of the currently existing miniwarehouses was in Texas and California, but hundreds had been built, or were being planned for construction in other parts of the country. Demand was demonstrated by the finding that several such operations had an assured occupancy of 70 percent even before they began operation, and the occupancy rate of established miniwarehouses was about 90 percent.

The Idea Behind the Miniwarehouse

A miniwarehouse is a facility that provides safe, convenient, self-storage units for individuals and businesses. The typical miniwarehouse complex consists of several buildings, usually of concrete block construction, surrounded by spacious paved driveways, and enclosed by a cyclone fence with only one gate-protected entrance. Storage units which are approximately eight feet in height range from closet size to bedroom size or larger. Each unit has its own door. Renters lock their own units and keep the keys. Storage space is rented on a monthly or annual basis, with monthly rentals typically ranging from $8 to $50 a unit.

There has been a latent demand for this type of storage for several years. Some of the reasons are trends toward smaller homes, increases in apartment and condominium living, and construction of newer homes without basements or attics. Further, a trend toward object accumulation, particularly in the more affluent metropolitan areas, has resulted in more personal effects than can be conveniently stored at home. Until the development of the miniwarehouse, the only solution for many people had been renting a private garage or leasing space in a conventional warehouse. In the latter case, storage costs were high, access to one's possessions was inconvenient and entailed additional charges, and the degree of privacy offered by the miniwarehouse was not available.

Previous studies indicated that a population of about 50,000 within a 5-mile radius of the warehouse site could support approximately 500 units encompassing about 50,000 square feet of storage space. Available information indicated the typical monthly rentals for various sized units. This information is shown in Table 15–1.

In addition to storage space, the miniwarehouse complex requires an apartment for a resident manager, plus ample driveway and parking facilities. Thus, a 50,000 square foot warehouse normally would require 100,000 square feet of land, and would provide about 49,000 square feet of storage, allowing approximately 1,000 square feet for the manager's apartment.

Site Location and Costs

Mesa City is a university town with approximately 35,000 population, excluding a student population of 12,000 during the academic year. Approximately one-half of the students live either in university dorms or married housing, with the remainder living in off-campus apartments, shared houses, and mobile homes. It seemed to Mr. Kile that the community could support a miniwarehouse, although he was uncertain of the size of the complex, and of the unit mix that should be offered.

Mr. Kile had located two sites which he could purchase, and which were zoned to permit the construction of a miniwarehouse. One, a 100,000 square foot site on the edge of town near the university could be acquired for $.75 per square foot, and would accommodate a 50,000 square foot complex. The other was a 45,000 square foot site in a centrally located industrial park; this site costs $1.25

Table   15–1
Typical Sizes and Rental Fees of
Selected Miniwarehouses

Unit size and square feet	Area A	Area B	Area C
4 x 6 (24)	$ 9	—	$ 9
5 x 10 (50)	13	$11	16
10 x 10 (100)	20	22	24
10 x 15 (150)	28	30	31
10 x 20 (200)	35	37	44
10 x 30 (300)	52	54	60

Table   15–2
Estimates of Building Costs

	50,000 sq. ft.	25,000 sq. ft.
Buildings @ $9 per sq. ft.	$450,000	$225,000
Land	75,000	56,250
Miscellaneous (estimated)	25,000	12,000
Total	$550,000	$293,250

Table   15–3
Estimated Annual Operating Expenses

Item	50,000 sq. ft.	25,000 sq. ft.
Real estate taxes	$14,000	$ 7,000
Insurance	3,500	1,750
Licenses/permits	300	300
Advertising	2,000	2,000
Telephone	350	350
Maintenance & repair	3,200	1,600
Refuse hauling	200	200
Water	225	225
Electricity	2,200	1,300
Accounting	1,800	1,800
Resident manager fee	9,000	9,000
Miscellaneous	2,500	1,500
Total	39,275	27,025

Table   15–4
Estimated Occupancy 1st Six Months

	1	2	3	4	5	6
50,000 sq. ft.	15%	30%	45%	60%	80%	90%
25,000 sq. ft.	20	30	50	70	90	90

per square foot, and could accommodate a 25,000 square foot complex. Other possible sites had been rejected because of cost, lack of easy access, or because of zoning restrictions. Estimates of building costs in these two areas are shown in Table 15–2.

Mr. Kile could arrange financing for about 75 percent of the appraised value of the project. The loan period was for 25 years at 10 percent. Thus, he required equity capital of about $137,000 for the 50,000 square foot complex, and $73,000 for the smaller complex. Mr. Kile had about $70,000 to $75,000 of his own to invest, and felt that he could easily raise another $75,000 to $100,000 by taking in a partner who had expressed interest in the venture, although he would prefer not to do so. From a study of local tax, utility, and service rates, combined with information obtained on miniwarehouse operations in other cities, Mr. Kile had assembled estimates of operating costs. These are shown in Table 15–3.

Loan amortization over 25 years at 10 percent would be $44,980 per year for the large complex, and $23,988 per year for the smaller one.

As a result of his greeting card shop experience, Mr. Kile recognized that it would be unrealistic to assume full occupancy of a miniwarehouse from the moment it opened. So, after a great deal of thought, he made estimates of occupancy for the first six months of operation. These estimates are shown in Table 15–4.

Market Demand

To assess market demand, Mr. Kile contracted with a marketing professor at the university to conduct a consumer survey in Mesa City. Although Mr. Kile thought the original estimate for the research was high, he was able to negotiate a satisfactory price, although it required some modifications in sample size and survey design.

Sample respondents living in apartments, mobile homes, single family dwelling units, duplexes, and business categories were selected from the 1977 city directory for Mesa City. Telephone interviews were used from Monday through Thursday from 7:00 to 9:00 pm for 2½ weeks. Sample telephone numbers were selected on a random and systematic basis by using a random starting point and recording every nth number. The calls were made from a central office and supervised by the marketing professor.

Since adequate lists of student telephone numbers were not available, personal

Table   15–5
Tentative Rate Schedule

Size unit	Rate
4 x 4	$ 6
5 x 8	11
5 x 10	13
10 x 15	32
10 x 20	40
10 x 30	60

interviews were used for student respondents. Students, both in university dorms and married housing, were selected on a random basis, starting at a randomly selected dorm room or housing unit, and taking every nth room.

The questionnaire was pretested, and the interviewers carefully trained by the marketing professor. A total of 3 percent of all dwelling units in the universe of Mesa City was interviewed, providing a total, usable sample of 370 interviews. One callback in addition to the original call was made at dwelling units where no respondent was found at home. Less than 2 percent of the sample contacted refused to participate in the survey.

Based on the research findings, modified by personal judgment, Mr. Kile developed a tentative rate schedule for the various units in the miniwarehouse complex. This schedule is shown in Table 15–5. In addition to rental income, Mr. Kile estimated additional income from the sale of locks and so forth of $3,420 for the 50,000 square foot complex and half of this amount for the smaller warehouse.

Other highlights of the research are summarized in the appendix.

Discussion Questions

1. Should Mr. Kile invest in a miniwarehouse in Mesa City?
2. If yes, which size complex? What should be his mix of unit sizes?
3. What is Mr. Kile's return on investment for each size complex?
4. What is Mr. Kile's cash flow return on investment for each size complex?

Table A

Comparison of Sample and Universe

Dwelling units	% of universe	% of sample
Single family	45.5%	40.0%
Multiple family	26.5	20.0
Mobile homes	13.0	12.9
University housing	14.0	20.8
Business firms	1.0	6.3
total	100.0%	100.0%

Table B

% of Sample Expressing Need for Space in Next 12 Months

	%	Projected number of dwelling units
Presently using storage outside of home	10.5%	1,319
Need additional space	17.4	2,185
No need for extra storage	72.1	9,056
Total	100.0%	12,560

Table   C

% of Various Housing Units
Requiring Storage

Type family unit	% requiring storage
Single family	8.4%
Multiple family	30.5
Mobile homes	18.3
University housing	40.3
Business firms	10.0

Table   D

Median Rate Respondents Indicated
They Would Be Willing to Pay for
Various Unit Sizes

Size unit	Monthly rate	Sq. ft. rate
4 x 4	$ 6.30	$.394
5 x 8	9.45	.236
5 x 10	12.60	.252
10 x 15	31.50	.210
10 x 20	39.38	.197
10 x 30	44.10	.147

Table   E

% of Sample Desiring Storage Space by Unit Size

UNIT DIMENSION	% REQUIRING UNIT*
4 x 4	35.0
5 x 8	45.4
5 x 10	10.6
10 x 15	4.5
10 x 20	3.0
10 x 30	1.5

Chapter 4

Pricing Strategies

Organizations are most concerned with price decisions when a new product which needs to be priced to meet some objectives is added to the product mix. Changes in environmental conditions such as competitors' changes in price also will cause management to reconsider its own price decisions. Unexpected customer demand (extremely high or low) may be another cause to consider a price change. The decision to reach new market segments will often direct management to change prices to enable the product to be acceptable to customers in these markets. Finally, the greater the likelihood of buyer-seller price bargaining, the greater the concern and complexity with pricing strategies. These conditions are likely to activate managers into pricing decision processes.

Pricing decision processes are the combination of objectives, information, and decision rules used by persons concerned with making price decisions. Pricing decision processes are likely to vary for industries, companies, and products even within companies.

One example of a pricing decision process, activated by a competitive change in price, is shown in Figure C—4–1. The firm's reaction to the competitive price change is determined by (1) perceived permanence of the change, (2) presence of workable alternatives to changing the firm's price, (3) the extent of the price change, and (4) the pricing objectives of the firm (maintain brand image in this case).

Four alternatives for the pricing decision process are shown in Figure C—4–1:

1. Hold price at present level and continue to watch the competitor's price.
2. Drop price to competitor's new price or to breakeven point, whichever is higher.
3. Make a nonprice reaction.
4. Consider dropping the product.

Thus, this process includes a number of input, process, and output variables. The

Figure   C—4–1
Decision Program for Meeting a Competitor's Price Cut

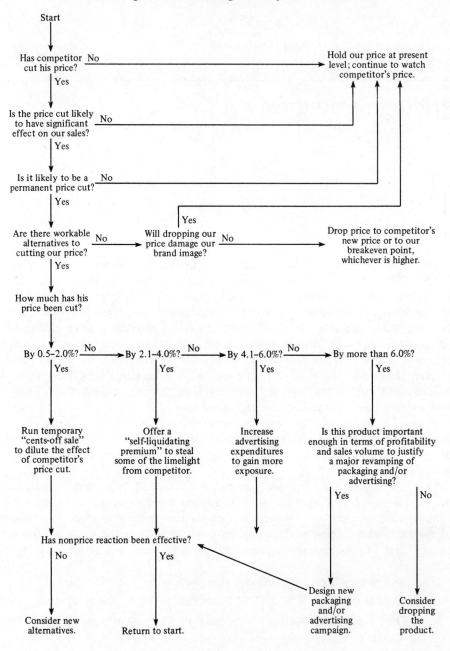

Source: Philip Kotler, *Marketing Management: Analysis, Planning, and Control* (Englewood Cliffs, NJ: Prentice Hall, 1976), p. 269. Original source: redrawn from published paper by Raymond J. Trapp, Northwestern University, 1964.

conditions causing the process to be initiated, the perceived alternative solutions available, and the pricing objectives of the firm are parts of pricing decision processes.

A General Price Decision Process

Pricing is one part of the marketing mix and a price can usually be related to a specific customer segment. Thus, knowledge of other parts of a firm's marketing mix and the intended customer segment is helpful in selecting a particular price.

A general price decision process should begin with the selection of particular market targets (customer segments) as shown in Figure C—4–2. Customer awareness and sensitivity to price changes should be seen to affect the general pricing strategy. Different prices may be appropriate for different customer segments. For example, a tourist attraction may have 2 entrance fees: one fee for tourists and one for local residents. Membership cards or special coupons with low prices might be made available to local residents to encourage repeat visitations and the tourist would pay a higher price since the price of admission is a small part of the cost of his or her vacation trip.

Brand Image

"We will not be undersold!" "Nobody offers lower prices." "Expensive and worth it." "Costs a little more but you're worth it." These are examples of sensitizing

Figure C—4–2
General Price Decision Process

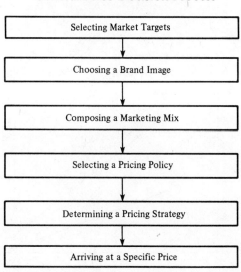

Source: Drawn from Alfred R. Oxenfeldt, "Multi-State Approach to Pricing," *Harvard Business Review,* **38** (July-August, 1960), pp. 125–133. Copyright © 1960 by the President and Fellows of Harvard College; all rights reserved.

buyers to price and particular brand images. Management may attempt to build a high quality brand image to enable a high price strategy and high price may be used to gain customers' perceptions of high quality. "Economy" and "savings" related to a brand image usually imply a low price relative to the majority of brands available. Some business firms follow a *price lining* strategy by providing brands with different images to appeal to different customer segments. For example, Anheuser-Busch offers Michelob (higher price), Budweiser (medium price), and Busch Bavarian (low price) to reach 3 different beer drinking markets (and sometimes the same beer drinkers in 3 or more different beer drinking situations).

Price and the Marketing Mix

Price is likely to interact significantly with other parts of the marketing mix to affect demand. For example, the use of a direct sales force, high quality, and no advertising may produce more sales volume and/or profits with a high versus a low price.

The results of a test market experiment for a new food product are shown in Figure C—4–3. Three price levels (base, +.10, +.20) and 2 advertising levels (low and high) were tested. The dependent variable was sales divided by a measure for store size (sales/ACV where ACV is all commodity value; the division by ACV is made to control for the effect of store size on the results of the study).

Notice in Figure C—4–3 that the effect of a low price on attracting buyers depends on the level of advertising. The high advertising plan produces sales 50 percent above the low plan at the base price. At the middle price, this percentage slips to 34 percent and at the highest price the high advertising level is ahead by

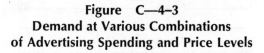

Figure   C—4–3
Demand at Various Combinations
of Advertising Spending and Price Levels

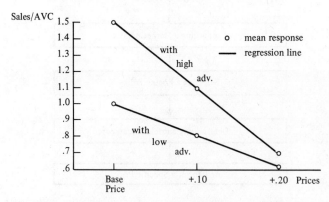

Source: Gerald J. Eskin, "A Case for Test Market Experiments," *Journal of Advertising Research,* **15** (April 1975), p. 31.

only 11 percent. Thus, an interaction effect of advertising and price on demand is present in Figure C—4–3.[1] These results are inconsistent with the conventional wisdom of classical economics in which the role of advertising is to reduce the effects of price changes on demand, hence allowing higher prices. "On the other hand, many marketers have always implicitly assumed the market works in the manner specified here. Grocery retailers who advertise only when there is a special price must believe in a negative price-advertising interaction." [2]

In another example of a market test experiment, demand was found to be greater for a cleaning kit for an 8-track music tape player for 4 substantially different prices when the salesperson delivered a sales message perceived to be high versus low in expertise. In this experiment, a high price ($3.98 instead of the suggested retail price of $1.98) with a high level of salesperson expertise produced the highest profits for the retailer.[3] Results of the study are shown in Figure C—4–4.

Thus, the specific price chosen should depend upon estimating the interaction effects of price, promotion, product, and distribution mixes. Counterintuitive effects on demand may occur if test market experiments are run. Unfortunately, few organizations experiment with different levels of price coupled with different levels of promotion, product types, and channels of distribution. Consequently, a new product may fail because of the poor selection of an untested marketing mix and not necessarily due to the lack of consumer demand.

---

[1] Gerald J. Eskin, "A Case for Test Market Experiments," *Journal of Advertising Research,* **15** (April 1975), p. 27–34.

[2] Ibid.

[3] Arch G. Woodside and J. William Davenport, Jr., "Effects of Price and Salesman Expertise on Customer Purchasing Behavior," *Journal of Business,* **49** (January 1976), pp. 51–59.

Figure   C—4–4
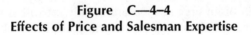
Effects of Price and Salesman Expertise

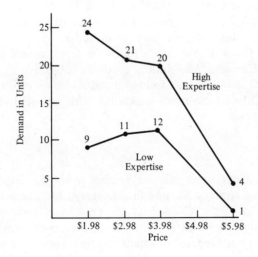

Selecting a Pricing Policy

Price policies are the general guidelines and rules which management uses when making strategic and tactical price decisions. Nearly all organizations will have written or unwritten price policies which one may quickly learn by observing the pricing behavior or by asking management the following questions:

• How do your prices compare with the average prices in the industry? Specifically, are your prices the same or 5, 10, 15, or 20 percent above or below competitors?

• How fast will you meet price reductions or increases by rivals?

• How frequently do you vary price? To what extent do you believe price stability to be advantageous?

• How frequently do you run price promotions?

• Do you follow a single price policy to all customers or do you negotiate price with different customers?

• Do you offer normal, higher, or lower prices to suppliers and resellers? For example, as a manufacturer, do you offer a 50 percent retail trade discount on a product with a suggested retail price of $1.98? If not, what trade discount do you offer retailers?

• What pricing objectives do you want to achieve? Do you want to maximize long-term or short-term profits, market share of sales volume, or customer loyalty?

• How do you relate your pricing mix with the rest of your marketing mix?

Pricing policies may be set in writing for particularly significant pricing situations. Customer desire to negotiate price, competitive price changes, and influences of firms in other levels of the marketing channel (suppliers and resellers) are examples of such situations.

The price policies of an organization are usually set within specified constraints by the pricing objectives. Examples of the principal pricing objectives of 20 large manufacturing organizations are listed in Table C—4-1. The pricing objectives can be classified into 3 major groups: profitability objectives, volume objectives, and social, ethical, status quo, and prestige objectives.

Notice in Table C—4-1 that Alcoa follows a target return on profitability objective, American Can and A&P follow a volume objective (market share maintenance or increase), and Gulf Oil follows a status quo objective. Thus, the pricing policies for Gulf Oil may be more concerned with competitive actions than are Alcoa's pricing policies.

Pricing Strategies

Specific pricing decision processes are *pricing strategies*. Figure C—4-1 is an example of a pricing strategy for one firm triggered by a competitive action. The strategy described in Figure C—4-5 is triggered by a customer's request for a temporary price reduction (Box 1). The first step after this environmental change is the development of a standard informational package by the sales representative

Table   C—4–1
Pricing Goals of 20 Large Industrial Corporations

COMPANY	PRINCIPAL PRICING GOAL	COLLATERAL PRICING GOALS
Alcoa	20 percent on investment (before taxes); higher on new products [about 10 percent effective rate after taxes]	a. "Promotive" policy on new products b. Price stabilization
American Can	Maintenance of market share	a. "Meeting" competition (using cost of substitute product to determine price) b. Price stabilization "General promotive" (low-margin policy)
A&P	Increasing market share	a. Charging what traffic will bear over long run
du Pont	Target return on investment —no specific figure given	b. Maximum return for new products—"life cycle" pricing
Exxon (Standard Oil of N. J.)	"Fair-return" target—no specific figure given	a. Maintaining market share b. Price stabilization
General Electric	20 percent on investment (after taxes); 7 percent on sales (after taxes)	a. Promotive policy on new products b. Price stabilization on nationally advertised products
General Foods	33⅓ percent gross margin ("⅓ to make, ⅓ to sell, and ⅓ for profit"); expectation of realizing target only on new products	a. Full line of food products and novelties b. Maintaining market share
General Motors	20 percent on investment (after taxes)	Maintaining market share
Goodyear	"Meeting competitors"	a. Maintain "position" b. Price stabilization
Gulf	Follow price of most important marketer in each area	a. Maintain market share b. Price stabilization
International Harvester	10 percent on investment (after taxes)	Market share: ceiling of "less than a dominant share of any market"
Johns-Manville	Return on investment greater than last 15-year average (about 15 percent after taxes); higher target for new products	a. Market share not greater than 20 percent b. Stabilization of prices

COMPANY	PRINCIPAL PRICING GOAL	COLLATERAL PRICING GOALS
Kennecott	Stabilization of prices	
Kroger	Maintaining market share	Target return of 20 percent on investment before taxes
National Steel	Matching the market—price follower	Increase market share
Sears, Roebuck	Increasing market share (8–10 percent regarded as satisfactory share)	a. Realization of traditional return on investment of 10–15 percent (after taxes) b. General promotive (low margin) policy
Standard Oil (Indiana)	Maintain market share	a. Stabilize prices b. Target return on investment (none specified)
Swift	Maintenance of market share in livestock buying and meat packing	
Union Carbide	Target return on investment	Promotive policy on new products; "life-cycle" pricing on chemicals generally
U. S. Steel	8 percent on investment (after taxes)	a. Target market share of 30 percent b. Stable price c. Stable margin

Source: Robert F. Lanzillotti, "Pricing Objectives in Large Companies," *American Economic Review* (December 1958), pp. 921–940.

(Box 2). This information is forwarded to the industry office (Box 3) which, organized by the end use and primarily responsible for market development, evaluates the information using appropriate critera as shown. The product office (Box 4)—organized by product line and responsible for costs, volumes, and coordination with manufacturing—employs different evaluative criteria. The augmented information (with recommendations) proceeds to the general manager (Box 6), who makes the decision—sometimes in conjunction with the vice-president (Box 7). The decision then is fed back to the sales representative, who negotiates with the customer (Boxes 8 and 9).[4]

By determining the actual decision processes within the organization, management is likely to discover methods to increase communication efficiency and reduce the time required to complete the strategy. For example, given the complexity of the decision process in Figure C—4–1, management may give the salesperson

---

[4] John A. Howard, James Hulbert, and John U. Farley, "Organizational Analysis and Information-System Design: A Decision Process Perspective," *Journal of Business Research,* **3** (April 1975), pp. 133–148.

Figure   C—4–5
A Feedback Decision Structure

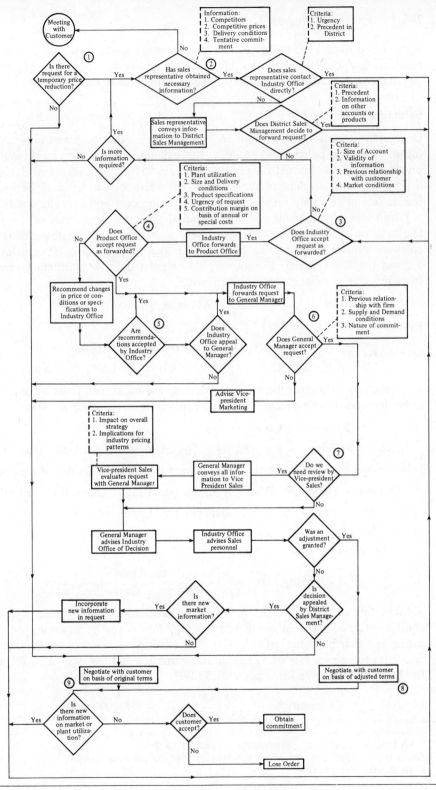

Source: John A. Howard, James Hulbert, and John U. Farley, "Organizational Analysis and Information-Systems Design: A Decision Process Perspective," *Journal of Business Research,* **3** (April 1975), p. 139.

authority to bypass the DSM (district sales management) with a price request and communicate directly with the industry office; conflict may be minimized by simultaneously informing the intermediate command channel (DSM).

Selecting a Specific Price

Once management has taken into account its market targets, brand image, marketing mix, pricing policy, and strategy, the calculations of costs and revenues for prices within a contrained range can be made. "The first 5 stages of decision are designed to take account of the business considerations which may be ignored if one selects price solely on the basis of prevailing cost and revenue conditions." [5]

Given that management operates within the pricing boundaries set by the first five decision stages, the revenues and costs associated with possible prices can be compared and a specific price selected to maximize sales, profits, or sales within a given profit constraint. Profits may be calculated from subtracting total costs from revenue associated with a given price:

$$\text{Profits} = \text{Revenue} - \text{Cost}$$

where Revenue = (Quantity) (Price)

$$\text{Cost} = \text{Fixed Costs} + \text{Total Variable Costs}$$

$$\text{Total Variable Costs} = (\text{Variable Costs per Unit}) (\text{Quantity})$$

This profit equation may be used to calculate the breakeven point in units needed to be demanded for a specific price. At breakeven, revenue equals costs.

$$\text{Revenue} = \text{Costs}$$

$$(\text{Quantity}) (\text{Price}) = \text{Fixed Costs} + [(\text{Variable Costs per Unit}) (\text{Quantity})]$$

Subtracting (Variable Costs per unit) (Quantity) from both sides of the equation:

$$(\text{Quantity}) (\text{Price}) - (\text{Variable Costs per Unit}) (\text{Quantity}) = \text{Fixed Costs}$$

or (Quantity) (Price − Variable Costs per Unit) = Fixed Costs

Dividing both sides of the equation by (Price − Variable Costs per Unit) results in the breakeven formula *in units:*

$$\text{Quantity} = \frac{\text{Fixed Costs}}{\text{Price} - \text{Variable Costs Per Unit}}$$

Marketing costs of advertising, marketing channel and sales force expenses are considered fixed costs in breakeven pricing. For example, assuming production expenses for a barbecue grill of $20,000, advertising costs of $40,000, channel and sales force expenses of $25,000, and variable costs per unit of $2.00, what is the breakeven in units for a price of $3.00?

$$\text{Quantity} = \frac{\$85,000}{\$3.00 - \$2.00} = 85,000 \text{ units}$$

---

[5] Alfred R. Oxenfeldt, "Multi-Stage Approach to Pricing," *Harvard Business Review,* **38** (July-August, 1960), p. 125–133. Copyright © 1960 by the President and Fellows of Harvard College; all rights reserved.

The breakeven point in units is 85,000:

The breakeven point is reduced as price is increased. This is shown for 3 prices for a manufacturer of barbecue grills in Figure C—4–6. Notice that the unit volume to recover full costs at factory prices of $3.00, $3.60, and $4.60 is reduced from 85,000 to 53,185 to 32,692, respectively. Profits are generated when volume exceeds the breakeven points and losses occur when volume fails to reach breakeven levels.

The break even volumes for 6 potential factory prices are shown in Table C—4–2. Each volume is calculated by dividing total fixed costs by the contribution to fixed costs (price − variable cost per unit) for each price. The table also includes the final prices consumers would pay when wholesale and retail margins are added to the manufacturer's selling prices. A price of $2.60 requires sales of

Figure   C—4–6
Multiple Breakeven Analysis for a Barbecue Grill

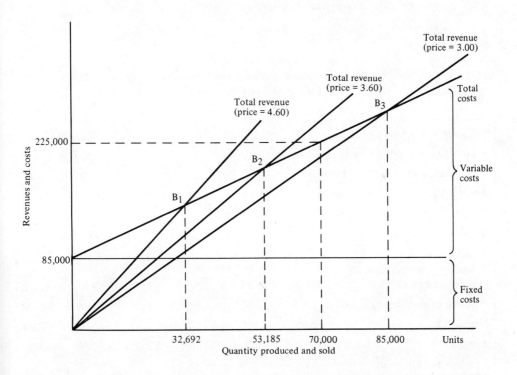

Source: Douglas J. Dalrymple and Leonard J. Parsons, *Marketing Management: Text and Cases* (New York: John Wiley & Sons, Inc., 1976), p. 346.

about 141,000 units to break even, whereas a price of $5 gives a profit after only 28,300 units have been sold.[6]

However, breakeven analysis is only half of the analyses necessary to determine a specific price. Some attempt to measure demand is needed if profits as well as demand will occur for the prices being considered.

Demand may be estimated using test market experiments, as discussed previously in this chapter, or some type of formal managerial judgment approach might be used to estimate demand for each price considered.

Price decision makers may be asked to estimate the most optimistic, realistic, and pessimistic demand levels for each price, using the managerial judgment approach. Then, the estimated quantity demanded for a given price and marketing mix might be estimated using the following formula and averaged across all managers surveyed:

$$Q_e = \frac{Q_p + 4Q_m + Q_o}{6}$$

---

[6] Douglas J. Dalrymple and Leonard J. Parsons, *Marketing Management: Text and Cases* (New York: John Wiley & Sons, Inc., 1976), p. 345.

Table C—4–2
Calculating Breakeven Volumes
Using Margin Per Unit

Salesmen's salary and expenses					$25,000	
Advertising and point of sale materials					40,000	
Amortization of R & D expenses					5,000	
Amortization of tooling expenses					5,000	
Overhead expense allocation					10,000	
Total					$85,000 [a]	
Retail price (Includes wholesale and retail margins)	$5.42	$6.25	$7.50	$8.33	$9.58	$10.42
Possible mfg. selling prices	2.60	3.00	3.60	4.00	4.60	5.00
Variable cost	−2.00	−2.00	−2.00	−2.00	−2.00	−2.00
Margin	$ .60	$1.00	$1.60	$2.00	$2.60	$ 3.00
Break-even volume in 1000's of units ($85,000/mfg's. margin)	141.7	85.0	53.2	42.5	32.7	28.3

[a] The fixed costs could be increased to include a profit so the break-even volumes would show the sales needed to return a planned profit.

Source: Douglas J. Dalrymple and Leonard J. Parsons, *Marketing Management: Text and Cases* (New York: John Wiley & Sons, Inc., 1976), p. 346.

where Q_e = estimated quantity demanded for a given price and given marketing mix

Q_p = pessimistic estimate of quantity demanded

Q_m = most realistic estimate of quantity demanded

Q_o = optimistic estimate of quantity demanded

This formula weights the most realistic estimate twice as heavy as the combined pessimistic and optimistic estimates.

Finally, profits or losses can be calculated by comparing the breakeven quantity (Q_b) with the demand quantity estimated. Such a comparison is shown in Table C—4–3 for 2 prices combined with 2 advertising (A) levels, and 2 sales force budgets (S). A total of 8 marketing mixes are examined. Thus, 8 estimates of demand (Q) and breakeven points (Q_b) are shown. The volume above breakeven ($Q - Q_p$) is used to calculate absolute profits (Z). Absolute profits is equal to price minus variable cost per unit ($P - V$) multiplied by ($Q - Q_b$).

The results indicate the following marketing mix should be selected to maximize profits at $18,998:

Price: $24

Advertising: $10,000

Sales Force Budget: $10,000

However, a different marketing mix might be selected if the objective was to maximize sales given a profit constraint of $10,000. In this second case, the first marketing mix would be selected resulting in an estimated profit of $16,398 and sales of 12,400 units (sales more than double the marketing mix which maximizes profits).

Pricing in Marketing Channels

Prices are also computed within marketing channels, usually after demand from consumers or industrial users has been estimated. The difference between the price the consumer pays and the price paid by the retailer to either the wholesaler or the manufacturer is called a *markup*. Markup is usually expressed as a *fixed percent of price above cost* of obtaining the product or service that the channel member keeps for his services and for profit. For example, the retailer price of $20 for a pair of men's shoes received direct from a manufacturer for $12 produces a markup or trade discount of $8, or 40 percent of the retail price for the retailer. The manufacturer receives 60 percent of the retail price of $12. Markup is always computed on price of products and services *of each channel level,* unless otherwise specified.

Let's assume a wholesaler is charged $3 for each shirt and the wholesaler wants a 10 percent markup; that is, the wholesaler wants to keep 10 percent of his selling price for each shirt sold. Therefore, 90 percent of his selling price is the wholesaler's cost ($3), and the wholesaler's selling price is $3.333.

Table C—4—3
A Comparison Of Expected Volume (Q) and
Breakeven Volume (Q_B) for Various Marketing Mixes

	(1)	(2)	(3)	(4)	(5)	(6)	(7)
		Marketing Mix				Volume above Break-even	Absolute Profits
	P	A	S	Q	Q_R	$Q - Q_B$	$Z = (P - V)(Q - Q_B)$
1.	$16	$10,000	$10,000	12,400	9,667	2,733	$16,398
2.	16	10,000	50,000	18,500	16,333	2,167	13,002
3.	16	50,000	10,000	15,100	16,333	-1,233	-7,398
4.	16	50,000	50,000	22,600	23,000	-400	-2,400
5.	24	10,000	10,000	5,500	4,143	1,357	18,998
6.	24	10,000	50,000	8,200	7,000	1,200	16,800
7.	24	50,000	10,000	6,700	7,000	-300	-4,200
8.	24	50,000	50,000	10,000	9,857	143	2,002

Source: Philip Kotler, "Marketing Mix Decisions for New Products," *Journal of Marketing Research,* **28** (February 1964), p. 43–49. Published by the American Marketing Association.

$$SP = \text{Selling price in dollars}$$

$$0.9(SP) = \$3 \quad SP = \frac{\$3}{0.9}$$

$$SP = \$3.333$$

Business firms relate the prices of their products and services to their costs. Most firms in the marketing channel make initial and, for many products, final price decisions based strictly on costs.

Many manufacturers compute their selling prices based upon markups and in relation to costs of materials and labor. Assume material and labor costs of $4 per unit for a manufacturer and the decision to price the product $5 above these costs. Therefore, price is equal to $9 and markup is 55.5 percent.

$$M = \text{Markup in percent}$$

$$M(\$9) = \$5$$

$$M = \frac{\$5}{\$9}$$

$$M = 55.5\%$$

Figure C—4–7 is an example of costs, markups, and prices for firms in different levels of a marketing channel. Notice that one level's price is another level's costs, and the markups for the manufacturer and retailer are greater than the markups for the jobber and the wholesaler.

Retail markups are usually greater than wholesale markups because of the savings in expenses associated with large wholesaler purchases and sales versus the smaller size purchases and sales of the retailer.

If you know the percent markup and cost of a product, you can compute the selling price by subtracting the percent markup from 100 percent and dividing the result into the cost.

General formula:

$$SP = \text{cost}/(100\% - M\%)$$
$$SP = \text{Selling Price}$$
$$M = \text{Markup}$$

Example: $SP = \$3/(100\% - 10\%) = \$3.333$

If you know the selling price and the percent markup, you can compute the markup in dollars and the cost.

General formula:

$$\$M = M\%(SP)$$

Example: $\$5 = 0.555(\$9)$

$$\text{Cost} = \$9 - \$5 = \$4$$

Figure C—4–7
Costs, Prices, and Markups of
Different Levels in a Marketing Channel

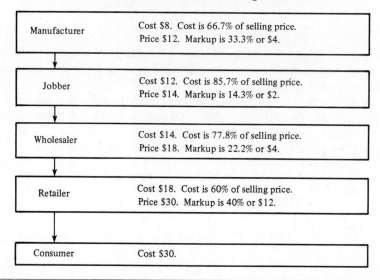

Source: J. Taylor Sims, J. Robert Foster, and Arch G. Woodside, *Marketing Channels: Systems and Strategies* (New York: Harper & Row, 1977), p. 275.

Markups vary substantially by type of product and across types of store and manufacturer within a channel level (as well as across channel levels). One study found the markups on the retail price in department stores to be 20 percent for tobacco goods, 28 percent for cameras, 34 percent for books, 41 percent for dresses, 46 percent for costume jewelry, and 50 percent for millinery.[7]

Large supermarket pricing strategists usually place only small markups on fast-selling products, for example, coffee, sugar, shortening, and milk may carry markups of less than 12 percent. These low markups may produce substantial profits for the supermarkets if the turnover per week or month is high. Turnover is the number of times the average inventory is sold in a given time period, such as a year.

Price Elasticity of Demand

How much of a change in demand is produced by a change in price? Price elasticity of demand is a measure of the change in demand produced by a change in price. Thus, the general formula for price elasticity (E_D) is the calculation of the percent change in demand divided by the percent change in price:

---

[7] *Department Merchandising and Operating Results of 1965* (New York: National Retail Merchants Association) 1965.

$$E_D = \frac{\text{Percent Change in Demand}}{\text{Percent Change in Price}}$$

If demand increases by 50 percent with a decrease in price by 20 percent, then E_D is -2.5:

$$E_D = \frac{.50}{.20} = -2.5$$

Price elasticities are usually negative with the quantity sold inversely related to changes in price. However, if price is positively related to demand, the E will be positive. For example, if demand increases by 20 percent with an increase in price by 30 percent, then $E_D = +.67$

The computational formula often used to measure E_D weights the amount of changes in demand and price by both the new and old levels:

$$E_D = \frac{\dfrac{Q_2 - Q_1}{Q_2 + Q_1}}{\dfrac{P_2 - P_1}{P_2 + P_1}}$$

This computational formula reduces the bias of computing a large or small E_D simply because of the choice of Q_2 or Q_1 and P_2 or P_1 in the demonstration of the equation.

E_D from 0 to 1.0 is named an *inelastic* price effect on demand. That is, the percent increase in price produced a smaller percent increase in demand. For example, a decrease in demand of 15 percent produced by an increase in price of 30 percent would be an inelastic change in demand $E_D = -.50$. A percent change in demand equal to the percent change in price is a *unitary* elastic price effect on demand and E_D is equal to -1.0. For example, a demand decrease in percent of 25 and a price increase of 25 percent results in $E_D = -1.0$. An *elastic* demand is represented by the percent change in demand being greater by the percent change in price, $E_D > -1.0$. For example, a percent increase in demand of 60 percent produced by a decrease in price of 10 percent results in $E_D = -6$.

The purpose of the marketing mix viewed from economic theory is to (1) shift the demand curve to the right, and (2) change the shape of the demand curve to *less* elastic or more inelastic. This is shown graphically in Figure C—4–8. The second demand curve (D_2) is shown to the right of the first (D_1) to represent the increase in sales resulting from the increase in marketing effort (e.g., dollars spent on advertising) for any given level of price. Thus, P_1 at D_d is greater than D_b at P_1 and D_c is greater than D_a at P_2.

Also notice in Figure C—4–8 that the change in demand ($D_d - D_c$) is less for D_2 compared with the change in demand ($D_b - D_a$) for D_1, given a price change from P_1 to P_2. Thus, the elasticity of demand for D_2 is *less* than the elasticity of demand for D_1:

$$E_{D_2} < E_{D_1}$$

Figure   C—4–8
Hypothesized Interaction Effect of
Price and Marketing Effort

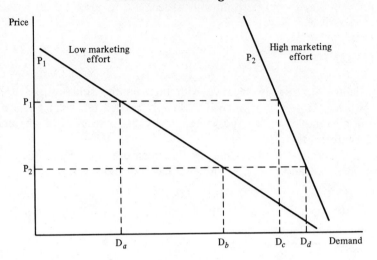

Figure   C—4–9
Example of Demand, Price, and
Marketing Effort Interaction

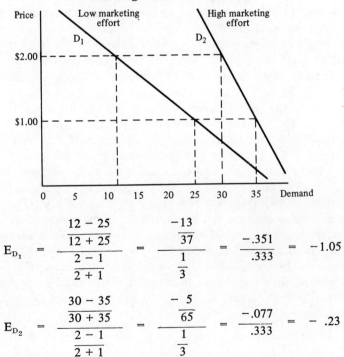

$$E_{D_1} = \cfrac{\cfrac{12 - 25}{12 + 25}}{\cfrac{2 - 1}{2 + 1}} = \cfrac{\cfrac{-13}{37}}{\cfrac{1}{3}} = \cfrac{-.351}{.333} = -1.05$$

$$E_{D_2} = \cfrac{\cfrac{30 - 35}{30 + 35}}{\cfrac{2 - 1}{2 + 1}} = \cfrac{\cfrac{-5}{65}}{\cfrac{1}{3}} = \cfrac{-.077}{.333} = -.23$$

Figure C—4–10
Perceived Carpet Quality As a
Function of Price, Store Image, and Type of Subject

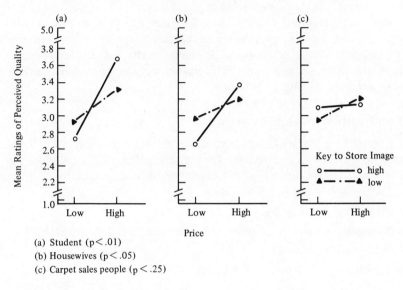

(a) Student (p < .01)

(b) Housewives (p < .05)

(c) Carpet sales people (p < .25)

Source: Arch G. Woodside, Jagdish N. Sheth, and Peter D. Bennett (eds.), *Consumer and Industrial Buying Behavior* (New York: North-Holland, 1977), p. 272.

A numerical example, Figure C—4–9, demonstrates the shift in demand and the changes in the shapes of demand due to differences in price and marketing effort. Notice that a substantial reduction in the price elasticity on demand is shown in the figure for the high compared to the low marketing effort conditions.

However, as described earlier in the test market experiments, real-life data may not always follow the proposed economic theory. It should be noted that consumers may perceive a positive price and perceived quality relationship which may affect the price and demand relationship.

Price and Perceived Quality

Research evidence has shown that consumers may use price as an information cue to judge the perceived quality in products.[8] Positive price-perceived quality relationships are shown graphically in Figure C—4–10. Perceived carpet quality is shown to increase with increases in price among students (Figure C—4–10a) and among housewives (Figure C—4–10b). Notice that the change in perceived quality is greater when the carpet is perceived to be from a store with a high

---

[8] Research evidence is reviewed by Jerry C. Olson, "Price As An Information Cue: Effects on Product Evaluations" and Kent B. Monroe, "Objective and Subjective Contextual Influences on Price Perception," both in Arch G. Woodside, Jagdish N. Sheth, and Peter D. Bennett, *Consumer and Industrial Buying Behavior* (New York: Elsevier North-Holland, 1977), pp. 267–296.

versus low image among both students and housewives. Among carpet salespersons the effects of price and store image in perceived quality were nonsignificant.

Assuming that students had the least amount of prior knowledge and experience with carpets and salespeople the most, a key factor in the relationship between price and perceived quality may be prior knowledge. Notice in Figure C—4–10 that the amount of changes in perceived quality decreased from one panel to the next—from low prior knowledge to high prior knowledge. Thus, consumers are likely to use other information besides price when available to judge the perceived quality in products.[9]

Legal Constraints in Pricing Decisions

Managers usually make price decisions within the legal frameworks of local, state (province or territory), and federal laws and regulations. Legislation has been passed in most western industrialized countries, including the United States and Canada, in the following 4 pricing areas:

1. Horizontal price fixing
2. Vertical price fixing ("fair trade" or resale price maintenance)
3. Price discrimination
4. Minimum price levels ("unfair trade")

Horizontal price agreements.   Price agreements among firms within the same marketing channel level (e.g., among manufacturers) are *horizontal price agreements*. The Sherman Antitrust Act of 1890 is the major U.S. legislation prohibiting almost all types of horizontal price agreements as restraints of trade. Horizontal price fixing is illegal per se regardless of how reasonable the resulting prices in such agreements.

The most famous court case in recent years concerning horizontal price agreements involved the General Electric price conspiracy case of 1962. General Electric, Westinghouse, Allis-Chalmers, and a number of other electrical equipment manufacturers pleaded guilty of collusive price fixing of heavy electrical machinery. As a result, 29 firms were fined a total of $11,800,000 and 7 executives were sent to prison as well as given personal fines. One pricing expert has reported that it is a fair guess that triple-damage suits and out-of-court settlements approached the quarter-billion-dollar mark following the court case.[10]

In 1975, American Cyanamid Company, Pfizer, Inc., Bristol-Myers Company, E. R. Squibbs & Sons, Inc., and Upjohn Company made rebates totaling more than $20 million to 888,371 antibiotic purchasers in an out-of-court settlement after 6 states sued the firms for conspiring to monopolize the market and restrain trade between 1951 and 1966. The firms agreed to a cash settlement, although they admitted no wrongdoing.[11]

---

[9] Arch G. Woodside and J. Taylor Sims, "Retail Experiment in Pricing a New Product," *Journal of Retailing,* **50** (Fall 1974), pp. 56–65.

[10] Kristin S. Palda, *Pricing Decisions and Marketing Policy* (Englewood Cliffs, NJ: Prentice-Hall, 1974), p. 97.

[11] "Antitrust Suits Bring Rebates to Consumers," *Consumer Reports,* **40, 10** (October 1975), pp. 585–586.

In the 1970s the American Medical Association, the Pharmaceutical Manufacturers Association, and other special interest representatives have gone to the courts in attempts to limit or prevent price competition among brands, products, services, and firms in retailing, wholesaling, or manufacturing.

Some firms and industries are legally permitted to engage in price fixing agreements. For example, the Webb-Pomarene Act allows cartels to be formed for selling in foreign markets.

Vertical price fixing. In the United States, the Miller-Tydings Act of 1937 and the McGuire Act of 1953 were federal laws exempting vertical price fixing from laws to prevent restraint of trade. These acts permitted state laws that allowed manufacturers to specify a price at or above which retailers must sell designated brand name products. A total of 36 states had such misnamed "fair trade" laws in the beginning of 1975.

The National Association of Retail Druggists has been a strong advocate of fair trade laws to protect its members' trade margins against price cutting by discounters.

From the manufacturer's viewpoint, resale price maintenance may serve as an indispensable part of collusive action. Given a horizontal pricing agreement and territorial market division among manufacturers, an efficient form of market division is to set up exclusive distribution networks and agree not to give franchises to new dealers without the consent of other manufacturers. To stabilize market shares of the retailers, and therefore the market shares of the manufacturers, retailers must not be allowed to compete, at least not on a price basis. Resale price maintenance (fair trade agreements) constitute one method of enforcing such agreements among manufacturers.[12]

Fortunately for consumers, President Gerald Ford signed federal legislation in 1975 making resale price maintenance laws illegal in the United States. The United States, Canada, Great Britain, France, and other countries now ban fair trade agreements. This should help increase price competition and promote lower consumer prices and greater demand for a number of products.

Price discrimination. *Price discrimination* is charging different prices to different firms or different consumers. Some price discrimination practices are illegal under certain conditions of the Robinson-Patman Act of 1936. Several states have enacted laws similar to the federal Robinson-Patman Act to limit or prevent price discrimination.

Trade discounts are legal forms of price discrimination if given to represent differences in costs to marketing channels in performing functions at different levels. Thus, a wholesaler may pay less than a retailer for the same product because the wholesaler performs different functions and *does not compete directly* with the retailer.

The following 4 possible defenses might be used by a firm for price discrimination practices:

1. Different prices charged to different firms were for physically different products.

---

[12] Lester G. Telser, "Why Should Manufacturers Want Fair Trade," *Journal of Law and Economics* (1960), pp. 89–100.

2. Buyers of the product are not competitors, nor are their customers.

3. Price differentials are caused by differences in the costs of manufacturing, sale, or delivery resulting from differing methods or quantities in which such products are sold or delivered.

4. Price differentials were made in good faith to meet a competitor's price on the service or facilities furnished by a competitor.

The third defense, cost justification, is usually raised for quantity discounts among channel levels. The fourth defense, the "good faith" justification, has been the most successful legal defense in price discrimination cases.

Minimum price levels ("unfair trade"). Several states have laws and regulations placing a floor on prices of certain products (e.g., milk) and preventing channel members from selling for less than the cost of the merchandise plus a minimum markup. Such laws and regulations are called *unfair trade laws,* and their original purpose was to protect small competitors from price competition by larger firms. Consumers are usually charged higher prices for products in states having unfair trade regulations compared with states without such regulations.

Summary

An organization decides on a specific price for a product by learning the actual pricing decision processes used, a useful step toward improving the outcomes of prices. A general price decision process is a multi-stage sequence of steps which an organization should take to select a specific price. Six steps are included in this general process. Only after reaching the sixth step (arriving at a specific price) should the costs and revenues of alternative prices be evaluated. The correct starting place in making a price decision is in the selection of market targets.

Breakeven analysis should be used with demand analysis to evaluate alternative prices. The calculation of breakeven in units and test market experiments can be used to compute profit and sales estimates of alternative marketing mixes.

Trade discounts, price elasticity, and the effects of price on perceived quality are often important to pricing decisions in many organizational settings. Finally, pricing decisions are affected by a number of legal constraints including 4 legislative and regulating actions affecting pricing strategies.

Discussion Questions

1. Interview a retail store manager and diagram the pricing decision process for a price reduction of a product in his or her store.

2. Explain price lining.

3. Is the "general price decision process" a descriptive or normative model of price decision? Explain.

4. What is a pricing policy? Offer an example of a pricing policy.

5. Compute the breakeven point given the following information. Compute estimated profit.

    Plant costs—$40,000
    Advertising—$30,000
    Sales Force Costs—$60,000
    Price—$1.50
    Variable Cost Per Unit—$.90
    Estimated demand with price of $1.50—240,000 units

6. Given the following data, evaluate the effect of price and salesperson expertise on demand. Compute the elasticities for the prices for both demand curves.

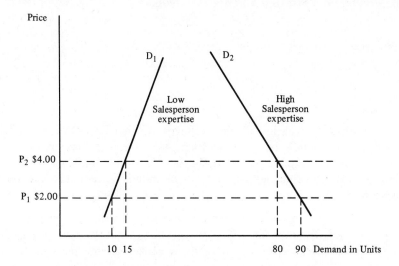

7. Explain the perceived quality and price relationships shown in the following figure.

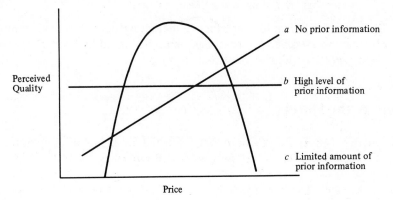

Executive Inn, Inc.

Kent B. Monroe
Virginia Polytechnic Institute and State University

Early in 1979, Mr. Charles Rabb, manager of the Executive Inn, had just completed reading a new book on pricing. As he leaned back in his chair, he pondered some pricing principles that the book's author had expounded. To be sure that he had the principles correctly in his mind, he reopened the book and reread the principles:

> The correct pricing of a product line should follow three principles:
>
> (1) Each product should be priced correctly in relation to all other products in the line. Specifically, perceptively noticeable differences in the products should be equivalent to perceived value differences.
>
> (2) The highest and lowest price in the product line have a special complementary relation to other products in the line and should be priced so as to facilitate desired buyer perceptions.
>
> (3) Price differentials between products in the product line should get wider as price increases over the product line. This principle follows the behavioral finding that price perception follows a logarithmic scale rather than an arithmetic or linear scale.[1]

Mr. Rabb realized that his director of marketing and sales had completed a study of room sales several weeks ago, and he asked his secretary to get a copy of the report for him to read that evening.

History of the Hotel

The Executive Inn is a 900-room hotel located in a major city in the southeastern United States. The hotel first opened for business in the spring of 1969,

---

[1] Kent B. Monroe, *Making Profitable Pricing Decisions* (McGraw-Hill forthcoming 1979).

and since that time has had an average room occupancy of 80 percent. Room occupancy had peaked at 87 percent in 1976. Part of the decline in the past 2 years was due to a number of new hotels that had been opened in the past few years. Indeed, about 1500 new hotel rooms had become available in 1977. Another 500-room hotel was under construction 3 blocks away, with an expected occupancy date of mid-1980.

Over the past seven years, the hotel had successfully attracted a major portion of its room business from traveling business and sales people. The hotel was located close to the downtown business district, and travelers had immediate access to the airport expressway. The drive to the airport took about 15 minutes in normal traffic. Also, the hotel was about five blocks away from the state university. Parents, alumni, and friends of the university have found the hotel a convenient place to stay when coming to sports, cultural, and other campus events. Although its location was not as attractive for tourists, many tourists stayed in the hotel when visiting the city.

Exhibit 16-1
Price and Room Classification Schedule

| | Room Price | |
Single Occupancy	Double Occupancy	Number of Rooms
$16.00	$19.50	30
16.50	20.00	40
17.00	20.50	30
17.50	21.00	300
18.00	21.50	200
18.50	22.00	50
19.00	22.50	30
19.50	23.00	30
20.00	23.50	60
21.00	24.50	10
22.00	25.50	10
24.00	27.50	25
26.00	29.50	10
27.00	30.50	5
27.50	31.00	5
28.00	31.50	10
29.00	32.50	5
29.50	33.00	20
30.00	33.50	5
32.00	35.50	15
35.00	38.50	10

Exhibit 16-2
Sample Occupancy Data
(Single Rate)

Room Price	Average Percentage Paying Price	Cumulative Percentage
$16.00	5.0%	5.0%
16.50	4.0	9.0
17.00	8.0	17.0
17.50	8.0	25.0
18.00	10.0	35.0
18.50	20.0	55.0
19.00	10.0	65.0
19.50	8.0	73.0
20.00	7.0	80.0
21.00	5.0	85.0
22.00	5.0	90.0
24.00	3.0	93.0
26.00	1.0	94.0
27.00	1.0	95.0
27.50	0.5	95.5
28.00	0.5	96.0
29.00	1.0	97.0
29.50	1.0	98.0
30.00	0.5	98.5
32.00	1.0	99.5
35.00	0.5	100.0

The Marketing and Sales Director's Report

That evening, Mr. Rabb read the report of the marketing and sales director. The report was organized into 3 parts: analysis of room demand, comparison of the supply of rooms with room demand, and ranking rooms according to noticeable physical attributes.

The first exhibit shows that the hotel had 900 rooms and 21 different single and double occupancy room rates. (See Exhibit 16–1.) The director had taken 2 samples of 14 days each, recording the number of persons paying each single room rate on each day. These data were converted into the average percentage of persons paying each rate, as shown in Exhibit 16–2. From Exhibit 16–2, a demand curve was developed showing the cumulative percentage of persons versus the rate paid. (See Exhibit 16–3.)

The director then assumed that if 5 percent of the guests occupied a $16 room,

Exhibit 16-3
Room Demand Curve

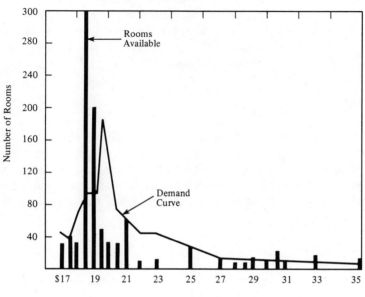

Price (Single Occupancy)

Exhibit 16-4
Room Demand at Current Prices

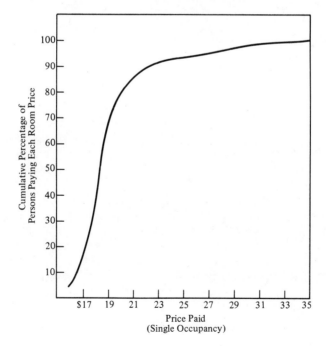

Price Paid
(Single Occupancy)

then 5 percent of 900, or 45 rooms, was the demand for a $16 room. Using this reasoning, he developed Exhibit 16–4.

Finally, all of the rooms in the hotel were evaluated according to factors of noticeable differences. The noticeable attributes were room size, location in terms of room floor and view, and facilities available: television, air conditioning, refrigerator, and size of bedding. This part of the study revealed that the hotel had 9 noticeably different types of rooms.

Room Prices

Mr. Rabb believed that the Executive Inn was not following the pricing principles he had just read about, and he decided to ask the marketing and sales director to recommend a new pricing schedule. Currently, the prices were competitive with other hotels in the city, but Mr. Rabb was concerned that the current pricing schedule was too complex and probably was not correct for his market.

Discussion Questions

1. What is wrong with the current pricing scheme used by Executive Inn, Inc.? Explain.
2. Using the pricing principles discussed in the case, develop a pricing strategy for Executive Inn, Inc.
3. How will the opening of additional rooms among competitors affect Executive Inn's pricing strategy? Explain.

The Guardian Life Insurance Company: A Strategic Pricing Case

Subhash C. Jain and Edwin C. Hackleman
The University of Connecticut

Early in 1977, Bob Williams, product manager for group dental insurance, was faced with a critical decision concerning future strategy. The potential market for group dental insurance was enormous and until recently Guardian Life Insurance Company (GL) had been one of the dominant factors in that market. However, in the recent awarding of National Telephone Company's group dental business, $114,100,000 in annual premium of which GL had expected to obtain 25 percent, the actual award to GL had been for only a little over $1 million. Because of this result, GL's management was calling for a complete review of their marketing strategy for group dental insurance, particularly in the area of pricing.

Background

GL is a large insurance company with revenues of $4.5 billion in 1976. It is made up of five major divisions: group insurance, individual insurance, group pension, property and casualty, and investments. In 1976, group insurance premiums were $1.5 billion of which $120 million were from dental insurance. In 1976, new group insurance premiums were $90 million of which $40 million (44 percent) were for dental insurance. Dental insurance was first offered by GL back in 1961 as part of their medical care policy. In the early 1970s, GL began writing dental insurance as a separate coverage. GL was very successful in the early 1970s selling dental insurance and established a reputation for giving quality service. This reputation enabled GL to obtain a very large share of a major automotive company's dental contract awarded in 1974. From this contract, GL received a great deal of praise from both the automotive management and UAW leaders for the quality of service they were providing. Because of this praise, GL had been very confident that they would come away with a large share of the National Telephone contract when it came up for bids in mid–1976.

Dental Insurance

The growth in voluntary dental benefit plans has been phenomenal, especially since much of the growth has taken place in a period of economic recession and inflationary cost for medical care benefits. Total enrollment now is probably approaching 40 million participants with perhaps a third of this total occurring over the last 18 months. Insurance companies have produced a majority of the enrollments, roughly 65 percent of the total. Dental service companies account for about 25 percent and the Reds around 8 percent. The balance is represented by independent programs, that is, self-administered private clinics and health maintenance organization programs. Some major group health insurance companies now have as many individuals insured for dental care as they have insured for hospitalization.

The outlook is for more of the same spectacular growth. Greater awareness of the relationship between oral health and general well being, rising affluence, cosmetic appeal of attractive teeth, and the advent of painless dentistry are helping to spark the grass roots popularity of dental care benefits. However, the biggest factors combining to push dental insurance into prominence are the maturity of many employee benefit programs and collective bargaining pressures. In the next few years, millions of additional people will be covered under dental plans. Enrollment in dental plans by 1980 has been projected by some experts to upwards of 80 million people.

Modern, independently structured dental benefit plans separate categories of treatment, assigning to each a different priority as to richness of benefits. Highest priority goes to *diagnostic* and *preventive* treatment. Most plans cover these treatments at 100 percent of reasonable and customary (R&C) charges, but this priority benefit richness concept can be applied under fully scheduled plans as well. Obviously, the intent is to encourage regular visits to the dentist.

Second in order of priority for richness of benefit are basic treatments for preservation of natural teeth, that is, principally amalgam fillings, root canal work, and treatment of gum disease. The benefit usually is 70 to 85 percent of reasonable and customary charges or a schedule amount usually in the range of 70 to 80 percent of *average* charges in the area.

Last in the order of priority for richness of benefit are major treatments for saving badly broken down teeth or replacing them with artificial teeth. These services tend to be more elective and expensive. Benefit levels are typically established at 50 to 60 percent of R&C charges or, in the case of scheduled benefits, average charges in the locality. Where dental benefits are being introduced for the first time, coverage for orthodontic expenses are included in about half of the plans. Generally, the benefit richness is the same or lower than that established for other major dental treatments.

Rarely are deductibles applied to diagnostic and preventive treatments. To do otherwise runs counter to the strategy of encouraging prevention to avoid the large expenses that tend to follow neglect. It is fairly common to see deductibles applied to other categories of treatment to cut cost by reducing the volume of small claims that the insured can budget easily. The deductible is on a calendar year or policy year basis, or, in rare instances, a lifetime basis. Most often the deductible is $25, but many are set at $50—and a very few are set at $100.

The single control on benefit payments is a yearly limit for an individual—most often $750 to $1,000. When orthodontia is covered the limit is lifetime—generally set at $500. Only a few plans limit total benefits over an individual's life.

Marketing Strategy

One of GL's group insurance division's major objectives was to concentrate on selling nonmedical insurance, mainly because of fear that a comprehensive national health program would strip all or part of the medical insurance premiums from GL (as well as other insurance companies). If the government took over all health insurance, GL would lose about $800 million in annual premiums and have thousands of employees whose services would not be needed. Of GL's group nonmedical products, the only one that could significantly offset this potential catastrophe is group dental. Because of this, GL (as are most major insurance companies) is very aggressive in trying to obtain group dental insurance for all companies for whom they currently provide medical insurance and to make a sales presentation to all other major companies whenever they decide they wish to purchase it.

GL's basic approach to marketing group dental is to be known as the carrier who provides the best claim service, who sees that the insured parties receive quality dental work, and whose product is competitively priced. To provide the service needed to substantiate this targeted image, GL has installed a special dental system which includes the following:

1. A network of regional claim offices around the country to handle dental claims, and only dental claims.

2. A proven computer system that pays claims accurately and on a timely basis.

3. A practicing dentist to act as a dental consultant for each office. The dentist is there as a liaison between the claims office and the dentist filing the claim and can help avoid a lot of misunderstanding.

4. The service of pretreatment review for claims over $100. After the dentist has described the work to be done, one of GL's consultants will decide if he agrees with that treatment plan and will advise both the dentist and the patient how much GL will pay for this work before any work has been performed.

5. An emphasis on preventive care with the intent of solving the problem before it becomes a big and expensive one.

6. A performance standard of processing claims without pretreatment review within five days and those with pretreatment review in ten days.

To make certain that their quality dental service system is recognized by prospective buyers and that they are getting maximum penetration in the market, GL took the following steps:

1. Lowered its profit objectives for dental insurance, but raised its sales objectives.

2. Began an intensive education of its sales force about dental insurance.

3. Provided its sales force with excellent sales promotion materials.

4. Changed its sales representatives' compensation system to make selling dental coverage significantly more profitable than selling other products.

5. Began advertising dental insurance over nationwide television during selected sports specials, such as the World Series.

Decisions That GL Must Make

After the National Telephone contracts had been awarded, GL was trying to determine if the approach taken by National Telephone's management was an aberration from the norm or a sign of things to come in the future. GL immediately sought input into the market's perception of them and their competitors. Valuable input was received from a follow-up with the broker who handled the National Telephone account (see appendix). This report told GL that certain major insurance companies had bought National's business by significantly underpricing GL. It also gave GL the broker's assessment of each of its major competitors.

After analyzing the information provided by its competitive analysis, GL was left with the following questions, the answers to which would have a tremendous effect on its future success in dental insurance:

Should GL lower its prices to the level its competitors used in obtaining National Telephone's business? Before this question can be answered, several more must be answered. Did the competitors expect to make money on the prices they charged or were they just interested in more sales? (The competitors were mutual insurance companies while GL is a stock insurance company and, therefore, much more concerned about profits.) If GL lowered their prices, would their competitors lower their prices further? Had competitors obtained all the business that they could currently handle and, therefore, didn't plan to be nearly so competitive in the next year?

Memorandum

From: J. C. Reynolds

Re: Postmortem National Telephone

I spent several hours with Bob Hill of E. F. Mutton, New York, yesterday, discussing the entire spectrum of the National Telephone dental quotations. Bob was reasonably frank during our discussions although he declined to give me many specific numbers. The salient points of our meeting follow:

To quote Bob, "If the only considerations had been National Telephone service/delivery and people, GL would have written a lot of the dental business . . ." Bob felt the GL divisions "weren't reading the newspapers" concerning the financial pinches which the National Telephone Companies were undergoing last fall and this spring. There was a lot of belt-tightening, including layoffs, and we should have sensed that cost factors would emerge as a major part of carrier determination.

Bob said that had he been us, he would have picked a few and "bought" them for down the road. We couldn't lose on this business. The mutuals obviously realized this and reacted accordingly. They made an "investment" in this business.

The Neopolitan Company could have written just about every company—they were that impressive in rate, retention, and automated/sophisticated delivery systems. They were consistently competitive, especially in rate. The Neo charged a little less than $2.00 for each claim draft. (Bob said he thought their standard charge was just about $2.00 per draft.)

The Neo people are "confident" their rates will hold up and that their approach to pricing was correct for the first year. They feel the rate components will turn around by the third year.

Neo has "regional dental offices" in Chicago (Aurora, Illinois), Detroit, Kingston, New York, and San Francisco. They plan to open offices in or around Atlanta (to serve Southern Telephone) and either Providence or maybe Springfield, Massachusetts to serve New England and the Northeast. To quote Bob again, "The Neopolitan is the biggest factor in the dental market today."

291

The Fairness Company was "mortal" low on retentions most of the time, and to a lesser degree on rates, but their claim system is "rough" and not very automated, and this hurt them. Being too low on retention also hurt their credibility in some quotes, but they still managed to write $25 million plus.

According to Bob, the Fairness Company is "always" low on big quotations no matter what the benefits. Bob is aware of our troubles on Union Department Stores and said it didn't surprise him they were chasing jumbo size cases—"they're tough on the big ones."

Gibraltor Company seemed to try harder on some quotations than others and seemed to be successful when they wanted to. The Gibraltor people admitted to being surprised by their number of successes. Gibraltor is getting quite good in their claim delivery although they're not as good as GL, "yet."

The Beta Life and Casualty was consistently high like GL—Beta's claim reputation and relations with dental societies hurt them from a general acceptance standpoint. They were never a real factor in the quotes. Beta's claim handling charge was about like ours—$3.00 plus.

The Followers Company was consistently in the middle of the pack on rate and retention but their lack of sophistication in claim handling (manual system) really hurt them. They made a "real run" at Western Bell and got it. Follower's claim handling charge is 5.5 percent of incurred claims.

Tom Jefferson Company was consistently second but nobody was terribly impressed. Their claim system is quite good, but their people didn't seem to exude much confidence in their know-how. Jefferson got so exotic on some of their funding ideas nobody could understand them.

Newark Life was "just out of it." They were either so low as to be ridiculous or way high—no credibility.

The Reds weren't really considered although they pushed hard, especially in New York. Their prices were always low, but their claim systems were poor or virtually nonexistent. They also had too much other medical coverage at National Telephone. Bob added this was another reason we could have "cleaned up" at National Telephone—we don't have much business.

It appears that most of the plans will be funded using a conventional insurance approach with deferred premium payment, along with terminal retro agreements on reserves.

Most all carriers quoted a deferred premium of *60 days plus the grace period*. Bob said we will have to go this route if we are going to compete on the big ones. *Our 30 days plus the grace period is not competitive.* The terminal retro on reserves also is a "must" in most cases. Bob said renewals are settled as if full reserves existed so carriers can't "cheat" on the size of rate increases to set up "hidden" reserves.

Generally we lost out on both rate and retention. The combination of higher going on costs (we were consistently in the upper third) and very high retentions (we were consistently the highest or in the top two or three) made it impossible for the buying carriers to justify GL even when they wanted to. In some instances our retentions were high by as much as $200,000 plus.

We were not only high on claim handling (Bob thinks we also hurt ourselves on our assumptions as to number of payments within the incurred claim figures given in the specifications—even though they tried to equate all carriers evenly), but also in our "other charges." I challenged Bob on this in view of our .5 percent risk, but he insisted other carriers (particularly the mutuals) were much lower than our charges.

A few specifics:
Western Telephone (our premium—$4,400,000): rates ranged from $6.15 to $8.75 (GL was $6.56). Retentions ranged from $369,000 to a high of $659,000. GL was at $550,000 on an "adjusted" basis as was Beta. The winning retention was less than $450,000.

Southern Telephone (GL premium—$1,600,000): Neopolitan's retention was $103,000 to our $150,000 with their premium being 20 percent below ours.

Newark Telephone (GL premium—$10,000,000): Low premium was $8 million, ours was highest. Follower's retention was $611,000 to our $816,000 (adjusted). High retention was $840,000. The net "all other" charges in the retention ranged from a low of $70,000 to a high of $180,000. The Fairness Company's retention on this one was $480,000 and too low to be believable.

Northeast Telephone (GL premium—$5,300,000): The Neopolitan's retention was $150,000 lower than our $500,000 (adjusted). Neopolitan was about 7 percent to our 9 percent. Bob said the Neo was "totally surprised" at getting Northeast Telephone.

In summary Bob said he was surprised and disappointed that we hadn't done better but the dollar differences were just too great. Bob wants to work with GL, thinks we really do know what we're doing in dental, and will support us to the extent possible. However, we have to be "in the ballpark" financially if he is to justify recommending GL—claim systems just aren't enough. I took the opportunity to reaffirm our intention of being a major factor in the dental market, financially and otherwise.

The Davenport Music Store: A Pricing Decision

Arch G. Woodside, University of South Carolina

Bill Davenport, owner and manager of the Davenport Music Company, Augusta, Georgia, recently purchased two cases (48 units) of HCC–2001, Head and Capstan Cleaner Kit for resale in his store. The kit included 2 felt pads, heading cleaning solution, and cartridge to be used to clean 8-track tape players. The product was manufactured by Becht Electronics, Burbank, California.

Bill Davenport made the following statement to his 2 salespeople in his store concerning the HCC–2001:

> All music tapes lose the oxide coating when being played, making the player dirty and harmful to tapes, so the item has real and universal utility to the owner of any 8-track player. A very small percentage (probably less than 5 percent) of tape player owners have a tape player cleaning cartridge, and these are the old abrasive type, which can scar the head and do so little for the capstan. Also, such devices do not have the selling appeal of a current hit recording, so most retail tape outlets do not offer such a device. Most outlet operators are not even aware of the need for periodic cleaning.
>
> It is normal for the user to play his unit until it becomes unusable and/or it begins to destroy expensive tapes one after another. Then, the unit is taken for repair to a shop, where it is repaired by a thorough scrubbing with a solvent.

Competition

None of the 6 competitors of the Davenport Music Store in Augusta, Georgia carried the HCC–2001 or a similar product. The competitors were visited by a "shopper" hired by Bill to buy "some type of cleaning stuff or kit" for his tape player. Two competitors knew of such devices but stated that demand was not great enough to carry them.

Product

The HCC–2001 was somewhat technically complex and its safe use was assumed to be important to a user since the product had to be connected to the tape player. The kit was mounted on cardboard, enclosed in a plastic container and had a suggested retail price of $1.98. Operating instructions were printed on one side of the cardboard.

Pricing Study

Bill Davenport expressed concern about the suggested retail price of $1.98 for the cleaning kit. The retail markup on the product was 50 per cent; his revenue was $.99 per unit sold.

Bill believed the kit was unlikely to sell in substantial numbers without active salesperson support. Bill wanted his salespeople to attempt to induce customers who had just purchased one or more tapes to make an additional purchase of the cleaning kit. However, the low price of the item did not appear to justify the time and effort to present a sales pitch to potential customers. Consequently, Bill decided to sales test different product prices in his store.

He noticed that the cleaning kit was similar in size and shape to 8-track music tapes priced between $3.00 and $5.00. He believed customers might be willing to pay a higher price for the cleaning kit since the customers might perceive the 2 products as similar.

Therefore, Bill decided to vary the price and also vary the salesperson's behavior in selling the cleaning kit. He knew from the marketing research course he had taken in college that he should randomly assign customers, each to one particular "price treatment." He decided to test 2 different selling pitches which he labeled "expert" and and "nonexpert" conditions.

Four prices were selected for testing: $1.98, $2.98, $3.98, and $5.98. Bill used this wide range of prices to ensure some significant price effects in the experiment. The complete research design is shown as Figure 18–1. He planned to use a total of 270 customers as participants in the study.

Procedure of Research Study

The salesperson attempted to induce customers who had just purchased one or more tapes to make an additional purchase of the cleaning kit. Selected customers were randomly assigned to one of the 8 treatment conditions or to the control group. Descriptions of treatments were typed and copies placed below the cash register in the store after the copies were randomly mixed. Space was available on the copies to record purchase information. Blank copies represented the control group assignment.

Customers examining 8-track tapes were selected unobtrusively as subjects in

Figure   18–1
Research Design for Cleaning Kit Study [1]
(n = Sample Size)

Price	Expertise		n
	Expert	Nonexpert	
$1.98	n = 30	n = 30	60
$2.98	n = 30	n = 30	60
$3.98	n = 30	n = 30	60
$5.98	n = 30	n = 30	60
Total	n = 120	n = 120	240

[1] Control group of n = 30 customers also used. Members of the control group were not given a sales pitch and the product was priced at $1.98.

the experiment. While a selected subject was examining the tapes, the salsperson looked at the top treatment copy under the register and administered that particular treatment. A display box containing 20 of the cleaning kits was placed near the cash register throughout the experiment. A 6 x 6-inch card appeared on the display box. The words "8-Track Tape Cleaner Kit" and the price were placed on the card. Different cards were used for the different price treatments. Prices were not listed on the cleaning kits. Purchase response was recorded immediately after the customer left the store. The copy of the treatment administered remained in its top position until the next subject was selected. The salesperson removed the previous customer's treatment copy at this time, noted the role for the new subject, changed the display card if necessary, and administered the treatment when the subject approached the cash register.

The treatments consisted of the 8 combinations of the 4 price levels and the 2 expert-nonexpert levels. A total of 30 customers was assigned to each combination and to the control group.

The salesperson asserted prior purchase of the musical tapes being bought by the customer in all treatment conditions except the control group. Levels of perceived expertise were defined as the salesperson's oral instructions on how to operate the tape cleaner versus expressed inability to operate the cleaner. Specifically, the following appeals were used:

Expert. I hope you enjoy the tapes. They are of very good quality. I have these same ones in my collection and play them often. Here is a device we have on special that will clean the dirt and tape oxide from the guides, the head, and especially the drive wheels of your tape player. You just put a few drops of this cleaner on these two pads, stick it in just like a tape, let it run for about 10 seconds while you wiggle this (pointing to head of cleaning bar). It will keep the music clear and keep the tapes from tearing up by winding up inside the player. It's only (price stated on card). Would you like one?

Nonexpert. I hope you enjoy the tapes. They are of very good quality. I have

Table   18–1
Results of Purchasing Behavior
For the Eight Treatment Groups in Percent

Price	Expertise	Purchase	No Purchase	Number of Customers
$1.98	Expert	80.0%	20.0%	30
1.98	Nonexpert	30.0	70.0	30
2.98	Expert	70.0	30.0	30
2.98	Nonexpert	36.7	63.3	30
3.98	Expert	66.7	33.3	30
3.98	Nonexpert	40.0	60.0	30
5.98	Expert	13.3	86.6	30
5.98	Nonexpert	3.3	96.7	30
1.98	Control	13.3	86.7	30

these same ones in my collection and play them often. Here is a thing we have on special that they tell me will keep your tape player clean. I don't really know how it works, but you can read the directions right here on the package as to how to use it and what it does. I never have used one, and really don't know anything about playing tapes except how to listen to them, but this thing is supposed to help the tape player a lot. It's only (price stated on card). Would you like one?

Customers in the control group did not receive any sales presentation but could purchase the product from the display box on the counter near the cash register. Any questions asked about the product by these customers were answered by the salesperson. No customer was rejected for requesting information. The salesperson responded to questions in the treatment role as required. The amount of additional information requested by the customer was recorded. Few customers requested further information.

Store policy was to accept cash, check, or charge card, and no discrimination was made for method of payment.

Results

The results for the 8 price and expertise combinations are shown in Table 18–1. Results for the control group also are shown in Table 18–1.

A total of 24 (80 percent) customers who received the expert and $1.98 price treatment purchased the product, although only 3.3 percent of those receiving the nonexpert and $5.98 treatment purchased the product. A total of 4 (13.3 percent) customers in the control group purchased the product.

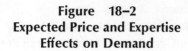

Figure   18–2
Expected Price and Expertise
Effects on Demand

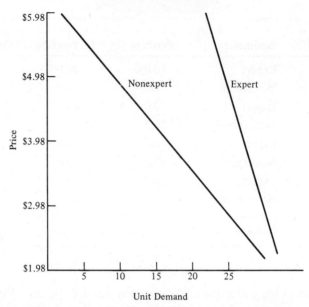

Unit Demand

The price and demand relationship for the 2 expertise conditions Bill *expected* to find are shown in Figure 18–2. He expected a shift to the right in the demand curve from the low expertise to the high expertise conditions. He also expected price to affect demand less in the high expertise versus low expertise conditions (a more vertical demand curve or a demand curve which is less elastic to price changes).

Bill wanted to know if the price changes produced much of an effect on demand. He also wanted to know if the expert sales pitch substantially increased sales compared with the nonexpert sales pitch. Looking at the data in Table 18–1, Bill thought he might set the retail price at $2.98 and offer his salespeople $.50 extra for each kit sold.

However, he first wanted to develop separate additional tables to study the effect of price alone and expertise alone on customer purchase behavior. He also wanted to graph the purchase behavior shown in Table 18–1 and compared his graph to Figure 18–2.

Discussion Questions

1. Construct a table showing purchase and nonpurchase percents for the 4 prices. Do not include the control group results.

2. Construct a table showing purchase and nonpurchase percents for the 2 expertise conditions (combine the price results for each expertise condition).

3. Graph the demand curves for the 2 expertise conditions and compare the observed results with the expected results shown in Figure 19–2.

4. What actions would you recommend to Bill Davenport? Should he price the kit at $2.98? Should the salesperson make a pitch to customers to buy the kit? If yes, what type of sales pitch?

5. What other factors should Bill Davenport consider in his evaluation of marketing the cleaning kit?

6. What general managerial implications are suggested from Bill's study?

Figure 18–3
Davenport Cleaning Cartridge

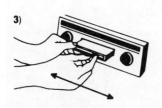

INSTRUCTIONS

1) Apply a few drops of Head Cleaning Solution to the two felt pads of the HCC-2001 Head and Capstan Cleaning Cartridge.

2) Insert Cartridge into player.

3) With a slight inward pressure, move the lever back and forth a few times.

NOTE: Extremely dirty heads may require a more positive inward pressure of the lever and longer cleaning time.

4) Remove the HCC-2001 Head and Capstan Cleaning Cartridge from player. The unit is now ready to play stereo tapes.
HCC-2001 Head and Capstan Cleaning Cartridge is the only nonabrasive cleaner, therefore it may be used as often as desired without the risk of damaging the delicate head surface. The wet felt pads safely dissolve all dirt and built up deposits from the tape head and capstan.

PATENT PENDING 222,535

 BECHT ELECTRONICS, BURBANK, CALIFORNIA

Figure 18–3 Cont'd.

Chapter 5

Channel and Distribution Strategies

Marketing channels are the activities, firms, and interactions among firms and customers in the exchange of products and services. *Activities* include the physical distribution and storage of products as well as transfer of ownership between firms and between firms and consumers. Manufacturing, wholesaling, retailing, and service firms are the major types of companies in marketing channels. Industrial users and consumers should also be considered as members of marketing channels. Verbal, nonverbal, and written communications between members of marketing channels are the *interactions* of marketing. Price, delivery, and service negotiations among manufacturers, wholesalers, retailers, and consumers are examples of interactions in marketing channels.

How firms and consumers organize and perform the activities and interactions in the exchange of products and services form the *structure of marketing channels*. For any product or service, a large number of channel structures can be used to exchange goods and services. However, a very limited number of channel structures are used for most transactions in most industries. Figure C—5–1 is an example of a channel structure for the exchange of drugs and physician services.

The flows of drugs and drug samples in Figure C—5–1 are part of the activities between firms and customers in marketing channels. The flows of money payments and credit (not shown in Figure C—5–1) are examples of financial activities.

Flows of information and word-of-mouth communication are interactions in the marketing channel of drugs and physician services. The flows of information are examples of formal communications and word-of-mouth flows are examples of informal communications between channel members.

The lines and arrows connecting the firms, customers, and services in Figure C—5–1 illustrate the structure of this marketing channel. A more complete analysis leads to the following conclusions:

    1. The most important sources of information for the physician are commer-

Figure   C—5–1

The Health Needs Environment as Perceived by the Physician

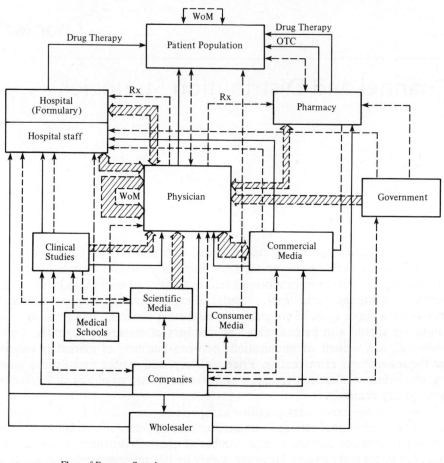

Source: Randall L. Schultz, Gerald Zaltman, and Philip C. Burger, *Cases in Marketing Research* (Hinsdale, Ill.: Dryden Press, 1975), p. 205.

cial media carrying promotion from pharmaceutical companies, and informal discussions physicians have with their colleagues.

2. Commercial media include the detailing activities of the pharmaceutical sales representative, the most effective means available for influencing physicians.

3. Word-of-mouth among physicians is particularly useful for the acceptance of new drugs.

4. With the possible exception of the patient, the pharmacy is the least influential among the several factors influencing the physician.[1]

Also notice in Figure C—5–1 that the physical flows of drugs and information
are not the same. Drugs reach the consumer (patient population) through three
intermediaries: (1) hospitals, (2) physicians, and (3) pharmacies. Information is
likely to reach the consumer through three intermediaries: (1) physicians, (2) consumer media (for example, *Consumer Reports*), television news reports, and
word-of-mouth communication from other consumers. This finding generally holds
true in most marketing channels; that is, the channel structure for product flows
are not necessarily the same as the channel structure for information flows within
the same marketing channel.

Payments for drugs and physician services are not shown in the marketing
channel in Figure C—5–1. Such payments would be likely to enlarge the structure
of the channel to include activities with insurance firms and banks. Sources of
supply also are not shown in Figure C—5–1. The study of most channel structures
focuses on part of the channel, and the student should be aware that not all of
the firms, activities, and interactions are being described. Be careful to ask yourself
if some important part of the structure should be added to complete your analysis.
However, remember that including all activities, firms, and interactions would be
difficult and unnecessarily complex.

The purposes of studying marketing channels are to increase efficiency performance and interactions between members of the channel and to satisfy customers.
Increasing efficiency includes reducing costs and increasing sales and market share
for firms in the marketing channel. Marketing channel strategies are decisions aimed
at increasing efficiency in channel structures and increasing the satisfactions of
consumers as integral members of the channel.

Basic Questions in Marketing Channel Strategy

Alternative courses of action should be developed and evaluated, and specific
actions chosen for several basic questions in marketing channel strategy. Such
questions include:

1. What are the objectives of the marketing program? Who are the ultimate
   customers?
2. How long a marketing channel is necessary to reach the ultimate customers?
3. How many firms are necessary at each channel level (channel width)?
4. What functions need to be performed between each channel level? Which
   firms will perform these functions?
5. What types of intermediary firms are available?

---

[1] Robert T. Dann and Charles D. Schewe, "Pharmatech Systems, Inc.," in Randall L.
Schultz, Gerald Zaltman, Philip C. Burger, *Cases in Marketing Research* (Hinsdale, IL:
Dryden Press, 1975); Raymond A. Bauer and Lawrence H. Wortzel, "Doctor's Choice: The
Physician and His Sources of Information About Drugs," *Journal of Marketing Research,* 3
(February 1966), pp. 40–47.

6. Are special concessions necessary to secure channel membership within existing channel structures?

7. What transportation and storage facilities are necessary?

8. What alternative flows of information, ownership, and payment are available?

9. What are the efficiencies and profits likely to be produced from each marketing channel alternative?

Figure   C—5–2

Decision Procedure for the Firm's Distribution System

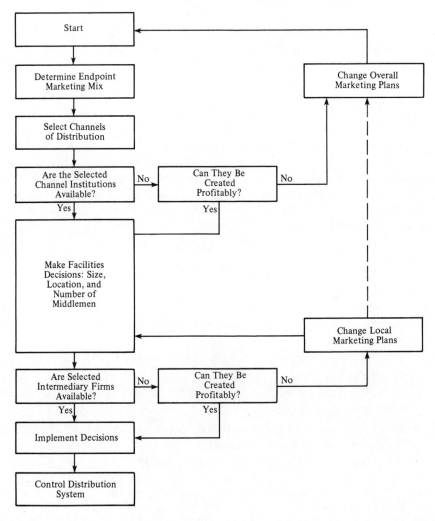

Source: David B. Montgomery and Glen L. Urban, *Management Science in Marketing,* © 1969, p. 217. Reprinted by permission of Prentice-Hall, Inc., Englewood Cliffs, New Jersey.

The first of these questions is the most basic. Marketing channel strategy is one of the marketing mix decisions of the firm. The financial resources necessary for a specific marketing channel depend on decisions related to price, promotion, and product features. The decision to price a new line of cosmetics in a low range to reach the young, single, working woman is likely to lead to a different marketing channel strategy compared with a high price range to reach the older, married housewife. The younger woman may need less assistance in learning how to use the product, less product variety, and, consequently, less (or no) sales clerk assistance. Thus, drugstores might be included in the marketing channel to reach the young woman and department stores may be necessary to reach the older woman. The important point is that the selection of a market target, price, product attributes, and promotion strategy are likely to interact and affect several marketing channel decisions.

Figure C—5–2 includes several basic questions in the development of a marketing channel strategy. Notice in Figure C—5–2 that alternative channels of distribution are selected for evaluation and action only after the endpoint (which is the market segment) and the marketing mix are evaluated. Sometimes, the selected channel institution may be unavailable. Given this situation, the firm would ask if such channel institutions can be created profitably. If not, a change in the overall marketing plan will be necessary.

Figure C—5–2 should serve as an example of the development of marketing channel strategy. Notice that the strategy chosen is affected by the answers to questions in a "network of processing rules." Thus, marketing channel strategies can be studied by the paths of decision choices available and chosen, available and not chosen, and unavailable to the firm. The questions in the rectangles in Figure C—5–2 are the processing rules, and the answers to the questions and connections between the rectangles form the network of the marketing channel strategy. Each of the processing rules and segments of the network may be divided into multiple steps to study details of the strategy. An example of this analysis is provided later in this chapter for a decision to change price in a marketing channel.

Length and Width of Marketing Channels

The length and width of marketing channels refer to the number of levels (length) and the number of firms at each level (width). Several basic questions of marketing strategy are concerned with channel length and width. Examples of 6 types of lengths of marketing channels to consumers and 4 types of industrial users are shown in Figure C—5–3.

The choice of channel length depends on the service requirements of the customer, perishability of the product, per unit value, financial resources of the firm, local customs, strength of existing channel structure to encourage and prevent channel use, order size, and several other factors (for example, management ability). Several criteria have been proposed to describe the relationship of these factors with channel length.

1. The greater the customer service requirements, the shorter the length of the marketing channel.

Figure C—5–3

Distribution Channel Alternatives

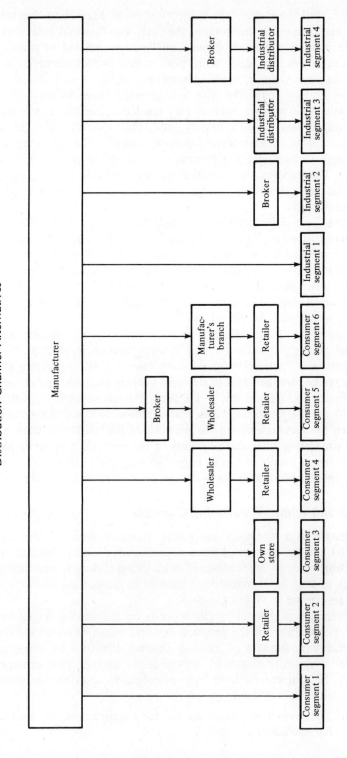

2. The greater the financial resources of the firm, the shorter the length of the marketing channel.

3. The greater the per unit value, the shorter the length of the marketing channel.

4. The larger the customer order size, the shorter the length of the marketing channel.

Manufacturer direct to consumer is an example of a very short marketing channel. Manufacturer to broker to wholesaler to wholesaler to retailer to consumer is an example of a long marketing channel.[2]

The length of the marketing channel selected also depends on the degree of market exposure desired. Although market exposure is a matter of degree, three basic levels of market exposure are usually evaluated:

1. *Intensive distribution*—marketing the product through any and every responsible wholesaler and retailer who will sell the product. A producer of convenience goods and industrial supplies would use intensive distribution.

2. *Selective distribution*—limited selection of intermediaries who agree to specific channel arrangements. A producer of shopping and specialty goods would use selective distribution.

3. *Exclusive distribution*—the choice of only one intermediary per geographic area. A producer of shopping and specialty goods, often desiring status or a unique image for its products would use exclusive distribution.

The desire for widespread distribution (for example, for *Playboy* and *Time* magazines) produces a need for an intensive distribution strategy. Otherwise, the effort needed to reach all desired retail outlets would be overwhelming. Assuming that each magazine publisher created 100 distribution branches and each branch serviced 300 regional centers and each regional center serviced 500 retail outlets, a total of 1,500,000 retail outlets would stock the magazines (this would include nearly all the retail stores in the United States)! Thus, the *major advantage of channel intermediaries* for the manufacturer and wholesaler is to reduce the number of transactions and, consequently, the cost of servicing larger number of customers.

Types of Intermediary Firms and Functions Performed

Intermediary firms are most often categorized into two main groups: wholesalers and retailers. Each group is further categorized according to their functions and the products they buy and sell.

Retailers are firms primarily engaged in transactions with ultimate consumers. Retail firms may be grouped into 11 major types as shown in Table C—5–1. Eating and drinking places are the largest group of retail stores in number of establishments (359,524 in 1972 and growing rapidly), and food stores have the largest percentage of total retail sales (21.9 percent in 1972 and decreasing).

---

[2] Based on local custom, this long channel is quite common in Japan as reported by William D. Hartley, "Cumbersome Japanese Distribution System Stumps U.S. Concerns," *Wall Street Journal* (March 2, 1972), pp. 1–12.

Table   C—5–1
Retail Trade by Type of Operation

Type of Operation	Number of Establishments	Sales (billions)	Percentage of Total Sales
Building Materials, hardware, garden supply, and mobile home dealers	83,842	23.8	5.2
General merchandise	56,245	65.1	14.2
Department stores	7,742	51.1	11.1
Variety stores	21,852	7.3	1.6
Other	26,651	6.7	1.5
Food stores	267,352	100.7	21.9
Automobile dealers	121,369	90.0	19.6
Gasoline service stations	226,459	33.7	7.3
Apparel and accessory stores	129,201	24.7	5.4
Furniture, home furnishings, and equipment stores	116,857	22.5	4.9
Eating and drinking places	359,524	36.9	8.0
Drugstores and proprietary stores	51,542	15.6	3.4
Other retailers*	338,359	34.4	7.5
Nonstore retailers	162,121	11.6	2.5
Mail-order houses	7,982	4.6	1.0
Automatic merchandising machine operators	12,845	3.0	0.7
Direct selling	141,294	4.0	0.9
Total retail trade	1,912,871	459.0	100.0

* Includes liquor, jewelry, and sporting goods stores, florists, etc.
Source: U. S. Bureau of the Census, *Census of Retail Trade,* 1972, *Establishment and Firm Size* (Washington, D. C.: U. S. Government Printing Office, 1976), pp. 1–8–1–36.

Some knowledge of the usual level of activities provided by each type of retail firm is needed to develop a marketing channel strategy. Walters has provided a summary of 16 activities performed and not performed by 13 types of retailers. This summary is shown in Table C—5–2.

Reading across the row for a particular activity provides insights into retail support likely to be received from specific types of retailers. For example, although department stores would likely support a marketing channel for clothing with heavy advertising, a clothing shop would not.

Reading down the column for a particular retail type you can see the strengths and weaknesses of the store. For example, department stores provide high levels of service across all activities whereas discount houses provide more selected levels of service activities. Thus, discount houses are more likely to be used for selected product categories and department stores would more likely be used for a wide range of products.

Wholesaling middlemen can be divided into two major categories: merchant middlemen and agent middlemen. *Merchant middlemen* take title (that is, legal ownership) to the goods whereas agent middlemen do not take title to but *might* take possession of the goods. Figure C—5–4 is a chart showing the different kinds of wholesaling intermediaries.

As shown in the figure, merchant middlemen are divided into 2 major categories: full function (or service) and limited function. Full function wholesalers provide a full range of services including (1) *carrying* a full stock and range of product lines, (2) performing the functions of *selling, handling,* and *delivery,* and (3) providing *credit* services to the trade.

Full-function wholesalers can be further classified as either *general merchandise, general line,* or *specialty* wholesalers. General merchandise wholesalers carry several unrelated product lines, such as food products, furniture, jewelry, and paper products. The assortment of lines is generally dependent upon the nature of the wholesaler's customers, for example, country stores. General line wholesalers are more specialized than general merchandise wholesalers. They tend to build a deep assortment of goods of related product lines, such as hardware (screwdrivers, hammers). Specialty wholesalers are further specialized in the products they carry. Their narrow assortment might include only springs, mattresses, and bedframes, and not all forms of household furniture, for example.

Limited-function wholesalers also take title (as does every merchant middleman), but perform only a few of the functions and services that full-function wholesalers do. The six limited-function wholesalers perform only those functions listed in Table C—5–3.

The primary functions provided by each limited-function wholesaler are the following:

1. *Cash and carry*—carries a limited line (mostly staples and fast-moving items), almost never extends to buyers, but instead, deals on a cash basis, has low risk and low investment, does not deliver, and tends to call on small firms.

2. *Drop shipper*—also known as "desk jobber," sells for direct delivery by producer to purchaser, mostly found in trades where goods are bulky; neither handles nor stores goods.

3. *Wagon or truck distribution*—performs sales and delivery functions simultaneously, carries limited assortment of fast-moving items of either a perishable or semi-perishable nature, and thus can reduce retailers' losses due to spoilage.

4. *Mail-order wholesaler*—performs selling functions by mail only.

5. *Producers' cooperatives*—provides large number of functions, emphasizes in particular the sorting function which provides higher-quality goods to consumers, also brands and promotes brand name; found in agricultural commodities, for example, California Fruit Growers Exchange.

6. *Rack jobber*—services small chain and independent grocers with nonfood items such as housewares, toiletries, and other products literally placed on in-store racks and displays; delivers and is usually paid by cash at

Table C—5—2
Important Activities of Some Major Retailer Types

	Department Store	Discount House	Supermarket	Variety Store	Specialty Stores Furniture	Convenience Grocery	Drug	Clothing Shop	Shoe Store	Auto Dealer	Gas Station	Jewelry Store	Hardware Store
Advertising	heavy	heavy	heavy	light	moderate	light	heavy	light	light	heavy	light	moderate	light
Personal Attention	yes	no	no	yes	yes	no	yes	yes	yes	yes	yes	yes	yes
Delivery	yes	varies	no	no	yes	yes	some	yes	no	yes	no	no	no
Width of Line	wide	wide	wide	wide	narrow	wide	narrow	narrow	narrow	narrow	narrow	narrow	wide
Product Quality	good	low	good	low	mixed	good	good	vary	vary	good	good	good	vary
Price	moderate	mixed and low	low	medium and low	mixed	mixed	high	vary	vary	high	vary	vary	vary
Special Service	yes	no	no	no	yes	some	no	vary	vary	yes	yes	yes	vary
Integrated	yes	yes	vary	yes	varies	yes	no	no	no	no	no	no	no
Customer Attention	yes	no	no	some	yes	some	no	yes	vary	yes	yes	yes	no
Warranty	yes	yes	yes	yes	yes	yes	yes	yes	yes	yes	yes	yes	yes
Parking	yes	yes	yes	no	yes	yes	yes	no	vary	yes	yes	no	vary
Fancy Fixtures	yes	no	no	no	mixed	yes	no	yes	vary	yes	yes	yes	no

	Department Store	Discount House	Supermarket	Variety Store	Specialty Stores Furniture	Convenience Grocery	Drug	Clothing Shop	Shoe Store	Auto Dealer	Gas Station	Jewelry Store	Hardware Store
Multiunit	yes	yes	yes	yes	some-times	often	yes	some	some	no	vary	vary	vary
Sales reps	yes	some	no	yes	yes	some	no	yes	vary	yes	yes	yes	no
Credit	yes	no	no	no	yes	yes	no	varies	no	yes	yes	yes	no
Location	central	central	area	central	central	area	neighbor-hood	area	area	central	neighbor-hood	central	area

Source. C. Glenn Walters, *Marketing Channels* (Santa Monica, CA.: Gooodyear Publishing Company, 1977), p. 124.

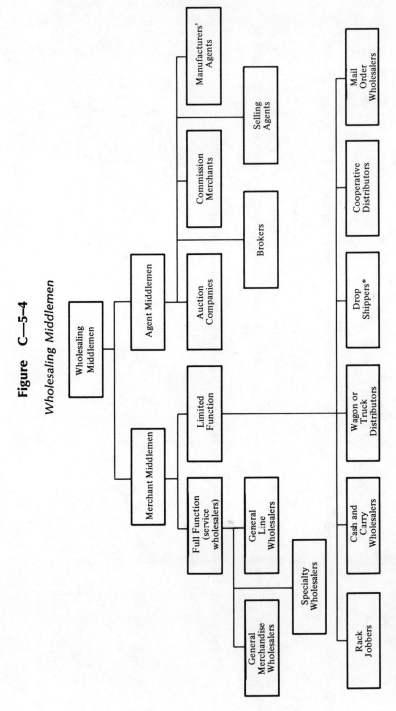

Figure C—5-4

Wholesaling Middlemen

Wholesaling Middlemen

Agent Middlemen

Merchant Middlemen

Manufacturers' Agents

Selling Agents

Commission Merchants

Brokers

Auction Companies

Limited Function

Full Function (service wholesalers)

General Line Wholesalers

Specialty Wholesalers

General Merchandise Wholesalers

Rack Jobbers

Cash and Carry Wholesalers

Wagon or Truck Distributors

Drop Shippers*

Cooperative Distributors

Mail Order Wholesalers

*Desk jobbers, or direct mill shippers.

Table   C—5–3
Functions provided by limited-function merchant wholesalers

	Limited-function or limited-service merchant wholesalers					
	Cash-and carry	Drop shipper (desk jobber)	Wagon or truck	Mail-order	Coopera-tives	Rack jobbers
Functions for customer						
Anticipates needs	X		X	X	X	X
Regroups goods (one or more of four steps)	X		X	X	X	X
Carries stocks	X		X	X	X	X
Delivers goods			X		X	X
Grants credit		X	maybe	maybe	maybe	consign-ment on some cases)
Provides information and advisory services		X	some	some	X	
Provides buying function		X	X	X	some	X
Owns and transfers title to goods	X	X	X	X	X	X
Functions for producers						
Provides producer's selling function	X	X	X	X	X	X
Stores inventory	X		X	X	X	X
Helps finance by owning stocks	X		X	X	X	X
Reduces credit risk	X	X	X	X	X	X
Provides market information	X	X	some	X	X	some

Source: E. Jerome McCarthy, *Basic Marketing: A Managerial Approach* (Homewood, Ill.: Richard D. Irwin, 1975), p. 351. Reprinted by permission of the publisher.

delivery; saves retailer from frequent reordering and maintenance of displays.[3]

The second major category of wholesaling middlemen is agent middlemen. Agent middlemen, as previously noted, do *not* take title although in some circumstances may facilitate title transfer. The functions of the five major agents and brokers are summarized in Table C—5–4. Although auction companies sometimes

---

[3] Jerome McCarthy, *Basic Marketing: A Managerial Approach* (Homewood, IL: Richard D. Irwin, 1975), p. 350–353. Reprinted by permission of the publisher.

carry inventory, their main activities are facilitating exchanges between buyers and sellers by providing a meeting place for both. Brokers do not provide a central meeting place but serve to locate buyers and sellers. Brokers receive a commission for providing this market information.

Commission merchants often are used for agricultural marketing channels. They often are used in livestock and grain sales. They handle the goods and are usually permitted to sell goods at the market price or a price above a stipulated minimum.

Manufacturers' agents usually work for 3 to 15 manufacturers as a sales person for each. This agent sells noncompeting product lines and recceives a 2 to 15 percent commission. The manufacturers' agent will travel to several cities, states, or provinces with product samples. Orders received by the agent are sent directly by the manufacturer to the buyer.

Selling agents have more authority than manufacturers' agents. Selling agents market the entire output of one or more producers and have almost complete control of pricing, service, and advertising decisions. Small manufacturing firms with financial problems often call upon selling agents to provide working capital

Table   C—5–4
Functions of agents and brokers

Functions	Auction companies	Brokers	Commission merchants	Manufacturers agents	Selling agents
Functions for customers					
Anticipates needs		some		sometimes	
Regroups goods (one or more of four stages)	X		X	some	
Carries stocks	sometimes		X	sometimes	
Delivers goods			X	sometimes	
Grants credit	some		sometimes		X
Provides information and advisory services		X	X	X	X
Provides buying function	X	some	X	X	X
Owns and transfers title to goods	transfers only		transfers only		
For producer					
Provides selling function	X	some	X	X	X
Stores inventory	X		X	sometimes	
Helps finance by owning stocks					
Reduces credit risk	some				X
Provides market information		X	X	X	X

and marketing expertise. Selling agents usually demand control of the marketing activities of the firm as a price for these services.

The relative size of wholesaling firms by number of establishments and sales are shown in Table C—5–5. Merchant wholesalers, full and limited function, comprise over 70 percent of these wholesale establishments and 50.9 percent of the total sales. Manufacturers' sales branches and offices are business entities owned solely by the manufacturer, and they comprise 36.8 percent of total sales. Although there are only 32,620 agents and brokers in the United States, they represent sales of 12.3 percent of $695.2 billion.

In comparing Tables C—5–1 and C—5–5, notice that total retail sales are less although the number of retail operations is 5 times greater than total wholesale sales and number, respectively. Thus, the average size retail operation is much smaller than the average size wholesale operation, and products are likely to be involved in more than one transaction at the wholesale level before reaching the retail level.

Industrial Distributors

The industrial distributor is a specific type of agent middleman selling primarily to manufacturers. The industrial distributor stocks the product he sells; has at least one outside salesperson as well as an inside telephone and/or counter salesperson; and performs a broad variety of marketing channel functions, including customer contact, credit, stocking, delivery, and providing a full product assortment.

There are three type of industrial distributors. *General-line distributors,* or "mill supply houses," stock a broad range of products and are often referred to as "the supermarket of industry." *Specialists firms* carry a narrow line of related products, such as bearings, power transmission equipment and supplies, and abrasives and cutting tools. The *combination house* is engaged in other forms of wholesaling in addition to industrial distribution, such as, an electrical distributor who sells to the construction firms and manufacturers, as well as to retailers and institutions.[4]

---

[4] Frederick E. Webster, Jr., "The Role of the Industrial Distributor in Marketing Strategy," *Journal of Marketing,* **40** (July 1976) pp. 10–16. Published by the American Marketing Association.

Table   C—5–5
Wholesale Trade by Type of Operation

Type of Operation	Number of Establishments	Sales (billions)	Percentage of Total Sales
Merchant wholesalers	289,974	$353.9	50.9
Manufacturers' sales branches and offices	47,197	255.7	36.8
Agents and brokers	32,620	85.6	12.3
Total wholesale trade	369,791	$695.2	100.0

Source: 1972 Census of Wholesale Trade, Establishment Size and Firm Data (Washington, D.C.: Government Printing Office, 1976).

Total volume of sales through industrial distributors was estimated at $23.5 billion for 1974.[5] A reasonable estimate of the total number of industrial distributors is 11,000–12,000, with the average firm having a sales volume of around $2 million.[6]

Webster identifies several issues which might result in conflict between industrial distributors and their suppliers.[7] The following conflicts might result:

1. A large customer of an industrial distributor may demand to deal directly with an industrial distributor's supplier to gain price concessions. Usually such a customer does receive some price concessions and the industrial distributor receives a reduced commission.

2. The industrial distributor often lacks growth motivation after reaching a comfortable sales volume. This represents the need for increased cooperation between the supplier and distributor.

3. The supplier and distributor often disagree over the necessary level of inventory at the distributor level. Solution: the manufacturer may find it necessary to finance distributor inventory by delaying billings, selling on consignment (payment received by producer when goods are sold by the distributor), or by providing cash loans.

4. Most distributors want a second product line to either have a broader price range or to get a wider variety of product types. Manufacturers cannot legally prohibit their distributors from carrying competing product lines. Solution: manufacturers can make major investments in distributor training programs and product line expansions.

5. Overlapping territories among distributors can produce conflicts over customers. This can, in fact, be the conscious intention of the supplier if he determines that different distributors have varying strengths in different market segments.

Channel Conflict

As implied in the discussion on industrial distributors, some amount of conflict is inevitable in marketing channels. *Channel conflict* is a situation in which one channel member perceives another channel member to be engaged in behavior that prevents or impedes the first channel member from achieving his goals. Channel conflict is a state of frustration brought about by a restriction of role performance.[8]

Does conflict have a negative, positive, or no effect on channel efficiency? Unfortunately, there is little empirical evidence currently to determine what effect channel conflict actually has. This issue remains to be settled. Rosenbloom has suggested that low levels of conflict are likely to be unrelated to channel efficiency

---

[5] *Industrial Distribution*, March 1975, pp. 31–38.
[6] Webster, *op. cit.*, p. 11.
[7] Ibid., pp. 14–15.
[8] Louis W. Stern and Adel I. El-Ansary, *Marketing Channels* (Englewood Cliffs, NJ: Prentice-Hall, 1977); J. Taylor Sims, J. Robert Foster, and Arch G. Woodside, *Marketing Channels* (New York: Harper & Row, 1977).

Figure C—5–5

Conflict and Channel Efficiency–General Curve.

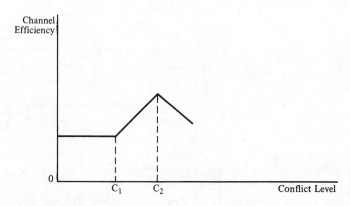

Source: Bert Rosenbloom, "Conflict and Channel Efficiency: Some Conceptual Models for the Decision Maker," *Journal of Marketing* (July 1973), pp. 26–30. Published by the American Marketing Association.

as shown in Figure C—5–5. Conflict within the range of OC_1 produces no effect on channel efficiency.

Over the range C_1 C_2, the effect of conflict is positive; although beyond C_2, the effect is negative. Conflict, then, is inherent in a marketing channel, and members of the channel need to recognize the need to manage conflict to increase channel efficiency.

The following marketing channel strategy for a price change decision includes examples of channel conflict and channel resolution built into the strategy.

Marketing Channel Strategy for a Price Decision

A specific channel strategy, processing rules to be answered by a decision maker (DM) and a district sales office, (DSO) is shown in Figure C—5–6. The strategy is based on watching the wholesale price of competitor i in the local market (l). If i does not change his price from our own product's price (P_{wslt}) in the present time period (t), we continue to watch i. If i increases his price (box 3 to box 4), the DSO is asked if our price should be increased (box 4). If yes, we increase our price (box 5) to match the price of i. If DSO says no, we go to box 6 and ask if the DM believes our price should be increased; if yes, there is a conflict between the DSO and DM over whether to increase price. In this case, the conflict is resolved by increasing the price.

Notice in Figure C—5–6 that the decision to increase price to match the competitor's wholesale price is less complicated than the decision to decrease price. The reason for this strategy is, in part, the likely increase in revenue resulting from a price increase if customers find it difficult to buy at the old price. Price decreases are more complicated and may take more time because of the threat to profits if demand does not increase to cover the potential loss in revenue. The DM has

Figure   C—5–6

Model I, Mark XI, Revised. A Binary Flow-Chart Depicting the Price Decision Process. Region W. Division W.

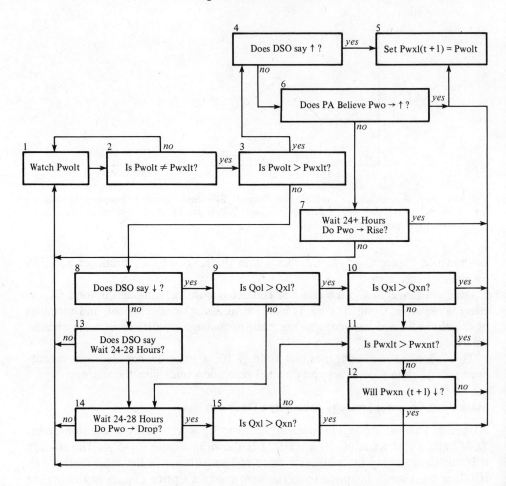

Symbols

P	— Price	t	— Time, at present	PA	— Price Analyst
r	— Retail	(t + 1)	— Time, subsequent to considering price change	=	— Is equal to
w	— Wholesale			≠	— is not equal to; or, is different from
x	— Our company	Q	— Quantity		
o→	— Other major competitors in local market	l	— Local market, wherein price change is being considered	>	— Is greater than
o	— Other major competitor initiator	n	— Nearby market with funnel influences	↑	— Raise price
				↓	— Drop price
		DSO	— District Sales Office (district sales manger)		

Source: William M. Morgenroth, "A Method for Understanding Price Determinants," *Journal of Marketing Research* **1, 3** (August 1964), p. 19. Published by the American Marketing Association.

some desire to prevent a price war between channels or at least contain price reductions to one local market.

Such marketing channel strategies can be developed to describe the decision processes at each level and between levels of marketing channels. Unfortunately, a limited amount of research is available on such strategies to help answer the basic questions of marketing channel management.

Vertical Marketing Systems

To increase channel efficiencies and manage channel conflicts, 3 types of vertical marketing systems have evolved. Vertical marketing systems (*VMSs*) are professionally managed and centrally programmed networks, preengineered to achieve operating economies and maximum sales impact. VMSs produce economies of scale through their size and elimination of duplicated services. The 3 types of *VMSs* include:

1. *Corporate vertical marketing system*—single ownership of each stage of the marketing channel, for example, Hart, Schaffner and Marx owns a retail chain of over 200 men's clothing stores.

2. *Administered vertical marketing system*—coordination of the marketing channel by a firm exercising economic and "political" power. Such a firm is often referred to as the "channel captain." Kodak Company obtains substantial shelf space, promotional support, and favorable retail word-of-mouth advertising from its retailers because of the trade discounts and turnover provided by its cameras and film.

3. *Contractual vertical marketing systems*—the most significant form of *VMSs* accounting for 40 percent of all retail sales. The franchise, wholesale-sponsored voluntary chain, and retail cooperative are examples of contractual *VMSs*. A franchise is an agreement whereby dealers (*franchises*) agree to meet the operating requirements of a manufacturer or other *franchisor*. The dealer typically receives a variety of marketing, management, technical, and financial services in exchange for a specified fee.[9] The soft-drink industry and most fast-food chains, for example, McDonald's, are examples of retail franchises.

The wholesaler-sponsored voluntary chain is a contractual *VMS* between a wholesaler and a group of retailers whereby the retailers agree to use a common name, have standardized facilities, and purchase the wholesaler's products. IGA Food Stores, with 5,000 retail stores, is an example of one of the largest wholesaler-sponsored, voluntary chains.

The retail cooperative is established by a group of retailers who set up a wholesaling operation to increase channel efficiencies, for example, purchase products in large lots at reduced prices. The retail members can also choose to use a common name, develop their own private brands, and use cooperative advertising.

---

[9] Louis E. Boone and David L. Kurtz, *Foundations of Marketing Channels* (Hinsdale, IL: Dryden Press, 1977), p. 239.

Physical Distribution Decisions

At the present time, the average manufacturer spends about 13 percent of every sales dollar on physical distribution.[10] Physical distribution costs average 25 percent of the cost of goods in inventory for wholesalers and retailers. These costs include transportation (.5 percent), handling and distribution (2.5 percent), taxes (.5 percent), storage facilities (.25 percent), insurance (.25 percent), depreciation (5.0 percent), interest (6.0 percent), and obsolescence (10.0 percent.)[11] Thus, physical distribution costs emphasize the importance of developing a physical distribution system.

Physical distribution costs may be grouped into 3 categories: (1) inventory holding, (2) inventory ordering, and (3) stockout. Details of these costs are shown in Figure C—5-7. There are several tradeoffs among the costs shown in the figure. For example, increases in product inventory (increasing inventory holding cost) will likely decrease stockout costs and decrease inventory ordering and transportation costs.

The tradeoff between inventory carrying cost per unit and order cost (including transportation costs) per unit is shown graphically in Figure C—5-8. Inventory carrying cost per unit (I) increases at an increasing rate with increases in quantity ordered (Q). Order processing cost per unit (S) decreases at a decreasing rate with increases in Q. Total cost of an order quantity is equal to the combination of I and S as shown in the following equation:

$$TC(Q) = \frac{D}{S}Q + IC\frac{Q}{2}$$

where $TC(Q)$ = total cost of order quantity Q
D = annual demand in units
S = order cost per unit
I = annual inventory carrying cost as a percent of C
C = value of a unit held in inventory (unit price in dollars).

For example, if D is equal to 2,000 units per year, I is equal to 10 percent, S equals \$10, and C equals \$5, then TC (Q) equals \$20,025 for 100 units per order.

$$TC(Q) = \frac{2,000}{100}(10) + 0.10(5)\frac{100}{2} = \$225.$$

Computer simulations and standardized formulas have been developed to determine optimum order quantities. Estimating annual demand in units (D) through the channel system poses one of the most substantial problems in managing physical distribution systems. One example of the changes in inventory caused by a 10 percent increase in retailers' orders from customers is described by Forrester and shown in Figure C—5-9.

---

[10] Stephen B. Oresman and Charles D. Scudder, "A Remedy for Maldistribution," *Business Horizons* (June 1974), p. 61.

[11] L. P. Alford and John R. Bangs (eds.), *Production Handbook* (New York: Ronald Press Company, 1955), pp. 396–97.

Figure   C—5–7

Tradeoffs Typically Found in Managing and Controlling Inventory Levels

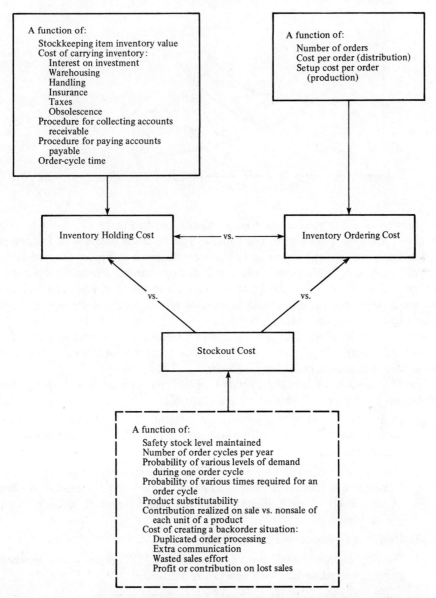

Source: James L. Heskett, Nicholas A. Glaskowsky, Jr., and Robert M. Ivie, *Business Logistics,* 2nd ed. (New York: The Ronald Press, 1973), p. 313.

The 10 percent increase in retailers' orders from customers is likely to produce a greater increase initially in retailers' orders to distributors (up to 28 percent as shown in Figure C—5–9). Consequent distributors' orders to factory warehouses

Figure   C—5–8

Tradeoffs Between Inventory Carrying Cost per Unit and Order Cost per Unit

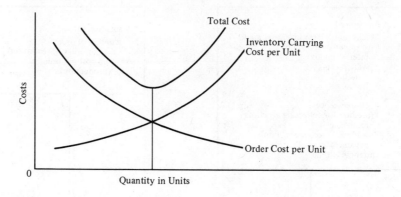

are likely to increase even more (up to 40 percent in Figure C—5–9) and then decrease (down by 3 percent in the figure). The resulting changes in factory production likely will change the most (52 percent increase in Figure C—5–9). Such data of retail and distributors' orders and factory output illustrate the need to monitor and adjust the physical flows of products in the marketing channel to reduce unnecessary costs and maintain acceptable service levels. A strategy to control the physical distribution system is needed.

Perreault and Russ delineated 15 elements to evaluate in developing a physical distribution system. These elements and the basic strategy of physical distribution management are shown in Figure C—5–10.

Figure C. 5–10 is a schematic overview of the management process for physical distribution service (*PDS*). Six steps are outlined.

1. *Define important PDS elements.* A total of 15 are shown and costs for each would be computed from in-house data and estimates of salespersons and channel members.

2. *Determine customers' viewpoints.* The stated importance of each element to customers (obtained from interviews), competitive potential of changing the levels of each element, and the relative cost of making changes are measured.

3. *Design a competitive PDS package.*

4. *Develop a promotional program to sell the PDS to the entire marketing channel including our own marketing personnel.*

5. *Market test the PDS package and promotional program.*

6. *Establish performance controls.*[12]

---

[12] William D. Perreault, Jr. and Frederick Russ, "Physical Distribution Service: A Neglected Aspect of Marketing Management," *MSU Business Topics,* **22** (Summer 1974), pp. 37–45. Reprinted by permission of the publisher, Division of Research, Graduate School of Business Administration, Michigan State University.

Figure C—5—9

Simulated Production Distribution System Response to a Sudden 10 per cent Increase in Sales at the Retail Level.

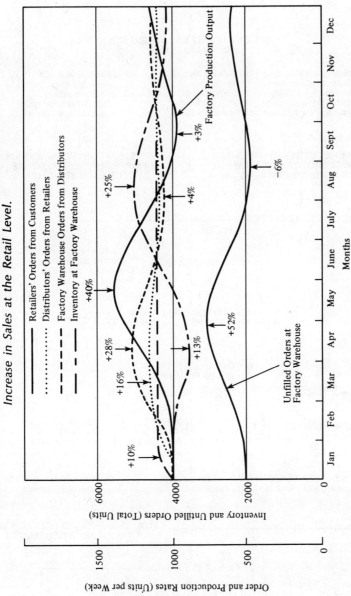

Retailers' Orders from Customers
Distributors' Orders from Retailers
Factory Warehouse Orders from Distributors
Inventory at Factory Warehouse

+10%

+16%

+28%

+40%

+25%

+3%

+4%

+13%

Factory Production Output

−6%

+52%

Unfilled Orders at Factory Warehouse

Inventory and Unfilled Orders (Total Units)

Order and Production Rates (Units per Week)

Months

Weeks

Figure   C—5–10

Schematic Overview of the Management Process for Physical Distribution Service (PDS)

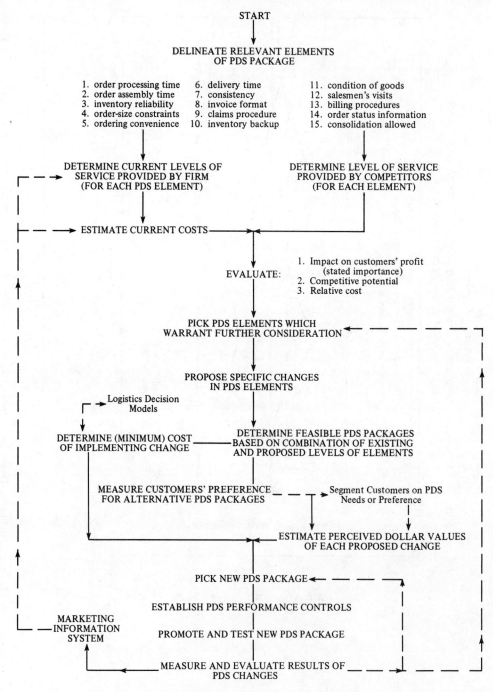

START

DELINEATE RELEVANT ELEMENTS
OF PDS PACKAGE

1. order processing time	6. delivery time	11. condition of goods
2. order assembly time	7. consistency	12. salesmen's visits
3. inventory reliability	8. invoice format	13. billing procedures
4. order-size constraints	9. claims procedure	14. order status information
5. ordering convenience	10. inventory backup	15. consolidation allowed

DETERMINE CURRENT LEVELS OF
SERVICE PROVIDED BY FIRM
(FOR EACH PDS ELEMENT)

DETERMINE LEVEL OF SERVICE
PROVIDED BY COMPETITORS
(FOR EACH ELEMENT)

ESTIMATE CURRENT COSTS

EVALUATE:

1. Impact on customers' profit
   (stated importance)
2. Competitive potential
3. Relative cost

PICK PDS ELEMENTS WHICH
WARRANT FURTHER CONSIDERATION

PROPOSE SPECIFIC CHANGES
IN PDS ELEMENTS

Logistics Decision
Models

DETERMINE (MINIMUM) COST
OF IMPLEMENTING CHANGE

DETERMINE FEASIBLE PDS PACKAGES
BASED ON COMBINATION OF EXISTING
AND PROPOSED LEVELS OF ELEMENTS

MEASURE CUSTOMERS' PREFERENCE
FOR ALTERNATIVE PDS PACKAGES

Segment Customers on PDS
Needs or Preference

ESTIMATE PERCEIVED DOLLAR VALUES
OF EACH PROPOSED CHANGE

PICK NEW PDS PACKAGE

ESTABLISH PDS PERFORMANCE CONTROLS

MARKETING
INFORMATION
SYSTEM

PROMOTE AND TEST NEW PDS PACKAGE

MEASURE AND EVALUATE RESULTS OF
PDS CHANGES

Source: William D. Perreault, Jr. and Frederick A. Russ, "Physical Distribution Service:
A Neglected Aspect of Marketing Management," p. 40, *MSU Business Topics,* Summer 1974.
Reprinted by permission of the publisher, Division of Research, Graduate School of Business
Administration, Michigan State University.

These six steps and the overview in Figure C—5–10 emphasize the need for systematic planning in developing physical distribution systems. This approach requires a marketing research program to measure channel members' perceptions at each level in the channel.

Summary

This chapter is intended as an overview to the structures, functions, and strategies of marketing channels. *Marketing channels* have been defined to include activities, firms, and interactions among firms and customers in the exchange of products and services. How firms and customers organize and perform the activities and interactions in the exchange of products and services form the *structure* of marketing channels. Specific marketing channels may involve different physical flows of products, financial flows, and information flows between firms and customers.

Nine basic questions in marketing channel strategy are identified. Several of these were analyzed in this chapter. The most important question includes idenification of the firm's marketing objectives and ultimate customers.

Figure C—5–2 provides a general framework for developing a marketing channel strategy. The decision processing rules in Figure C—5–2 are directly related to the basic questions of marketing channel management.

The number of firms, sales volumes, and activities performed among several types of retail and wholesale firms are analyzed in this chapter. Such analysis provides helpful input in developing and choosing alternative channel structures.

Channel conflict is an inherent part of marketing channels. The causes of channel conflict should be determined and conflict should be managed to increase channel efficiencies. Three types of vertical marketing systems (*VMSs*) have been developed to increase channel efficiencies and manage channel conflicts.

Physical distribution strategy is an integral part of managing marketing channels. Such strategy includes an analysis of tradeoffs between inventory holding cost, inventory ordering cost, and stockout cost. Physical distribution strategy involves multiple stages of delineating and evaluating elements of physical distribution services.

Discussion Questions

1. Define marketing channels. Distinguish between activities and interactions.

2. Diagram the marketing channel for a used college textbook. Include information flows, word-of-mouth communication, and physical flows.

3. Which basic questions in marketing channel strategy are analyzed in this chapter? Which are not discussed?

4. What are processing rules? Provide two connected examples.

5. What is the major advantage provided by channel intermediaries for the manufacturer?

6. Distinguish between selling agents and manufacturer's agents.

7. Distinguish between agents/brokers and merchant wholesalers.

8. Using the information in Table C—5–2, which type of retail store would you recommend for nylon stockings for the young woman desiring a low price, durability, and a "sheer look." Why?

9. What is a *VMS*? What types of *VMSs* exist in marketing channels?

10. Define marketing channel efficiency.

11. Draw vertical lines in Figure C—5–9 for 0, 10, and 20 weeks. Calculate retailers' orders from customers, distributors' orders from retailers, factory warehouse orders from distributors, inventory at factory warehouse and unfilled orders at factory warehouse at 0, 10, and 20 weeks. Construct a table showing your data. Provide five conclusions to your analysis.

12. Calculate TC (Q) for $Q = 50$, 150, 200, 400, and 600 using the cost information given in the text. Provide 2 conclusions from your calculations.

Readings

Johan Arndt, "Temporal Lags in Comparative Retailing," *Journal of Marketing* (October 1972), p. 40–45.

Louis P. Bucklin, "A Theory of Channel Control," *Journal of Marketing* (January 1973), p. 39–47.

Adel I. El-Ansary and Robert A. Robicheaux, "A Theory of Channel Control: Revisited," *Journal of Marketing* (January 1974), p. 2–7.

J. Robert Foster and F. Kelly Shuptrine, "Using Retailers' Perceptions of Channel Performance to Detect Potential Conflict," *1973 Combined Proceedings* (American Marketing Association), p. 118–23.

Shelby B. Hunt and John R. Nevin, "Power in Channels of Distribution: Sources and Consequences," *Journal of Marketing Research* (May 1974), 186–193.

Bert C. McCammon and William L. Hammer, "A Frame of Reference for Improving Productivity in Distribution," *1974 Combined Proceedings* (American Marketing Association), p. 455–459.

William D. Perreault, Jr. and Frederick A. Russ, "Physical Distribution Service and Industrial Purchase Decisions," *Journal of Marketing* (April 1976), p. 53–62.

Frederick W. Webster, "The Role of the Industrial Distributor in Marketing Strategy," *Journal of Marketing* (July 1976), p. 10–16.

William G. Zikmund and William J. Stanton, "Recycling Solid Wastes: A Channels of Distribution Problem," *Journal of Marketing* (July 1971), p. 34–39.

Some Major Channel and Distribution Information Sources

Census of Business—lists retail and wholesale rates by type of outlet and geographic area.

Census of Manufacturers—lists geographic and industry data on manufacturers, including costs of materials and production quantities.

Census of Retail Trade—provides data for over 2,400 retail centers. Includes a separate report for each state having one or more standard metropolitan statistical area (SMSAs) and for the District of Columbia. Statistics are presented on the number of establishments, sales, payroll, and employment for each SMSA, for each city of 100,000 inhabitants or more and its central business district (CBD), and for other major retail centers in the SMSA that have 100 or more retail establishments. In addition, for smaller major retail centers (MRC), the number of stores is shown by kind of business, and sales are shown for three major kind-of-business categories. Maps in each report show the total area covered, define the CBDs, and locate the MRCs in the SMSA.

Census of Transportation—provides an enumeration of personal travel, the characteristics and use of trucks, and the long-distance shipment of commodities by manufacturers.

Census of Wholesale Trade—presents data for each state, the United States, and the District of Columbia on the number of establishments, sales, payroll, employment, and end-of-year inventories for all wholesale trade establishments. Data on the number of establishments and sales also are presented separately for the following types of wholesale operation: merchant wholesalers, manufacturers' sales branches and offices, and merchandise agents and brokers. Detailed statistics are presented for SMSAs also.

Current Retail Trade Reports—provides weekly, monthly, and annual retail sales estimates for current period and final estimates for preceeding periods for the United States by major kind-of-business categories and for selected kinds of business. Includes estimates on monthly accounts receivables and year-end inventories.

Marketing Channel Strategy: A Selected Bibliography—edited by Ronald D.

Michman, Myron Gable, and Taylor Sims, 1976. There are five sections to this study: (1) functions of channel management; (2) channel development and evolution; (3) role of channel participants in the marketing channel environment; (4) channel management and strategy; and (5) evaluation and control of channel performance.

Monthly Department Store Sales for Selected Areas—provides monthly sales for about 200 selected areas, including standard metropolitan statistical areas (SMSAs), cities, and other selected areas.

Monthly Wholesale Trade Reports—provides preliminary estimates for the current month and final estimates for the preceding month of sales, end-of-month inventory, and stock-sales ratios of merchant wholesalers by kind of business. Estimates in more limited detail also are provided for geographic divisions.

Progressive Grocer—presents data and information for decision makers in the retail food industry who control buying, merchandising, administration, and operation of supermarkets. Articles cover trends in the field, and case histories of successful merchandising and operating activities. Designed to make more money for supermarkets through "how to" information, it has special quarterly merchandising reviews, and a store-of-the-month column. It has many idea departments such as "Profit Talk" and "Pointers on Perishables."

Rand McNally Commercial Atlas and Marketing Guide—Maps and statistics on retail sales, agriculture, manufacturers, population, bank deposits, automobile registrations, and other market data. (annual)

Sales Management's "Annual Survey of Buying Power"—an index to the relative buying power of various counties and cities in the United States. Computed by using a formula which weights (1) the percentage of national disposable income for an area [wt. = .5], (2) the percentage of national retail sales in the area [wt. = .3], and (3) the percentage of national population contained in the area [wt. = .2].

Standard Industrial Classification (S.I.C.) System—provides number of establishments, their sales volumes, and number of employees, given by county and SMSA, for all types of businesses in the United States. Businesses are divided into 10 groups, using a range of 2-digit classification code numbers. A 2-digit number is assigned to a major industry (e.g., Wholesale and Retail Trade, S.I.C. numbers ranging from 50 to 59). Third and fourth digits subdivide the industry into finer segments within the industry.

Mason's Hardware:
Market Analysis of a Retail Store Location

William R. Darden, University of Arkansas
James Williams, Lindenwood College

Introduction

Jim Mason has always wanted to own a hardware store. As a young boy in Bloomington, Illinois, he spent his after-school hours working in his father's hardware store. Recently, he became interested in a promising retail site along Highway 71 in Rogers, Arkansas. He understood that the Rogers trade area was one of the fastest growing in the country.

Wanting to know the investment potential of the project but having a very limited time in which to make a decision, he asked two marketing consultants to evaluate the site of the proposed hardware store. He outlined to the consultants the kind of hardware store he felt to be appropriate to the market of the area and to his own interests.

The store's orientation is defined by the factors below:

1. The hardware stores would cater to suburbanite markets and include a home and garden center.

2. The store was *not* to handle bulk building materials, such as lumber, cement, sash and doors, and bricks. Some building materials for the do-it-yourselfer, such as nuts, bolts, nails, cabinet and kitchen fixtures as well as limited lines of trim and paneling, would be included.

3. Quality merchandise would be emphasized for home repair and the do-it-yourselfer.

4. Minor appliances, hand power tools, and kitchenware would be carried.

5. Some major appliances, such as stoves, refrigerators, and air conditioners would be stocked.

The Market

Rogers is located in the center of the recent population boom in NW Arkansas. North of Rogers on Highway 71 is Bentonville, a rapidly developing retirement community. The Beaver Lake recreation area is located immediately east of Rogers and is the major attraction of the area. It is a drawing point for tourists and a major contributor to the housing boom in NW Arkansas. The Rogers market area has been able to capitalize on the back-to-nature trend of city dwellers in search of the "good life."

Because of these factors, there is a growing retirement contingent within and surrounding the community. Many of these retirees are white-collar workers and executives who see NW Arkansas as an ideal place to spend their later years. The locale is picturesque, the leisure activities varied, and each season mild.

South of Rogers are the cities of Springdale and Fayetteville, both in Washington County. Fayetteville is the home of the main campus of the University of Arkansas, with approximately 13,000 students.

Springdale is a vigorous city of over 20,000 residents, displaying substantial population growth while retaining much of its rural charm.

Tables 19–1 and 19–2 testify to the rapid growth of the city of Rogers and Benton County.

In particular, it demonstrates a clear trend toward increases in expenditures on both new housing and conversions or alterations of old housing. These data suggest that the demand for home improvement and home repair products also are increasing for the Benton County area.

Tables 19–2 and 19–3 indicate the population of the City of Rogers and Benton County is increasing proportionately faster relative to the state. It is fair to say that a disproportionately large number of new arrivals are retirees. Because of the fixed nature of the incomes from their pensions, retirees tend to vote against new tax

Table 19–1
Building Permits for the City of Rogers

Year	Number of Housing Units	Housing (000s)	Conversions and Alterations (000s)	Total Construction (000s)
1971	320	3,679	845	6,993
1972	465	7,003	284	8,710
1973	363	5,319	234	12,742
1974	182	3,737	810	6,229
1975	229	4,653	355	7,773
1976	325	5,556	852	9,480

Source: City Inspector

Table   19–2
Population Trends

Year	City of Rogers	Benton County	State of Arkansas
1930	3,554	35,523	1,854,482
1940	3,550	36,148	1,949,387
1950	4,962	38,076	1,090,511
1960	5,700	36,272	1,786,272
1965	8,284		
1968	8,861		
1970	11,050	50,476	1,923,259
1971			1,965,000
1972		53,600	2,007,800
1973	13,189	55,700	2,034,700
1974		57,700	2,061,500
1975		59,100	
1976	14,942		

Table   19–3
Postal Receipts
Rogers Chamber of Commerce
Rogers, Arkansas
Revised January 1976

1960	$189,693.38
1961	229,391.00
1962	244,145.86
1963	292,343.09
1964	297,036.42
1965	323,072.33
1967	348,188.68
1968	403,192.00
1969	439,926.10
1970	481,484.70
1971	523,107.30
1972	588,825.00
1973	596,613.00
1974	810,927.00
1975	716,214.00

Table 19–4
Income Trends

Year	Total Personal Income (000s)			Per Capita Personal Income		
	SMSA, Fayetteville, Springdale, Rogers	Benton County	Washington County	SMSA, Fayetteville, Springdale, Rogers	Benton County	Washington County
1970	$382.4	$153.5	$228.9	$2,978	$3,027	$2,946
1971	416.2	164.5	251.7	3,159	3,129	3,180
1972	482.5	195.6	286.9	3,476	3,519	3,448
1973	581.3	234.3	347.0	4,094	4,112	4,082
1974	598.5	243.3	355.2	4,130	4,159	4,113

measures of all kinds. It also is fair to say that they exert considerable political clout.

From Table 19–4, it can be seen that both total personal income and per capita personal income are increasing in the Fayetteville-Springdale-Rogers SMSA. From 1970 to 1974, however, total personal income increased slightly faster for Benton County than for the total SMSA,[1] and, in particular, Washington County (both Springdale and Fayetteville are in Washington County).

Table 19–5 shows retailing trends in Benton County; some factors are projected for 1980. Total retail sales for 1980 are expected to double over 1974 sales figures. Sales of general merchandise and furniture and appliances all show signs of increasing substantially through 1980. A vigorous retail market is indicated by the upward trends for the media Effective Buying Power and the Buyer Power Index.

---

[1] *Editor's note:* SMSA is the Standard Metropolitan Statistical Area.

Table   19–5
Retailing Trends in Benton County

	1980	1975	1974	1973	1972
Population (000s)	65.7	59.1	57.7	55.7	53.6
Households (000s)	23.5	20.7	20.7	19.9	18.8
Total Retail Sales (000s)	262,728	154,303	136,829	107,499'	86,762
General Merchandise (000s)	—	27,575	25,221	14,658	12,074
Furniture and Appliances (000s)	—	7,272	6,844	4,309	3,127
Lumber, Building Materials, Hardware (000s)	—	—	—	6,362	8,855
Effective Buying Income (000s)	396,076	236,498	212,568	188,074	160,362
Median Effective Buying Income	—	10,295	8,660	7,131	6,222
Buying Power Index	.0273	.0243	.0236	.0226	.0212
Percent by Effective Buying Income Group					
$ 8,000– 9,999		11.0%	11.9%	11.8%	11.8%
$10,000–14,999		22.5	22.3	17.9	15.3
$15,000–24,000		19.7	15.7	9.9	6.6
$25,000+		5.8	4.1	4.0	2.4

Exhibit 19-1
Store Survey (eight stores)

	1	2	3	4	5	6	7	8
Gardening Tools								
Hand		X[a]	X	X	X	X	X	X
Power		X	X				X	
Rototiller			X					
Mowers								
Push		X	X					
Ride			X					
Tractors			X					
Seed & Supplies								
Trees and Shrubs								
Sporting Goods		X						
Tools								
Hand								
Carpentry	X	X	X	X	X	X	X	X
Masonry	X	X	X	X		X	X	
Power								
Hand	X	X	X	X			X	X
Tablesaw, etc.							X	X
Houseware								
Appliances		X	X					
Major		X	X					
Minor		X	X		X		X	X
Kitchenware		X	X		X	X		
Building Supplies								
Nails, Nuts, Bolts	X	X	X	X	X	X	X	X
Paint	X	X	X	X		X	X	X
Painting Supplies								
Ladders	X	X	X			X	X	
Paneling	X		X	X			X	X
Sash & Door	X		X				X	X
Wood	X		X	X			X	X
Plumbing								
Fixtures					X			
Pipe	X				X	X		
Electrical								
Fixtures					X			
Supplies	X	X		X	X	X		

[a] An "x" indicates that store carries the indicated line of product.

Exhibit 19-2
Store Locations
and
Traffic Counts

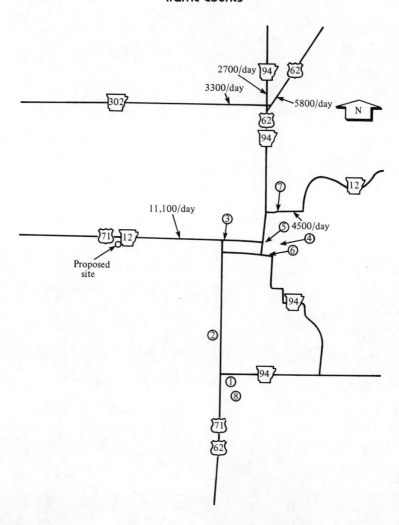

Competition

In 1977, at the time Jim Mason is considering his decision (see Exhibit 19–1), Rogers has eight stoers which are hardware suppliers. However, some of these are primarily suppliers of building materials and do not represent direct competition for the suburban home repair or addition market. Other hardware stores represent more direct competition. In fact, one hardware store is planned across the highway from the proposed site. However, Exhibit 19–2 shows that most of them are located in

Table   19–6
1975 Hardware Store Industry Norms:
West-South Central Region (29 Stores)
(in percentages)

Net Sales ($527,672)		100.00%	
Cost of Goods Sold		66.16	
Margin			33.84%
Payroll and Other Employee Expenses		17.62	
Occupancy Expenses			
Heat, light, power, water	.68%		
Repairs to building	.36		
Rent or ownership in real estate	2.73	3.77	
Other Costs			
Advertising	.94		
Depreciation (other than real estate)	.43		
Insurance (other than real estate of group)	.55		
Taxes (other than real estate or payroll)	.43		
Other expenses	3.01	5.36	
Total Operating Expense			26.15
Net Operating Profit			7.69%

the eastern and southern parts of town. The proposed site is to be in the northwest sector.

A survey of Exhibit 19–1 reveals that there is little competition for roto-tillers, seeds and supplies, and trees and shrubs. Undoubtedly, this lack of competition is because of the large number of commercial nurseries adjacent to the area. It does suggest, however, that the idea of a "home center" may be feasible for this particular market.

Characteristics of Proposed Site

Two spot traffic counts were taken at the proposed site. On Friday afternoon, May 13, the traffic count was 1166/hr. and on the following Tuesday morning it was 764/hr. Exhibit 19–2 also gives daily traffic counts taken in 1970 for various points in the city. The site is to be located across the street from the Dixieland Mall on a 4-lane thoroughfare. The mall already contains a department store catering to the upper-middle class. The site is to cost $133,000 and, at present, Mr. Mason is planning a total investment of $300,000 to include land, building, and inventory.

He feels that the land is an excellent investment because of the rising property values in the area.

Industry Norms

Table 19–6 contains 1975 hardware operating information from the National Retail Hardware Association for the West-South Central Region of the United States. In general, it shows low operating costs with a high net operating profit. The average store has 6,000 square feet with approximately 4,800 square feet of sales area. The Mason hardware store is to have a total of 7,500 square feet. The average inventory turnover for this region is from 2.5 to 3.0. Average investment per square foot of sales area is about $12.50 in this region.

However, costs for building were some what vague. Mason feels a metal building might suit his purposes. However, these costs ranged from $12 to $17 per square foot in construction costs. Mason wonders if the $300,000 projected for this venture would be sufficient.

The Decision

Although the prospects seem bright, Jim Mason feels that there are several factors which might make the project unfeasible. First, the national energy problems could well cause a recession. Thus, timing for the new store could be wrong. Second, the market analysis could be misleading, since he would be catering to a "special" market. With respect to the second problem, he suspects that the increasing elderly market, along with inflation, could affect his business either positively or negatively (inflation and recession could stimulate or discourage improvements of any kind). In addition, he is unsure of the nature of future cash flows. Also, if the real estate boom in NW Arkansas were to subside, he could not be sure of his future financial position.

Selmer's Department Store: The Dynamics of Retail Location

Dale M. Lewison and John E. Mertes
University of Arkansas at Little Rock

Retail management constantly is faced with decisions regarding adjustments to its dynamic operating environment. Changing consumer and retail structure patterns create a continuing need for reevaluation of market positions and merchandising strategies. The director of stores of Selmer's Department Store and his staff are faced with a series of merchandising decisions as a result of the planned introduction of a large regional shopping mall into the firm's local retail market. A recently-completed impact study conducted at the University of South Carolina intensifies the need for decisions.

The City: Columbia, South Carolina

Centrally located within the state, Columbia reaps the economic and political benefits associated with that position. The pleasant physical environment (climate, terrain, and vegetation) of the uplands area of South Carolina provide highly desirable "quality of life" factors that contribute greatly to the population and economic growth of the area. As the capital of South Carolina, Columbia has evolved into the cultural, political, and economic hub of the state.

The Columbia SMSA's current population of 313,200 is expected to continue its steady growth rate of the last decade. This continuing growth rate is predicated on a strong and balanced economy. The city's economic base is reasonably well balanced among primary and secondary production, distribution, and service sectors of the economy. As the seat of state government, Columbia enjoys the benefits of a stable state and federal employment sector. In addition, this governmental employment sector is enhanced by the presence of the University of South Carolina and a major federal military base, Fort Jackson.

The diverse production sector is illustrated by the presence of such industries as chemicals, electronics, textiles, wood and paper products, machine tools, food processing, component parts, subassemblies, and apparels and accessories. The national trend of southern migration of industry is having a positive impact on the Columbia area.

Columbia's centrality makes it ideal for local and statewide distribution activities. In recent years, the percent of labor force employed in the distributive trades has shown a sharp increase. In addition, some distributors have found Columbia ideally suited for interstate distribution. The area has experienced a slow but steady increase in district and regional distribution facilities.

The growth rate of both Columbia and South Carolina has produced a great need for services. Columbia has become the state's hub for medical, social, cultural, legal, and educational services. The natural beauty of the area and of the state has increased the need for recreation and entertainment services; these services are becoming a mainstay of the economy.

Population Structure

Demographic characteristics of Columbia's population are shown in Exhibits 20–1, 20–2, and 20–3. The demographic variables shown are total population, racial composition, median family income, age composition, occupational status, and employment status. Exhibit 20–4 is a map of census tracts.

Retail Structure

Columbia's retailing structure consists of the following: (1) regional shopping clusters, (2) community and neighborhood shopping centers, and (3) free-standing string developments along major traffic arteries. Due to the limited sales potential of the localized trading areas of the latter two, Selmer Department Store has limited its store locations to those clusterings having regional attraction. Four regional shopping clusters exist in the Columbia area. They are (1) downtown, (2) Dutch Square, (3) Richland Mall, and (4) Five Points Shopping Center. Currently, Selmer's operates a store in each of the four. Although the size (square foot of selling space) of each store varies, the percentage of selling space devoted to a given product line remains constant. The location of each major cluster is shown in Exhibit 20–4.

Downtown

Currently, the largest shopping cluster is the downtown area with 102 retailing establishments. Three "full-line" department stores, including J. C. Penney, Belk, and Davidson's, are the principal retail attraction for the downtown area. Several quality soft-goods retailers with local and regional reputations are an important attraction for the area. They include Tapps Department Store, Berry's on Main, Britton's, Lourie's, and Selmer's Department Stores. In addition, downtown has the largest concentration of furniture and appliance, as well as specialty, stores in the area. Consumer willingness to spend considerable time, money, and effort in making price and quality comparisons relative to these goods should make shopping in the downtown area even more attractive. In general, the tenant mix of retailers downtown is quite conducive to consumer trip generation and comparison shopping.

Exhibit 20-1
Population Characteristics:
Total Population and Racial Composition

Census Tract	Total Population		Racial Composition			
			% White		% Black	
	1960	1970	1960	1970	1960	1970
1	1,050	900	26	18	74	82
2	2,800	2,100	18	18	82	82
3	5,400	4,300	32	30	68	70
4	6,100	6,200	34	14	66	86
5	4,900	4,950	38	36	62	64
6*	—	—	—	—	—	—
7	6,400	6,950	64	68	36	32
8	5,700	5,700	72	72	28	28
9	5,350	5,400	70	70	30	30
10	4,750	4,700	72	71	28	29
11	6,200	6,300	35	34	65	66
12	5,750	5,700	81	80	19	20
13	4,900	4,900	77	77	23	23
14	5,100	5,000	83	81	17	19
15	6,540	6,350	74	70	26	30
16	6,100	6,700	52	46	48	54
17	5,200	5,300	50	39	50	61
18	7,400	7,300	21	7	79	93
19	6,700	6,900	58	58	42	42
20	4,100	4,100	64	62	36	38
21	5,350	5,250	94	94	6	6
22	6,100	6,050	63	62	37	38
23	5,100	5,250	97	97	3	3
24	3,000	3,400	69	68	31	32
25	3,100	3,300	70	70	30	30
26	2,200	2,900	74	73	26	27
27	3,900	4,700	84	84	26	26
28	1,900	3,400	83	82	17	18
29	1,200	5,100	84	90	16	10
30	1,700	3,900	87	89	13	11
31	2,100	6,300	95	98	5	2
32	2,600	4,900	92	96	8	4
33	3,700	5,650	94	94	6	6
34	3,650	5,100	88	88	12	12
35	1,200	2,900	74	75	26	25
36	800	7,000	50	95	50	5
37	200	800	100	100	0	0
38	1,700	3,700	98	99	2	1
39	2,300	5,250	99	99	1	1
40	1,800	6,100	100	100	0	0

Exhibit 20-1
Population Characteristics:
Total Population and Racial Composition

Census Tract	Total Population		Racial Composition			
			% White		% Black	
	1960	1970	1960	1970	1960	1970
41	1,250	2,700	98	99	2	1
42	1,600	8,200	96	99	4	1
43	1,000	4,800	90	96	10	4
44	1,200	6,400	94	99	6	1
45	800	5,100	98	99	2	1
46	1,400	5,400	92	99	8	1
47	1,300	4,900	94	99	6	1
48	1,300	3,900	81	87	19	13
49	1,200	4,100	87	97	13	3
50	1,700	3,700	96	98	4	2
51	1,100	4,400	96	99	4	1
52	1,400	7,100	99	99	1	1
53	1,000	6,100	100	100	0	0
54	300	4,100	100	100	0	0
55	1,300	8,000	96	99	4	1
56	2,100	7,000	97	99	3	1
57	800	6,000	99	99	1	1
58	1,100	4,000	100	100	0	0
59	1,600	8,700	100	100	0	0
60	900	6,900	99	100	1	0
61	1,700	4,700	96	100	4	0
62	1,900	6,300	99	100	1	0
TOTAL	181,900	313,200				

* Census tract 6 is the University of South Carolina consisting of 16,000 full-time students. Approximately one-third of the student body resides in campus housing in census tract 6.

The downtown has several positional strengths from a retailing perspective: (1) centrality to the entire city's population, (2) proximity to the federal, state, and local government office complex, (3) proximity to the city's major complex of business offices, and (4) proximity to the University. In addition the downtown area is adjacent to the city's sports and convention complex and the associated hotel complex. With the completion of the new Main Street pedestrian mall, the shopping atmosphere of the downtown area should be greatly enhanced.

The downtown area is not without its retailing weaknesses. External and internal accessibility to and within the area is extremely limited. Accessibility is further complicated by a lack of sufficient parking in the immediate area. Although the new pedestrian mall should improve the shopping atmosphere, it could well

Exhibit 20-2
Population Characteristics:
Median Family Income and Age Compositon

Census Tract	Median Family Income		Age Composition			
			% Under 18		% Over 65	
	1960	1970	1960	1970	1960	1970
1	$4,500	$ 4,900	22	16	12	28
2	4,750	5,150	26	21	10	29
3	5,100	5,450	20	20	8	12
4	5,700	6,100	21	16	7	10
5	5,500	6,350	16	12	9	14
6*	—	—	—	—	—	—
7	6,900	6,300	28	16	12	8
8	5,500	6,000	26	21	15	15
9	6,600	8,100	21	20	14	16
10	8,100	7,400	19	10	12	26
11	7,300	8,100	18	13	10	18
12	7,400	9,300	23	23	11	13
13	7,000	9,100	21	21	9	9
14	7,100	10,700	22	26	7	7
15	7,700	9,600	20	23	6	10
16	7,000	7,900	18	20	6	14
17	6,700	7,400	16	17	7	19
18	5,100	6,100	17	22	6	10
19	5,900	6,700	14	14	7	14
20	5,700	6,900	17	16	8	17
21	6,200	8,300	19	19	10	10
22	6,500	7,900	16	18	7	8
23	6,800	9,100	24	24	4	3
24	5,900	8,300	23	22	3	5
25	6,100	8,100	21	22	3	4
26	6,300	8,200	20	21	5	5
27	7,100	9,600	18	19	3	3
28	7,200	9,400	19	20	4	5
29	7,000	10,200	18	19	4	3
30	6,800	9,600	17	17	5	5
31	7,300	10,300	16	16	4	4
32	7,000	10,400	14	18	6	5
33	7,400	10,500	16	19	2	2
34	7,000	9,300	19	21	2	4
35	6,800	8,900	21	21	1	4
36	5,800	8,900	20	21	4	3
37	6,100	8,800	20	24	6	1
38	6,400	9,300	19	21	1	1
39	6,300	9,400	18	22	2	1
40	6,400	9,700	18	23	3	1

Exhibit 20-2
Population Characteristics:
Median Family Income and Age Compositon

Census Tract	Median Family Income		Age Composition			
			% Under 18		% Over 65	
	1960	1970	1960	1970	1960	1970
41	6,500	10,000	14	20	2	2
42	6,900	11,200	13	20	2	0
43	7,000	10,100	14	18	3	2
44	6,800	11,300	15	18	3	1
45	7,500	12,900	14	19	2	0
46	7,000	11,900	15	18	1	1
47	8,100	14,500	10	16	0	0
48	8,300	15,200	14	18	1	1
49	6,200	9,900	20	20	2	2
50	6,800	9,700	21	20	2	3
51	7,100	10,000	20	20	3	3
52	6,900	10,800	21	21	2	1
53	6,400	11,700	16	23	2	0
54	6,800	14,300	10	21	4	1
55	6,000	16,800	11	19	3	0
56	6,400	16,200	12	18	4	1
57	7,100	15,900	13	18	5	2
58	7,100	16,000	11	17	5	3
59	7,800	18,200	14	19	5	1
60	7,700	21,000	14	16	4	0
61	6,900	19,100	12	20	8	2
62	7,700	20,300	11	17	6	1

* Census tract 6 is the University of South Carolina consisting of 16,000 full-time students. Approximately one-third of the student body resides in campus housing in census tract 6.

mean further deterioration in the accessibility and parking problems. Shopper security, especially during the evening and weekends, creates additional problems. Muggings, robberies, and auto vandalism have had a serious adverse effect on consumer willingness to shop in the downtown area. The security problem has resulted in most stores closing at 6:00 p.m. except during annual holiday seasons or for special events. With the slow but steady increase in the number of low-status retailers in and around the downtown area, the consumer security problem could easily worsen.

The general shopping atmosphere of the downtown area also places certain limitations on consumer attraction. Even with the new pedestrian mall, many of the buildings are old and in need of extensive repair. Numerous vacant buildings have taken their psychological toll on consumer purchase motivation. For the white, middle-class suburban shopper, the minorities-majority makeup of the

Exhibit 20-3
Population Characteristics:
Occupation and Employment Status

Census Tract	Occupation (Head of Household)				(Head of Household) % Unemployed	
	% Blue Collar		% White Collar		Employment Status	
	1970	1960	1960	1970	1960	1970
1	64	88	36	12	18	21
2	66	90	34	10	12	14
3	70	88	30	12	10	10
4	50	74	50	26	8	12
5	58	70	42	30	10	10
6*	—	—	—	—	—	—
7	34	58	66	42	7	6
8	52	56	48	44	6	4
9	53	63	47	37	5	5
10	49	59	51	41	3	3
11	46	63	54	37	3	4
12	70	70	30	30	4	2
13	60	65	40	35	4	3
14	34	40	66	60	4	3
15	33	48	67	52	1	1
16	74	80	26	20	2	5
17	90	91	10	9	4	5
18	83	92	17	8	4	8
19	75	79	25	21	5	4
20	68	70	32	30	4	4
21	75	78	25	23	4	3
22	70	70	30	30	4	4
23	68	72	32	28	2	2
24	58	52	42	48	3	2
25	50	52	50	48	3	3
26	40	36	60	64	3	4
27	38	32	62	68	2	1
28	42	42	58	58	2	1
29	22	20	78	80	2	1
30	30	26	70	74	2	2
31	12	10	88	90	1	0
32	20	20	80	80	1	1
33	18	17	82	83	0	0
34	34	36	66	64	2	1
35	48	50	52	50	2	2
36	37	35	63	65	4	1
37	55	60	45	40	1	1
38	70	75	30	25	0	0
39	80	78	20	22	0	1

Exhibit 20-3
Population Characteristics:
Occupation and Employment Status

Census Tract	Occupation (Head of Household)				(Head of Household) % Unemployed	
	% Blue Collar		% White Collar		Employment Status	
	1970	1960	1960	1970	1960	1970
40	78	82	22	18	0	0
41	60	61	40	39	1	0
42	60	32	40	68	0	1
43	24	22	76	78	3	1
44	30	30	70	70	1	1
45	35	30	70	65	0	0
46	30	25	70	75	2	1
47	22	21	78	79	1	1
48	39	37	61	63	3	1
49	42	43	58	57	2	1
50	58	57	42	43	1	1
51	59	67	41	33	1	0
52	70	70	30	30	3	4
53	80	82	20	18	3	3
54	74	70	26	30	3	5
55	52	24	48	76	2	0
56	27	27	73	73	2	2
57	25	27	75	73	2	3
58	27	16	73	84	2	1
59	21	10	79	90	0	0
60	18	17	82	83	0	0
61	23	20	77	80	0	0
62	14	12	86	88	0	0

* Census tract 6 is the University of South Carolina consisting of 16,000 full-time students. Approximately one-third of the student body resides in campus housing in census tract 6.

downtown shopper is psychologically discomforting and results in a poor shopping "frame of mind." According to rumor, some of the major department stores plan to adjust downward their pricing points and carry a lower quality of goods in order to appeal to the low-income minorities consumer.

Finally, the "cost of doing business" in the downtown area currently is the highest in the city. High rent, extra security, and high storage rates all add to this cost. In addition, with very defined daily peak shopping periods (noon hour, coffee hours, and postworkday), labor costs are necessarily higher to meet these peak demand periods.

Exhibit 20-4
Census Tract Map

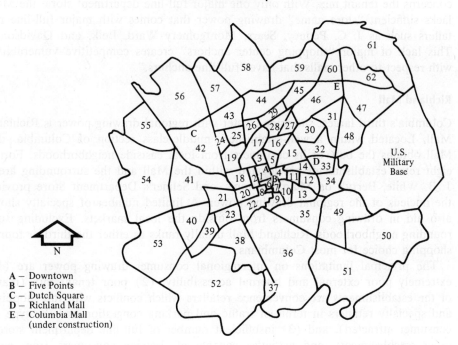

A – Downtown
B – Five Points
C – Dutch Square
D – Richland Mall
E – Columbia Mall
(under construction)

Dutch Square

The Dutch Square Mall and its adjacent area is the second largest retailing cluster in the Columbia SMSA. When completed in 1973, the Mall consisted of 48 retailing establishments. In 4 years, it has grown to its present size of 89 retailing establishments. The tenant mix of the cluster is: (1) one full-line department store, J. B. White, (2) 3 discount department stores, Woolco, K-Mart, and Richway, (3) 2 catalog showrooms, Sam Solomon's and Key Wholesalers, and (4) 5 major soft goods retailers, Tapp's Department Store, Berry's on Main, Britton's, Lourie's, and Selmer's Department Store. In addition, there is the usual mix of specialty, shopping and convenience goods retailers.

Located in South Carolina's fastest growing upper-middle class suburban areas, Dutch Square has been extremely successful. Sales per square foot are among the highest in the Columbia area. Lack of competition is the reason most often cited for the success of the cluster. With good external accessibility, the Mall attracts the entire metro area, as well as numerous surrounding communities. The recent addition of several office complexes should also enhance the cluster's drawing power.

Retailing weaknesses are relatively few, but two are noteworthy. First, with the last four years' rapid expansion, internal accessibility within the shopping cluster has been severely retarded. Long-term effects are certain to be felt as consumers seek more convenient and accessible shopping opportunities. The second weakness concerns the tenant mix. With only one major full-line department store, the Mall lacks sufficient "store name" drawing power that comes with major full-line retailers such as J. C. Penney, Sears, Montgomery Ward, Belk, and Davidson's. This lack of major "shopping center anchors" creates competitive vulnerability with respect to other malls that have "full-line anchors."

Richland Mall

Columbia's third largest shopping cluster with regional drawing power is Richland Mall. Located within a well-established, middle-class section of Columbia, the Mall obtains the bulk of its customers from local eastside neighborhoods. Forty-eight retail establishments are located within the Mall and the surrounding area. J. B. White, Berry's on Main, Britton's, and Selmer's Department Store provide the nucleus of the regional drawing power. A limited number of specialty shops also aid in drawing consumers from outside the local markets. Excluding surrounding neighborhoods, Richland Mall usually ranks as either the third or fourth shopping choice for most Columbians.

The principal limitations on interregional consumer drawing power are (1) extremely poor external and internal accessibility, (2) poor tenant mix (many of the establishments are convenience retailers which conflicts with the shopping and specialty retailers in terms of traffic and parking congestion and the type of consumer attracted), and (3) insufficient number of full-line department stores, other establishments, and activities capable of drawing consumers from considerable distances. As a matter of fact, there are rumors that J. B. White is considering relocating.

Five Points Shopping Center

Next to the downtown area, the Five Points Shopping Center is the oldest shopping cluster in Columbia. Consisting of approximately 3 dozen shopping, specialty, and convenience goods retailers, the center's ability to attract regional consumers is based on 2 factors. First, Columbia's only Sears store is located adjacent to the cluster. In Columbia, Sears, by itself, is capable of drawing consumers from considerable distances. Second, historically, all of Columbia's old-line specialty and shopping goods retailers (Berry's on Main, Britton's, Tapp's, Lourie's, and Selmer's Department Store) have branch locations within the center.

Located adjacent to what was Columbia's most exclusive residential area (University Heights), Five Points was once the exclusive shopping district of the upper-income Columbia consumer. With the migration to the suburbs in the 1950s and 1960s, University Heights subsequently evolved into a low-income multidwelling residential area populated with University students and minority groups. Conversion of many of the single-family dwellings into multiple-family units hastened the physical deterioration of the area. Recently, however, restoration of the area and its dwellings has become a passion for many young, middle-class professionals. Since it is adjacent to the University, it is a highly desirable place of residence for the University administration, faculty, and staff.

The advantages associated with the cluster's location with respect to the University and the downtown area are far outweighed by the disadvantages of reduced external and internal accessibility and increased competition. In terms of the Columbia metro area, Five Points is by far the least accessible. Internal traffic conjestion and the lack of parking facilities is an extreme limitation. Perhaps, with the closing of Sears (effective at the end of the year), conjestion will be reduced. In addition, there has been some talk about refurbishing the Center's many older buildings.

Columbia Mall

The opening of the new Columbia Mall, scheduled for the fall, will signal a new era in retailing for the greater Columbia area. Located in the northeastern section of Columbia (see Exhibit 20–4), the 2-story, 1.5 million square-foot development will contain 145 retailing establishments. Success of the venture is almost certain, given the consumer drawing power associated with such noted shopping center "anchors" as Belk, J. C. Penney, Sears, and Rich's. What is certain are some profound changes in the retailing structure of the Columbia metropolitan area. To the Columbia area consumer, it will offer new and exciting shopping opportunities. To the existing and would-be Columbia area retailer, it will represent a business opportunity and/or a source of potential competition.

A recent study completed by the Marketing Research Division of the University examined the potential impact of the Columbia Mall on existing major shopping clusters. Four shopping clusters (Downtown, Dutch Square, Richland Mall, and Five Points) and 7 product categories (clothing, footwear, apparel accessories, furniture and appliances, household accessories, recreation and entertainment, and personal) were included in the study. The study estimated the probability of a consumer in a given census tract traveling to a particular shopping cluster for a given product category. To ascertain the impact of the new mall, a "before" and "after" research design was employed. The conclusions of the study are as follows:

> Of the 7 product categories considered, the new mall should assume the dominant market share position in the 5 areas of clothing, footwear, household accessories, recreation and entertainment, and personal products. In addition, Columbia Mall's market share in apparel accessories should be second only to the downtown area. Only in the furniture and appliance product category is the Columbia Mall's market share expected to be of a limited scope . . . If the market share positions projected here are assumed to be valid, then it would be appropriate to expect the Columbia Mall to become the dominant force in the retailing activities of the Columbia area . . . Further, these projections would indicate that the impact of the Columbia Mall would not be evenly distributed. Substantial differences, given these conditions, would occur between product categories and shopping clusters.

For most of the 4 existing clusters, substantial decreases in market share would be expected for most product categories. Overall, most of the existing clusters would experience their largest market share decreases in clothing and footwear product categories . . . The entrance of the mall into the retailing structure of the Columbia area poses several difficult problems for existing and potential retailers. Initially, decisions regarding locational strategies will need to be made. Later, as the effects of the new mall become apparent, marketing strategies relative to product, promotion, and price will require adjustment.

The impact of the Columbia Mall already is being felt. In the area surrounding

Exhibit 20-5
Columbia Mall Lower Level*

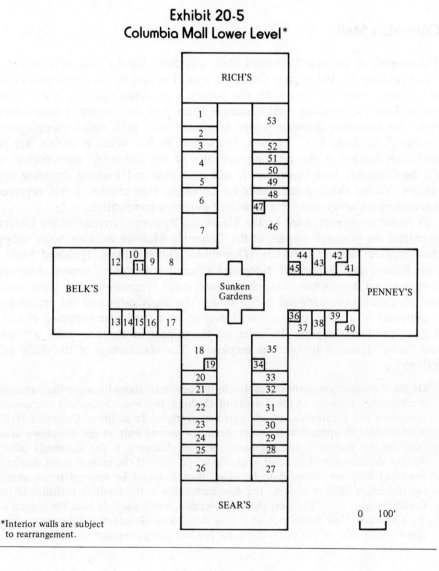

*Interior walls are subject
  to rearrangement.

Columbia Mall Upper Level

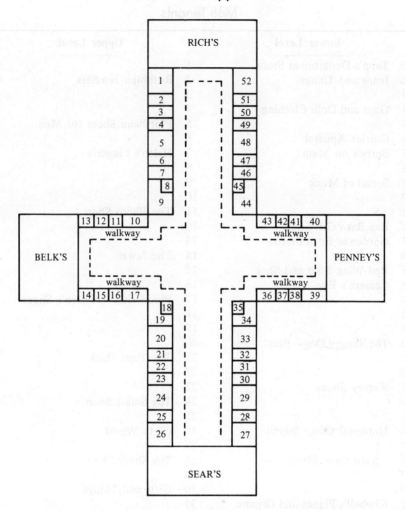

the mall, several firms have announced that they have purchased land and plan to build within the next year. Among these are 2 major discount-department stores, a major catalog showroom, a developer who specializes in small (10–15 stores) specialty shopping clusters, and a firm that specializes in 4-screen theaters. In addition, there are rumors that 2 major department stores have purchased adjacent properties.

The layout of the mall is shown in Exhibit 20–5. The mall will be completely enclosed and, therefore, climatically controlled. Sunken gardens and a lower level walkway have been designed to provide customers with an excellent shopping atmosphere. The planned activities for the garden and walkways include concerts, exhibits, shows, and displays.

Tenants of the mall are listed in Exhibit 20–6. The list includes most of the

Exhibit 20-6
Mall Tenants

Lower Level		Upper Level	
1	Tapp's Department Store	1	
2	Jeans and Things	2	Rothman Jewelers
3		3	
4	Guys and Dolls Clothing	4	
5		5	Florsheim Shoes for Men
6	Curries Apparel	6	
7	Berry's on Main	7	Helen's Lingerie
8		8	
9	Sound of Music	9	
10		10	
11		11	The Photo Shop
12	Red Barn Gift Shop	12	
13	Garden of Eden Florist	13	
14		14	The Jewel
15	Red Wing Boot and Shoe	15	
16	Camera's Eye	16	
17		17	Woodside's Children's Shoes
18		18	
19		19	
20	The Shaggy Dog—Pets	20	
21		21	The Tape Deck
22		22	
23	Kinney Shoes	23	
24		24	The Smart Shop
25		25	
26	Universal Office Supply	26	Cloth World
27		27	
28	United Shoe Store	28	The Shade Shop
29		29	
30		30	Gifts and Things
31	Kimball's Pianos and Organs	31	
32	Stride Rite Shoes	32	
33		33	Thom McAnn Shoes
34		34	
35	Fillene Jewelers	35	
36		36	
37	National Shirt Shop	37	Batterman's Men's Shop
38		38	
39		39	Tandy Leathercraft
40		40	
41	Shade and Blind	41	
42		42	The Fireplace Shop
43	Interior Decorators	43	
44		44	The Levi Place
45		45	

46	————	46	
47		47	Stitch and Sew
48		48	
49	Edward's Women Shoes	49	The Green Thumb
50		50	
51		51	
52	World of Gifts	52	Big and Tall Men's Store

major local retailers, as well as many nationally known retailers. The developers are attempting to control the tenant mix in terms of product, price, and promotional mix. Hopefully, the tenant mix will be such that it will attract consumers from many income categories ranging from upper-lower to upper-upper income groups.

The Firm: Selmer's Department Store

Selmer's Department Store, a leading soft-goods merchandiser in the Columbia area for over 80 years, was first established by William L. Selmer in 1889. Over the years, the name Selmer's has become synonymous with quality and style in the Columbia area. Appealing to the upper 40 percent of the market, Selmer's product, pricing, and promotional strategy is directed toward those consumers whose principal purchase motives are high quality, high style, and excellent service. For the last two decades, Selmer's merchandising strategy has been to offer high quality merchandise in a limited number of product lines at various pricing points. Sales departments, product lines, sales areas, pricing ranges, and annual sales are shown for each store in Exhibits 20–7, 20–8, 20–9, and 20–10. This standardized mix has proven to be quite successful for the last 20 years. However, ultraurban population shifts have created considerable sales variation from one store to another. These variations become more pronounced when reviewed in terms of sales per square foot. Perhaps some changes in the standardized mix are needed.

Gross margin characteristics and operating expenses by department for each store also are shown in Exhibits 20–7, 20–8, 20–9, and 20–10.

The Problem

Should Selmer's Department Stores engage in new facilities expansion by locating within the new Columbia Mall? If affirmative, follow Decision Path A; if negative, follow Decision Path B. (See Exhibit 20–11.)

Decision Path A	Decision Path B
A1—Justify decision to locate within the new mall.	B1—Justify decision not to locate within the new mall.

Exhibit 20-11

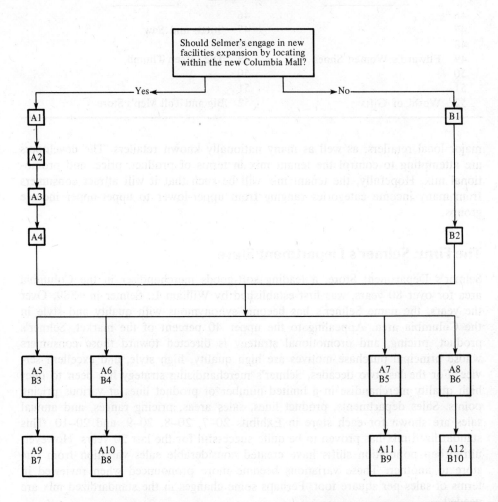

Should Selmer's engage in new facilities expansion by locating within the new Columbia Mall?

Yes◄ ── No►

Decision Path A	Decision Path B
A2—Determine where Selmers should locate within the new mall and justify the location decision.	B2—Without a new location, will the new mall have an impact on Selmer's current locations (stores)?
A3—Determine whether the new mall location will require adjustments in Selmer's standardized merchandising strategy (price, promotion, product mix, and facilities).	B3—What are the potential positive and negative impact factors of the new mall on the downtown location?
	B4—What are the potential positive and negative impact factors of the new mall on the Dutch Square location?
A4—Given a new mall location, will the new mall have an impact on Selmer's current locations (stores)?	
	B5—What are the potential positive and negative impact factors of

Decision Path A	Decision Path B

A5—What are the potential positive and negative impact factors of the new mall on the downtown location?

A6—What are the potential positive and negative impact factors of the new mall on the Dutch Square location?

A7—What are the potential positive and negative impact factors of the new mall on the Richland Mall location?

A8—What are the potential positive and negative impact factors of the new mall on the Five Points location?

A9—Should the downtown location be abandoned? Justify decision. If the Downtown location is to continue operations, then justify decision and determine what, if any, adjustments are required in Selmer's merchandising strategy (price, promotion, product mix, and facilities).

A10—Should the Dutch Square location be abandoned? Justify decision. If the Dutch Square location is to continue operations, then justify decision and determine what, if any, adjustments are required in Selmer's merchandising strategy (price, promotion, product mix and facilities).

A11—Should the Richland Mall location be abandoned? Justify decision. If the Richland Mall location is to continue operations, then justify decision and determine what, if any, adjustments are required in Selmer's merchandising strategy (price, promotion, product mix, and facilities).

the new mall on the Richland Mall location?

B6—What are the potential positive and negative impact factors of the new mall on the Five Points location?

B7—Should the downtown location be abandoned? Justify decision. If the downtown location is to continue operations, then justify decision and determine what, if any, adjustments are required in Selmer's merchandising strategy (price, promotion, product mix, and facilities).

B8—Should the Dutch Square location be abandoned? Justify decision. If the Dutch Square location is to continue operations, then justify decision and determine what, if any, adjustments are required in Selmer's merchandising strategy (price, promotion, product mix, and facilities).

B9—Should the Richland Mall location be abandoned? Justify decision. If the Richland Mall location is to continue operations, then justify decision and determine what, if any, adjustments are required in Selmer's merchandising strategy (price, promotion, product mix and facilities).

B10—Should the Five Points location be abandoned? Justify decision. If the Five Points location is to continue operations, then justify decision and determine what, if any, adjustments are required in Selmer's merchandising strategy (price, promotion, product mix, and facilities).

Decision Path A	Decision Path B
A12—Should the Five Points location be abandoned? Justify decision. If the Five Points location is to continue operations, then justify decision and determine what, if any, adjustments are required in Selmer's merchandising strategy (price, promotion, product mix, and facilities.)	

Exhibit 20-7

Sales Operations by Departments:
Downtown Store

Sales Departments	Price Range ($)	Sales Area (sq. ft.)	1977 Sales ($)	1976 Sales ($)	1975 Sales ($)	1977 Gross Margin % of Sales	1977 Operating Expenses % of Sales
Men's Department							
Suits	100–400	1,500	321,000	220,000	191,750		
Sportswear	15–100	3,800	345,000	222,750	188,500		
Accessories	10–100	1,500	243,000	178,750	136,500		
Total	*10–400*	*6,800*	*909,000*	*621,500*	*516,750*	*44.1*	*40.3*
Women's Department							
Moderate Dresses	25–100	6,350	417,000	371,250	347,750		
Moderate Sportswear	15–100	3,050	252,000	222,750	227,500		
Better Dresses	50–800	5,750	75,000	178,750	315,250		
Better Sportswear	30–900	2,250	33,000	167,750	312,000		
Lingerie	10–90	3,350	90,000	88,000	123,500		
Cosmetics	1–50	3,000	333,000	327,250	357,500		
Accessories	1–100	3,500	285,000	231,000	256,750		
Total	*1–900*	*27,250*	*1,485,000*	*1,586,750*	*1,940,250*	*46.2*	*41.5*
Junior's Department							
Sportswear	15–100	2,250	183,000	173,250	217,750		
Dresses	20–100	2,250	69,000	74,250	94,250		
Coats	20–200	500	33,000	27,500	32,500		
Total	*15–200*	*2,400*	*123,200*	*275,000*	*344,500*	*45.8*	*41.7*

Sales Departments	Price Range ($)	Sales Area (sq. ft.)	1977 Sales ($)	1976 Sales ($)	1975 Sales ($)	1977 Gross Margin % of Sales	1977 Operating Expenses % of Sales
Children's Department							
Boys	10–100	2,250	24,000	35,750	100,750		
Girls	10–100	2,250	12,000	30,250	94,250		
Infants	3–40	1,100	18,000	49,500	123,500		
Total	*3–100*	*5,600*	*54,000*	*115,500*	*318,500*	*46.5*	*41.8*
Gifts-Linen Department							
Total	*5–500*	*5,350*	*267,000*	*151,250*	*130,000*	*47.4*	*42.0*
Total	1–900	50,000	3,000,000	2,750,000	3,250,000		

Exhibit 20-8
Sales Operations by Departments: Dutch Square

Sales Departments	Price Range ($)	Sales Area (sq. ft.)	1977 Sales ($)	1976 Sales ($)	1975 Sales ($)	1977 Gross Margin % of Sales	1977 Operating Expenses % of Sales
Men's Department							
Suits	100–400	1,000	125,100	130,000	133,000		
Sportswear	15–100	2,500	213,800	190,000	127,000		
Accessories	10–100	1,000	150,100	155,000	126,000		
Total	*10–400*	*4,500*	*489,000*	*475,000*	*386,000*	*47.1*	*38.1*
Women's Department							
Moderate Dresses	25–100	4,200	377,100	380,000	401,000		
Moderate Sportswear	15–100	2,000	210,100	185,000	129,000		
Better Dresses	50–800	3,800	299,800	315,000	377,000		
Better Sportswear	30–900	1,500	171,100	165,000	119,000		
Lingerie	10–90	2,200	116,900	120,000	90,000		
Cosmetics	1–50	2,000	379,500	367,000	316,000		
Accessories	1–100	2,300	281,500	289,000	230,000		
Total	*1–900*	*18,000*	*1,836,000*	*1,821,000*	*1,662,000*	*48.2*	*38.6*
Junior's Department							
Sportswear	15–100	1,500	414,300	374,000	301,000		
Dresses	20–100	1,500	134,900	153,000	167,000		
Coats	20–200	300	45,000	46,000	36,000		
Total	*15–200*	*3,300*	*594,200*	*573,000*	*504,000*	*47.8*	*39.7*

Sales Departments	Price Range ($)	Sales Area (sq. ft.)	1977 Sales ($)	1976 Sales ($)	1975 Sales ($)	1977 Gross Margin % of Sales	1977 Operating Expenses % of Sales
Children's Department							
Boys	10–100	1,500	87,900	60,000	52,000		
Girls	10–100	1,500	104,000	77,000	66,000		
Infants	3–40	700	84,900	82,000	53,000		
Total	*3–100*	*3,700*	*276,800*	*219,000*	*171,000*	*48.5*	*38.8*
Gifts-Linen Department							
Total	*5,500*	*3,500*	*209,600*	*208,000*	*180,000*	*49.4*	*40.3*
Total	1–900	33,000	3,405,600	3,295,000	2,903,000		

Exhibit 20-9
Sales Operations by Departments: Richland Mall

Sales Departments	Price Range ($)	Sales Area (sq. ft.)	1977 Sales ($)	1976 Sales ($)	1975 Sales ($)	1977 Gross Margin % of Sales	1977 Operating Expenses % of Sales
Men's Department							
Suits	100–400	1,000	69,000	78,750	82,080		
Sportswear	15–100	2,500	94,300	114,750	118,560		
Accessories	10–100	1,000	94,300	114,750	118,560		
Total	*10–400*	*4,500*	*257,600*	*308,250*	*319,200*	*45.1*	*38.0*
Women's Department							
Moderate Dresses	25–100	4,200	292,900	297,000	321,480		
Moderate Sportswear	15–100	2,000	200,100	155,250	114,000		
Better Dresses	50–800	3,800	115,000	137,250	143,640		
Better Sportswear	30–900	1,500	135,700	114,750	70,680		
Lingerie	10–90	2,200	73,600	69,750	57,000		
Cosmetics	1–50	2,000	232,300	229,500	280,440		
Accessories	1–100	2,300	186,300	186,750	214,320		
Total	*1–900*	*18,000*	*1,225,900*	*1,190,250*	*1,201,560*	*47.2*	*38.4*
Junior's Department							
Sportswear	15–100	1,500	257,600	234,000	228,000		
Dresses	20–100	1,500	94,300	92,250	91,200		
Coats	20–200	300	29,900	22,500	22,800		
Total	*15–200*	*3,300*	*381,800*	*348,750*	*342,000*	*46.8*	*39.2*

Sales Departments	Price Range ($)	Sales Area (sq. ft.)	1977 Sales ($)	1976 Sales ($)	1975 Sales ($)	1977 Gross Margin % of Sales	1977 Operating Expenses % of Sales
Children's Department							
Boys	10–100	1,500	71,300	63,000	61,560		
Girls	10–100	1,500	73,600	67,500	63,840		
Infants	3–40	700	69,000	45,000	41,040		
Total	3–100	3,700	213,900	175,500	166,440	47.5	38.8
Gifts-Linen Department							
Total	5–500	3,500	220,800	227,250	250,800	48.4	39.9
Total	1–900	33,000	2,300,000	2,250,000	2,280,000		

Exhibit 20-10
Sales Operations by Departments: Five Points

Sales Departments	Price Range ($)	Sales Area (sq. ft.)	1977 Sales ($)	1976 Sales ($)	1975 Sales ($)	1977 Gross Margin % of Sales	1977 Operating Expenses % of Sales
Men's Department							
Suits	100–400	1,200	1,200	58,500	66,600		
Sportswear	15–100	3,040	109,200	105 000	86,400		
Accessories	10–15	1,200	72,800	70,500	66,600		
Total	*10–400*	*5,440*	*235,200*	*234,000*	*219,600*	*41.1*	*37.5*
Women's Department							
Moderate Dresses	25–100	5,080	114,800	160,500	219,600		
Moderate Sportswear	15–100	2,440	114,800	120,000	95,400		
Better Dresses	50–800	4,600	29,400	55,500	95,400		
Better Sportswear	30–900	1,800	75,600	61,500	66,600		
Lingerie	10–90	2,680	35,000	39,000	48,600		
Cosmetics	1–50	2,400	123,200	120,000	198,000		
Accessories	1–100	2,800	95,200	90,000	118,800		
Total	*1–900*	*21,800*	*588,000*	*646,500*	*842,400*	*45.2*	*38.0*
Junior's Department							
Sportswear	15–100	1,800	260,400	255,000	253,800		
Dresses	20–100	1,800	128,800	120,000	104,400		
Coats	20–200	400	43,400	48,000	46,800		
Total	*15–200*	*4,000*	*432,600*	*423,000*	*405,000*	*42.8*	*38.8*
Children's Department							
Boys	10–100	1,800	14,000	30,000	86,400		

Sales Departments	Price Range ($)	Sales Area (sq. ft.)	1977 Sales ($)	1976 Sales ($)	1975 Sales ($)	1977 Gross Margin % of Sales	1977 Operating Expenses % of Sales
Girls	10–100	1,800	22,400	43,500	95,400		
Infants	3–40	880	11,200	33,000	66,600		
Total	3–100	4,480	47,600	106,500	248,400	42.5	38.1
Gifts-Linen Department							
Total	5–500	4,280	96,600	90,000	86,600	44.4	38.9
Total	1–900	40,000	1,400,000	1,500,000	1,800,000		

The Hindman Stores:
The Addition of a Customer Service*

Michael J. Etzel, Utah State University

Hindman's is a 4-store chain of women's ready-to-wear establishments located in shopping centers in widely scattered areas of suburban Denver. Major management functions and bookkeeping for the 4 stores are conducted in a central location. The parent store is incorporated although each of the other three are operated as a sole proprietorship.

The owner of the stores has an extensive retail background in the Denver area, beginning with a single downtown store in the late 1940s. By the middle 1950s, though the downtown location was successful, the owner recognized a trend away from the core city and toward the suburbs, so the original store was relocated in a shopping center. In the next four years, the owner opened two additional stores, and in 1965 added a fourth operation, all in shopping centers.

The stores are designated 1, 2, 3, and 4 by the owner according to the order in which they were opened. The owner is concerned about store 4's declining sales.

Store 4 is a family-held corporation that began operation in January 1965. The store carrries a full line of women's ready-to-wear clothes with sales in the store divided among product lines as follows: 50 percent dresses and suits, 30 percent sportswear (slacks, blouses, swimwear), 10 percent coats, and 10 percent lingerie and sleepwear. The dresses in the store range from casual to cocktail styles and are priced from $15 to $75 with most sales in the $20 to $40 category. Coats range in price from $20 to $60 with $40 being the median sale.

The sales staff consists of the equivalent of five full-time people (four full-time and two part-time). One of the employees acts as store manager responsible for supervising store personnel, interviewing prospective employees, opening and closing the store, handling general housekeeping, and completing daily report sheets. The store also has the part-time services of a stock clerk and a bookkeeper.

---

* This case is adapted from an actual situation. The names have been changed to protect confidentiality.

The store is located in a shopping center which has a total floor area in excess of 400,000 square feet and a parking area for 3,000 cars. In 1968 there were 46 merchants in the center, including three additional women's ready-to-wear outlets. Two of these are larger than store 4 and one is smaller. There also are two major department stores in the center that have women's ready-to-wear departments larger than store 4. The center is approximately 4 miles from the downtown area. Three small (less than 100,000 square feet) shopping centers with 2 additional competitors are located within 3 miles. Store 4, situated on the edge of the shopping center without exposure to the main shopping mall, has 1,800 square feet of selling space with additional area for storage and dressing rooms.

Operating Data and Analysis—Store 4

Table 22–1 shows the total monthly sales figures for store 4 for years 1965 through 1968. Total sales show a constant decline over the four-year period. A closer examination of the figures indicates that the high sales months (characteristic of the first two years), April, May, August, and December declined considerably in 1967 and 1968. This is contrary to industry trends in retail clothing for the same period. Discussion with the owner produced a number of reasons for the annual decline. Three department stores in or near the shopping center in which

Table   21–1
Store 4—Total Sales by Month
1965–1968

Month	1965	1966	1967	1968
January	$ 4,387	$ 4,611	$ 3,396	$ 3,800
February	4,412	5,501	5,171	4,387
March	9,245	7,755	9,138[a]	7,429
April	13,160	10,226	8,664	8,907
May	10,266	10,125	8,625	8,659
June	7,262	7,782	7,410	6,753
July	8,474	8,282	6,003	6,341
August	12,958	11,719	9,282	10,149
September	9,921	8,057	9,556	7,889
October	9,196	7,263	6,028	6,883
November	7,784	6,032	5,573	5,702
December	12,785	9,678	10,840	8,061
Total	**$109,850**	**$97,031**	**$89,686**	**$84,960**

[a] Introduction of BankAmericard.

store 4 is located remodeled and improved the departments that provide competition. In addition, during this period three new specialty stores that produce direct competition were opened in the neighborhood. The owner also feels that the opening of a large department-discount store and a large grocery store nearby has considerably decreased the pedestrian traffic in the center. A final problem is a large shopping center which opened in 1967 that draws from part of the same market area as store 4's shopping center. Though all of these factors are present, the owner concedes that part of the decline also may be due to managerial error, specifically the failure to develop a significant differential advantage. In hopes of rectifying the problem, the owner was among the first merchants in the area to adopt the BankAmericard.

Credit Operations in the Hindman Stores

Credit Programs

Each of the stores offered internally financed credit since starting business. The internal credit program is relatively standard and includes two types of accounts: 30-day accounts and 90-day extended payment accounts. The 30-day accounts require no down payment with full payment due on or before the end of the month following the purchase. If full payment is not made within this time period, the account becomes delinquent and a 1.5 percent monthly service charge is added to the balance.

The second type of account is a 90-day extended payment account. Under this plan, the customer pays one-fourth of the total amount of the purchase price at the time of the sale. The remaining balance is due in one-third installments on the first day of each month of the three months following the purchase. A charge of 1.5 percent a month is made on the unpaid balance of all 90-day accounts.

Credit Applications

For customers who desire credit, the stores provide a standard credit application, requiring such information as home ownership, husband's employment, personal references, credit references, and bank accounts. All applications are reviewed by the owner who decides if further investigation is necessary before ruling on the request. Often the owner contacts personal and/or credit references by phone to collect all available pertinent information before ruling on the account and setting the credit limit. The normal limit on ordinary accounts is a maximum balance of $125 outstanding at any time. Although this is an unwritten rule, accounts are handled on a more personal basis, with considerable flexibility in this figure.

The owner does not make use of a credit bureau in checking applications because he feels an account can be personally processed for less than the $.90 charged by the credit bureau. The owner also feels that personal consideration of the applications is a special service that gives him the opportunity to consider unusual circumstances which might be ignored in an impersonal credit bureau check.

Handling Credit Sales

At the time of every cash or credit sale, a 2-copy sales slip is completed. The slip provides information on the item purchased, the amount of the sale, the name of the customer (for credit sales), and the amount received from the customer. At the end of the day, the information from the accumulated sales slips is transferred to a daily report sheet which, together with the sales slips, is sent to the bookkeeper. On receiving the package, the bookkeeper verifies the accuracy of the report sheet, posts credit sales to the appropriate ledger cards and credit statements, and prepares the bank deposit.

During 1969, the stores had approximately 2,445 accounts open-to-buy. However, the account file was not regularly purged, and a number of these accounts were no longer active. Management had made no effort to segregate active from inactive accounts or to develop any measure of the amount of activity in each account. According to the owner, the primary value of such an activity was as a source for direct mail lists. However, he felt the cost of direct mail advertising eliminates it as a promotional tool.

Bank Credit Card Operations

Reasons for Adopting the Bank Plan

According to the owner, the principal reason for adopting the credit plan was to attract additional sales. Another reason for adding the plan is the convenience it provides customers. The owner commented that the bank credit card gives the consumers the opportunity to shop without carrying cash, thus making unplanned purchases easier and therefore more frequent. A final rationale for accepting the credit card is that other stores provide it. In order to be competitive, the store owner feels a complete package of service must be offered to consumers including accepting bank credit cards.

The major disadvantage of the credit card, as seen by the owner, is that its use dilutes the loyalty of the credit buyer toward the store. He commented, "Credit customers have a habit of buying where they have an account due to either better service, recognition, or special service they receive." This objection has been overcome by mentally or intuitively weighing the trade-off between increases in potential customers and sales provided by the credit card against dilution of store loyalty produced by the general acceptability of the card.

When asked how much the plan might dilute store loyalty, the owner stated:

> I would guess that our account openings may be reduced by 25 percent (because of the bank plan), but BankAmericard brought us additional business. It made it easier for people to shop on a charge plan. Of course, it is impossible to determine how many or how few of the BankAmericard customers would open accounts or pay cash if we didn't accept it.

Though the store owner contends that no special effort has been made to encourage the use of credit, employees are given a cash incentive for each credit

Table 21–2
Store 4—Cash Sales, Internal Credit Sales,
And Bank Plan Sales by Month,
1965–1968

Month	1965		1966		1967			1968		
	Cash Sales	Internal Credit Sales	Cash Sales	Internal Credit Sales	Cash Sales	Internal Credit Sales	Bank Plan Sales	Cash Sales	Internal Credit Sales	Bank Plan Sales
January	$ 2,867	$ 1,520	$ 2,813	$ 1,798	$ 1,735	$ 1,661	—	$ 2,364	$ 1,030	$ 406
February	2,606	1,806	3,034	2,467	2,504	2,667	—	2,675	1,293	419
March	6,320	2,925	4,906	2,838	5,965	3,056ᵃ	$ 117	4,503	2,365	561
April	9,418	3,742	6,439	3,787	5,600	2,835	229	6,002	2,760	145
May	7,568	2,698	6,618	3,507	6,252	2,210	163	5,441	2,753	465
June	5,599	1,663	5,409	2,373	5,230	1,945	235	4,903	1,167	683
July	5,603	2,871	5,727	2,555	4,093	1,769	141	4,398	1,567	376
August	8,977	3,981	7,599	4,120	5,834	2,999	449	6,303	3,500	346
September	7,094	2,872	4,934	3,123	6,078	2,767	711	5,168	1,907	814
October	6,527	2,669	4,899	2,364	3,771	1,914	343	3,835	2,772	276
November	6,205	1,579	4,553	1,479	3,740	1,349	484	3,737	1,176	789
December	8,370	4,370	6,391	3,297	6,884	3,264	692	5,554	1,861	646
Total	$77,154	$32,696	$63,323	$33,708	$57,686	$28,436	$3,564	$54,883	$24,151	$5,927

ᵃ Introduction of bank credit card.

application taken. Possibly the owner's feelings are revealed in the statement, ". . . credit customers are better than cash customers, in a sense, because psychologically they are freer to spend, whether they know it or not."

Promotion of Credit

Media promotion of the stores' credit plans is limited to a one-line statement in printed advertisements stating that credit is available. There also is a sign in each of the store's dressing rooms to the same effect. The most expensive promotion is the bonus paid to employees for each completed credit application they secure.

Promotion of the bank plan is equally limited. The only visible notice of the plan is the standard window decal advertising the credit card's acceptability.

The stores do not employ the seasonal promotions—mobiles and stand-up signs—provided by the bank. An employee explained that these are not viewed by the management as merchandising aids but as unnecessary clutter that distracts from the clothing display.

Handling Bank Plan Sales

The stores do not submit credit sales slips to the bank daily in the manner envisoned by the plan's promoters. Instead of frequently mailing the sales slips to receive cash for sales, one deposit is made each month. The owner offers two reasons for doing this. First, he does not feel a need for the working capital the bank plan sales could provide since he currently receives the maximum discount on merchandise purchases without resorting to these funds. Secondly, the owner feels that a daily or even weekly submission of credit sales slips would take too much time for the volume of sales involved. Rather than take some fraction of every day to prepare the deposit, he feels it is more efficient to prepare and submit all of the month's bank credit card transactions at once.

Table 21–2 presents total sales divided into cash, internal credit, and bank plan sales. The table indicates that a decline in sales was experienced in both cash and internal credit sales. However, when bank credit card sales are added to internal credit sales, an element of stability appears. In 1967, total credit

Table   21–3
Store 4—Cash and Credit
Sales Ratios by Year,
1965–1968

Year	Cash Sales / Total Sales	Internal Credit Sales / Total Sales	Total Credit Sales [a] / Total Sales
1965	70.24%	29.77%	29.77%
1966	65.26	34.74	34.74
1967	64.32	31.71	35.68
1968	64.60	28.43	35.43

[a] Total credit includes BankAmericard sales.

Table   21–4
Store 4—Number of BankAmericard Sales,
Sales Volume, Average Amount of Each Sale,
And the Discount Income to the Bank, by Month,
1967–1968

Year/ Month	Number of Sales	Dollar Volume of Sales	Average Sales	Discount Income to Bank
1967				
March	5	117	$23.31	$ 5.85
April	9	229	25.43	11.40
May	8	163	20.35	8.10
June	14	235	16.80	11.80
July	10	141	14.13	7.10
August	28	449	16.02	22.40
September	29	711	24.53	35.55
October	12	343	28.61	17.15
November	19	484	25.45	24.10
December	30	692	23.08	34.55
Total	164	3,564	$21.77	$178.00
1968				
January	20	406	$20.31	$ 20.30
February	20	419	20.95	20.95
March	27	561	20.77	28.00
April	10	145	14.49	7.25
May	30	465	15.52	34.15
June	35	683	19.51	34.15
July	19	376	19.78	18.80
August	20	346	16.29	17.25
September	38	814	21.43	40.70
October	9	276	30.68	13.80
November	27	789	29.21	39.45
December	34	646	19.01	32.25
Total	289	5,927	$20.51	$296.15

sales became $32,000, and in 1968, $30,078; a relationship clearly shown in Table 21–3.

Table 21–3 shows that from 1965 to 1966, prior to the adoption of the bank credit card, internal credit sales increased as a proportion of total sales. However, from 1966 to 1967 and 1967 to 1968, internal credit sales showed a decline while total credit sales, including the bank credit card sales, continued to increase.

A breakdown of BankAmericard sales for store 4 is shown in Table 21–4 by month since the inception of the plan.

Table 21–5 brings together the sales activity of 1967 and 1968 in order to compare bank plan sales with other sales figures. Bank plan sales are a significant portion of total sales in both years, rising 2.34 percent in 1968 to total 6.98 percent of total sales in that year.

Table 21–6 portrays the role the bank plan has played in the sales decline experienced by store 4. Finally, when bank plan sales are added to internal credit sales, the decline in total credit sales is much more consistent with changes in total sales and cash sales. Table 21–7 shows the decline in sales from 1967 to 1968 with bank plan sales included and excluded. Thus, if one considers the change in total sales from 1967 to 1968 including bank plan sales, which is what actually occurred, the decline is 5.27 percent. On the other hand, if bank sales

Table   21–5
Store 4—Bankamericard Sales As a Percentage of
Total Sales, Cash Sales, Total Credit Sales
And Internal Credit Sales by Year,
1967–1968

Year	$\dfrac{\text{BAC Sales}}{\text{Total Sales}}$	$\dfrac{\text{BAC Sales}}{\text{Cash Sales}}$	$\dfrac{\text{BAC Sales}}{\text{Internal Credit Sales}}$	$\dfrac{\text{BAC Sales}}{\text{Total Credit}}$
1967[a]	4.64%	6.50%	14.76%	12.86%
1968	6.98	10.80	24.54	19.71

[a] The percentages of 1967 are calculated using the ten months of data that correspond to the presence of the bank plan.

Table   21–6
Store 4—Yearly Percentage Change in Total
Sales, Cash Sales, Internal Credit Sales, Total
Credit Sales, and Bank Plan Sales,
1965–68

Year	Total Sales	Cash Sales	Internal Credit Sales	Total[a] Credit Sales	Bank Plan Sales
1965–66	−11.66%	−17.93%	+ 3.10%	+3.10%	—
1966–67	− 7.57	− 8.89	−15.64	−5.07	—
1967–68	− 5.27	− 4.85	−15.07	−6.01	+66.30%
TOTAL	−24.50	−31.67	−27.61	−7.98	

[a] Total credit includes BankAmericard sales.

Table 21–7
Store 4—Change in Total Sales
And Credit Sales from 1967 to 1968 When
BankAmericard Sales Are Included and Excluded

Year	Total Sales	Cash Sales	Credit Sales	BAC Sales
1967				
with credit card	$89,686	$57,686	$32,000	
without credit card	86,122	57,686	28,436	$3,564
1968				
with credit card	$84,960	$54,883	$30,078	
without credit card	79,033	54,883	24,151	$5,927
Change 1967 to 1968				
with credit card	−5.27%	−4.85%	− 6.01%	
without credit card	−8.23	−4.85	−15.07	

are deleted from both years, total sales show a decline of 8.23 percent. It is particularly interesting to note the accentuation of the decline in credit sales—from 6.01 percent to 15.07 percent—when bank plan sales are excluded.

Table 21–8 presents a breakdown of returns on bank plan sales showing the number of returns, the amount of returns, and the average return on a monthly basis. Data on internal credit sales returns are not available for comparison. However, Table 21–9 compares bank plan returns with bank plan sales.

In addition to its impact on sales, the cost of the bank credit plan must be considered. Table 21–10 is the result of an analysis of internal credit costs. The comparable costs for bank credit card sales including operating costs and the discount paid to the bank, 15.4 percent of bank credit card sales.

Hindman is faced with a decision about the new credit service. He has several options including dropping the bank credit card completely, adding it to the service package at his other stores, and/or attempting to replace internal credit with the bank plan.

Discussion Questions

1. Based on the data provided, does the bank credit card plan produce significant benefits for Hindman? Why or why not?

2. The promoters of the bank credit card claim that the plans will:
(*a*) reduce management time in credit

Table   21–8
Store 4—Number of BankAmericard
Sales Returns, Amount of Returns, and
Average Amount of Returns by Month, 1967–1968

Year/ Month	Number of Returns	Amount of Returns	Average Return
1967			
March	—	—	—
April	—	—	—
May	—	—	—
June	3	$ 61.95	$20.65
July	1	9.45	9.45
August	—	—	—
September	—	—	—
October	1	21.52	21.52
November	1	47.25	47.25
December	—	—	—
Total	6	$140.17	$23.36
1968			
January	—	—	—
February	—	—	—
March	1	$ 24.15	$24.15
April	1	18.90	18.90
May	—	—	—
June	—	—	—
July	—	—	—
August	—	—	—
September	3	75.60	25.20
October	—	—	—
November	5	57.75	11.55
December	—	—	—
Total	10	$176.40	$17.64

(*b*) provide increased working capital
(*c*) offer protection from bad debt losses
(*d*) result in a lower cost of doing credit business
(*e*) increase sales

Has Hindman experienced these benefits?

3. Would you consider the addition of the bank credit card in 1967 a potentially significant differential advantage?

4. What do you recommend Hindman do with the bank credit card plan and why?

Table   21–9
Store 4—The Number and Amount of Bank
Plan Sales Returns As a Percentage of the
Number and Volume of Bank Plan Sales,
1967–1968

	1967	1968
Number of Sales	164	289
Number of Returns	6	10
# Returns/ # Sales	3.66%	3.46%
Amount of Sales	$3,564	$5,927
Amount of Returns	$140	$176
Amount Returns/Amount Sales	3.93%	2.97%

Table   21–10
Store 4—Direct Cost of Offering
Internal Credit During 1968

Credit Expenses

1. Solicitation of new accounts	$ 21.00
2. Checking credit applications	75.18
3. Preparation and issuance of identification cards	253.50
4. Preparation and handling of monthly statements	257.28
5. Receiving correspondence from customers	341.55
6. Contacting and tracing delinquent accounts	190.80
7. Cost of capital invested in accounts receivable (calculated at 7.0%)	223.65
8. Bad debt expense	798.08
Total Cost of Credit	$ 2,161.04

Credit Income

9. Income from services charges	−222.75
Net Cost of Credit	$ 1,938.29

Total credit sales during 1968 $24,151.00

Direct cost of internal credit as a percentage of internal credit sales at a cost of capital of:

7%	8.02%
9	8.29
12	8.69
15	9.87

Amway Corporation: Direct Marketing System

J. Taylor Sims, Wright State University

Amway Corporation is one of the fastest growing companies in North America. In only a few years it has grown from a small distributor of household products into a complete manufacturing and sales organization with a multi-million dollar annual sales volume. This growth includes all areas of operation. The company has completed several phases of a continuing program of increasing facilities for research, production, warehousing, and selling. Distributors have rapidly multiplied, until today, over 80,000 people are engaged in selling Amway products to homes and industry throughout the United States and Canada.

The corporation was founded by two men with broad experience in direct selling. Jay Van Andel and Richard DeVos each have over 15 years experience developing direct sales distributorships. As president, Mr. DeVos is in charge of personnel, aviation, and sales divisions (including training, conventions, and sales meetings). Mr. Van Andel, board chairman, handles the finance, manufacturing, operations, marketing, and legal divisions. In effect, these two men serve as co-chief executive officers of the corporation.

Amway's U. S. home office and main manufacturing facilities are located on a 250 acre tract of land at Ada, Michigan, about 9 miles east of Grand Rapids. In Amway's multi-million dollar complex is housed a modern, efficient manufacturing operation, including the most up-to-date equipment for formulating, packaging, bottling, and labeling powder and liquid products. Due to the importance of aerosol packages in the Amway line, the plant includes one of the most completely automatic aerosol filling facilities in existence.

Laboratories at the Ada plant are staffed with specialized chemists who carry out extensive testing programs on both raw materials and finished products to assure rigid standards of quality control. In addition, these laboratories are used for research on new and improved products.

Other departments at the Ada plant include: offices where the details and correspondence connected with millions of dollars worth of annual sales are handled; the creative and printing production department, which turns out hundreds of thousands of price lists, bulletins, brochures, and other printed pieces each month; and extensive storage facilities for inventories of raw materials and finished goods. Over 20 regional warehouses in strategically located cities in the United States and Canada serve distributors. Amway home products include such items as pesticides, auto care products, clothing care products, floor and furniture care products, laundry and kitchen care products, room fresheners, and personal care products. Amway also manufactures a line of commercial cleaning products. (See Exhibit 22–1.)

Amway Distribution System

Physical Distribution

In the Amway system products are produced and then sent to a central warehouse on location at the Ada plant facility. From this warehouse Amway products are shipped to private warehouses all over the United States. In other words, the central warehouse handles orders from all of these individual warehouses. The central warehouse performs the transportation function of goods from the manufacturer to the private warehouses. Transportation of goods from the private warehouses are handled in two ways. The individual salesperson placing an order can furnish transportation or, if this is not feasible, the warehouse can handle the transportation in the most cost efficient manner available.

The Amway Marketing Plan

The following points summarize the Amway marketing plan:

(1) Each Amway distributor is either an independent business person or husband-wife partnership. Each distributorship is authorized to sell Amway products by Amway Corporation.

(2) This independent business that an Amway distributor builds, distributing Amway products, belongs to the distributor. In the event of the distributor's death, the business can be passed to legal heirs or estate as directed by applicable laws.

(3) Amway distributors may sponsor new applicants for Amway distributorships. In exchange for motivating, training, and acting as wholesale supplier, the sponsor earns financial rewards through higher bonuses or "refunds" earned by combining the sponsor's purchase volume with that of the distributors sponsored.

(4) Amway distributors can develop income through retail sales as a result of their own sales efforts or in the form of bonuses based on total business volume, including wholesale sales to sponsored distributors.

(5) Amway distributors have exclusive rights to the distributors and their

Exhibit 22-1

Safety Care

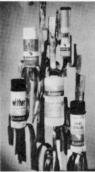

Pesticides, Germicides,
Herbicides

Auto Care

Clothing and Clothing Care

Floor and Furniture Care

Laundry Care

AMWAY HOME CARE PRODUCTS

Room Fresheners

Personal Care

Kitchen Care

customers. As long as they are properly serviced, customers cannot be switched from one Amway distributor to another without consent of both parties.

(6) Amway distributors who sponsor other distributors have the right to continue that sponsorship without change as long as basic sponsorship requirements are met.

(7) Because of the customer and distributor protection system, it is not necessary to restrict the general operations of Amway distributors to territories, and thus each Amway distributor has the entire nation as field for development.

(8) The Amway Corporation distributes Amway products only through Amway distributors and does not solicit business except through distributors. All prospective customer leads coming to the Amway office are passed on to the nearest direct distributor; there are no "house accounts."

The Amway Profit Plan

Basic Discount

The person selling Amway products can earn gross income 2 ways—the first of these is through "basic discount." The salesperson buys products from a sponsor at a wholesale price and sells them to customers at a retail price. The basic discount on most home-size products is 35 percent with a few at 25 percent. That percentage is the salesperson's gross profit—the basic discount received when the salesperson is paid by a customer. (The basic discount on larger size commercial products is usually 15 percent.) Most distributors *average* about 30 percent immediate profit. The sponsor sells the products to his sponsored distributors at the same price at which the products are bought, making no "basic discount" for the sponsor.

Refund

The second way the salesperson earns income is through monthly refund on *all* Amway products purchased for resale—home products, cookware, and commercial products (but not including literature or sales aids). In addition to the immediate "basic discount," the salesperson receives a refund each month based on the total combined purchase volume (PV) of all products sold for the month. The refund varies from 3 to 25 percent, depending upon a salesperson's PV as shown in Table 22–1.

Example of Part-Time Group Sponsorship Profits

To see how the Amway salesperson earns part-time profits as a sponsor, take this example: The sponsor is selling on a part-time basis to personal customers who purchase $320 worth of Amway products per month. She also sponsors 5 other part-time distributors who add a total of $2,400 of monthly combined PV. Table 22–2 shows how each of the distributors she sponsors earns his full discount and refund, while the sponsor earns her full discount on her personal sales, plus a

Table   22–1
Personal PV
Basic Discount + Refund = Gross Profit

Total Monthly PV*		Basic Discount on Personal PV	Refund	% of Gross Profit on Personal PV
$ 1.00 to $ 99.99		up to 35%	0	up to 35%
100.00 to 299.99		up to 35%	3%	up to 38%
300.00 to 599.99		up to 35%	6%	up to 41%
600.00 to 999.99		up to 35%	9%	up to 44%
1,000.00 to 1,499.99		up to 35%	12%	up to 47%
1,500.00 to 2,499.99		up to 35%	15%	up to 50%
2,500.00 to 3,999.99		up to 35%	18%	up to 53%
4,000.00 to 5,999.99		up to 35%	21%	up to 56%
6,000.00 to 7,499.99		up to 35%	23%	up to 58%
7,500.00 and up		up to 35%	25%	up to 60%

* Total monthly PV includes both personal PV and PV of others you sponsor

Table   22–2
Distribution of Refund on $2,720 Total Group PV—
18 Percent Refund $489.60

	Individual PV	Individual Refund %	Individual Refund $	% Refund Left for Sponsor	$ Refund Left for Sponsor
A	$640	9%	$ 57.60	9%	$ 57.60
B	560	6	33.60	12	67.20
C	480	6	28.80	12	57.60
D	400	6	24.00	12	48.00
E	320	6	19.20	12	38.40
Sponsor	320	—	—	18	57.60
Total	$2,720		$163.20		$326.40

Total Refund: $489.60
Paid Out: 163.20
Sponsor Maximum Basic Discount: $112.00
Sponsor Maximum Total Earnings: $438.40

Note: A, B, C, D, and E also sponsor distributors under them.

refund of 18 percent on her personal sales, plus the difference between 18 percent and the percentage refund earned by each of her distributors on his sales. If she were *not* a sponsor, her income would be $131.60—6 percent refund plus 35 percent discount. In this case, as a sponsor, she earns a total of $438.40 from part-time selling and sponsoring.

Example of Full-Time Group Sponsorship Profits

The following example shows how an Amway salesperson might earn even greater income as a full-time sponsor of a group of distributors. In this instance she is selling to a larger personal customer clientele who make purchases from her totaling $500 of Amway products monthly. Also, the distributors she sponsors have increased their sales and have recruited some distributors of their own until they contribute an additional $5,000 to the sponsor's total PV. Now she is in the 21 percent refund bracket and gets the full basic discount on her personal sales, plus 21 percent refund on her personal sales, plus the difference between 21 percent and the percentage refund earned by each of her distributors on his sales. As a sponsor, she earns $736. In this example, as well as in the previous one, *note that she does not reduce the regular profits of the distributor she sponsors, and her sponsor does not reduce his regular profits.* Every distributor receives the full amount she has earned on the discount and refund schedule, which will also include an override on the sales of those sponsored either directly or indirectly when her combined refund percentage is greater than theirs. (See Table 22–3.)

Table 22–3
Distribution of Refund on $5,500 Total Group PV—
21 Percent Refund $1,155

	Individual PV	Individual Refund %	Individual Refund $	% Refund Left for Sponsor	$ Refund Left for Sponsor
A	1,000	12%	$120	9%	$ 90
B	900	9	81	12	108
C	1,200	12	144	9	108
D	1,500	15	225	6	90
E	400	6	24	15	60
Sponsor	500	—	—	21	105
Total	$5,500		$594		$561

Sponsor's Maximum Basic Discount: $175
Sponsor's Maximum Total Earnings: $736

Note: A, B, C, D, and E also have distributors under them helping to make total. From here it is only a short step to direct distributor.

The Direct Distributor

At the head of every distributor group there is a direct distributor. This distributor has reached the maximum PV bracket and, thereby, the maximum refund bracket of 25 percent. There is no limit to the number of direct distributors; anyone can become one by reaching the qualifying PV of $7,500 monthly. Direct distributors buy directly from Amway Corporation, they can also become voting members of the

ADA, and they may serve on the board. They enjoy other privileges as the sales leaders in the Amway sales system. Among these benefits are the added bonuses for which they qualify, which are described briefly below.

When a person sponsors a direct distributor, then both the sponsor of the direct distributor and the direct distributor are in the same refund percentage bracket. In order that the sponsor of a direct distributor may enjoy a profit also, Amway pays a special 3 percent bonus. To qualify for the 3 percent, the sponsor must either have at least $2500 personal group PV, in addition to sponsoring the direct distributor below him, or sponsor 2 or more direct distributors. (See Table 22–4.)

"Sub-Direct" Distributor

A "sub-direct" distributor is one who sponsors only one direct distributor (25 percent) group but does not have a minimum of $2500 personal group PV. Such a person does get the 25 percent refund on whatever personal group PV he may have but does not qualify for the 3 percent bonus. Since it is the purpose of the Amway sales plan to compensate the distributor in proportion to the production resulting from the time and effort he has put forth, the direct distributor bonus is computed in such a way that it is more profitable to sponsor several direct distributors than

Table   22–4
Direct Distributor Income

Distributor Groups	Volume	Distributor Group: % Earned	Total Refund Paid
A	$ 1,000	12%	$ 120
B	500	6	30
C	1,500	15	225
D	2,000	15	300
E	100	3	3
F	200	3	6
G	200	3	6
H	1,500	15	225
I	2,000	15	300
J	1,000	12	120
Total	$10,000		$1,335

Refund Received: $2,500
Refund Paid Out: $1,335
Profit From Group: $1,165

Note: In this example personal sales are not shown. If the sponsor had $500 in personal sales, his earnings would increase by $300 making a total of $1,465.

just one. If a sponsor does happen to sponsor just one direct distributor, it is more profitable for the sponsor to have a sizeable personal group PV in addition to sponsoring that one direct distributor than it is to have little or no personal group PV or personal retail PV and sponsor only one direct distributor.

Sponsoring two or more direct distributors usually is the result of the direct distributor's sponsor having spent considerably more time and effort than her sponsoring of just one direct distributor, with little or no personal group PV maintained in addition. Therefore, the direct distributor bonus brings the most compensation to the direct distributor's sponsor who has put in the most time and effort and produced the *best balanced* groups.

The 3 Percent Bonus

Although a direct distributor collects a 3 percent bonus on the personal group PV of the direct distributor she sponsors, she also must remember that her sponsor collects a 3 percent bonus on her personal group PV. Therefore, each direct distributor will collect a 3 percent direct distributor bonus on the personal group PV of the direct distributor she sponsors and will maintain sufficient personal group or personal retail PV himself to guarantee that her sponsor receives a 3 percent direct distributor bonus on her personal group PV of:

(1) At least equal to the amount of the bonus collected if she sponsors only one direct distributor, but not more than $225,

(2) Equal to at least one-half of the combined 3 percent bonus collected if she sponsors 2 direct distributors, but not more than $225,

(3) Equal to at least one-third of the combined 3 percent bonus collected if she sponsors 3 direct distributors, but not more than $225,

and so on, always guaranteeing to her sponsor a bonus equal to the total bonus received, divided by the total number of direct distributors sponsored but never more than $225 per month.

If a direct distributor sponsor's personal group PV is such that the sponsor would not receive a 3 percent bonus of at least the amount specified in the above paragraph, the difference between the amount that the 3 percent actually amounted to, and what it should amount to, is deducted from the direct distributor bonus of the *first* direct distributor sponsor and added to the direct distributor bonus of her sponsor. This same adjustment applies up a group sponsorship. The adjustment is limited to a maximum of $225, however. An example of how the 3 percent bonus system works is shown in Figure 22–1.

In the example, A sponsors B who in turn sponsors distributors C, D, E, and F. B receives a 3 percent bonus on the sales of each of his distributors. According to Amway's bonus guarantee structure, B must guarantee A the average of $217.50 ($870 divided by 4). Since B has no personal group PV, the $217.50 is deducted from his $870, leaving him a net profit of $652.50. Remember that each direct distributor deals directly with Amway so the $652.50 is paid to B even if he were sick, retired, or traveling around the world.

Figure   22–1
Example of a 3 Percent Bonus*
Each circle represents a direct distributor

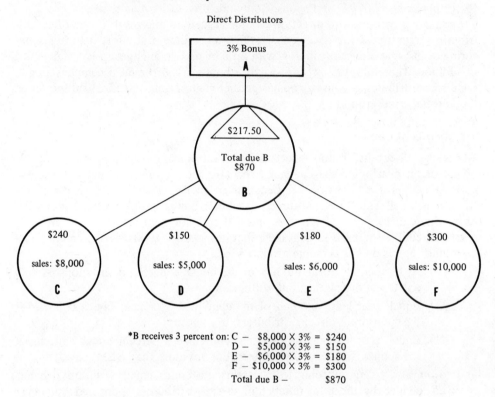

Direct Distributors

*B receives 3 percent on: C — $8,000 × 3% = $240
D — $5,000 × 3% = $150
E — $6,000 × 3% = $180
F — $10,000 × 3% = $300
Total due B — $870

Sales Training Bonus

The sales training bonus is designed to reward sponsors of multiple groups of direct distributors. Direct distributors who sponsor personally 3 or more groups of direct distributors share a fund consisting of one-fourth of 1 percent of the national PV, which is distributed to them annually. This, in effect, gives them a percentage on all the volume in their total group, regardless of depth.

Profit Sharing Bonus

At the end of each year that Amway has been in business, a percentage of Amway's corporate net profit has been divided among the direct distributor voting members of ADA as a profit-sharing bonus. The bonus currently is paid in the form of 7-year interest bearing debenture bonds. The bonus is not guaranteed since it is discretionary with Amway.

Product Quality and Pricing

Amway Corporation is known for its quality products. No product is released for distribution until it has been exhaustively tested for quality and performance. Each Amway product carries a 100 percent money-back guarantee. See Exhibit 22–2.

Amway products are priced slightly higher (about 10 percent) than competitive products. The policy of "best quality," however, generally justifies the price differences in the minds of consumers. In addition, the in-the-home selling environment tends to make Amway competition more indirect than direct. The Amway salesperson who is invited into a customer's home to discuss Amway products does not have to compete with either the loyalty or the impulse factors exhibited by competitive products in the store.

Advertising and Promotion

National Advertising

Amway Corporation supports its sales program on the national level through radio and magazine advertising. "Paul Harvey News," a staple of the ABC Radio network since 1951, was chosen by Amway in 1968 to present a nationwide radio program to bring the Amway home care message to America's radio-listening public.

According to Jay Van Andel, chairman of the board, Amway's entrance into radio advertising media is designed to support and strengthen the firm's national magazine advertising program initiated in the spring of 1965. One example of

Exhibit 22-2
Amway Guarantee

Guarantee

Amway Corporation guarantees the quality of any product which bears the Amway label, and is confident that you will find its products satisfactory in every respect.

If for any reason, however, you are not completely satisfied with any Amway product purchased by you, you may return it, or the unused portion thereof, to the Amway Distributor who sold it to you. The Distributor will offer you the choice of replacement or repair without charge, or full credit toward the purchase of another Amway product, or refund of the full purchase price.

This Guarantee is limited only by the terms of certain specific warranties attached to or packaged with certain products (such as hosiery), and does not apply to any products intentionally damaged or misused.

AMWAY CORPORATION

Amway's magazine advertising program is its *TV Guide* campaign. See Exhibit 22-3. Featuring illustrations by Norman Rockwell, America's best-known artist, Amway's *TV Guide* ads are seen by over 12 million subscribers and newsstand buyers—an estimated 26 million readers! The entire *TV Guide* series is distributor oriented. The products are mentioned, but the distributor receives the major emphasis.

Regional and Local Promotion

In addition to national advertising, Amway has developed a great variety of promotional material which the distributor may display to customers. Point-of-purchase advertising and aids have been most effective in retail sales. All sales literature and advertising material is printed by Amway for sale to their distributors. Direct distributors buy this material from Amway and resell it to the distributors in their groups at cost. The general types of advertising and promotional materials provided by Amway include:

(1) Outdoor billboards

(2) Slide films, records, tapes

(3) Catalogs and manuals

(4) Annual international convention

(5) Sales rallies

(6) Home care demonstration kit

(7) Fund raising brochure

Exhibit 22-3
TV Guide Campaign

Exhibit 22-4
Amway Trademark

AMWAY TRADEMARKS

Amway Trademarks Not To Be Used On Any Item:
Literature, Premium, Or Product Of Any Sort,
Without Advance Approval, In Writing, From Amway

(8) Portable tape recorder

(9) Personal shoppers service catalog

(10) Company trademark decals

(11) Newsgrams

(12) Personal sales award plaques

(13) Point-of-purchase display kit

(14) Meeting badges

(15) Gift boxes for customers

Discussion Questions

1. Evaluate the direct distribution system used by Amway. Do you feel that this is the most efficient type of channel that could be used given the types of products Amway manufactures? What other distribution systems might Amway consider? Why?

2. Does the type of distribution system employed by Amway allow for adequate control of product distribution by the manufacturer? Why or why not?

3. What are the sources of conflict in this type of channel? How important are such conflicts likely to be as a deterrent to Amway's sales and profit policies?

4. Evaluate the Amway sales and profit plan. How attractive are the plans from

the point of view of the manufacturer? From the point of view of the resellers? From the point of view of the ultimate consumer?

5. Critically assess the advertising and promotional support supplied by Amway to its distributors. What changes would you make, if any?

Leisure Products, Inc.

Robert A. Robicheaux, University of Alabama

"You know, Jim, I'm beginning to think that our success really is going to depend, more than any other factor, upon the channel system we develop to market our products. When our consultant told me that several weeks ago I didn't believe him. But, the more I think about it, the more I tend to agree." Avery Norwood, president and majority stockholder of Leisure Products, Inc. (LPI), a new Tennessee-based small appliance manufacturer, was talking to James Phillips, vice-president and plant foreman for LPI. This was June 1976, and the two men were on their way to a working session with their CPA and marketing consultant to discuss the marketing program for their proposed new company.

Between 1972 and 1975, Norwood and Phillips gave considerable thought to breaking away from their current comfortable positions and striking out on their own. Norwood is currently plant manager of the Munsey Products plant in Lenoir City, Tennessee. Phillips is plant foreman. The plant produces component parts for a variety of small appliances that are assembled at other Munsey plants. Norwood is considered by many in the industry to be a tooling design genius. He personally designed many of the labor-saving production line machines in the Munsey plant. Phillips, on the other hand, has the capacity to get the most out of his workers in a most amiable manner. He literally runs the production operations at the Lenoir City plant.

Background

In 1975, Norwood completed the tooling design on the equipment to mass produce two-burner hotplates/buffet ranges and outdoor electric grills. These are the two items with which Norwood feels his new company could enjoy the greatest differential advantages in terms of product styling, durability, performance,

389

and cost (price to consumers). The hotplate/buffet range products were designed to be used as warming trays for hot *hor d'oeuvres* at parties as well as free standing cooking/warming elements for patio cooking. The production plans call for the development of hotplates that are far more attractive and durable than those currently on the market. Recognizing the advantages of a multiple item product line, Norwood added an outdoor electric grill to the product line. This, he thought, would be his first step toward the development of a full line of entertainment/leisure/convenience (ELC) cooking appliances.

Norwood and Phillips examined the trade publication reports of industry sales of hotplates/buffet ranges throughout the early seventies. They reasoned that in an industry with sales of nearly one million units (hotplates), they would have to secure only a very small share of the market to succeed financially. They determined that they would have to make an initial fixed capital outlay of approximately $207,000 during the first year of their new company's operation. The company already has entered into negotiations with the Small Business Administration (SBA) to secure a loan to supplement their equity. They currently plan to invest approximately $149,000 in land, building, tools, and equipment. Other anticipated fixed costs include an annual administrative overhead expense of approximately $38,000 and annual interest payments of $10,000 on the SBA loan. Variable unit production costs on the two-burner hotplates have been estimated to be $10.00 (including a 5 percent agent's selling commission). The hotplates would list at retail for about $29.99 and be sold to wholesalers for $20.50. Wholesalers were expected to sell the hotplates at $22.50 each to retailers. Variable production costs on the electric outdoor grill have been estimated to be $20.00 (also including a 5 percent agent's selling commission). The grills would list at retail for $69.99 and be sold to wholesalers for $35.00. LPI expected wholesalers to sell the grills to retailers for about $40.00 each. Selling expenses had been estimated quite liberally at 10 percent of gross invoice value of annual sales to support the normally high marketing program start-up costs.

The two men have been optimistic throughout the past several years that they could produce superior products at lower costs than their competitors. They both recognize that they have a "production orientation" and look upon marketing as a necessary evil. During the 1974–1975 recession, they witnessed the rapid demise of many small and medium-size companies in the appliance industry, however, and recently have begun to have second thoughts about the wisdom of leaving their secure positions with Munsey to form their own company.

A discussion of several critical topics was planned for the working session to which they were headed. Most importantly, Norwood wanted to learn from his consultants how they assessed the market opportunity for LPI's entry into the small appliance industry. He felt that this required a detailed appraisal of industry and consumer market trends as well as a rational assessment of LPI's probable competitive strengths and weaknesses. A second major area of interest to Norwood was a determination of unit sales volume and market share that LPI would have to achieve to break even. Finally, he was anxious to begin detailed discussions of the marketing channels program that was going to serve as the framework for the new company's entire marketing program. This discussion was to encompass such topics as:

(*a*) extent of LPI's distribution throughout the U.S.

(*b*) type(s) of channel(s) to be employed to distribute LPI products

(*c*) intensity of distribution most appropriate at each level of the firm's channel(s)

(*d*) extent to which LPI should attempt to control resale prices and limit agent and/or distributor territories

(*e*) extent and character of inventory protection and marketing assistance that LPI should extend to members of its channel(s)

As Norwood and Phillips continued on their drive, they silently reviewed the results of their recent months' research.

Short-Term Economic Outlook

The probability of the success of LPI will be at least partially dependent upon the health of the U.S. economy. Established firms can weather the hard times of a recession much better than fledgling newcomers. The U.S. economy suffered through the most severe slump experienced in several decades during the early seventies. Forecasters and analysts in mid-1976 predicted that the upturn that began during the second half of 1975 would continue at least through 1977. The deceleration in the rate of inflation, tremendous decline in wholesale prices, drop in unemployment, and jump in retail sales during the second half of 1975 appeared to confirm those optimistic forecasts. Further, during the spring of 1975, the Gross National Product showed a substantial increase, the first real dollar increase in over a year. GNP continued to rise steadily through the winter of 1976 and the Survey Research Center of the University of Michigan forecast continued, steady GNP growth throughout the remainder of 1976.[1]

The national unemployment picture also made a dramatic turnaround during the second half of 1975. The percent of the U.S. workforce unemployed fell from almost 9 percent in mid-1975 to about 7.5 percent at the end of the first quarter of 1976. Although this was still high in absolute terms, it was the lowest level reached in 15 months. The Michigan Survey Research Center forecast unemployment to continue to decline slowly but steadily throughout 1976.[2]

In early 1975, the Survey Research Center's Index of Consumer Sentiment, a measure of consumer confidence, reached its lowest level in over 15 years. By early 1976, however, the Index had climbed to moderately healthy, early-1973 levels. Still, however, consumers' long-term (five year) expectations about business conditions in general remained much less optimistic than they were during the mid-1960s.[3]

---

[1] *Economic Outlook USA* (Spring 1976).

[2] Ibid.

[3] Jay Schmiedeskamp, "Recovery Sentiment Gains Strength," *Economic Outlook USA* **3** No. 2, (Spring 1976), p. 26

Important Consumer Market Trends

Small appliance sales in the United States depend heavily upon the level of income, the number of people in the "appliance buying age groups," the number of housing starts, and rate of household formation. Trends in these demographics suggest a promising outlook for small appliance sales through 1980. The 25–34 year age group will grow at a rate four times faster than the total U.S. population, and the number of households will reach record heights. Most importantly, rising incomes, smaller families (fewer children per family), and new life styles should yield significant opportunities for leisure, entertainment, and convenience-related products.[4]

Income

Family incomes will increase substantially between 1976 and 1980. In 1972, approximately 25.5 percent of all U.S. households had incomes over $15,000. The most conservative estimates predict that by 1980, 30 percent of American households will fall in the $15,000 and over class. (Department of Commerce high series projections indicate that up to 35 percent may fall in this category). Real income grew at an average annual rate of 3.75 percent between 1950 and 1965—a period of rapidly rising American affluence. Between 1976 and 1980, real income is expected to climb at an average annual rate of 4.5 percent. This figure suggests that Americans can expect to enjoy higher levels of living over the next few years.[5]

Population

The population of the United States will grow by almost 10 million over 1976 levels by 1980. The absolute level of this increase alone is significant. More important to small appliance manufacturers, however, is the growth expected in key age categories. In 1973, 28.6 million persons or 13.5 percent of the U.S. population were between 25 and 34 years of age. By 1980, this group will jump to 37 million—an increase of 8.4 million—and will account for 16.5 precent of the entire U.S. population. More dramatically, the increase in the number of persons 25–34 years will account for over half of the entire increase in the number of persons in the United States between 1973 and 1980. (See Table 23–1.) Since persons between 25 and 34 buy the largest share of new houses and appliances, this shift should affect appliance sales very positively.

Although the entire U.S. population will grow by about 10 million persons between 1976 and 1980, the populations of different states will grow at widely different rates. The Pacific, Mountain, and South Atlantic states, for example, will grow at rates considerably larger than the total population. Other areas, notably the Middle Atlantic, East North Central and East South Central states,

---

[4] "The Consumer Market: Demand is Soft," *Standard and Poor's Industry Surveys,* 1 (July 1975) pp. E–23 to E–29.

[5] *Consumer Environments and Lifestyles of the Seventies: A Whirlpool Corporation Report* (Whirlpool Corporation: Benton Harbor, Mich.), August 31, 1971, p. 11.

Table 23–1
Projections of the Population
By Age Group to 1985 [1]
(millions of persons)

Year	Population Total	Age Group					
		Under 20	20–24	25–34	35–44	45–54	55 and Over
Estimates:							
1970	204.9	77.2	17.2	25.3	23.1	23.3	38.7
1971	207.0	77.2	18.1	25.8	23.0	23.5	39.4
1972	208.8	76.9	18.0	27.1	22.9	23.7	40.0
1973	210.4	76.2	18.3	28.6	22.8	23.8	40.6
Projections:							
1974	212.2	75.7	19.0	29.9	22.7	23.7	41.3
1975	213.9	75.1	19.4	31.1	22.7	23.6	42.0
1976	215.8	74.6	19.8	32.4	22.9	23.4	42.7
1977	217.7	74.1	20.2	33.5	23.4	23.1	43.4
1978	219.8	73.7	20.6	34.5	24.1	22.9	44.0
1979	221.9	73.4	20.9	35.7	24.8	22.6	44.6
1980	224.1	73.2	21.1	37.0	25.4	22.4	45.1
1981	226.4	73.1	21.2	38.3	25.9	22.2	45.6
1982	228.7	73.2	21.1	38.8	27.5	22.1	46.1
1983	231.0	73.3	21.0	39.5	28.7	22.0	46.5
1984	223.4	73.6	20.8	40.2	29.9	22.0	46.9
1985	235.7	74.0	20.4	40.8	31.2	22.0	47.3

[1] Note: Series E or low projections as of July 1, 1974.
Source: *A Guide to Consumer Markets, 1974–75,* Conference Board Report No. 638 (The Conference Board, Inc.: New York, NY 1974).

will grow at rates substantially below the national average. Particular states which will exhibit above average growth rates are located along the southern border of the United States, including Texas, Florida, California, and Arizona. Lower-than-average rates of growth are expected in most states located between the Mississippi River and the Rockies. These projections suggest growing market opportunities for products associated with leisure and outdoor entertainment-oriented life styles common in warmer climates.[6] State populations as of 1975, projections for 1980, and average annual rates of growth are noted in Table 23–2.

[6] David T. Kollat, Roger D. Blackwell, and James F. Robeson, *Strategic Marketing* (Holt, Rinehart and Winston: New York, 1972), pp. 103–106.

Table   23–2
Population Growth Rates by States
1975 to 1980
(in thousands)

State	Population 1975	Population 1980 [1]	Projected Average Annual Rate of Growth
Alabama	3,500	3,565	.37
Alaska	328	352	1.42
Arizona	1,974	2,164	1.86
Arkansas	1,986	2,052	.66
California	22,077	24,226	1.88
Colorado	2,423	2,636	1.70
Connecticut	2,288	3,551	1.56
Delaware	601	655	1.74
Florida	7,557	8,280	1.84
Georgia	4,887	5,191	1.21
Hawaii	828	874	1.09
Idaho	735	761	.70
Illinois	11,666	12,256	.99
Indiana	5,483	5,782	1.07
Iowa	2,861	2,908	.33
Kansas	2,287	2,334	.41
Kentucky	3,290	3,372	.49
Louisiana	3,807	3,975	.87
Maine	1,003	1,016	.26
Maryland	4,348	4,782	1.92
Massachusetts	5,977	6,277	.98
Michigan	9,445	10,031	1.21
Minnesota	4,021	4,245	1.09
Mississippi	2,227	2,245	.16
Missouri	4,866	5,070	.83
Montana	706	721	.42
Nebraska	1,525	1,570	.58
Nevada	584	673	2.88
New Hampshire	807	878	1.70
New Jersey	7,725	8,300	1.45
New Mexico	1,052	1,088	.68
New York	18,964	19,789	.86
North Carolina	5,277	5,482	.77
North Dakota	607	600	−.23
Ohio	11,152	11,675	.92
Oklahoma	2,669	2,787	.87
Oregon	2,257	2,421	1.41
Pennsylvania	11,964	12,157	.32
Rhode Island	985	1,027	.84
South Carolina	2,658	2,731	.54
South Dakota	600	658	−.06

State	Population 1975	Population 1980 [1]	Projected Average Annual Rate of Growth
Tennessee	4,089	4,259	.82
Texas	12,002	12,812	1.32
Utah	1,146	1,234	1.49
Vermont	474	504	1.24
Virginia	4,936	5,229	1.16
Washington	3,682	3,958	1.46
West Virginia	1,681	1,634	−.57
Wisconsin	4,669	4,931	1.09
Wyoming	336	342	.36

[1] Based on Series E (low) projections.
Source: *A Guide to Consumer Markets, 1974–1975*, Conference Board Report Number 638, (Conference Board: New York, NY 1974).

Households and Housing Starts

Two factors which have affected appliance sales in the past are household formations and housing starts. For small electric appliances, household formations should affect sales more directly than housing starts. Sales of refrigerators, freezers, and ranges are more highly correlated with new housing construction. The short-term outlook for new housing starts is moderately optimistic. It calls for a recovery to pre-1974 levels of new private housing starts by the second half of 1976. The outlook for household formations between 1976 and 1980 is much more optimistic and probable. Households are expected to increase by nearly 1.5 million units per year, a substantially higher rate than in recent years, and should result in the formation of over 7.2 million new households by 1980. This last projection suggests a growing opportunity for small appliances even if the housing industry does not recover as rapidly as anticipated.

Life-style Trends

Several life-style trends will contribute to increased sales for many different types of electric leisure/entertainment/convenience products. Successes during the early seventies for slow cookers, electric drip coffee pots, and many personal care electric appliances illustrate this point. Among the market trends that contribute favorably to the opportunity for marketing electric hotplates/buffet ranges and electric outdoor grills are:

(*a*) Americans will be spending a larger share of their disposable income between 1976 and 1980 for leisure/entertainment related products.

(*b*) The American family is increasingly forsaking the "family meal" in favor of more casual and "quickie" eating habits.

(*c*) As the woman's domination of the task of food preparation continues to diminish, the husband/father and children are demanding simplified food preparation appliances.

(*d*) As fuel costs continue to rise, Americans will be encouraged to shop more carefully for energy saving appliances.[7]

Appliance Industry Trends and Forecasts

The household appliance industry is comprised of manufacturers of a wide variety of products.[8] The Bureau of Census includes in this industry firms which produce household cooking equipment (stoves, ovens, and ranges), refrigerators and freezers, laundry equipment, housewares and fans (blenders, broilers, hotplates), vacuum cleaners, sewing machines, and other appliances not classified elsewhere. A summary of important trends for the household appliance industry, producers of electric housewares and fans, and manufacturers of hotplates and disc stoves is provided below.

Household Appliances

The anticipated population increases in the 25 to 34 year age groups, the resurgence of housing starts, and the expected boom in household formations favor an upward trend in appliance industry sales throughout the second half of the seventies.[9] Between 1967 and 1974 the value of shipments of all firms in the household appliance industry grew at an average annual rate of 7.8 percent. The industry experienced a moderate decline in sales growth during 1974 and early 1975, however, because of the substantial decline in the housing industry.

Between 1964 and 1973, appliance sales were directly linked to the growth in disposable personal income. One measure of this relationship is the coefficient of income elasticity which defines the relationship between consumption expenditures for a product class and consumers' disposable income. Between 1960 and 1972, consumers' expenditures for all durable goods rose and fell in proportions greater than changes in consumers' real disposable income (1.61 percent changes in consumption for 1.0 percent changes in income). Expenditures for kitchen and other household appliances were particularly responsive to income changes as evidenced by an elasticity coefficient of 1.63. Disposable personal income in the United States is expected to increase to about $1.2 trillion by 1980, which is up from less than $700 billion in 1970.[10]

With expected increases in real income, new housing, and consumer durable expenditures identified in the economic outlook to 1980, household appliance demand can be expected to increase at a moderately high pace over the next several

---

[7] *Consumer Environments and Lifestyles of the Seventies: A Whirlpool Corporation Report,* *op, cit.,* pp. 24–25.

[8] The Standard Industrial Classification (SIC) code is used to classify firms engaged in the manufacture and/or sale of similar types of products. Household appliance manufacturers are included in SIC code categories 3631 to 3636 and 3639.

[9] "The Consumer Market: Demand is Soft," *op. cit.,* p. E–29.

[10] Kollat, Blackwell and Robeson, *op. cit.,* p. 111.

years. In fact, industry shipments are expected to grow at an annual rate of 6.7 percent reaching $11.3 billion in 1980.[11] This rate is below the 7.8 percent growth rate enjoyed between 1967 and 1974, however.

Housewares and Fans

The housewares and fans industry (SIC 3634) consists of firms engaged in the production of electric fans, electric razors, small electric household appliances (hotplates, toasters, space heaters, corn poppers) and parts, and attachments for small electric appliances. This segment of the entire household appliance industry has been substantially less responsive to the vagaries of the economy. In fact, housewares was the segment of the appliance industry least affected by the downturn of the economy in 1974. Following a boom year for the appliance industry in 1973, household electronics unit sales fell by nearly 13 percent in 1974. In contrast, housewares unit sales showed a minimal dip of 3.2 percent.[12] Although this is encouraging news for manufacturers during an economic downslide, it suggests that housewares marketers may not enjoy dramatic sales bursts during periods of economic recovery, as the electric range and refrigerator manufacturers can expect.

Hotplates/Buffet Ranges

Between 1965 and 1974, U.S. hotplate/buffet range unit sales expanded at an average annual rate of 4.5 percent, from about 700,000 units to over one million units. (See Table 23–3.) Throughout this period, the percentage of U.S. wired homes with hotplates advanced slowly but steadily from a level of 22.5 percent in 1964 to 25.5 percent in 1974. In contrast, *Merchandising Week* estimated that as of December 31, 1974, 56 percent of U.S. wired homes had electric blankets, up from 32 percent in 1964; 43.8 percent had electric blenders, up from 11 percent in 1964; and 49 percent had free-standing electric ranges, up from 32 percent in 1964.[13] In 1975, however, hotplate sales plummeted 28 percent to 740,000 units. Unit sales are forecast to rise 5.4 percent in 1976 to 780,000 units and to grow an average annual rate of 4.01 percent through 1980. (Total household appliance sales are expected to increase at an average annual rate of 6.7 percent up to 1980; however, this trend will be influenced primarily by the recovery of the housing industry.)

Outdoor Barbecue Grill Unit Sales

Little published information is available about past years' sales of outdoor barbecue grills. The Research Department of *Merchandising Magazine* published information about 1974 and 1975 industry sales with a forecast for 1976. However, data for earlier years was not available. In 1975, 2,800,000 outdoor barbecue

---

[11] "Household Appliances," *U.S. Industrial Outlook 1975* (U.S. Department of Commerce: Washington, 1975), p. 225.
[12] "1975 Statistical and Marketing Report," *Merchandising Week* (February 24, 1975), p. 22.
[13] "1975 Statistical and Marketing Report," *op. cit.*, pp. 31–32.

Table   23–3
Unit Sales of Electric
Hotplates/Buffet Ranges
1965–1975 [1]

Year	Hot Plate Sales (000s units)	Annual Net Change in Unit Sales (000s units)	Percent Change in Unit Sales
1965	705	—	—
1966	690	− 15	− 2.1
1967	680	− 10	− 1.5
1968	775	+ 95	+14.0
1969	880	+105	+13.5
1970	810	− 70	− 7.9
1971	825	+ 15	+ 1.9
1972	890	+ 65	+ 7.9
1973	950	+ 60	+ 6.7
1974	1,025	+ 75	+ 7.9
1975	740	−285	−28.0

[1] 1965–1974 sales estimates from: "10 Year Tables: Housewares," *Merchandising* (February 24, 1975), pp. 26–27. 1975 sales estimates and 1976 forecast are from: "Housewares: Forecast '76," *Merchandising Magazine* (May 1976), p. 72.

grills were sold in the United States. Unit sales in 1975 were up nearly 8 percent over 1974 figures in spite of the mild slump in other housewares products. (See Table 23–4.) Unit sales of electric outdoor barbecue grills grew by over 11 percent in 1975 over the previous year's sales. *Merchandising Magazine* forecasts that the sales of all types of outdoor barbecue grills (electric, gas, charcoal, and hibachi) would grow by 7 percent in 1976. Electric unit sales are predicted to expand by only 5 percent, however. Gas fired outdoor grills are expected to lead the way with a 10 percent increase, although hibachi sales seem to be leveling off. It appears that the electric outdoor barbecue grills have not yet caught the attention of the majority of American consumers. Their lagging sales growth may be due to consumers' fears of cooking with electricity outdoors, concerns about high energy consumption, or simply unfamiliarity with electric grills. The electric outdoor grill remains in the early stages of its product life cycle and requires a great deal of information transfer to consumers before sales will reach their potential.

The shares of the total outdoor grill market captured by electric, gas, charcoal, and hibachi units remained fairly stable during 1974 and 1975, and no great change is expected for 1976. With the expected slowdown in the growth of the hibachi units, the market will no longer be dominated by any particularly impressive growth item. Thus, there appears to be no serious threats of any other type of outdoor grill unit cutting deeply into the electric grill market share. As

Table 23–4 shows, electric outdoor barbecue grills are forecast to rise to a 1976 unit sales level of 105,000, up 5 percent over 1975 sales.

Leisure Products' Competition

LPI in 1976 is contemplating entry into two moderately competitive sectors of the appliance industry. Competitors for hotplate sales are to include such entrenched giants as General Electric, Dominion Electric (Scovill and Hamilton Beach brands), Sunbeam, Salton, National Presto, and Hoover. For outdoor electric grills sales, LPI will encounter competition from companies like W. C. Bradley, Toastmaster Division of McGraw-Edison, Dominion, and the Charo-O Corporation, in addition to stiff competition from makers of gas and charcoal units. Additionally, Sears, Penney's, Montgomery Ward, and other private label retailers have their own hotplate and grill brands.[14] In 1973, only 9 companies were reported to have sales of hotplates/buffet ranges in excess of $100,000. The sales trend of the early 1970s is expected to attract new entrants and to encourage existing competitors to devote more marketing effort to hotplates, however.

Table   23–4
Outdoor Barbecue Grill Sales by Type

Type	1974 Units	1975 Units	1976 Units (est.)	% Change 1976/75	% Change 1975/74
Electric	90,000	100,000	105,000	+ 5.0	+11.1
Gas	180,000	200,000	220,000	+10.0	+11.1
Charcoal	1,900,000	2,000,000	2,160,000	+ 8.0	+ 5.3
Hibachi	425,000	400,000	510,000	+ 2.0	+17.6
Total	2,595,000	2,800,000	2,995,000	+ 7.0	+ 7.9

Source: *Merchandising Magazine* (May, 1976), p. 82.

Marketing Hotplates/Buffet Ranges And Electric Outdoor Grills

Manufacturers of electric housewares, in general, and hotplate/buffet ranges and outdoor grills, in particular, engaged in aggressive marketing practices throughout the early 1970s. By the mid-1970s, however, most manufacturers had begun to curtail services provided to distributors and retailers. The principal characteristics

---

[14] *Appliance Manufacturer* (June 1975), pp. 46 and 52.

of consumers and several of the marketing practices that were developing in 1976 are summarized in the following sections.

Characteristics of Consumers

The largest share of all appliance sales in 1974 and 1975 were made to persons between 25 and 34 years of age in households with incomes over $10,000. These consumers have been and are expected to continue to be more value conscious and cautious in their purchases of appliances. They have exhibited a willingness to pay for quality and guarantees of services (warranties). Industry sources indicate that price and brand name are no more important than product features in their sales generating impact. Consumers in 1975 tended to shun those retailers who carried narrow assortments in favor of those with wide and deep product mixes.

Monthly Sales Patterns

Retail sales of hotplates/buffet ranges have been distributed unevenly throughout the year. The months of July through October were the biggest months of unit sales. Nearly half of all sales in 1975, for example, were made during that 4-month period. The complete pattern of 1975 unit sales is shown in Table 23–5. Also shown in Table 23–5 is the monthly pattern of retail sales of outdoor grills. Notable is the fact that while 47 percent of the 1975 hotplate sales were made at retail between July and October, 86 percent of the outdoor grill sales were

Table   23–5

1975 Monthly Retail Sales Pattern of Hotplates

Month	Percent of Annual Hotplate Unit Sales	Percent of Annual Grill Unit Sales
January	4	1
February	6	3
March	9	17
April	8	25
May	4	24
June	9	20
July	13	3
August	11	1
September	13	1
October	10	1
November	7	1
December	6	3

Source: *Merchandising Magazine* (March 1976), pp. 114, 126.

made at retail between March and June. Wholesalers' orders from manufacturers normally anticipate retail orders by 60 days.

Geographic Sales Distribution

No published estimates are available of the geographic distribution of recent years' sales of either hotplate/buffet ranges or electric outdoor grills. Estimates of each continental U.S. state's Effective Buying Income might be used by LPI to approximate statewide hotplate and outdoor grill market potentials. Effective Buying Income (EBI) is defined as personal income (wages, salaries, interest, dividends, profits, and property income) minus federal, state, and local taxes. It generally is equivalent to the government's measure of disposable personal income. It can be used as a bulk measure of the market potential of a particular geographic region because it indicates the general ability to buy in the region. EBI is often used in comparing, grouping, and selecting markets on the basis of their ability to buy.[15] Effective buying indices are calculated for each continental U.S. state. Then the 48 continental states are grouped into 8 territories consistent with boundaries suggested by the Manufacturers' Agents National Association.[16] By summing the EBIs of the states in each territory and dividing the sum by the total U.S. EBI for 1974, territorial effective buying income indices are determined. LPI is considering using these indices to estimate the percent of annual hotplate and electric grill sales potential in each territory.[17] The territorial EBI index estimates are in Table 23–6.

Housewares Distribution [18]

Most housewares manufacturers contract with independent agents to market their products to wholesale distributors and large retailers. The agents typically represent several noncompeting manufacturers of complementary products for an extended period of time. Contracts with agents normally are cancellable by either party on 30 days notice. The manufacturer-agent Short Form Agency Agreement (contract) and the Manufacturers' Agents National Association Code of Ethics is contained in the appendix to this case.

Presently, most housewares manufacturers (80 percent) market their products through independent wholesale distributors. The other 20 percent sell directly to retailers. Of the sales made by manufacturers who belong to the National Housewares Manufacturers Association (NHMA), 61 percent were made directly to retailers and 39 percent to wholesalers. These NHMA member manufacturers are typically larger and offer more complete product lines, however, than the smaller manufacturers who do not belong to NHMA.

---

[15] *Sales Management's Survey of Buying Power* (July 21, 1975).

[16] Manufacturers' Agents National Association, *1976 Membership Directory* (Los Angeles, CA).

[17] Norwood knew that the estimates would have to be adjusted to recognize, for example, that more grills are likely to be made in states with warmer climates. However, he did not know the exact adjustments to make.

[18] This and the following sections are based upon material contained in several articles in various 1975 and 1976 editions of *Merchandising Week* and *Merchandising Magazine*.

Table   23–6
Territory Effective Buying Power

Territory	States Included [1]	Effective Buying Income Index Percent [2]
1	ME, NH, MA, CN, RI, VT, NY, NJ	19.6
2	OH, KY, IN, MI	13.7
3	MD, VA, DE, NC, SC, TN, AR, LA, MS	12.9
4	GA, AL, FL	7.3
5	TX, OK, CO, UT, MT, ID, WY, NV, CA, AZ, NM	21.5
6	IL, KS, MO	9.3
7	PA, NV, WI	8.3
8	MN, ND, SD, IA, NE, WA, OR	7.3

[1] These nine territories are consistent with territorial boundaries suggested by the Manufacturers' Agents National Association, *1976 Membership Directory,* MANA (Los Angeles, CA).

[2] Effective Buying Index for each territory was calculated as the percentage of the included states' effective buying income (as defined in *Sales Management's Survey of Buying Power,* July 21, 1975) to the total U.S. effective buying income. Effective buying income is a bulk measure of market potential. It is a measure of a market's ability to buy. It does not account for the market's willingness to buy which might depend more upon sellers' marketing efforts than upon ability to buy.

At the retail level, electric cookware is sold primarily through department, discount, and hardware stores. In 1974, for example, 29 percent of all sales were made through discount stores, 25 percent through department stores, and 20 percent through hardware stores. Outdoor products, including electric outdoor grills, are distributed through essentially the same types of retail outlets as are electric cookware products (see Figure 23–1).

The traditional structure of trade discounts on small housewares has been 40/15/5 percent. This means that an item that would list for $100 retail would be sold to the retailer by a wholesaler for $60 ($100 less 40 percent), the wholesaler would pay $51 ($60 less 15 percent). The manufacturer would collect $48.45 (minus 2 percent of $51 if the wholesaler pays within 10 days since average cash terms are 2/10 net 20).

In recent years, the wholesale distributor has grown in significance to manufacturers in the appliance marketing channels. In response to the rising costs of carrying inventories, both retailers and manufacturers have become more dependent upon the distributors. Manufacturers expect in the future to profit from their greater dependence upon wholesalers who can often provide market information which helps in anticipating sales trends. Such information can be used to establish appropriate production schedules. In the past, manufacturers have used early order discounts very effectively to get confirmed orders, which has helped to stabilize pro-

Figure 23–1
Where Outdoor Products and Electric Cookware Are Sold

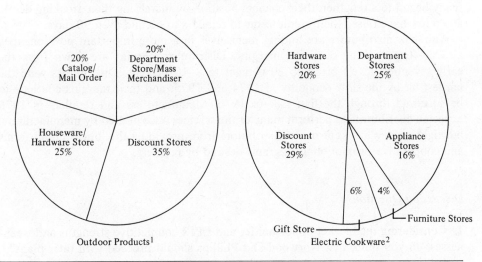

Outdoor Products[1]   Electric Cookware[2]

Source: [1] *Merchandising Week*, September 29, 1975, p. 43.
[2] *Merchandising Week*, February 24, 1976, p. 87.

duction schedules. Many manufacturers have, in recent months, begun cutting their dating terms and tightening their credit terms to distributors and retailers. Also, many have curtailed their promotional support to retailers. It is uncertain at this time if these changes are permanent or temporary.

Retailers in 1976 have shortened their order cycle from 60 to 30 days. They increasingly are buying in smaller quantities, carrying smaller inventories, focusing on fast-moving items, and narrowing their product assortments. If these trends persist, the retailers' reliance upon wholesale distributors who maintain adequate inventories of housewares is likely to increase. Competition has forced retail margins down from 40 percent to 30 to 35 percent. Many retailers are already relying more heavily upon wholesalers who offer programmed merchandising packages—carefully designed product assortment suggestions with programmed promotions. Retailers who have been able to effectively use the services of distributors have enjoyed lower warehousing and inventory costs. With retail margins on housewares down to 30 to 35 percent, these savings are crucial.

Although many retailers are increasing their reliance on selected distributors, most wish to avoid linking themselves very closely with any small group of manufacturers' product lines or sales promotion programs. Retailers, for the most part, have tended throughout 1975–1976 to switch back and forth between manufacturer brands depending upon the level and types of services offered at each point in time. It is expected by some in the industry that with the expected recovery in 1977 retailers will begin to align themselves more closely with those distributors and manufacturers who offer more consistent product availability and promotional programs.

To meet new demands placed upon them by manufacturers and retailers, distributors will have to carry larger uncommitted inventories of housewares in 1977 to provide retailers with their desired order flexibility. Some distributors have already begun to strengthen their channel position by increasing their stocking depth, and a few have raised their credit terms to retailers to 60 and even 90 days.

Although distributors are finding themselves in a more important position, they also are experiencing declining margins. Distributor margins are down from the early seventies' levels of 15 to 20 percent to 8–10 percent. Distributors were the hardest hit by the slow economy of 1974 and 1975, and their margins continue to be squeezed through the first half of 1976. Manufacturers and retailers in 1976 expected distributors to perform many of the services once offered by manufacturers, but tight money has kept many distributors from providing the longer credit terms and cooperative promotional programs desired by retailers.

Discussion Questions

1. Considering the market opportunities and LPI's competitive strengths and weaknesses, do you think that Norwood and Phillips should proceed with their plans?

2. What sales volume (dollars and units) must LPI attain to break even?

3. What plans for geographic market coverage and distribution intensity do you believe are appropriate for LPI?

4. Characterize the distribution channel structure and channel relationships that LPI should strive to achieve.

MANA

CODE OF ETHICS

1. TO BE ACCORDED THE MANUFACTURER BY THE AGENT:

☐ Comply with established policies of the manufacturer

☐ Conscientiously cover the territory assigned

☐ Avoid misrepresentation in any form or manner

☐ Restrict lines or accounts with principals to those which can well be handled and

☐ Give the manufacturer the same loyal service as the agent, operating his own business, expects from his own employees.

2. TO BE ACCORDED THE AGENT BY THE MANUFACTURER:

☐ Enter into a fair and clearly worded agreement with the Manufacturers' Agent

☐ Make the agreement cancellable by either party during its first year on suitable advanced written notice, but subsequently only for failure of either party to comply with its terms, or by mutual consent

☐ Refrain from any modification whatever of the terms of such agreement, except by mutual consent after full and friendly discussion of the reasons for such desired modification

☐ Extend to the Manufacturers' Agent the same benefits available to the manufacturer's own salaried employees, wherever possible

☐ Refrain from absorbing, refusing or cutting the Manufacturers' Agent's established commissions for any reason whatever and

☐ Provide practical and dignified means for friendly arbitration of all controversial points that may arise, between agent and principal.

3. TO BE ACCORDED ONE MANUFACTURERS' AGENT BY ANOTHER:

☐ Exchange trade information, in the mutual interest

☐ Avoid any suggestion or agreement to divide commissions with those representing other than the agent's own principals

☐ Refrain from soliciting from manufacturers the known lines or accounts of other established Manufacturers' Agents by unfair methods and

☐ Cooperate to upbuild the profession of the Manufacturers' Agent—by supporting the National Association established for that purpose, subscribing to its aims and objectives, and in every practical way working to advance the interests of all Manufacturers' Agents and Representatives.

Source: Manufacturers' Agents National Association, 3130 Wilshire Boulevard, Suite 509, Los Angeles, California 90010.

Standard Agency Agreement

SHORT FORM AGENCY AGREEMENT

This Agreement is made on the date shown below by and between _____

("Principal") and _____ ("Agent").

1. **Exclusive Representative.** Principal grants to Agent the exclusive right (to the exclusion of Principal and all claiming under or through Principal), by acting as Principal's sales representative, to solicit orders for those goods, equipment and/or services ("Products") described on Exhibit A attached hereto and hereby incorporated by reference herein, within the geographical area ("Territory") described on Exhibit B attached hereto and hereby incorporated by reference herein.

2. **Sales Policies.** The prices, charges and terms of sale of the Products ("Sales Policies") shall be established by Principal. The Sales Policies shall be those currently in effect and established from time to time by Principal in its price books, bulletins and other authorized releases. Written notice of each Sales Policy's change shall be given by Principal to Agent at least 30 days in advance of such change.

3. **Orders and Collections.** Orders for Products solicited by Agent shall be forwarded to and subject to acceptance by Principal. All invoices in connection with orders solicited by Agent shall be rendered by Principal, direct to the customer, and full responsibility for all collections and bad debts rests with Principal.

4. **Agent's Commissions.** The commissions payable by Principal to Agent on orders solicited within or delivered to the Territory shall be as determined in accordance with Exhibit C attached hereto and hereby incorporated by reference herein. Commissions shall be deemed earned by Agent upon acceptance or delivery of the order by Principal, whichever occurs first. Commissions earned by Agent shall be computed on the net amount of the invoice rendered for each order or part of an order, exclusive of freight and transportation costs (including insurance), normal and recurring bona fide trade discounts and any applicable sales or similar taxes. All commissions earned by Agent hereunder shall be due and payable to Agent at Agent's address for receiving notices on or before the twentieth (20th) day of the month immediately following the calendar month during which the invoice applicable to an order solicited by Agent is sent by Principal.

5. **Relationship Created.** Agent is not an employee of Principal for any purpose whatsoever, but is an independent contractor. Principal is interested only in the results obtained by Agent, who shall have sole control of the manner and means of performing under this Agreement. Principal shall not have the right to require Agent to do anything which would jeopardize the relationship of independent contractor between Principal and Agent. All expenses and disbursements incurred by Agent in connection with this Agreement shall be borne wholly and completely by Agent. Agent does not have, nor shall he hold himself out as having, any right, power or authority to create any contract or obligation, either express or implied, on behalf of, in the name of, or binding upon Principal, unless Principal shall consent thereto in writing. Agent shall have the right to appoint and shall be solely responsible for his own salesmen, employees, agents and representatives, who shall be at Agent's own risk, expense and supervision and shall not have any claim against Principal for compensation or reimbursement.

6. **Term.** This Agreement shall continue in full force and effect until the date ("Termination Date") set forth in a notice given by one party, to the other indicating such party's election to terminate this Agreement, which Termination Date shall be at least one hundred twenty (120) days after the date notice of such election is given. If this Agreement shall terminate for any reason whatsoever, Agent shall be entitled to receive his full fees determined in accordance with provisions of Exhibit C with respect to orders solicited prior to the effective date of such termination, regardless of when such orders are accepted by Principal (provided Agent can demonstrate such orders were solicited prior to the effective date of such termination) and regardless of when such shipments are made or invoices rendered.

(Alternate)

6. **Term.** This Agreement shall continue in full force and effect until the first to occur of the following events, at which time it shall terminate:

    6.1 The expiration of thirty (30) days after Agent gives written notice to Principal of Agent's election to terminate this Agreement, which right Agent is hereby granted and which shall be within Agent's sole discretion;

    6.2 The election by one party ("The Aggrieved Party") to terminate this Agreement upon (1) the breach or default by the other party ("The Defaulting Party") in the reasonable performance of the Defaulting Party's obligations and duties under this Agreement and (2) the failure of the Defaulting Party to cure the same within fifteen (15) days (the "Cure Period") after receipt by the Defaulting Party of written notice from the Aggrieved Party specifying such breach or default, provided that the Aggrieved Party gives written notice of his or its election to terminate within ten (10) days after expiration of the Cure Period; or

    6.3 By mutual written Agreement between both of the parties hereto.

7. **Hold Harmless.** Principal shall save Agent harmless from and against and indemnify Agent for all liability, loss, costs, expenses or damages howsoever caused by reason of any Products (whether or not defective) or any act or omission of Principal, including but not limited to any injury (whether to body, property or personal or business character or reputation) sustained by any person or to any person or to property, and for infringement of any patent rights or other rights of third parties, and for any violation of municipal, state or federal laws or regulations governing the Products or their sale, which may result from the sale or distribution of the Products by the Agent hereunder. This Agreement shall be subject to and shall be enforced and construed pursuant to the laws of the State ("Agent's State") where the Agent's principal office is located, as set forth below. Principal hereby appoints as its agent for service for process in connection with any action brought by Agent against Principal hereunder the Secretary of State of Agent's state of residence at the time such action is brought. In the event of litigation, the prevailing party may recover court costs and reasonable attorneys' fees.

8. **Notices.** Any notice, demand or request required or permitted to be given hereunder shall be in writing and shall be deemed effective twenty-four (24) hours after having been deposited in the United States mail, postage pre-paid, registered or certified, and addressed to the addressee at his or its main office, as set forth below. Any party may change his or its address for purposes of this agreement by written notice given in accordance herewith.

DATE:_____   (Principal) _____

                                 By: _____

                                 Title: _____

        Address of Principal's Main Office: _____

                                 (Agent): _____

The Brockman Company, Inc.: Health Care Marketing

P. Ronald Stephenson, Indiana University

Background Information

In 1956, Kenneth Brockman left his position as a leading salesman for a medical products manufacturer and started the Brockman Company, a wholesale distributor of medical/surgical supplies and equipment. He was 32 at the time. The first few years were rough, due largely to the necessity of repaying substantial personal debts incurred getting the business going. Brockman had worked very hard at building the business and was quite proud when last year's sales reached $5 million for the first time.

Through 1964, Brockman concentrated almost exclusively on generating sales in the physician market segment, although the firm did some limited business with a few small hospitals outside its major metropolitan market. However, by 1962 the rate of sales growth had slowed substantially. In 1962, 1963, and 1964, sales grew at an average rate of just under 2 percent per year. As a consequence, in 1965 Brockman began to move aggressively to gain business from hospitals located in his metropolitan market. Today, he estimates that his sales volume breaks down as follows: 50 percent from hospitals and extended care (nursing home) facilities; 45 percent from doctors; and 5 percent from lay sales (sales and equipment rental direct to consumers).

Brockman is not displeased with the results of his 20-year effort. However, he feels now that his business is at a stage where he needs to make a careful assessment of management to see if some major changes would be appropriate and profitable. He has two sons who will soon enter the business, and he wants very much to present them with a significant business opportunity in which to invest their futures.

Brockman feels that his primary problem is one of financial control. His business is no longer small, and he knows he cannot continue to run it as loosely as in the past. His own skill and his primary emphasis have been on sales. The sales force reports directly to him, and he sold to key accounts himself until 1970.

407

The Medical Supply Industry

The channel in which Brockman operates is one segment of the total United States health care industry. It consists of firms involved in the wholesale distribution of supplies and equipment used in human health care. Customers include all major health care delivery agencies, that is, hospitals, physicians, clinics, nursing homes and laboratories. Medical supply distributors are independent wholesalers that dominate performance of wholesale distribution functions in the medical supply channel.

Key characteristics of the medical supply industry are summarized in Exhibit 24–1. Other important characteristics include:

(1) Most medical supply wholesalers are closely held, owner-managed firms. Relatively few firms in the industry have publicly traded stocks or are divisions of other major companies.

(2) Medical supply wholesalers range in size from less than $1 million to $100 million annual sales. Average size is approximately $3 million annual sales volume. American Hospital Supply, the industry giant, is not included in these figures.

(3) Due to expansion of the U.S. health care system, medical supply wholesalers have experienced significant market growth. Compounded annual growth rates during the last decade have ranged between 15 and 20 percent.

(4) Economic recession has little impact on the industry due to the emergency character of health care and growth of third-party payment plans, that is, private insurance programs, such as Blue Cross/Blue Shield and government payment programs, such as Medicare.

(5) The medical supply industry does not typically include distribution of drugs or dental supplies. Separate distribution channels have evolved for the latter products.

The industry's key market segments and their characteristics are summarized in Exhibit 24–2. Of the markets listed, the hospital and physician segments dominate. Hospitals are the largest segment with the greatest recent and future projected growth. Gross margin possibilities for wholesalers selling to hospitals are quite low (median = 20 percent) as a result of intense price competition, buyer price sensitivity, large volume purchasing, and competitive bid purchases. Recent and projected expansion of the physician market is much more protracted. However, gross margins available in the physician segment are relatively high (median = 32 percent) as a result of small volume purchasing, relatively low price sensitivity, and high service requirements.

Medical Supply Industry Financial Performance

Brockman is a member of the American Surgical Trade Association, a trade association of United States medical supply wholesalers. A major service of the associa-

Exhibit 24-1
The Medical Supply Industry Measures of 1976 Activity
(estimates)

Number of wholesalers	1,100
Value of wholesaler shipments	3,000,000,000
Number of manufacturers	2,000
Value of manufacturer shipments	$3,125,000
Number of hospitals	7,200
Number of hospital beds	1,600,000
Number of practicing physicians	330,000

Sources: American Surgical Trade Association, Health Industries Manufacturers Association, and author's calculations.

Exhibit 24-2
Market Segment Characteristics
The Medical Supply Industry

Market segment	Market size ranks	Relative growth rate	Degree of competitive intensity	Gross margin possibilities
Hospitals	1	Rapid	High	Low
Physicians	2	Slow	Moderate	High
Extended care facilities	3	Moderate	Moderate	Low/Moderate
Laboratories	4	Moderate	Moderate	High
Lay [a]	5	Rapid	Low	Very high
Government	6	Moderate	High	Low
Industrial	7	Slow	Low	High

[a] Refers to sales and rentals direct to consumers.
Source: P. Ronald Stephenson, "Strategic Analysis of Wholesale Distribution: A Study of the Medical Supply Industry," *Industrial Marketing Management*, **5** (1976), pp. 37–44. Modified to reflect market changes.

tion is an annual study of the financial performance and condition of its member firms. The report is distributed to members in the form of median percentage data. Brockman finds this data very useful as it allows him to compare his performance with that of his industry.

Excerpts from the most recent industry study are summarized in Exhibits 24–3 through 24–6. Exhibits 24–3 through 24–5 summarize profit and loss performance, balance sheet condition, and key industry ratios. The first column contains median data for all firms in the industry. The second column describes firms that specialize in the doctor market segment. The third column contains data describing firms that specialize in the hospital segment. Data in the fourth column describes the "profit makers." These are the top 25 percent of the firms in the industry in terms of return on total assets. Exhibit 24–6 summarizes return on investment performance in the industry.

Physical Facilities

The Brockman Company operates out of a relatively modern one-story warehouse constructed in 1971. The building is self-contained providing all warehouse and

Exhibit 24-3
Summary of Medical Supply Industry
Profit and Loss Performance
1976
(Net Sales Equals 100%)

| | Medical Supply Dealer Performance* | | | |
	Average Dealer** Performance	Dealers Selling Primarily to Doctors	Dealers Selling Primarily to Hospitals	The Profit Makers
Net Sales	100%	100%	100%	100%
Cost of Goods Sold	76.97	67.79	79.91	76.94
Gross Margin	23.03	32.21	20.09	23.06
Other Income	0.42	0.47	0.30	0.17
Gross Operating Income	24.04	32.56	20.92	23.40
Warehouse and Delivery Expenses	3.14	4.52	2.59	2.38
Selling Expenses	6.49	8.41	5.50	6.08
General & Administrative Expenses	10.70	14.26	8.26	8.21
Total Operating Expenses	20.87	27.22	16.72	17.14
Pretax Profit	3.66	3.66	3.82	6.50
Taxes	1.35	0.97	1.76	3.27
After-tax Profit	2.18%	2.52%	2.18%	3.46%

* Note that the average is the median rather than the arithmetic mean. Thus the percentages do not precisely "add up" as an income statement normally would.

** Like Brockman, a number of firms in the industry do not specialize in either the doctor or hospital market segments. Their profit performance is included in the average and tends to be lower than that of dealers who do concentrate on one of the two key market segments.

Exhibit 24-4
Summary of Medical Supply Industry
Balance Sheet Data
1976
(Total Assets Equals 100%)

	Medical Supply Dealer Porformance*			
Condition	% Average Dealer	% Dealers Selling Primarily to Doctors	% Dealers Selling Primarily to Hospitals	% The Profit Makers
Cash	1.77	2.38	1.16	5.43
Accounts Receivable	42.14	40.09	44.91	43.12
Inventories	45.44	39.92	45.31	34.62
Other Current Assets	0.94	1.40	0.59	1.27
Total Current Assets	95.47	90.53	96.02	94.09
Total Fixed Assets	4.53	9.47	3.98	5.91
Total Assets	100	100	100	100
Total Liabilities	56.89	57.50	58.85	52.11
Net Worth	43.11	42.30	41.15	47.89
Total Liabilities and Net Worth	100	100	100	100

* Note that the average is the median rather than the arithmetic mean. Thus the percentages do not precisely "add up" as a balance sheet normally would.

Exhibit 24-5
Summary of Medical Supply Industry
Key Peformance Ratios
1976

	Medical Supply Dealer Performance			
	Average Dealer Performance	Dealers Selling Primarily to Doctors	Dealers Selling Primarily to Hospitals	The Profit Makers
Inventory turnover	5.41x	5.77x	6.38x	7.27x
Average number of days accounts receivable are outstanding	50 days	46 days	50 days	47 days
Sales per sales rep	$410,000	$208,000	$529,000	$539,000
Sales per employee	$100,000	$70,000	$121,000	$121,000

Exhibit 24-6
Summary of Medical Supply Industry
Strategic Profit Formula Results*
1976

SPF*—Average Dealer

Profit Margin	×	Asset Turnover	=	Return on Assets	×	Leverage Ratio	=	Return on Net Worth
2.2%	×	3.1	=	6.8%	×	2.2	=	15.0%

SPF*—Doctor Dealers

Profit Margin	×	Asset Turnover	=	Return on Assets	×	Leverage Ratio	=	Return on Net Worth
2.5%	×	3.2	=	8.0%	×	2.4	=	19.2%

SPF*—Hospital Dealers

Profit Margin	×	Asset Turnover	=	Return on Assets	×	Leverage Ratio	=	Return on Net Worth
2.2%	×	3.4	=	7.5%	×	2.3	=	17.3%

SPF*—Profit Makers

Profit Margin	×	Asset Turnover	=	Return on Assets	×	Leverage Ratio	=	Return on Net Worth
3.5%	×	3.4	=	11.9%	×	2.1	=	25.0%

---

* Strategic Profit Formula (SPF) is calculated as follows:

$$\frac{\text{Net Profit}}{\text{Net Sales}} \times \frac{\text{Net Sales}}{\text{Total Assets}} = \frac{\text{Return}}{\text{on Assets}} \times \frac{\text{Total Assets}}{\text{Net Worth}} = \frac{\text{Return on}}{\text{Net Worth}}$$

Profit Margin	×	Asset Turnover	=	Return on Assets	×	Leverage Ratio	=	Return on Net Worth

---

office space, as well as a small lay (retail) outlet located at the front of the building. The site is nicely located on an access road near a major interstate highway. Brockman arranged for construction with a local investor. His lease arrangement has four years to run and includes renewal options.

Market Conditions

The company currently serves a major metropolitan market, approximately 1 million population. In addition, sales representatives call in a surrounding area (75-mile radius) of smaller towns and cities with a combined population of over 400,000. At the end of 1976, the market area contained 1,500 active physicians, 30 hospitals with approximately 7,500 beds, 8 independent diagnostic labs, and about 2,200 beds in extended care facilities. Two of the hospitals are large state-owned operations that make a substantial number of their purchases on a bid basis.

Brockman's primary competition comes from two additional medical distributors based in the area. One is smaller than Brockman. However, he considers it to be a fairly well-run, aggressive competitor. One firm is a branch of American Hospital Supply, the giant of the industry. Outside sales representatives working in the area offer some additional competition, but they do not have branch facilities.

Merchandising Practices

Brockman considers himself a full-line distributor. He attempts to stock an item whenever he feels demand is sufficient, and he does not concentrate on any selected merchandise categories. However, several aspects of his inventory practices worry him at this point. First, he feels that he has never had good control over his inventory either in terms of investment or units. His turnover is too low, and he frequently has old, unsalable stock in inventory. On the other hand, he frequently is out-of-stock on key items and faced with back-order situations. He also is concerned that he may be carrying too many brands of essentially similar items. His inventory consists of approximately 14,000 items and the industry average is 8,000 items in stock.

A minimum order size has never been imposed on the firm's customers. The result is that many customers make frequent small orders, often in broken case quantities. This appears to be a problem particularly in the physician segment. Brockman has been worried about the lack of a policy in this area, but because of considerable resistance among sales representatives, he has not yet acted on the problem. Indeed, he suspects that some of his sales representatives may be calling on physician accounts too frequently.

Brockman is becoming increasingly concerned about his handling of the firm's growing hospital business. The physician and hospital market segments are treated essentially alike. He wonders if this really makes sense, particularly in light of somewhat different service requirements and clearly smaller gross margins on hospital sales.

Virtually all of Brockman's sales are on credit and his credit terms are 1/15, net 30. No service charge is made for late payment. Brockman wonders if the cash discount is really useful. He is not sure that it really speeds up payment from doctors, and many hospitals frequently take unearned discounts.

Computer Operations

Like many firms of similar size, Brockman recently has acquired a computer and now has to figure out what to do with it. Currently, the computer is being used only for clerical functions—that is, payroll, accounts receivable, and accounts payable. Brockman hopes to use the machine for inventory control and in his buying operation. In addition, he would like to be able to generate some useful management control reports.

The Sales Organization

The company has a sales force of thirteen people, and Brockman himself handles all sales management activities. Because he always has tried to hire experienced sales representatives, his training procedure has included only company indoctrination and teaching the product line. Information regarding product changes usually is given either by memo or informal discussions with sales representatives, one at a time.

Sales representatives are given as much freedom as possible to run their territory in tune with customer and competitive conditions. For example, they are allowed to adjust (within reason) prices to customers. Brockman believes that sales representatives are in the best position to determine the price necessary to get the business. He monitors the gross margin produced by each sales representatives and sometimes asks for explanations from individual representatives if he thinks the percentage is dropping too low.

Representatives also are expected to control collection for all their accounts. Each representative has the authority to drop an account if he or she feels that collection is too great a problem, or to demand COD shipments. Representatives also have the authority to allow continued selling to so-called good accounts that are substantially overdue.

In line with their pricing freedom, Brockman feels that it is best to compensate his sales representatives on the basis of the gross margin each produces. He pays 30 percent of the gross margin each representative generates, and sales representatives pay their own expenses.

Brockman is concerned about whether he ought to try to develop any specialization within the sales force. His sales people currently are organized on a territory basis. All the representatives sell to all types of customers and handle all the items in the company's line. He wonders, for example, whether he should try to develop hospital specialists and how he should train and compensate such people.

Specifically, Brockman is concerned over the situation of two of his reps whose territories include the largest area hospitals. Most of their sales now come from these hospitals, and their gross margin percentages are very low. Brockman wonders if his hospital business is really profitable. After the sales representatives take their 30 percent, not many gross margin dollars are left for the company. He has toyed with the idea of setting up a separate compensation system for the hospital business. For example, he considered putting the hospital business exclusively in the hands of specialists and paying these people a salary plus a reduced commission rate. He has not come to any conclusion about this idea. Indeed, he keeps putting it off since he expects any such change to be met by considerable resistance from his representatives.

An additional problem is the discrepancy in performance among his sales representatives. Brockman's best rep generates sales of over $800,000 per year. The weakest person sells less than $200,000. Brockman is convinced that the territories are of nearly equal potential and that the weak rep has certainly been on the job long enough to gain adequate experience. Brockman as yet has taken no action regarding the weak rep because he feels he is not really losing money. He pays only for sales productivity, and the rep covers his own expenses.

Brockman also is worried about the performance of one of his older sales reps who seems to have topped out at about $600,000 annual sales. Additional income does not seem to be a motivator. This sales representatives has been successful for a number of years, owns some good commercial real estate, and is part owner of an auto dealership with a brother. The thing that concerns Brockman most is that the sales person appears to be covering only about half the potential accounts in his territory. Obviously, this rep does a very good job with these customers, but Brockman would like to have some of the rest of the available business.

In light of the above problems, Brockman has toyed with the idea of using some type of quota system. Indeed, he tried it once in the past, but his sales representatives tended to ignore it since their income was not tied to achievement of quota.

Financial Performance

Exhibits 24–7, 24–8, and 24–9 summarize the Brockman Company's recent financial picture. Kenneth Brockman was not totally dissatisfied with his firm's financial

Exhibit 24-7
The Brockman Company, Inc.
Profit and Loss Statement
1976

Net Sales		$5,000,000
Base cost of goods sold		$3,755,000
Plus: freight in		$50,000
Less: cash discounts taken		$30,000
Total cost of goods sold		$3,775,000
Gross margin		$1,225,000
Other income		$25,000
Gross operating income		$1,250,000
Operating expenses:		
warehouse & delivery expenses	$200,000	
selling expenses	$400,000	
general and administrative expenses	$550,000	
Total operating expenses		$1,150,000
Pretax profit		$100,000
Income taxes		$40,000
Net profit		$60,000

Exhibit 24-8
The Brockman Company, Inc.
Balance Sheet
1976

Assets	
Current Assets:	
Cash	$40,000
Accounts Receivable	$830,000
Inventory	$940,000
Misc. Current Assets	$10,000
Total Current Assets	$1,820,000
Fixed Assets	$180,000
Total Assets	$2,000,000
Liabilities and Net Worth	
Liabilities:	
Current Liabilities	$1,200,000
Long-Term Liabilities	$100,000
Total Liabilities	$1,300,000
Net Worth:	
Invested Capital	$100,000
Retained Earnings	$600,000
Total Net Worth	$700,000
Total Liabilities and Net Worth	$2,000,000

performance. Over the years, the business has made him a moderately comfortable man financially. However, he is convinced that profits could be improved and perhaps substantially. Also, he is genuinely concerned about some specific problems.

Recently, the firm has consistently generated good sales increases (12 to 15 percent annually). However, the growth of dollar profits has been much smaller and profit as a percentage of sales has actually declined. He considers this situation to be at least partially an industry-wide problem resulting from decreasing gross margins and inflated operating costs.

Like many firms of similar size, the Brockman Company frequently is pinched for cash. Brockman's business has required relatively heavy investments in accounts receivable, and he also is somewhat concerned about the average size of his investment in inventory. In recent years he has had to compensate by stretching his credit from suppliers as much as possible. As a result, the firm was able to take advantage of only about half of its available cash discounts last year.

The cash problem worries Brockman even more when he considers it in terms of requirements for future growth. He definitely is concerned about the source of funds for some of the expansion programs he is considering. He has not been able to at-

Exhibit 24-9
The Brockman Company, Inc.
Key Ratios

Inventory Turnover				
$\dfrac{\text{Cost of Goods Sold}}{\text{Inventory}}$	=	Turnover	$\dfrac{\$3,775,000}{\$940,000}$	= 4.0

Average Number of Days Accounts Receivable are Outstanding

Step 1	$\dfrac{\text{Credit Sales}}{\text{Accounts Receivable}}$	= Accounts Receivable Turnover	$\dfrac{\$830,000}{\$5,000,000}$	= 6.0
Step 2	$\dfrac{\text{Number of Days in Year}}{\text{Accounts Receivable Turnover}}$	= Days outstanding	$\dfrac{360}{6}$	= 60

Strategic Profit Formula

Profit Margin	×	Asset Turnover	=	Return on Assets	×	Leverage Ratio	=	Return on Net Worth
$\dfrac{\text{Net Profit}}{\text{Net Sales}}$	×	$\dfrac{\text{Net Sales}}{\text{Total Assets}}$	=	Return on Assets	×	$\dfrac{\text{Total Assets}}{\text{Net Worth}}$	=	Return on Net Worth
$\dfrac{\$60,000}{\$5,000,000}$	×	$\dfrac{\$5,000,000}{\$2,000,000}$	= 3.0%		×	$\dfrac{\$2,000,000}{\$700,000}$	=	8.7%
1.2%	×	2.5	= 3.0%		×	2.9	=	8.7%

tract significant outside investment funds, short of selling his business. Although he has a good line of credit with a local bank, the bank is reluctant to expand the line. They feel he is too highly leveraged. In other words, he has too much debt relative to his net worth. In short, money for growth programs probably will have to be generated internally.

Discussion Questions

1. Do a complete evaluation of the Brockman Company's profit performance and financial condition. Identify key problems and opportunities for improvement.

2. Analyze the significance of market segmentation to the management of the Brockman Company.

3. Analyze and make recommendations regarding management of the field sales force.

4. Analyze and make recommendations regarding Brockman's inventory management processes.

5. Evaluate Brockman's credit management activities. What are your recommendations?

6. Develop plans to provide adequate financing to support a 3-year growth goal of 15 percent per year.

7. Assume you bought the Brockman Company. Develop a detailed strategy designed to significantly increase profit.

Chapter 6

Advertising Strategy

This chapter focuses on developing and implementing advertising strategy, its supporting role and interaction with other marketing mix variables, and its relationship to corporate and marketing objectives and strategies.

Development and Implementation

Developing and creating an effective advertising strategy is a complex project requiring identification of advertising opportunities, product analysis and clear statements of objectives and strategy alternatives. Quite often vast amounts of money, time, effort, planning, and creativity are required to implement the selected strategy.

Identify Advertising Opportunities

Because of many changes in consumer attitudes, values, life styles, economic conditions, advertising legislation, and environmental changes, once successful advertising strategies might no longer be effective. Thus, it is important for advertisers to continously monitor changes in the business environment and in consumer tastes, preferences, and life styles.

To develop effective advertising strategy, advertisers must continually survey changes in such business factors as government regulation, consumerism, the economy, socio-cultural attitudes, and technology. These factors both create and destroy opportunities for advertisers.

Government Regulation. Government regulation can either create or destroy advertising opportunities. For example, the FTC created an opportunity for advertisers by encouraging product comparison advertising such as, the Datril versus

Tylenol advertisements (price comparison). Government regulations and mandates also destroy advertising opportunities. The ban on cigarette broadcast advertising continues to affect the tobacco industry's advertising programs.

Consumerism.   Consumer groups have had a substantial impact upon recent federal and state legislation on advertising and upon corporate decisions regarding advertising campaigns.

Several years ago, Campbell's showed a bowl of soup with an abundance of thick vegetables and meat at the top. Because marbles were dropped into the bowl, the vegetables and meat were forced to the top, looking as though the soup had a greater proportion of vegetables and meat than it actually had. As a result, the FTC issued an order stopping this form of advertising. A group of law students petitioned the court requesting that corrective advertising be required of Campbell's. Although the court did not feel that Campbell's case required corrective advertising, they did feel that the idea of corrective advertising had merit. As a result, the FTC developed criteria to determine when corrective advertising was needed.[1]

Consumerism and consumer groups are having a greater impact on business in general and advertising in particular than ever before. A citizens' group which has had a substantial impact on advertisers is the National Citizens' Committee for Broadcasting (NCCB). Their objective is to rid television of violent programs and to "expose" companies who advertise on programs that display violence. Over a 12-week period during the fall of 1976, the NCCB ranked the five most violent prime time television shows and the least violent shows. The most "violent sponsors" were (1) Chevrolet, (2) Whitehall Labs—Anacin, (3) American Motors, (4) Sears, (5) Eastman Kodak, (6) Schlitz, (7) Proctor and Gamble, and (8) General Foods. The least "violent sponsors" were (1) Peter Paul candy, (2) Hallmark, (3) Texaco, (4) Whirlpool, (5) Prudential Insurance, (6) Jean Naté, and (7) Schaper toys. In addition, NCCB publicizes the names and addresses of the sponsors and strongly urges citizens to write and "raise their voices against violence." [2]

Economic Factors.   Both national and international economies affect advertising decisions. The oil crisis of 1973–74 created an opportunity for some automobile manufacturers to advertise their cars' fuel economy. During recessions, much advertising is directed at "value," "savings," and "economy." During "boom" periods "status," "elegance," and "quality" are themes which frequently appear.

Technological Factors.   Changes in technology affect advertising decisions in a variety of ways. The advent of television, color television, micro-fragrance and vinyl sound sheets in magazines, color in newspapers, and video-talkers in department stores and shopping malls has changed the way companies advertise. The boom in video games and predictions of sophisticated computerized games and

---

[1] Robert E. Freer, Jr., "The Federal Trade Commission—A Study in Survival," *The Business Lawyer,* July 1971, p. 1516.

[2] A pamphlet published by National Citizens' Committee for Broadcasting, Washington, D.C. No date of publication.

even computers which attach to the TV screen have affected and should continue to affect audience viewer time. Moreover, cable television has provided home audiences with entertainment free from commercials. And, according to the newspaper industry, a day is coming in the not too distant future when subscribers will read their daily "newspapers" over cable television. It is evident that media technology can both create and destroy opportunities for television advertisers and networks.

Sociocultural factors. Within the last several years, products have been advertised which a decade ago were not even considered for advertising such as sanitary napkins, feminine hygiene deodorants, and contraceptives. Also, appeals used today for a variety of products are much more provocative than a decade ago. Advertisers must monitor social attitudes to determine what can be advertised and how.

Perform a Market Analysis

Market analysis involves a comprehensive evaluation and analysis of total market sales, company sales (if not a new product), each competitor's sales and product position, and potential market segments. General sources of information to perform a market analysis are (1) consumer research, (2) government sources (e.g., *Census of Business* and *Census of Manufacturers*), (3) retail audits (actual sales from purchase records and/or inventories from a sample of retail stores), (4) trade associations, (5) trade publications (*Advertising Age, Business Week*), and research sources (Nielson, Simmons, TGI, AIS/Marketronics, Starch). These sources can be helpful in answering questions that bear directly on product positioning, media mix composition, advertising budgeting, and scheduling advertising delivery.

Two of the more complex areas of market analysis are consumer research and identification of consumer groups (segments).

Conduct Consumer Research

Advertisers must have a basic understanding of human behavior in order to conduct good consumer research. Among the behavioral concepts advertisers must understand are human attention and perception processes, learning theory, attitude formation and change, diffusion and adoption processes, personality and self-concept theory, psychographics and life-style analysis, group behavior, consumer decision processes, and postpurchase behavior.

Most consumer research begins with these basic questions: "What do consumers need or want?" "What are the benefits, both instrumental and psychological, sought by our consumers?" To illustrate the kinds of information advertisers seek in their consumer research, study the question areas for after-shave lotions and colognes presented in Exhibit C—6–1.

After questions of need and want, the question of how to *motivate* the consumer to purchase the product arises. A well-established axiom of human behavior is that unsatisfied needs are motivators of behavior. Discovering these unfulfilled

Exhibit C-6-1

Questions in a Market Study For After-Shave Lotions and Colognes:

a. Who uses after shaves and colognes?
   How many men used these products in the past six months?
   What types of products do they use?
   How much of an overlap is there in use of after shaves, colognes, and all-purpose lotions?
   How often do men use these products?
   What are the users' demographic profiles?

b. What types and brands do they use?
   How do people classify brands?
   What are the main types?
   What types do they use?
   What brands do they use?
   How often do men use each type?
   Where do they apply each type?

c. Who buys these products?
   Do people buy these products as gifts or for regular use?
   How much of the total volume do gift brands account for?
   Who buys the regular brands?
   Who selects the regular brands?
   Where are the regular brands bought?
   Who buys the gifts?
   What types are bought as gifts?
   What brands are bought as gifts?
   What product combinations are bought as gifts?
   Do women select gifts in the store?
   How often are gift brands used?
   How often are gift types used?
   Are users likely to start buying brands they've received as gifts?

d. What are people looking for in after shaves and colognes?
   What dimensions of the product are people concerned with?
   What after shave dimensions are most important?
   Which cologne dimensions are most important?
   How do the dimensions compare in importance?
   Are men and women looking for the same things?
   How different are after shave and colognes?

Source: Alvin A. Achenbaum, "Statement in behalf of the Joint A.N.A./A.A.A.A. Committee (before the Federal Trade Commission, October 28, 1971).

needs provides the key to advertising strategies and message appeals. In some cases, advertising strategy might be devised to make consumers *aware* of latent needs. In other cases, the strategy might attempt to *intensify* current consumer needs which the consumer might not recognize as a strong need. In both cases, advertisers can develop strategies to motivate consumer trial use of the advertised product.[3]

Motivation research attempts to reveal subconscious needs. Ernest Dichter is a pioneer in this field and has conducted studies for such firms as Alcoa, Colgate-Palmolive, DuPont, General Mills, Johnson and Johnson, and Proctor and Gamble.[4] Among his findings are the following:

(1) Typists regard typewriters as feminine and yielding objects. Based on this finding, a major typewriter company has developed a model with a "more concave keyboard in a receiving configuration." [5]

(2) People hold deep attachment to their first car because it is a "puberty symbol." It represents escape and freedom from parents. As a result of this finding, Chrysler Corporation developed the theme "Do you still remember when . . . ?" depicting an old Plymouth with a new one.

Other motivational research suggests that men desire their cigars to be strong in order to prove their masculinity; "consumers prefer vegetable shortening because animal fats stimulate a sense of sin;" [6] and women prefer "revealing" clothes due to an unsatisfied (and unconscious) need for exhibitionism.

Motivation research certainly is not without its critics. Achenbaum points out that it is highly subjective and unscientific, uses samples which are too small, and yields conflicting interpretations of data.[7]

Advertisers also collect data on consumer attitudes, learning, self-concepts, personalities, psychographics, and media behavior. These studies help advertisers to set advertising objectives and to segment markets (a topic discussed in Chapter 2).

Analyze Resources

In developing a total advertising program, the decision maker should analyze available resources such as money, time, creativity, expertise, consumer franchises, relationships with the business community (particularly advertising agencies, media), and company products. The first part of the analysis should focus on the product(s) for which the advertising campaign is being developed.

Product Analysis

Consumers do not buy products, they buy bundles of satisfaction. Charles Revson of Revlon, Inc. commented, "In the factory we make cosmetics; in the store we sell hope." Women do not buy a chemical formulation, but a promise of beauty.

---

[3] See M. Wayne DeLozier and Denis F. Healy, "A Theoretical Framework Relating the Concepts of Need, Want, Drive, and Motivation," in Henry W. Nash and Donald P. Robin (eds.), *Proceedings: Southern Marketing Association, 1976 Conference*, pp. 118–120; and John B. Stewart, "Product Development," in George Schwartz (ed.), *Science in Marketing* (New York: John Wiley & Sons, Inc., 1965), pp. 163–211.

[4] Roger Ricklefs, "Ernest Dichter Thrives Selling Firms on 'Hidden Emotions,'" *The Wall Street Journal*, November 20, 1972, p. 1.

[5] Ibid.

[6] Philip Kotler, *Marketing Management: Analysis, Planning, and Control* (Englewood Cliffs, NJ: Prentice-Hall, 1976), p. 76.

[7] Ricklefs, *loc. cit.*

Consumers buy benefits—the satisfactions they perceive the physical object gives them. Theodore Levitt said:

> The product is not what the engineer explicitly says it is, but what the consumer implicitly demands that it shall be. Thus, the consumer consumes not things, but expected benefits—not cosmetics, but the satisfactions of the allurements they promise; not quarter-inch drills, but quarter-inch holes; not stock in companies, but capital gains; not numerically controlled milling machines, but trouble-free and accurately smooth metal parts; not low-cal whipped cream, but self-rewarding indulgence combined with sophisticated convenience.[8]

Therefore, in developing an advertising strategy advertisers should examine the consumers' perceived benefits and how the product can fulfill consumers' hopes and dreams.

Specific areas to examine in a product analysis include package testing, consumer price perception, consumer usage behavior, and consumer perceptions of stores in which the product is (or will be) bought. Although these areas are not physically a part of the product, they all contribute to the consumer's perception of the *total product offering*.

A final area to consider is the product life cycle. In developing an advertising strategy, advertisers should determine whether the product is in its introduction, growth, maturity, or decline stage. If the product is in its *introductory* stage, advertising should be designed to create generic product awareness. The promotional effort should be directed at stimulating *primary* demand, rather than *secondary* (or selective) demand. During the *growth* stage, advertisers should emphasize brand name recognition and brand benefit recall. Their objective should be one of creating a selective demand and hopefully a loyal consumer group. In the *maturity* stage, competition becomes fierce and the advertiser must shift from a growth strategy to a highly competitive strategy. Positioning the brand becomes critical. It usually becomes necessary to allocate more dollars to the advertising effort to retain market share, dealer and consumer loyalty, and shelf space.

Finally, when a product enters its *decline* stage, advertising expenditures decline drastically. The advertising strategy aims at retaining the "hard core," highly loyal consumer. Little effort, if any, is made to locate new consumers.

Set Advertising Objectives

After assessing advertising opportunities and evaluating advertising resources, the advertiser delineates the boundaries within which to set realistic and attainable goals. The advertisers' appraisal of opportunities provides a set of potentially fruitful areas to exploit; the resource analysis sets the boundaries within which and the levels at which the advertiser can work. With this analysis done, the advertiser should set forth operationally defined objectives for the company's advertising effort.

---

[8] Theodore Levitt, "The Morality of Advertising," *Harvard Business Review*, July-August, 1970, p. 91. Copyright © 1970 by the President and Fellows of Harvard College; all rights reserved.

Three functions of advertising objectives are to (1) communicate to lower-level decision makers what their task is, (2) provide a criterion for choosing among alternative advertising plans, and (3) act as a standard in evaluating the results of an advertising campaign.[9]

Advertising goals can be stated in terms of sales-related goals or as communications-related goals. Sales-related goals generally are:

(1) To increase company sales by 30 percent by year-end 197*x*.

(2) To increase company market share to 20 percent by year-end 197*x*.

(3) To increase company profits by 25 percent by year-end 197*x*.

Sales- and profit-related goals, however, are generally unrealistic since advertising is only one of several marketing variables that influence sales. Price, packaging, product configuration, sales promotion, personal selling, favorable and unfavorable publicity, channel selection, competitor activity, and economic, technological, and sociocultural changes are among the many influences affecting sales.

Advertisers are beginning to look at advertising's role in producing certain desired behavioral changes. In particular, they are beginning to state advertising objectives in terms of desired communications effects. A general statement of advertising objectives using a communications perspective could include the following:

(1) Attain a 60 percent level of *awareness* among consumers within our target market by year-end 197*x*.

(2) Achieve a 40 percent level of brand comprehension (stated brand attributes, functions, and benefits predetermined by management) among consumers within our target market by year-end 197*x*.

(3) Create a favorable attitude (or conviction to purchase, buying intention, preference) among 20 percent of consumers within our target market by year-end 197*x*.

(4) Stimulate favorable word-of-mouth advertising from 15 percent of our current purchasers over the next 12 months. (Example, Firestone: "Ask a friend about us.")[10]

Professor John B. Stewart has created a rather extensive list of advertising objectives stated in terms of (1) achieving desired conditions in the consumer's mind, (2) achieving desired conditions in the consumer's overt behavior, and (3) achieving desired conditions in the corporate position. This set of objectives is shown in Exhibit C—6–2.

Although these objectives are stated in general terms, they present ideas that can be stated in specific and operational terms.

---

[9] David A. Aaker and John G. Myers, *Advertising Management* (Englewood Cliffs, NJ: Prentice-Hall, Inc., 1975), pp. 85–86.

[10] M. Wayne DeLozier, *The Marketing Communications Process* (New York: McGraw-Hill Book Company, 1976), p. 278.

Exhibit C-6-2
A Statement of Some Possible
Marketing Communications Objectives

I.   Desired conditions to achieve in the consumer's mind

    A.   Clarify needs

       1. Make the consumer conscious of the difference between his objectives and present position

       2. Clarify the nature of this difference in his mind

       3. Increase the magnitude of the differences in his mind

       4. Provide some urgency about eliminating the difference

       5. Make him feel more certain that a difference does exist now or in the future

    B.   Increase brand awareness

       1. Increase the breadth of awareness (the number of people aware)

       2. Increase the intensity of awareness (near the surface of consciousness)

       3. Improve the timing of initial awareness in relation to purchase

       4. Increase the duration of awareness

       5. Improve the quality of the prospects made aware

       6. Increase the closeness of association between the need felt and this brand as a solution to it

    C.   Increase product knowledge

       1. Increase the consumer's total knowledge about this brand

       2. Increase the ratio of favorable knowledge to unfavorable knowledge about this brand

       3. Improve the accessibility of this knowledge in the consumer's mind

       4. Improve the accuracy of knowledge about the product in the consumer's mind (eliminate unfavorable myths)

       5. Improve the appropriateness of consumer knowledge—especially on unique points of product differentiation and hidden qualities

       6. Improve the credibility of consumer knowledge

    D.   Improve the brand image

       1. Improve consumer attitudes toward the product attributes (design, capacity, expense, quality, etc.)

       2. Improve consumer attitudes toward the personality attributes (age, status, gender, etc.)

    E.   Improve the company image

       1. Progressiveness

       2. Honesty

       3. Reliability

       4. Competence

       5. Friendliness

    F.   Increase brand preference

       1. Increase the breadth (the number of consumers that prefer the brand)

       2. Increase the intensity (the strength of preference)

       3. Extend the time period

II. Desired conditions to achieve in the consumer's behavior

    A. Stimulate search behavior

        1. Increase store traffic

        2. Increase telephone inquiries

        3. Increase other forms of product inquiries

    B. Increase brand trial purchase

        1. Increase the number of triers

        2. Increase the quality of triers (i.e., triers with the greatest probability of repurchase)

    C. Increase repurchases

        1. Increase the frequency of purchase

        2. Increase the volume of repurchase (decrease cognitive dissonance)

        3. Extend the period of time over which repurchases continue to be made

    D. Increase voluntary promotion by consumers of the brand

        1. Increase the quality and the amount of word-of-mouth communications among consumers

        2. Increase favorable consumer feedback to dealers

III. Desired conditions to achieve for corporate position

    A. Improve the financial position

        1. Increase the sales volume per year

        2. Reduce the cost of sales per year

        3. Increase the profits per year and/or return on investment

        4. Extend the period of profit flow

        5. Increase the period of profit flow (the certainty of)

    B. Increase the flexibility of the corporate image to facilitate future growth and/or diversification

    C. Increase cooperation from the trade

        1. Stimulate the enthusiasm of company sales representatives

        2. Increase the shelf space at retail outlets

        3. Increase the completeness of inventory

    D. Enhance the company's reputation in the financial community

    E. Enhance the company's reputation among present and potential employees

    F. Increase the influence of public opinion concerning political issues related to corporate welfare

    G. Build up management ego

Criteria for Stating Advertising Objectives

There are several criteria for developing a set of advertising objectives. Some essential characteristics are: [11]

    (1) Stating objectives in terms supportive of other promotional efforts and in line with overall marketing and corporate objectives.

---

[11] David W. Nylen, *Advertising: Planning, Implementation, and Control* (Cincinnati, OH: South-Western Publishing Co., 1975), pp. 208–211.

(2) Stating objectives in "problem-related" terms.

(3) Stating objectives in terms of *"what* is to be accomplished, not how it is to be accomplished." [12]

(4) "Advertising objectives should provide specific guidelines to people designing programs to accomplish objectives." [13] Objectives should be stated in a way to provide direction for media planners and creative people.

(5) "Advertising objectives should be stated in measureable terms," [14] to evaluate the success of a campaign. These terms include the time period within which the desired result must be obtained and the level of performance desired.

Develop Alternative Advertising Strategies

Depending upon a company's objectives, several *specific* advertising strategies can be generated from 4 *broad* categories. These categories are product-benefit, image-identification, product positioning, and attitude.

Product-benefit strategies communicate specific product features, uses, and customer benefits. The advertiser attempts to communicate to prospective buyers feaures, uses, or benefits that successfully differentiate the company's brand from those of competitors and that will satisfy a consumer need, for example, Crest toothpaste stressing cavity prevention, and MacLean's stressing whiter teeth.

Image-identification strategies focus on either projecting a personality (image) for a brand, such as the Jolly Green Giant (image strategy) or on developing a brand image with which consumers can identify, such as the "Winchester Man." Although these strategies stress brand image, the former builds the image around the brand, whereas the latter creates the image based on the consumer.

Image strategies emerged in the 1960s as a popular advertising approach. Some strategies ascribe human personality traits to brands, whereas others stress elegance, prestige, and other nonphysical traits of the products. Two purposes of image strategies are (1) to create a mental picture of a brand which consumers can more easily recall and (2) to develop a psychological differentiation of the brand in the minds of consumers. The latter purpose is particularly important for physically similar products, such as cigarettes, beer, and colas.

Identification strategies create images for products based on consumer self-images or life-styles. Self-image theory is based primarily upon two premises:

(1) An individual strives to maintain and enhance his self image. [15]

(2) Individuals endeavor to maintain harmony and internal consistency of the self. [16]

---

[12] Ibid., p. 209.
[13] Ibid.
[14] Ibid.
[15] Arthur W. Combs and Donald Snygg, *Individual Behavior* (New York: Harper & Brothers, 1959), p. 45.
[16] Prescott Lecky, *Self Consistency* (Hamden, CT: The Shoe String Press, Inc., 1961), p. 155.

According to this theory, consumers should prefer those brands which they *perceive* will either maintain or enhance their self-image. Research supports this idea for some product areas. As examples, beer drinkers have shown preferences for brands which they perceive maintain or enhance their self-concepts.[17] Women express preferences for shampoos and perfumes which they perceive as most consistent with their self-images.[18]

Grubbs and Grathwohl summarized several self-theoretic concepts and their relationship to purchase behavior in the following qualitative model:

(1) An individual has a self-concept.

(2) The self-concept is of value to him.

(3) Because this self-concept is of value to him, an individual's behavior will be directed toward furthering and enhancing his self-concept.

(4) An individual's self-concept is formed through interaction with parents, peers, teachers, and significant others.

(5) Goods serve as social symbols and, therefore, are communication devices.

(6) The use of these good-symbols communicates meaning to the individual and to others causing an impact and/or the interaction processes, and, therefore, an effect on the individual's self-concept.

(7) The individual's consuming behavior will be directed toward furthering and enhancing his self-concept through the consumption of goods as symbols.[19]

The implication for advertising strategy is that through self-image research, profiles of consumer self-concepts can be developed to aid advertisers.

In recent years *life-style* and psychographic research have provided advertisers with another approach for developing advertising strategies. Life style is a distinct way of living generally described in terms of a person's (1) activities (2) interests (3) opinions, and (4) demographics.[20]

Psychographics includes life-style variables with one or more of the following: personality traits, consumer self-images, media habits, brand usage behavior, brand benefits desired, brand perceptions, consumer needs and values, and shopping behavior. Ruth Ziff simplifies psychographic terminology by describing consumer group characteristics as follows:

• Life-style variables, needs, values, and personality characteristics related to the product under study.

---

[17] Edward L. Grubb, "Consumer Perception of 'Self Concept' and Its Relationship to Brand Choice of Selected Product Types," unpublished D.B.A. dissertation, University of Washington, 1975, pp. 120–124.

[18] Wayne DeLozier and Rollie Tillman, "Self Image Concepts—Can They Be Used to Design Marketing Programs?" *The Southern Journal of Business,* **7** No. 4, November 1972, pp. 9–15.

[19] Edward L. Grubb and Harrison L. Grathwohl, "Consumer Self-Concept Symbolism and Market Behavior: A Theoretical Approach," *Journal of Marketing,* **31** October 1967, pp. 25–26. Published by the American Marketing Association.

[20] Joseph Plummer, "Applications of Life Style Research to the Creation of Advertising Campaigns," in William D. Wells (ed.), *Life Style and Psychographics* (Chicago: American Marketing Association, 1974), p. 160.

- Products' characteristics or benefits.
- Age, sex, and other demographic variables.
- Consumer purchase and usage.

And *if* the study is extensive,

- Consumer views of current brands on the market.
- Consumer media habits.[21]

An example of the kinds of output from psychographic research is summarized in Figures C—6-1 and C—6-2. Figure C—6-1 describes a group referred to as the

---

[21] Ruth Ziff, "The Role of Psychographics in the Development of Advertising Strategy and Copy," Ibid., pp. 145–146.

Figure   C—6-1
Dependent Driver

WHO THEY ARE LIKE
- Know little about cars
- Uninvolved in cars, driving, maintenance
- Apprehensive about cars
- Need reassurance that car will run well
- Car make & dealer important
- Get pleasure from appearance of car

WHAT THEY WANT
- Trust in manufacturer and dealer
- Dependable car
- Good engine performance
- Good handling qualities
- Good styling
- Minimum maintenance

WHO THEY ARE
- Older
- Better educated
- Higher incomes

WHAT THEY DO
- More own Chevrolets, Pontiacs, Oldsmobile
- Choose on trust in make; styling
- Own more cars; recent models

Source: Ruth Ziff, "The Role of Psychographics in the Development of Advertising Strategy and Copy" in William D. Wells (ed.), *Life Style and Psychographics* (Chicago, IL: American Marketing Association, 1974), p. 145.

Figure   C—6–2
Active   Driver

WHAT THEY ARE LIKE
- Know a lot about cars
- Involved in cars and maintenance
- Enjoy driving
- Are power oriented in driving
- Want to be in control when driving
- Believe in differences between makes

WHAT THEY WANT
- Powerful cars for driving control
- Top engine performance
- Good handling qualities
- Cars made by major companies

WHO THEY ARE
- Younger
- Middle class in income and education

WHAT THEY DO
- More own a Ford, fewer a Chevrolet/AM
- Drive more powerful cars
- Choose on engine performance; styling

Source: Ruth Ziff, "The Role of Psychographics in the Development of Advertising Strategy and Copy" in William D. Wells (ed.), *Life Style and Psychographics* (Chicago, IL: American Marketing Association, 1974), p. 146.

"dependent driver." Figure C—6–2 profiles a group called the "active driver." Once the advertiser has a complete picture of the consumer for the product, an advertising strategy can be developed which fits the consumer's life-style.

Product Positioning Strategies
A company's brand is only one of several brands in a "competitive field" within the minds of consumers.[22] Consumers "position" brands within the "field" among dimensions they deem as most relevant to the product category. A product positioning strategy, therefore, is one which attempts to either create or change a brand's position in the consumers' competitive field. Figure C—6–3 illustrates the positions consumers perceive for brands of toothpaste with respect to their abilities to whiten

---

[22] Kotler, *op. cit.,* p. 425.

teeth and to prevent tooth decay. The letters A through H represent hypothetical brands. The letters I_1 through I_4 represent consumers' perceptions of the ideal brands of toothpaste. I_1, for example, represents the ideal brand for consumer group one.

Given the positions of the ideal points and the various brand positions, an advertiser for brand H may decide to emphasize the toothpaste's whitening power and re-position H toward I_2 since there are no competitors close to that ideal point. Of course, the ultimate success of the company's campaign will depend upon the toothpaste's ability to deliver the promised benefit. In some cases a producer may need to reformulate the product.

Another approach to product positioning is advocated by Trout and Ries.[23] They suggest that the advertised brand must in some way either be related to its competitors or linked to something else already in consumers' minds. For example,

7-Up was competing head-on with Pepsi and Coke in the soft drink market and not making much progress. Consumers viewed 7-Up as one of the soft drinks they

Figure   C—6–3
Hypothetical Map of Consumer Perceptions of Toothpaste Brands According to Ability to Whiten Teeth and Prevent Tooth Decay

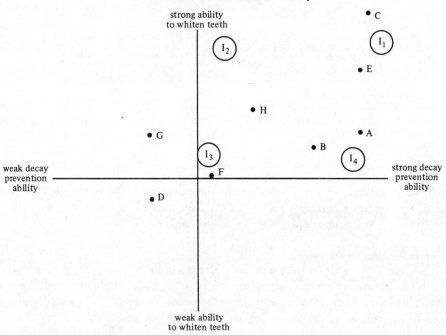

[23] Jack Trout and Al Ries, "The Positioning Era Cometh," a reprint from *Advertising Age* (Chicago, IL: Crain Communications, Inc. 1972). The article originally appeared in three parts, April 29, May 1, and May 8, 1972.

had to choose from, and colas were enjoying by far the greater preference. Then 7-Up came up with the un-cola campaign. This campaign, in effect, separated the soft drink market in the minds of consumers into the "cola" market and the "un-cola" market, where 7-Up 'moved' from being the third or fourth most preferred soft drink to being the most preferred "un-cola." [24]

This campaign was designed to make 7-Up an *alternative* to the colas and thereby establish its own position within its own newly-created "product category."

Another example is the Avis campaign in the 1960s in which Avis positioned itself *against* Hertz by using the theme that "We're number 2, but we try harder," creating the "underdog" position. Since many Americans traditionally have pulled for the underdog, the company produced a positive emotional reaction and Avis rentals increased.

Attitude Strategies

Boyd, Ray, and Strong suggest an attitudinal framework to generate advertising strategies. Their attitudinal framework is based largely upon the work of Amstutz [25] and is diagrammed in Figure C—6–4.

Out of this framework, the authors suggest the following five strategies:

(1) Affect *those* forces which influence strongly the choice criteria for evaluating brands belonging to the product class.

(2) Add characteristic(s) to those considered salient for the product class.

(3) Increase/decrease the rating for a salient product class characteristic.

(4) Change perception of the company's brand with regard to some particular salient product characteristic.

(5) Change perception of competitive brands with regard to some particular salient product characteristic.[26]

Strategy 1 is directed at stimulating primary demand for a product by affecting consumers' generic needs and values. Strategies 2 and 3 are directed at the choice criteria consumers use to evaluate brands within a product class. Strategy 2 attempts to add an important criterion to the consumers' decision-making process. This strategy is particularly important in the maturity stage of the product's life cycle.

Strategy 3 is also directed at consumers' choice criteria. It is not concerned with adding an important choice criterion, but *changing* consumers' perceptions of existing criteria. The strategy is to make consumers believe that the brand's highly rated attribute *is* very important in making a brand selection. For example, consumers might believe that the car a company produces has disc brakes and rack and pinion steering, but they do not feel rack and pinion steering is important (they might not even know what rack and pinion steering is). However, if the

---

[24] DeLozier, *op. cit.*, p. 287.

[25] Arnold E. Amstutz, *Computer Simulation of Competitive Market Response* (Cambridge, MA: M.I.T. Press, 1967).

[26] Harper W. Boyd, Jr., Michael L. Ray, and Edward C. Strong, "An Attitudinal Framework for Advertising Strategy," *Journal of Marketing,* **36** (April 1972), pp. 29–30. Published by the American Marketing Association.

Figure   C—6–4
A Simple Attitudinal Framework for
Developing Advertising Strategies

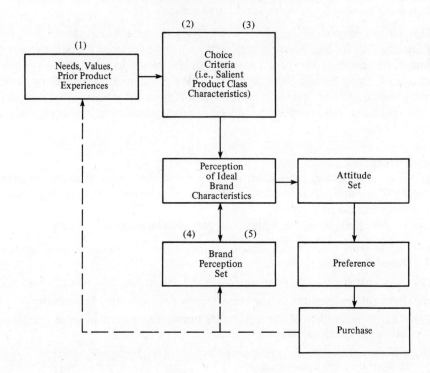

auto manufacturer can show the importance of rack and pinion steering in safe driving and manueverability, then the company might be able to attract more customers.

Strategy 4 is directed at the consumer's brand perception set for the purpose of bringing the company's brand "in line" with the consumer's perception of the "ideal" brand. However, this advertising strategy will fail if the brand does not "live up" to the promised features.

Strategy 5 also is directed at the consumer's brand perception set. However, the purpose of strategy 5 is to reposition competitors' brands by altering consumers' perceptions of them. One example is the campaign conducted for Beck's beer. Beck's objective was to reposition Lowenbrau by advertising "You've tasted the German beer that's the most popular in America; now taste the German beer that's the most popular in Germany." U. S. consumers mistakenly assumed that Lowenbrau was *the most popular beer in Germany* and therefore must be good-tasting beer. However, Beck's advertising repositioned Lowenbrau from the most popular German beer in America, *not Germany,* and positioned themselves as the *most popular beer* in Germany.

Tactical Considerations

Once an advertiser has selected a strategy, tactical decisions must be made to create the message appeal and develop a media plan (including media selection, media scheduling, and media budgets).

Creating the Message Appeal

Ultimately, all advertising messages appeal either directly or indirectly to human needs. Although there are many classifications of basic human needs, the most widely recognized list is that of A. H. Maslow. Maslow envisions a hierarchy of needs, where the most prepotent needs must be satisfied (or nearly so) before an individual becomes fully aware of the next needs. Maslow's needs hierarchy is as follows:

(1) Physiological (hunger, thirst, reproduction, etc.)

(2) Safety (security, protection, etc.)

(3) Love (affection, belongingness, etc.)

(4) Esteem (self-respect, prestige, social approval, achievement, etc.)

(5) Self-actualization (self-fulfillment, self-expression, artistic creation, etc.)[27]

Physiological needs are the basic elements of life—food, water, and physical sex. Once they are satisfied, safety becomes the individual's predominate concern. At this need level, the primary concern is for physical safety and protection—freedom from bodily harm. In the United States, most people are relatively unconcerned about the first two need levels, although these needs are of prime importance in other parts of the world.

With satisfaction of the first two needs, love needs dominate. The love need includes both the love *for* others as well as the love *of* others. People wish to give and to receive affections.

The fourth need level is *esteem*. Esteem refers to how a person evaluates himself. These needs are concerned with adequacy, self-confidence, and personal achievement, and how *others* see oneself based upon personal recognition, reputation, and prestige.

Finally, self-actualization, the highest need in the hierarchy, refers to what a person can be, he must be. It is the need to be the "ideal" and completely fulfilled self.

Many need schemes have been devised and can be used as the basis for developing an advertising message appeal;[28] however, Maslow's hierarchy is the most widely known and accepted and serves as the basis of the following discussion.

An understanding of needs and need theory is imperative for advertisers since

---

[27] A. H. Maslow, "A Theory of Human Motivation," *Psychological Review,* **50** 1943, pp. 370–396.

[28] For other need classifications, see Arthur Combs and Donald Snygg, *Individual Behavior* (New York: Harper & Brothers, 1959), p. 49; G. A. Steiner and B. Berelson, *Human Behavior: An Inventory of Scientific Findings* (New York: Harcourt, Brace & World, Inc., 1964), pp. 241–242; and Henry A. Murray (ed.), *Explorations in Personality* (Oxford University Press, 1938).

it is widely recognized that unsatisfied needs motivate behavior and that satisfied needs do not motivate behavior. Thus, advertising appeals, media selection, and scheduling should be based heavily upon consumer needs.

Advertising appeals are of 2 general types—direct appeals to human needs and indirect appeals to human needs.[29]

Direct appeals mention the need in the advertisement and show how the advertised brand can fully satisfy that need. For example, "When you have a man-size thirst, drink Gatorade." The advertisement addresses the need directly. If the ad is visual, such as a television commercial or a magazine advertisement, it may use a nonverbal message such as a hot, perspiring athlete to support the verbal message.

Indirect appeals allude to a human need rather than emphasize it. Consumers must interpret for themselves what need the product can fulfill for them.

Figure C—6–5 shows a framework for classifying general kinds of advertising appeals used in generating advertising messages. Advertisers use (1) product-oriented approaches and (2) consumer-oriented approaches. Product-oriented approaches emphasize either a product *feature,* a product *use,* or a *comparison* of the advertised brand with a competing brand. Consumer-oriented approaches focus on either consumers' attitudes, groups important to consumers (reference groups, parents, etc.), consumers' life styles, or consumers' subconscious desires.

---

[29] Much of this section is based upon DeLozier, *op. cit.,* pp. 232–234.

Figure   C—6–5
A Framework for Developing Advertising Appeals*

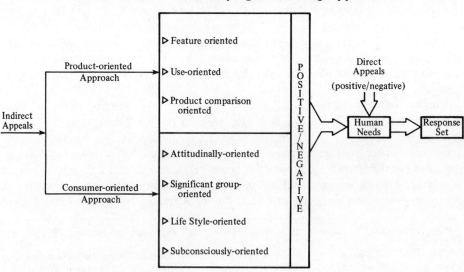

---

*Adapted from M. Wayne DeLozier, *The Marketing Communications Process* (New York: McGraw-Hill Book Company, 1976), p. 232.

Product-Oriented Approaches. *Feature-oriented appeals* are one in which the basic message emphasizes a brand's attributes and characteristics. "Schlitz Light Beer has approximately ⅓ fewer calories than our other fine quality beer." This message focuses on the low-calorie feature of Schlitz Light. Beer consumers might interpret the message as an appeal to a safety or survival need or as an indirect appeal to a love need.

Use-oriented appeals focus on a brand's in-operation and/or postoperation advantages. For example, "Trim hedges in half the time with 'Hedge Clipper.' " This message might appeal indirectly to consumers' needs for either achievement or esteem.

Product-comparison appeals focus on differences between the advertised brand and one or more competing brands, such as Granada rides as smoothly as a Mercedes.

Consumer-Oriented Approaches. Whereas product-oriented appeals focus directly upon the product, consumer-oriented appeals focus directly upon the consumer.

Attitudinally-oriented appeals are ones which present an attitude consistent with the target audience's attitude, followed by a request to act in a manner favorable to a company or organization. For example, "A wasted mind is a terrible thing. Please contribute generously to the United Negro Education Fund, so that our children can have a better life." This message may be appealing to the love need (affection, belongingness) of some target audience members, or even to a safety need (the future security of Black Americans).

Significant group-oriented appeals focus on the kinds of groups which either use or endorse the use of the advertised brand. Parents, friends, athletes, religious institutions, organizations, and reference groups which are influential on consumers' purchase behavior are used in this approach. A mother discussing with her daughter why she used Pampers instead of cloth diapers might appeal to the young mother who respects an experienced mother's advice. An Italian family shown sitting around the table at mealtime eating "Italiana" pizza might be an appropriate reference group for pizza lovers. These are generally appeals to love needs (belongingness, in particular). Advertisers use this strategy for products and brands whose purchase is strongly influenced by groups important to the purchaser.

Life style-oriented appeals stress a life-style with which the target audience can identify. For example, the Schlitz advertising campaign stresses "You only go around once in life, so grab for all the gusto you can get." This appeal was aimed at the heavy beer drinker whom Schlitz had identified as a dreamer, a hero worshiper, a pleasure seeker, a sports enthusiast, and a person with a male-dominant orientation to life.[30]

Subconsciously-oriented appeals are messages whose primary appeal is disguised and directed at the subconscious needs of the target audience. The basic message is aimed at the buyer's fantasy but is often veiled by an appeal to the consumer's

---

[30] Joseph T. Plummer, "Applications of Life Style Research to the Creation of Advertising Campaigns," in William D. Wells (ed.), *Life Style and Psychographics* (Chicago: American Marketing Association, 1974), pp. 159–168.

conscious mind. Examples of this form of advertising were given in a previous section on motivation research.

Positive Versus Negative Presentations.   Appeals can either be positive and supportive or negative and threatening. A positive presentation places the members of the target audience in a favorable mood by showing them the benefits they will experience by using the advertised brand. A negative presentation presents a threatening or saddening message to the target audience followed by a conclusion which shows how the advertised brand can help the purchaser either avoid or correct the negative situation.

The presentation form which will be most effective will depend upon the target market for which the advertiser is shooting and the nature of the product. Negative forms of presentation are used frequently by advertisers of personal products (deodorants, mouthwashes, toothpaste).

Developing the Media Plan

A media plan involves decisions regarding media selection, scheduling, and budgeting. Before discussing each of these decisions, we will look at the kinds of media available and the strengths and weaknesses of each.

Print Media.   Print media have characteristics that distinguish them from broadcast media and provide advantages over television and radio such as:

(1) Allow readers to control the time, pace, and direction of their exposure.

(2) Permit consumer retention of complex materials better than oral presentations.

(3) Reach small, specialized audiences, allowing the advertiser to create and tailor a message to the needs of the target audience.

(4) Permit easy reexposures since print is always readily available and not "fleeting."

(5) Have many publications which are high in status and prestige due to their authoritative, expert, and specialized nature.[31]

The newspaper medium. Among all media, newspapers rank first in advertising revenue. Newspapers are very much preferred by retailers. Several reasons for their popularity as an advertising medium can be cited:

(1) High geographic flexibility.

(2) High readership (77 percent).

(3) Heaviest readership is among better-educated and "upscale" consumers.

(4) Newspaper reading is a daily activity.

(5) A newspaper page (excepting classified ad pages) has an 84 percent chance of being opened.

---

[31] A synthesis of Joseph T. Klapper, *The Effects of Mass Communication* (New York: The Free Press of Glencoe, Inc., 1960), p. 11; and Joseph T. Klapper, "The Comparative Effects of the Various Media," in Harper W. Boyd, Jr. and Joseph W. Newman (eds.), *Advertising Management: Selected Readings* (Homewood, IL: Richard D. Irwin, Inc., 1965), pp. 431–432.

(6) Newspaper readers are *actively* involved in their reading, including clipping out articles and advertisements and discussing with friends what they read.[32]

In *scheduling* advertisements, newspapers have a major advantage over other advertising media. A short notice time (closing time) of usually 20 hours gives newspapers a high degree of flexibility that other media do not have. Newspapers also have geographic flexibility. For example, Delta Airlines uses different ad copy for different geographic markets.

Like every medium, newspapers have disadvantages—poor reproduction quality, numerous errors, and a short life span.

Magazines. The nature of magazines has changed over the past 10 to 15 years. In the past there were many general magazines such as *Life* and *Look;* today magazines are more specialized and cater to special interest audiences.

Major advertising advantages for magazines are "(1) *high quality* in reproduction (2) *credibility and prestige* of specific magazines, and (3) the *long life*.[33] Another advantage is the geographic flexibility created by national magazines producing regional editions. However, magazines do not offer the degree of geographical flexibility of newspapers.

Other print media. Other print media include the *Yellow Pages, outdoor* advertising, *transit* advertising, and *point-of-purchase* advertising. Consumers consult the yellow pages once they recognize some need or problem. Thus, they use the yellow pages most often at or very near the time of their purchase decision.[34] Two very inexpensive media are outdoor advertising (average cost per thousand exposure at about $.26)[35] and transit advertising (average cost per thousand exposures between $.15 and $.20 for inside-car exposure and $.07 for outside posters).[36] Both outdoor and transit provide geographic flexibility but generally are low in message impact and often have a short exposure time.

Point-of-purchase advertising comes in many forms, such as posters, banners, in-store displays, clocks, window displays, etc. Because they are close in time and space at the point of the actual purchase decision, they can be very effective in influencing impulse purchases.

Broadcast Media.   There are two major broadcast media which advertisers employ in delivering messages to audiences, television and radio.

Television.   In general, people spend more of their time with television than with any other medium. Average viewing time is approximately 5.5 hours per day. Consumers spend more than twice as much time watching television than on all other mass media combined.[37]

---

[32] *Advertising Age*, Nov. 21, 1973, p. 66.

[33] DeLozier, *op. cit.*, p. 240.

[34] *The Yellow Pages in Marketing and Advertising* (American Telephone and Telegraph Company, 1970), pp. 6–7.

[35] *Advertising Age*, November 21, 1973, p. 112.

[36] Ibid., p. 126.

[37] John P. Robinson, "Television Leisure Time: Yesterday, Today, and (Maybe) Tomorrow," *Public Opinion Quarterly*, **33** 1969, pp. 210–222.

The benefits which television offers advertisers are:

(1) Ability to reach a large audience with a single message.

(2) Relatively low cost per exposure.

(3) Uses sight, sound, motion, and color to provide a realistic and high impact message.

(4) Excludes competing message at instant of exposure.

(5) Ability to reach select audiences.

(6) Influential in gaining dealer support.[38]

(7) "Psychology of attention" (i.e., a viewer tends to continue to watch television through a commercial instead of changing to another program.)[39]

Three disadvantages are:

(1) *Absolute* cost is very high for a national commercial.

(2) Lack of availability of the desired time or program.

(3) An audience does not have the ease and convenience of re-exposure, since the television message is "fleeting."

Radio. Although radio does not have the impact it had three decades ago, it remains a very pervasive advertising medium. Today more than 98 percent of all homes in the United States have one or more radios totalling nearly 370 million working radios of which 93 million are found in automobiles.[40]

Radio has several advantages:

(1) It has a larger audience than television up to 6:00 p.m.

(2) It is a highly selective medium due to the 11 basic program formats which appeal to particular listening interests of people with different socioeconomic profiles.

(3) It offers geographic flexibility.

(4) It delivers an advertising message at less expense than either television or newspapers.

Disadvantages of radio are:

(1) It lacks the prestige of television and magazines.

(2) It has no visual impact.

(3) Its message is "fleeting" and does not permit easy re-exposure.

Because each advertising medium has its own characteristics and performs different functions, an advertiser should judge the usefulness of each medium in terms of its ability to deliver advertising messages to achieve the firm's advertising objectives most efficiently and effectively.

Selection of Media Vehicles. Media vehicles are specific versions, such as *Business Week, Playboy,* and *Cosmopolitan,* within a media class, such as maga-

---

[38] Dorothy Cohen, *Advertising* (New York: Wiley & Sons, Inc., 1972), pp. 564–565.

[39] J. F. Engel, H. G. Wales, and M. R. Warshaw, *Promotional Strategy* (Homewood, IL: Richard D. Irwin, Inc., 1971), p. 261.

[40] *Advertising Age, op. cit.,* p. 100.

zines. The selection of the right media vehicle is dependent upon (1) a definition of the target audience, (2) the kinds of media and media vehicles which best reach the target audience, (3) the advertising objectives of the company, (4) the available advertising budget, (5) the nature of the product, and (6) media costs.

Defining the Target Market.   The prerequisite of any advertising or marketing plan is to develop a clear profile of who the target market or audience is. Most companies develop profiles of target audiences. Although a demographic profile is useful in some instances, psychographic profiles have shown to be better indicators in most cases. Douglas Tigert found a strong relationship between consumers' life-styles and their exposure to media.[41] His work suggests that a match between purchaser (or better, heavy purchaser) psychographic profiles and media consumption habits can be useful to advertisers in selecting media.

As an example, demographic analysis of *Time* only readers and *Newsweek* only readers indicated the following:

(1) *Time* readers generally are "upscale" compared with *Newsweek* readers.

(2) A greater proportion of *Time* readers are college graduates compared with *Newsweek*.

(3) A greater proportion of *Time* readers have either professional or semi-professional occupations compared with *Newsweek*.

(4) *Time* only readers are in a higher income bracket than *Newsweek* only readers.

(5) *Time* only readers own homes which have higher market value than *Newsweek* only readers.[42]

However, many *Time* only and *Newsweek* only readers fall between these generalizations. Some of the differences a life-style analysis showed were that *Newsweek* only readers:

(1) Preferred job security to money.

(2) Exhibited greater concern about the power of government and labor unions.

(3) Were more concerned about religion.

(4) Believed "hippies" should be drafted.

(5) Believed more strongly that Communism is a great threat to the world today.

(6) Tend to be more old-fashioned in tastes and habits.

(7) Felt that if Americans worked harder and complained less, the United States would be a better place to live.

Tigert also shows how psychographic profiles of television viewers differ. Tigert's research suggests that the selection of media vehicles should depend more heavily

---

[41] Douglas J. Tigert, "Life Style As A Basis For Media Selection," in William D. Wells (ed.) *Life Style and Psychographics* (Chicago: American Marketing Association, 1974), pp. 173–201.
[42] Ibid., pp. 185–187.

on the life-styles of audience readers (or viewers) and that the firm's advertising messages should be placed in media whose audiences exhibit the life-style characteristics of the advertiser's intended target market.

Other media selection criteria are: [43]

(1) *Reputation.* The degree of credibility, trustworthiness, and prestige of each medium vehicle relative to other media vehicles.

(2) *Life Span.* The length of time which medium vehicle exposure remains in the home can vary from a 5-second radio commercial to several months for a magazine advertisement. Easy accessibility to repeat exposure to an advertising message is an important media vehicle selection criterion.

(3) *Target Market/Total Audience.* The ratio of target market to target audience is an expression of the proportion of prime prospects for a company's brand relative to the total audience for a medium vehicle. This figure aids media decision makers in determining the most efficient means of delivering an advertising message.

(4) *Cost.* Advertisers must look at both the *relative* cost (such as cost per thousand figures) and the *absolute* cost of advertising in a media vehicle. Although the cost per contact might be low for a national network spot, the *absolute* cost (for example, $150,000 per minute) may be prohibitive for most companies' advertising budgets.

(5) *Flexibility.* The medium vehicle should offer the *geographic* and *timing* flexibilities the advertiser needs to achieve the company's advertising objectives.

(6) *Reseller Support.* How effective is each medium in gaining reseller support? Newspaper, radio, and spot television are the most effective media for gaining reseller support at the local level. Gaining reseller support is important in obtaining shelf space and enthusiastic selling support.

(7) *Message Reproduction.* The media vary in their capabilities to physically deliver an advertising message.

(8) *Editorial Climate.* This phrase refers to the programs or articles presented in each media vehicle alongside the advertisements. If the programs or articles are supportive of the products advertised within that vehicle, then the editorial climate is said to be favorable.

(9) *Availability.* How easy or difficult is it for an advertiser to gain access to advertising space and broadcast time? It is very difficult to get a national network spot, whereas it is much easier to get space in a newspaper.

(10) *Psychological Impact.* Which media are better at achieving desired psychological impressions? If the objective is to create a favorable brand image, magazines and television generally are better media than newspapers and billboards.

---

[43] These criteria are based primarily upon DeLozier, *op. cit.*, pp. 245–257.

(11) *Reach.* Reach refers to "the number of different homes or individuals exposed to a given medium or combination of media over a period of time."[44] Reach generally refers to an *unduplicated* audience over the time span considered.

(12) *Frequency.* Frequency refers to the average number of times different households or individuals are reached by a specified media schedule over some time period. Frequency provides the impact necessary to facilitate consumer learning of product benefits and company identification. Repetition is an essential ingredient in successful advertising.

(13) *Gross Rating Points* (GRP). GRP is a gross weight or total impact measurement of message delivery over some stated period of time. GRP is calculated by multiplying reach times frequency. Thus, if a media plan delivers a reach of 40 percent to a target market 4 times, the GRP is 160 (40 x 4). GRP levels provide the advertising decision maker with comparisons which can be used to select among media alternatives. However, it should be noted that a GRP of 160 can be arrived at by either hitting 1 percent of the target market 160 times, by reaching 80 percent of the target market twice, or by any other combination of reach and frequency which yields 160 GRP.

Media Models. Many models have been developed to aid decision makers in selecting the best advertising media plan. At least five forms have been and are being used.

Linear Programming Models. Linear programming is a mathematical technique which allocates resources to their optimal uses, subject to certain constraints. Figure C—6–6 shows the general form of a linear programming model and a sample statement as they apply to selecting the number of media vehicle insertions to maximize total exposure value.

In the same statement, the total advertising budget for media insertions is $1,750,000 and the cost per insertion in medium vehicle 1 through n is $38,000, $29,000, $31,000 . . . and $23,000, respectively. Medium vehicle 1 gives 6100 (in thousands) effective exposures, medium vehicle 2 gives 4800 (in thousands), etc. Media vehicles 1 and 2 are published weekly and can therefore run from 0 to 52 ads over a year (assumes one ad per issue); medium vehicle 3 is published biweekly and can have up to 26 ad insertions per year, and medium vehicle *n* is published monthly, permitting up to 12 ad insertions. Finally, the lower limits (or minimum) ads which can be inserted must be nonnegative and therefore zero or greater. The lower limit for media vehicles 1 and 2 is set at zero, and at 2 and 6 for media vehicles 3 and *n*, respectively. Management might have either particular reasons or a certain preference for making sure that there are at least 2 and 6 insertions for media vehicles 3 and *n*.

Once the problem is set up as in the sample statement, the LP model locates the optimal number of insertions to place in each vehicle to maximize total effective exposures (E). An example set of solutions would appear as follows:

---

[44] C. H. Sandage and Vernon Fryburger, *Advertising Theory and Practice* (Homewood, IL: Richard D. Irwin, Inc., 1975), p. 419.

$$X_1 = 32$$
$$X_2 = 18$$
$$X_3 = 2$$
$$\bullet = ..$$
$$\bullet = ..$$
$$X_n = 12$$

Many times one or more variables within the set of solutions will contain a fraction such as 13.137. In these cases integer programming, a valuable extension

Figure   C—6–6
Linear Programming Model for Media Selection
General Model

Maximize $E = e_1x_1 \;+\; e_2x_2 \;+\; e_3x_3 \;+\; \ldots \; e_nx_n$
Subject to $c_1x_1 \;+\; c_2x_2 \;+\; c_3x_3 \;=\; \ldots \; c_nx_n \le B$

$$x_1 \ge l_1$$
$$x_1 \le u_1$$
$$x_2 \ge l_2$$
$$x_2 \le u_2$$
$$x_3 \ge l_3$$
$$x_3 \le u_3$$
$$x_n \ge l_n$$
$$x_n \le u_n$$

Where,
   $E \;\sim\;$ Total exposure value (number of rated exposures).
   $e_i \;\sim\;$ Exposure value of one ad in one medium.
   $x_i \;\sim\;$ Number of ads to be placed in medium i.
   $c_i \;\sim\;$ Cost of placing one ad in medium i.
   $B \;\sim\;$ Total advertising budget.
   $l_i \;\sim\;$ Lower limit for (minimum) number of ad insertions in medium i.
   $u_i \;\sim\;$ Upper limit for (maximum) number of ad insertions in medium i.

Sample Statement

Max $E = 6,100x_1 \;+\; 4,800x_2 \;+\; 5,300x_3 \;+\; \ldots \; 4,700X_n$
S.T. $38,000x_1 \;+\; 29,000x_2 \;+\; 31,000x_3 \;+\; \ldots \; 23,000x_n \le 1,750,000$

$$x_1 \ge 0 \qquad x_1 \le 52$$
$$x_2 \ge 0 \qquad x_2 \le 52$$
$$x_3 \ge 2 \qquad x_3 \le 26$$

$$x_n \ge 6 \qquad x_n \le 12$$

of the linear programming technique, can be used. This technique is the linear programming model with the additional requirement that the optimal set of solutions be integers.

Four major limitations in using linear programming for media selection are:

(1) It assumes constant marginal effects for repeat exposures.

(2) It assumes that a medium's cost per insertion is constant (not accounting for discounts accruing to multiple time and space purchases).

(3) It does not handle the problem of audience duplication (10,000 exposures to one person is treated by LP as equivalent to one exposure to 10,000 people).

(4) It does not determine *when* the ad should be scheduled.

Although not a limitation to the model itself, the exactness of the solutions generated by LP can lead some advertising decision makers into thinking they have *the* best media plan.[45] However, the solutions are only as good as the data and the assumptions built into the model. Good managerial experience and judgment must be used in arriving at a final media schedule, and linear programming should be viewed as only one input into making the final decision.

Heuristic Models. Whereas linear programming uses an algorithm designed to reach mathematically optimal solutions, heuristic uses rules of thumb, often trial and error procedures, to arrive at near-optimal solutions. Although there are many heuristic models, the "High Assay" model developed by Young and Rubican provides an illustration. (See Figure C—6–7.)

The "High Assay" model uses a *sequential* procedure to select media, rather than the *simultaneous* selection procedure of the LP model. The decision criterion is to choose the one medium vehicle with the lowest cost per prospect during week t (the first week). If the achieved exposure rate of the first selection does not reach the optimum advertising rate, the model recycles to make a second selection taking into account audience duplication and potential media discounts. This procedure continues until the optimal exposure rate is reached for week t, at which time the model begins to reiterate the procedure for week t + 1 until either the budget is exhausted or week 52 is reached.

The critical part of the model is the optimum exposure rate which is a function of the number of customer prospects, brand switching rates, product purchase cycle, and multiple exposure coefficients. The high assay model handles two of the limitations of the LP model, specifically audience duplication and media discounts.

Simulation Models. Simulation models are used to systematically evaluate the impact (or consequences) of a set of factors or events upon a system. In media selection, simulation is used to examine the question "what is likely to happen if we use this media plan?" The Simulmatics Corporation has developed a model which has 2,944 imaginary media users, described by an assortment of demographic data, socioeconomic data, and media exposure habits. The simulated audience is exposed to a media schedule and the computer provides output in

---

[45] Engel, Wales, and Warshaw, *op. cit.,* pp. 298–299.

Figure   C—6–7
The High Assay Model for Media Selection

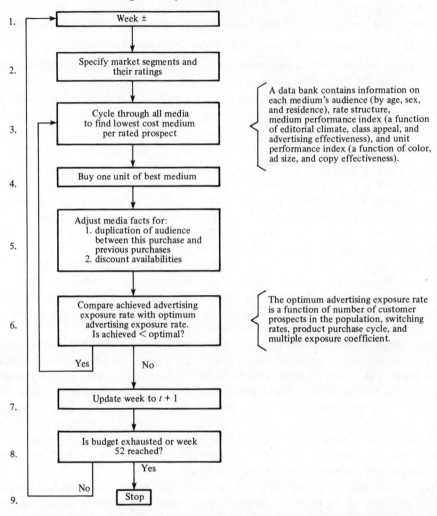

Source: Taken from Kotler adaptation of description in William T. Moran, "Practical Media Decisions and the Computer," *Journal of Marketing,* July 1963, pp. 26–30. Published by the American Marketing Association.

terms of the number of "audience" members reached, frequency of exposure, audience profile, and total cost.

Whereas the previous models are optimizing models, simulation is not. It merely attempts to examine probable outcomes from introducing media plans to an audience which approximates a cross-section of the U.S. population. Thus, simulation should be viewed as complementary to and not a substitute for the previously discussed models.[46]

MEDIAC. A more complex model of media scheduling has been developed by Little and Lodish which they call MEDIAC.[48] The objective of MEDIAC is to maximize sales. The advertising decision maker first divides the population into several market segments each of which has its own sales potential and media habits. Good prospects or heavy users are given higher weights than light users or poor prospects. It is assumed that an insertion in a particular magazine, for example, causes exposure in all market segments. Because people are subject to forgetting, a decay function is built into MEDIAC. Finally, the MEDIAC model operates under the assumption that with increased exposures, sales will increase but at a decreasing rate. The objective for MEDIAC is to find the number of insertions which maximizes sales in each media option during a specified time period. The model takes into account the exposure value per capita in each market segment, advertising wear out over time, the amount of exposure value retained from previous periods, expected number of exposures per person in each market segment for each media option, and a media option source effect (a measure of the qualitative value of a media vehicle, e.g., a sports car ad in *Road and Track* might have greater impact than the same ad in *Field and Stream*).

ADMOD. Another sophisticated model recently developed to determine a media plan is ADMOD (Advertising Decision Model).[48] ADMOD differs in several ways from MEDIAC. The major difference is that ADMOD "focuses on specific cognition changes or decisions that advertising is attempting to precipitate . . ."[49] ADMOD examines media plans in terms of (1) creating maximum brand awareness, (2) changing consumer attitudes, (3) generating new trial purchasers, or (4) stimulating consumers to try a brand in a new way. The ADMOD problem, therefore, is to find the optimal set of media insertions for each media vehicle to maximize the value sought (awareness, attitude change, etc.). The major steps are (1) divide the population into segments, (2) select a sample from each segment, (3) derive the probability that an individual will be exposed to a particular media vehicle, and (4) derive the probability that if an individual is exposed to a particular vehicle that he will also see the ad. ADMOD considers the exposure probabilities at the *individual level* instead of at the aggregate level, as is the case for MEDIAC. The results from this model are then projected to the real population.

Media Scheduling. Determining the timing of advertising messages is a critical

---

[46] Kotler, *op. cit.,* pp. 690–691.

[47] John D. C. Little and Leonard M. Lodish, "A Media Selection Model and Its Optimization by Dynamic Programming," *Industrial Management Review,* **8** fall, 1966, pp. 15–23. An improved and more complex version can be found in John D. C. Little and Leonard M. Lodish, "A Media Planning Calculus," *Operations Research,* **17** January-February, 1969, pp. 1–35.

[48] Daniel A. Aaker and John G. Myers, *Advertising Management* (Englewood Cliffs, NJ: Prentice-Hall, Inc., 1975), pp. 483–489.

[49] Ibid., p. 492.

decision which can be viewed in 2 parts, allocation of advertising exposures over the year, and allocation of exposures over periods shorter than a year.

In considering the advertising schedule over a year, the advertiser first considers whether demand is seasonal. If so, then he must consider whether to allocate advertising exposures to follow seasonal patterns, to run opposite of seasonal patterns, or to hold exposure constant over the entire year.[50] The decision rests on whether there is an advertising carryover effect and whether habitual purchasing is involved. If there is neither advertising carryover nor habitual purchasing behavior, then the best timing pattern for advertising exposures is one which coincides with the seasonal pattern. If there is advertising carryover and/or habitual purchasing, heavy advertising exposure should *lead* the peak seasons and be curtailed just before the slack seasons. Furthermore, the greater the carryover effect, the longer the lead time should be. And, finally, the greater the degree of habitual purchasing, the more constant advertising exposures should be over the year.[51]

Allocation of advertising exposures over short periods of time can either be *intermittent* or *continuous*. Over a period of a month, for example, an advertising message can be scheduled only on Saturday mornings of each week (such as advertising for young children's products). This form of advertising represents *intermittent* advertising. On the other hand, advertising a new model of automobile every day of a particular month represents *continuous* advertising. Additionally, advertising can be high to low in *concentration* (or saturation) for either intermittent or continuous advertising. For example, an advertiser can run either 10 television spots or one spot each day.

Over the long run, advertising is considered in terms of continuity and size. *Continuity* refers to the delivery pattern of a message over time. That is, a message may be distributed over a particular time period or concentrated at certain times throughout the year, such as particular seasons. *Flighting* refers to a concentrated advertising effort in a short period of time, such as a 4-week period, and is illustrated in Figure C—6–8.

As shown in Figure C—6–8, flighting involves several short bursts (4 weeks, for example) of concentrated advertising followed by no advertising for some period of time (for example, 4 weeks). *Continuous* advertising refers to advertising evenly over a period of time, such as a year. Figure C—6–9 illustrates continuous advertising.

Size of an advertising message refers to either the length of time it is broadcast on radio and television or the amount of space it uses in print media. The longer the ad is broadcast or the larger the size of the print ad, the greater the impression-making value. It has been shown that a full-page ad in a magazine develops greater awareness among readers than a half-page ad. However, a full-page ad which is *twice* the size of a half-page ad does *not* create twice the awareness of the advertising message. Rudolph learned from his studies that an advertisement twice the size of another will not double the amount of attention the ad receives. Rather,

---

[50] Kotler, *op. cit.*, pp. 364–365.

[51] See Alfred A. Kuehn, "How Advertising Performance Depends on Other Marketing Factors", *Journal of Advertising Research*, March 1962, pp. 2–10.

Figure   C—6–8
An Example of Flighting

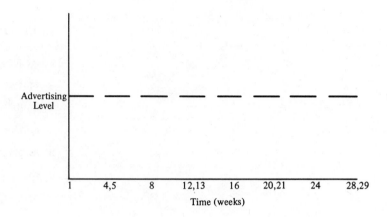

Figure   C—6–9
An Illustration of Continuous Advertising

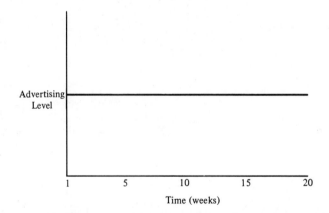

according to Rudolph, the ad must be 4 times the size of the smaller to attract twice the attention. This statement has become known as the "square root law." This "law" says that attention value of an ad increases as the square root of the size of the ad increases.[52] Thus, there are trade-offs between costs of an advertisement and its attention value.

An advertiser must be concerned about reader frequency, continuity, and size in developing the media mix. These elements are interrelated and interdependent and pose several alternatives for a media planner depending upon the firm's objectives. These alternatives are shown in Figure C—6–10.

---

[52] H. J. Rudolph, *Attention and Interest Factors in Advertising* (New York: Funk and Wagnall Company, 1947). This finding applies primarily to print media.

Figure   C—6–10
Possible Media Plan Alternatives Using Reach, Frequency,
Continuity, and Size, Given a Budget Constraint*

Major Objective	At Expense Of
	a. frequency
	and/or
I. Large reach	b. continuity
	and/or
	c. message size
	a. reach
	and/or
II. High frequency	b. continuity
	and/or
	c. message size
	a. reach
	and/or
III. More continuity	b. frequency
	and/or
	c. message size
	a. reach
	and/or
IV. Larger message size (impact)	b. frequency
	and/or
	c. continuity

*Adapted from C. H. Sandage and Vernon Fryburger, *Advertising Theory and Practice*, (Homewood, IL: Richard D. Irwin, Inc., 1975), pp. 420–421.

Figure C—6–10 points out that a major media objective must be set, after which trade-offs begin to occur among the 3 other media elements. These elements also should be ranked to arrive at a plan which achieves the advertising and marketing objectives of the firm, given the budget constraint.

Developing the Advertising Budget (Budgeting Strategy).   Several approaches are used in developing advertising budgets. Six methods are discussed briefly.

Arbitrary Allocation.   Budgets based upon arbitrary allocations are ones which involve management intuition, emotions, or whim. This method is quite common, particularly among retailers. Their budgeting decisions may be based upon a talk with a friend, the influence of a media sales representative, or because of something they read. Their advertising budget is therefore very likely to be the result of the personality traits, ego, or self-expression of the decision maker.

Percentage of Sales.   Probably the most commonly used budgeting approach among U.S. businesses is the percentage of sales method. The method typically involves taking a fixed percentage of either last year's sales or of forecasted sales for the coming year and allocating that amount to advertising. This reasoning is typical. Business decision makers have long looked for "rules of thumb" to guide their decisions. The percentage of sales method is simple to use, which is why it is so appealing. However, this method has no scientific basis, has poor logic, and expresses no relationship with achieving advertising objectives.

Competitive Parity.   The competitive parity approach to advertising is to spend what the competitors spend. This approach takes into account competitive activity, but assumes that how much competitors allocate to advertising is an appropriate level of expenditures. Obviously, this approach neglects to consider whether competitors are at an optimal level of expenditures, or that competitors may be at a different point in their product life cycle, and the advertising expenditures necessary to achieve the firm's advertising and marketing objectives.

All You Can Afford.   In some cases, companies budget their advertising expenditures on what they can afford or what is left over after all other costs and expenditures. This approach is typical of firms introducing new products to regional markets. Their purpose is to generate high sales volume regardless of advertising efficiency or profits. The approach suffers from the same lack of logic or scientific basis as the previous budgeting methods. It neither relates advertising expenditures to marketing and advertising objectives, nor to long-term profits.

Objective and Task.   Although not an ideal method, the objective and task method is the best of the practical methods for budgeting advertising expenditures. Simply stated, the objective and task method involves 3 steps:

(1) Set up operational advertising objectives.

(2) Determine the tasks which must be performed to attain these objectives.

(3) Determine the costs of the tasks and total them. This total is the advertising budget.

If one of the advertising objectives is to increase brand awareness by 30 percent over the next 12 months, the advertiser must determine what media mix will create the reach and frequency necessary to increase brand awareness by 30 percent. The tasks would involve the "right" media with the "right" number of insertions at the "right" time. Other costs might include advertising production costs. Quite often, the budget which is determined by this method will be in excess of what the company can afford. In such cases, the advertising objectives must be revised downward.

This budgeting method has several merits. First, advertising expenditures are tied to advertising objectives, not to arbitrary allocations or to competitors' spending levels or as a percentage of sales. Instead, this method views advertising expenditures as one of the *causes* of sales, not as a result of sales. Second, this method becomes a part of advertising strategy and is useful in planning the strategy. Third, it often forces management to conduct research to determine which tasks need to be performed and how they can be performed most efficiently to attain the stated objectives. Fourth, it provides criteria on which management can measure performance.

Although this approach has several merits over most other budgeting methods, the question arises whether the stated objectives are worth attaining. Also, it is difficult to specify exactly which combination of media, frequency, and reach is best to achieve the objectives, such as 30 percent increase in brand awareness. Even with these shortcomings, the objective and task method is a sound managerial approach to budgeting for all but the largest companies who can afford elaborate experimentation and model building.

The "Ideal" Approach—Marginal Analysis.   The field of economics provides us several excellent analytical tools and concepts in developing marketing and advertising models. Joel Dean suggests that the ideal method for budgeting advertising in the short run is to use the concept of marginal analysis. Figure C—6–11 shows how marginal analysis can be used to determine the optimal advertising budget.

In terms of economic analysis, maximum profits occur where marginal cost equals marginal revenue. The ideal level of advertising expenditures is where the marginal advertising cost (after other costs have been taken into account) equals marginal revenue. Dean uses the assumption that such things as price (marginal revenue), costs of production, and physical distribution remain constant over the

Figure   C—6–11
A Marginal Analysis Determination of the Optimal Advertising Budget

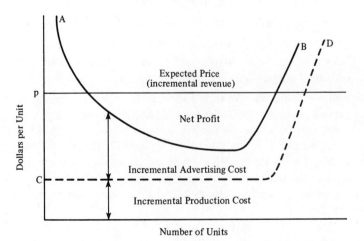

short run. These assumptions are reasonable, but can be relaxed in a more sophisticated analysis using curvilinearity for cost and price functions. The simple assumptions used in Figure C—6–11, however, facilitate the basic explanation of the concept.

In Figure C—6–11 the advertising cost per unit is shown as the difference between line AB (marginal advertising cost per unit) and line CD (marginal production, physical distribution costs, etc.). Line AB is curvilinear because: (1) The initial amount of advertising dollars spent generates brand awareness, but few sales; thus, advertising costs per unit are high; (2) As more people become aware of the brand and learn of its benefits, additional advertising generates a greater number of unit sales and reduces the advertising cost per unit; and (3) Eventually, fewer additional purchases result from more advertising expenditures and diminishing returns set in.

Where line AB (marginal advertising costs) intersects line **P** (marginal revenue) on the right side of the graph, total profits are maximized. Although in the latter part of the net profit curve, per unit profit is decreasing, total profit is increasing up to the point where the last dollar spent on advertising equals the marginal revenue (price) generated by that unit of sale.

Marginal analysis is sound conceptually, but in practice companies are unable to discern changes in per unit demand generated by each marginal dollar spent in advertising. However, several large firms have been able to approximate this approach by using incremental analysis.

Incremental analysis involves *large* changes in expenditures (as opposed to the minute changes in marginal analysis) to determine effects of advertising expenditure levels upon demand and profits. Several large companies have used experimentation to approximate how variations in advertising expenditure levels affected their sales. This research is conducted using several experimental and control cities. The control cities receive the same amount and kind of advertising as before the experiment. The experimental cities receive either lower advertising expenditure levels or higher expenditure levels. The effects on sales are observed and the most profitable level (in a gross sense) is determined. As examples, DuPont found that they needed heavy advertising for their Teflon cookware to achieve higher market share and profits,[53] and Anheuser-Busch found that *less* advertising expenditures on Budweiser produced higher profits.[54]

Although experimentation can be helpful in finding the best incremental level of advertising expenditures, there are several shortcomings. Specifically, experimentation is very expensive, usually involves long periods of time to get results, cannot be controlled well enough to be considered scientific, and results can be disrupted by competitor actions during the experiment. With all these shortcomings, advertising sales experiments can be useful inputs to managerial decision making if tempered with sound judgment.

---

[53] James C. Becknell, Jr. and Robert W. McIssac, "Test Marketing Cookware Coated With Teflon," *Journal of Advertising Research,* **3** September 1963, pp. 4–5.

[54] Thomas M. Newell, "What is the Right Amount to Spend on Advertising?" An address to the 1968 Western Regional Convention, American Association of Advertising Agencies, Palm Springs, CA, October 6–9, 1968, p. 28.

Coordinating Advertising with Other Promotion and Marketing Decisions

Advertising decisions must be coordinated with other promotion and marketing decisions. For example, advertising is useful in making prospective clients aware of a company product offering and can "open doors" for and make more efficient the sales representatives' calls. A summary of a study published by McGraw-Hill illustrates the point. See Table C—6–1.

Advertising can be used effectively with sales promotion activities. First, advertising can direct consumers' attention to sales displays in their local retail outlets. Second, it can inform retailers through trade advertising of forthcoming promotions and provide retailers with ideas for displays (sales representatives may not have the time to "make the rounds" to all retail customers prior to upcoming sales promotion activities). Third, retailers may be more willing to provide manufacturers with display space if national and cooperative advertising is present. Fourth, special deals, such as coupons, sweepstakes, trading stamps, contests, and other sales promotion devices, can be aided through advertising to make them more effective.

Advertising and public relations must be coordinated to assure that an inconsistent message is not presented to the consuming public. Advertising should contribute to good public relations by creating goodwill among consumers, government, and the trade.

Getting shelf space in retail outlets often can be a difficult task, particularly for many small- and medium-sized producers. Advertising can assist companies in obtaining space by using one of 2 advertising strategies. One approach is to use a push strategy, which directs advertising (and often other promotional efforts) at members of the channels of distribution. In this strategy, the company uses an intense effort directed at wholesalers, retailers, and other middlemen in their

Table   C—6–1
Results of Combining Business-Publication Advertising with Personal Selling

Industry Class	Percentage Increase in Sales-Per-Call When Ads Are Added	Reduced Selling Costs As a Percentage of Sales When Ads Are Added
Utilities products	6.4%	− 7.5%
Commodities	23.6	−19.6
Electrical	12.6	−11.4
Metalworking	20.8	−18.6
Chemicals	6.9	− 6.3

Source: How Advertising Works in Today's Marketplace: The Morrill Study (New York: McGraw-Hill, 1971), p. 4.

channel. The idea is to "push" the company's brand through the distribution channel to the retailer where consumers will be exposed to the company's brand and thus have opportunity to choose between it and those of competitors.

A second approach is to use a "pull" strategy. This strategy uses intense advertising directed at *ultimate* consumers to encourage them to seek the brand and to ask for the brand at their local retail store. The idea is to encourage consumers to ask retailers for a brand which is not stocked, so that the retailers in turn will call their local distributors who in turn will call the producer to supply the asked-for brand.

Advertising plays an important role in supporting a firm's pricing strategy. Advertising can emphasize discount, value, or prestige. Naturally, the advertising message must support the pricing strategy for a brand. For example, many products which are conspicuous in nature are advertised using prestigious, status, or regal themes. This advertising strategy will support a higher price for a brand especially when consumers desire either a status good or high product quality. In effect, advertising is desensitizing consumers to the higher-than-competitive price by establishing a high quality image and reputation for the brand.[55]

Discussion Questions

1. Distinguish between product-oriented and consumer-oriented appeals. What kinds of products lend themselves to one kind of approach versus the other? Explain.

2. From among the 4 major media which one(s) do you believe would be most important as an advertising medium for the following:

a. a local retailer putting summer clothes "on sale"

b. a large manufacturer of women's colognes and perfumes attempting to convey a sensual image for a brand of cologne

c. an airline advertising flight departure and arrival times and cost information

d. a manufacturer of office furniture, shop equipment, and steel shelving.

3. Given the following information, set up the linear programming (LP) model to maximize advertising exposures:

Magazine	Cost/Insertion	Issue/Year	Reach (in 000s)
A	$22,000	26	8,113
B	18,000	52	5,896
C	62,000	12	21,492
D	26,500	52	9,122
E	34,000	52	10,214

Advertising budget for media allocation = $2,200,000.

[55] See Richard T. Sampson, "Sense and Sensitivity in Pricing," *Harvard Business Review*, November-December 1964, pp. 101–103. Copyright © 1960 by the President and Fellows of Harvard College; all rights reserved.

What are the advantages and disadvantages of using LP in media planning? (*Note:* if a computer is available, run the program to solve the above problem.)

4. Compare the 5 attitude strategies discussed in the text. Under what conditions could each be used?

5. Describe how marginal analysis can be adapted to determine appropriate advertising expenditures.

6. A company is introducing a new brand of toothpaste. Advise them on scheduling their advertising.

7. Distinguish between sales-oriented and communications-oriented advertising objectives. How can an advertising planner determine the best levels at which to set the objectives (60 percent awareness? 20 percent increase in sales? etc.)

8. Using the criteria for selecting media vehicles discussed in this chapter, rate the following media vehicles on a scale of 1 (highest) to 5 (lowest):

a. New York Times
b. The Johnny Carson Show
c. A local rock radio station
d. *Playboy* magazine
e. The campus newspaper

How can a rating procedure such as the one above help media planners in selecting media vehicles?

9. Describe how synergy occurs between advertising and other elements in the promotional and marketing mixes.

Summary

We have examined how advertising strategies are developed, the difference between sales and communications objectives, and types of advertising strategies. In addition, media characteristics and strategies, the criteria for advertising media selection, and advertising's role in enhancing the efforts of other marketing and promotional mix variables were discussed.

In this chapter, we presented arguments to show why sales objectives are unrealistic advertising objectives, and we talked about several specific communications objectives within the realm of achievement for advertisers.

Advertising strategies create awareness, shape product positioning, and encourage attitude formation and change. Advertising themes are based upon consumer needs. Criteria for selecting media vehicles mathematically and nonmathematically and principles for media scheduling (timing of an ad) were given. Finally, several practical and ideal methods of developing an advertising budget were discussed in detail.

Advertisng decisions require both art and science. Judgment and logical quantitative techniques should be used in arriving at the best appeal, media selection, and timing based upon a careful analysis of the target market matched to the target audience.

Some Major Advertising Information Sources

Advertising Age—the title of this weekly paper is deceptive; it presents more than advertising. Most issues include articles, data, and brief reports on all aspects of the nation's business. More importantly, it has considerable information on trends in television, broadcasting, newspapers, and other media. All that is recent and upcoming in the field of national sales and advertising and international news is presented. Personnel shifts, account changes, important rating figures, new products, and convention news are given through regular columns. There is often coverage of controversial subjects, interviews, and speeches. During the year, 6–8 large topical issues concentrate on a single subject, such as "Market Data" or "Leading Advertisers."

Audit Bureau of Circulation—provides circulation data for magazines.

A Guide to Marketing/Advertising Information—Charles F. Steilen and Roy Altizer, 1972. A bibliography covering general and specific secondary sources of marketing and advertising information.

National Advertising Investments—Leading National Advertisers, Inc. A record of the advertising expenditures of national advertisers broken down by media. (annual)

Standard Rate and Data Services—publishes reports detailing rates and specifications for buying advertising space or time in different media.

"Sprite" Soft Drink:
Developing an Advertising Campaign

Leonard Lanfranco and Ralph Morgan
University of South Carolina

The Coca-Cola Company: A Brief Profile

The Coca-Cola Company is the world's leading manufacturer of soft drink beverages. From its meager beginnings in Atlanta in 1886, Coca-Cola is now sold around the world at a rate of 190 million servings a day.

Syrup, concentrate, and beverage bases for Coca-Cola and the Company's other soft drinks are manufactured and sold by The Coca-Cola Company and its subsidiaries to more than 1,400 bottlers in over 130 countries.

These bottling plants are, with few exceptions, owned and operated by independent businesspeople native to the countries in which they are located. By contract with The Coca-Cola Company or its local subsidiaries, these local businesses are authorized to bottle and sell Coca-Cola and other soft drinks within certain territorial boundaries and other conditions that insure the highest standards of quality and uniformity.

The independent bottler provides the required capital investments for land, buildings, machinery and equipment, trucks, bottles, and cases. Most supplies are purchased from indigenous sources where possible, often creating new supply industries and areas of employment within the local economy.

Coca-Cola USA, the operating division for the United States, participates with the independent bottlers in funding many marketing functions like advertising, promotion, and merchandising. Coca-Cola USA is responsible for the development of all advertising strategy and through its agencies develops the creativity necessary to support the strategies. All materials using any of The Coca-Cola Company trademarks must be approved by the company.

The company supplies the bottler not only with syrup or concentrate and beverage bases, but also actively engages in management guidance to help insure the profitable growth of the bottler's business, thus enhancing the value of the franchise. The management counseling covers a broad spectrum of business experience such as product quality control, marketing, advertising, engineering, financial, and personnel training.

The company's operations are managed by geographical subdivisions primarily known as zones, areas, and districts, each with its own resident manager responsible for operations within a particular country or group of countries. In addition to maintaining zone, area, and district offices, the company also owns and operates syrup, concentrate, and beverage base manufacturing plants, as well as a few bottling plants.

Despite field decentralization and the need for programs indigenous to a specific locale, there is a certain degree of uniformity in the methods used to market the products around the world. This uniformity is achieved through a program of services coordinated by The Coca-Cola Company's headquarters offices in Atlanta, Georgia.

Advertising for Coca-Cola around the world projects a uniform brand image to promote a strong consumer appeal for this successful, respected product with a world-wide reputation for quality. Uniformity in advertising also establishes the image of the same pure, refreshing product in each country.

Sprite

The First "Specialty" Drink from the Coca-Cola Company

The specialty green-bottled drink, "Sprite," a trademark since 1955, was made available to all Coca-Cola bottlers in February 1961 by Fanta Beverage Company, a division of The Coca-Cola Company.

Extensive market studies over the previous 10 years had indicated that one-third of the growing soft drink market was consistently made up of flavors. On this rationale, The Coca-Cola Company had moved from its long standing one-product policy to launch the Fanta line of flavors throughout the nation in 1958. Sprite followed shortly thereafter, providing Coca-Cola bottlers the opportunity to serve the total soft drink market with beverages produced under the same strict standards traditional to Coca-Cola and recognized by the consuming public.

Phenomenal Acceptance

Sprite received its first major market introduction at Houston, Texas, in March 1961. Two thousand outlets for the new drink opened the first week. In the first 5 months, the Houston bottler sold 70 percent of the total first year's sales estimate. At Baltimore, sales in the first 20 weeks after introduction were 97 percent of their estimate for the entire year.

Ten months after the introductory announcement, Sprite was on sale in 40 states and available to 27 percent of the total U.S. population. Three hundred thirty-four bottlers had requested contracts to bottle and sell Sprite, and 241 were already on the market with Sprite.

At the beginning of its fourth year in 1964, Sprite had become the fastest growing product in the green bottle field, having reached 60 percent of the national per capita in areas where it was on sale. By the end of 1965, 797 bottlers serving 83 percent of the U.S. population were selling Sprite. It had then become the nation's second largest selling lemon-lime soft drink. Sprite has consistently increased its share of the total soft drink market since its introduction in 1961.

The phenomenal reception can be attributed to a careful combination of product, name, packaging, and advertising. Prior to market tests, Sprite underwent three-and-a-half years of product development, and the record it has made is a reflection of its inherent quality appeal to the consumer. The name—short, sharp-sounding, and memorable—reflects the beverage's brisk and bracing characteristics. The bright green bottle with the refreshing bubbles decorating its surface is considered one of the most distinctive soft drink packages ever introduced.

Sprite is available today in 7, 10, 12, 16, 28, 32, and 64-ounce returnable bottles, and in 10, 12, 16, 28, 32, and 64-ounce one-way bottles. A 12 oz. can also is available. It also is available in one- and two-liter metric sizes in both returnable and nonreturnable bottles.

Advertising Strategies

The advertising strategy for Sprite has been to position the brand with the young adult with somewhat sophisticated appeal. From its introduction it has been promoted as a soft drink and a mixer; the company's first bid for the mixer trade (second was Fresca, registered as a trademark in 1963, and achieved national distribution in 1966).

The advertising strategy, which has been outstandingly successful, has from its inception allowed the product to dominate the picture. In the introductory period, this was in opposition to the prevailing school of sociability in soft drink copy. Nevertheless, ads for Sprite capitalized on the inherent product drama, making use of pouring shots, quick cuts, close-ups, and other photographic and lighting devices, which since have become standard.

In the beginning, copy adhered to the "tart and tingling" theme. Introductory television commercials featured humorous "egghead" figurines and the "tingling tartness" jingle to reflect the sparkling, tingling qualities of the drink.

The second year's ad material retained the theme but introduced refreshment images and product in-use sequences in coolness scenes. Maintaining the self-imposed discipline of the original copy philosophy, the creative experts continued to talk about the product in succeeding years with no radical departure except to emphasize the dimension of sound to communicate the subtlety of taste. Both print and electronic media developed visually and phonetically the sound and taste excitement.

The new copy in 1966 popped, poured, and fizzed: "So tart and tingling, we just couldn't keep it quiet," "Heard any good soft drinks lately?" "Sprite is a roaring good drink." Magazine copy headlined "gin and sonic."

In 1968, a new ad theme began associating the taste of Sprite with the freshness of springtime, introducing consumers to "a new season for soft drinks." This creative strategy, which carried through all visual and electronic media for the soft drink, conveyed in their different ways the single theme, "Open a bottle of Sprite and springtime breaks loose. Sprite . . . it's a natural."

The new approach repositioned Sprite in the all-family market with emphasis on America's young families. Along with the new creative strategy for the ad was the implementation of a completely new package design, both reflecting 1969 marketing plans for Sprite.

In 1972, a new "Lymon" campaign was created to give Sprite a distinct product difference. Research indicated that emphasizing lime with lemon reinforcement (i.e., "Lymon") maximized the attractive appeal that lime had for consumers (thirst-quenching, refreshing, tart) and provided a preemptive position for the brand. Additionally, research further showed that the mnemonic device of "Lymon" had appeal to Sprite's target audience.

The campaign has evolved through 4 phases. Initially, the campaign was designed to introduce and explain the Sprite mnemonic device, "The Lymon," symbolizing Sprite's taste of lime and lemon. The visual Lymon device was "leaves" (sound from lemon and lime tree leaves).

The campaign was altered slightly in 1975 to give additional attention to the "lime" part of the lime/lemon taste sensation and its thirst-quenching ability, as well as to its compatibility with food. The visual Lymon device continued to be "leaves."

In 1976, "The One and Only Lymon Taste" campaign was introduced to explain that the only way you could get the taste of a Lymon was to get Sprite. Visual device was changed to the Lymon fruit (half lemons/half limes).

The 1977 campaign, "Lymon is the Secret of Sprite" was developed for Sprite to increase the product's intrinsic and extrinsic image ratings (traditional soft drink images), while continuing to communicate the brand's unique taste called "Lymon." The visual device continues to be "Lymon"—half lemon and half lime fruit.

The Soft Drink Industry

Two major firms—The Coca-Cola Company and Pepsico—dominate the soft-drink industry, and 70 percent of the soft drink market is held by 10 brands representing the 5 largest soft drink manufacturers. See Table 25–1.

The soft drink industry is characterized primarily by 4 "types" of products:

1. Colas
2. Lemon-lime (this is a category of the "green bottle" type which includes Fresca, Mountain Dew, and 7-Up)
3. Peppers (i.e., Dr. Pepper, Mr. Pibb)
4. Flavors

A percent of market share by flavor is presented in Table 25–2.

A major impact on the soft drink industry has been the introduction of the diet soft drink. The diet soft drink market has been growing much faster than either the total soft drink market or the regular soft drink market. Since 1970, diet soft drinks have grown at an estimated rate of 15 to 20 percent annually. Diet soft drinks should continue to grow at a 10 to 15 percent rate beyond 1976 and

Table   25–1
Top 1976 Brands

Rank	Brand	Million Cases	Percentage of Market
1	Coca-Cola	1294.0	26.5
2	Pepsi-Cola	864.0	17.7
3	7-Up	305.8	6.3
4	Dr. Pepper	243.0	5.0
5	Royal Crown Cola	162.2	3.3
6	Tab (Coca-Cola Co.)	142.0	2.9
7	Sprite (Coca-Cola Co.)	136.0	2.8
8	Diet Pepsi-Cola	91.5	1.9
9	Mountain Dew (PepsiCo)	73.0	1.5
10	Sugar Free 7-Up	60.0	1.2

Source: Beverage Industry, April 15, 1977.

regular soft drinks should expand at a rate of 2 to 3 percent annually, resulting in a long-term domestic industry volume increase of about 4 percent annually. Table 25–3 presents data regarding the growth in the domestic soft drink market by regular and diet soft drink segments.

Table 25–4 provides data on the lemon-lime consumption for 1973–1976 by the 3 major lemon-lime bottlers.

In the soft drink industry, a major component of a firm's marketing mix is advertising. Table 25–5 presents data on the advertising expenditures in the lemon-lime category for 1974–1976.

Consumption and expenditure data indicate that the lemon-lime category of the soft drink industry is primarily the property of the "Un-Cola" and the "Lymon," with 7-Up and Sprite holding over 80 percent of the market.

Sugar-free and diet beverages are not considered as important at this time in the "greenbottle" market as they are in the "cola" and "pepper" markets. Therefore, data concerning sugar-free sprite and 7-Up has not been separated from the data for the regular beverages.

Demographic data on purchases of lemon-lime soft drinks are presented by region of country, household income, age of female head-of-household, age of male head-of-household, education of female head-of-household, education of male head-of-household, size of household, children in household, occupation of male head-of-household, container types, purchase outlets, season of the year, and weekly consumption by yearly household income. These data are shown in Table 25–6.

Table   25–2
Market Share by Flavor [a]

Flavor	1971	1972	1973	1974	1975	1976 [b]
Cola, regular	52.0 %	51.5 %	51.0 %	51.0%	50.7 %	50.5%
Diet cola	5.6	6.0	6.2	6.6	7.3	7.8
Total cola	57.6	57.5	57.2	57.6	58.0	58.3
Lemon-lime, regular	11.4	11.3	11.4	11.3	11.0	10.9
Sugar-free lemon-lime	0.6	0.7	0.8	1.2	1.7	2.0
Total lemon-lime	12.0	12.0	12.2	12.5	12.7	12.9
Regular orange	4.8	4.7	4.6	4.4	3.9	3.6
Regular root beer	4.4	4.4	4.0	3.9	4.1	4.2
Regular peppers	3.9	4.3	5.0	5.2	5.7	6.0
Diet/sugar free peppers	0.27	0.45	0.55	0.7	0.95	1.2
Total pepper	4.17	4.75	5.55	5.9	7.65	7.2
Ginger ale, tonic, carbonated water and soda	4.4	4.6	4.7	4.8	4.9	5.0
All other (regular grape, Mountain Dew, chocolate, black cherry, etc.)	9.6	9.0	8.3	7.4	6.0	4.8
All other diet (including diet orange, root beer, etc.)	2.93	3.05	3.45	3.6	3.85	4.0
Total regular	90.6	89.8	89.0	87.9	86.2	85.0
Total diet	9.4	10.2	11.0	12.1	13.8	15.0
Total	100.0	100.0	100.0	100.0	100.0	100.0

[a] Numbers may not add due to rounding.
[b] Estimated
Source: Oppenheimer Soft Drink Industry Share Data, November 1976.

Other Relevant Information

1. The Coca-Cola Company does not direct Sprite advertising toward persons under 13 years of age.
2. No alterations are permitted of the Sprite trademark or package design or in the packages (bottle or cases) themselves.

Table   25–3
Domestic Soft Drink Market Growth
By Regular and Diet Segments

% Total Soft Drink Market	1971	1972	1973	1974	1975	1976*
Regular	10.6%	89.8%	89.0%	87.9%	86.2%	85.0%
Diet	9.4	10.2	11.0	12.1	13.8	15.0
% change total soft drink market	—	+ 5.0	+ 6.5	+ .8	− .9	+10.0
% change regular	—	+ 4.1	+ 5.6	− .2	− 3.0	+ 8.3
% change diet	—	+14.0	+14.5	+ 9.0	+14.0	+22.0
% Growth By Flavor Type						
Regular cola	—	+ .14	+ 4.6	− 0.2	− 2.0	+ 9.5
Regular lemon-lime	—	+ 3.2	+ 6.5	− 0.2	− 5.3	+ 7.7
Regular pepper	—	+14.8	+22.8	+ 3.9	+ 6.3	+14.0
Diet cola	—	+12.5	+10.0	+ 6.5	+11.0	+19.0
Diet lemon-lime	—	+22.5	+21.7	+50.0	+40.0	+26.4
Diet pepper	—	+75.0	+ 30.2	+40.0	+30.7	+30.0

* Estimated.
Source: Oppenheimer Soft Drink Industry Share Data, November 1976.

Table   25–4
The Lemon-Lime Product Category by Major Bottlers*

	7-Up	Coca-Cola	Pepsi-Cola	Subtotal	All Others	Total
Million Cases	330.4	95.0	14.8	440.2	116.8	557.0
1973 % total	59.3	17.0	2.7	79.0	21.0	100.0
% change	+10.2	+17.3	+5.7	+11.5	+6.8	+10.5
Million Cases	338.6	105.0	14.0	457.6	112.4	570.0
1974 % total	59.4	18.4	2.5	80.3	19.7	100.0
% change	+ 2.5	+10.5	−5.4	+ 4.0	−3.8	+ 2.3
Million Cases	339.1	115.3	13.5	467.9	109.1	577.0
1975 % total	59.8	20.3	2.4	82.5	17.5	100.0
% change	+ 0.1	+ 9.8	−3.6	+ 2.3	−2.9	+ 1.2
Million Cases	365.8	136.0	13.8	515.6	105.0	620.6
1976 % total	59.0	21.9	2.2	83.1	16.9	100.0
% change	+ 7.9	+18.0	+2.2	+10.2	−3.8	+ 7.6

* Estimated.
Source: Beverage Industry, 1977.

Table 25–5

Advertising Expenditures in Lemon-Lime Category (000s)

Brand	Magazines	Newspaper Supplements	Net TV	Spot TV	Net Radio	Outdoor	6 Media Total
Sprite*							
1974	—	$48.9	—	$2,340.3	—	$ 33.9	$ 2,423.1
1975	—	—	—	2,596.2	—	16.6	2,612.8
1976	—	—	$ 396.0	2,029.3	—	16.4	2,441.7
7-Up**							
1974	—	—	1,693.2	9,347.7	$119.0	1,224.2	12,404.1
1975	$22.0	—	2,143.7	9,751.6	—	1,414.1	13,331.4
1976	79.6	—	2,465.7	9,721.3	66.3	1,379.9	13,712.8
Teem							
1974	—	—	—	—	—	—	—
1975	—	—	—	61.2	—	—	61.2
1976	—	—	—	62.8	—	0.7	63.5

* Includes sugar-free Sprite.
**Includes sugar-free and diet 7-Up.
Source: Leading National Advertisers, Inc. Multi Media Reports, 1974, 1975, and 1976.

Table   25–6
Lemon-Lime Market Data
(multiple responses; in percentages)

A. Carbonated beverage brands usually purchased by census region

Brand	Total	North East	North Central	South	West
Sprite	2.0	.9	1.9	3.8	.6
7-up	16.9	12.6	24.4	9.3	24.8
Millions of Households	72.4	16.7	19.5	22.4	13.8

B. Carbonated beverage brands usually purchased by yearly household income

Brand	Total	Under $10,000	$10,000 –15,000	$15,000 –20,000	$20,000 –30,000	$30,000 & More
Sprite	2.0	2.0	3.5	2.1	2.2	1.4
7-Up	16.9	16.4	18.0	19.7	20.3	16.2
Millions of Households	72.4	26.1	17.4	12.3	12.3	4.3

C. Carbonated beverage brands usually purchased by age of female head-of-household

Brand	Total	Under 25 yrs.	25–34	35–49	50–64	65+	No Female H-of-H
Sprite	2.0	2.9	1.8	2.5	2.3	1.1	1.7
7-up	16.9	17.0	16.8	16.7	17.2	17.5	18.3
Millions of Households	72.4	7.8	14.3	17.1	15.6	10.4	7.2

D. Carbonated beverage brands usually purchased by age of male head-of-household

Brand	Total	Under 25 yrs.	25–34	35–49	50–64	65+	No Male H-of-H
Sprite	2.0	1.8	1.0	3.0	2.4	1.6	1.4
7-Up	16.9	15.7	17.5	17.6	16.4	20.0	14.7
Millions of Households	72.4	4.4	12.8	15.5	14.4	8.3	17.0

E. Carbonated beverage brands usually purchased by education of female head-of-household

Brand	Total	Not H/S Graduate	H/S Graduate	Attended College	College Graduate	No Female H-of-H
Sprite	2.0	2.4	2.2	1.4	2.1	1.2
7-Up	16.9	14.7	18.3	16.3	19.7	16.9
Millions of Households	72.4	24.8	25.4	7.8	7.2	7.2

F. Carbonated beverage brands usually purchased by education of male head-of-household

Brand	Total	Not H/S Graduate	H/S Graduate	Attended College	College Graduate	No Male H-of-H
Sprite	2.0	2.4	2.6	1.8	1.4	1.4
7-Up	16.9	17.9	18.6	20.4	13.9	14.8
Millions of Households	72.4	20.4	17.7	7.2	10.1	17.0

G. Carbonated beverage brands usually purchased by size of household

Brand	Total	One	Two	Three	Four	Five	Six	Seven or More
Sprite	2.0	1.1	1.2	3.2	2.4	1.8	2.3	5.0
7-Up	16.9	17.6	16.9	17.3	16.9	19.9	15.1	13.2
Millions of Households	72.4	14.2	22.2	12.6	11.3	6.5	3.1	2.5

H. Carbonated beverage brands usually purchased by children under 12 in household

Brand	Total	Children Under 12	No Children Under 12
Sprite	2.0	2.4	1.8
7-Up	16.9	16.0	17.5
Millions of Households	72.4	22.9	49.5

I. Carbonated beverage brands usually purchased by 12 to 17-year-olds in households

Brand	Total	Children 12 to 17	No Children 12 to 17
Sprite	2.0	4.2	1.4
7-Up	16.9	17.1	16.9
Millions of Households	72.4	16.3	56.1

J. Carbonated beverage brands usually purchased by occupations of male head-of-household

Occupation	Sprite	7-Up	Millions of Households
Professional	1.1	12.9	6.7
Managers and owners	2.9	17.6	8.5
Sales	4.8	20.8	2.7
Clerical	5.4	23.2	2.5
Craftsman	1.0	21.0	9.5
Operatives	2.7	17.6	7.2
Laborers	7.4	16.9	7.2
Service workers	1.0	17.9	3.5
Retired/unemployed	1.6	17.4	2.7
No male head-of-household	1.4	15.1	12.1

K. Container types usually purchased by census regions

Container	Total	North East	North Central	South	West
Cans	18.9	15.1	17.1	14.9	33.2
Nonreturn 16 oz/less	12.9	21.8	10.1	10.3	9.4
Nonreturn 32 oz/plus	14.1	34.6	7.6	8.7	5.1
Return bottle 16 oz/less	26.0	8.5	39.1	30.2	22.1
Return bottle 32 oz/plus	16.3	6.0	17.3	21.7	19.4
All plastic	1.8	1.2	1.3	3.4	.7
Don't know	.6	.8	.5	.8	.4
Miscellaneous	.6	1.4	.3	.2	.5
None purchased	20.9	21.3	21.6	20.0	20.9
Millions of Households	72.4	16.7	19.5	22.4	13.8

L. Usual outlet for carbonated beverages by census regions

Outlet	Total	North East	North Central	South	West
Supermarkets	70.3	67.4	71.9	71.1	70.6
Convenience stores	2.6	4.2	2.3	2.3	1.3
Beverage stores	2.9	4.9	2.9	1.9	1.6
No special outlet	1.1	.8	.1	2.0	1.4
None purchased	20.6	20.9	21.2	19.8	20.6
Millions of households	72.4	16.7	19.5	22.4	13.8

M. Average weekly consumption of carbonated beverages in winter by census region

Consumption	Total	North East	North Central	South	West
One quart or less	18.9	24.2	18.1	12.5	24.5
1 to 4 quarts	36.8	35.7	38.2	28.1	33.5
4 to 8 quarts	13.4	10.2	13.5	16.3	12.7
More than 8 quarts	7.7	6.0	6.5	10.8	6.2
Don't know	2.7	3.1	2.5	2.5	2.5
Do not purchase	20.6	20.9	21.2	19.7	20.6
Millions of households	72.4	16.7	19.5	22.4	13.8

N. Average weekly consumption of carbonated beverages in summer by census region

Consumption	Total	North East	North Central	South	West
One quart or less	10.9	14.6	8.5	7.5	15.8
1 to 4 quarts	31.4	32.8	32.4	31.5	27.4
4 to 8 quarts	19.5	16.9	21.4	20.1	19.3
More than 8 quarts	14.8	12.2	13.8	18.0	14.2
Don't know	2.8	2.7	2.6	3.0	2.6
Do not purchase	20.7	20.9	21.2	19.9	20.7
Millions of households	72.4	16.7	19.5	22.4	13.8

O. Average weekly consumption of carbonated beverages in winter by yearly household income

Consumption	Total	Under $10,000	$10,000 –15,000	$15,000 –20,000	$20,000 –30,000	$30,000 & More
One quart or less	18.9	22.2	17.4	14.9	15.4	22.9
1 to 4 quarts	36.8	32.3	42.2	39.0	42.6	40.5
4 to 8 quarts	13.4	9.5	15.4	19.5	17.3	11.4
More than 8 quarts	7.7	4.6	9.6	9.5	9.1	11.4
Don't know	2.7	2.6	1.7	2.2	1.7	1.0
Do not purchase	20.6	28.9	13.7	14.9	13.9	12.9
Millions of households	72.4	26.1	17.4	12.3	12.3	4.3

P. Average weekly consumption of carbonated beverages in summer by yearly household income

Consumption	Total	Under $10,000	$10,000 –15,000	$15,000 –20,000	$20,000 –30,000	$30,000 & More
One quart or less	10.9	11.9	10.7	8.5	6.9	14.3
1 to 4 quarts	31.4	29.6	32.8	30.2	35.5	40.0
4 to 8 quarts	19.5	16.5	23.3	25.1	25.1	13.8
More than 8 quarts	14.8	10.3	17.6	18.8	16.2	18.1
Don't know	2.8	2.8	1.9	2.4	2.2	1.0
Do not purchase	20.7	28.9	13.7	15.0	14.1	12.9
Millions of households	72.4	26.1	17.4	12.3	12.3	4.3

Q. Average weekly consumption of carbonated beverages in winter by size of household

Consumption	Total	One	Two	Three	Four	Five	Six	Seven or More
One quart or less	18.9	28.9	21.9	18.4	15.2	13.8	5.4	11.8
1 to 4 quarts	36.8	26.1	39.0	40.9	37.8	38.5	37.6	27.7
4 to 8 quarts	13.4	3.9	8.6	14.6	22.4	15.8	20.9	22.3
More than 8 quarts	7.7	1.2	4.6	6.7	9.0	13.4	19.0	20.5
Don't know	2.7	3.1	2.4	3.3	2.6	1.4	2.7	2.7
Do not purchase	20.6	36.8	23.6	16.2	12.9	17.0	14.3	15.0
Millions of households	72.4	14.2	22.2	12.6	11.3	6.5	3.1	2.5

R. Average weekly consumption of carbonated beverages in summer by size of household

Consumption	Total	One	Two	Three	Four	Five	Six	Seven or More
One quart or less	10.9	18.6	13.1	10.3	7.6	7.3	1.9	7.3
1 to 4 quarts	31.4	28.6	37.4	33.3	29.0	27.8	20.5	15.5
4 to 8 quarts	19.5	11.0	13.1	24.8	25.8	24.3	32.2	23.2
More than 8 quarts	14.8	2.5	9.8	13.1	21.4	21.7	27.5	36.4
Don't know	2.8	2.5	3.0	1.8	3.3	1.8	3.5	2.7
Do not purchase	20.7	36.8	23.6	16.6	12.9	17.0	14.3	15.0
Millions of households	72.4	14.2	22.2	12.6	11.3	6.5	3.1	2.5

3. New or modified trademark or package designs or package sizes will not be considered.

4. Recommendations for product revisions or line extensions will not be considered.

Sprite "Target Market"

Presently, Coca-Cola considers persons between the ages of 13 and 39 years to be the principal market for Sprite. However, they do not make the mistake of considering this market a homogeneous group in terms of its perception and use of Sprite.

Competition

Obviously, any beverage can be considered a logical competitor to Sprite. However, from a practical standpoint, management is only concerned with those beverages in the lemon-lime category. Sprite and 7-Up account for over 80 percent of this category. Also, due to distinctive taste preferences in the market, management is not concerned about the possibility of significant "cannibalism" between soft drink categories.

Your Assignment

Simply speaking, the problem (or the opportunity) is to develop a total national advertising campaign to help increase the purchase and consumption of brand Sprite in the United States. Think of yourselves as the "potential new advertising agency" for Coca-Cola USA for the business on brand Sprite.

You should develop the marketing and research basis to support your recommendations for the new advertising campaign for Sprite. What are the advertising strategies and objectives? What should we be saying to our target audience(s) about this brand and exactly how (executionally) should we be saying it? What should the media mix, strategy, objectives, and plans consist of?

These and other pertinent questions should be addressed to abet the development of the most effective advertising campaign in the history of brand Sprite.

All objectives, budgets, media selection, and creative strategy should be directed toward the *national program* in the *mass media*. Local campaigns and merchandising recommendations are not to be included. However, you may wish to present a *few* representative *creative* executions that demonstrate how the national campaign strategy will work for franchises in local advertising and merchandising (i.e., point-of-sale).

The Agency Dilemma for a Food Chain*

Richard W. Skinner, Kent State University
Terence A. Shimp, University of South Carolina

The Portage Grocery Company (PGC) is a dynamic company situated in a midwestern state. The company, which experienced a growth rate in retail sales during the past year of approximately 18 percent, operates 80 stores throughout the state. Approximately one-half of the stores are corporate-owned, and the remainder are franchised carrying the corporate identity of Portage.

Many of the franchised stores are located in the small rural sectors of the state, with most of the corporate-owned stores in metropolitan areas. The Portage stores had combined sales in 1973 of approximately $180 million; the major competitor in the metropolitan areas has 60 stores and sales of approximately $280 million. The Portage Grocery Company is relatively young and innovative. Its growth during the past decade has exceeded the growth of most regional chain grocery companies in the United States. All stores are supplied from one warehouse situated in the largest metropolitan area of the state. Although 4 new stores are on the drawing boards, it is anticipated that during the 1970s all future stores will continue to be supplied and operated from one central warehouse.

The stores are jointly advertised by a program developed and implemented from corporate headquarters. All stores, including franchised stores, are assessed .8 percent of retail sales for advertising. Added to this amount are all forms of co-op advertising. Next year, it is anticipated that the advertising budget will approximate $1.7 million. It also is anticipated that next year's advertising budget will be allocated similar to the current budget—that is, one-third spent on newspapers in the smaller market areas (including rural), one-third spent on newspapers in the metropolitan markets within the state, and approximately one-fourth on TV and radio advertising. The remainder is spent on outdoor and direct mail advertising.

The company, several years ago, began to use TV advertising. Approximately one-fourth of the budget for the past two or three years has been allocated to TV

* All names have been disguised to protect confidentiality.

production and placement (including radio). Management is convinced that the dollars spent have been worthwhile; however, they do not expect to increase expenditures on this medium in the foreseeable future. No formal research program evaluating the TV advertising has been conducted; however, the company has won awards for its TV commercials.

Much of the credit for the success of their TV advertising must go to Tom Wilson, director of advertising. He has been with the company for 18 years and in his present position over six years. Wilson is an extremely inventive and imaginative individual. His efforts to sell top management some of his ideas have been supported by one of the directors of the company who is a vice-president of a very large advertising agency. This director has been very helpful to Wilson and has instructed him in contacting the right people to produce commercials. The agency of which the director is vice-president has no interest in the PGC account since it concentrates exclusively on industrial accounts.

Richard Helms, the president of Portage Grocery Company, has for some time been concerned that there is a need for more formalized outside advertising assistance. He believes that Tom Wilson works too long and hard, and that he needs to learn some other aspects of the business; additionally, perhaps real savings could be effected by outside professional help. The president, however, has not been displeased with the quality of the past TV advertising.

A few days ago during an informal lunch, several of PGC's executives discussed the broadcast advertising being done by retail food chains. After some discussion there was a general consensus that larger grocery chains had increased their broadcast advertising. Someone remarked that Food Fair, which had left TV, returned during 1973. Somebody else commented that they had read that all of the top ten chains were using TV to some extent. The conversation prompted the president to give some additional thought to the future regarding the PGC's advertising. He also began to do more reading in advertising trade publications.

The president learned in *Advertising Age* of a recent study by the Newspaper Advertising Bureau which indicated the following:

- That a number of supermarket companies have taken to the airwaves to bring customers into the store since A&P introduced WEO.
- That supermarket executives basically attribute the reasons for the changes in ad strategies to the pressure on prices as well as the consumer movement.
- That price and item advertising in newspapers will continue to represent the biggest dollar volume in supermarket advertising; however, the chains realize advertising must begin to reflect the company's image and philosophies.

The study also offered suggestions concerning the future of supermarket advertising:

- An information revolution will transform some of the consumerist ideas, such as open dating and nutrition into good solid advertising.
- A more institutional approach to discounting.
- An increase in games and promotions.

- Increasing efforts to personalize ads by use of spokespeople, household hints, and so on.
- More creative logos and ad campaigns due to increased use of ad agencies.
- More and better departmental promotions, and, despite price rises, meat will be the most promoted department.
- More line extension advertising to promote the one-stop shopping concept.

Concerning allocation of annual budget to various media, the Bureau noted that 71.6 percent was devoted to newspapers, 17.4 percent (among those that use TV) were devoted to TV, 9.1 percent to radio, 8.0 percent to direct mail, and 17.1 percent to other.

Almost 90 percent of the supermarkets said they budget advertising as a percent of sales, and of those, 45 percent designated a normal rate as 1 to 1.5 percent; 36 percent said 0.5 to 1.0 percent; and 11 percent said 2 percent or more.

The findings of this study and other readings prompted the president to request a meeting in one week with Tom Wilson and Bill Green, vice-president of retail operations. Both men were instructed to be prepared to defend their position regarding the efficacy of employing an advertising agency to be responsible for all broadcast (TV and radio) advertising. The president indicated that he had a definite opinion about the matter but certainly would be receptive to changing his opinion if logical arguments could be presented.

Green welcomed this opportunity as he had for some time advocated retaining a full-service ad agency to handle the broadcast portion of the budget. Green, however, had not been able to sell Wilson on the idea, and the president had seen no reason to persuade Wilson to change in view of the good work he was doing. Wilson disagreed with Green and maintained that no one understood the food retail business like those involved in it; he believed that the "in-house" agency that he had been operating should continue.

Presidential Meeting on the Future of PGC Broadcast Advertising

The president opens the meeting with the following statement:

> Tom and Bill, I just finished looking over some figures for the last three years. I want to commend both of you for the job you have done. I know that much of the success must be credited to the two of you. I take great pride in our team effort. Despite inflation and the energy crisis, the future for the Portage Grocery Company looks bright.
>
> Now, to the main issue of our meeting, a discussion during lunch and some reading started me to thinking about the advertising program. In what I am about to recommend, I am in no way implying or suggesting that I am anything but pleased with the results of our advertising program. However, I recommend that we obtain some outside help for Tom in developing and implementing our broadcast advertising program. Note that I only said broadcast advertising. It is my conviction that our own advertising staff can do the newspaper advertising more effectively and efficiently than any outsider.
>
> I have read in *Advertising Age* about the increasing development of 'boutique

shops.' These are creative specialists who probably could aid us significantly in creating and producing our broadcast messages. In addition, we could utilize 'media-buying services' which would negotiate and place our broadcast advertising. These are options that are available today that were not a few years ago. The opponents to these types of specialists call this approach to advertising 'piecemealism.' It is my understanding, however, that many advertisers are experimenting with piecemealism.

There are several reasons for my recommendation. Basically, they consist of the following:

(1) Tom has more work than he can be expected to handle effectively. I would like for Tom to have more time to plan and to keep abreast of changes in the industry.

(2) The creative specialists or boutique people should be able to add a fresh dimension to our broadcast advertising which our own staff could not achieve. They may be able to do this without the higher cost that would come with a full-service agency, as the full-service agency is likely to have more overhead.

(3) The media-buying agency provides a specialized service which negotiates and places broadcast advertising. It is a matter of fact according to the Association of National Advertisers that independent media services have been a desirable development for advertisers since more efficient buying practices resulted from their advent.

(4) The fee structure for the media-buying services of some of them is 5 percent for spot TV buying, 5 percent for radio, and 1.85 percent for network TV buys. For a total media job which includes newspapers and magazines, the fee is about 3.75 percent. This, of course, is significantly less than the 15 percent received by a full-service agency.

(5) According to trade publications, we can expect increased competition from our competitors via the broadcast media; thus, we must continue to do an outstanding advertising job. The creative specialists should enable us to do this job more effectively and efficiently as we only employ them when we need them, and creativity is their business.

(6) E. G. Weiss predicts that advertisers in the future will tend to rely not so much on internal capabilities as on limited internal capabilities plus wide outside services.

In summary, Tom is overworked—needs more time for planning, etc. The boutique people and media-buying specialists will permit us to continue an excellent broadcast advertising program at an efficient cost figure.

There is a pause, then the president looks at the vice-president of retail operations. Bill Green seizes this opportunity to speak:

I agree with you in principle; however, I sincerely believe you are only taking half a step when we should go the full way—that is, a full-service agency.

Tom and I have discussed this several times, but I have never had support from anyone else in management. Tom, I know, does not agree with me; however, I am pleased that the subject has emerged again. I think that Tom understands that my desire for a full-service agency in no way reflects upon the job that he and his staff have done. My concern is lack of continuity that would exist if Tom should leave the company, get sick, or be promoted.

There are a number of factors which I believe support my position. These factors are:

1. We spend approximately $400,000 in broadcast advertising. This is a significant amount and requires skills in production and placement that are not comparable to newspaper advertising. I agree with the concept that an agency is probably not adequately staffed to handle a retail food chain's newspaper advertising. It also seems logical that a retail food chain could not be expected to be adequately staffed to produce and place broadcast advertising. The point is that while our TV commercials have been good, they perhaps could have been better.

2. A full-service agency generally has the following departments and people:
   (a) Copywriters—skilled writers who develop ideas and write advertisements exclusively for broadcast media.
   (b) Art directors and artists—people who supply the visual framework for the advertising message.
   (c) Media department—this department places the advertising messages developed by creative departments.
   (d) Production department—responsible for mechanical production of ads.
   (e) Account people—responsible for detailing problems, development, and implementation of plans.
   (f) Research department—researchers who may be trained statisticians, psychologists, economists, etc., to provide facts that will form a basis for themes and image development.
   It just does not seem logical that we, specialists in food merchandising, could satisfactorily perform the tasks that I just defined, nor could we be expected to seek out and retain, on our own staff, the people who could effectively perform the tasks.

3. Champion athletic teams usually are champions because of their bench strength. A good agency will have a depth of manpower that our own advertising staff could not expect nor afford to maintain.

4. The 1960s saw a strong movement by agencies toward compensation by fees such as cost-plus with commissions rebated to the client. Under this type of arrangement we only have to pay for what we get. This results (I think) in greater objectivity by the agency and more complete service.

5. A very significant advantage of using an agency over establishing an in-house agency is the greater flexibility that would be possible with an outside agency. It would be difficult if not impossible to temporarily abandon TV or reduce it drastically for one year with an in-house agency as the overhead would be too great. We would have this flexibility with an outside agency.

6. Also, a full-service agency with research capabilities would provide us considerable input for formulating effective merchandising strategy that would appeal to the ever-changing consumer tastes, and enable us to be one step ahead of our competitors, or in step with those competitors who also have a full-service advertising agency.

I recognize that many of my arguments in favor of a full-service agency are equally applicable to the use of creative specialists and media-buying specialists to supplement our own advertising staff. I seriously question that we have the expertise or know-how to seek out and, even more importantly, to effectively control these specialists. It would be very difficult to coordinate the use of these specialists with the overall image we desire. A full-service agency would not only tell us via research what image we should strive for but how to obtain that image.

I doubt that we could find a boutique shop that really understands the retail food business. Also, I seriously doubt that the size of our broadcast budget would impress the media-buying people sufficiently to take a real interest in our company based on the relatively small commission.

The advertising director for PGC, Tom Wilson, was becoming increasingly impatient as the vice-president spoke, since he had heard many of the arguments from Bill Green before. However, he would have to agree that Green had spent some time preparing for the meeting.

Tom liked Bill, and they had worked together for the company for several years. They were golf partners in the company's golf league, and their families frequently socialized. However, on the point of retaining a full-service advertising agency, they seemed to widen the gap in their thinking each time it had been discussed, so much so that recently they tended to avoid the issue.

When the vice-president paused, the director of advertising quickly interjected:

The last two points you just made are equally applicable to a full-service agency. I seriously doubt that we could find a full-service advertising agency with the expertise or knowledge of food retailing; and, even if we could, I doubt that a good agency with all the departments and people that you made reference to would be interested in our company with a total broadcast budget of $400,000.

I appreciate the concern of both of you as to my work load; however, I don't think either of you have heard me complain. I have heard you (the president) say on more than one occasion that the principal reason for the success of the company is the combination of ability, experience, and youthful enthusiasm of the officers and department heads. I like to consider myself a part of that team. I sincerely believe that I can be most effective and contribute more to the growth and profit of this company by continuing with what might be called an in-house agency. I like my work. My only request is that I be permitted to add the necessary staff when needed and to use the people my staff believes will do the best job in production.

According to the Association of National Advertisers (ANA), about one-half of all large advertisers now have at least letterhead agencies on the premises. The ANA reported in the March 1971 survey of 104 of its member companies that many advertisers have made changes in their methods of managing advertising, including creating in-house advertising capabilities and using outside creative services and media-buying specialists. The reasons for these changes were such factors as desire for greater economy, disenchantment with the 15 percent commission system, desire for faster action, and greater flexibility.

According to *Advertising Age*, for many years following World War II, the average number of employees per $1 million in billings for an agency was 10; today it is near 5.5. Does this mean that with only a $400,000 budget that we might expect an average of two people to work on our account? Perhaps a more appropriate question would be why do we need an average of two employees devoted to our relatively small budget?

Perhaps one of the most significant arguments I can advance in favor of an in-house agency is the obvious need to coordinate broadcast advertising with print advertising. It is difficult to comprehend how we would do this effectively with a full-service agency. Under our present arrangement, coordination is quite simple since the same people work on both forms of advertising.

I also am quite concerned as to whether an outisde advertising agency would devote sufficient time and money to learn the food retailing industry (assuming they do not now have a food retail account). More importantly, how long will it take them to become familiar with us, our stores, and our market area?

Before we make a decision, I strongly encourage Bill to think about the flexibility that we now have which, most probably, would be lost with a full-service agency. There are a lot of things that we take for granted that would necessitate additional communication with and approval from the agency.

I agree with the president that food chains will use more broadcast advertising in the future; however, I think we have a jump on our competitors by two or three years, and I also believe we can maintain this leadership by continuing as we have operated. My impression of the 'boutique' people is that they become overly concerned with the creative process so as to impress their peers and to aid in obtaining new accounts. In other words, they would tend to use us to advance their prestige. I do not think the media-buying services would be interested in us either. It is my impression they tend to operate for nationwide accounts and that we would be too small to justify their time and expense. Frankly, I sincerely believe we do as well as they could in our market. It is my understanding that the media-buying specialists have not delivered the miracles once promised. As you are aware, we devote considerable time to our placement and buying functions. We know the people, they know us, there is a mutual trust. We have and should continue to have buying and placement expertise within the company.

With an in-house agency, when our people have ideas, they will fight for them; they will talk up and talk back. I guess what I'm really saying is that communications is a critical management tool. With an in-house agency we can provide this communications more efficiently, directly from the firm to the consumer and, at the same time, be in a position to interpret the consumer's reaction. Thus, we can identify problems and make adjustments so much quicker than we could if we relied on outside advertising assistance—whether full-service or boutique.

Do you realize that if we were to use a full-service agency, and let's assume an agency of some size that would have other accounts, what might happen if the agency lost one or two sizeable accounts! The result might cause the agency to almost disintegrate or at least retrench drastically. In effect, we no sooner get one account executive trained to the retail grocery business than we have to start all over and retrain another one.

In addition, agencies, buying services, and creative specialists are all accustomed to persuading consumers to buy products—anywhere they can. We in retail advertising urge the consumers to buy products from us, not elsewhere. The large department stores' in-house agencies turn out more advertisements than many full-service advertising agencies. Our problems are unique to food retailing; agencies do not understand them. Thus, we can do the job, I believe, more effectively and efficiently.

At this point in the meeting the president's secretary knocks at the door and indicates that the warehouse union steward wants to see him now; thus, the meeting is quickly adjourned.

PennTex Gas Corporation

Ronald F. Bush, University of Mississippi

Background

PennTex Gas Corporation was founded in 1920. Its service area includes four mid-Atlantic states. Company sales had steadily increased over a 50-year period until the early seventies. Beginning in 1970 sales growth rates dropped and by 1972, sales had actually declined. The company president, H. W. Sims, had not been overly alarmed with decreasing sales because his firm had been experiencing difficulty supplying natural gas. More recently, however, increasing future gas supplies and decreasing profits drew Sims' attention to the declining sales projections.

Situation Analysis

Mr. Sims called a meeting of the company officers to discuss the problem. C. F. Yarbrough, vice-president of marketing, went over the sales figures and pointed out that since 1972, sales had declined at an annual average rate of about 6 percent (see Exhibit 27–1). Mr. Yarbrough indicated that his main concern was the faster rates of decline in recent years. "The company simply has been so concerned with obtaining supplies and pricing that we're not putting proper emphasis on marketing." Mr. Yarbrough provided the officers with expense figures which demonstrated that marketing expenses, as a percentage of sales, had gone down dramatically in the past five years. "Marketing simply does not have enough funds to do its job properly." Finance vice-president, J. Rogers, commented that he felt that marketing expenditures had been reduced because, in a situation of limited supply and excess demand, there was virtually no need for marketing. Mr. Yarbrough stated that regardless of the reason, the present environment called for a more aggressive marketing program if the company wanted sales to increase.

Exhibit 27-1
Operating Revenues, Operating Expenses,
and Net Income for Penntex Gas Corporation
(1975-1978)

	1975	1976	1977	1978
Operating Revenue	$120,433,000	$118,024,340	$110,942,879	$102,067,449
Operating Expenses	88,884,056	87,902,073	81,879,992	75,328,533
Net Income	$ 6,250,988	$ 6,125,968	$ 5,758,410	$ 5,429,237

Exhibit 27-2
Residential and Industrial Customers,
(1975-1978)

	1975	1976	1977	1978
Residential	55,987	55,821	55,803	54,996
Industrial	15,342	15,426	15,938	15,471

Mr. Sims asked the other officers if they could suggest other reasons for the sales decline. Engineering vice-president, M. T. Arnold, stated that the company's industrial installations had steadily increased over the years but residential installations had gone down (see Exhibit 27–2). Mr. Arnold suggested that conversion of more family homes to electricity was probably responsible for the decrease in sales and profits. He also stated that, from his perspective, he did not understand why customers were demanding electricity, when gas is a much more efficient fuel. Mr. Yarbrough commented that consumers had to be aware of this because most of the company's promotional material contained a slogan widely used in the gas industry—"Gas—Your Most Efficient Fuel!" At this point, Mr. Rogers stated that advertising probably did not mean anything in this situation because the residential fuel decision is usually made by building contractors. "Perhaps the company should find out why the builders are not installing gas appliances and gas heating and cooling systems."

Mr. Sims asked Mr. Yarbrough if he had any measure of the effects of the advertising the company had been doing. Yarbrough said that advertising effectiveness studies were costly and that he was spending every available dollar on this "limited budget" already. Sims then mentioned some business articles he had read recently and wondered whether the ideas were applicable to PennTex. The articles discussed growing consumer discontent with utility companies in this country. An article reported the results of a public opinion survey which found that consumers felt utility companies were too large and impersonal, that they were owned by a government agency and, therefore, their rates were "set." Sims wondered just how customers in the PennTex service area felt. "Do you know, I often run into people who ask why PennTex advertises? They say we are a monopoly and monopolies waste money when they advertise." Sims then told the officers that he knew these kinds of attitudes were not the sole reason for declining sales, but he felt that they certainly contributed to the problem.

Mr. Rogers said that he really did not think these opinions mattered much. The surveys were conducted in other areas of the country and the PennTex customers he knew seemed very positive toward the company and its operations. "Besides, if customers in our service area felt this way about utilities, why haven't the electricity firms in our area experienced the same sales decline we have?" Yarbrough said that perhaps these negative attitudes are associated more with PennTex than with competing energy companies. "After all, our competitive electric companies do about four times more image-building promotion than we do!"

Mr. Arnold believed that the problem had to be more concrete. He suggested that "something is wrong with our appliances." Appliance sales had fallen off much more dramatically than total company sales. Arnold referred to the obvious link between gas appliance sales and sales of natural gas and stated that he felt the problem could be associated with the low appliance sales.

President Sims thanked the officers for their comments and asked them to come up with some "firm suggestions" after they had had more time to think. Mr. Sims called for another meeting the following week.

Areas for Investigation

The following week a lengthy meeting took place and the following statements were made:

1. There was a need for PennTex to better understand its image among consumers. Since "big businesses," especially utilities, have received growing consumer criticism, PennTex should know the extent to which this criticism was prevalent in their service area. Furthermore, there was evidence to indicate that consumers in other parts of the country inaccurately perceived the operation of regulated utility companies, such as PennTex.

2. There was a need for PennTex to better understand consumer perceptions of sources of energy (gas versus electricity).

3. There was a need to determine what consumers' appliance-buying intentions were and why.

4. There was a need to assess the impact of PennTex's promotion.

During the meeting the officers discussed several alternative actions, but decided they should continue their first attempt at solving their declining sales problem to an analysis of consumer perceptions.

Consumer Information Corporation

PennTex had a staff group to plan promotional strategy for the firm, but the officers decided that they needed to call on an outside marketing research firm with experience in consumer research. A decision was made to ask Mr. Yarbrough to contact several research firms and to recommend one for the survey. With the approval of other officers, Yarbrough acquired the services of Consumer Information Corporation (CIC). The firm was fairly new but specialized in consumer surveys, and Yarbrough believed CIC to be competent. PennTex agreed to pay CIC $50,000 for the survey. One third of the amount was requested by CIC after PennTex had approved the survey design and the remainder was due upon presentation of the final report. CIC agreed to have a tentative research proposal to PennTex officers within two months. The proposal would contain a copy of the survey questionnaire, and a complete description of the research design, including a timetable for its completion.

Review of Past Operations

A team of three members from CIC started the consumer survey by first visiting the company and making an in-depth review of past operations of both PennTex and the gas industry. The object of this research was to establish the primary criteria that consumers use to judge utility firms. Since no previous information was available, it was difficult for the researchers to develop a complete list of criteria. They had to resort to past situations and events in the PennTex service area which they thought may have influenced consumers' attitudes about utility companies.

Safety

One area which concerned the researchers was safety. For example, a few years earlier PennTex had experienced a problem with gas leakages. The company's storage facilities in a small town within the service area had developed a structural tank leak and the gas ignited, resulting in a large fire which burned out of control for approximately 24 hours. The researchers felt that this event, coupled with a slightly above average accident rate during the last few years, may have caused consumers to perceive a safety problem with the use of natural gas.

Employees

Though the CIC researchers did not find any information to lead them to believe that the utility companies in the PennTex service area had experienced problems with their employees, the researchers felt that the employees of a firm were a vital component of a firm's image. Consequently, the researchers firmly felt they should include some measure of the utility companies' employees' image of the company in the survey.

The researchers wanted to measure employee image because past records indicated that PennTex had put very few dollars into employee training and development programs. The researchers were also concerned about providing information which would not be used by a company. If their survey indicated that PennTex employees had a poor image they were concerned that the corporation would not do anything to remedy the situation.

Services

A review of the records of the various state public service commissions, the regulatory agencies for the utility companies, revealed that the electric companies had experienced frequent isolated power failures in various communities. Consequently, a substantial number of residential and industrial electricity users were constantly relying on the service provided by the electric companies. The researchers were very interested to know how the consumers perceived this service. Did they feel that the electric companies were adequate? Did they feel the electric companies could provide better service than gas companies?

Future Energy Supply

By this time, every citizen was aware of the country's finite energy supply. The researchers wondered what consumers thought about the future supply of natural gas versus electricity. If consumers felt that the future supply of natural gas was more limited than electricity, they would probably prefer to have electrical appliances and heating and cooling systems installed in their homes. This, perhaps, could explain why many of the residential customers seemed to be changing from natural gas to electricity. The researchers were fully aware that most consumers probably do not understand the complex ways in which electricity is generated. For example, substantial portions of the electricity generating plants are actually powered by natural gas. Although most consumers understand that natural gas is a finite source of energy, they do not understand electric energy supplies. Consequently, the CIC researchers decided to include several questions regarding the future supply of both gas and electricity.

Energy Rates

At the same time energy supplies shortened, the energy companies raised their rates in an effort to curtail demand. Over the last several years, energy rates have increased dramatically causing consumers to become more sensitive to rates and the efficiency of energy. The researchers were basically interested in two issues regarding rates. First, they believe that many consumers do not fully understand the rate structure in the utility industry, and many consumers apparently believe that utility companies artificially raised their rate by intentionally withholding supplies. Secondly, in dealing with energy rates, it is difficult to equate the cost of one source of energy with another. The basic rate measure for electricity is the kilowatt hour; the basic rate measure for natural gas is 1,000 cubic feet. Since these measures are different, few consumers can evaluate which is the more efficient energy source. Furthermore, the researchers did not know how to provide adequate information about consumers' perception of rates since both electric and gas rates varied substantially throughout the PennTex service area.

Analysis of Former Advertising

As part of their overall promotional campaign, PennTex had been doing a substantial amount of advertising over the years. The CIC researchers wanted to know what kind of impact this advertising had on PennTex customers. Also, the CIC researchers wanted to get some baseline measure of company name awareness, recall of past advertising, recall of out of which media consumers had either seen or heard the ads, and recall of the advertising theme. The researchers felt that these areas would establish certain baseline measures which PennTex could use to evaluate its future advertising efforts.

Mr. Sims had told the researchers that he believed that many consumers did not believe utility companies should advertise. He substantiated his claims by showing the researchers several articles which discussed this issue and, in general, criticized the industry. Sims was very interested in finding out whether consumers in the PennTex trading area believed that advertising by utility companies was appropriate. One of the researchers mentioned that this information may be difficult to obtain because consumers may believe one type of advertising was appropriate whereas another type would not be. Mr. Sims, however, strongly urged the researchers to investigate this issue.

Proposal Meeting

After two months of background research, the CIC researchers met with PennTex officers to present the research proposal. The research proposal contained a detailed description of the research methodology to be used in conducting a consumer survey in the PennTex service area. The proposal also contained a detailed timetable and a copy of the research questionnaire (see Exhibit 27–3). CIC explained that the survey would be conducted on a selected sample of consumers in the PennTex service area. They also pointed out that the questions they had selected to include in the questionnaire were obtained from a variety of sources. First, several questions were obtained from an analysis of the secondary information available on utility companies. Secondly, several questions were directed at finding answers to questions that the PennTex officers had raised during interviews with the researchers.

After reviewing the methodology and the survey instrument, the officers began discussing the questionnaire. Mr. Yarbrough pointed out that there were several questions included which would help him establish bench marks upon which to evaluate the company's promotional efforts. He recalled the earlier discussion and stated that Mr. Sims had asked him during the meeting several months ago whether he had developed any measures of the effects of the advertising the company had been doing. He stated that several of the questions in the survey would

Exhibit 27-3
Questionnaire
Consumer Survey

Introduction

Good Morning (Afternoon)

My name is_____ and I am collecting information for an Opinion Survey Company. We are interested in your opinions about the energy companies serving you here in the City of _____. This is part of a regional study which is designed to obtain information which help your energy companies serve you better. Your name will not be identified in any way and this will take only about _____ minutes. Would you mind helping us to learn how your energy companies can serve you better?

1. What is the name of the electric utility that serves you?
    Knows name of company _____ (1)
    Does not know name of company _____ (2)

2. What is the name of the natural gas company that serves you?
    PennTex _____ (1)
    Does not know name of company _____ (2)

3. Is your natural gas company privately owned by stockholders or publicly owned by a governmental agency?
    Privately owned _____ (1)   Does not know _____ (3)
    Publicly owned _____ (2)

4. Do you remember any advertising by either your electric utility or your gas company?
    Yes _____ (1)   No _____ (2)   (If "no," go to question #7)

5. If yes to question 4, ask which media (check as many as stated).
    Radio _____ (1)   TV _____ (3)   Don't Know _____ (5)
    Newspaper _____ (2)   Other _____ (4)   More than 1 media _____ (6)

6. If yes to question 4, ask if they remember what the advertisement was about. (Prompt if necessary—all categories.)

	Gas	Electric	Both
Conservation	_____ (1)	_____ (1)	_____ (1)
Availability (supply)	_____ (2)	_____ (2)	_____ (2)
Appliances	_____ (3)	_____ (3)	_____ (3)
Cost of Service	_____ (4)	_____ (4)	_____ (4)
Other _____	_____ (5)	_____ (5)	_____ (5)
Don't know _____ (6)			

7. Most utility companies generally use several different messages in advertising. We would like to know which advertising you feel is appropriate for energy companies to use. For example, should energy companies:

Advertise to sell their
appliances   Yes _____ (1)   No _____ (2)   Don't know _____ (3)

Advertise to sell their
energy   Yes _____ (1)   No _____ (2)   Don't know _____ (3)

Advertise to tell how
to conserve energy   Yes _____ (1)   No _____ (2)   Don't know _____ (3)

Advertise to tell you general things about the company (such as why rates have changed, what the company is doing for the benefit of the community)

                     Yes _____ (1)   No _____ (2)   Don't know _____ (3)

Advertise ways to save money on your utility bill

                     Yes _____ (1)   No _____ (2)   Don't know _____ (3)

8. Which source of energy do you believe is the most efficient for home use—natural gas or electricity?

      Natural gas _____ (1)

      Electricity _____ (2)

      Don't know _____ (3)

      Both the same _____ (4) (both high, both low)

INTERVIEWER: ASSIST SUBJECT IN RESPONDING TO OPINION QUESTIONS

Thank you. We have just a few more questions we would like for you to answer.

APPLIANCE AND ENERGY PREFERENCES

1. What was the last major appliance you purchased?

Stove	_____ (1)	Air Conditioner	_____ (5)
Clothes Dryer	_____ (2)	Heating Unit	_____ (6)
Water Heater	_____ (3)	Central AC & H	_____ (7)
Refrigerator	_____ (4)	Other	_____ (8)

        Purchased 2 or more appliances _____ (9)

2. What types of energy does this appliance use?

    a. electricity   _____ (1)

    b. natural gas   _____ (2)

    c. other   _____ (3)

    d. more than one _____ (4)

3.   Why did you buy a (gas or electric) appliance? _____

      (1) _____ Advertising   (5) _____ Cheaper to operate

      (2) _____ Know appliance dealer   (6) _____ Efficiency

      (3) _____ House not wired for it   (7) _____ Price

      (4) _____ My mother used it   (8) _____ Replacement of same kind of energy

            (9) _____ Other—Write answer above.

4.   Do you plan to purchase a new major appliance in the next year?

      Yes _____ (1)   No _____ (2) (If no, go to General Information section.)

5.   If yes, what is the planned appliance purchase?

      _____

6.   Is this _____ (planned appliance purchase) _____ going to be an electric ap-plance or a gas appliance?

      Electric _____ (1)

      Gas   _____ (2)

      Both   _____ (3)

7.   Why are you going to purchase an (electric or gas) appliance?

      _____

      _____

      (1) _____ Advertising   (5) _____ Cheaper to operate

      (2) _____ Know appliance dealer   (6) _____ Efficiency

      (3) _____ House not wired for it   (7) _____ Price

      (4) _____ My mother used it   (8) _____ Replacement of same kind of energy

            (9) _____ Other—Write answer above.

GENERAL INFORMATION

1.   Do you feel that your electric utility is trying hard to keep their rates as low as possible?

      Yes _____ (1)   No _____ (2)   Don't know _____(3)

2.   Do you feel that your natural gas company is trying hard to keep their rates as low as possible?

      Yes _____ (1)   No _____ (2)   Don't know _____(3)

3. When was the last time that you had a personal contact with your gas or electric company. By personal contact we mean such things as a telephone conversation, a visit to the utility company or a visit by a repairman, etc. (Please check only one.)

    Within the last month ————— (1)   Five to six months ago ————— (4)

    One to two months ago ————— (2)   Over 7 months ago ————— (5)

    Three or four months ago ————— (3)

4. What is the specific position or occupation of the head of your household? (If retired or unemployed, last job held.)

    _____

5. What is the highest grade level of school completed by the head of your household?

    INTERVIEWER: From the num-
    ber at the right, circle the last year
    of school that the head of house-
    hold completed

1	2	3	4	Elementary school
5	6	7	8	Elementary school
9	10	11	12	High School
13	14	15	16	College/tech school
17	18	19	20	Graduate school

6. (Interviewer: Show subject the following question as you ask it.)
    Which of the following letters is beside the category that shows your age?

    A. Under 26 ————— (1)   D. 51–60 years ————— (4)

    B. 25–35 years ————— (2)   E. Over 60 ————— (5)

    C. 36–50 years ————— (3)

7. Please tell me the letter beside the income category which indicates your approximate family income in thousands of dollars.

    A. ————— Under $4,000

    B. ————— $ 4,000–$ 7,000

    C. ————— $ 7,001–$10,000

    D. ————— $10,001–$13,000

    E. ————— $13,001–$16,000

    F. ————— $16,001–$19,000

    G. ————— $19,001–$22,000

    H. ————— $22,001–$25,000

    I. ————— $25,001–$28,000

    J. ————— $28,001–$30,000

    K. ————— Over $30,000

8. Although you will remain anonymous, you may be called at a later date simply to ask if I have interviewed you. Therefore, could you please tell me your phone number.

    Phone No. —————————

9.   Lastly, is there anything you believe your electric or gas company can do to help provide you with better service.

Gas Company _____

_____

_____

Electric Company _____

_____

_____

10.   INTERVIEWER: Record the following for the respondent:

Sex of subject: M _____ (1)   F _____ (2)

Race of subject: B _____ (1)   W _____ (2)

11.   Interviewer's Signature _____

OPINION QUESTIONS

Part I

Instructions

Below is a list of characteristics related to utility companies. We would like for you to rank the characteristics from 1 (most important) to 7 (least important). Place the number one (1) beside the most important characteristic, the number two (2) by the second most important, and so on. The number seven (7) should be placed beside the characteristic which is least important of the seven characteristics. Please be sure to place a different number in *each* blank. Please read *all* seven characteristics before you begin to rank them.

_____ Friendly Employees
_____ Emergency Repair Services
_____ Competent Employees
_____ Rates
_____ Future Supply
_____ Clean Source of Energy
_____ Safety

OPINION QUESTIONS

Part II

Instructions

We would like for you to tell us how you feel about certain characteristics of energy companies (gas and electric utilities). We would like for you to tell us to what extent you believe the following statements are true by putting an "X" on the following scales in a position which best describes your feelings. There are no right or wrong answers. We simply want your own personal opinion. You will be rating two companies in your city—the electric company and the gas company.

EXAMPLE: Suppose we want you to tell us your feelings about a company's office location.

We would state:

> Company A has a convenient office location.
>
> How true do you think this is?
>
> LIKELY ___:___:___:___:___:___:___ UNLIKELY
>
>   7   6   5   4   3   2   1

If you believe the office location is *definitely* in a convenient location you would place your X as shown below:

> LIKELY __X__:___:___:___:___:___:___ UNLIKELY
>
>   7   6   5   4   3   2   1

PENNTEX GAS CORPORATION

1. PennTex Gas Corporation has *friendly employees.*

   How true do you think this is?

   LIKELY ___:___:___:___:___:___:___ UNLIKELY

       7   6   5   4   3   2   1

2. PennTex Gas Corporation provides *emergency repair* services.

   How true do you think this is?

   LIKELY ___:___:___:___:___:___:___ UNLIKELY

       7   6   5   4   3   2   1

3. PennTex Gas Corporation has *competent employees.*

   How true do you think this is?

   LIKELY ___:___:___:___:___:___:___ UNLIKELY

       7   6   5   4   3   2   1

4. PennTex Gas Corporation provides natural gas at reasonable rates.

   How true do you think this is?

   LIKELY ___:___:___:___:___:___:___ UNLIKELY

       7   6   5   4   3   2   1

5. PennTex Gas Corporation has an adequate *future supply* of natural gas.

   How true do you think this is?

   LIKELY ___:___:___:___:___:___:___ UNLIKELY

       7   6   5   4   3   2   1

6. PennTex Gas Corporation, as a supplier of natural gas, is a *safe* source of energy.
    How true do you think this is?
    LIKELY ____:____:____:____:____:____:____ UNLIKELY
    　　　　 7   6   5   4   3   2   1

7. PennTex Gas Corporation provides a *clean* source of energy.
    How true do you think this is?
    LIKELY ____:____:____:____:____:____:____ UNLIKELY
    　　　　 7   6   5   4   3   2   1

NAME OF COMPETING ELECTRIC COMPANY IN THIS AREA

1. *Electric Company* has *friendly employees.*
    How true do you think this is?
    LIKELY ____:____:____:____:____:____:____ UNLIKELY
    　　　　 7   6   5   4   3   2   1

2. *Electric Company* provides *emergency repair* services.
    How true do you think this is?
    LIKELY ____:____:____:____:____:____:____ UNLIKELY
    　　　　 7   6   5   4   3   2   1

3. *Electric Company* has *competent employees.*
    How true do you think this is?
    LIKELY ____:____:____:____:____:____:____ UNLIKELY
    　　　　 7   6   5   4   3   2   1

4. *Electric Company* provides electricity at reasonable *rates.*
    How true do you think this is?
    LIKELY ____:____:____:____:____:____:____ UNLIKELY
    　　　　 7   6   5   4   3   2   1

5. *Electric Company* has an adequate *future supply* of electricity.
    How true do you think this is?
    LIKELY ____:____:____:____:____:____:____ UNLIKELY
    　　　　 7   6   5   4   3   2   1

6. *Electric Company,* as a supplier of electricity, is a *safe* source of energy.
    How true do you think this is?
    LIKELY ____:____:____:____:____:____:____ UNLIKELY
    　　　　 7   6   5   4   3   2   1

7. *Electric Company* provides a *clean* source of energy.
    How true do you think this is?
    LIKELY ____:____:____:____:____:____:____ UNLIKELY
    　　　　 7   6   5   4   3   2   1

enable him to develop some means of measuring the effects of the PennTex promotional efforts.

Mr. Rogers, vice-president of finance, asked why the survey contained questions regarding the types of appliances that consumers had purchased in the past or intended to purchase in the future. Mr. Yarbrough responded by saying that these questions should enable PennTex to determine what percent of the consumers were buying gas or electric appliances and the reasons for those purchases. Yarbrough pointed out that many consumers were changing from gas appliances to electric and this changeover, of course, affected the consumption rate of these two energy sources. Also, Yarbrough noted that appliance sales were drastically down and any information on appliance purchase intentions would help the company to understand this sales problem.

Mr. Arnold did not fully understand the differences between Part I of the opinion questions and Part II. He said that it seemed that these two sections were really measuring the same things. A CIC researcher responded, saying that he should not really be concerned since this format was a new method of measuring opinions which would provide PennTex with useful information.

Mr. Sims spoke up and said he was pleased to see several questions which were apparently designed to measure PennTex's corporate image. He felt that the PennTex image could be contributing to the sales problem. He specifically referred to the questions on the appropriateness of utility companies' advertising, whether they were sincerely trying to provide reasonable rates, and consumers' perceptions of the ownership of utility companies. Sims then went over the timetable with the CIC researchers and asked the other officers to vote on whether they wished to proceed with the remainder of the survey. The officers voted unanimously to allow CIC to complete the survey and each expressed his eagerness to review the results.

Discussion Questions

1. Was finance vice-president, Rogers, correct in stating that there is no role for marketing in conditions where demand exceeds supply? Why?

2. Were the four areas of investigation adequate? Explain.

3. Do you think the CIC researchers did an adequate job in presenting the marketing research proposal? Why?

4. How do you think the information collected in the survey will help PennTex? Explain.

R. J. Reynolds Industries, Inc.: Advertising and Social Responsibility*

John E. Mertes and Dale M. Lewison
University of Arkansas/Little Rock

Company Background

In 1875, Richard Joshua Reynolds left a partnership with his father in tobacco farming and manufacturing in Virginia, moved to Winston, North Carolina, and invested $2,400 in a plot of ground, a factory, and equipment.

By 1906, Reynolds was producing one-seventh of the nation's plug (chewing) tobacco, and by 1912, one-fourth. In 1907, Reynolds developed Prince Albert Smoking tobacco, now the largest selling smoking tobacco in the country.

Camel was introduced as the company's first major cigarette brand in 1913. Four years after introduction, Camel was the nation's largest selling cigarette and in the next half-century went on to become the most popular cigarette ever produced, selling more than 132 million packs. Winston cigarettes, first introduced in 1954, has continuously ranked as one of the sales leaders in the United States; and Salem, introduced in 1956, is among the leaders in the menthol category.

Diversification began in the 1950s when the company's Archer Aluminum Division started making packaging products for customers other than Reynolds Tobacco. During the 1960s, the company continued to diversify by acquiring companies in foods, fruit juice beverages, and containerized freight transportation. In June 1970, a new parent company, R. J. Reynolds Industries, Inc., was formed. Under a corporate-wide reorganization, R. J. Reynolds Tobacco Company became the largest subsidiary of R. J. Reynolds Industries, Inc.

Currently, the R. J. Reynolds Tobacco Company leads the tobacco industry in sales. Reynolds' brands account for approximately one-third of all domestic cigarette sales. Three of the top-selling brands in their categories—Winston, Salem, and Camel—are all Reynolds' products. Reynolds' first cigar product, Winchester, is a leader in the little cigar market; Prince Albert continues to be one of the

---

nation's leading smoking tobaccos, and Days Work remains a leader among plug chewing tobacco brands. A listing of the company's brands is shown in Exhibit 28–1.

Research on Cigarette Smoking and Health

Through the years, cigarette industry advertising has been subjected to criticism. Much of the criticism stems from research that indicates that cigarette smoking is a health hazard. In an effort to find out the answers to this concern, the industry is continuing to support, through unrestricted grants, the scientific research vitally needed to learn the true facts about smoking and health. For example, the industry has set up a $2.8 million grant to the Harvard Medical School for a 5-year investigation of any specific effects cigarette smoking may have in the development of lung and heart diseases. The industry is providing more financial help for such research than all the private agencies combined.

The Advertising Policy

To assist in making advertising decisions, the tobacco company set up its initial guidelines in 1964. In 1972, the guidelines and procedures were revised in accor-

Exhibit 28-1
R. J. Reynolds Tobacco Company Brands

Cigarettes

WINSTON King Size	DORAL King Size Menthol
WINSTON Super King Size	VANTAGE King Size
WINSTON Super King Size Menthol	VANTAGE King Size Menthol
SALEM King Size Menthol	VANTAGE Super King Size
SALEM Super King Size Menthol	MORE 120s
CAMEL Regular (nonfilter)	MORE 120s Menthol
CAMEL King Size Filter	REAL King Size
TEMPO King Size	REAL King Size Menthol
DORAL King Size	

Smoking Tobaccos	**Chewing Tobaccos**
PRINCE ALBERT	DAYS WORK
CARTER HALL	BROWN MULE
GEORGE WASHINGTON	APPLE SUN CURED
MADERIA GOD	REYNOLDS NATURAL LEAF
TOP	

Exhibit 28-2
Personnel Policy & Procedure Manual*
R. J. Reynolds Tobacco Company

Advertising and Sales Promotion Standards

I. POLICY

It is the philosophy, intent and commitment of the R. J. Reynolds Tobacco Company that each and every advertising and sales promotion effort be a truthful and factual representation of the product; be presented in good taste and with adult appeal; be in the best interest of the consumer and the company; not degrading or belittling to competing products; and, further, be in accordance with the standards set forth hereinafter.

II. PRACTICE

A. Purpose

All advertising and sales promotion activity shall be conducted in such a way as to ensure that all company products are honestly represented to the consumer.

B. Obligation

The company recognizes its obligation to its stockholders, employees, consumers, and the public at large to manufacture products of high quality and market such products at fair prices. The company also recognizes its obligation to make all reasonable efforts to increase the market share for its products through aggressive efforts.

C. Standards

All advertising and sales promotion efforts shall comply to the following standards.

1. Cigarette advertising shall not appear in school, college, or university media (including athletic, theatrical and other programs).
2. Cigarette advertising shall not appear in comic books or comic supplements to newspapers.
3. Sample cigarettes shall not be distributed to persons under twenty-one years of age.
4. No sample cigarettes shall be distributed or promotional efforts conducted on school, college or university campuses, or in fraternity or sorority houses.
5. Natural persons depicted as smokers in cigarette advertising shall be at least twenty-five years of age and shall not be dressed or otherwise made to appear to be less than twenty-five years of age.
6. Fictitious persons so depicted in the form of drawings, sketches or any other manner shall appear to be at least twenty-five years of age in dress and otherwise.
7. Cigarette advertising may use attractive, healthy looking models, or illus-

---

* Revised January 1, 1972, Number 9.06. Original date of issuance April 27, 1964, pp. 1–3 of 3.

trations or drawings of persons who appear to be attractive and healthy, provided that there is no suggestion that their attractive appearance or good health is due to cigarette smoking.

8. No cigarette advertising shall contain a picture or an illustration of a person smoking in an exaggerated manner.

9. Cigarette advertising shall not depict as a smoker any person that might have a specific appeal to youth.

10. Cigarette advertising shall not depict as a smoker any person participating in physical activity requiring stamina or athletic conditioning beyond that of normal recreation.

11. Testimonials from athletes or celebrities in the entertainment world, or testimonials from other persons who would have special appeal to the persons under twenty-one years of age, shall not be used in cigarette advertising.

III. PROCEDURE

Responsibility for Implementation

A. Vice-presidents—Advertising and Sales

The vice-presidents responsible for advertising and sales shall be responsible for:

1. Ensuring that this policy is communicated to all members of management and, through appropriate management procedures, to all employees, and to all company agents and agencies responsible for advertising and sales promotion activities.

2. Ensuring that all product advertising and sales promotion materials are submitted to legal counsel for review prior to their use.

B. Chief Executive Officer

The Chief Executive Officer is responsible for assuring the implementation of, and compliance with, this policy.

C. Delegation of Authority and Responsibility

Delegation of authority and responsibility is not authorized.

---

dance with suggestions made by the National Business Council for Consumer Affairs through its Sub-Council on Advertising and Promotion. The policy, practice, and procedure manual is presented in Exhibit 28–2.

Problem

Assume you are the marketing research manager and chairperson of the Marketing Policy and Procedure Committee for the R.J. Reynolds Tobacco Company. The executive vice-president of marketing has assigned you and the committee the task of evaluating the advertising and sales promotion standards set forth in the revision of January 1, 1972. He has instructed you to submit a full report on the adequacy of the advertising and sales promotion standards in view of current governmental and societal expectations. Are the standards adequate to meet the company's obligations as stated in Part II, Section A of the Personnel Policy and Procedure Manual?

Chapter 7

Strategies in Sales Management and Buyer/Seller Interactions

What sales messages should be used by salespersons when interacting with buyers to produce sales? How many salespeople should an organization hire? What training programs should a firm have for its salespeople? How should salespeople be paid? How does the organization's personal selling activities interact with other marketing mix elements of the firm? How should the performance of salespeople be evaluated? These are a few of the key questions in sales management.

Sales management is the recruitment, training, allocating, supervising, compensating, and evaluating the sales force of an organization. Each of these decision-making areas are related to answering a central question in sales management: What actions of the sales force should be taken to influence buyers' purchase behavior? Actions may be selected to increase, maintain, or decrease buyer purchases. (Most sales managers are concerned with maintaining and increasing buyer purchases; however, in situations of shortages and delivery problems, actions may be selected to attempt to decrease buyer purchases.)

A sales force is one part of an organization's marketing system. Most organizations select objectives, market segments, products, and prices before making sales management decisions. Then, marketing communications decisions, including advertising and sales promotion, and sales force decisions are made. Outputs of the system which usually are measured for business firms include profit, ROI (return on investment), and market share achieved by the firm. This marketing system is shown as Figure C—7–1.

In Figure C—7–1 feedback is shown as a measure of the output of the marketing results. The corporation uses feedback to adjust the inputs to the sales force. Notice in Figure C—7–1 that external forces, such as a labor strike, are recognized as affecting the outputs of the system.

The sales force itself may be viewed as a subsystem in an organization. As a system, sales management and sales force behavior has input, process, and output variables. These variables are shown in detail in Figure C—7–2. The sales man-

Figure   C—7–1
The Sales Force As Part of
The Corporation's Marketing System

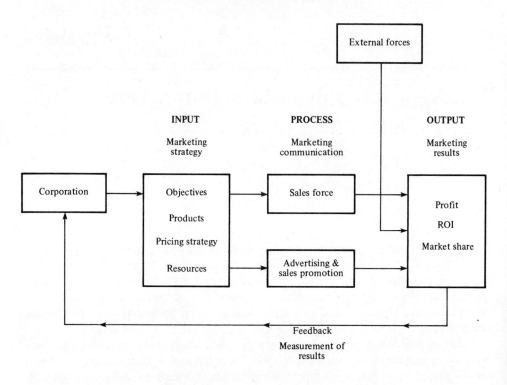

ager's activities are outputs *to* salespersons' input variables. Changes to 3 *salespersons' output variables* can occur to improve sales force performance:

1. An increase in total *sales volume,* without any change in the product mix or sales cost ratio.

2. A more *profitable product mix,* in which the products producing a higher profit represent a larger percentage of total sales volume.

3. A reduction in the *sales volume cost* ratio, which can result from increasing sales without a corresponding increase in costs, or from decreasing sales costs.[1]

The decisions and actions of sales management affect the 3 salespersons' input variables in the figure. Each salesperson might be motivated by sales management

---

[1] Porter Henry, "Manage Your Sales Force As A System," *Harvard Business Review,* March-April 1975. Copyright © 1975 by the President and Fellows of Harvard College; all rights reserved.

to increase the number of sales calls per week or the organization might increase the number of calls by hiring more salespeople. The quality of sales calls can be measured by such yardsticks as calls per order, dollar sales or profits per call, or percentage of calls that achieve specific objectives. Call quality in Figure C—7–2 consists of 3 elements:

1. The information content of the call. Is the salesperson adequately informed about the customer's problems or plans, as well as about his or her own products and their applications?

2. The effectiveness of the calls as an act of communication. Does the salesperson deliver the message in an understandable and convincing manner? Is the salesperson a good listener and questioner?

3. The interpersonal aspects of the call. Does the salesperson rub the customer the wrong way without being aware of it? When the customer's "inner child" speaks, does the salesperson's "inner child" respond? [2]

Salespersons' *allocations* of sales effort refers to the frequency of calls to large, medium, and small customers. The allocation mix to each of these customer groups is important in affecting the output of the sales force system. A typical problem among salespeople is spending too much time with little customers and losing some of the additional potential volume from key large customers. Sometimes, a salesperson may call on a large customer so often that profitability is reduced because of noncontacts with smaller customers.

A total of 22 sales managers' control variables are shown in Figure C—7–2. These control variables are divided into 7 categories which affect different salespeople's input variables. For example, the number of salespeople hired affects the number of calls the sales force can make but no other salespersons' input variable. Motivation and compensation affect both the salespeople's input variables of quality of calls and allocation of sales effort.

Sales Manager's Activities

How does the sales manager spend his or her time to change salespersons' input variables (number, quality, and allocation of calls)? Although no studies of observing the day-to-day behavior of sales managers may be available, some data are available based on self reports and reports by salespeople and top management. The allocation of job activities by field sales managers is shown in Table C—7–1 divided into five areas. Over one-third (36.6 percent) of the activities relate directly to selling, such as making sales calls with salespeople and personal selling to the sales manager's own accounts. Notice that several of the activities listed in the table are shown as sales manager's control variables in Figure C—7–2.

A Sales Manager's Meeting with the Sales Force

Several activities of a sales manager to influence the behavior of salespeople can be learned by studying the interactions between sales managers and salespeople

---

[2] Ibid.

Figure   C—7–2
The Sales Force As A System

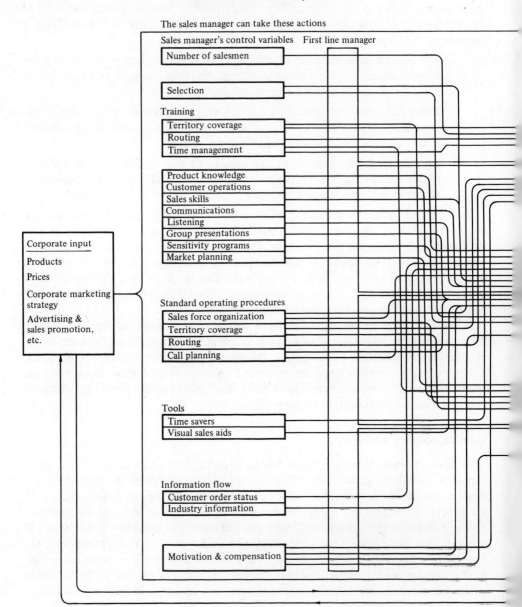

se these behavioral changes. . .   achieve these results

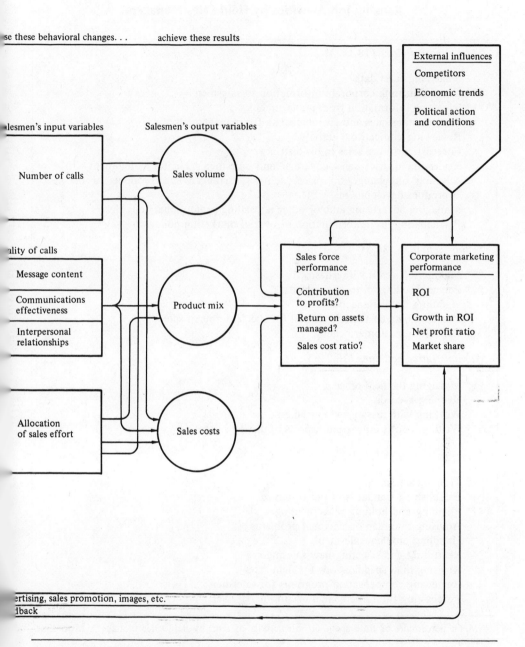

Salesmen's input variables   Salesmen's output variables

External influences
Competitors
Economic trends
Political action
and conditions

Number of calls   Sales volume

ality of calls

Message content
Communications
effectiveness   Product mix
Interpersonal
relationships

Sales force
performance

Contribution
to profits?
Return on assets
managed?
Sales cost ratio?

Corporate marketing
performance

ROI

Growth in ROI
Net profit ratio
Market share

Allocation
of sales effort   Sales costs

ertising, sales promotion, images, etc.
dback

Source: Porter Henry, "Manage Your Sales Force As A System," in Marvin A. Jolson (ed.), *Contemporary Readings in Sales Management* (New York: Petrocelli/Charter, 1977), pp. 48–49.

Table   C—7–1
Ranking Job Activities by Field Sales Managers

Marketing activities (18.1%)[a]

† * Analyzing sales data
φ † * Communicating corporate information to salesmen
φ † * Digesting information from management
    Summarizing sales and customer data for management
  † Reviewing competitive activity
    Forecasting future sales in his district
    Reviewing district sales coverage and salesmen's territory alignment
    Advising on changes in price, delivery, arrangements, products or on new
       product development
    Managing advertising and/or other nonselling promotional activities
    Participating in the formulation of overall marketing policy

Selling activities (36.6%)

φ † * Making sales calls with salesmen
φ † * Personal selling to his own accounts
  * Handling problem accounts
    Deciding on a customer's request for special terms of sale
    Expediting customer orders

Administrative activities (18.2%)

φ † * Managing the field office
    Keeping records
    Working with dissatisfied customers
  φ † Writing reports on various aspects of district operations

Personnel activities (20.4%)

φ † * Training salesmen
  † * Establishing standards of performance
φ † * Planning and holding sales meeting
    Advising salesmen on personal problems
    Handling problem salesmen
  φ Recruiting and selecting new salesmen
    Revising man specifications for field sales
    Reviewing compensation programs for salesmen
    Forecasting future personnel need in his district

---

[a] Mean percentage of time spent on job activity as seen by field sales managers. Most time-consuming activities:
  * As seen by field sales managers
  † As seen by salesmen
  φ As seen by top management
Source: Adapted from Rodney Earl Evans, *An Empirical Analysis of the Function and Role of the Field Sales Manager* (East Lansing, Mich.: Michigan State University, 1968), unpublished dissertation, appropriate pages.

Financial activities (7.4%)

†* Analyzing selling expense data
 * Controlling inventory and warehousing costs
 * Controlling costs of branch office operation
   Watching trend of costs expended in relation to profits generated in his district
   Preparing budgets
   Advising on the need for additional capital expenditure in his district

---

during sales meetings. The following excerpt from one such meeting provides insights into the motivation and evaluation actions of the sales manager.

The meeting taking place is the regular weekly meeting for the sales manager (SM) and 6 salespeople for a life insurance firm, Protection Life.[3]

SM: Well, we don't have anything big to go over today; we'll just cover the routine things. I put here on display the objectives for the year in order to keep it in front of everybody. That's the whole secret, as you all know, is having objectives and staying on time with them. Based on last week's results, though, I don't—I think, *we* might have a shortage of energy because we didn't have too much expended last week, so it must be a shortage. But it's the next to the last week of "Get Your Wife in the Picture Contest" and the only people who had applications turned in were Jed—his net was highest in the company last week. Keith Stuckey had a zero week. So, Jed's two and one for the week were the extent of the results last week.

SP1:   Do the wives get a copy—do they get sent home?

SM: Your wife should have gotten a copy instead of you, Jim. What are you opening her mail for? (humorous tone)

SP1:   No, I just said she got one at home.

SP2:   I didn't get one.

SM: Well, blame your mail service. It'll be there today. Now, back in December out at the house, you took objectives for January and paid business. So these are the results. Jed got 120 percent of his objective—15 paid premiums. Keith got 97 percent of his objective of 1937. Bert got 800 percent or something like that, 8000. Jim, you got 60 percent. David got 17 percent, and Rod got 5 percent. Now, based on the projection—if that continued for the rest of the year—Jed would have earnings from that business of $25,000 and, with our commission being half the next year and half the next year, that much business would be worth to him $40,800. In other words, just that business alone in the next 3 years would be worth—if he continued that each month this year—that would value $40,838. Bert's would be $84,000. Keith's would be $18,660. Now the Protection Life Bulletin for this past week showed Jed being #2 for

---

[3] Names are disguised. Data provided by James L. Taylor, Texas A&M University, from tape recordings of the sales meeting.

the week of January 24 and Keith being #9 and both coming in. For the month to date, Jed was third and Keith was eighth. So it shows what happened—the same two people that are leading in "Get Your Wife in the Picture" are leading the company. And for what it might be worth, there's a correlation—the only two activity reports that I have up to this point are these same two people.

That can tell you something; in other words, staying on what's #1 and getting it done. I'm not going to preach a sermon, but you're all familiar with the beatitudes in the Bible. So I just thought a little correlation there—blessed is he who isolates a problem and takes action to solve the problem. In order not to be anti-bible, you could just say *attitude,* instead of beatitude—for blessed is he who isolates a problem and then takes action to solve the problem. Now, you stop and think about it. That's about the most important approach to life and to business— whatever your problem is, just isolate it and then get on it, whether it be sales or whether it be in your own personal life.

Now, as far as our problem is concerned—what we've been trying to do this year, as you know, is to ask everybody to have 10 more-than-qualified prospects; prospects who have some reason in your mind that they ought to buy this particular week. So, that to me is isolating the problem as far as sales go—to have at least 10 people each week that you expect to sell. An example here were Keith's down below and there are Jed's. That's what you've been doing—taking those 10 each week on your report, and then trying to get sales from those 10 people. Now, we should use this same procedure to isolate the problem for today; in other words, if you don't right now know what 2 people you expect sales to come from today, then you haven't taken that step toward isolating the problem. You're already behind unless you've done that. If you don't have 2 people today, or you don't have 10 for the week, then your #1 problem is to get the 10. That's the problem you've got to first isolate in order to go from there to the people you'll sell. Once you've done that, of course, then you've got to move into these 2 people —if you don't already know their problem—and isolate it again. You should already know the problem; otherwise they shouldn't be the type people you'd expect to sell today. Otherwise, I don't think we'd have to read names.

I'm not going to go through this entire sheet, but just the steps in isolating the problem of the person. I'm just going to read 2 or 3 paragraphs from this particular article. People will remain names unless converted into prospects by an interview under favorable conditions. The key to determine that they recognize a need, have the money, and are receptive to a solution and will buy from you. We don't ever want to forget that "will buy from you." Sometimes people realize they've got a problem and they are going to buy, *but* their brother is in business. Some of you have already established the habit of, when you're talking to someone, finding out in the beginning if you like what I have to offer and if you buy, would it be from me or is your next door neighbor in the business or do you have a brother. Get that out of the way right in the beginning, particularly if it's the type of case that's going to take a lot of time. Don't hesitate to come right out and ask them and get a commitment that, if they buy, they will buy from you.

And, of course, the preapproach—the purpose of it is to get an interview under favorable conditions using either in-person contact call as Jim, you and Jed did Friday afternoon or Thursday—quite a number of those types of calls, a telephone call or a letter or combination. Jim, I know you sent out several orphan policy letters; of course, that fits in this category. You are making your preapproach. Then your opening interview approach will bridge the gap between greeting the person and conducting the opening interview. Of course, use the time wisely, create a relaxed atmosphere, present your business and personal credentials, and set the stage through the interview. Strategic questions are used as a qualifying procedure through which we determine if there is a need. In other words, is there a problem to isolate in the first place? We can find out only through asking strategic questions. Once you've done that, is money available for him to be able to solve his problem? And can he be motivated to buy? And this author says then, and only then, can he be said to be a prospect. In other words, then and only then can he qualify to be one of these 10 people who you're supposed to see this week. Not only does he have the money to buy—proper questions can often give you the solution to that. A man may have an endowment or he ought to have a whole life—one that he's had for 10 years—that you can change to a whole life with this same company. We've gone over that before. Many techniques of obtaining money to buy. If you find that his wife is working and they're saving all that money, and that's something else that you should determine in the interview, then there is a source of money. So a part of this, of course, is to obtain a source of money. This is just a step-by-step—nothing new to any of us but a few things we have to be reminded of a little—step-by-step procedure in arriving at these 10 that we are trying to line up this week.

Now once you get into the sale and once you get this qualified prospect in the sales interview, we—all of us—are guilty of certain violations that prevent us from making a sale. It's not recognizing the prospect's buying signals. By lacking flexibility in the sales presentation— I could hear part of it and Rod heard part of it the other day when Mrs. Pittman was up here and, Jim, you and Jed were talking to her. It looked like at the beginning of that interview that the sale was lost, didn't it, Rod? You remember?

SP2:   Sure did.

SM: Rod said that Jed's got to work that out. That lady has backed out since yesterday. But if it had not been for flexibility in the interview, it would have been shot. But she changed from wanting to buy life insurance to wanting disability income and without some flexibility, right quick, the sale would have been lost. By not being prepared to close, quite often we go into an interview and we can even violate basic things, like not having an application with us, for that matter.

SP1:   I did that.

SM: I've done that, too. I did it when the office was 20 miles away, one time. I looked and the agent looked at me and I looked at him and neither one had an application. But this is referring to something more—not quite that basic, by not being prepared to close. If we go and expect to sell whole life, we ought to be prepared to offer terms, if that's what it takes. We ought to be prepared to shift to a different type of sale on some other member of the family. In other words, we ought to be prepared to shift gears right in the middle of the interview if we have to— by being more interested in talking than making a sale. I told y'all about the time, one time, when I was on a program when I first came into the business and we had this training expert from New York, and told me right quick when I got through. He said you did one hell of a job of educating, but a sorry job of selling. Quite often, we're all guilty of that. After years and years and years in the business, I am still conscious of that problem of sticking with the sale rather than trying to educate a person to what the problem is. So that's a right quick coverage of the points I wanted to go over this morning. We're talking about the selling conduct to the sale, the flexibility and all this sort of thing.

This excerpt is not intended as representative of most sales meetings but it does serve as an example of the contents of communications between sales managers and salespeople and how interactions occur between people.

The interactions and contents of communications between the sales manager and salespeople are likely to be similar for similar types of firms but different between industries. In industrial marketing, face-to-face interactions between the sales manager and salespeople are less likely to occur weekly compared with an insurance sales meeting. The purchase behavior activities and problems of key customers are likely to take up most of the time and communications content between the sales manager and salespeople in industrial marketing.

Selling Costs and Sales Volume

Some measures of the compensation for sales and how compensation is related to sales volume should be made to determine if problems exist in an organization. Table C—7–2 is an example of data on compensation and sales volume made available from the American Supply Association, which serves plumbing distributors.

Notice that the typical rates of sales compensation cost to sales has been very close to 3.0 percent over a long period of time. "Looking at 1980, if the rate of inflation continues at 10 percent, then the average level of compensation will be

$25,865 per salesman. The salesman, in turn, will have to generate sales per territory of $862,000 if his cost ratio is to be 3.0 percent." [4]

Sales cost ratios are likely to fluctuate by organizations within industries which means that some organizations are receiving more return in sales per dollar spent in selling. An example of this is shown in Figure C—7–3 for 4 firms carrying roughly the same product lines. A reasonable conclusion from the figure is that Company D should take some action to reduce its sales cost ratio.

Company D might attempt to increase sales volume while maintaining the same costs and thereby reducing the cost ratio. Or, another possibility maintain sales and decrease the number of salespeople. Such comparisons between firms are useful inputs (feedback) to making changes in sales management control variables. Unfortunately, comparisons between firms within industries are difficult to make. Data on sales volume and cost ratios are not readily available.

Salesperson Compensation Plans

Salesperson compensation takes one of 3 forms: straight salary, straight commission, and combination of salary and commission. In the straight salary plan, the salesperson receives a fixed income at regular intervals plus money to defray part or all expenses. Persons on fixed salaries are likely to be more willing to engage in activities not directly related to meeting with present customers, for example, completing reports, and attempting to open new accounts. However, the straight salary plan does not provide any incentive for the salesperson to out-perform previous sales levels or other salespeople.

The straight commission plan pays the salesperson a fixed percent of sales (the percent may be scheduled to decrease at certain sales levels). The straight com-

---

[4] William P. Hall, "Improving Sales Force Productivity," *Business Horizons*, August 1975.

Table   C—7–2
Trend in Sales Representative's Compensation
Cost Ratios
1959–1974

Year	Average Sales Per Territory	Average Compensation	Compensation As Percent of Sales
1959	$200,000	$ 6,000	3.0%
1962	238,600	7,200	3.0
1970	322,900	11,000	3.4
1974	536,900	14,600	2.7

Source: William P. Hall, "Improving Sales Force Productivity," *Business Horizons*, August 1975. Original source: American Supply Association.

Figure   C—7–3
Cost/Volume Relationship

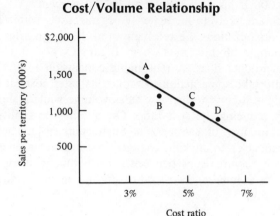

Source: William P. Hall, "Improving Sales Force Productivity," *Business Horizons,* August 1975, p. 34.

mission plan ties selling expenses directly to sales volume and permits management to relate sales goals for specific products to financial incentives to salespeople. Salespeople may be given special financial incentives to sell products with particularly high profit margins. However, the straight commission plan may reduce the salesperson's morale when sales fall due to external influences. Straight commission plans may be more costly to administer if sales volumes are high per territory.

The majority of business firms use a combination of salary and commission or bonus incentives. This plan is most attractive to management when sales volume depends upon motivating the salesperson and mangement wants more control over the salesperson's performance of nonselling duties.

Yearly evaluations should be made of the relationships between the cost ratios on sales alternative compensation plans.

As shown in Table C—7–3 and Figure C—7–4, a commission plan can be considered a "variable" expense from an accounting standpoint in that the expense dollars rise and fall directly with sales volume. However, when looked at as an expense ratio, it can be considered just the opposite—the ratio remains fixed as sales rise or fall. Conversely, the fixed cost plan (salary) or fixed plus variable plan (salary plus incentive) results in significant changes in the cost ratio as sales volume rises or falls.[5]

Thus, reducing the sales cost ratio is very different with a straight commission plan. However, the ratio is most responsive to a salary plan; and the ratio responds to a salary plus incentive plan. In general, substantial increases in the sales volume in an organization may imply a need to change salary compensation plans, and vice versa.

---

[5] Ibid.

Table C—7–3
Cost Impact of 3 Compensation at
Various Sales Levels

	Sales Volume (Thousands)		
Type of Plan	$250	$500	$750
Salary @ $25,000	$25,000	$25,000	$25,000
Commission @ 5% of sales	12,500	25,000	37,500
Salary @ $12,500 plus commission of 2.5%	18,750	25,000	31,250
Cost Ratios			
Salary plan	10.0%	5.0%	3.3%
Commission plan	5.0	5.0	5.0
Salary plus incentive plan	7.5	5.0	4.2

Source: William P. Hall, "Improving Sales Force Productivity," *Business Horizons,* August 1975, p. 34.

Figure C—7–4
Sales/Cost Relationship Based on
Various Compensation Plans

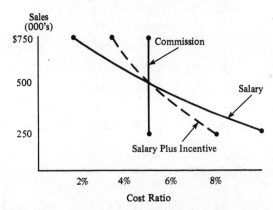

Source: William P. Hall, "Improving Sales Force Productivity," *Business Horizons,* August 1975, p. 36.

Salespeople's Activities

What activities of salespeople relate to selling products? Selling activities can be grouped into 5 categories: finding prospects, contacting prospects, stimulating desire for ownership, closing sales, and retaining customers. Some of the specific activities and approaches which can be used within each of these categories are listed in Table C—7–4.

A salesperson needs to perform well each of the 6 general activities. The following case illustrates why.

> Conrad Nave does a very poor job of finding prospects. However, once he acquires a prospect's name, he visits him promptly, delivers an excellent sales presentation, and closes a high proportion of sales after his demonstrations. His customers like him very much, especially since he visits them often after the equipment has been delivered to make sure the employees know how to operate it.
>
> Nave is one of the most likeable people in his organization and is always encouraging new salespeople and helping his peers improve their sales demonstrations. At the same time, Nave is looking around for another job since his commissions do not provide him with adequate earnings.[6]

Thus, a salesperson's performance is a multiplicative function of his or her performance in a number of selling activities. That is, if the salesperson's performance is low in prospecting, the salesperson's sales performance will be low no matter how high the performance in the other selling activities. This may be shown mathematically as

$$SP = (P) (C) (S) (F) (R)$$

where

$$SP = \text{sales performance}$$
$$P = \text{prospecting}$$
$$C = \text{contacting prospects}$$
$$S = \text{stimulating desire}$$
$$F = \text{closing sales (finish)}$$
$$R = \text{retaining customers}$$

If P is 5 percent of the norm, then SP will be low even if the other variables are all 200 percent above the norm: $SP = (.05)(2)(2)(2)(2) = .80$ or 80 percent.

Buyer/Seller Interactions

What are the contents of the communications between buyers and sellers? Is there a pattern of verbal behavior between buyers and sellers during sales meetings? Who is likely to be involved in buying and selling products? How can salespeople modify their interactions with customers to increase sales? These are some of the questions important in buyer/seller interactions.

Research on buyer/seller interactions has shown that one of a limited number of patterns of verbal behavior occur during such meetings. The general pattern of verbal behavior likely to occur is shown in Figure C—7–5, including 5 stages

---

[6] Marvin A. Jolson, *Sales Management: A Tactical Approach* (New York: Petrocelli/ Charter, 1977), p. 46.

Table   C—7–4
**Major Techniques Used by Salespeople
to Accomplish the 5 Promotional Tasks**

Finding prospects

Cold canvass
Telephone solicitation
Referrals from customers and other sources
Responses to mass-media advertising
Responses to direct mail or circulars passed out
Follow-up of will-call letters [a]
Past call-backs
Voluntary inquiries
Outside bird dogs [b]
Recommendations by suppliers
Contacting customers who have already purchased another company product
Trade shows and exhibits
Specialty-advertising responses (matchboxes, pens, calendars)
Friends and associates

Contacting prospects

Unsolicited visit
Announced periodic visit
Visit following telephone appointment
Visit following will-call letter
Visit by prospect to salesman's place of business on voluntary, invited, or ad-
    response basis

Stimulating desire for ownership

Personal sales presentation and demonstration
    Problem solving
    Demonstration of benefits
    Persuasion
Preconditioning literature and materials
Free-trial approach
Sales presentation by telephone

Closing sales

Demonstration of "now" needs
Price inducements
Product-scarcity approach
Two-man close [c]

---

[a] An unsolicited announcement that salesman will call at some future date. Promotional literature may or may not be included.

[b] Outside canvasser or lead-getting organization paid to locate prospects for the firm.

[c] A salesman who is unable to close an order due to inexperience or a perceived personality conflict can solicit the aid of an associate or supervisor.

Source: Marvin A. Jolson, *Sales Management: A Tactical Approach* (New York: Petrocelli/ Charter, 1977), p. 47.

Trial order
Selling oneself
High pressure and gimmicks

Retaining customers

Posttransactional service
Supplying market intelligence
Warmth and social contacts
Return and exchange privileges
Continuous customer contact

**Figure   C—7–5
A Dyadic Sales Process Model**

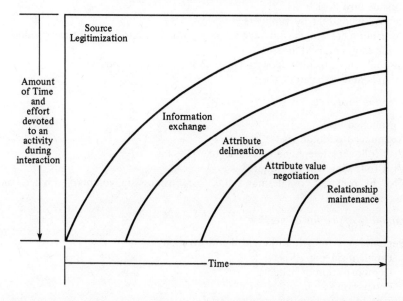

Source: David T. Wilson, "Dyadic Interaction," in Arch G. Woodside, Jagdish N. Sheth, and Peter D. Bennett, *Consumer and Industrial Buying Behavior* (New York: North-Holland, 1977), p. 361.

of interaction. The figure represents developmental or long terms as opposed to one-shot selling and buying situations.

The first few minutes of a meeting between buyer and seller are likely to be devoted to attempts by the salesperson to legitimize himself and the company as a useful and honest source of information. Unless this basic source acceptability is developed in the buyer, further communication tends to become ineffective if not impossible.

In the next stage (information exchange and problem identification), problems of the buyer through purchase are identified. The amount and nature of the

Figure C—7–6
Types of Contacts Between Buying and Selling Centers

a. Buying and Selling Centers for the Household

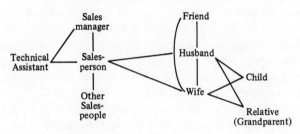

b. Buying and Selling Centers for the Firm

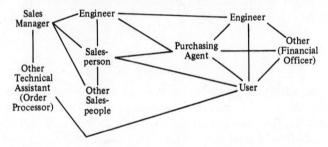

information exchanged is probably a function of the relationship established in the source legitimization stage. A salesperson perceived as an expert and similar to the buyer is likely to be given more information more quickly than other salespeople. All salespeople may obtain the standard type of information, but the more favored salesperson may get additional data (e.g., which attributes are important and who is the key decision maker in the buying center).

The buying center are all the people involved in the decisions to buy the product. For important purchases and products purchased for the first time (often called extensive problem solving or new task buying situations), several persons are likely to be part of the buying center. Similarly, the selling center may include several persons. Persons likely to be involved in the buying and selling centers for important purchase situations are shown in Figure C—7–6. Notice in the figure that persons are shown to be involved in the centers for both consumers and industrial buying situations. However, the number of types of contacts between centers is shown to be greater in the industrial situation.

In the attribute delineation stage, the selling and buying center develops the bundle of attributes that will be exchanged. Many of these will be discussed explicitly, for example, product features and credit terms. The salesperson clearly influences attribute determination and evaluation.[7]

[7] Richard W. Olshavsky, "Customer-Salesman Interaction in Appliance Retailing," *Journal of Marketing Research* **10** (1973), pp. 208–212 Published by the American Marketing Association. Jacobo A. Varela, *Psychological Solutions to Social Problems* (New York: Academic Press. 1971)

Determining the attribute set and the exchange rate (attribute value negotiation) of each attribute can be viewed as the *bargaining process*. The bargaining process may not be overwhelming in frequency or volume but it is likely to exert an important influence on the ultimate purchase outcome.

Relationship maintenance is the last stage in the interaction. New personnel attributes related to sentiments (friendship) is likely to occur in this stage. Some salespeople use the relationship maintenance stage to reduce the buyer's tendency toward *postdecision regret*. Postdecision regret is the tendency of buyers to want to back out of their decision to buy. To overcome this tendency, the salesperson may use one of 2 strategies: over-persuasion and innoculation.

Over-persuasion is the verbal behavior of the salesperson to get more commitments in as many areas as possible after the buyer has agreed to purchase the product. An innoculation is a direct attempt to prevent other salespeople from convincing the buyer to change his or her mind and cancel the prior order for the product.

Reactance

Salespeople may attempt to provoke as well as avoid reactance on the part of the buyer during the sales encounter. *Reactance* is the state where "as the pressure to comply increases, the pressure not to comply also increases and the result and effect on the individual's final response is difficult to predict. In addition, where the magnitude of reactance is less than the pressure to comply, the individual will do what is suggested but less enthusiastically than if no reactance were experienced." [8] Thus, the freer the buyer feels in making a commitment, the greater the buyer's strength to commitment.

A seller may initially provoke reactance to help establish the buyer's freedom of choice as perceived by the buyer. The seller may use selected questions likely to elicit a negative response from the buyer to provoke reactance in the direction desired by the seller. Later, the seller can avoid negative answers by asking questions likely to elicit a positive response. Such approaches have been used in a number of situations. The following case is an example of such an approach.

The selling firm is a small manufacturing company attempting to market textile products in a new market to retailers. The following persuasion design was developed and applied in the buyer's stores. Mr. Sales is a salesperson for the manufacturer and Mr. Lopez is the store owner.

Sales: Good afternoon, Mr. Lopez.

Lopez: Good afternoon. Pardon me, sir, but how do you know my name? I don't believe I know you.

Sales: You are right, Mr. Lopez. You don't know me, and I shall introduce myself—Juan Perez, and it's a pleasure meeting you. I am one of the representatives of PQX. The truth is I have heard a lot about you from some of your colleagues. When I called on them, many

---

[8] J. W. Brehm, *A Theory of Psychological Reactance* (New York: Academic Press, 1966).

suggested I see you. You are supposed to be very experienced in these lines, and that's the reason for my visit.

Lopez: That's nice of them. Of what use can I be to you? What do you people make?

Sales: Well, we're new in the market. We are probably going to start out with beddings, although our major interest will be in home decoration and furnishing in general.

Lopez: What do you plan to do in the way of beddings?

Sales: Our outlook is rather broad. We'll probably go into sheets, pillows, and pillowcases, and even into quilted and other bedspreads.

Lopez: Sounds fine. Bring me some samples, and we'll see. If your prices are right, maybe we'll be able to make a deal.

Sales: Excuse me, Mr. Lopez, but perhaps I didn't make myself clear. I am not planning on selling you anything. Although before too long we will be manufacturing, what I would like from you, if it's at all possible, is to obtain some technical and commercial advice—something that can be of use to my firm. I ask for this based on the experience and reputation you have in this field.

Lopez: All right. Go ahead and ask anything you want.

Sales: Tell me, Mr. Lopez, is it true that quilted bedspreads give you a large profit margin?

Lopez: Why? Are you thinking of going into that first?

Sales: Well, it's one of the lines we are considering, but the reason I ask is that you seem to be carrying a very profitable line of these.

Lopez: No! I have to carry these because clients ask for them, but the markup is very low. It's often below 10 percent, and there are some in which there is no profit at all. They're no good commercially, and the competition has all but wrecked the prices and profits.

Sales: I suppose you make up for the low margin by having a high turnover due to massive sales.

Lopez: Not on your life! Everyone has them. Take the case of Kase: They cost 5.3 and they are selling them all over the place for 5.5. Do you think that's good business?

Sales: I suppose that looked at from that angle, you are right, but I bet you don't have any problems in deliveries. You probably order today and have the goods delivered in a day or two.

Lopez: What? Never! You don't seem to be too knowledgeable about these things. I have an urgent order placed a month and a half ago, and here we are right in the middle of the season with no signs yet of delivery! How does that sound to you?

Sales: Gee, I appreciate these facts. I certainly see you are right, we do need advice.

Lopez: Yes, one has to have been in the market for sometime to know things, and if you wish to get ahead you had better have more information.

Sales: Well, you see now Mr. Lopez why I came to see you. Any advice you give me will certainly be useful to my firm. Tell me, Mr. Lopez, in your estimation what are the conditions that a quilted bedspread must fulfill in order to fulfill usefulness and still be easy for you to sell?

Lopez: To begin with, it must be competitively priced. It should be neatly made, should come in exclusive colors, have lots of filling, and especially not be sold to just anyone.

Sales: Do you think that a new firm could be successful if it did things well, that is, if it acted in the way you suggest?

Lopez: I can assure you. Besides, I'd be one of the first to buy.

Sales: Well, Mr. Lopez, you can be sure that I'll make your comments known to our management, and I would like to invite you in the future to see our plant so that you can tell if we have followed your advice. May I count on your paying us a call when we are ready to start production?

Lopez: You sure can, Mr. Perez. That's what we're all here for, to help one another to do more and work better.

Sales: Thank you very much, Mr. Lopez, for the time you've afforded me. As soon as things take shape, I'll be glad to call on you so we can set a date for your visit to us.

Lopez: All right. Thank you very much, Mr. Perez, I'll be very glad to pay you a call.[9]

With slight variations with different store managers, this persuasive design was successful in over 90 percent of the cases, compared with less than 5 percent success with previous straight persuasion attempts. The salesperson, of course, already knew of the drawbacks that Mr. Lopez mentioned. By making reactance-provoking statements, he got the store owner to find fault with his present products and suppliers. Afterward, the conversation led naturally to a request for a definition of what the distinguishing attributes should be for an acceptable product. The prior reactance led Mr. Lopez to make a definition of exactly the characteristics that the sales firm was going to incorporate into its product. This constituted a tremendous commitment on the client's part. If he defined so clearly what the product should be, it would be hard for him not to buy when offered goods having exactly those qualifications.

Summary

Sales management involves several related decisions—recruitment, training, allocating, supervising, compensating, and evaluating. At the same time, sales man-

---

[9] Varela, *op. cit.,* pp. 130–131.

agement should be recognized as a subsystem of the promotion mix and as an element in the marketing mix of an organization.

Several sales management decisions should be directly tied to measures of sales force performance, that is, sales volume, profitable product mix, and sales volume cost. These measures can be used as units of measurement to provide feedback for sales management decisions.

The level of sales performance for salespeople is a multiplicative function of several selling activities which are prospecting, contacting prospects, stimulating desire, closing sales, and retaining customers. Poor performance in any one of these activities will produce low sales no matter how high the salesperson's performance on the other activities.

Buyer/seller interactions tend to follow a limited number of set patterns. The seller can direct the pattern of interactions to affect the outcome of the sales encounter. Over-persuasion, innoculation, and reactance provocation and avoidance are examples of effective persuasion techniques in selling.

Discussion Questions

1. What salesperson's output variables can be changed to improve sales force performance?

2. How can the quality of sales calls be measured?

3. Fill in the blocks for the following diagram and identify the dependent variables in the system.

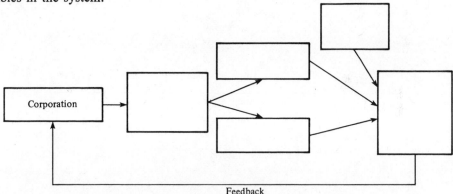

4. What is wrong with the following diagram? Explain.

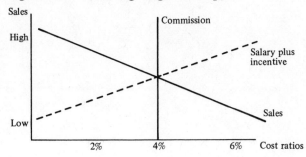

5. What is the difference between attribute delineation and attribute value negotiation?

6. Complete the following diagrams and list 2 similarities and 2 differences between the diagrams.

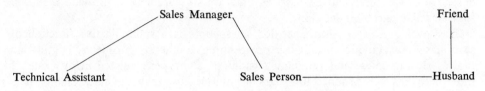

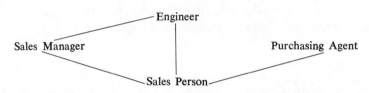

7. Explain reactance theory and describe how it might be applied to improve the effectiveness of a sales presentation.

Hollywood-At-Home, Inc.: Promoting In-Home Movies

Marvin A. Jolson, University of Maryland

The Industry and Company

Hollywood-At-Home, Inc. (HAH) was incorporated in January 1976, to engage in the subscription TV business. The public had been exposed to current, unedited, commercial-free movies in hotels and motels, and early tests disclosed that apartment and condominium dwellers were willing to pay a fee to receive these films in their homes.

Television programming has moved increasingly to movies since 1961 when they were first shown regularly in prime time. Industry spokespersons were of the opinion that uninterrupted, more up-to-date, uncensored movies would cut into free-TV audiences or else force a change in programming. Television did not kill radio, as many people predicted it would, but it forced a change in programming. Apparently, the same is proving true of pay versus free TV.

In mid-1975, 10 million homes were hooked up to one or another of the nation's 3,240 cable systems. But cable penetration in each market—the proportion of people who can sign up for cable who actually do—was not what cable operators had hoped for. In New York, it was about 30 percent. As with "load factors" in the airline industry, "penetration" is crucial in the cable business. "Once you rip up the streets, lay the cable, and endure additional costs of central overhead, the cost of hooking up new subscribers—particularly in an already-wired building—is minimal." [1]

A major objective of the cable system is to provide acceptable TV reception in areas where the reception of conventional TV signals is less than satisfactory, or where consumers perceive the number of available channels as inadequate. These problems are not as prevalent in major metropolitan areas as they are in rural or

[1] Andrew Tobias, "Are You Ready for Super-TV?" *New York Magazine*, August 4, 1973, pp. 25–32.

remote locations. Yet when *Home Box Office* introduced its current, unedited movie offerings in 1972, cable subscriptions increased drastically in affluent New York areas.

At the time of inception of HAH, the home TV movie industry was in its infancy, dating back approximately 4 years. Accordingly, there was no substantial track record upon which to rely and no reliable record of profitability in the industry. The HAH operation was typical of similar organizations throughout the country who placed major emphasis on the hotel/motel market and subsequently found that the greatest potential for expansion lay in the residential apartment/ condominium market.

Transmission Methods

The company had a choice of transmitting programs by use of in-house cassette units placed in each building or microwave transmission from a centrally-located broadcast studio. After considering the advantages and disadvantages of each system, as summarized in Figure 29–1, HAH's founder and president, Henry Newhouse, decided in favor of the microwave approach. HAH was located in a major metropolitan western city and contracted for transmission rights with Microband Corporation of America, a New York-based firm that holds the FCC common carrier license.

Thus, the subscriber in a multi-dwelling building receives a program on the TV receiver transmitted from a central point via microwave broadcast transmission and not via cable. However, the signal can also be transmitted to the receiving equipment of a cable system for distribution to private homes. HAH contracts with movie studios to rent 35 mm film transcribed onto video tape then transmitted in scrambled form to receiving antennas erected by HAH on the roofs of apartment buildings.

Selling Problems

HAH's most optimistic forecast was that it could ultimately acquire 60,000 subscribers, 12 percent of the 500,000 apartment units in the greater metropolitan area. By mid-1977, the firm had approximately 3,500 subscribers and revenues of nearly $550,000 per year. Profits were at the breakeven point. In July 1977, Henry Newhouse was in the process of coordinating the elements of the firm's promotional program, especially the personal selling effort. In particular, Newhouse was concerned with formulation of the optimal remarketing program, for example, the method of obtaining additional subscribers in buildings where the HAH system had been operative for some time.

For reasons that will be explained in the following section, sales force turnover was excessively high and recruiting and training new sales force members was a continuous process. Sales manager Lucy Mora reported to work each weekday at noon, performed administrative and planning functions during the day, recruited and trained salespeople during the late afternoon and early evening, and was out in the field with her salespeople each evening. She was also quite active most Saturdays and Sundays since prospective subscribers were available for contact

Table 29–1
Comparison of Microwave System
With In-House Cassettes

Microwave	In-House Cassettes
1. Personnel not needed to operate equipment.	1. Personnel needed to operate equipment.
2. Uses one tape for entire city which means less repeated usage.	2. Cassette tapes are bicycled from building to building, thus reducing quality with each play.
3. Microwave programming is more versatile and can be expanded because it broadcasts from a single location to all parts of the city.	3. Cassette programming is limited to that which must be physically placed into the machine by an attendant.
4. Microwave equipment is maintained daily at broadcasting studio.	4. Cassette decks have to be lubricated, demagnetized and their heads cleaned frequently.
5. One-inch tape provides superior image.	5. Three-quarter-inch tape used in cassette machines.
6. Reel-to-reel machines provide more uniform transport.	6. Cassette machines used in-house operations.
7. Initial investment for broadcast studio and transmitter is approximately $250,000. In addition, the cost of installing an antenna on each building is approximately $400.	7. Each in-house cassette console costs $4,000. No antenna is required.

on weekends. Lucy had the authority to control her own working hours but because of her conscientious nature, she seldom took time off. Yet she was both physically and mentally exhausted and was giving serious thought to submitting her resignation.

The Promotional System

Company marketing efforts were aimed at two distinct groups: (1) individuals who reside in "fresh" buildings, that is, buildings in which the HAH television network is being introduced for the first time, and (2) individuals who reside in "exposed" buildings, that is, buildings in which HAH already has a substantial number of subscribers.

Fresh Buildings

At the time the company was formed, Henry Newhouse, the founder, had enjoyed 25 successful years as a builder, developer, and property manager in the local area. Because of his established contacts, the company was immediately successful in convincing apartment building owners and managers that it would be to their advantage to equip their properties with the unique HAH network.

After receiving formal permission from building management, HAH erects a parabolic receiving dish on the building roof. The system is then connected into the "head end" of the building's master antenna. This connection technically permits each resident to receive HAH programs assuming the resident's TV set is connected to the building's master antenna. The resident is offered a choice of subscribing or not. A subscriber pays a small installation charge and a $10.00 deposit for a small box on his TV set that "unscrambles" or "decodes" the HAH signal. The programs appear on an unused TV channel during specified hours each day, usually 6:00 pm to 2:00 am. An added benefit to the subscriber is that installation usually improves TV reception on all channels.

The monthly subscription rate is $12.00 and the subscriber may view current, uncut movies without commercials. *Uncut* movies are those with the same explicit materials that appear in theaters. The decoder box is equipped with a parental guidance key that permits parents to prevent children from viewing the private channel.

Prior to any personal selling activities, HAH places attractive signs in strategic building locations to advise residents that the service will be available. A notice is then mailed to each resident, on the letterhead of the building, advising the prospective subscriber that a HAH representative will call to explain the service and respond to questions. Representatives are well-trained, well-dressed young men and women who make evening sales calls to prospective subscribers who have been sent the prenotification letter.

The in-home sales presentation is brief (about ten minutes in duration) but quite exciting due to the unique appeal of the product. Every evening on the HAH television network, two and sometimes three features are presented. Each month, 8 premiere feature films and 4 previously-shown films are available. In addition, a number of monthly specials—including music, cultural, sports, and night club events—are offered. Salespeople emphasize that subscribers can enjoy the same movies currently showing at local theaters while avoiding the hassle of driving, parking, standing in line, paying babysitters, and spending $3.00 or more per person. Moreover, the subscriber is not involved in a lease or long-term commitment. The service may be cancelled with a 30-day written notice, and the decoder box will be removed and the $10.00 deposit refunded.

Aside from supplying an initial list of occupants and a monthly list of new move-ins, building personnel are not involved in the operation. In some buildings, the maintenance man removes the decoder box a day or two before the tenant moves. For this courtesy, both the resident manager and maintenance man receive free HAH service. HAH handles all transmitting, distribution of movie programs and announcements, collections of monies, and processing of complaints.

HAH salespeople are either students or young men and women who are employed elsewhere during the day. They represent HAH several evenings a week and often on weekends. Salespeople earn between $100 and $200 per month based on an average sales commission of $7.00 per order.

Typical door-to-door selling problems prevail. It is the policy of some buildings to forbid such direct solicitation or to require that the salesperson be announced from the lobby. At least 30 percent of the prospective subscribers are not at home when first contacted. Recruiting is difficult due to the perceived negative features of a job that requires door-to-door contacts on a straight commission basis. Sales force turnover is high since those who do not experience immediate success terminate quickly. Therefore, recruiting and training are never-ending processes frustrating to management.

Exposed Buildings

Company records show that the initial concentrated selling effort in a fresh building results in sales of 8 to 20 percent of the tenants depending upon building demographics. The remaining residents do not subscribe either because the sales proposal is rejected or because the salesperson, for one or more reasons, fails to make contact with the prospect in order to deliver a sales presentation. Moreover, approximately 6 percent of all subscribers terminate their service each month because of move-outs, dissatisfaction with the movies, financial, or other personal reasons.

Clearly, then, there are a large number of nonsubscribers in all exposed buildings at all times. Due to the limited number of available fresh buildings, and HAH's substantial capital and labor costs in "opening" a fresh building, the remarketing program in exposed buildings is of paramount importance.

In July 1977, HAH is operating in more than eighty apartment buildings, approximately 25,000 apartment units. Using a 3 percent monthly move rate, 750 fresh prospects are available each month in exposed buildings.

Mr. Newhouse noted that new move-ins (NMI's) are unusually good prospects for company offerings:

> NMI's possess all three characteristics of a great prospect for our product. They have *buying power* since in most cases they are working couples with double incomes. Second, since the wife works all day, she has *less sales resistance* than the typical housewife who is confronted by numerous door-knockers every day of the week. Moreover, many NMI's are often new-marrieds or singles who have had *limited exposure to salespeople* and therefore are not canvass-wise as yet. Finally, young people under the age of 36 *welcome modern films that strike at realism in all forms.* They enjoy westerns, crime dramas, and story lines that involve intellectually mature content.

Despite the perceived high quality of NMI's as HAH prospects, there are certain sales logistics problems when 750 prospects are spread throughout 80 or more buildings. The salesperson must drive from building to building, park, ride up and down elevators, and suffer disappointment when many of these prospects are not at home or will not answer the door. Thus, despite a relatively high rate of conversion of presentations into sales, fewer presentations and sales are possible in a given evening.

Incumbent tenants in an exposed building represent an even more formidable selling hurdle. These people either rejected the HAH proposition at an earlier date or could not be reached previously. Unlike NMI's or those who live in a fresh building, these people may already know the HAH story. They may have been exposed to the negative comments of former subscribers who have since discontinued the service. They may know the price of the service and may have developed firm reasons opposing the subscription. A high level of sales resistance by this group may require persuasive selling efforts which, in Mr. Newhouse's opinion, may not lead to a satisfied subscriber over a long period of time. Furthermore, many salespeople are not cut out for persuasive or creative selling.

Previous Remarketing Efforts

When Lucy Mora came to work for HAH, she was convinced by Mr. Newhouse that the door-to-door selling method would be appropriate for the HAH operation. For more than a year she devoted herself completely to the task of building a sales force. She visualized the ultimate development of two or three unit field managers, each of whom would work with small groups of salespeople.

To date, Lucy has not been successful in developing a single dependable assistant. She finds it more difficult to "sell recruits the job" than to sell subscriptions for the HAH program. She has read many articles and reports about successful direct-selling companies, but she now is quite doubtful that direct-to-consumer personal selling is the correct approach for HAH:

> 'No Canvassing' signs are now posted in most buildings. Residents are reluctant to open doors because of high crime rates or unwillingness to talk to salespeople. The unit sale and earned commission are so small that the sales agent's gasoline costs often exceed earnings. It is getting so that applicants will not even answer our ads and it is like pulling teeth to get someone to try out the job for a few days. Our product is great but there must be a better way to sell it.

Mr. Newhouse did not overtly agree with Lucy, but since he had no direct-selling experience himself, he was not in a position to make any suggestions to ease her burden. He did, however, agree to experiment with other selling methods that would be supplementary to the direct-to-consumer approach. He felt, inwardly, that direct selling was suitable for selling in "fresh" buildings but difficult, to say the least, in "exposed" buildings.

HAH attempted to employ building resident managers, rental clerks, and other apartment building employees as part-time salespeople. In general, these people exhibited a major reluctance to sell. They felt that efforts to sell to tenants would interfere with their primary occupations and that there should be a sharp separation between building services and HAH programs.

The company spent several thousand dollars to create a multi-color direct mailing piece which includes a postage-free return card. The return rate was a minuscule 4 percent. The company then attempted to improve the response rate by directing a telephone call to individuals who had failed to return the reply card. The phone message included mention of a 50 percent reduction of the installation fee. The telephone follow-up did little to improve the return rate.

The company even spent more than thirty days experimenting with several phone solicitation approaches. The method was mildly successful in "fresh" buildings but completely unsuccessful in "exposed" buildings. Excessive costs soon resulted in termination of telephone solicitation efforts.

The Free Trial

Following some amount of dissatisfaction with the ventures described above, HAH executives were convinced that the remarketing program should be spearheaded by an offer to expose nonsubscribers to seven days of HAH movies without charge. The underlying assumption is that once exposed to theater-like movies on a living room level, residents would be reluctant to give up this luxury.

Two types of free trial hookups are possible. The first is a *private connection* including a decoder, the same currently used by present subscribers. This type of hookup includes a special wall plate and involves a company cost of $13.00 per unit including labor, supplies, and equipment. The resident is required to put up a refundable deposit of $27.00. At the conclusion of the free trial, the prospect can elect to:

1. Subscribe at the standard rate of $12.00 per month, plus a $15.00 installation charge. These charges have been covered by the $27.00 deposit. An additional deposit of $10.00 for the decoder box is billed the following month.

2. Reject the subscription and receive a refund of $27.00 when the decoder box is returned and the connection to the wall plate is removed.

3. Reject the subscription but retain the wall plate and private connection in order to improve TV reception on all channels. The previously collected $27.00 pays for installation.

The second type of free trial hookup is a *mass connection* whereby all TV sets in the building that are connected to the master antenna would automatically receive HAH programs on a predetermined channel. For example, for a 7-day period, all regular programs on Channel 45 would be aborted between the hours of 6:00 pm and 2:00 am, so that HAH programs could be shown. In these cases, HAH programs could be viewed without the need for a special wall plate or decoder box. The company unit cost of installation is negligible and tenants would not be subject to installation charges or deposits. Following the free trial period, the HAH signal is removed and those who wish to subscribe must have the private connection.

Clearly, the private connection requires prior permission of the tenant along with payment of an installation fee and deposit for a decoder box. This permission may be obtained by a personal sales visit, a telephone call, or mail.

The mass connection requires permission from the building management but not from the resident. However, its effectiveness as a promotional tactic requires that the prospective subscriber is aware of and responsive to the promotion. This responsiveness may be solicited by a personal visit or a telephone call [2] and, to a lesser degree, by mailing the resident an announcement of the impending free trial.

Additionally, each month attractive program guides are left at the desk of each exposed building to be taken. Large (10 x 16) promotional displays are put in laundry rooms, bulletin boards, and the reception desk in the lobby.

Remarketing Suggestions

Following a series of meetings of HAH executives and their advisors, the following promotional ideas were under consideration:

1. New move-ins (NMIs) would be telephoned and notified that the HAH program is active in their building, and that they are eligible for 7-day free trial on a private connection basis. The telephone correspondent would inform NMIs that information describing the HAH program and the free trial will be mailed along with a guide of current movies being shown. The NMI is told that he/she will be recontacted by telephone in a few days to see if he/she is willing to authorize a free trial.

2. If the NMI completely rejects the HAH program and the free trial, no literature is mailed. It is estimated that about 80 percent of those contacted by telephone will be willing to look over the literature.

3. The second phone call would inform the NMI about the enthusiastic response to the free trial offer, and the phone correspondent would offer to answer any questions the NMI might have. Assuming the prospect wishes to authorize the free trial, he/she may return the free trial agreement along with a credit card number or check for $27.00. A private connection will be made within a few days. It is estimated that about half of those who receive the literature and the second phone call will authorize the free trial.

The agreement indicates that if the NMI decides not to subscribe to HAH service after the free trial, the NMI may so notify the company and receive a refund of $27.00 when the decoder and installation material are recovered or may purchase the installation only. HAH will recover the decoder, and the deposit ($27.00) will pay for that installation. The company estimates that of those authorizing the free trial, 50 percent will subscribe, 20 percent will retain the private connection, and 30 percent will buy nothing. Thus, the forecast calls for subscriptions from 20 percent of those who received the original phone call.

4. Incumbent tenants (ITs) in exposed buildings would be approached in a parallel but somewhat different way than that used to promote subscriptions from NMIs. Since ITs in a given building far outnumber NMIs, the former could

---

[2] HAH's experience with telephone promotional programs has not been satisfactory because phone number are difficult and costly to obtain. Lists supplied by buildings do not include phone numbers. Many phone numbers are not listed in the directory, especially those of NMI's and people who desire unlisted numbers. Telephone company information operators will give out only one or two phone numbers at a time.

be best converted into subscribers by use of a mass connection approach. ITs would be telephoned and informed that on a given date the entire building will have the benefit of a 7-day free showing of HAH programs. The purpose of the phone call is to announce the event and to inform the tenant that information describing the HAH program, including a movie guide, is being mailed. The ITs are told that they will be recontacted at or near the conclusion of the trial period so that questions pertaining to HAH service can be answered.

5. The literature is mailed and a second phone call is made as the trial period nears completion. Those who wish to subscribe would be asked to fill in a brief agreement and return it along with a credit card number or check for an installation fee, decoder box deposit, and the first month's subscription.

6. When the payment has been received, a private connection will be made. HAH officials predict that 12 percent of the contacted ITs will subscribe.

Sales Force Recruitment

The telephone selling system would be manned by part-time people to be recruited from the following sources:

1. Salespeople who are presently contacting residents of fresh buildings on a door-to-door basis.

2. Newspaper ads.

3. On-site representatives to be enlisted by advertisements on the HAH TV screen. These are satisfied customers who are familiar with the HAH service. Each person will be assigned a logistically acceptable area within 5 to 10 minutes driving time of their own apartment house.

Discussion Questions

1. Is HAH's product offering well conceived?

2. Evaluate the proposed remarketing suggestions.

3. HAH management has identified three separate and distinct market segments: residents of fresh buildings, NMIs, and ITs. Do you agree that three separate and distinct selling approaches should be used to reach these segments?

4. What is your appraisal of the future potential of the HAH operation?

Whitmore Brick and Block Company

James M. Clapper, Wake Forest University

Early in October, 1975, Bill Hollingsworth, marketing manager at Whitmore Brick and Block Company, was reviewing his first draft of the proposed revision in the compensation plan for the company's salespeople. With just under $15 million annual sales, Whitmore was one of the largest brick manufacturers both in North Carolina and in the country. Recently, however, the company had been affected by the general slump in the brick industry and was not experiencing the sales growth it had in the recent past and which was still expected by management. Management felt that the failure of the firm to meet earnings expectations was due only in part to a general industry slump and that much could be done to correct the situation by improving Whitmore's marketing effort. In particular there was some concern that the company's personal selling effort could be improved. Jack Johnson, Whitmore's controller, recently completed a review of sales representatives' salaries and sales performance figures which indicated there was little relationship between the representatives' earnings and their productivity. After discussion between Johnson and company marketing executives, the decision was made to examine whether changes to the existing sales compensation scheme should be made in an effort to both increase performance motivation and establish a clearer relationship between performance and compensation. Accordingly, Bill Hollingsworth was given the assignment of reviewing the compensation scheme and making recommendations for changes that would introduce an effective incentive element. Hollingsworth was reviewing his initial work on this project to determine whether he was on the right track.

The Brick Industry

Brick manufacturing is a $360 million a year industry nationwide. Manufacturers, located throughout the country, are most heavily concentrated in the Southeast. Historically, firms in this capital intensive industry have been small, family-owned and managed operations. This is still largely true today with approximately 65 percent of the firms having annual sales of less than $3 million. A strong production orientation has been a tradition in the industry with the result that today the industry enjoys perhaps the highest level of production efficiency that can be found among any of the building material industries.

Because of the comparatively high cost of shipping finished brick, manufacturers have found it largely uneconomical to compete for business in markets better served by firms located closer to the market in question. As a result, the brick industry is characterized by high levels of intraregional competition but significantly lower levels of interregional competition.

Brick is widely recognized in the construction industry as a high-quality building material. Available in a wide variety of colors, sizes, and forms and with a variety of performance characteristics, brick has many diverse uses. Despite the recognized quality and versatility of brick products, total demand for brick has not grown at the same pace as has the demand for competitive products. Many people, both within and outside the industry, believe that the cause of this poor competitive performance is the fact that marketing practices in the industry have remained rather primitive compared to those of other industries. According to a report by Arthur D. Little, Inc.:

> Few efforts have been made to discover the real needs of the consumer or specifier, and even today the industry is fairly remote from the decision-making process that effects its sales. Although companies have increased their sales force in the recent past and a few use advertising and other promotional methods, the production orientation still predominates. Informal conversations between two or more brick manufacturers are invariably centered upon machine design, plant labor problems, production costs, and other manufacturing considerations. The industry has long operated, and continues to operate, in a marketing vacuum and has abdicated its promotional responsibilities to the dealer and distributor and to the regional and national association.[1]

Relying on dealers and distributors for marketing and promoting brick has not been a particularly effective strategy. Building material dealers and distributors commonly carry a wide variety of competing lines, serving as outlets not only for brick but also for such commodities as concrete brick and wood products as well. Thus, dealers do not perceive their interests as being directly aligned with those of the brick industry. Further, dealers in the building materials field typically play very passive, order-taker roles, dispensing technical price information but making little effort to influence customer choices.

The promotional efforts that have been carried on in the industry have been directed at contractors and design professionals. These efforts have taken 2 basic forms, promotion of the various uses of brick and promotion of the quality of brick construction. Nonbuilding uses of brick such as patio paving, have especially been singled out for promotion by the industry. The primary quality themes used include brick's low maintenance, permanence, and the aesthetic appeal.

---

[1] *The Brick Industry: An Industry at the Crossroads,* Arthur D. Little, Inc., Report C–73958 (Cambridge, MA, March 1972), p. 64.

Pricing among firms in the industry has been very competitive. When "in-place" costs are compared, brick also is competitively priced with most other building materials, the major exception being wood siding. In the residential housing segment of the market, the competition from wood siding is an important factor. Costs vary widely from area to area and fluctuate rapidly over time, but the in-place cost for wood per square foot of wall area is roughly half that of brick. However, at late 1975 prices, for a home with 2,000 sq ft of floor space, the initial cost differential between brick and wood siding would be less than $1,800. In addition, this cost would be more than recovered in maintenance savings over the life of the house.

The Industry in North Carolina

North Carolina is known as "Brick Capital of the Nation" because of the state's preeminence in the industry. Twenty-two manufacturers located in the state produce approximately one billion brick annually for roughly 15 percent of the entire nation's output. North Carolina has been the nation's leading brick producer for over 20 years. Although the industry situation in North Carolina largely parallels that of the industry at large, there is one major difference: North Carolina manufacturers have not relied as heavily on dealers and distributors to sell their product. The 22 firms in the state employ among them over 100 salespeople and secure approximately 90 percent of their sales as direct sales. This figure compares with the national average of approximately 30 percent direct sales.

The Company

Whitmore Brick Company, as it was known then, was founded in 1938 by John Whitmore. Whitmore was able to capitalize on his 15 years experience in the brick industry and progress for the new firm was rapid. By 1957 the Whitmore plant had an annual capacity of 100 million brick per year.

In 1964, Whitmore Brick bought the Thomasville Block Company at Thomasville in an effort to diversify the holdings of the company and to be able to offer a complete line of masonary products to its customers. At this time the firm's name was changed to its present form. During the 1960s and early 1970s, Whitmore continued to expand both by acquiring other firms and by building new plants. By 1975, Whitmore possessed a total production capacity of 400 million brick per year and 10 million concrete block.

Whitmore's Marketing Effort

Whitmore's primary market area is the Carolinas and south central Virginia. This area accounts for approximately 80 percent of the company's sales with the remaining 20 percent distributed throughout the eastern half of the United States.

Whitmore has traditionally been a leader in marketing brick and concrete block in its market area. The firm has one of the most extensive product lines in the business, manufacturing a wide variety of different styles and handling the products of other firms to meet customer needs where there are gaps in the Whitmore line.

In its marketing area, the firm has been a leader in consumer advertising and promotion. Whitmore was the first brick company in the Carolinas to use mass media ads, starting this practice in the late 1950s. Today the firm uses a mix of radio, television, newspaper, and outdoor advertising to make the public aware of the advantages brick has over wood and to sell Whitmore brands of brick. Although Whitmore's consumer marketing effort is among the largest in the industry when measured in dollars, this effort is still small in comparison to the firm's effort to influence the building trades; and the strength of this effort has been the company's sales force.

The Sales Force

As indicated in Exhibit 30–1, the cost of the company's sales organization represents the bulk of Whitmore's marketing expenditures. The firm employs 19 field sales representatives to cover its direct sale marketing area in the Carolinas and Virginia. One additional sales representative handles what are termed "foreign sales"—sales outside the direct marketing area.

The company's method of absorbing acquisitions resulted in a divisional structure for the firm. Administratively, the 19 company sales representatives are assigned to the different divisions according to the scheme outlined in Exhibit 30–2. However, each salesperson is assigned an exclusive geographic territory and is responsible for sales of all the firm's products within that area, not just the products of the division. The firm's 19 direct sales territories are indicated in Exhibit 30–3.

Sales Force Characteristics

Most of Whitmore's salespeople are high school graduates although some have college degrees. They range in age from the mid-20s to early-60s with a median age between 35 and 40 years old. Tenure with the firm varies from 4 months to 18 years, with 8 years being the median. Turnover is low. In the recent past, the primary cause of turnover has been company dissatisfaction with the sales representatives' performance.

Whitmore traditionally has acquired new salespeople either by promotion of personnel in a division's customer service operation or by hiring people with sales experience gained either with other brick companies or in related industries. Advancement opportunities are available for interested and qualified salespeople. All of the 6 current sales management personnel in the firm began their service in sales organization as field sales representatives. In addition, some former salespeople have been promoted to administrative staff positions in other areas of the business.

Job Responsibilities

Salespeople are responsible for sales and field service of accounts. They call on a variety of individuals in their efforts to sell Whitmore brick. As a group, home builders, general contractors, and masons buying their own brick represent the great bulk of actual purchases. However, sales representatives also pay calls on building supply dealers and people who influence the design specifications of buildings or who may have some influence in the actual brand or style of brick to be purchased for a particular building. Such people include engineers and

Exhibit 30-1
Whitmore Brick and Block Company
Budgeted Sales and Marketing Expenditures

Advertising	
Agency Fees	$ 2,000
Trade Publications	500
Consumer Magazines	7,000
Newspaper	1,000
Outdoor	10,000
Radio	20,000
Television	25,000
Other	5,000
Total	$ 70,500
Sales Promotion	
Conventions	$ 1,500
Customer Group Functions	3,000
Home Builders Associations	1,000
Novelties	1,000
Samples and Displays	45,000
Other	1,000
Total	$ 52,500
Personal Selling Expense [1]	
Sales Salaries	$420,000
Fringe Benefits	65,000
Sales Meetings	5,000
Travel and Entertainment	100,000
Car Rental	20,000
Total	$610,000
Administrative Expense	
Direct Office Costs	$ 50,000
General Overhead	30,000
Total	$ 80,000
Total Sales and Marketing Expense	**$813,000**

[1] Includes Sales Management Salaries and Fringes.

Exhibit 30-2
Partial Organization Chart

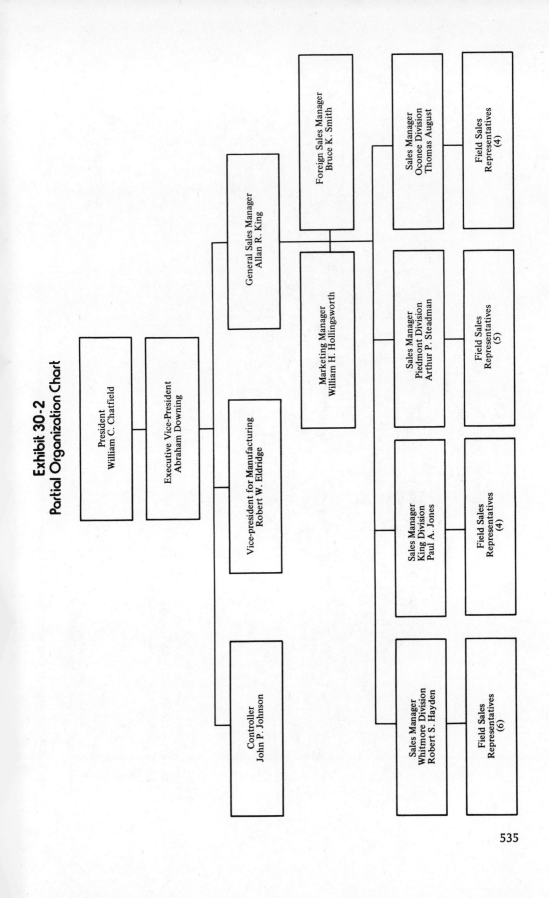

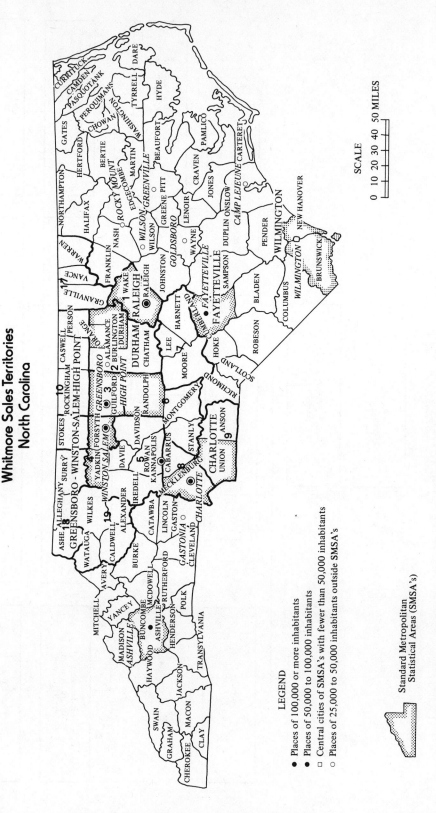

Exhibit 30-3

Whitmore Sales Territories
North Carolina

LEGEND

● Places of 100,000 or more inhabitants

● Places of 50,000 to 100,000 inhabitants

□ Central cities of SMSA's with fewer than 50,000 inhabitants

○ Places of 25,000 to 50,000 inhabitants outside SMSA's

Standard Metropolitan
Statistical Areas (SMSA's)

Source: U.S. Department of Commerce Social and Economic Statistics Administration Bureau of the Census

SCALE

0 10 20 30 40 50 MILES

Whitmore Sales Territories
South Carolina

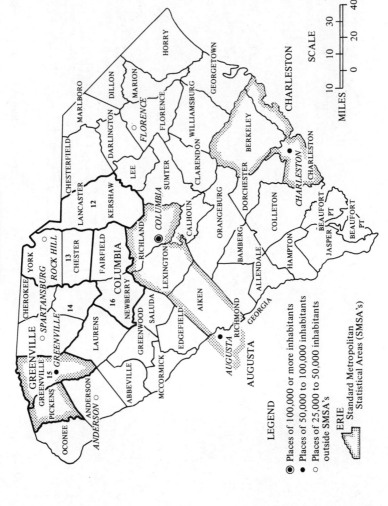

LEGEND

- ◉ Places of 100,000 or more inhabitants
- ● Places of 50,000 to 100,000 inhabitants
- ○ Places of 25,000 to 50,000 inhabitants outside SMSA's

ERIE — Standard Metropolitan Statistical Areas (SMSA's)

Source: U.S. Department of Commerce Social and Economic Statistics Administration Bureau of the Census

537

Whitmore Sales Territories
Virginia

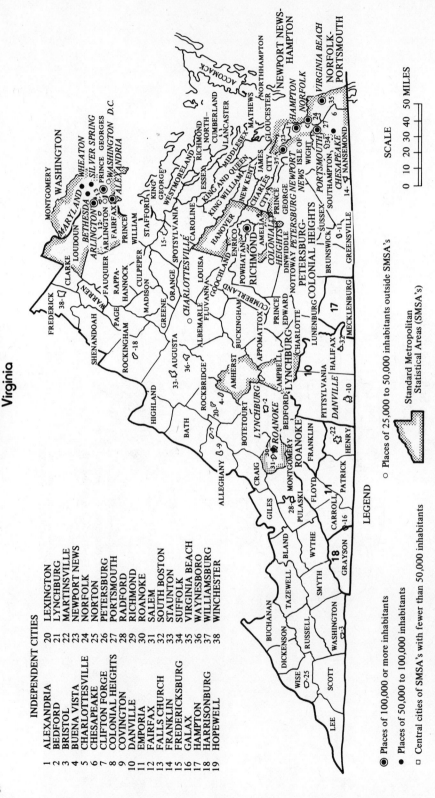

INDEPENDENT CITIES

1 ALEXANDRIA	20 LEXINGTON
2 BEDFORD	21 LYNCHBURG
3 BRISTOL	22 MARTINSVILLE
4 BUENA VISTA	23 NEWPORT NEWS
5 CHARLOTTESVILLE	24 NORFOLK
6 CHESAPEAKE	25 NORTON
7 CLIFTON FORGE	26 PETERSBURG
8 COLONIAL HEIGHTS	27 PORTSMOUTH
9 COVINGTON	28 RADFORD
10 DANVILLE	29 RICHMOND
11 EMPORIA	30 ROANOKE
12 FAIRFAX	31 SALEM
13 FALLS CHURCH	32 SOUTH BOSTON
14 FRANKLIN	33 STAUNTON
15 FREDERICKSBURG	34 SUFFOLK
16 GALAX	35 VIRGINIA BEACH
17 HAMPTON	36 WAYNESBORO
18 HARRISONBURG	37 WILLIAMSBURG
19 HOPEWELL	38 WINCHESTER

LEGEND

◉ Places of 100,000 or more inhabitants

● Places of 50,000 to 100,000 inhabitants

□ Central cities of SMSA's with fewer than 50,000 inhabitants

○ Places of 25,000 to 50,000 inhabitants outside SMSA's

Standard Metropolitan
Statistical Areas (SMSA's)

SCALE

0 10 20 30 40 50 MILES

Source: U.S. Department of Commerce Social and Economic Statistics Administration Bureau of the Census

538

architects, public officials such as building committee members, executives of firms with building plans, and so forth. In order to deal effectively with these people, the salesperson must be totally conversant with the entire Whitmore product line and competitor offerings. Salespeople are not engineers but must be reasonably knowledgeable and able to talk effectively about aesthetics, structural qualities, energy efficiency, price, and life-cycle costs.

Because the business is so competitive, salespeople often encounter potential customers who want to bargain on price. Whitmore sales representatives can and do negotiate price but must receive final approval for concessions from their sales managers.

Closing a sale often requires the efforts of more than one salesperson. As an example, a salesperson may become aware of plans for construction of a new building in his territory. He may then ask that another salesperson call on key executives of the firm which will own the building since these executives are physically located in the latter sales representative's territory. Depending on their location, the building's architect and general contractor may be called on by yet another sales representative. Once a sale is made, though, it is the responsibility of the salesperson in whose territory the building is to be located to coordinate with production and shipping to provide the best service possible for that particular job. Brick in existing structures may have to be matched or changes in original quantities and delivery schedules may be requested by the customer, and so forth.

Selection, Training, and Supervision of Sales Representatives

Selection of sales representatives is done on an "as needed" basis. When a vacancy occurs or is anticipated, the sales manager together with the marketing manager initiate a search for a new person. Preference is given to qualified employees within the firm who would like to have the job. If no interested and qualified people are found within the firm, the scope of the search is widened by taking out blind employment ads in the large daily newspapers within Whitmore's marketing area and by letting it be known to the trade through the grapevine that the firm has an opening. People with a background in some aspect of building industry sales are preferred although people with sales backgrounds from other industries are also given consideration. The final decision as to who will be hired is made by the sales manager, the marketing manager, and the general sales manager, with the general sales manager having final say if there is some dispute.

Whitmore has no formal sales training program. The company does, however, make extensive use of the training programs and meetings run by the Brick Association of North Carolina and the Brick Institute of America. These programs generally are designed to increase the participant's knowledge of brick and of industry conditions, but the meetings typically contain very little information or guidance on sales technique.

When a new salesperson joins the firm, the first 3 months are considered a trial period. The sales manager typically will take the representative around the new territory, introducing the firm's regular customers. In addition, the sales manager will spend between 4 and 6 days making calls with the new salesperson during the first 3 months on the job. The sales manager will also solicit information from valued and trusted customers as to their perceptions of the new representative's job performance. Beyond this, the sales representative is evaluated largely by the level of business the territory produces and by the impressions the sales manager gains from normal business-related contact. At the end of the 3-month period, a decision is made whether to retain the salesperson on a permanent basis.

The same informal pattern is used to evaluate veteran salespeople. In addition to normal business contact, sales managers occasionally accompany salespeople on calls, primarily at the salesperson's request, either to participate in negotiations with new customers or to lend support at what is anticipated to be a difficult call. In these instances, evaluation is a by-product rather than an objective. For evaluation, more weight is put on the salesperson's performance against quota than on anything else.

Each sales representative has a yearly performance evaluation interview with

Exhibit 30 - 4
Whitmore Brick and Block Company
Salesman Annual Performance Review

Sales Representative ——————   Review Date: ——————
Rated By: ——————————   Distribution: Original—Sales Representative
                                     Copy—Sales Representative's
                                     Personal File

	Excel.	Avg.	Unsat.	Comments (required for all below average ratings)
Territory Management:				
Routing				
Account Coverage				
Call Planning				
Overall Territory Knowledge				
Adherence to Policies & Procedures				
Time & Effort Distribution				
Thoroughness				
Administration & Organization:				
Reporting—Completeness, Accuracy, Etc.				
Record Maintenance				
Expense Control				

Correspondence

Priority Setting

Selling:

Quality of Presentations

Customer Education

Account Cooperation

Special Promotions

Sales Volume

Orders vs. Calls

Knowledge:

Products

Competition

Customers

Territory Trends

Customer Interests & Needs

Business Practices

Company Policies & Procedures

Personal Characteristics:

Attitude

Enthusiasm

Judgment

Inspirational Abilities

Industry

Resourcefulness

Appearance

Flexibility

Acceptance of Suggestions

Objectives and Recommendations for Performance Improvement:

Sales Rep's Signature ——————   Rater's Signature ——————

the manager. At this meeting, the manager discusses impressions of the salesperson's performance and explains the entries made on his annual performance review sheet (see Exhibit 30–4). The annual performance review sheet then is placed in the personnel file and becomes part of the permanent employment record.

As noted above, sales quotas are used in evaluations. Annually, management makes a forecast of company sales by geographic territory. This territorial forecast becomes the quota for the sales representative in that territory who is then expected either to meet or exceed the established quota. A representative is considered to be doing a good job for the company as long as the quota is met consistently. Those people who fail to meet their quota repeatedly are counseled by their sales managers and encouraged to do a better job. Sales managers may spend extra time with those who are having difficulty meeting their quotas and may make sales calls with them. Constructive suggestions for improved performance are usually forthcoming from these contacts.

Sales Representative Compensation

As is almost exclusively the case among the firms in the Carolinas, Whitmore sales representatives are compensated on a straight salary basis and are reimbursed for expenses incurred performing their job. Supplementing their salary is a fringe benefit package worth approximately $2,200 annually. The fringe benefit package is considered better-than-average in the industry. The average annual salary among company salespeople is $14,200, but there is tremendous variation from person to person with the top earner making $18,900 and the bottom one earning only $10,200 per year. In general, Whitmore's salary levels are competitive with those of other brick companies in the Southeast. In addition to their salary and fringe benefits, each salesperson is provided a company car which may also be used for personal travel. The sales representatives are expected to pay for the gasoline consumed in personal use of their assigned vehicle, but otherwise are free to use the car for any purpose that will not damage it.

Exhibit 30-5

To: Al King

From: Jack Johnson

Subject: Sales Productivity Analysis

Date: August 20, 1975

As we all know, overall sales performance year-to-date has been disappointing. Certainly the economic climate has not been as favorable as it was a few years ago, but it is better than last year and yet our sales are lagging. If we continue at the pace set year-to-date, and if foreign sales perform as expected, total sales for this year will be only about $150,000 greater than last year. This is far short of our target of $400,000 in growth and still leaves us over $1.5 million below our record 1972 sales performance.

In doing some research, I've found very uneven performance among sales representatives. As you can see from the following figures, some people are doing a great job, most are doing what we ask of them, but three sales people are far below quota. More disturbing is that Alquist and Williams are 2 of our highest paid representatives.

I also checked back as far as 1971 and found that Alquist was marginally under quota in 1971 and just marginally over quota in 1972, our record year. In 1973, like everyone else, he was under quota and in 1974 he exceeded his quota by only $50. The historical picture for Williams is little better. He did have a good year in 1972 but in 1973 he was below quota and in 1974 he was just about even, exceeding his quota by about $1,000. Walters joined the firm in April 1973. In 1974, the first full year of history for him, he was $15,000 below quota. Considering his performance to date, I wonder if Walters wasn't a hiring mistake.

In a capital intensive business like ours, shifts in total sales have a dramatic impact on profitability. As a result, we can't afford to miss any sales opportunities. We've got to make sure we have people in the field who are giving us 100–110 percent when times are difficult. Look over the following numbers and see if you don't agree we need to make changes.

Salesman	Territory	1975 7/12 Quota	1975 Sales thru July (7 months)	1974 Sales thru July (7 months)	1975 Salary
Alquist	5	$379	$347	$370	$17,400
Brannen	8	365	363	356	16,000
Douglas	7	373	366	371	12,600
Edwards	18	350	351	347	12,000
Elbertson	15	408	397	396	18,400
Hair	10	379	376	385	13,200
Hughes	3	394	388	386	18,900
Longworth	9	365	356	362	14,900
Mendenhall	14	379	374	376	12,100
Miles	4	385	375	387	14,200
Noseworthy	17	362	354	352	12,400
Parent	19	338	340	n/a (new hire)	10,200
Richards	1	368	371	361	12,400
Solen	12	373	362	364	13,100
Thomas	16	365	357	362	11,400
Tilden	2	379	382	385	13,400
Walters	13	368	349	368	11,400
Williams	11	379	351	373	17,600
Young	6	388	391	389	18,200

Quotas and sales figures to the nearest $1,000.

The Problem

The motivation for examining sales compensation was a slowdown in brick sales and the accompanying increase in the per unit cost of sales. This situation prompted Jack Johnson, the company's controller, to examine the firm's sales on a territory by territory basis in an effort to determine key areas in which improvement should be sought. The results of Johnson's investigation were transmitted to Allen King, Whitmore's general sales manager, in memo form on August 20. See Exhibit 30–5 for Johnson's memo.

After reading Johnson's memo, King called in Bill Hollingsworth to discuss the memo. As marketing manager, Hollingsworth was responsible for a wide variety of sales and marketing administrative functions including market and sales analysis. King felt Hollingsworth would be in the best position to help him evaluate the arguments in Johnson's memo.

After reading the memo, Hollingsworth pointed out to King that the firm's method of reporting sales in a territory where the brick was delivered regardless of who was involved in the sale was in part responsible for the apparent lack of relationship between sales representative productivity and compensation. Some salespeople, notably those in the Raleigh, Durham, and Charlotte areas, had high concentrations of architects and other purchase influencers in their territory and, through calls on these people, were involved in a great many sales for which they received no explicit credit. Hollingsworth also pointed out that to a great extent, the productivity level of the salespeople was determined by the sales potential in the area served. This in turn was influenced in large part by the level of building activity in the area. Sales potential tended to vary greatly from territory to territory and within a single territory varied over time. Hollingsworth did agree, however, that even considering these factors, there did appear to be inequities in compensation when each salesperson's contribution to the firm was considered. Hollingsworth and King had the following exchange.

Hollingsworth: "As you know, Al, each year at annual review time, Bob Haden or Paul Jones is bound to complain that one or two of their good young salespeople are not earning a fair salary for their contributions compared to some of the older people who have been here longer. They don't think it's fair that the older guys are paid more just because they've been with us longer even though their sales are no better, and in some cases worse, than some of the young guys coming along."

King: "Yes, I know. We do hear that just about every year and every year the answer is the same. To management, longevity counts. Those who have served the firm faithfully deserve to be rewarded. Also, we've got to keep in mind the total salary structure of the company. Some guy who has been working in production in one of the plants for 15 years is going to be real upset if he sees some young guy who just joined the firm a couple of years ago in sales is making as much as he is. Besides, according to the analysis in Jack's memo, our productivity problems aren't related to the length of service either. It's just that, even allowing for your objections, some people do not appear to be pulling their weight."

Hollingsworth:	"Well, you've heard Bob Hayden say we teach people that kind of behavior. Because we pay a man for the time he's been with us more than for the job he's doing, we teach him that extra effort doesn't pay."
King:	"Yes, I've heard him but he overstates the case. Anyway, this whole discussion is drifting from the point. I've got to get with Jack to be sure, but it sounds like he wants some drastic action taken. Before I do anything though, I want to be sure of the situation. I'm not going to fire some guy or put him on probation just because he's at the bottom of the productivity list. Hell, there will always be somebody at the bottom, even when everybody is doing well. What I want to know is whether these guys are doing what we expect. If these sales results are due to poor performance, we'll certainly act; but if they're due to external influences beyond the sales representative's control, we'll just have to live with it for now and hope the sales climate improves.
	Take Jack's memo back to your office and look it over again. See what you think of his analysis and do whatever analysis of your own you think is appropriate. Get back to me on Friday if you can on this so that we can sit down with Jack and hash this out."

After two weeks of analysis and discussion, the men concluded little other than that changes needed to be made. It was decided to do nothing about the specific individuals cited in John's August 20 memo until some overall plan for coping with the issues of motivation and performance had been devised. Considering some of the arguments they had heard from sales managers over the past few years, it was agreed that the possibility of instituting some sort of incentive compensation scheme as a means of both stimulating performance and insuring some relationship between performance and compensation should be investigated. Accordingly, Bill Hollingsworth was given the task of developing a preliminary plan for review by King and Johnson and eventual presentation to senior management for acceptance and implementation. Hollingsworth was asked to report back by October 16.

Exhibit 30-6
Whitmore Brick and Block Company
Proposed Incentive Compensation Plan for
Field Sales Representatives

This proposed plan is designed to reward sales representatives for achieving sales objectives and will hold and attract high-producing sales representatives. The plan will reward only those producing a profit for the company.

In designing this proposed compensation plan, the following criteria were taken into consideration:

    a. Must be competitive with other employers in order to attract and hold top quality sales representatives

    b. Easy to understand

  c. Easy to administer
  d. Fair and equitable to individual and company
  e. Provide incentives to reach sales objectives
  f. Place importance on top dollar as well as high brick and block volume

The plan will consist of a base salary and commission on brick and block dollar sales net of discount.

  1. Base salaries will average $8,000 per year. Actual base salaries will be determined individually considering experience, length of service and type of territory or customer mix.
  2. Commissions will be paid at 4 different rates, depending upon the level of monthly sales, according to the chart below:

Brick and Block Dollar Volume for the Month	Commission Rate for the Month
Less than $50,000	.0085 (.85%)
Between $50,000 and $60,399	.01 (1.0%)
Between $60,400 and $70,833	.0115 (1.15%)
Over $70,833	.0130 (1.3%)

  3. Commissions will be paid on a split basis. One-third of the commission will be paid to the sales representative responsible for specification, one-third to the sales representative responsible for the purchase order, and one-third to the sales representative responsible for servicing the job. In the case where there is no specification involved, the split will be one-half for the sales representative initiating the order and one-half for the sales representative servicing the job. Sales representatives performing multiple tasks on a single sale will receive all the commissions attributable to the activities in which they were involved.

      It will be the responsibility of the sales representative entering the order to make sure that the correct split is entered on the order edit form. Sales managers will provide guidance in the area of exceptional situations.
  4. Commissions will be paid in the middle of the month following actual shipments.

As an example of how the proposed plan will work, the plan's framework was used to compute commissions that would have been paid on sales during the first 9 months of 1975. Total sales in the direct market area during this period were $8,935,740. Field sales representatives' salary and commission would have been $203,357 approximately. Actual salaries paid during the first nine months of 1975 were $206,625.

If the proposed plan is put into effect for 1976 and Whitmore reaches the proposed minimal goal of $12.4 million in sales in the direct market area, total compensation for the 19 field sales representatives would be approximately $276,000. In this case field representatives' salary compensation will amount to 2.23 percent of sales.

Two hypothetical examples of individual compensation under the proposed plan are shown on the following chart. As can be seen, the plan insures that a sales representative's level of compensation will be directly related to sales productivity.

In conclusion, the proposed plan is felt to meet all the criteria outlined earlier in the proposal. In particular, it is felt that this plan provides attractive incentives for sales representatives to achieve sales objectives while at the same time insuring a reasonable cost of sales for the company.

1. John Doe

Month	Actual Month Sales: Brick			Actual Month Sales: Block			$ Volume and Total Commission		
	M Units	Net Price	$	Units	Net Price	$	$	Rate	$
January	704	$52.00	$ 36,608	11,560	.3565	$ 4,121	$ 50,729	.0085	$ 346.20
February	660	52.00	34,320	11,560	.3565	4,121	38,441	.0085	326.75
March	800	52.00	41,600	11,560	.3565	4,121	45,721	.0085	388.63
April	968	52.50	50,820	18,480	.3765	6,956	57,776	.01	577.76
May	1,012	52.50	53,130	18,140	.3765	6,830	59,960	.01	699.60
June	1,056	52.50	55,440	20,200	.3765	7,613	63,053	.0115	725.11
July	1,056	53.00	55,968	20,220	.3765	7,613	63,581	.0115	731.18
August	1,056	53.00	55,968	20,220	.3765	7,613	63,581	.0115	731.18
Sept.	1,144	53.00	60,632	20,220	.3765	7,613	68,245	.0115	784.82
October	924	51.50	47,586	20,800	.3565	7,415	55,001	.01	550.01
November	792	51.50	40,788	15,360	.3565	5,476	46,264	.0085	393.24
December	748	51.50	38,522	11,560	.3565	4,121	42,643	.0085	362.47
Total	11,000	$51.94	$571,382	200,000	.3680	$73,613	$644,995	.0101	$6,516.95

2. Albert Anyman

Month	Actual Month Sales: Brick			Actual Month Sales: Block			$ Volume and Total Commission		
	M Units	Net Price	$	Units	Net Price	$	$	Rate	$
January	700	$50.00	$ 35,000	20,000	.38	$ 7,600	$ 42,600	.0085	$ 362.10
February	750	50.50	37,875	20,000	.38	7,600	45,475	.0085	386.54
March	800	51.00	40,800	30,000	.38	11,400	52,200	.01	522.00
April	900	51.00	45,900	35,000	.39	13,650	59,550	.01	595.50
May	1,000	51.00	51,000	35,000	.39	13,650	64,650	.0115	743.48
June	1,000	51.50	51,500	40,000	.39	15,600	66,600	.0115	765.90
July	1,000	51.50	51,500	40,000	.40	16,000	67,500	.0115	776.15
August	950	52.00	49,400	35,000	.40	14,000	63,400	.0115	729.10
Sept.	1,050	52.50	55,125	37,000	.40	14,800	69,925	.0115	804.14
October	800	50.00	40,000	30,000	.37	11,100	51,100	.01	511.00
November	800	50.00	40,000	28,000	.37	10,360	50,360	.01	503.60
December	750	50.50	37,875	25,000	.37	9,250	47,125	.0085	400.56
Total	10,500	$51.00	$535,475	375,000	.3867	$145,010	$680,485	.0104	$7,100.62

In the process of developing his proposal, Hollingsworth gave consideration to such issues as the desired income level for good performers, the division of compensation among base salary, individual incentive, and group incentive, and the effect of the proposed plan on total sales costs to the firm. Doing a good job was defined as exceeding quota, and a direct compensation level of $15,000 to $16,000 was felt to be appropriate for this type of performance. It was further decided that base salary should amount to approximately $8,000 per year for the average sales representative. This figure, of course, could be adjusted upward or downward to account for such things as length of service, and to correct for any fundamental inequities resulting from the imbalance of sales territory, or the assignment of additional responsibilities.

Hollingsworth also attempted to design a proposal that, if it had been in effect during the first 9 months of 1975, total compensation expense for the firm would have been no greater than that actually incurred. Also, as sales rose above those 1975 levels, Hollingsworth wanted no more than 1.5 percent of additional sales to be paid to sales representatives as compensation.

As he sat at his desk this early October morning, Hollingsworth gave one last reading to the report he planned to submit to King and Johnson. Moving to an incentive based salary program represented a radical departure from past practice for the firm, and Hollingsworth was aware that the plan would receive close scrutiny both by King and Johnson and later by senior management. Yet, Hollingsworth was convinced that an incentive program was necessary. He hoped that the program he had devised was favorable to management and salespeople alike, and that in practice it would deliver the promised benefits. The issue was sensitive enough, he felt, that if a false start was made the whole concept of incentive sales compensation might be abandoned. The proposal Hollingsworth intended to present to King and Johnson is contained in Exhibit 30–6.

Protection Life*

James L. Taylor, Texas A&M University
Arch G. Woodside, University of South Carolina

Peter Bennett has just been appointed sales manager of District 5 of Protection Life Insurance Company. He has been working for Protection Life for 12 years since graduating from Midwest State University. Peter had achieved $1 million in life insurance production for the past 6 years. His insurance premiums produced for Protection had been among the top 5 for all the firm's salespeople.

Peter, who has had no prior management experience at Protection Life or at other business firms, wanted to learn the selling behavior of the salespeople in his new district. Five salespeople were based in District 5 which included Columbia, South Carolina, and 8 counties in the midlands of the state.

Peter moved to Columbia in September of this year. After one week studying the sales history of the district and the sales production records of the 5 salespeople, he requested that each sales representative tape record several meetings with different clients. He wanted to learn the actual selling and buying behavior of the sales representative and the clients, and he thought that the tape recordings would provide useful information to evaluate selling techniques.

Peter and the sales representatives discussed this idea. Two salespeople believed strongly that their clients would object to the tape recordings. Peter did not push his plan with these agents. Three agents agreed to try the recording provided the clients would agree to participate.

A total of 17 of 18 clients meeting with the 3 agents in early October agreed to have their meetings recorded. Peter had transcripts of the tapes typed. Excerpts of the tapes of 2 meetings with 2 different clients are included here. One meeting produced an insurance sale and the other meeting did not.

Peter was attempting to analyze these tape recordings to find clues on effective and ineffective features of each encounter. He wanted to identify key points and

---

*This case has been prepared for class discussion and is not intended to imply correct or incorrect exchange behavior in sales management. The names of the participants and certain facts have been disguised.

decisions in each tape relevant to a successful and an unsuccessful sale. Peter planned to present his beliefs and recommendations based on his analysis at the next sales meeting of agents in his district.

Case 1: Mr. and Mrs. Charles C. Shaw and Bill Johnson

The husband, Charles Shaw, had been insured by Protection Life through his parents. Neither the wife nor the husband had insurance with the company that they had purchased themselves. Since the husband's parents had been the sales agent's (Bill Johnson) clients, the agent decided to approach the prospect of discussing a policy of their own.

Bill Johnson is a 34 year-old black male who is married and has two children. His children are girls aged one and four years old. Bill has been a sales agent with Protection Life for 4 years.

Educational experience includes a Bachelor of Science degree from Rutgers University. Bill's major field of study at Rutgers was business management. After graduating from college, he joined the U.S. Army and was commissioned as an aviation and armory officer. He remained in the Army for 9 years and served 2 tours in Viet Nam. He obtained the rank of Captain. After leaving the Army, Bill was employed by Protection Life. He has been working for this company ever since.

Mr. and Mrs. Shaw are a white upper-lower social class couple with no children. Mr. Shaw is 26 years old and his wife is 25. Mr. Shaw is employed as a steel worker but has ambitions of becoming a professional bowler. Mrs. Shaw works in the customer complaint department of a South Carolina insurance company. They presently are renting a 2-bedroom apartment in the northeast part of Columbia, South Carolina.

Situation: Bill Johnson is meeting with Mr. and Mrs. Shaw after setting the appointment by telephone the previous week. The meeting takes place in the Shaws' home.

S: *   How long you guys been married?

W: It'll be two years this month.

H: The 26th.

S: Let me tell you, the Johnson family has been insured with The Protection Life Company for quite a while. And, unfortunately, we've had a succession of agents kind of switch over on you, and we're sorry that's happened. I've been with Protection Life about 5 years now. Are you familiar with Protection Life?

W: More or less.

S: OK. Protection is a company out of Madisonville and they've been in

---

* H   husband
  S   sales representative
  W wife

business since 1905. And they're one of the largest corporations in S. C. They own such things as Roadway Mall and WAC-TV and a lot of other pretty good size . . . (salesman establishes credibility).

W: I didn't know that.

S: You didn't know that? They try to keep some things not too much before the public notice, but they are a good, strong, substantial company. And the people that have been policy holders of theirs for years, they like to take good care of them. So, they assigned the Johnson family to me, so that's why I called C.C. and asked him if I could come out and sit down with you and go over what you presently have and maybe talk about some things you might want to accomplish in the future. OK? And to do that I've got a little questionnaire that takes a few minutes to answer (solicits compliance with small request). Now we might discuss some things that are somewhat confidential. If you'd care not to divulge something say so, OK? But it's basic stuff. For instance, Linda, where do you work?

W: S. C. Farm Owner's Insurance.

S: You work for an insurance department? Uh oh. Big trouble already.

W: I work in the Complaint Department.

S: What is that gentleman's name? I met a gentleman up there not too long ago.

W: Which department?

S: Mr. Sam Kay. Kahn.

W: Mr. Conners?

S: Conners. Yeah. Fine gentleman (salesman establishes common ground between prospects and himself).

S: C.C. you work where?

H: Boyd and Loy Corporation.

S: What exactly do you do?

H: I'm a steelworker of sorts, I guess.

S: OK, and how long have you been there?

H: A year in June.

S: You like it or . . .

H: It's hard work, but it's ok. It's different.

S: Let me ask you this. You're a pretty young fellow and you've got your whole career ahead of you and everything. What do you envision for yourself in about 5 years?

H: I would like to think that I'd be a professional bowler within 5 years.

S: Oh, good. How's it coming? You have a specific program geared toward that end? Do you have any advice?

H: Really, I know several pros and they've given me different ideas and suggestions on how to get there, but I haven't sat down and mapped out a plan. But hopefully within the next 3 years that's what I will be doing.

S: That's interesting. I wish you all the luck in the world, and I'm going to follow your progress very attentively. My wife is a big bowling fan. I used to bowl when I was smaller. I used to do a lot of pin setting (salesman establishes similarity).

S: What we try to do is—we ask you to let us sit down with you at least once a year to review your program so we're never more than a year away from the solution to the problem (solicits commitment). We hope that you'll continue to improve your program year by year as you go along— always within, in fact under, what you consider you can do at the particular time. I'd much rather you under do a little bit than to burden yourself. The priority for you is to live and enjoy life and all those good things. But your insurance program, of course, saves you from what? Catastrophe, being wiped out financially, and just living a life of misery (dissonance creation). So this is what your insurance program is supposed to do. OK. What other coverage do you have, C.C.? Do you have any other coverage?

H: I thought that my mother and father had taken out a policy.

S: They do. They have one on you. They're paying the premiums on it. I discussed that with your mother. Almost all parents have a little coverage on their children, and she's paid for it and I say just let it lie. That's her wish so I would continue to do that but I think you should consider that separate and apart from your own personal program.

W: Yeah, that's hers.

S: So this is your extent of coverage. Linda, what do you have?

W: Nothing.

S: You don't have a thing?

W: Well, what I've got at work.

S: OK. Let me explain something to you. You may have a little more than you think. As a state employee you have at least a year's salary, plus $3,000 in your Blue Cross-Blue Shield program. So that gives you $9,300 a year (establishes expertise). C.C., right now you've got about $10,000 coverage and roughly, Linda, you've got about $10,000. I think a young family on the start—my basic recommendation is to accomplish just what you want to accomplish, to provide either partner with a readjustment sum and to pay off any final expenses. I think you both need somewhere in the neighborhood of $25,000 each. I don't think that's unrealistic for today's society. Of course, as you grow, you're going to have a need for additional coverage. We have some real good programs where we have what we call family type program policies where we cover both partners for a like amount. In this instance, I think something around $15,000 at least is needed.

Now you indicated that you were saving a little bit of money in the credit union. I don't want to disrupt your life style or whatever. Approximately what are you saving in the credit union?

W: About $200.

S: $200 a month? OK. One suggestion you might do—you're putting that away for your house payment. Most house payments—I don't want to shock you, but $200 is not going to be enough.

H: We've been looking.

W: That's what I know.

S: Let me take a look at something. . . . Let me show you something. This is what we call our Protection Life savings type program. This comes in amounts from $20,000 to $5 million. But, for instance, this is $50,000. The reason I showed you this is that it would provide $25,000 coverage for each one; but we can scale this down to the amount you need. I just use this as an illustrative program. This would be $25,000 on Linda and $25,000 on yourself; if you paid that annually, you'd have to deposit $646.50 per year through the program. The first year it's just a small cash value; that means just like savings with the credit union—that's the amount you can take out, if you need it. Now, this is a little bit unusual. Most insurance companies don't give you any cash value the first year. This is a new policy; it's a little bit unusual. You deposit the $646.50 the first year; the first year you have a $100 cash increase in the policy. So the net cost to you in the first year is $546.50. That's pretty expensive in the first year, but let's look at what happens after that. Let's look at the second year. You deposit $646.50; the cash value increases the second year $600.00, so the cost of insurance for both of you is only $46.50 for that whole year. That means if you decided to stop the policy, that all it would have cost you for that year was $46.50 (traditional persuasion).

S: Now, what you could do so it wouldn't disrupt your life style is just reduce the amount to the credit union to $160 and take that extra money and put it in your checking account. So you really don't disrupt your life style. You don't have to take it from your disposable income. It will be a different type of savings.

H: I could stop it any time? And give you a call and say, "Hey, I need the money."

S: All you have to do is call the bank and say don't honor the draft and it could be the same minute.

H: I do need more coverage than just that one thing.

S: You do. I think it's imperative that you have additional coverage on your wife.

W: It bothers me that I don't have anything on me, because $10,000 wouldn't be a drop in the bucket to me. Of course, it would be worse on me, because he makes a heck of a lot more money than I do.

H: The reason I'm not worried about that is because if anything ever did happen to her, I could live on what I make and I wouldn't see a need . . .

W: Unless we had a bunch of kids (wife helps salesman by exerting social pressure).

S: Let me point this out to you. You're not only buying for right now. As I indicated, your needs won't decrease—they're going to increase as you go along (dissonance creation).

H: Right.

S: You'll have more obligations. This is why I recommend that you do something substantial now. Really, I think you can get by on a $15,000 right now. But, you'll find out that these years are going to fly so fast and we're going to sit here—maybe not in this apartment, but at this same table—and you're going to say, Bill, I wish I'd bought $50,000 that night. Because you're going to need the coverage later on and it's going to be terribly expensive and I'm going to say, well, I wanted you to live within your means but I wanted you to at least get that program started. I've seen both ends of the spectrum (expertise). I've seen those that have bought it and got by pretty good and then I've seen some that made a decision of trying to save $10 a month and that cut off $10,000 in protection and so I come back with a check for $10,000 instead of $20,000. I feel terrible, she feels terrible (dissonance creation). And that's why we try to ascertain what's comfortable for you and then you go from there.

H: Insurance is one of the worse things I could buy . . . as far as having to make a decision. It's hard for me on that. I can go out and buy me a new bowling ball right now.

S: We're talking about what, about $8 a week? You tell me what family doesn't take $8 and look in your wallet at the end of the week and . . .

H: I know one that does—this one right here.

S: This is a good investment in your family's future (creates cognitive dissonance). I think this is important to you.

H: Well, I'll go along with you about that . . . (pause) . . . about that right now.

S: Who's the one in the family that takes care of the money?

H: Me.

S: You? OK. Would you give me a check to Protection Life for $36.75 (solicits commitment)?

H: Right now?

S: I need to get some information from your wife while you're doing that.

H: Boy, you cut me short this time.

S: Well, let me point this out to you. I need to have that in my hands in case I walk out the door and something happens. You can postdate it whenever you want to (solicits commitment).

H: I get paid tomorrow.

W: We wouldn't be covered in this tomorrow.

S: Yes, ma'am. That's why I get that check, because the policy is in force as soon as he writes out that check.

H: No matter what the date is on the check.

S: That's right. As long as I have it in my possession. You may pay one month and then decide to stop it, then you made a $36 mistake. We all make a lot of those. But I'd hate to be the one who made a $25,000 mistake. We don't make too many of those and get away with it (dissonance creation).

H: What date do I have it withdrawn?

W: Whenever you want it; it's up to you.

S: What is your social security number? (salesperson fills out the application and Mr. Shaw writes the check).

S: Once the policy is issued, I'll come back and we'll sit down and go over the policy provisions and everything about it. At that particular time, if you don't like anything in the policy or if you're dissatisfied in any way, I'll give you your money back. No hasty decision—don't want you to feel like that. I think you realize the importance of what we covered. I think we're getting an adequate amount and I think it's something that you can work within your budget, tomorrow you might say, "I don't know if I made the right decision." Well, you're not out anything. Wait 'til you get the policy back. We'll sit down. We'll go over it and you'll see that it's good coverage by law and by contract. You ask anybody in the insurance commissioner's office. Ask them about Protection Life (salesperson attempts to reduce postpurchase regret by validating decision).

S: Let me mention a couple of things and I'll get out of your hair. Number 1: I hope this will be the start of a long and enjoyable relationship. I'll do those things to keep you informed of any age changes, any new rules, etc. If anything, God forbid, should happen to either one of you, I will do whatever is required to help get your lives straightened out. And that's the last time I will say anything about that. I promise to come by and do all those things and renew your program every year. In return, this is what I ask (cultivates the long-term relationship). I ask you to at least be a little bit loyal to me. You'll probably be bothered with every insurance guy in the world coming by and wanting to talk to you. You don't have all that time to sit down and spend a lot of evenings with insurance people. If they come by, tell them, look, I've got a pretty good agent named Bill Johnson. If you've got any ideas you think I could use, give him a call. I'll look it over for you and if I am able to see something of value to it, I'll get back in touch with you and let you know and I'll give you an impartial answer. I think that way you save a lot of time and effort, problems and everything else. Then you won't be jumping into hasty decisions, getting all confused by every guy that comes. There are 1800 companies. If you'd let 1800 different people come in here and explain things to you, you'd go wacky. The minute I don't do my job, fire me. Say, you're fired and go on out and get yourselves another agent. So I have earned the right to continue doing business with you.

H: I have no complaints from the last 4 years.

S: Anytime anything comes up that you don't understand or you don't agree with me, call me. That's why I've got my home number and my office number there. Call me; I'm at your service.

Case 2: Law Firm and Mr. Sutton and Mr. Jones

Situation: In this case, 2 sales agents made a "cold call" on a legal firm. A cold call is where the salesperson makes an unannounced visit on a prospect. The S. C. Bar Association had provided many legal firms in the state with group health insurance through Blue Cross-Blue Shield prior to this recorded transaction. Blue Cross-Blue Shield had raised their premium rates, thus the sales agents thought that they might provide this firm with a less costly purchase alternative. With this hope, the agents approached the firm. The representatives introduced themselves and asked to talk with one of the lawyers for a few minutes.

SP1: * As you may know, the S. C. Bar Association recently went up on their rates as far as group health insurance is concerned. I just wanted to drop by and see if you were interested in discussing some alternatives or group health plans one can get under a group employee trust.

L: Yeah, I don't know too much about our present plan. I know we have it through a general agency and that's about all I know. (calls secretary) Joyce, do you have a minute? Could you come in here a minute?

S: (comes in) Oops! I am sorry.

L: Joyce, this is Mr. Sutton, Mr. Jones. This is Joyce Dowd.

S: Hello, how are you?

SP1&2: Hello, how are you?

S: What do you need?

L: These gentlemen have an alternative proposition of health insurance and they are with Protection Life. Is that right?

SP1: Yes.

L: And the other thing was group life and health and since you pay the premiums and know about that sort of thing, I thought there was no point of me sitting over here discussing it and not knowing a thing.

---

* L   lawyer
  SP1   salesperson 1
  SP2   salesperson 2
  S   secretary

	(pause) Let's establish a few things first. We have it through a general agency and we also have our life policies through them.
S:	No. Our life insurance is through Pilot Life.
L:	And that doesn't go through general agency? That's directly through Pilot?
S:	Right.
SP1:	So you have your health with Blue Cross-Blue Shield through the S. C. Bar Association which is run through a general agency.
S:	Right. (pause) Did y'all come in mass to give us a hard sell?
SP1:	No, we just came by to . . .
L:	You see why I called you. I had to have some help back here.
SP1:	Well, we figured that by bringing 2 people, if it came to a vote, we would have 2 "yes" votes.
S:	Yeah, but I pay the money.
SP1:	Usually we don't go to this many people but Jim wanted to do this study.
L:	(changes subject) You probably know their (Blue Cross-Blue Shield) premium rates and Joyce writes out the checks to them every month.
SP1:	How many people do you have participating?
S:	In the health insurance?
SP1:	Yes.
S:	Six lawyers and 4, no 3 secretaries.
SP1:	Six lawyers? 3 secretaries?
S:	Yes, at present. Sometimes it goes to 5 secretaries.
SP1:	Three to 5, but never lower than 3. Is that right?
S:	Yes.
SP1:	What is the total number of your employees?
S:	Usually you are not going to have less than 10 employees.
SP2:	What type of group coverage do you have and how much is it?
L:	It varies.
S:	Yeah, it does vary.
L:	In other words, some people have like 40 and some have 10.
S:	Some have five.
L:	I have 10.
S:	You may have 20.
L:	This isn't like under an employees trust or anything. I don't know how you (speaking to secretary) have it set up.
S:	It's just straight life insurance. All the partners would have $40,000

except one who has 10 or 20. (pause) I am not sure. The secretaries have $5,000.

SP1:   Well, there are several ways you could go with this. You could try, with 10 employees, a true group plan. A true group plan is 10 people or more. Anything below that you get into a franchise. In a franchise group, there are 4 people. Four to 10 people for a franchise group. Two to 4 is a group employee trust.

S: Are you speaking of just health policies or are you speaking of combination health and life.

SP1:   Combination of both. Now you can go—I know what Blue Cross' rates are and I also know that Protection Life group life rates are much more reasonable. You could probably get it for the same thing you are paying now just for health. Additionally (pause) let me see if I can explain why. It is not that we are going out buying business or anything like that. It is just that Protection Life has never gone into the group life and health areas without adopting the philosophy that one should make money on it. The philosophy these days is to break even on the health and make a little bit on the life. And because they took that philosophy 3 years ago, Blue Shield was underbidding everybody. Protection Life, Pilot Life, and all the rest of them were overbidding and the bids were just not there. But now, Blue Cross-Blue Shield has started to lose their rear ends in the health business, so they had to raise their rates substantially where the other companies have just remained level—they started higher and are just sort of hanging in there. And that is where the diversion started. So what I would like to do is if I could just get the data on your people. All you need is the date of birth, age, sex, and whether they want single or family coverage.

S: All right. (secretary leaves the room)

SP1:   Additionally, it might be a good idea to not only get this information as far as Protection Life but to look at several other companies as well, such as Western Life, Occidental, Travelers, and a few others.

L: Well, it never hurts to compare. (secretary returns)

SP2:   On your Pilot rates, are you paying so many cents per thousand, or just a straight rate?

S: I don't really know. I think it is on a thousand unit. But you know, all I am concerned with every month is paying the premium. Periodically, I look at it and I don't pay too much attention to it because it doesn't really vary. (pause) All right. Are you ready (to receive the information)?

SP1:   Yes.

S: OK. What do you want?

SP1:   Let's start with sex first.

S: OK. Uh. You have 6 men. (pause) All right, now I have to know if you are computing on health or computing on life insurance or a combination of 2. Because right at the moment I have 2 girls that aren't covered; they are covered with life insurance but they are not covered with health insurance. Health insurance coverage with one is nonexisting and the other has it through her husband.

SP1:   Do they have any children?

S: Yes. They both have children.

SP1:   We can use either method.

S: OK. Good enough.

SP1:   Why don't you just prepare it on what you have now.

S: Six males and 3 females. Two possibles.

SP1:   Six males, 3 females, and 2 possibles. And their ages and dates of birth?

S: OK. Men are January 23, 1946; May 12, 1941; May 20, 1945; August 7, 1929, September 27, 1925; November 27, 1941.

L: Did you say '45? I think you have it wrong because I don't know anyone born in '45.

S: No, that's right. OK, the females: February 23, 1950; May 13, 1950; May 31, 1954. The two possibles are June 31, 1950 and August 31, 1947. (pause) There is a very wide range.

SP1:   OK. I have the sex and date of birth. Now, I need to know whether they want single or family coverage.

S: OK. Men will want family coverage. Six family, 3 single, and 2 question marks.

SP1:   Six family and 3 singles and 2 question marks?

S: If they (the 2 questionables) were going to opt for any, one definitely would be a family and one may or may not.

SP1:   Let's say that this one girl's husband has group coverage. If they don't have any children the best way to handle it is for his employer to pay for his coverage and her employer pay for her coverage and that way you wouldn't have to pay anything. If there are children involved, then go with the employer who is picking up most of the bill for the family coverage.

L: Now, they have one child and he works for the state. Is that right? And the way we do around here is to split 50/50.

S: For health. The firm picks up the tab for life. It should be the other way around.

SP1:   Let's see. Why don't we say in all probability the lady born June 31, 1950 would probably want single coverage.

S: Well, let's see. I don't know. She has a little boy and she also has a husband, but not right at the moment (Sic).

SP1:   Well, that's no problem.

S: Well, I am telling you that I don't know if she is going single or married. It is incorrect to make the assumption that she would go on the family plan.

SP1:   Well, for the purpose of calculation, we just need to go with one thing or another. We can always take that out and later reduce the portion and just take the family out.

L: But as basis for comparison, you might as well go with what she has now.

SP1:   OK.

S: And when you give me the computer rates on those and you have worked up a tally sheet on them, are you going to also give me what your policy covers?

SP1:   Yes.

L: We have had all sorts of experiences finding out what Blue Cross-Blue Shield covers in our office and through our clients. We may not be familiar, however, with your policy.

S: Well, I know where AEtna comes from and where Travelers comes from. Now we have another one as input into the pot.

SP1:   Have you gotten rates from AEtna and Travelers?

S: Yes. I have AEtna's rates.

SP1:   Do you have Travelers?

S: No. Are you finished with me?

L: Do you need to find out anymore about the health and the life?

SP1:   Well, I am assuming (pause) how many partners are there?

L: There are 5.

SP1:   Which is the one person who doesn't have the $40,000 coverage?

L: January 23, 1946.

SP1:   And everyone else has $40,000 and the secretaries have $5,000.

S: Yeah, the pecking order is reflected in the coverage. (laughs)

L: But that is not set up as a trust fund. That is just payable to the beneficiary.

S: Just flat out. (pause) There is not a double indemnity or anything else.

L: It's not keyed into a partnership agreement or anything.

SP1:   Would you be interested in increasing your secretaries' coverage to $10,000?

S: That is a decision that I am not eligible to make at the moment. If you can give me a cost mark up on it and tell me the difference between the 5 and 10 and how much difference it is going to cost the firm, then we might be able to talk a little bit more definitely. Right at the moment it's hard to say, but an increase to 10 would be super. Everybody would like that.

SP1:　　It would probably be about .39 a thousand. About $3.90.

S:　　We might be able to afford that. But sometimes I wonder . . .

L:　　Yet, we can't afford to be without insurance.

SP1:　　Thank you. I appreciate it.

S:　　OK. (secretary leaves)

L:　　Did I give y'all all the information that you need?

SP1:　　One other thing, I noticed that you mentioned that you had a partnership agreement.

L:　　I don't know. I have never been party to the discussion on this. There may be a written agreement, but if there is, the life insurance is not hooked into it so that the partnership is the recipient of the fund. I don't know that they looked that far ahead. None of them anticipate dying this week.

SP2:　　How old is the firm?

L:　　I guess the longest it has been under the same name is 20 years, if that long. And that was under Gene Rogers.

SP1:　　Are y'all thinking about anything like this?

L:　　I don't think they want to do it. That is something that they are aware of but it is something that you do when you are ready and I don't think they are ready to do it. (someone knocks on door; lawyer signs papers and then continues conversation)

SP1:　　OK. I guess that's all I need. By the way, do y'all practice a little bit of everything?

L:　　We do more of some things than not, but we do generally everything.

SP1:　　(tells joke) (inaudible)

L:　　Well, it was nice meeting you.

SP1:　　It was nice meeting you.

L:　　Are you going to send us a letter or . . .

SP1:　　As soon as I get all the information. It will probably be about a week—I will give you a call.

L:　　Thank you so much. As you can see, Joyce knows this stuff, and I don't.

This case was concluded when the sales representatives went back to the firm 2 months later with the figures on the cost of providing the same coverage that the firm presently had. It took a considerable amount of time to get the information back from the home office as far as the cost of the coverage. This was somewhat unusual because similar cases did not take that long for information return. It never was really clear what the holdup was. The firm rejected the proposal presented by the sales representatives in favor of an alternative proposal submitted by a competitor who was not revealed to the salespeople. In essence, the competitor's proposal provided the same amount of coverage at a lower cost.

Data Products International

Barbara A. Pletcher
California State University at Sacramento

Fred Johnson was turning into a true believer in Gumperson's Law which states that the probability of any given event is inversely proportional to its desirability. Not only are those things you wish to avoid most likely to occur, but the events you anxiously anticipate never seem to materialize. Fred was feeling somewhat depressed because equal opportunity had finally come to roost in his office. He is the manager of the San Francisco sales office of Data Products International. One of his primary responsibilities is recruiting and hiring new sales representatives. Up to now, he had managed to avoid the issue of women.

Data Products International (DPI) is a large firm, although dwarfed by some of the giants in the data processing industry. It is headquartered on the East Coast and has sales offices in almost every major U.S. city. Several of the larger metropolitan markets are serviced by multiple sales offices. DPI was growing rapidly as primary demand for the industry's products expanded. This rapid growth brought about constant pressure to recruit new salespeople.

DPI followed a fairly established recruiting pattern. Almost all of its recruiting activities involved college placement offices and most candidates were recent college graduates. Although DPI preferred business graduates with some math or science background, a few of the more recent recruits had degrees in political science and economics. Each September Fred prepared a forecast of his hiring requirements for the next spring. This included both new positions and replacements for people who either left the company or were transferred. On the basis of this forecast, he scheduled visits to area colleges. He had several favorite schools from which he had hired a number of successful sales representatives in the past. He liked to visit the University of the Pacific in Stockton, San Luis Obispo, California State University, Sacramento, Chico State, and the University of Nevada at Reno. On-campus interviewing usually took place between January and March. Until now, he had conducted all the on-campus interviews personally, so he also was responsible for initial screening. After seeing between 25 and 35 students over the normal campus season, he would invite as many as three students per antici-pated position to a follow-up interview in San Francisco. The purpose of the office interview was to get a better look at the person in an actual business setting, complete a few tests, and give the potential employee a better chance to evaluate the company. Fred always gave the student some time alone with one of the newer sales representatives. He hoped that the student would ask some questions which might seem too frivolous or dangerous to ask the sales manager. He often was surprised that these young people asked so few questions when they had such important decisions to make, both about the company and the nature of the selling job. Finally, after conferring with any people who had met the applicants and reviewing the applicant's qualifications, he would rank order them and start to make offers. The first offers usually went out during the first week of May.

Although the recruiting process was long and sometimes frustrating, Fred was proud of his record. He could point to a number of young men he had brought into the company who had continued on to management positions. Although mak-ing decisions that directly affect the future of others can be a heavy burden, Fred assumed that he must be doing something right. It was not easy to decide who would be successful in sales and who would not. Fred had read lots of books on the subject over the years. Most of the advice boiled down to two simple terms: ego drive and empathy. Ego drive has been described as the need to make the sale, the need to succeed, and the need to win. Empathy is the ability to under-stand another person's position and feelings. Although Fred never doubted that these were important qualities, he often wished someone would come up with a foolproof way to measure them in people. Not only did he worry that he might damage some other person either by hiring a person who was not qualified and would fail or by failing to hire someone who would have been successful. He worried about his own future.

Fred's effectiveness in the hiring process affected his future in two very direct ways. First, as manager of the San Francisco office, he was held responsible for productivity. If his people were not good in the field, he would hear about it from headquarters. Secondly, his compensation was directly tied to his sales force. He received a small base salary; however, the majority of his compensation was an override on his salespeople's commissions. If his people didn't sell, he didn't get paid.

This year things were different. A new position had been created that had brought about some significant changes in the recruiting process. All of the DPI sales offices were clustered into regions. San Francisco was part of the Western Region which included 11 western states. In a move to ease some of the sales manager's recruiting burden, a staff person from the regional office had assumed the college interviewing duties. There was some justification for this in that the manager typically saw as many as 10 students for each person hired. If the initial screening process could be completed by someone else, the sales manager would have more time to devote to developing new salespeople. Although like many of the sales managers in the district, Fred could see both advantages and disadvantages to this system, he had not anticipated the difficulty which developed. In effect, he was brought face-to-face with a fact which to this point he had chosen to ignore.

He knew that DPI was under pressure to implement affirmative action. All of the advertisements of job openings included the phrase "We are an equal opportunity employer M/F." He had always hoped that managers of the other offices would hire enough minority people so that he would not have to move in that direction. It was not that he had any evidence that women could not do the job as sales representatives, it was just that all his experience proved to him that men could. After all, his livelihood depended on his sales force.

The Staff Recruiter

Jack Cartwright had been with DPI for almost 30 years. He had started out as a salesman in the Philadelphia office and had managed the Cleveland, Ohio office for 12 years. After a recent heart attack, he had been ordered to cut back on his levels of activity and stress. His needs dovetailed with the DPI plan to introduce a regional staff recruiter. Management decided that it might be a good idea to test this concept using a person with experience in selling, and sales management, and years of knowledge about the company and the industry. Jack looked upon his new position as an opportunity to give the careful attention to screening applicants that he had always hoped for but never had time to accomplish while managing the Cleveland office.

Having some organizational sense and recognizing that innovation often collides with vested interest, one of Jack's first activities was to meet with each of the managers of each of the offices in the Western district to assure them that his only purpose was to save them time by screening applicants so that only qualified people would be seen by the individual managers. He emphasized that the final decision, as always, would rest with the individual manager. He stressed the advantages of the new system. He honestly felt that this would save time and result in a more efficient recruiting process. Under the former system, each manager visited a few schools. There were some schools that never were covered and others that were visited by more than one manager. Not only was the company in competition with itself, but it was somewhat confusing for the student, who was never sure whether to schedule interviews with each manager.

Another of Jack's important objectives for the initial meeting with each manager was to determine the manager's needs for people for the coming year and to encourage the manager to discuss preferences and priorities regarding the selection process. He summarized the responses for future reference. (See Exhibit 32–1.) Since the managers' opinions seemed consistent with his own, he moved to the next step and scheduled interviews at campus placement centers across the region.

Candidates for the San Francisco Openings

Fred Johnson anticipated two openings on his sales staff. Growth in the sales volume in the mini-computer line justified one position, and one of the men in the office products area would be retiring in June justifying the other position.

Exhibit 32-1
Managers' Responses

1.	Appropriate education	Business degree, MBA preferred Some science or math courses Economics or Political Science is acceptable
2.	Work experience	Sales experience preferred Work should have involved people contact
3.	Drive	Should be involved in extra activities Should have earned part of school expenses Should show leadership experience Sports is a good indication
4.	Enthusiasm	Interest in sales Confidence in abilities Adventuresome spirit Should have ventured off the safe paths
5.	Self Reliance	Demonstrated ability to take care of oneself Independent spirit
6.	Interpersonal skills	Some group activities Preference for "people jobs"

At the end of February, he received a telephone call from Jack Cartwright who asked about the best schedule for follow-up interviews in San Francisco for the 5 students he had selected as most qualified for the positions. Fred was pleased that the recruiting process was ahead of schedule and that Jack had delivered on his promise to leave the final choice up to the individual manager. Since all 5 people were from the Northern California area, they decided to schedule the interviews on 5 consecutive days during the second week in March. Jack promised to send the papers on each candidate immediately so that Fred could be prepared for the interviews. They agreed that Jack might as well schedule the interviews with the candidates since there was no apparent reason to see them in any particular order and they all knew Jack. (See Exhibit 32–2.)

When Fred received the materials on the candidates, his initial reaction was surprise. For a few moments, he had the urge to call Jack to see if the interviews had been scheduled. If they had not, he intended to suggest that Jack need not bother to schedule one for Joan Channell. It did not take long for him to realize that he could not do that. It is one thing to avoid women, but it is an altogether different matter to reject them once they have passed the initial screening. When *he* had been doing the interviewing, he had avoided this problem. He decided he would have to go through with the interviews, but he believed that there was little chance that he would offer one of the positions to Ms. Channell.

The issue of Joan Channel stuck with him throughout the day, and he spent some time thinking about the objections he had heard whenever the topic of women in sales had come up in managers' meetings. Absentmindedly, he jotted

Exhibit 32-2
Application Materials

DATA PRODUCTS INTERNATIONAL
EMPLOYMENT APPLICATION

Applicant's Name — *Please Type or Print*

Channell	Joan	Linda
Last	First	Middle

POSITION APPLIED FOR	REASON FOR APPLYING
sales representative	my qualifications meet your requirements and I think this position represents an excellent opportunity

an Equal Opportunity Employer who hires without regard to race, religion, sex, color, national origin, or age.

Home Address 22346 Burt Road
Number   Street

Fairfield   California   94533
City   State   ZIP Code

Home Phone 353-4063   Business Phone 362-1986

Referred By ☐ employee ☐ newspaper ☐ agency

☒ other college placement center

Social Security Number |4|0|2|—|2|3|—|1|7|5|2|

Do you have the right to work in the United States on a permanent basis? ☒ Yes ☐ No

Do you have relatives employed by DPI?
☐ Yes ☒ No   If yes, who?_____
where?_____

Have you ever been employed by DPI?
☐ Yes ☒ No   If yes, when?_____
where?_____

RECORD OF EMPLOYMENT

Employer Business and Address	Dates FROM (Mo.-Yr.)	Dates TO (Mo.-Yr.)	BASIC MONTHLY SALARY OR DRAW ACCOUNT	OVERTIME BONUS COMMISSION	Position and Basic Duties	Reason for Leaving
MacDonalds 3065 N. Main, Fairfield	6/72	5/73	$2.30/hr		Counter clerk	better job
Stereo Record Center 29375 Elm, Fairfield	6/73	8/74	$2.65/hr		Sales clerk	better job school
Macy's Sacramento,	9/74	6/76	$3.25/hr		Sales clerk	graduate school
California State U. Sacramento	7/76	12/77	$320		graduate assistant	graduation

Have you any income in addition to your salary? ☐ Yes ☒ No   If yes, explain_____

EDUCATION

	Name	Dates Attended From	To	Major	Minor	Degree
HIGH SCHOOL	Howard Taft, Dayton, OH	9/69	6/72	College prep		diploma
COLLEGE	Solano County C.C.	9/72	9/74	communications		A.A.
	Cal. State. U., Sacramento	9/74	12/77	Marketing	Finance	B.A., M.B.A.
OTHER TRAINING						

MISCELLANEOUS INFORMATION

List honors, awards, extra-curricular activities (school or community), and grades Delta Sigma Pi, Treasurer
Inter-collegiate Business Games team, 1976; Jerry Lewis Telethon volunteer, 1975-77

What part of expenses did you earn during high school?_____ college? 25%
List any hobbies, including sports tennis, water skiing, snow skiing

---

Draft Status -- _____ Have you been in the United States military service? ☐ Yes ☒ No
If no, explain Not eligible for draft and did not volunteer

_____ Branch of Service _____
Date of entry into active duty -- _____ Date of release from active duty _____
Rank on release from active duty _____ Completion date of Reserve commitment _____

Have you ever been convicted of any criminal action? ☐ Yes ☒ No   If yes, explain _____

List health disabilities none
Are you willing to go to work in any DATA PRODUCTS INTERNATIONAL office in the United States? ☒ Yes ☐ No
List preferences San Francisco, Sacramento, Los Angeles, Seat __ , Denver, Phoenix

Tell something about yourself, including reasons you feel you are qualified for the position.

As the youngest of four children in a military family I have had numerous opportunities to develop skills in interpersonal relations and personal adjustment. I have had to make new friends and understand different types of people each time we have moved. I feel that these experiences would make me more able to assume a selling position. I have researched the data processing industry in connection with a term paper and understand the requirements of a sales representative in that industry. I know that I would be diligent in that rewards are related to performance and the possibility exists for advancing into a management position.

The information given herein is true and accurate to the best of my knowledge and belief; I understand that all information given will be verified.

Date 2-2-77   Signature Joan Channell

HIRING COMMITMENT (For Official Use Only)

Interviewer's Comments/Name _____

Department/Office _____   Organization Code _____
Starting Date _____   Expense Allocation Code _____
Bi-weekly Salary _____   Job Title _____
Job Code _____   Date _____
Designated Signature _____   Name (printed) _____

Code 169 Rev. 4/74

DATA PRODUCTS INTERNATIONAL

EMPLOYMENT APPLICATION

Applicant's Name — *Please Type or Print*

Greenfile	David	Alexander
Last	First	Middle

POSITION APPLIED FOR	REASON FOR APPLYING
Sales	Father's recommendation

an Equal Opportunity Employer who hires without regard to race, religion, sex, color, national origin, or age.

Home Address 16236 San Ysidro
            Number   Street

San Jose   CA   95119
City   State   ZIP Code

Home Phone 219-8385 Business Phone --

Referred By ☒ employee ☐ newspaper ☐ agency

☐ other_____

Social
Security Number 4 1216 — 1 18 — 2 12 17 17

Do you have the right to work in the United States on a permanent basis? ☒ Yes ☐ No

Do you have relatives employed by DPI?
☒ Yes ☐ No If yes, who? Donald Greenfil
                          where? San Jose

Have you ever been employed by DPI?
☐ Yes ☒ No If yes, when?_____
                         where?_____

RECORD OF EMPLOYMENT

Employer Business and Address	Dates FROM (Mo.-Yr.)	Dates TO (Mo.-Yr.)	Salaries BASIC MONTHLY SALARY OR DRAW ACCOUNT	OVERTIME BONUS COMMISSION	Position and Basic Duties	Reason for Leaving
Safeway, 2336 Cooper San Jose	6/64	9/69	4.65 per hour	none	stock clerk checker	military
San Jose Bee 312 12th street, west	1/73	3/7	4.25/per hour	none	copy assistant	school

Have you any income in addition to your salary? ☒ Yes ☐ No If yes, explain G.I. benefits

EDUCATION

	Name	Dates Attended From	To	Major	Minor	Degree
HIGH SCHOOL	San Gabriel, San Jose	9/63	6/67	--		graduated
COLLEGE	San Jose State	9/67	6/69	physical education	psychology	--
	San Jose State	9/74	6/77	business	communications	B.A.
OTHER TRAINING						

MISCELLANEOUS INFORMATION

List honors, awards, extra-curricular activities (school or community), and grades __Vet's Club, San Jose State__

What part of expenses did you earn during high school? __25%_____ college? __100% inc. GI Bill__

List any hobbies, including sports __flying, jogging,__

Draft Status __served_____ Have you been in the United States military service?   [X] Yes   [ ] No

If no, explain _____

_____ Branch of Service __army__

Date of entry into active duty __12/69_____ Date of release from active duty __11/73__

Rank on release from active duty __sp. 4th_____ Completion date of Reserve commitment __--__

Have you ever been convicted of any criminal action? [ ] Yes [X] No   If yes, explain _____

List health disabilities __none__

Are you willing to go to work in any DATA PRODUCTS INTERNATIONAL office in the United States? [X] Yes [ ] No

List preferences __San Francisco, Portland, San Diego__

Tell something about yourself, including reasons you feel you are qualified for the position.

It has taken me a while to decide what I want to do but now I've decided that I want to work in the data processing industry. I've completed both school and my military obligations and am ready to get serious about my career. I know that I can earn a good living in sales and I'm sure that I would be a good representative of Data Products International.

The information given herein is true and accurate to the best of my knowledge and belief; I understand that all information given will be verified.

Date __2/16/77_____ Signature __David Greenfield__

HIRING COMMITMENT (For Official Use Only)

Interviewer's Comments/Name _____

Department/Office _____ Organization Code _____

Starting Date _____ Expense Allocation Code _____

Bi-weekly Salary _____ Job Title _____

Job Code _____ Date _____

Designated Signature _____ Name (printed) _____

Code 169 Rev. 4/74

DATA PRODUCTS INTERNATIONAL
EMPLOYMENT APPLICATION

Applicant's Name – *Please Type or Print*

PLOWE	EUGENE	J.
Last	First	Middle

POSITION APPLIED FOR	REASON FOR APPLYING

an Equal Opportunity Employer who hires without regard to race, religion, sex, color, national origin, or age.

Home Address __899__ __Delaware__
                 Number   Street
__Vacaville__   __Ca__   __98275__
 City   State   ZIP Code

Home Phone _541-5871_ Business Phone _____

Referred By ☐ employee ☐ newspaper ☐ agency

☒ other_ Vocational Counsellor_

Social Security Number | 4 | 8 | 2 | – | 6 | 5 | – | 9 | 8 | 7 | 2 |

Do you have the right to work in the United States on a permanent basis? ☒ Yes ☐ No

Do you have relatives employed by DPI?
☐ Yes ☒ No   If yes, who?___
                where?___

Have you ever been employed by DPI?
☐ Yes ☒ No   If yes, when?___
                where?___

RECORD OF EMPLOYMENT

Employer Business and Address	Dates FROM (Mo.-Yr.)	Dates TO (Mo.-Yr.)	Salaries BASIC MONTHLY SALARY OR DRAW ACCOUNT	OVERTIME BONUS COMMISSION	Position and Basic Duties	Reason for Leaving
Galt, Ca. Motor Industries	9/69	8/70	P.T. $5.20/hr.		Production Line	Military Service
Long Beach Long's Drugs	10/73	6/74	$4.00/hr.		Clerk & Stock	Better job w/Compa
Long Beach State	6/74	9/75	5.00/hr.		Campus Security	Wanted experience
Liberty Dept. Store	7/75		P.T. $1.50/hr. F.T. $250/wk.		Office Records	

Have you any income in addition to your salary? ☒ Yes ☐ No   If yes, explain _Dividends on inherited stocks_

EDUCATION

	Name	Dates Attended From	Dates Attended To	Major	Minor	Degree
HIGH SCHOOL	Vacaville High	1965	1969			
COLLEGE	Consumnes River	1969	1970			
	Long Beach State	1973	1976	Business	Finance	B.A.
OTHER TRAINING						

MISCELLANEOUS INFORMATION

List honors, awards, extra-curricular activities (school or community), and grades _____

Football letter 11, 12   Jr. Achievement 9, 10

What part of expenses did you earn during high school? _*NONE*_ college? _*50%*_

List any hobbies, including sports *Football, Soccer, Boating*

_____

_____

Draft Status _____ Have you been in the United States military service? ☒ Yes ☐ No

If no, explain _____

Branch of Service *Army*

Date of entry into active duty *Aug. 1970*   Date of release from active duty *Aug. 1973*

Rank on release from active duty *Sergeant*   Completion date of Reserve commitment _—_

Have you ever been convicted of any criminal action? ☐ Yes ☒ No   If yes, explain _____

_____

List health disabilities _*None*_

Are you willing to go to work in any   DATA PRODUCTS INTERNATIONAL office in the United States? ☒ Yes ☐ No

List preferences *California — San Francisco Area, or Los Angeles*

Tell something about yourself, including reasons you feel you are qualified for the position.

I work well with machines and people. I am interested in modern technology and its potential for the future. Being unmarried, I am able to concentrate my energy to the job at hand. As my college transcript shows, I have received excellent grades along with continuing outside employment.

The information given herein is true and accurate to the best of my knowledge and belief; I understand that all information given will be verified.

Date *2/10/77* _____ Signature *Eugene J. Pearce*

HIRING COMMITMENT (For Official Use Only)

Interviewer's Comments/Name _____

Department/Office _____ Organization Code _____

Starting Date _____ Expense Allocation Code _____

Bi-weekly Salary _____ Job Title _____

Job Code ___ _____ Date _____

Designated Signature _____ Name (printed) _____

Code 169 Rev. 4/74

DATA PRODUCTS INTERNATIONAL
EMPLOYMENT APPLICATION

Applicant's Name – *Please Type or Print*

Goldner	Alan	Henry
Last	First	Middle

POSITION APPLIED FOR	REASON FOR APPLYING
Selling	good opportunity

an Equal Opportunity Employer who hires without regard to race, religion, sex, color, national origin, or age.

Home Address __3635 E. Parkway, Apt. 16__
                        Number   Street

__Chico__   __CA__
City   State   ZIP Code

Home Phone __232-9098__ Business Phone __--__

Referred By ☐ employee ☐ newspaper ☐ agency

☐ other __instructor__

Social
Security Number |5|2|5| — |1|1| — |1|3|3|2|

Do you have the right to work in the United States on a permanent basis? ☒ Yes ☐ No

Do you have relatives employed by DPI?
☐ Yes ☒ No   If yes, who?____
                                    where?____

Have you ever been employed by DPI?
☐ Yes ☒ No   If yes, when?____
                                    where?____

RECORD OF EMPLOYMENT

Employer Business and Address	Dates FROM (Mo.-Yr.)	TO (Mo.-Yr.)	BASIC MONTHLY SALARY OR DRAW ACCOUNT	OVERTIME BONUS COMMISSION*	Position and Basic Duties	Reason for Leaving
K-Mart, Chico	6-73	9-73	2.85		clerk	school
Shasta Center Hasting's Menswear	6-75	10-75	3.10		clerk	school

Have you any income in addition to your salary? ☒ Yes ☐ No   If yes, explain __scholarship__

EDUCATION

	Name	Dates Attended From	To	Major	Minor	Degree
HIGH SCHOOL	Oroville High	9-70	6-73			graduate
COLLEGE	Chico State U.	9-73	6-77	Marketing	Org. Behav.	B.S.
OTHER TRAINING						

MISCELLANEOUS INFORMATION

List honors, awards, extra-curricular activities (school or community), and grades _K-Club scholarship, Chico_
State Varsity Football, 1973-76, Fellowship for Cristian Athletes

What part of expenses did you earn during high school? _0_   college? _10%_
List any hobbies, including sports _Football, track, tennis, golf, model railroads_

Draft Status _1Y_ _____ Have you been in the United States military service? ☐ Yes ☒ No
If no, explain _colorblind_

_____ Branch of Service _____
Date of entry into active duty_____ Date of release from active duty _____
Rank on release from active duty_____ Completion date of Reserve commitment _____

Have you ever been convicted of any criminal action? ☐ Yes ☒ No   If yes, explain _____

List health disabilities _none_
Are you willing to go to work in any   DATA PRODUCTS INTERNATIONAL office in the United States? ☒ Yes ☐ No
List preferences _San Francisco, Atlanta, New Orleans_

Tell something about yourself, including reasons you feel you are qualified for the position.

I've spent all of my life in Northern California and am anxious to undertake a position
which will allow me to live in a metropolitan community. I think leadership and
responsibility are important experiences and I feel that I have had many opportunities
to demonstrate these qualities. I have been a athlete and understand the value of a
team effort. I think I work well with people. While my selling experience has been
limited to retail sales, I know that I will enjoy the opportunity to help people to
meet their needs.

The information given herein is true and accurate to the best of my knowledge and belief; I understand that all information given
will be verified.

Date _2/10/77_ _____ Signature _Alan Goldner_

HIRING COMMITMENT (For Official Use Only)

Interviewer's Comments/Name _____

Department/Office _____ Organization Code_____
Starting Date _____ Expense Allocation Code _____
Bi-weekly Salary _____ Job Title _____
Job Code_____ Date _____
Designated Signature _____ Name (printed) _____

Code 169 Rev. 4/74

DATA PRODUCTS INTERNATIONAL
EMPLOYMENT APPLICATION

Applicant's Name — *Please Type or Print*

Mc Namarra	Brian	Douglas
Last	First	Middle

POSITION APPLIED FOR: Account representative

REASON FOR APPLYING: Sales is the entry level position leading to marketing management.

an Equal Opportunity Employer who hires without regard to race, religion, sex, color, national origin, or age.

Home Address 10404 Bobolink Lane
Number / Street
Walnut Creek　CA　94596
City / State / ZIP Code
Home Phone 726-2104　Business Phone ___

Referred By ☐ employee ☐ newspaper ☐ agency
☒ other marketing professor

Social Security Number 219 - 64 - 6362

Do you have the right to work in the United States on a permanent basis? ☒ Yes ☐ No

Do you have relatives employed by DPI?
☐ Yes ☒ No　If yes, who?___
where?___

Have you ever been employed by DPI?
☐ Yes ☒ No　If yes, when?___
where?___

RECORD OF EMPLOYMENT

Employer Business and Address	Dates FROM (Mo.-Yr.)	Dates TO (Mo.-Yr.)	BASIC MONTHLY SALARY OR DRAW ACCOUNT	OVERTIME BONUS COMMISSION	Position and Basic Duties	Reason for Leaving
C&I construction	Summers 1969-73		$625		carpenters assistant	graduation — new job
State of California Dept. Motor Vehicles	6-74	9-75	1110	—	staff researcher	graduate school

Have you any income in addition to your salary? ☐ Yes ☐ No　If yes, explain___

EDUCATION

	Name	Dates Attended From	Dates Attended To	Major	Minor	Degree
HIGH SCHOOL	Walnut Creek	1967	1970	regular program	yes	
COLLEGE	San Francisco St.	1970	1974	business	social science	B.A.
	San Francisco St	1975	1977	Management	Marketing	MBA
OTHER TRAINING	none					

MISCELLANEOUS INFORMATION

List honors, awards, extra-curricular activities (school or community), and grades _____

_____

What part of expenses did you earn during high school? *10%* _____ college? *40%*

List any hobbies, including sports _____

_____

_____

Draft Status *1A* _____ Have you been in the United States military service? ☐ Yes ☒ No

If no, explain _____

Branch of Service _____

Date of entry into active duty _____ Date of release from active duty _____

Rank on release from active duty _____ Completion date of Reserve commitment _____

Have you ever been convicted of any criminal action? ☐ Yes ☒ No   If yes, explain _____

_____

List health disabilities *none* _____

Are you willing to go to work in any DATA PRODUCTS INTERNATIONAL office in the United States? ☒ Yes ☐ No

List preferences *San Francisco, Oakland, Fresno, Stockton* _____

Tell something about yourself, including reasons you feel you are qualified for the position.
I get along well with people. I used to work for the state and didnt see much opportunity to advance. This would offer more opportunity for me to use my skills and education.

The information given herein is true and accurate to the best of my knowledge and belief; I understand that all information given will be verified.

Date *February 15, 1977* Signature *Brian L. McNamara*

HIRING COMMITMENT (For Official Use Only)

Interviewer's Comments/Name _____

_____

Department/Office _____ Organization Code _____

Starting Date _____ Expense Allocation Code _____

Bi-weekly Salary _____ Job Title _____

Job Code _____ Date _____

Designated Signature _____ Name (printed) _____

Code 169 Rev. 4/74

down a list of comments (See Exhibit 32–3.) As he looked at his list, he realized that he was in a vulnerable position. If he did not treat this female properly in the interviewing process, he could open up the possibility of action against himself and/or the company. He resolved that he would read some materials on interviewing women and set up some standard questions to avoid problems.

To prepare for the interviews, Fred called in several of his salesmen and told them than since a woman would be coming in for an interview, he felt it was time to standardize the interviewing process. Until now, most interviews had been considered an opportunity to get to know the candidate. In the past, he had encouraged applicants to discuss the job with one of his salesmen but felt that this would no longer be possible. Fred prepared a list of standardized questions, carefully avoiding taboo topics, such as family plans. When the big week of interviews came, he was ready. (See Exhibit 32–4.)

The Interviews

By Wednesday afternoon Fred was quite pleased. He had seen 3 of the young men recommended by Jack Cartwright and although there were distinct differences, two of them seemed to be serious about a career in sales with DPI. Brian McNamarra was probably the weakest of the 3. He had had little work experience,

Exhibit 32-3
Managers' Comments on Females in Sales

---

1. They won't get along with the salesmen.

2. It will turn this place into a party instead of an office.

3. What would the wives think?

4. What would our customers think?

5. What if they cry?

6. Women aren't dependable.

7. Women won't relocate if we try to transfer or promote them.

8. They will get married and have babies.

9. Women aren't interested in machines.

10. We know that men can do the job. Why mess with success?

11. We can't find any with sales experience.

12. They don't like to travel.

13. They won't be able to take care of themselves on the road.

14. Women aren't really serious about careers.

Exhibit 32 - 4
Fred Johnson's Interview Plan

ASK:

1. Why are you interested in this type of work?
2. How did you select Data Product International?
3. Why do you feel that you are qualified for this job?
4. Where do you plan to be in your career five years from now?
5. Tell me about something you have done where the results were particularly pleasing to you.
6. How important is money to you?
7. What questions do you have about this position or this company?

DON'T ASK:

1. Are you married or do you plan to get married?
2. Does it bother you that all of our salespeople are men?
3. Are you willing to travel?
4. How old are you?
5. How do you handle your home responsibilities and a job?
6. Do you type (HA HA)?

---

none of which was in selling. He seemed quite nervous and had no questions to ask when Fred finished describing the job and the company. Although he had a graduate degree, he seemed to place a lot of value on security.

Eugene Plowe seemed like a serious young man with a strong career orientation. He had made an effort to work his way through school in areas related to his field of study. He was full of questions about the company and the job. Fred was impressed that he not only asked questions, but probed for more complete answers. He seemed quite mature and handled himself with confidence.

Alan Goldner seemed a bit less mature than Eugene Plowe, but Fred attributed that to his lack of military experience. A few months in the field would probably buff off any rough edges. His experience in team sports showed through. He was quite easy to converse with and would get along well with the other men and the customers as well. He had asked fewer questions, but seemed very sincere and listened to the answers with care.

On Thursday, Fred faced Joan Channell. She was wearing a threepiece suit. It occurred to Fred that he had never considered what a saleswoman would wear. He wondered what his customers would think if a saleswoman called on them. The interview did not last quite as long as the others. After he finished his list of questions, he asked if she had any questions or concerns. She asked several questions about the training program. He explained that the company sent each new salesman to Long Beach for eight 2-week training sessions during the first year. He pointed out that the training cost the company a great deal of money and that, in a normal situation, the salesman had started to earn his own way sometime near the end of his second year with the company. Every time he said the word "salesman" he felt uncomfortable, but Joan did not seem to notice. He was glad when the interview was over and congratulated himself on his preparation and avoidance of dangerous subjects.

He was glad when Friday's interview was over, too. David Greenfile was a nice young man, but Fred did not share his idea that he had finally decided what to do with his life. After a few questions, it became obvious that Dave's father had decided for him. He had all the raw materials. He was bright and presentable and understood the requirements of selling. He answered all of the questions appropriately, but did so in a mechanical manner. He showed little enthusiasm for the job. Fred had always felt that a salesman had to like his work. Fred went home Friday night having made up his mind to offer the positions to Eugene and Alan. He hadn't quite figured out how to justify not hiring Joan, but figured that Jack could send her to interview for a position in another office. She was a bright young woman and she would manage.

Bright and early Monday morning Jack called to ask how the interviews had gone. He listened quietly while Fred gave brief descriptions and indicated what he intended to do. Then Jack calmly pointed out that rejection of a qualified minority applicant was a serious move when DPI faced the government-imposed affirmative action requirements. He urged Fred to reconsider his decision.

Discussion Questions

1. If you were Fred, what would you do?

2. Given the application materials shown in Exhibit 32–2 and the case discussion, how would you rank the applicants for a position with DPI?

3. Discuss hiring practices and laws pertaining to hiring "minority" groups. Are they fair? How do such practices and laws affect a company's business?

4. What are some behavioral principles you learned from this case about hiring practices? Explain.

Chapter 8

International Marketing Strategies

Applications of marketing strategies in markets within other countries involve the same 2 basic questions of marketing management: What market segments should be selected by the organization? What marketing mix should be developed to stimulate demand from the market segment to reach sales, profits, and social goals? However, international marketing strategies are complicated by 3 additional dimensions. First, there are government laws and regulations at the national level for all countries concerning importing and exporting products and services. Special taxes (tariffs), quotas, and invisible trade barriers (e.g., competing firms located elsewhere may receive benefits from a "favored nation" arrangement between governments) often are used to restrict international marketing. Second, 2 or more markets are involved in international marketing often resulting in using different marketing mixes for different domestic markets in different countries. Third, the marketing structure or system will often be different in different countries (e.g., unavailability of commercial television in most socialist nations and the custom of using long channels of distribution for consumer durables in Japan). Thus, government actions, market behavior, and marketing structure affect international marketing strategies, and more than one marketing mix often will be used in international marketing.

Scope of International Marketing Operations

The size and impact of international marketing operations vary by country, industries, and organizations within industries. For the United States, international trade represents less than 10 percent of its gross national product (GNP) but the country is the largest importer and exporter of products. International marketing represents over 50 percent of the GNP for some other industrialized countries, for example, Japan and Belgium.

The scope and impact of international marketing for different industries and firms within industries may be seen by studying Table C—8–1. A total of the 11 largest business firms in the world by sales volume are listed. Each firm had sales of over $2 billion in 1971. General Motors (GM) is the largest firm with $28 billion sales of which 19 percent came from sales outside of the United States. GM operates in 21 "subsidiary countries" with 15 percent of its assets located outside of the United States.

Compare GM's international operations with Nestle. A total of 98 percent of Nestle's sales are outside of Switzerland, 90 percent of the firm's assets are located in other countries, the firm has marketing operations in 15 "subsidiary countries." Foreign marketing operations are more important for Nestle than for GM in a relative sense, even though the total sales volume of foreign sales is larger for GM ($5.4 billion) than for Nestle ($3.5 billion).

For firms within an industry, comparisions can be made between GM, Ford, Volkswagen, and Standard Oil (N.J.), Royal Dutch Shell, and British Petroleum in Table C—8–1. Substantial differences in the relative scope of foreign operations are apparent, for example, 40 percent of the assets of Ford versus 15 percent of the assets of GM are in foreign locations with Ford operating in 30 "subsidiary countries."

Thus, international marketing operations should be studied at the national, industrial, and organizational levels to learn the scope and impact of international versus domestic sales, earnings, and assets. The *relative* size of international marketing's operations for a firm is most likely to affect the marketing strategies of the firm. For example, international marketing operations will dominate the planning and direction of marketing strategy at Nestle but not at GM.

International Marketing Decisions

Several related decisions must be made by an organization entering international markets. The first decision is whether to enter into foreign marketing. A firm may enter into international marketing in an unplanned manner—simply at the request of an order for products from a foreign customer. An organization may also plan ahead to enter markets because of sales and profit opportunities, unused production capacity, competitive preemptions in domestic markets, competitive entry into foreign markets, and reciprocal purchase arrangements with foreign suppliers.

Market Selection Decision

The market selection decision is the second major decision for an organization which has decided to develop an international marketing strategy. Market selection should be viewed as a sequence of steps to estimate market potential, costs, and rate of return on investment for a firm.

The five steps in this sequence include the following: [1]

---

[1] See David S. R. Leighton, "Deciding When to Enter International Markets," in *Handbook of Modern Marketing,* ed. Victor P. Buell (New York: McGraw-Hill Book Company, 1970), section 20, pp. 23–28.

Table C—8—1
Foreign Content of Operations and Assets of
Selected Manufacturing Corporations
1971

Company	Nationality	Total Sales (Millions of Dollars)	Foreign Content* as a Percentage of			Number of Subsidiary Countries
			Sales	Earnings	Assets	
General Motors	United States	28,264	19	19	15	21
Standard Oil (N.J.)	United States	18,701	50	52	52	25
Ford Motor Company	United States	16,433	26	na	40	30
Royal Dutch Shell	The Netherlands United Kingdom	12,734	79	na	na	43
IBM	United States	8,274	39	50	27	80
IT&T	United States	7,346	42	35	61	40
British Petroleum	United Kingdom	5,191	88	na	na	52
Volkswagen	Federal Republic of Germany	4,967	69	na	na	12
Nestle	Switzerland	3,541	98	na	90	15
British-American Tobacco	United Kingdom	2,262	93	92	82	54
Singer	United States	2,099	37	75	54	30

Source: United Nations, *Multinational Corporations in World Development,* Table 3, pp. 130–137.
* Foreign content percentages refer to years 1967, 1968, 1969, or 1970.

(1) *Estimate of current market potential.*   The first step is to estimate current market potential in each candidate market. This marketing research task calls for using existing published data supplemented by primary data collection through company surveys and studies. The obstacle is that foreign marketing research is more difficult, as a general rule, than domestic market research, for at least 4 reasons.

(*a*) Published census and market data are usually scarce and somewhat unreliable in several countries, especially the poorer ones.

(*b*) Many trade associations do not make their data public.

(*c*) Marketing research firms are not always of high quality.

(*d*) Buyers in other countries are less used to cooperating in interviews.

Yet there are some signs of improvement. The U. S. Department of Commerce and several large banks are increasing the amount of information available about foreign markets. The United Nations publishes statistical data and market information. Foreign governments, banks, chambers of commerce, and private companies are increasingly responding to the problem of better market information.

(2) *Forecast of future market potential.*   The firm also needs a forecast of future market potential. This is complicated because the market analyst is usually insufficiently versed in the economic, political, cultural, and business currents of another country. Many foreign countries do not show the stability of government, currency, or law that the analyst's own country may show.

(3) *Forecast of market share.*   The normal difficulties of forecasting market shares are compounded in a foreign marketing environment. The foreign marketer will be competing against other foreign marketers as well as against home-country firms. The foreign marketer has to estimate how the buyers will feel about the relative merits of a different product, selling methods, and company. Even if the buyers are impartial, their government may put up barriers in the form of quotas, tariffs, taxes, specifications, or even outright boycotts.

(4) *Forecast of costs and profits.*   Costs will depend on the marketer's contemplated entry strategy. If the marketer resorts to exporting or licensing, costs will be spelled out in the contracts. If the marketer decides to locate manufacturing facilities abroad, the cost estimation will require an understanding of local labor conditions, taxes, trade practices, and stipulations regarding the hiring of nationals as key employees. After estimating future costs, the marketer subtracts them from estimated company sales to find company profits for each year of the planning horizon.

(5) *Estimate of rate of return on investment.*   The forecasted income stream must be related to the investment stream to derive an implicit rate of return. The estimated rate of return should be high enough to cover

(*a*) the company's normal target return on its investment

(*b*) the risk and uncertainty of marketing in that country

The risk premium has to cover not only the chance that the basic estimates of sales and costs may be wrong but also the chance that unanticipated monetary changes (devaluation, blocked currency) and political changes (future discrimination against foreign business firms, or even expropriation) may occur.

Markets may be grouped at the national level by several environmental and societal factors. The following factors are likely to be important in affecting the marketing structure of local markets in international marketing and, consequently, the marketing mixes selected to reach such markets.

I. Environmental Factors

   1. Total population

   2. Population density

   3. Annual percentage rate of increase in population

   4. Percentage of population of working age (15 to 64)

   5. Literacy: literate percentage of population aged 15 and over

   6. Agricultural population as a percentage of total population

   7. Urbanization: percentage of population in cities over 20,000 population

   8. Primacy: population of the primate city as a percentage of the total population of the four largest cities

II. Societal Factors

   9. Ethnic diversity: number of ethnic groups which amount to 1 percent of the population or more

   10. Religious homogeneity and identification
Homogeneous—75 percent of the population with one religion

   11. Racial homogeneity and identification
Homogeneous—90 percent of the population belonging to one racial stock

   12. Linguistic homogeneity: percentage of the adult population which speaks a common language
Homogeneous—a common language spoken by at least 85 percent of the adult population.[2]

Countries have been grouped according to the similarities and differences in their environmental and societal profiles. A substantial majority of countries can be placed into one of 5 such groups:

(1) *Most highly developed countries,* for example, the United Kingdom, West Germany, Belgium, the United States, France, Canada, Sweden, Netherlands, Italy, and Australia. All have a very high literacy rate and relatively high urbanization. None has an overwhelmingly predominant metropolis. Almost all have a very large measure of cultural homogeneity and possess a dominant language.

(2) *Developed countries,* for example, Finland, South Africa, Ireland, Mexico, Portugal, Israel, and Brazil. These countries do not possess a single com-

---

[2] A. A. Sherbini, "Classifying and Comparing Countries," in B. Leander, ed., *Comparative Analysis for International Marketing* (Boston: Allyn and Bacon, 1967), p. 4–376.

mon attribute. Most are highly literate, highly urbanized, not densely populated, and not overwhelmingly agricultural. They show wide variances in population increase. Most have a dominant language and are heterogeneous in religion and race.

(3) *Semideveloped countries,* for example, Lebanon, Greece, United Arab Republic, Turkey, Colombia, Peru, India, and Iraq. A majority of these countries are literate, have a predominantly agricultural population with a high annual population increase, possess a low working age/dependency ratio, and a dominant language, race, and religion. They vary substantially in population size.

(4) *Underdeveloped countries,* for example, Tunisia, Ghana, Syria, Bolivia, Iran, and Indonesia. Most of these countries contain largely illerate rural (agricultural) populations, have high annual rates of population increase, and are reasonably homogeneous with respect to race and religion. They vary a great deal in size of population.

(5) *Very underdeveloped countries,* for example, Nigeria, Burma, Thailand, Sudan, Jordan, Mali, Haiti, Liberia, and Ethiopia. The size of population in these countries varies widely, but almost all have a low population density. Most have a high dependency ratio and a high population rate increase. There is considerable heterogeneity in race, religion, and language.[3]

Entry and Operating Decisions

Different methods of entry and operations may be used once a firm has decided to enter foreign markets. These methods may be grouped into 3 main types: (1) exporting (domestic production and foreign selling), (2) joint venturing (joining with foreign companies in some way), and (3) direct investment abroad.

Exporting is the simplest way for a manufacturer to get involved in a foreign market. Several different exporting arrangements can be developed. Indirect export using export merchants (who take title to the product), agents (who do not take title), and cooperative organizations within an industry are popular arrangements for small firms or firms new to international marketing. Direct export arrangements are frequently found for large scale international operations. Direct export arrangements include a domestic-based export department, overseas sales branch, and foreign-based distributors, agents, or salespersons.[4]

Joint venturing with foreign firms or other organizations (e.g., governments) may take the form of licensing, contract manufacturing, management contracting, and joint-ownership ventures. Each of these forms of joint ventures require some type of long-term contractural arrangement with a foreign firm. Joint ventures offer the advantages of speed of entry into foreign markets, low capital risks, and an increase in marketing expertise compared with other operating arrangements. However, joint ventures usually reduce the control a firm has over its foreign operations compared to investing directly into foreign manufacturing facilities.

---

[3] Ibid.
[4] Philip Kotler, *Marketing Management* (Englewood Cliffs, NJ: Prentice-Hall, 1976), pp. 473–474.

Also, profits, if any, from manufacturing in foreign locations are not realized from joint venture arrangements.

Several large manufacturing firms have become multinational organizations due to the size of their direct investment in foreign-based assembly or manufacturing facilities. The *multinational corporation* has been defined as a company which has a direct investment base in several companies, which generally derives 20 to 50 percent or more of its net profits from foreign operations, and whose management makes policy decisions based on the alternatives available anywhere in the world. Approximately 300 such companies are operating and most of these are American.[5]

Marketing Mix Decisions

Most firms operating in international markets attempt to standardize some of the elements of their marketing mixes where possible. For example, similar pricing on product components policies might be used for several international markets. However, some adjustments to the marketing mix are usually necessary to satisfy different local environmental and societal factors or because of unavailability of the domestically available market structure.

Five combinations of product and promotion strategies are identified and summarized in Table C—8–2.[6] The first strategy is a straight extension of both domestic product and communication mixes. It has been used successfully by Pepsi-Cola to introduce its soft drinks everywhere in the world, but it has failed for some other producers such as Philip Morris in the Canadian market and Campbell's tomato soup in the British market (not bitter enough for Britains). This product communications extension strategy has great appeal to most international companies because of the enormous cost savings associated with the approach. For example, the substantial costs of producing alternative television and print advertisements and product models are eliminated.

The second strategy is the use of product extension and communication adaptation mix. When a product fills a different need or serves a different function under use conditions identical with or similar to those in the home market, the only adjustment required is in marketing communications. Bicycles, for example, satisfy needs mainly for recreation in the United States but provide basic transportation in countries like India. The appeal of the product extension communications adaptation strategy is that savings in manufacturing, research and development, and inventory costs can still result. The additional costs are in identifying the different product functions the product will service in foreign markets and in reformulating advertising, sales promotion, and other dimensions of market communications around the newly identified function.

A third international product strategy is to extend without change the basic communications strategy developed for the central market but to adapt the product

---

[5] James C. Baker, "Multinational Marketing: A Comparative Case Study," in Bernard A. Morin, ed., *Marketing in a Changing World*, (Chicago: American Marketing Association, 1969), p. 6.

[6] Warren J. Keegan, "Multinational Product Planning: Strategic Alternatives," *Journal of Marketing* (January 1969), p. 59. Published by the American Marketing Association.

Table C—8–2
Multinational Product-Communications Mix:
Strategic Alternatives

Strategy	Product Function or Need Satisfied	Conditions of Product Use	Ability to Buy Product	Recommended Product Strategy	Recommended Communications Strategy	Relative Cost of Adjustments	Product Examples
1	Same	Same	Yes	Extension	Extension	1	Soft drinks
2	Different	Same	Yes	Extension	Adaptation	2	Bicycles, motor-scooters
3	Same	Different	Yes	Adaptation	Extension	3	Gasoline, detergents
4	Different	Different	Yes	Adaptation	Adaptation	4	Clothing, greeting cards
5	Same	—	No	Invention	Develop new communications	5	Motor vehicles

Source: Warren J. Keegan, "Multinational Product Planning, Strategic Alternatives," *Journal of Marketing* (January 1969), p. 59. Published by the American Marketing Association.

to different use conditions. The product adaptation communications extension strategy assumes that the product will serve the same function in foreign markets under different use conditions. Esso followed this approach when it adapted the physical characteristics of its gasoline to the different climatic and user conditions of various countries while continuing to use on a worldwide basis the invitation to "Put a tiger in your tank." International companies in the soap and detergent fields have adjusted their product formulation to meet local water conditions and the characteristics of local washing machines, with no change in the companies' basic communications approach.

Strategy four is to adapt both the product and the communications approach when there are differences in environmental conditions of use and in the function that a product serves. In essence, this is a combination of strategies two and three. U.S. greeting-card companies have faced these circumstances in Europe, where the occasions for using greeting cards differ from those in the United States. Also, in Europe the function of a greeting card has been to provide a space for the sender to write her own message in contrast to the United States where cards contain prepared messages.

A final strategy is that of product invention. When potential customers cannot afford one of the firm's products, there may be an opportunity to invent or design an entirely new product that satisfies the identified need or function at a price that the consumer can afford. If product-development costs are not excessive, this may be a potentially rewarding product strategy for the mass markets in the less developed countries.[7]

Pricing decisions are often affected differently in different international markets. Ultimate prices are usually raised by shipping costs, tariffs, longer channels of distribution, larger middlemen margins, and special taxes in international markets.

Some of the possible effects of these factors on the end price of a consumer item are illustrated in Table C—8–3. Because costs and tariffs vary so widely from country to country, a hypothetical but realistic example is used: it assumes (1) that a constant net price is received by the manufacturer, (2) that all domestic transportation costs are absorbed by the various middlemen and reflected in their margins, and (3) that the foreign middlemen have the same margins as the domestic middlemen in the first 3 foreign examples. In some instances, foreign middleman margins will be lower, but it is equally probable that foreign middlemen margins will be greater (as is assumed at the retail level in the fourth foreign example). In fact, in many instances middlemen will use higher wholesale and retail margins for foreign goods than for similar domestic goods.

Notice that the retail prices in Table C—8–3 range widely, illustrating the difficulty of price control by manufacturers in overseas retail markets. No matter how much the manufacturers may wish to market a product in a foreign country for a price equivalent to $1.90 U.S., they may find they have little opportunity for such control. Even assuming the most optimistic conditions of Foreign Example 1, the producer would need to cut his net by nearly one-third to absorb freight-plus-tariff so that the goods could be priced the same on the foreign and domestic markets. To compute, work backward from the retail price. Retail price minus retail margin, wholesaler margin, transportation and tariffs equals manufacturers' net. Price escalation is everywhere; the landed price of Cutty Sark Scotch whiskey in Japan, including transportation, is $1.28. To this add $1.16 of standard tariff, a 220 percent tax (on cost *plus* tariff), and a $.33 customs and handling fee. To the resultant $8.14 distributor price, add wholesale and retail margins for a typical retail price of about $14.00. The dominant domestic brand, Suntory, offers whiskeys from $.95 to $30.00 a fifth, with a comparable product retailing for about $8.00. One study of European housewares provides numerous examples of price escalation. A $10 (U.S.) electric can opener is priced in Milan at $24; a $15 (U.S.) automatic toaster is priced at $22 in France.[8]

A manufacturer may attempt to offset tariffs and transportation charges by accepting a lower net price for goods sold in foreign markets, but this may be viewed as "dumping" by local firms in the foreign markets who may request government action to nullify the price reduction. Several distribution alternatives might be considered in an attempt to keep prices under control. Some countries charge a tax for each transaction through a marketing channel. If a channel can be shortened and the total taxes reduced on the product, price decreases may be realized.

---

[7] Ibid.

[8] Philip R. Cateora and John M. Hess, *International Marketing* (Homewood, IL: Richard D. Irwin, 1975), p. 435.

Table C—8–3
Sample Causes and Effects of Price Escalation

	Domestic Example	Foreign Example 1: Assuming the Same Channels with Wholesaler Importing Directly	Foreign Example 2: Importer and Same Margins and Same Channels	Foreign Example 3: Same as 2 but with 10% Cumulative Turnover Tax	Foreign Example 4: Long Channels, Larger Retail Margins, No Turnover Tax
Mfg. net	$ .95	$ .95	$ .95	$ .95	$ .95
Transport, c.i.f.	x	.15	.15	.15	.15
Tariff (20%)	x	.19	.19	.19	.19
Importer pays	x	x	1.29	1.29	1.29
				.32	
Importer margin when sold to wholesaler z (25% on cost)	x	x	.32	+ .13 turnover tax % .45	.32
Wholesaler pays landed cost	.95	1.29	1.61	1.74	1.61
				.58	
Wholesaler margin (33⅓% on cost)	.32	.43	.54	+ .17 turnover tax = .75	.54
Local foreign jobber pays	x	x	x	x	2.15
Jobber margin (33⅓% on cost)	x	x	x	x	.72
Retailer pays	*1.27*	*1.72*	*2.15*	*2.49*	*2.87*
				1.25	
Retail margin (50% on cost)	.63	.86	1.08	+ .25 turnover tax =1.50	1.92 (66⅔% on cost)
Retail Price	*1.90*	*2.58*	*3.23*	*3.99*	*4.79*

Notes: All figures in $U.S.

x = not applicable.

The exhibit assumes that all domestic transportation costs are absorbed by the middlemen. Transportation, tariffs, and middleman margins vary from country, but for purposes of comparison only a few of the possible variations are shown.

Source: Philip R. Cateora and John M. Hess, *International Marketing* (Homewood, IL: Richard D. Irwin, 1975). Reprinted by permission of the publisher.

Figure C—8–1
Levels of Distribution in Selected Countries

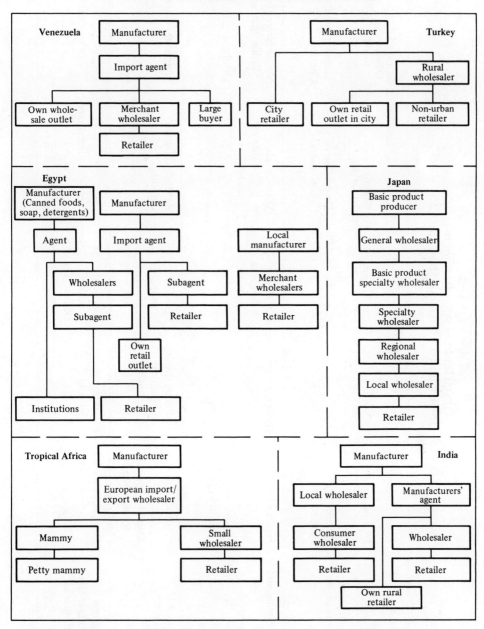

Source: George Wadinambiaratchi, "Channels of Distribution in Developing Economies," *The Business Quarterly,* **30** (Winter, 1965), pp. 74–82.

Table C—8–4
Obstacles to Standardization in
International Marketing Strategies

Factors Limiting Standardization	Elements of Marketing Program				
	Product Design	Pricing	Distribution	Sales Force	Advertising & Promotion; Branding & Packaging
Market characteristics					
Physical environment	Climate Product use conditions		Customer mobility	Dispersion of customers	Access to media Climate
Stage of economic and Industrial development	Income levels Labor costs in relation to capital costs	Income levels	Consumer shopping patterns	Wage levels, availability of manpower	Needs for convenience rather than economy Purchase quantities
Cultural factors	"Custom and tradition" Attitudes toward foreign goods	Attitudes toward bargaining	Consumer shopping patterns	Attitudes toward selling	Language, literacy Symbolism
Industry conditions					
Stage of product life cycle in each market	Extent of product differentiation	Elasticity of demand	Availability of outlets Desirability of private brands	Need for missionary sales effort	Awareness, experience with products

Competition	Quality levels	Local costs / Prices of substitutes	Competitors' control of outlets	Competitors' sales forces	Competitive expenditures, messages
Marketing institutions / Distributive system	Availability of outlets	Prevailing margins	Number and variety of outlets available	Number, size dispersion of outlets	Extent of self-service
Advertising media and agencies			Ability to "force" distribution	Effectiveness of advertising, need for substitutes	Media availability, costs, overlaps
Legal restrictions	Product standards / Patent laws / Tariffs & taxes	Tariffs & taxes / Antitrust laws / Resale price maintenance	Restrictions on product lines / Resale price maintenance	General employment restrictions / Specific restrictions on selling	Specific restrictions on message, costs / Trademark laws

Source: Robert E. Buzzell, "Can You Standard Multinational Marketing?" *Harvard Business Review,* **36** (November-December, 1968), p. 102–113.

Marketing channels available for selection often vary by different international markets. Several typical marketing channels for 6 countries are shown in Figure C—8–1. A firm may be forced to use the existing channel structure whether or not the channel is desired.

For example, consider a can of Del Monte peach halves in a Japanese marketing channel. The peaches arrive in Yokohama at .26 a can. Immediately, customs and handling charges add .09 to the price. Then the importer sticks on a bit more than a penny and sells it to a wholesaler, who adds another .03; the wholesaler sells it to another wholesaler, who adds a further .02 then sells it to a grocery store, which adds an additional .11.

The retail price: .52 a can—a far cry from the .30 or so the 15-ounce can might command in a suburban U.S. supermarket. So it is no surprise that in a typical Japanese city, some 90 percent of the imported canned peaches are sold wrapped as expensive gifts.

The peaches are victims of a phenomenon stumping many American business people there these days: the Japanese distribution system. Those who have encountered the Japanese system say it may well rank as the most inefficient, most complex, and most costly of any in the industrialized world—a lesson in how not to do it. So many eager middlemen handle each item that the wholesale volume runs about 5 times retail volume, one expert calculates. In the United States, the comparable wholesale figure is only twice the retail volume.[9]

Summary

International marketing strategy is not likely to be a carbon copy of a domestic marketing program. Several legal, market behavior, and market structure factors are likely to prevent standardization of one marketing mix across many international markets. Table C—8–4 is a summary of factors likely to prevent standardization of international marketing strategies. Thus, management should plan on some adaptations to its marketing mix for different international markets.

The scope and impact of international marketing varies by country, industry, and firms within industries. Consequently, few generalizations or standard operating procedures can be concluded by studying international marketing at an aggregate level. Case analyses of individual firms and international marketing situations are needed to improve management expertise in international marketing strategy.

Discussion Questions

1. What 3 dimensions are the special concern of international marketing strategists?

---

[9] William D. Hartley, "Cumbersome Japanese Distribution System Stumps U. S. Concerns," *Wall Street Journal* (March 2, 1972), pp. 1, 12.

2. What problems in marketing strategy would a manager likely be faced with in Japan?

3. What 5 product and communication strategies have been used in international marketing? Explain each briefly.

4. Provide a one-page summary of findings to Table C—8–1.

5. What questions would you want answered before deciding on specific international market segments?

6. Explain the additions to the $1.90 domestic price in Table C—8–3 to reach the $4.79 international market price shown in the last column of the table.

Some International Marketing Information Sources

Statistics Africa: Sources for Market Research—by Joan M. Harvey, CBD Research, Ltd., 1970. Provides information on statistics sources for the whole of the African continent and its adjacent islands. The statistical publications are arranged in groups covering general, production, external trade, internal distribution, population and standard of living statistics.

Statistics America: Sources for Market Research—by Joan M. Harvey, CBD Research, Ltd., 1973. Describes the main sources of statistical information for each country in North, Central, and South America and adjacent islands. The publications are arranged in the same groups as in *Statistics Africa* above.

Statistics Europe: Sources for Market Research—by Joan M. Harvey, CBD Research, Ltd., 2nd ed., 1972. Describes the main sources of statistical information for each country in Europe. The publications are arranged in the same groups as in *Statistics Africa* above.

Statistical Yearbook—United Nations (annual) updated by *Monthly Bulletin of Statistics,* 1961-date (yearbook); also, *Monthly Bulletin.* World economic statistics covering population, national income, agricultural and industrial production, energy, external trade and transport.

Yearbook of International Trade Statistics—United Nations. Provides basic information on individual countries' external trade performances in terms of the overall trends in current value as well as in volume and price, the importance of trading partners and the significance of individual commodities imported and exported. (annual)

Yearbook of National Accounts Statistics—United Nations. Published in 3 volumes, Vols. I and II, *Individual Country Data,* gives detailed national accounts data for 121 countries and areas on gross domestic product and expenditure, national income and national disposable income, capital transaction of the nation. Volume III, *International Tables,* gives estimates of total and per capita gross domestic product, national income, and national disposable income, etc. for about 154 countries. (1967-date)

Worldcasts—Predicasts, Inc. Published in 2 sections, regional and product. It includes abstracts of published international forecasts for series such as population, production, and consumption. (quarterly, 1974-date)

Advertising Strategy: Introduction of New Sanitary Napkins in a Different Culture*

Prakash Sethi, University of Texas at Dallas

Stille-Werner, Sweden

Stille-Werner is a Swedish company primarily engaged in manufacturing and distributing infirmary supplies and paper products in the Swedish market. The company had 750 employees and an annual turnover of 60 million Swedish Kronas in 1969.

Stille had manufactured and sold sanitary napkins in Sweden before World War II but had not been in the market since then. However, in 1967, Stille found an opportunity to enter the market in a dramatic manner. The company's new products group had developed a new sanitary napkin. Based on an invention by SPA, a paper mill company, this napkin had two important features for convenient use and disposal distinguishing it from and making it superior to other sanitary napkins on the market. One, it could be attached to the underwear with a tape and therefore no belt was needed to wear it. Two, it could be flushed in the toilet.

At first Stilles' management doubted the product's marketing possibilities in view of the competitive structure of the market and novel product design. However, before making a decision, they decided to conduct a market survey to make a more realistic assessment.

General Market Conditions

As a first step, Stille conducted a study to determine the market size of sanitary protection (SP) items and the nature of existing competition. Their findings are briefly summarized here:

* Reprinted from *Advanced Cases in Multinational Business Operations* (Santa Monica, CA: Goodyear Publishing, 1972) pp. 435–445. Permission granted by Goodyear Publishing Co.

The SP market in Sweden amounted to 68 million SwKrs. In 1968 (in retail prices), of which SwKrs. 42 million were for sanitary napkins and SwKr 18 million for tampons. The SP market has grown about 10 percent during the sixties. The napkin market has been growing at the rate of 5 to 6 percent, and the tampon market at 15 to 20 percent a year.

The number of consumers has been somewhat constant, there being about 1.8 million females between the ages of 13 and 50. However, the market size may increase through more intensive use. On an average, a consumer changed protection 2 to 3 times a day with 18 to 20 changes per menstruation period. Gynecologists, however, recommended twice this rate. About 95 percent of all consumers used industry produced SP products.

Grocery stores are the principal outlets for SP, handling about 65 percent of total retail sales, with the remaining 35 percent sold through department stores and cosmetic shops. In 1968, SP worth SwKrs. 6 million were sold through grocery stores (including supermarkets), SwKrs. 15 million through department stores, and SwKrs. 9 million through cosmetics and other shops. The independent food stores (noncooperative) have 50 percent of the sanitary napkin and 40 percent of the tampon sales.

Mölnlycke is the major brand in the market and accounted for 75 percent of the napkin market and 95 percent of the tampon market in 1968. Co-op brand, Lady, was number two. Other brands like Silkesept, Formita, and Tampax had smaller shares. In 1965, Mölnlycke had sold 25 million ten-unit packages of SP of which 18 million were napkins and 9 million tampons.

Market Research—Attitude Study

The next step for Stilles was to do a consumer study about product acceptability. This research was conducted in Stockholm and in a small religious town. The study found that 54 percent of the consumers interviewed liked the product and 82 percent of the latter group said that they were willing to pay a higher price for this napkin. The research also showed that the SP consumption was proportionally much higher in the small town. The explanation was that the women in Stockholm consumed more birth control pills which caused lighter menstruations.

Buying Habits
The attitude study showed that women buy SP only when they need it and are, accordingly, not very open for low-price campaigns or other such promotions.

Information Need
The research told that there was practically no communication among women about SP products. It was found that the women preferred real information and not victorian language. This was especially true for women in the below-25 age group.

Package
Market research showed that women normally kept the SP package in a concealed place.

Results of this survey were quite encouraging and Stilles decided to test-market the product. The choice of location, however, presented some problems. Stilles was afraid that if the product was test-marketed anywhere in Sweden, Mölnlycke was likely to interfere with the test by reducing prices of their products in the test-market area, thereby distorting test findings. Consequently, the product was test-marketed in 1968 in Tammersfors, Finland. Results showed a somewhat higher repurchase disposition than the consumer test had indicated.

Introduction of Stilles Sanisept

Stilles was now ready to introduce its brand, Stilles Sanisept, in the Swedish market. To market its product, it made the following basic decisions concerning marketing and promotional strategies:

1. Distribution—National: all channels carrying SP products were to be used.
2. Pricing—Price Stilles Sanisept slightly lower than the premium brand of the major competitor. The price of Stilles Sanisept compared with Mölnlycke follows:

Brand	Package	Average Retail Price (including 10% purchase tax) SwKrs.
Mimosept Mölnlycke	10 in a plastic bag	2.70
Mimosept Lady (low price)	10 in a plastic bag	1.97
Mimosept Lady (low price)	20 in a plastic bag	3.32
OB Tampon	10 in a plastic bag	2.88
Stilles Sanisept	10 in a plastic bag	2.44

There were to be no price promotions or rebates.

3. Package—To give the product a high visibility, a package was designed that could be hung on a bathroom hook. Stilles used a base design and color combination found on the most widely sold brand of bathroom towels, that is, Cannon (made by a Swedish subsidiary of the U.S. textile company of the same name). See Exhibit 33–1.
4. Advertising—To be the heart of their sales campaign, advertising was primarily concentrated in women's magazines. The basic theme was to emphasize the functional aspect of the product and provide information in a no-nonsense manner.

The advertising campaign hammered at the superiority of Stilles Sanisept over the competitors' products by showing the two products side-by-side. Although rules for such advertising had been relaxed during the last few years, Stilles ads were nevertheless extreme examples of comparative advertising. Four examples of ads used in the campaign are reproduced in Exhibits 33–2 to 33–5.

Exhibit 33–2 is an ad from a woman's magazine. It describes the qualities of the napkin. Headline: "You can apply the new sanitary napkin Stilles Sanisept in this simple manner and it can be flushed down." The text informs the reader that a belt is unnecessary, a tape attaches it to the underwear, the napkin is only 12 mm thick and not 25 mm as ordinary sanitary napkins, and that it is the only napkin that is permitted by the Stockholm Health Department for flushing in the toilet (ordinary sanitary napkins are prohibited from being flushed down). Exhibit 33–3 is an ad from a teenage magazine directed at young women. The text gives in a summarized form the same information as in Exhibit 33–2. Exhibit 33–4 is an ad published in a women's magazine in April 1969. Headline: "No more tangled

Exhibit 33-1

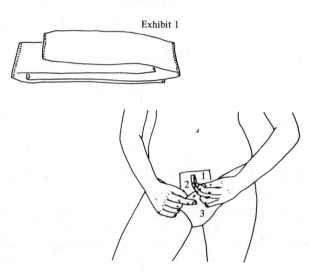

Exhibit 1

Exhibit 33-2

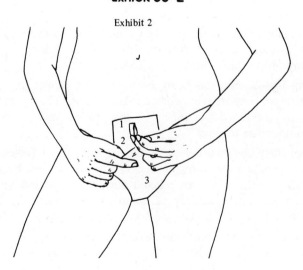

Exhibit 2

Exhibit 33-3

Exhibit 3

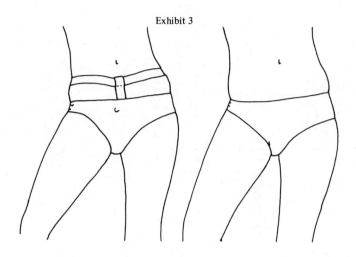

Exhibit 33-4

Exhibit 4

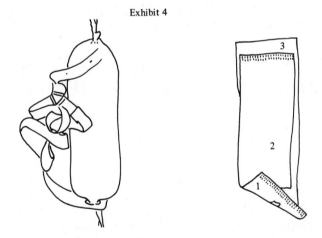

belt, troublesome ropes, ties and clasps which rub, this is the new sanitary napkin Stilles Sanisept and it can be flushed down." The text gives the same information as in Exhibit 33–2. Exhibit 33–5 is an ad from a women's fashion magazine published in November 1969. It describes the possibilities for combining the layers of wadding.

Stilles spent heavily on mass advertising in promoting Stilles Sanisept. The brand was introduced nationally in March 1969. During the period March to December 1969, Stilles spent about SwKrs. 824,000, approximately 46 percent of the total press advertising done by all manufacturers on all SP products during 1969 (Tables 33–1 and 33–2).

Exhibit 33-5

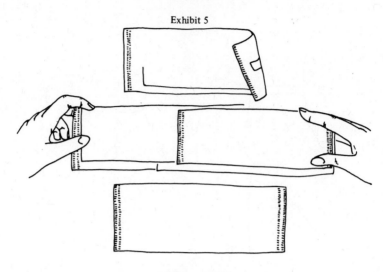

Exhibit 5

Table   33-1

**Sanitary Protection Advertising
Expenditures—Sweden
(space costs in thousands of SwKrs.)**

Brand	1967	1968	1969
Formita	227	15	31
Kronosept	12	0.4	0.3
Mölnlycke:			
Mimosept	100	140	77
Mimosept Lady	233	103	166
OB	527	542	175
Mölnlycke Others	78	14	104
Sanetta (co-op)	3	—	—
Silkesept	100	63	—
Stilles Sanisept	—	—	824
Tampax	295	374	413
Total	1,575	1,249	1,794

Results

By January 1970, ten months after the market introduction Stilles Sanisept had gained 22 percent of the *total* SP market. The market shares for various brands

Table 33–2
Breakdown of Advertising Expenditures
For Sanitary Products—Sweden

Brand Name and Nature of Medium	1967			1968			1969		
	No. of Ads	Column Space Centimeters	Total Space Cost SwKrs.	No. of Ads	Column Space Centimeters	Total Space Cost SwKrs.	No. of Ads	Column Space Centimeters	Total Space Cost SwKrs.
Formita									
Daily Press, Stockholm, Gothenburg, Malmo	4	1,260	45,060	—	—	—	8	629	11,781
Daily Press, provincial	—	—	—	—	—	—	24	1,869	18,866
Magazines	31	3,049	155,075	2	159	11,670	—	—	—
Trade Press	7	1,160	26,546	3	212	3,440	—	—	—
Total	42	5,469	226,681	5	371	15,110	32	2,498	30,647
Kronosept									
Daily Press, Stockholm, Gothenburg, Malmo	14	606	11,681	1	27	378	2	146	3,281
Daily Press, provincial	1	77	704	—	—	—	—	—	—
Total	15	683	12,385	1	27	378	2	146	3,281
Mimosept									
Daily Press, Stockholm, Gothenburg, Malmo	66	1,517	35,403	—	—	—	—	—	—
Daily Press, provincial	1	12	60	1	7	35	1	7	35
Magazines	18	968	57,760	14	1,298	128,923	8	971	77,015
Trade Press	2	308	7,223	2	445	11,030	—	—	—
Total	87	2,804	100,446	17	1,750	139,968	9	978	77,050

Table 33–2
(continued)

Brand Name and Nature of Medium	1967			1968			1969		
	No. of Ads	Column Space Centimeters	Total Space Cost SwKrs.	No. of Ads	Column Space Centimeters	Total Space Cost SwKrs.	No. of Ads	Column Space Centimeters	Total Space Cost SwKrs.
Mimosept Lady									
Daily Press, Stockholm, Gothenburg, Malmo	1	193	2,754	14	2,366	61,638	—	—	—
Daily Press, provincial	—	—	—	1	8	40	—	—	—
Magazines	49	3,246	221,655	2	212	17,990	19	2,254	166,365
Trade Press	2	305	7,168	4	890	22,060	—	—	—
Total	52	3,743	232,577	21	3,476	101,728	19	2,254	166,365
Mölnlycke Others									
Daily Press, provincial	—	—	—	1	8	40	—	—	—
Magazines	13	356	270,095	1	86	13,500	14	1,548	94,920
Trade Press	13	2,530	50,506	—	—	—	2	445	9,068
Total	26	2,886	277,601	2	94	13,540	16	1,993	103,988
Mölnlycke, Ob									
Daily Press, Stockholm, Gothenburg, Malmo	1	28	434	—	—	—	—	—	—
Daily Press, provincial	16	455	3,738	—	—	—	—	—	—
Magazines	69	6,893	464,350	69	8,033	511,043	27	2,873	175,440
Trade Press	23	2,653	58,960	10	1,291	30,510	—	—	—
Total	109	10,029	527,482	79	9,324	541,553	27	2,873	175,440

Sanetta									
Daily Press, provincial	6	363	3,360	—	—	—	—	—	—
Total	6	363	3,360	—	—	—	—	—	—
Silkesept									
Magazines	19	2,044	99,940	—	—	—	—	—	—
Total	19	2,044	99,940	—	—	—	—	—	—
Tampax									
Magazines	179	5,039	29,765	210	6,940	374,115	198	7,617	409,260
Trade Press	—	—	—	—	—	—	1	220	4,180
Total	179	5,039	29,765	210	6,940	374,115	199	7,837	413,440
Stilles Sanisept									
Daily Press, Stockholm, Gothenburg, Malmo	—	—	—	—	—	—	1	195	13,790
Daily Press, provincial	—	—	—	—	—	—	2	25	232
Magazines	—	—	—	—	—	—	62	14,325	742,380
Trade Press	—	—	—	—	—	—	11	1,964	62,781
Total	—	—	—	—	—	—	76	16,509	823,683
All SP Products									
Daily Press, Stockholm, Gothenburg, Malmo	86	3,604	96,332	15	2,393	62,016	11	969	28,852
Daily Press, provincial	24	907	7,862	3	23	115	27	1,901	19,133
Magazines	378	21,594	1,320,640	311	18,089	1,120,270	328	29,587	1,665,380
Trade Press	47	6,956	150,403	19	2,838	67,040	14	2,629	80,529
Total	535	33,060	1,575,237	348	23,343	1,249,442	380	35,086	1,793,894

of SP in *grocery stores* (which account for 65 percent of the total SP retail sales) during September 1969 to February 1970 were as follows:

Brand	Market Share
Mölnlycke	69 percent
Stilles Sanisept	12 percent
KF Sanetta (co-op)	11 percent
Tampax	2 percent
Other	6 percent

The total consumption of SP products in Sweden in 1970 was expected to be worth 70 million Swkrs. Another important change in the market was the increased frequency of use. This was expected to rise to 25 changes per menstruation period in 1970 as against 18 to 20 during 1968.

The Stilles Sanisept ads were adjudged among the best in Sweden in 1969 by a jury of the Association of Advertising Agencies and were awarded a prize for excellence.

Mölnlycke reported the Stilles Sanisept ads to Naringslivets Opinions-namnd, a court of honor with the task of improving Swedish advertising. Mölnlycke complained that this kind of comparative advertising insulted Mölnlycke and other producers of ordinary sanitary napkins. After an inquiry, Naringslivets Opinion-namnd declared that the ad contained in Exhibit 33–4 gave a wrong and insulting description of the ordinary napkins. The data about the thickness of the napkins was wrong. They said that the ads did not follow the rules of the International Chamber of Commerce.

Sweden has since passed a new law concerning unfair competition which will come into force in 1971. It is likely that ads like Stilles Sanisept will be prohibited under the new law.

Bacardi Rum

James H. Sood, American University
Arch G. Woodside, University of South Carolina

Effects of Government Policies on International Marketing Strategies

The Federal Alcohol Administration Act is the principal legislation that regulates the production and marketing of alcoholic beverages in the United States. This act defines rum as "an alcoholic distillate from the fermented juice of sugar cane, sugar cane syrup, sugar molasses, or other sugar cane by-products, produced at less than 190 proof and in such manner that the distillate possesses the taste, aroma, and characteristics generally attributed to rum, and bottled at not less than 80 proof; and also includes mixtures solely of such distillates."

The Market

The growth of the whiskey market in the United States has been decreasing in recent years. Whiskey blends, straights, and bonds have actually decreased while Scotch and Canadian whiskeys are increasing at a decreasing rate. The consumption of nonwhiskeys such as vodka, gin, and rum, however, has been increasing markedly. See Figures 34–1 and 34–2.

Industry analysts have observed that the predominant trend is away from the traditional whiskeys and toward the lighter (in color), more bland (in taste), lower proof (around 80°) distilled spirits. In addition, there has been a significant movement of trading down or switching to lower priced brands that were lightly advertised or not advertised at all. A large youth market (20s and early 30s) also has emerged rather suddenly, together with a diversification or broader buying of different types of distilled spirits by consumers. The consensus of the industry is that the U.S. rum market will continue to grow at an annual rate of 4 to 6 percent until 1985. The relative growth of the rum market is shown in Table 34–1. The sources of supply of rum in the U.S. market are shown in Tables 34–2 and 34–3.

The rum industry in the United States and most other countries is dominated by Bacardi which has between 65 and 70 percent of the market. Bacardi has established this position by the development of an effective distribution system of over 200 wholesalers, by an extensive advertising program, and by a considerable marketing research effort. The success of Bacardi's marketing program is illustrated by the fact that Bacardi is almost synonymous with rum. Bacardi produces all of its rum for the U.S. market in Puerto Rico. Most of the rum is shipped in bulk containers to Jacksonville, Florida where it is aged, blended, and bottled. Bacardi rum for the West Coast is bottled in Puerto Rico and shipped directly to that area.

Figure   34–1
Whiskey Consumption Trend—1955 to 1975
(Expressed as a three year moving average)

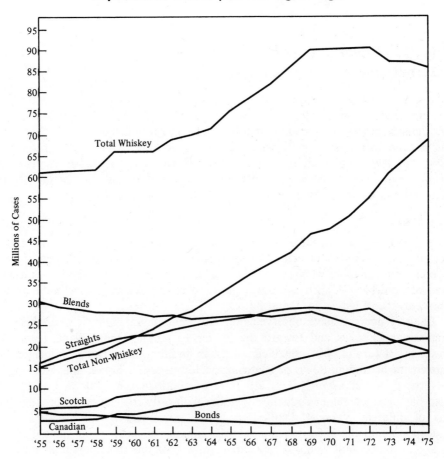

Source: Liquor Handbook, 1976

Figure 34–2
Nonwhiskey Consumption Trend—1955 to 1975
(Expressed as a three year moving average)

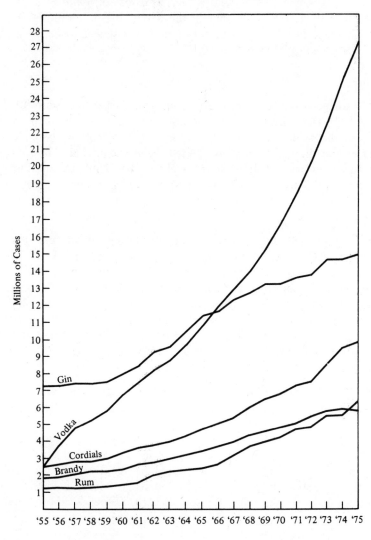

Source: Liquor Handbook, 1976

Pricing

Of course, the price of the product to the consumer reflects the import duty, to some degree. Table 34–4 shows the percentage of total demand for each type of distilled spirits, by price range, in 1975.

The dominance of Bacardi and the difficulty of increasing market share is demonstrated by a project undertaken by a Jamaican rum producer in 1974.

This producer and its import agent lowered the bottle price of their rum from .90 higher to within $.25 (per fifth) of Bacardi throughout the State of Texas. At the same time, they heavily increased the display promotion in the retail stores. This effort was continued for an entire year, at a loss of about $200,000 without increasing their market share. Although the result was disappointing to the producer, the demand curve for this brand of rum was shown to be inelastic in this price range. See Tables 34–5 and 34–6.

The Product

The vast majority of bottled rum products on the market today are "light" rums. The heavy, dark rums are essentially products of the past. About the only difference between the white rums and the golden rums is that the latter are colored with caramel and the former usually filtered through charcoal. The ratio of white to golden rum sold in the United States is about 3–1. Thus, the product has been designed to meet the present needs of the market which are light, bland, 80° rums.

Distribution

All imported rum, including Puerto Rican and Virgin Island rum, pass through the same type of distribution channel. The one exception is Bacardi which does its own importing and bottling. (See Figure 34–3.) Because of the many economies in handling, shipping, bottling, and taxes, there is a decided trend toward shipping rum in bulk (usually at about 150° and in 4,500 gallon steel containers) from the producing countries to the importers in the United States. The importers age, blend, bottle, label, and distribute the rum to wholesalers and the control states.

Promotion

Government regulations prohibit advertising distilled spirits on radio or television. Most of the national advertising is in magaznes and is sponsored by the producers and importers, usually on a joint basis. Local advertising primarily uses the newspaper medium, and private retailers use this form of promotion to announce specific sales. The major national advertiser in the rum industry is "Rums of Puerto Rico." This organization is supported by the Puerto Rican government and it currently spends about $3 million annually to advertise Puerto Rican rum in an institutional manner. The Bacardi Company spends approximately $2.5 million per year on advertising. The other companies in the industry allocate

Table 34–1
Rum Sales in U.S. As Percentage of All Distilled Spirits Sales

1970	1971	1972	1973	1974	1975
3.1%	3.3%	3.4%	3.8%	3.7%	3.9%

Source: Time, *Marketing Report #1940,* 1976.

Table 34–2
Estimated Rum Entering Trade Channels in U.S. Market
(000's of wine gallons)

	1970	1971	1972	1973	1974	1975
Puerto Rico	9,049 (73.2%)	10,591 (76.8)	9,623 (70.4)	11,931 (79.0)	11,895 (76.7)	13,601 (77.6)
Virgin Islands	249 (2.0)	199 (1.4)	401 (2.9)	872 (5.8)	1,012 (6.5)	1,309 (7.5)
Other Domestic	2,909 (23.6)	2,448 (17.8)	3,083 (22.5)	1,662 (11.0)	1,905 (12.3)	1,902 (10.9)
Total Domestic	12,207 (98.6)	13,238 (96.0)	13,107 (95.9)	14,465 (95.8)	14,812 (95.5)	16,812 (95.9)
Imported	141 (1.1)	546 (4.0)	566 (4.1)	638 (4.2)	694 (4.5)	714 (4.1)
Total	12,348	13,784	13,673	15,103	15,506	17,526

Percentages of total for each year are in parentheses.
Source: Distilled Spirits Council of U.S. Washington, D.C. *1975 Annual Statistical Review.*

Annual Change (%) by Source

	1970–71	1971–72	1972–73	1973–74	1974–75
Puerto Rico	17.0%	(−)9.1%	24.0%	(−)0.3%	14.3%
Virgin Islands	(−)20.1	101.5	117.5	16.1	29.3
Other Domestic	(−)15.8	25.9	(−)46.1	14.6	(−)0.2
Total Domestic	8.4	(−)1.0	10.4	2.4	13.5
Imported	287.2	3.7	12.7	8.8	2.9
Total	11.6	(−)0.8	10.5	2.7	13.0

Calculated from above table

Table 34-3
U.S. Rum Imports from Selected Countries
(000's of proof gallons)

	1970	1971	1972	1973	1974	1975
Barbados	35.9	16.9	16.7	34.8	35.9	37.9
Brazil	0.2	0.2	—	0.2	0.2	98.0
Guyana	48.5	53.4	98.5	60.6	63.3	63.7
Jamaica	322.9	255.4	446.6	515.2	579.4	504.9
Trinidad	2.2	1.2	2.4	7.3	3.0	10.1

Source: U.S. Department of Commerce, Bureau of the Census, *Schedule A: U.S. Imports by Country of Origin.*

Other Sources of U.S. Rum Imports

Antigua	Dominican Republic
Bahamas	French West Indies
British Virgin Islands	Haiti
Canada	Mexico
Cayman Islands	Netherlands Antilles
Columbia	Turks & Caicos Islands

Table 34-4
Distilled Spirits
Percentage of Total Demand, by Price Range, By Type—1975

	Straight Whiskey	Bonded Whiskey	Light Whiskey	Blended Whiskey	Scotch Whiskey	Canadian Whiskey	Irish Whiskey
less than $5.14	17.5%	—	4.4%	14.9%	—	—	—
$5.15–5.65	7.0	—	87.5	43.2	—	—	—
$5.66–6.00	32.6	—	—	—	—	—	—
$6.01–6.60	19.4	65.6%	8.1	41.9	39.2%	49.0%	—
$6.61–7.65	19.4	0.8	—	—	0.8	8.4	69.7%
$7.66–8.60	4.1	33.6	—	—	52.2	41.7	30.3
over $8.60	—	—	—	—	7.8	0.9	—

	Vodka	Gin	Rum	Brandy & Cognac	Cordials & Liqueurs	Prepared Cocktails	Tequila
less than $5.14	73.8%	25.8%	18.6%	—	—	51.6%	5.0%
$5.15–5.65	5.6	61.4	—	—	35.5%	48.4	5.4
$5.66–6.00	20.6	—	80.5	83.2%	38.4	—	66.6
$6.01–6.60	—	—	—	—	—	—	—
$6.61–7.65	—	12.8	0.9	—	7.1	—	23.0
$7.66–8.60	—	—	—	—	—	—	—
over $8.60	—	—	—	16.8	19.0	—	—

Source: Liquor Handbook, 1976. New York: Gavin-Jobson Associates, Inc.

Table   34–5
Retail Rum Prices (per fifth)
Selected Locations

	Virginia State Stores	Montgomery County Md.	Private Store Washington D.C.
Bacardi (Puerto Rico)	$4.75	$4.45	$4.69
Ronrico (Puerto Rico)	4.60	4.45	3.99
Don Q (Puerto Rico)	—	4.45	4.69
Appleton (Jamaica)	5.45	—	4.89
Myers (Jamaica)	6.65	6.05	5.79
Mt. Gay (Barbados)	—	6.05	5.99
Cockspur (Barbados)	—	—	5.99
Fernandes (Trinidad)	—	—	5.99
St. James (Martinique)	—	—	7.99
Barbancourt (Haiti)	—	—	7.59
Old Sea Dog (Guyana)	—	—	6.59
Ron Virgin (Virgin Is.)	—	—	3.79

Table   34–6
Rum Pricing in the U.S. Market [a]
(Examples with present tariff and tariff reduction)
Costs, Markups, and Prices Per Case (2.4 gallons)

	present tariff ($1.75 per P.G.)	tariff reduced 60% ($.70 per P.G.)
Rum cost	$ 2.80	$ 2.80
Importer and Bottler (50%)	1.40	1.40
Costs to wholesaler	4.20	4.20
Tariff	4.20	1.68
Federal excise tax	25.20	25.20
State tax (Washington, D.C.)	4.80	4.80
	38.40	35.88
Wholesaler (18%)	6.90	6.45
Cost to Retailer	45.30	42.33
Retailer (30%)	13.60	12.70
Retail price per case	$58.90	$55.03 [b]
Retail price per fifth	$ 4.91	$ 4.58 [b]

[a] For rum shipped in bulk containers from country of origin to U.S.
[b] A tariff reduction of 60% could be applied to provide a 6.7% ($.33 per fifth) price reduction, or the difference ($3.87 per case) could be used for additional promotion.

Figure   34–3
Distribution Channels for Rum

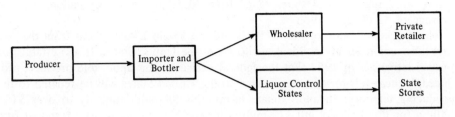

relatively much smaller amounts to this form of promotion. Personal selling, or pushing the product through the channel, is still a major form of promotion in the rum business.

Taxes and Regulations

The federal excise tax is $10.50 per proof gallon if the alcohol content is 100 proof or more and $10.50 per wine gallon if the proof is less than 100. The proof gallon is calculated by dividing the proof of the distilled spirits by 100, when the proof is 100 or more. When the proof is less than 100, it is considered to be the same as 100 proof and equals one proof gallon. The wine gallon is simply the same as the liquid volume of measure; that is, one gallon equals 231 cubic inches. For example, one gallon at 150 proof equals 1.5 proof gallons, and one gallon at 80 (or 86 or 90, etc) proof equals one proof gallon. Both of these examples equal one wine gallon.

The federal excise tax is on all alcoholic beverages produced or imported in the United States. The amount of the excise tax has not been changed since 1951. The historical level of the federal excise tax is shown in Table 34–7. U.S. Senators Jacob Javits and Charles Percy sponsored a bill in the 1975 Congress which would raise the federal excise tax by 50 percent. This bill did not clear the Senate Finance Committee, but there is a chance that this bill in some form will be passed in the coming session of congress.

The distribution and sale of alcoholic beverages are controlled by the state governments in 18 states: Alabama, Idaho, Iowa, Maine, Michigan, Montana, Mississippi, New Hampshire, North Carolina, Ohio, Oregon, Pennsylvania, Utah, Vermont, Virginia, Washington, West Virginia, Wyoming, and Montgomery County in Maryland. The approval of that state's alcoholic beverage control board is required to sell a particular brand of alcoholic beverage in one of the former states. The requirements to obtain this approval vary by state, but essentially the

Table   34–7
The Federal Excise Tax on Alcoholic Beverages

1933	1934	1938	1940	1941	1942	1944	1951
$1.10	$2.00	$2.25	$3.00	$4.00	$6.00	$9.00	$10.50

seller must convince the board that the brand will satisfy a need not being satisfied by the brands the state is presently offering its customers. The state taxes in the states other than control states range from $1.50 to $4.30 per gallon, with an average of $2.60 per gallon.

The special situation of Puerto Rico and the Virgin Islands stems from the fact that these countries are political territories of the United States. It was established by legislative act in 1954 that the federal excise tax on applicable products produced in these territories and exported to the United States will be rebated to the producing territory. In approximate terms, this amounts annually to over $100 million for Puerto Rico and $20 million for the Virgin Islands as a result of rum shipments to the United States. These revenues are about 10 percent and 15 percent respectively of the total government budgets of these territories. The rebate of the federal excise tax is the singular aspect of the industry that makes it a unique situation for negotiation.

The Tariff

Table 34–8 shows that the tariffs on all other alcoholic beverages have been reduced substantially, particularly since the Kennedy Round, although the tariff on rum has been held constant at $1.75 per proof gallon. The present position of the United States on this question is that it is highly sensitive to the interests of all parties concerned with the tariff on rum imports in the United States. On one hand is a strong desire to work with the countries in the Western Hemisphere, and on the other is the special consideration of Puerto Rico and the Virgin Islands.

All potential negotiations concerning the tariff on rum imports would be held within the framework of the Multilateral Trade Negotiations in Geneva, Switzerland. Under the authority of the Trade Act of 1974, the president can negotiate tariff reductions up to 60 percent of the tariff without specific approval of Congress if the tariff is greater than 5 percent ad valorem, and he can eliminate the tariff completely if the tariff is 5 percent ad valorem or less. The U.S. tariff on rum would fall into the former category. All concessions on nontariff barriers must be approved by Congress.

One other possibility is the Generalized System of Preference (GSP). By executive order, the United States could eliminate the tariff on rum for 5 years to all Most Favored Nations, except a country which supplies more than 50 percent of the imports of that product.

Perhaps the only nontariff barrier to the U.S. rum market is the method of assessing the federal excise tax and the duty on imported bottle spirits. Both of these levies are calculated on a proof gallon basis if the product imported for consumption is 100 proof or more and on a wine gallon if less than 100 proof. Since most bottled rum is imported at 80 proof (40 percent alcohol) rather than 100 proof (50 percent alcohol), this means that 10 percent water is subjected to the federal excise tax and the tariff. If this assessment were applied to the domestic producers, there would not be a nontariff barrier. However, U.S. producers (and bulk importers) pay the tax on withdrawal from bonded warehouses at a time when the spirits are usually about 100 proof. This method of assessment provides the domestic producers and bulk importers with a relative 10 percent advantage in the excise tax, and also a 10 percent advantage in the tariff in the case of the bulk importers, vis-à-vis the bottled rum importers. This has been one of the motivating factors behind the increased importation of alcoholic beverages in bulk in the United States.

Another regulation that has probably had some effect on the rum market in the United States is that American tourists can bring back only one quart of spirits duty free, although before 1965 they could bring back one gallon duty free. One effect of this is shown by the following example from Barbados a few years ago. One of the Bajan (Barbardian) rum producers heavily promoted its rum to a large group of tourists from Winnipeg. Without any additional advertising or sales promotion, sales to the Province of Manitoba increased substantially since the initial promotion effort.

Although Puerto Rico and the Virgin Islands can ship goods to the United States without tariff, other countries have similar opportunities with other regional or national markets. For example, the former British Commonwealth countries can export rum to the European Economic Community (EEC) countries duty free, within prescribed import quotas, under the Lome Convention of 1975. The French Caribbean countries of Martinique and Guadalupe also have this advantage since they are French Departments. The multinational operational approach of the Bacardi Company illustrates the importance of tariff and nontariff barriers. In order to avoid these difficulties, Bacardi supplies the French market from its facility in Martinique; the English market from its operations in the Bahamas and Bermuda; the U.S. market from Puerto Rico; and so on. Of course, there are many other factors that influence the trend and level of exports. For example, West Germany has defined rum as a very heavy product in order to protect its domestic industry. France also has decreed that the distillation process for rum must be limited to 4 or fewer stages to protect the obsolete (other than Bacardi) operations in Martinique and Guadalupe.

The tariff and principal nontariff barriers for rum for selected countries are listed in the appendix. It is apparent that the barriers to the U.S. maket are considerably less than the barriers to the rum markets of other countries. Nevertheless, rum has not received equal treatment with the other alcoholic beverages in past multilateral negotiations.

The cause of this unequal treatment in the case of rum is that the United States cannot negotiate concessions that would undermine the Puerto Rican economy. Most probably, any U.S. gain in negotiations would tend to help the overall U.S. economy, although any U.S. concession would tend to hurt the Puerto Rican economy. It is not a quid pro quo negotiating situation. There is no possible concession to Puerto Rico that would compensate them for a reduction of Puerto Rican rum sales in the U.S. market, since this would mean, in effect, a reduction in government revenue because of the decreased rebate of the excise tax. Since there is no other likely source for this amount of revenue, the U.S. reluctance to jeopardize the situation is understandable.

Bacardi, which represents about 75 to 80 percent of the Puerto Rican rum industry, was initially a Cuban company that moved its primary operations to

Table 34-8
Import Duties on Distilled Spirits
(per proof gallon if 100 proof or more, wine gallon if less than 100 proof)

Class and Type	1951–1955	1956	1957	1958–1961	1962	1963	1964–1966	1967	1968	1969	1970	1971	1972–1973	1974–1975
WHISKEY—(Scotch and Irish)	$1.50	$1.42	$1.35	$1.25	$1.14	$1.02	$1.02	$1.02	$ .91	$ .81	$ .71	$ .61	$ .51	$ .51
OTHER WHISKEY—(Canadian, etc.)	1.25	1.25	1.25	1.25	1.25	1.25	1.25	1.25	1.12	1.00	.87	.75	.62	.62
RUM	1.75	1.75	1.75	1.75	1.75	1.75	1.75	1.75	1.75	1.75	1.75	1.75	1.75	1.75
GIN	1.25	1.25	1.25	1.25	1.12	1.00	1.00	1.00	.90	.80	.70	.60	.50	.50
BRANDY in containers each holding:														
One gallon or less valued not over $9.00	1.25	1.25	1.25	1.25	1.25	1.25	1.25	1.25	1.12	1.00	.87	.75	.62	.62
Valued $9.00 to $17.00							5.00	5.00	5.00	5.00	5.00	5.00	5.00	1.25
More than one gallon valued not over $9.00					1.12	1.00	1.00	1.00	.90	.80	.70	.60	.50	.50
Valued $9.00 to $17.00							5.00	5.00	5.00	5.00	5.00	5.00	5.00	1.00
Valued over $17.00							5.00	5.00	5.00	5.00	5.00	5.00	5.00	5.00
CORDIALS	1.25	1.25	1.25	1.25	1.12	1.00	1.00	1.00	.90	.80	.70	.60	.50	.50
BITTERS fit for beverage purposes				1.25	1.12	1.00	1.00	1.00	.90	.80	.70	.60	.50	.50
Other	2.50	2.50	2.50	2.50	2.29	2.08	1.88	1.88	1.69	1.50	1.31	1.12	.94	.94

ETHYL ALCOHOL for beverages	2.25	2.25	2.25	2.25	2.25	2.25	2.25	2.25	2.25	2.02	1.80	1.57	1.35	1.12	1.12
BEVERAGE SPIRITS other than above:															
Arrack	2.50	2.50	2.50	2.50	2.25	2.00	2.00	2.00	2.00	1.80	1.60	1.40	1.20	1.00	1.00
Aquavit	1.25	1.18	1.12	1.06	.95	.85	.85	.85	.85	.76	.68	.59	.51	.42	.42
OTHER spirits and preparations: Chief value of distilled spirits:															
Spirits	1.25	1.25	1.25	1.25	1.25	1.25	1.25	1.25	1.25	1.25	1.25	1.25	1.25	1.25	1.25
Other	5.00	4.16	3.33	2.50	2.50	2.50	2.50	2.50	2.25	2.00	1.75	1.50	1.25	1.25	

Source: U.S. Tariff Commission, 1976.

Puerto Rico after the revolution. The company is now a multinational operation with production facilities in 9 countries and bottling plants in 6 countries. Bacardi cannot be considered a Puerto Rican company, either in ownership or management, and thus would appear to have little allegiance to Puerto Rico. Although it appears that Puerto Rico and the Virgin Islands are in a position of strength in the rum industry, these countries are actually in a vulnerable and sensitive situation. See Table 34–9 for rum industries in other selected countries.

Discussion Questions

1. Should Puerto Rico attempt to maintain the present import tax situation with respect to rum? If yes, why? If no, what new policies should Puerto Rico attempt to achieve from the U.S. government?

2. Should the U.S. government revise existing import tax laws with respect to rum? Explain the reasons for your answer.

3. How should the Carribean nations attempt to change the existing rum laws in the United States?

4. What is the relevance of the present U.S. government import laws on rum to France and Portugal?

Approximate Import Duties on Rum in Major Rum Markets (per gallon at 80 proof)

Country	Tariff	Other Import Taxes	Total Duty
Australia	$22.30	—	$22.30
Belgium	2.40	—	2.40
Canada	2.00	—	2.00
Central America	2.50 to 10.00 (varies)	—	2.50 to 10.00 (varies)
France	1.41	$2 04	3.45
Greece	6.40	—	5.92
Italy	1.41	2.88	4.29
Japan	2.25	—	2.25
Luxemburg	2.40	—	2.40
Netherlands	1.40	1.26	2.66
Portugal	20.00	—	20.00
South Africa	1.91	—	1.91
South America	7.00 to 10.00 (varies)	—	7.00 to 10.00 (varies)
Spain	2.73	3.18	5.91

Common Nontariff Barriers in Major Rum Markets

— Import Quotas

— Special tariffs if import quotas are exceeded

— Discretionary licensing

— Discriminatory product standards

— Subject to availability of foreign currency

Chapter 9

Marketing Strategy

Sound strategic planning is essential to the long-term survival and profitability of any business firm. "Strategy provides the orderly plan for adapting a company's resources to market opportunities" [1] and for guiding the course of a company's activities. This chapter examines fundamental concepts of strategy, the planning process for developing a marketing strategy, and the kinds of marketing strategies which firms use to grow and to compete in the complex world of business.

Fundamental Concepts of Strategy

Strategy is a term which has been defined in many different ways throughout history. Perhaps the first people to plan strategies were generals of armies and heads of state. The early Greeks referred to the large-scale planning efforts of their generals as *strategia,* "the art of the general." This definition, however, is not very useful since the scope of and steps in developing strategies varied among individual generals.

In this chapter, strategy is defined in two ways, both of which are useful:

1. "The art of distributing and applying military [or business] means to fulfill the ends of policy." [2]

2. "The art and science of adapting and coordinating resources to the attainment of an objective." [3]

These two definitions define strategy at 2 levels. The first defines *grand strategy,* a very broad, long-term plan designed to achieve the highest level organizational

---

[1] M. Wayne DeLozier, *The Marketing Communications Process* (New York: McGraw-Hill Book Company, 1976), p. 270.

[2] B. H. Liddell Hart, *Strategy,* 2nd rev. ed. (New York: Frederick A. Praeger, Inc., 1967), p. 335.

[3] DeLozier, *op. cit.,* p. 271.

goals or ends of policy.[4] The "end" for any business or nonbusiness organization is referred to as the *corporate mission,* which "is a long-term vision of what the business is or is striving to become." [5] Thus, grand strategy is concerned with fulfilling an organization's corporate mission.

How should an organization decide what its corporate mission is or should be? The answer is to determine the *generic* need which the organization is attempting to satisfy. IBM views itself as meeting people's problem-solving needs, not as computer producers. Exxon defines its corporate mission as satisfying people's energy needs, not as oil and gas producers. These companies are successful and should continue to be for a long time because they have taken a broad look at the generic needs they are trying to satisfy. Such a broad definition of what an organization is or is striving to become provides impetus for the organization to search for new and better alternatives to satisfy their customers' needs.

Buggy companies did not view themselves as transportation companies, rather as producers of horse-drawn carriages. As a result, they are no longer in business. Had they understood the generic need they were fulfilling, they may very well have been in business today producing automobiles, trucks, and other modes of transportation.

The second definition of strategy refers to *functional strategy,* which is concerned with meeting intermediate-term functional objectives. Functional strategy, a middle management responsibility, is more narrow in scope and shorter in time span than grand strategy. These strategies are designed to achieve marketing objectives, production objectives, financial objectives, sales objectives, and so on. Functional objectives and strategies should be an outgrowth of, and thus consistent with, an organization's corporate mission and grand strategy.

Tactics on the other hand involve "the specific activity of resources on a moment-to-moment or day-to-day basis. Two specific examples of tactics in business are (1) the advertising copywriter who operationalizes marketing strategy through his development of appropriate copy and (2) the sales representative who prepares (and adjusts) his sales presentation to the needs of prospective clients. These tactics represent 'in-the-field' activities carried out for marketing personnel." [6]

The success of any level of strategy or tactic to achieve an objective depends on how well a strategist adapts resources to an identifiable opportunity. Figure C—9–1 summarizes this idea.

The general plan for adapting an organization's resources to a perceived opportunity for the purpose of achieving a stated objective (or set of objectives) is the strategy. Tactics are simply short-term plans to operationalize strategy. The "movement" of adapted resources toward the identified opportunity is the *implementation* of strategic and tactical plans.

The 3 levels of planning activities discussed so far and their relationships are

---

[4] See Hart, *op. cit.,* pp. 335–372.

[5] David T. Kollat, Roger D. Blackwell, and James F. Robeson, *Strategic Marketing* (New York: Holt, Rinehart and Winston, Inc., 1972), p. 14.

[6] DeLozier, *op. cit.,* p. 272.

Figure　C—9–1
A Simple Model of Strategic Planning

Figure　C—9–2
A Simple Model of an Organization's Planning System

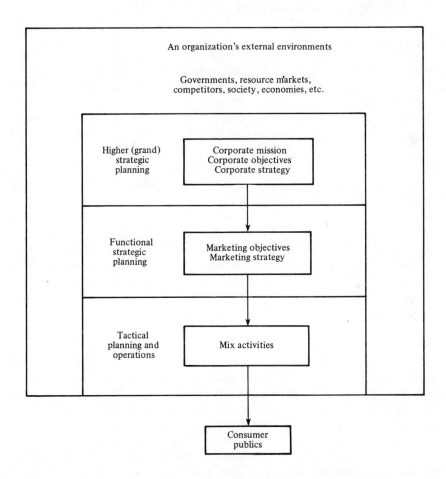

shown in Figure C—9–2. This figure shows that an organization's objectives, strategies, and tactical plans and operations are influenced by several external environments, such as governments (local, state, federal, international) resource markets, competitors, and economies. Examples of environmental factors which affect strategic planning are presented in the next section.

Steps in Developing a Marketing Strategy

The 5 basic steps which a marketing planner uses in developing a marketing strategy are:

1. Identify and assess market opportunities.
2. Analyze the firm's marketing resources.
3. Set marketing objectives.
4. Develop and evaluate alternative marketing strategies.
5. Assign specific marketing tasks.

Identify Market Opportunities

The first step in developing a marketing strategy is to identify and to evaluate market opportunities. Market opportunities either can be created or destroyed by changes in environmental factors external to the firm. Some of these major environmental factors affecting the availability of opportunities to an organization are technological, economic, social, and government (or legal/political) factors.

Technological factors.   Today technological change is more rapid than ever before. This statement is particularly true for the electronics field. For example, advances in micro-electronic circuitry has led the way for the introduction of inexpensive calculators, in-home computers, and video-games. These advances have created market opportunities for some firms and their suppliers, while destroying others (for example, slide rules). Video counter displays and counter talkers have created opportunities for advertisers, and new packaging technology has aided companies in creating novel, interesting, eye-appealing, and better protecting packages. New product developments have created everything from Teflon for greaseless, nonstick cooking to portable telephones.

Economic factors.   Changes in local, state, national, and international economies create and destroy market opportunities. The levels of inflation and unemployment affect how goods are produced, packaged, priced, advertised, and bought. For example, the Arab oil embargo of 1973–74 brought about obvious changes in prices, as well as changes in product offerings and advertising. A greater number of smaller cars were introduced to the automobile market, automobile advertising themes began to focus on gas mileage to a much greater extent, new products designed to prevent gasoline theft from automobiles appeared, and "long-mileage" oil lubricants became popular. Also Bell Telephone System advertised the cost savings of long-distance conferences with customers as opposed to the fuel waste involved in travel.

Generally speaking, when an economy such as the United States is prosperous, consumers begin to purchase prestige brands and products, spend more money on recreation and entertainment, and replace worn-out durable products. These changes in consumption offer the marketing strategist several opportunities.

Social factors. Changes in sociocultural attitudes and values create and destroy opportunities for marketers. As examples, some prognosticators foresee changing values and expectations among consumers to include attitudes of antimaterialism, anti-big business, more ecological concern, less pride of ownership and more use from rentals, greater use of debt-financing of goods and services, and disenchantment of growth.[7]

Sociocultural attitudes in the United States and other countries toward limiting childbirths has lowered population growth and affected many industries. Baby food producers have realized a tremendous drop in sales in baby foods and have sought new markets. Home game manufacturers who traditionally marketed their games to children have now expanded into the adult game market. The "fashionableness" of debt has created a burdgeoning of credit cards among banks, department stores, airlines, oil companies, and others which are becoming more widely accepted by retailers and consumers.

Changing life styles have created and destroyed market opportunities. During the mid-1960s men in our society began to use what had once been exclusively "feminine" products. Hair sprays, hair dryers, necklaces, and earrings became acceptable to "traditional" males.

Changing social attitudes have also affected opportunities for advertisers. In recent years, advertisers have found that it is acceptable among most people to advertise condoms, feminine and male hygiene deodorants, feminine hygiene napkins, abortion services and clinics, and drugs for diarrhea and constipation. Social attitudes toward minorities has also opened up new opportunities for advertisers. Blacks and other non-whites are now seen in a greater number of commercial advertisements and in more prominent roles. Also, women are shown increasingly in "traditional" male roles in advertising. These examples show how vigilant marketers have adapted marketing programs to meet social changes in the market place.

Legal-Political Factors

Government legislation and government agencies create and destroy marketing objectives. Federal agencies have affected the sale of hair dyes, cigarettes, children's toys, foods and beverages containing saccharin, and drugs, among many other products. The Federal Trade Commission (FTC), for example, has issued complaints against producers of several products stating that their product claims have no scientific bases (analgesics and mouthwashes, for example). Ads for these products have come under severe criticism and demands for corrective advertising affected many products.

Governments also affect sales for a product through blue laws, taxation, and public announcements. Government announcements on the health hazards of cigarette smoking, for example, has reduced the percentage of the United States population who smoke from approximately 50 percent to 38 percent. Additionally,

---

[7] W. J. E. Crissy, "Selling in the Seventies—Change, Challenge, Opportunity," in Eugene J. Kelly and William Lazar, *Managerial Marketing: Policies, Strategies, and Decisions* (Homewood, IL: Richard D. Irwin, 1973), pp. 435–436.

current cigarette smokers are rapidly changing to low tar cigarettes with approximately 25 percent of all cigarette purchasers smoking low tar brands.

The government also has powerful influences over the press. Through publicity releases, news services pick up news stories about such things as botulism in one company's mushrooms, excess radiation in a firm's television sets, and cancer-producing agents in foods using a particular ingredient.

Governments are pervasive forces which have tremendous impacts upon industries. Specific industries affected are those engaged in the production of foods, drugs, cosmetics, and other health-related products. Pronouncements on products produced by these and other industries both create and destroy market opportunities.

As you can see, external environments are powerful agents which can open or close profitable opportunities to business. These opportunities are generally broad in scope. Thus, a particular firm must refine identified opportunities. This can be done through market segmentation as discussed in Chapter 2. For example, a company might find that men are increasingly using what were "female" products, such as hair sprays, hair dryers, and necklaces, and find that men are susceptible to other traditional female products. Specifically, they may find that some men recognize the need to cover bad facial features and accentuate their positive features by using makeup. Since all men are not a market for "male" makeup, the firm must identify whether there is a substantial market for male makeup and whether it is accessible. If a substantial, accessible, and measurable market segment can be identified, a company who produces makeup might try to cultivate this market target.

In general, identification and evaluation of market opportunities involves examination of environmental factors which change and create marketing opportunities. Once a broad opportunity has been identified, a company must further examine the opportunity by identifying a potentially profitable market segment. If convinced that a profitable market target exists, the company must determine whether it has the resources to exploit the identified market.

Analyze Marketing Resources

The second step in developing a marketing strategy is to analyze the company's marketing resources. Resources might include sales force skills, innovative marketing services, creative merchandising, financial posture, channel strength, advertising expertise, corporate reputation, quality-price combinations, and managerial talent and competence, among others.[8] In analyzing its resources, a firm should attempt to identify its *distinctive competence*. "The 'distinctive competence' of an organization is more than what it can do; it is what it can do particularly well." [9] A firm should consider further those market opportunities for which it can match its distinctive competence or at least its resource strengths, and eliminate those

---

[8] DeLozier, *op. cit.*, p. 277.
[9] Kenneth R. Andrews, *The Concept of Corporate Strategy* (Homewood, IL: Dow Jones-Irwin, Inc., 1971), p. 97. The phrase "distinctive competence" is used by Philip Selznick, *Leadership in Administration* (Evanston, IL: Row, Peterson, and Company, 1957), p. 42.

market opportunities for which it has no resource strengths. Thus, a firm's resources impose limitations upon which opportunities can be given further consideration.

Setting Marketing Objectives

> "Cheshire Puss," she (Alice) began . .
> "Would you please tell me which way I ought
> to go from here?" "That depends on where you
> want to get to," said the cat.
>
> —Lewis Carroll

Objectives are statements of where a company wants to be at some point in the future. Objectives are essential to problem statements and strategic planning. Figure C—9–3 is a diagram of the relationships among these elements.

In order for a company to determine where it wants to go, it must first determine where it is; that is, conduct a situation analysis and determine where it is going—determine its current course or direction. A situation analysis is, in a sense, like taking a snapshot at a point in time—it is static. Determining where a company is moving is, in another sense, like taking a moving picture; it involves a look at past trends (a series of snapshots) and predicted future trends or movements. Realistic objectives cannot be set until a company has a clear understanding of its current situation and direction.

A company's problem or set of problems is *how to* move from its current situation (and perhaps alter its direction) to a desired situation. The selected strategy is the plan which mobilizes the resources and sets the course and speed to attain the company's desired situation (objective[s]) within a stated time frame.

As discussed earlier, strategies can be stated at various levels in the business hierarchy. Similarly, objectives can be stated at different levels within the corporate or organizational framework. Figure C—9–4 shows the relationship between objectives and strategies within a business hierarchy.

This diagram suggests several important ideas. "First, it is not feasible to define a strategy in the absence of any objective. Second, lower-level objectives and

Figure   C—9–3
Relationships of Objectives,
Problems, and Strategies

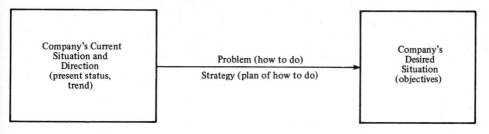

Figure C—9–4
A Hierarchy of Objectives and Strategies

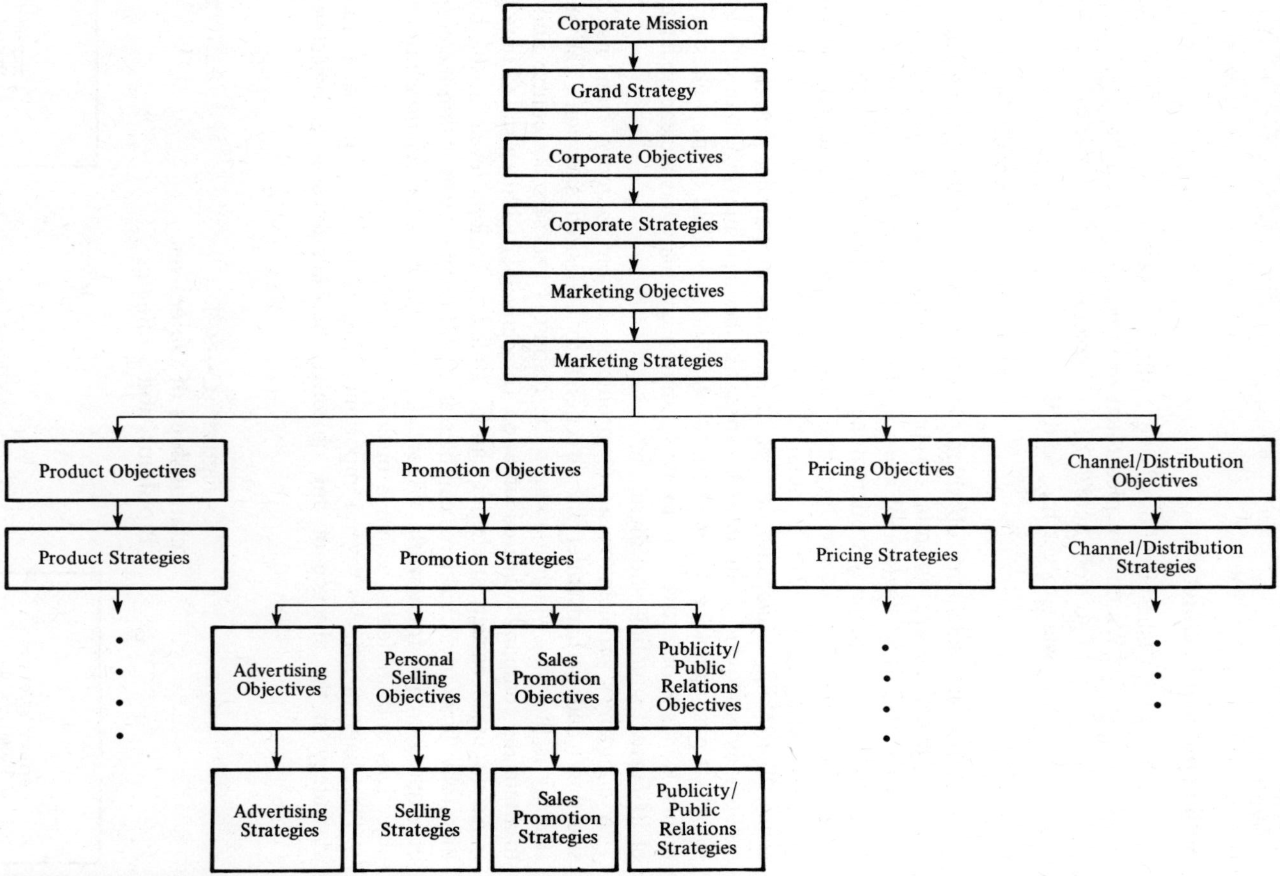

strategies will depend upon higher-level objectives and strategies." [10] Third, all objectives and strategies must ultimately be directed toward achievement of (or at least movement toward) the corporate mission. Further, the product, promotion, price, and channel/distribution objectives and strategies must be consistent with the overall marketing strategy and objectives.

Any statement of objectives must specify the level of attainment, such as a 20 percent increase in sales over last year's sales; a specific time frame, such as 12 months; and an acceptable level of risk subjectively determined by current market conditions. Some of the objectives stated by marketing managers are (1) to increase sales by X percent over the next 12 months, (2) to increase market share by Y percent over the next 12 months, (3) to attain Q percent return on investment over the next 12 months, (4) to achieve R percent return on stockholders' equity over the next 12 months, and so on. These stated objectives are really statements of yardstick performance; that is, these objectives are stated in terms of increases along a yardstick or measuring instrument, not in terms of achieving the corporate mission of the firm or matching corporate resources to market opportunities. In ideal terms, the marketing and corporate objectives are to match corporate resources to the best possible market opportunities in order to maximize the benefits to the organization or business firm and its consuming publics. The yardstick of success is long-term profits.

Develop and Evaluate Alternative Marketing Strategies

Given stated corporate and marketing objectives, the next step is to arrive at a marketing strategy. This phase of the strategic planning process involves alternative statements of plans which will move an organization from its present situation to a more desirable position. From the enumeration of different plans, management must decide upon the best approach, based upon strengths and weaknesses of each to attain its marketing objectives. Among the several potential strategies management proposes, each must be evaluated in terms of probable outcome, competitor reactions, risk, time frames, and management's personal value system.

Specific marketing strategies are ultimately based upon an analysis of market opportunities, specific consumer needs, and the firm's ability to satisfy the identified consumer needs at a long-term profit.

Assign Specific Marketing Tasks

Once a broad strategic plan has been selected, the marketing decision maker must make specific decisions regarding the specific roles and tasks to be performed by advertising, the sales force, sales promotion, price, and packaging. Also, specific decisions must be made regarding channel selection, distribution, branding, the physical product, and the level of service. All of these tactical decisions must be blended into a consistent *total product offering*. A systems approach can be useful in this regard. A systems approach can aid the decision maker in recognizing the

---

[10] Kenneth R. Davis, *Marketing Management*, 3rd ed. (New York: The Ronald Press Company, 1972), p. 17.

interaction of the mix activities and how external environments impact on specific task decisions (e.g., government agencies on product formation and on the specific advertising message; and for another, competitors' reactions to price, etc.). A final consideration in tactical decision making is to build flexibility into the final plan so that a company might react quickly to changing market conditions while still being able to carry out the overall strategy.

Marketing Strategies

Marketing strategies are inextricably linked to corporate strategies and corporate mission. In most cases, they appear similar. Figure C—9–5 shows 11 marketing strategies which relate to corporate growth. Ten of these strategies involve either penetration of or growth in current and new markets using either current, reformulated, or completely new product offerings. The eleventh strategy involves changes in the firm's distribution network through forward and/or backward integration to increase control, efficiency, and profitability.

These strategies are described as follows: [11]

1. *Market penetration.* The company attempts to increase sales of present products in present markets. This strategy may take several forms. The strategy (1) might be directed at either increasing the rate of usage among present customers by showing how the product can be used in different ways (e.g., put Arm & Hammer Baking Soda in your refrigerator to absorb odors), increasing the size of the product purchased (e.g., 16-ounce cans of beer or soda, 8-paks, etc.), creating faster product obsolescence, and providing customers with cents-off coupons, premiums, etc.; (2) entice competitors' consumers to buy the product, and (3) stimulate trial purchasers among nonusers. Both attracting competitor's customers and nonusers could be accomplished through such methods as comparative advertising, product sampling, price changes, and advertising new ways to use the product. A market penetration strategy relies upon intensifying efforts in advertising, personal selling, sales promotion, channels/distribution, and pricing. All or a combination of these marketing mix variables might be used. However, there are no changes in the product.

2. *Market development.* In using this strategy a company attempts to market its current product(s) in new markets. "New" markets can be viewed in several ways, such as new geographic markets or new market segments within an existing market. For example, Texize might market its industrial cleaning liquid in new regional and/or international markets (geographic) or introduce the product to household consumers, which it did in the form of "Janitor in a Drum." This

---

[11] Kollat, Blackwell, and Robeson, *op. cit.,* pp. 21–22; influenced by Samuel C. Johnson and Conrad Jones, "How to Organize for New Products," *Harvard Business Review,* 35 (May-June 1957), pp. 49–62; Lee Adler, ed., *Plotting Marketing Strategy* (New York: Simon and Schuster, Inc., 1967); H. Igor Ansoff, *Corporate Strategy* (New York: McGraw-Hill, Inc., 1965), pp. 123–138; Philip Kotler, *Marketing Management: Analysis, Planning, and Control,* 2nd ed. (Englewood Cliffs, NJ: Prentice-Hall, Inc., 1972), pp. 236–240.

Figure C—9—5
Marketing Strategies for Corporate Growth

Products / Markets	Present Products	Improvements in Present Products	New Products with Related Technology		New Products With Unrelated Technology
			Assortment Manipulation	Expansion of the Variety of the Product Line	
Consumption Markets: Same markets	(1) Market-penetration strategies	(3) Reformulation strategies	(5) Replacement strategies	(7) Product-line extension strategies	(9) Horizontal diversification strategies
New Markets	(2) Market development strategies	(4) Market extension strategies	(6) Market segmentation product differentiation strategies	(8) Concentric diversification strategies	(10) Conglomerate diversification strategies
Resource and/or Distribution Markets	(11) Forward and/or backward integration strategies				

Source: David T. Kollat, Roger D. Blackwell, and James F. Robeson, *Strategic Marketing* (New York: Holt, Rinehart and Winston, Inc., 1972), p. 22.

strategy requires no alterations in the basic product, but usually requires a change in packaging (especially for new market segments and international markets), channels of distribution, pricing, and promotion.

3. *Reformulation.*   This strategy emphasizes changes in product formulation to appeal to present consumers. The addition of fluoride to toothpastes, enzymes to detergents, and filters to cigarettes are examples. The major change in the marketing mix is the product. Advertising is affected only to the extent that the theme or appeal changes and that expenditures might be higher for the "new" product introduction. Reformulation may take several forms, such as changes in color, style, odor, shape, power, volume, size, ingredients, and weight. This strategy involves changes not only in the product, but very likely in price and promotion.

4. *Market extension.*   This strategy is used to reach new classes of consumers with modifications in current company products. For example, nylon was used initially in making hosiery for women but has subsequently been used to make ball bearings, parachutes, and thread, among other uses.

5. *Replacement.*   This strategy replaces present products with new products having better structures, formulations, or ingredients. Producers of razors have replaced double-edged razors with single-blade razors, twin-blade razors, and disposable twin-blade razors.

6. *Market segmentation/product differentiation.*   These terms are interrelated. When a company differentiates a product, it usually appeals to a different market segment whether intentional or not. This strategy attempts to attract new customers by varying its product offering and offering assortments in its existing product lines. Producers of shampoos have introduced brands for oily hair, extra oily hair, normal hair, dry hair, and extra dry hair. Psychological differentiation can be introduced by companies by advertising psychological differences, such as shampoo for the aristocratic woman, the sexy woman, and the down-to-earth woman. Product differentiation is either an alteration in the physical product or the marketing communications messages which create a difference in the minds of consumers for the same product in the same market.

7. *Product-line extension.*   This strategy uses the company's perceived distinctive competence in a related technology to extend its line of products offered to present customers. For example, Texas Instruments markets electronic calculators, electronic watches, and video games, among other products using their electronic technologies.

8. *Concentric diversification.*   This strategy attracts new classes of customers by adding new products that have technological and/or marketing synergies with the existing product line. The Coca-Cola Company, through acquisition of the Minute Maid Corporation, diversified into the citrus-processing and coffee industries." [12]

9. *Horizontal diversification.*   This strategy seeks increased sales by adding product lines technologically unrelated to the company's current product lines to sell to the same type of consumer. This strategy is often used after a company has expanded its market geographically to the point where it would be unprofitable

---

[12] Kollat, Blackwell, and Robeson, *op. cit.* p. 23.

to expand further and where the company already has an extensive mix of related product lines.

10. *Conglomerate diversification.* This strategy attempts "to attract new classes of customers by diversifying into products that have no relationship to the company's current technology, products or markets." [13] To illustrate, Pepsico not only produces and markets soft drinks but also snack foods (Frito Lay), sporting goods equipment (Wilson Sporting Goods), and transportation (North American Van Lines, National Trailer Convoy—mobile homes, and Lee Way Motor Freight).

11. *Integration strategies.* Another growth strategy is backward and/or forward integration. A producer can either move backward by acquiring suppliers or forward by acquiring channel members, or both. An example is oil companies which are fully integrated from the oil wells to the gasoline stations. The advantages of this strategy are increased control over the channels of distribution and supply, greater efficiency and certainty of supplies and intermediate customers, and reduced channel conflict.

In considering a strategy to adopt management should be concerned with the synergistic effects of the adopted strategy with respect to the "fit between the firm and its new product-market entries." [14] Synergy in a business sense denotes that the combined performance among the firm's product-market entries is greater than the sum of its individual entries.

Several types of business synergy are the following: [15]

1. *Sales synergy* occurs when products use common channels of distribution, common warehouses, common sales offices, common services offices, common sales forces, common sales promotion, related products for tie-in sales, among others.

2. *Operating synergy* results from large lot purchasing, spreading of overhead, and greater use of common facilities and personnel.

3. *Investment synergy* results from combined use of plant and equipment, common raw materials inventories, and a carryover effect of research and development for one product to others.

4. *Management synergy* occurs when management's experience with past strategic, administrative, and/or operating problems with present product-market entries are similar to ones they encounter with new product-market entries, even when the new entries may be totally unrelated to past entries.

Evaluating Alternative Marketing Strategies

To assist the decision maker in evaluating alternative strategies, several mathematical approaches have evolved to handle logically the selection process.

---

[13] Ibid.

[14] H. Igor Ansoff, *Corporate Strategy* (New York: McGraw-Hill Book Company, 1965), p. 25.

[15] Ibid., p. 80, 98–99.

Statistical Decision Theory [16]

Decision theory has emerged in recent years as a means of helping marketing managers to evaluate alternative courses of action. First, it forces the marketing strategist to explicitly state alternative strategies and possible outcomes for each. Second, it forces the strategist to evaluate each alternative within a logical framework. And, third, decision theory helps the strategist recognize which are controllable variables and which are uncontrollable variables. The controllable variables are the marketing mix elements and the target market. The uncontrollable variables represent states-of-nature and competitive-actions.

States-of-nature are essentially environmental conditions that are likely to influence the outcomes of each alternative strategy. Thus, the marketing decision maker must estimate the probabilities that a set of strategic alternatives will lead to given outcomes. These various estimates provide the necessary elements for calculating the expected values for each alternative. An expected value is a weighted mean of a set of payoffs, where the weights are the probability estimates.

A general equation for computing expected value is

$$EV = p_1Z_1 + p_2Z_2 + \ldots p_nZ_n$$

where EV is the expected value of an alternative strategy; p_1, p_2, $\ldots$ p_n are the probabilities that a given set of events will occur, and Z_1, Z_2, $\ldots$ Z_n are a set of payoffs corresponding to n events. Suppose a company is deciding between introducing one of its present products to a new market (market-development strategy) and modifying a present product to reach a new class of consumers (market-extension strategy). The outcomes of these strategies will be affected significantly by whether the economy experiences a recession or prosperity (events or states of nature) in the coming year. If the economy experiences a recession, which the marketing strategist estimates at an 0.6 probability, the market-development is expected to yield a $4 million profit over three years, whereas a prosperous economy would provide an expected $8 million over the 3-year period. The market extension strategy, on the other hand, would provide an expected $1 million loss if recession occurs, but an expected $12 million profit if the economy prospers.

Using statistical decision theory, the decision maker would make the following calculations of expected value for each strategy (see payoff matrix in Table C—9–1).

Expected Value (EV) for
market-development strategy   =   0.6 ($4 million) + 0.4 ($8 million)

    = $5.6 million

Expected Value (EV) for
market-extension strategy   =   0.6 (−$1 million) + 0.4 ($12 million)

    = $4.2 million

---

[16] See Robert O. Schlaifer, *Analysis of Decisions Under Uncertainty* (New York: McGraw-Hill Book Company, 1969) and Howard Raifta, *Decision Analysis* (Reading, MA: Addison-Wesley Publishing Company, Inc., 1968).

Table   C—9–1
Payoff Matrix for Two Strategies

	Recession (0.6)	Prosperity (0.4)
Market-development strategy	$4 million	$ 8 million
Market-extension strategy	−$1 million	$12 million

In this example, the marketing strategist should select the market-development strategy if using the decision criterion of expected value. However, a strategist should recognize the underlying assumptions of this approach. Expected value assumes that over the long run using repeated plays the expected payoffs would result in the values calculated above. Also, the strategist must recognize that such things as goodwill, synergy, sales, and market share are ignored. Finally, the strategist must have *confidence* in her probability estimates that events will occur and in her estimates of payoffs for each strategy given each event.

Game Theory

Game theory, like statistical decision theory, assumes that the strategist can identify alternative strategies, uncertain variables, and the payoffs for different outcomes. However, game theory deals with situations where a strategist makes assumptions about how a *competitor* will react to his strategies. Further, it does not consider the likelihood of an event occuring. The competitor is assumed in each instance to maximize his own welfare (i.e., select the best solution from his point of view). Many models have been developed which suggest that different courses of action can be taken under conditions of uncertainty, depending upon the model used. Only 2 models are discussed briefly to illustrate game theory.

One model uses a maximax criterion, which says "choose the best of the best payoffs" (maximize the maximum payoff). A second model, minimax, uses a criterion to select the "least worst" strategy (i.e., minimize the maximum loss). The first criterion, maximax, is a go-for-broke solution, whereas minimax assumes both opponents are conservative or pessimistic. Table C—9–2 shows how the decision criterion used alters strategy selection.

If a maximax criterion is used, the correct strategy selection is S_2: market-extension. If a minimax criterion is used, the correct solution is S_1: market-development. And if an expected value solution is used (where competitor reaction one is 0.3), S_3: market-penetration is the strategy which should be selected. Thus, the company's managerial philosophy based on experience determines the strategy selection using these different criteria.

The Bayesian Approach*

The Bayesian approach is another statistical decision model which simply is an extension of the expected value approach discussed earlier. In the Bayesian ap-

---

*This section may be skipped without interrupting continuity.

Table   C—9–2
Alternative Decision Criteria
For Strategy Selection

Strategy Alternative	Payoff Matrix (in millions)		
	Competitor's Reaction One	Competitor's Reaction Two	Expected Value
S_1: Market-development	−0.5	3.0	1.95
S_2: Market-extension	−2.0	5.0	2.90
S_3: Market-penetration	−0.8	4.7	3.05

proach an estimate is made on the value of collecting additional information before selecting a strategy. The estimate is made using the Bayes theorem, which shows how sample information might affect the decision maker's estimated probabilities of the states-of-nature. In light of new information, prior probabilities (the initial ones subjectively estimated by the decision maker) are revised. The revised probabilities are then applied to the original problem. By collecting new information a decision maker may be able to reduce the risk of making a wrong decision. The following case illustrates how Bayesian analysis can be useful to the strategic planner. A mathematical and graphic solution are presented.

A company is considering the introduction of a new coffee maker into the market. They believe they face three different states-of-nature (market conditions) —S_1, S_2, S_3. If they introduce the new maker and S_1 is the true state-of-nature, they can make a profit of $500,000; if S_2 exists, they will make $300,000 profit; and if S_3 exists they will incur a loss of $500,000. In the manager's judgment, the probabilities of each state-of-nature is 30 percent for S_1, 40 percent for S_2, and 30 percent for S_3. If they buy information about the state of the market the possible research outcomes would be as shown in Table C—9–3.

Table   C—9–3
Table of Conditional Probabilities, $P(E_i/S_j)$

Market Information	Possible States of Nature		
	S_1: 6% of Mkt.	S_2: 3% of Mkt.	S_3: 0% of Mkt.
E_1: Below 2%	0.20	0.30	0.50
E_3: 2% to 5%	0.30	0.40	0.30
E_2: Above 5%	0.50	0.30	0.20
	1.00	1.00	1.00

Table C—9–3 represents the probability of obtaining a certain piece of information in a test market given that a particular state-of-nature exists. Table C—9–3 is a table of conditional probabilities $P(E_i/S_j)$; that is, specific statements E_1, E_2, or E_3 will be made given the true situation S_1, S_2, or S_3. These probabilities are presumed built on past experiences of similar situations.

Given the above set of facts, there are several questions which can be answered. First, what new estimates of the true state of nature can be made given each piece of information? Second, how much should the company be willing to pay for that information?

The following procedure can be used to answer these questions. First, what is the probability of getting each single piece of information? The answer can be found by computing joint probabilities, i.e., $P(S_j) \cdot P(E_i/S_j)$. Table C—9–4 provides the results of these computations. One can see that by adding across the rows that the probability for getting any particular piece of information can be obtained. These are referred to as *marginal probabilities*.

At this point, we now have enough information to compute our new estimates for the true states-of-nature conditional, of course, upon which piece of information our research turns up. These revised estimates are called *posterior* probabilities, as opposed to our first estimates called *prior* probabilities.

The posterior probabilities are calculated by dividing each joint probability by its respective marginal probability;

$$P(S_1/E_1) \;=\; \frac{P(S_1) \cdot P(E_1/S_1)}{\displaystyle\sum_{j=1}^{3} P(S_j) \cdot P(Z_1/S_j)}$$

or: $\dfrac{\text{a given joint probability}}{\text{the respective marginal probability}}$

Table C—9–5 shows the calculations and results.

Table C—9–4
Display of Joint and Marginal Probabilities

Information	Joint Probabilities $P(S_1) \cdot P(E_i/S_1)$	$P(S_2) \cdot P(E_i/S_2)$	$P(S_3) \cdot P(E_i/S_3)$	Marginal Probabilities $P(E_i)$
E_1	0.06	0.12	0.15	0.33
E_2	0.09	0.16	0.09	0.34
E_3	0.15	0.12	0.06	0.33
$P(S_j)$	0.30	0.40	0.30	

Table   C—9–5
Posterior Probabilities

Information	Posterior Probabilities		
	$P(S_1/E_i)$	$P(S_2/E_i)$	$P(S_3/E_i)$
E_1	$\dfrac{.06}{.33} = 0.181$	$\dfrac{.12}{.33} = 0.365$	$\dfrac{.15}{.33} = 0.454$
E_2	$\dfrac{.09}{.34} = 0.265$	$\dfrac{.16}{.34} = 0.470$	$\dfrac{.09}{.34} = 0.265$
E_3	$\dfrac{.15}{.33} = 0.454$	$\dfrac{.12}{.33} = 0.365$	$\dfrac{.06}{.33} = 0.181$

Table   C—9–6
Expected Value of Introducing
Without Information

Alternative Decisions	States of Nature					
	S_1		S_2		S_3	
	$P(S_1)$		$P(S_2)$		$P(S_3)$	
Introduce	30%	$500,000	40%	$300,000	30%	($500,000)
Do not introduce	30%	0	40%	0	30%	0

$EV_u = 0.30\ (\$500,000) + 0.40\ (\$300,000) + 0.30\ (-\$500,000)$
$= \$120,000.$

Each cell tells us the probability of a state-of-nature, given the appearance of some sample event (a piece of market information). We can now say, for example, *if* we get information E_2 that we will estimate the true state-of-nature as being 0.265, 0.470, and 0.265 for S_1 through S_3, respectively.

Now we have the needed information for determining how much the company should be willing to pay for their market information. To determine the *value of information,* we must calculate the expected value of making a decision without information versus the expected value of making a decision with information. The *difference* is the value of information. We can calculate the expected value without information by multiplying the subjective (or prior) probability of each state of nature times the profit for each state of nature. Table C—9–6 shows these calculations.

Now if we are given information E_1 by the research department, the expected value of introducing or not introducing the new brand is shown in Table C—9–7.

If, however, the research department gives us E_2 as market information, then the EV of our decision to introduce would be calculated as shown in Table C—9–8.

And, similarly, if the research department gives us E_3 as market information, then the EV of our decision is shown in Table C—9–9.

Now we have the expected value of making a decision about introducing the new maker or not introducing, given each piece of information. If we receive E_1, we would not introduce the new product since the EV of not introducing (i.e., EV = 0) is greater than the EV of introducing (i.e. EV = −$27,000). If we receive E_2 piece of information, we would make the decision to introduce since the EV of introducing is greater than the EV of not introducing, i.e., $141,000 > 0. And, finally, if we were to receive E_3 piece of information, we would introduce the product since the EV of introducing ($246,000) is greater than the EV of not introducing (0).

We can calculate all of these things in advance of actually collecting information. Is it worth collecting? To answer this question we must compare the expected value of making a decision without information to that of making a decision with information. We already know that the expected value of introducing without information is $120,000. (See Table C—9–6.)

Now we want to calculate the expected value of a decision given that we buy the needed information. We already know that if we have E_1 our EV will be zero.

Table C—9–7
Expected Value of Decision Given E_1

Alternative Decisions	$P(S_1/E_1) = 0.181$	$P(S_2/E_1) = 0.365$	$P(S_3/E_1) = 0.454$	EV
Introduce	$500,000	$300,000	($500,000)	$27,000
Do Not Introduce	0	0	0	

Table C—9–8
Expected Value of Decision Given E_2

Alternative Decisions	$P(S_1/E_2) = 0.265$	$P(S_2/E_2) = 0.470$	$P(S_3/E_2) = 0.265$	EV
Introduce	$500,000	$300,000	($500,000)	$141,000
Do Not Introduce	0	0	0	0

Table C—9–9
Expected Value of Decision Given E_3

Alternative Decisions	$P(S_1/E_3) = 0.454$	$P(S_2/E_3) = 0.365$	$P(S_3/E_3) = 0.181$	EV
Introduce	$500,000	$300,000	($500,000)	$246,000
Do Not Introduce	0	0	0	0

If we have E_2 our EV will be $141,000. And if we have E_3 our EV will be $246,000. However, we don't really know which information we will get. But we do know the probabilities attached to getting each piece of information (see Table C—9–4). The probability of getting E_1—$P(E_1)$—is 0.34; $P(E_2) = 0.34$; $P(E_3) = 0.33$. These are our marginal probabilities in Table C—9–4. Since we have the expected value of making a decision with each information piece and we have the probabilities of getting each piece of information, $P(E_i)$, we have the necessary elements for computing the expected value of having market information. More specifically, the expected value of decision if research is conducted is:

$$0.33\ (0) + 0.34\ (\$141,000) + 0.33\ (\$246,000) = \$129,120$$

or $9,120 greater than the EV without information. The company, therefore, should be willing to spend up to $9,120 for information, but no more.

At this point, let us take a nonmathematical view of this problem. We will look at the problem in a graphical way and also from a pictorial viewpoint. Both of these approaches should give a better intuitive grasp of the Bayesian approach. See Figure C—9–6 and Table C—9–10.

Figure C—9–6 shows a tree diagram summarizing all of the previous calculations. Table C—9–10 is a pictorial display of the total probability space. Column one, $P(S_1)$, takes up 30 percent of total probability space, column 2, 40 percent, and column 3, 30 percent. Looking at the upper left cell, we know that $P(E_1/S_1)$, the probability of getting information E_1 given the estimated state of nature S_1, is 20 percent. Thus, that portion of total probability space represented by $P(S_1) \cdot P(E_1/S_1)$, the joint probability of both occurring, is .20 times .30, or .06. Similar calculations can be made for all joint probabilities, the total of which is 100 percent of the total probability space. Marginal probabilities are then calculated by adding the joint probability spaces for each E_i. For example, $P(E_1) = .06 + .12 + .15 = .33$. Having arrived at the marginal probabilities, then posterior (revised) probabilities, $P(S_i/E_i)$, can be calculated by dividing the joint probabilities by their respective marginal probabilities. The pictorial display eliminates the need for either memorizing a formula or simply plugging numbers into a formula to arrive at a solution.

Only a few models have been described to illustrate their usefulness in helping the marketing decision maker evaluate strategic alternatives. However, the decision maker is cautioned to use these and other quantitative models as inputs to her strategy selection and not as ultimate solutions. Often decision makers are dazzled by the precision of mathematical models. However, in the final analysis the decision-maker's judgment based upon experience and intuition must be exercised in strategy selection.

Summary

This chapter has discussed the meaning of strategy, the steps involved in its development, the kinds of marketing and corporate strategies, and some examples of mathematical criteria that can be applied to the evaluation of alternative marketing strategies. In particular, strategy was defined as a plan for adapting resources to the opportunity to attain a stated objective. In developing a market strategy, the strategic planner follows the following steps.

Figure   C—9–6
Tree Diagram Showing Value of Information

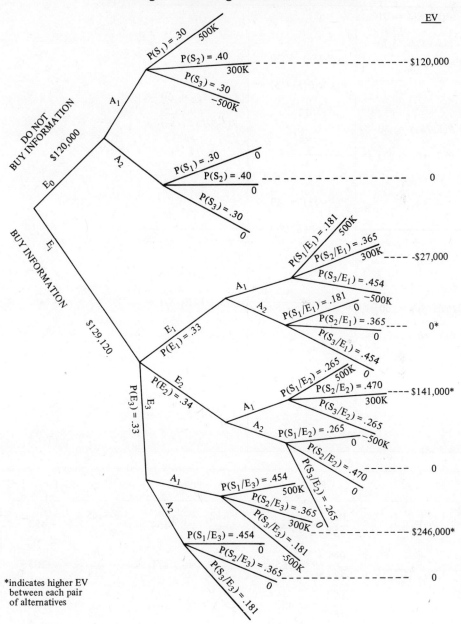

*indicates higher EV
  between each pair
  of alternatives

Table   C—9–10
Pictorial Display of Calculations of
Posterior Probabilities

Total Probability Space

$P(S_1) = .30$	$P(S_2) = .40$	$P(S_3) = .30$	$P(E_i)$ Marginal
$P(E_1/S_1) = .20$ $P(S_1) \cdot P(E_1/S_1) =$ .06	$P(E_1/S_2) = .30$ $P(S_2) \cdot P(E_1/S_2) =$ .12	$P(E_1/S_3) = .50$ $P(S_3) \cdot P(E_1/S_3) =$ .15	= .33
$P(E_2/S_1) = .30$ $P(S_1) \cdot P(E_2/S_1) =$ .09	$P(E_2/S_2) = .40$ $P(S_2) \cdot P(E_2/S_2) =$ .16	$P(E_2/S_3) = .30$ $P(S_3) \cdot P(E_2/S_3) =$ .09	= .34
$P(E_3/S_1) = .50$ $P(S_1) \cdot P(E_2/S_1) =$ .15	$P(E_3/S_2) = .30$ $P(S_2) \cdot P(E_2/S_2) =$ .12	$P(E_3/S_3) = .20$ $P(S_3) \cdot P(E_3/S_3) =$ .06	= .33 1.00

	$P(S_1/E_i)$	$P(S_2/E_i)$	(PS_3/E_i)
E_1	$\dfrac{.06}{.33} = .181$	$\dfrac{.12}{.33} = .364$	$\dfrac{.15}{.33} = .455$
E_2	$\dfrac{.09}{.34} = .265$	$\dfrac{.16}{.34} = .471$	$\dfrac{.09}{.34} = .265$
E_3	$\dfrac{.15}{.33} = .455$	$\dfrac{.12}{.33} = .364$	$\dfrac{.06}{.33} = .181$

1. Identify market opportunities.
2. Analyze the firm's corporate and marketing resources.
3. Set objectives.
4. Develop and evaluate alternative strategies.
5. Assign specific tasks.

In addition, contingency plans should be developed to adapt to changing environmental conditions, and specified feedback and control mechanisms should be stated and implemented.

Several different corporate/marketing strategies dealing with various combinations of product/market mixes were discussed. And several quantitative criteria, such as expected value, game theory (e.g., maximax and minimax), and the Bayesian theorem provide examples of how matematical techniques can aid decision makers in evaluating alternative solutions to a problem. However, the decision maker must keep in mind that these quantitative criteria and others must by tempered by managerial judgment.

Discussion Questions

1. What are some benefits a company derives from defining its corporate mission? Explain. How would you define the corporate mission for Revlon, Inc.?

2. Discuss several environmental factors that affect, and in the future might seriously affect, network television viewership. Explain.

3. Discuss several strategies producers of video games might use to increase company sales and profits. Explain.

4. Identify new product-market growth strategies for a college textbook publisher. Explain and defend.

5. Discuss the kinds of synergies which Texas Instruments achieves in its various product/market strategies. Explain.

6. You are the vice-president of marketing for Zilch, Inc. and must decide whether to introduce a new toothpaste called "Wow" or intensify the company's marketing efforts for the current toothpaste "Zowie." You have concluded from your research information that an intensified effort with Zowie will increase *profits* by $70,000 over the coming 3 years. Some preliminary consumer studies for Wow have been made and you appraise the situation as shown in Table 1.

Table 1
Possible Market Shares, Profits, and Probability
Assessments for "Wow" Over the Next 3 Years

Market Shares (possible states of nature)	Discounted Profits	Probabilities
O_1 = Capture 10 percent of market	$10,000,000	0.7
O_2 = Capture 3 percent of market	1,000,000	0.1
O_3 = Capture 0 percent of market	−5,000,000	0.2

At this point you feel it might be advantageous to obtain additional information about the true probabilities of each state-of-nature for Wow. You know that you can obtain information through a test-market study at a cost of $20,000. Table 2 describes the probabilities attached to each outcome of the test market given a state-of-nature is the true state.

Table 2
Conditional Probabilities of Possible
Outcomes of Test Market

States	Sell 10% or More of Market in Test (Z_1)	Sell 5-10% or More of Market in Test (Z_2)	Sell Less Than 5% in Test (Z_3)	Total
Market share = 10% − 0_1	0.6	0.3	0.1	1.0
Market share = 3% − 0_2	0.3	0.6	0.1	1.0
Market share = 0% − 0_3	0.1	0.1	0.8	1.0

Using Bayesian analysis, do the following:

a. Draw a decision tree which describes the "Wow" problem.

b. Set up a table of the joint, marginal, and posterior probabilities.

c. Compute the expected values of introducing versus not introducing the new product if no information is bought.

d. Compute the expected values if the test market information is bought at $20,000.

e. Based on the information, would you (1) intensify market efforts for "Zowie" or (2) would you introduce "Wow?"

7. Suppose a textile company is deciding between introducing a new fabric for high-styled men's suits and ladies' dresses (a product extension strategy) or intensifying its efforts selling its current fabrics for the blue jeans market (a market penetration strategy). The outcomes of these strategies will be significantly affected by whether the economy experiences recession or prosperity (states-of-nature). The expected payoffs and the probabilities of its states-of-nature are shown below.

	Recession (0.3)	Prosperity (0.7)
Product-extension (high-styled suits)	−$3 million	$15 million
Market-penetration (intensified effort for jeans)	0	$ 8 million

Based upon *expected value* which decision should the company choose? Explain.

8. The Firmex Company is considering several strategic alternatives to increase corporate profits. One alternative is to introduce a new product to a new market; another alternative is to introduce a present product to a new market. The success or failure of each marketing strategy depends upon whether recession or prosperity comes in the following 3 years. The following table provides a payoff matrix for each strategy, given economic conditions.

Strategy	Payoff Matrix in Millions	
	Recession	Prosperity
New product/new market	−2.0	4.2
Present product/new market	−3.0	7.0

a. If the company uses a maximax criterion, which alternatives should be selected?

b. If the company uses a minimax criterion, which alternative should be selected?

c. Which of these two criteria would you use? Explain.

D/M Inc.—A Marketing Case Study*

Denis F. Healy, University of Delaware

General Background

John Gilbert is one of several industry managers (*IMs*) for a well-known West Coast chemical company, D/M Inc., which produces basic chemical products for industrial processors. At the moment he is faced simultaneously with several conflicting and difficult marketing situations confronting his industry group, part of the Noxxe Division. The products for which he is responsible are being sold in several market segments within a broad industry area.

One of Gilbert's major concerns rises out of a series of actions being taken by one of D/M's strongest competitors (Macronite) in the market served by his industry group. That competitor apparently is relinquishing market position in one of Gilbert's major markets (market A). At the same time, there are some indications that Macronite has its eye on some of Gilbert's other markets. The opportunity for D/M to capture some of the forfeited share in market A on the one hand, coupled with the Macronite threat to other established market segments on the other, poses several immediate problems for John Gilbert especially because of his short tenure in the IM role.

As shown in Exhibit 35–1, Gilbert was promoted to industry manager about 8 months ago. He had been with D/M for several years, but had not worked previously for the Noxxe division. His predecessor in the IM assignment left D/M for another management position and, as a result, had not been available for consultation. The organization structure of D/M is shown in Figure 35–1. In addition to his own newness in the IM position, Gilbert's marketing coordinator, Maxine Watkins (see Exhibit 35–2), had been promoted into marketing from the marketing research group less than a year ago.

Exhibit 35-1
John Gilbert
Biographical Sketch

Personal:	Age 41, married, two children.
Education:	B.S., Chemical Engineering, Purdue, 1958
	Advanced studies, Chemical Engineering
	MBA in progress (3/4 finished), nights at UCLA (began in 1972)
	Other various management seminars and sales training programs
Experience:	January 1977 to present—Industry Manager, Noxxe
	1973–1976—Sales Manager, Oxxen Division
	1969–1973—Field Sales, Enoxx Division
	1965–1969—U.S. Army, Engineers
	1958–1965—Various product development technical service and sales assignments in other companies.

Figure 35–1
D/M Company—Organization Chart

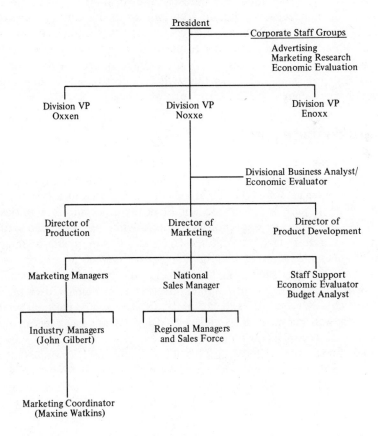

Exhibit 35-2
Maxine Watkins
Biographical Sketch

Personal:	Age 32, single.
Education:	MBA, Columbia University, 1970
	BS, Chemistry, UCLA, 1966
	Other various management and marketing research seminars and sales training sessions.
Experience:	September 1976 to present—Marketing Coordinator, Noxxe
	1973–1976—Marketing Research Analyst, D/M Corporate
	1970–1973—Sales Representative, Enoxx Division
	1968–1970—Staff Research Assistant, Port of New York Authority
	1966–1968—Vista Volunteer, Watts, California

Gilbert's Situation

Gilbert's inexperience in the new position coupled with the incomplete records and programs prepared by his predecessors are imposing considerable strains. He still is trying to learn about the industry and to build rapport with the other members of his management team. In addition, up to this time, he has only been able to meet a few of the buying influences in his key accounts. In spite of these obstacles, Gilbert feels that it is his responsibility to identify the "real" nature of the situations facing his industry, both present and future. He also is responsible for developing programs and plans that will be effective in meeting those situations, and that are convincing to other decision makers at D/M.

D/M's Marketing Approach

D/M serves its markets largely by direct sales from the manufacturer. (The Noxxe channel is diagrammed in Figure 35–2.) Part of the reason for this practice is tradition. The other reason is that D/M's products are used in a variety of finished products which require sophisticated and delicate processing conditions. In addition, there are shelf life and processing considerations associated with D/M's material. As a result, D/M executives feel that it is particularly important to understand the manufacturing and handling processes of its customers. To accomplish this, producers such as D/M, invest heavily in technical service personnel training their sales forces about manufacturing systems employed in the industry. D/M is particularly proud of its technical capabilities and of the high quality of its products. It is well known in the industry that D/M's line can meet or exceed the specifications of any of its customers.

Although competitive shifts within his markets are in full swing, Gilbert is involved in reviewing and reacting to a market research report initiated ten months ago but delayed because of a realignment of priorities in the marketing research group. The report, summarized in Exhibit 35–3, suggests that market A is nearing

Figure   35–2
NOXXE Division's Distribution Channel

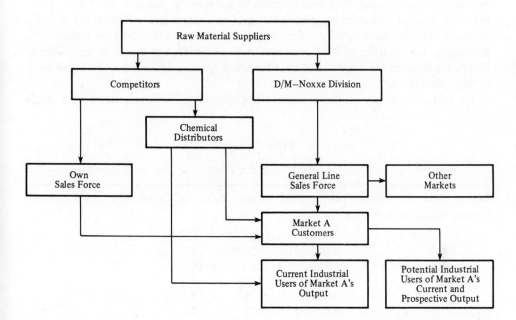

the peak of its growth and that declines in the rate of growth can be expected to appear at an increasing rate in the future. In addition to a slowdown in usage rates, several substitute products using different technologies already are beginning to take away market shares from the established producers.

Gilbert does not know precisely the nature of competitive marketing activities in market A. However, Ms. Watkins has prepared some sketchy profiles of the six major participants (D/M—Noxxe Division, and the five major competitors) as presented in Exhibit 35–4. It looks as if three of the five competitors, Minitrol, Oletrop, and Effersil, have resorted to price competition to alter their market share levels. Sincromil, in an atypical move, appears to have invested heavily in journal advertising and trade show exhibits but has kept prices about the same as D/M. The two remaining companies, Macronite and another minor firm, have either dropped out of the market or cut back on marketing efforts to explore alternative target markets. The few records available suggest that pricing has not been a major competitive weapon in market A until the last 12–18 months.

The advertising and promotional efforts used by Gilbert's predecessor had been largely limited to expensive journal advertising as well as exhibits at some of the major trade shows. Since the objectives for these efforts had either not been written down or could not be found, Gilbert has been unable to identify either their real purpose or their effectiveness. All he knows is that they are expensive. Similarly, field sales activities are continuing, but it is unclear whether specific objectives (if any) have been established for the total field sales effort or for the different regional sales groups.

Growth Opportunities and Impediments

Although market A's growth rate appears to be slowing down, Gilbert feels there are still several outstanding profitable growth opportunities open for D/M's products. To tap these opportunities, he believes that modifications in technology, packaging, and pricing will be required. And although not precisely determined, it appears that other markets (outside of market A) might be available for products of this general type.

To take advantage of these market opportunities, however, there is a need

Exhibit 35-3
Profile of Market A

Market size—the current annual total industry sales to Market A are $80 million.
Growth rate (based on units)—

	Industry	D/M
1965–1970	20%	25%
1970–1974	15	18
1974–1975	10	9
1975–1976	8	7
1976–1977	7	6

Number of Competitors and Estimated Shares ($ basis, 1976)—

D/M—Noxxe Division	34–40%
Macronite	25–30
Minitrol	15–20
Oletrop	10–15
Effersil	5–10
Sincromil	5–10

Number of New Competitive Products—three new materials have been presented to the market since early 1976.

Level of Pricing Activity—generally erratic and downward at annual rate of 5 percent since 1974. In 1977 there have been 3 price reductions of 5 percent each by several suppliers.

Product Modification Trends—minor activity with mostly product line pruning taking place. Some formulation alterations have appeared but were basically done to cut costs, not to improve process-ability for the customer.

Channel of Distribution Trends—some distributors are expanding their sales of product to market A and are attempting to purchase in larger quantities. There also is a tendency for several large customers to purchase the production process from producers.

Technical and Sales Service Trends—demand for technical service is diminishing in market A but appears to be growing in other markets. Sales service requirements are about the same as always, if not growing slightly, as customers attempt to "fine tune" their purchasing and production operations.

Exhibit 35 - 4
Competitive Profiles and Strategies

D/M—Noxxe Division

Profile:

1. The largest competitor in terms of financial and technical resources.

2. Conservative in terms of rate of market entry, new product development and withdrawal from established markets.

3. Viewed by customers and competitors as a "quality" producer but somewhat slow to respond to change.

4. Part of a much larger corporate organization.

Strategies:

1. Emphasizes market penetration during the late growth and maturity stages of market development.

2. Employs technical service activity to secure and hold market shares.

3. Uses skimming price strategy until market shares drop more than 5 percent.

Macronite

Profile:

1. Second in size to D/M with resource base of 80 percent of D/M's and a market share of 25 to 30 percent.

2. Aggressive in developing new products and markets. Active in shifting marketing effort from one area to another.

3. Viewed by customers and competitors as the most dynamic and innovative organization in the industry.

4. Has difficulty maintaining momentum in areas after it has opened the market.

5. Part of a much larger corporate organization.

Strategies:

1. Emphasize market and product development.

2. Develop channels of distribution employing key chemicals distributors and sales representatives in addition to its own sales and distribution organization.

3. Capture, control, and milk markets during growth and early maturity stages, then move on to other markets.

4. Avoid mature markets.

Minitrol

Profile:

1. Third in size with a 15 to 20 percent market share and a resource base about 10 percent the size of D/M's.

2. Limited technical development ability but strong marketing organization.

3. Has limited resources for product or market development, but excellent market information system for tracking developments.

4. Viewed by customers as a good second source supplier and by competitors as a disruptive force on market stability.

5. A growth-oriented organization.

Strategies:

1. Concentrate on selected markets newly developed by others. Tries to be a fast second into the marketplace.

2. Emphasize price flexibility and distribution capabilities to distinguish from other competitors.

3. Capitalize on small size to maneuver within and between markets—especially those in early growth stages.

4. Minimize expenses to participate in selected mature markets at profitable levels.

Oletrop, Effersil, Sincromil (three different companies with similar profiles and strategies)

Profile:

1. One of several smaller competitors sharing 20 to 30 percent of the market.

2. A small division of a larger organization which apparently is using this group as a "cash cow."

3. Has an image of smallness and as a highly specialized supplier.

4. Frequently purchases some products from major suppliers to supplement its own production.

5. Viewed as a last resort as a supplier or as producer for established and declining markets.

Strategies:

1. Established position as dependable supplier in very specific product lines and market segments.

2. Achieve market position in late maturity—early decline markets.

3. Minimize all expenses, especially marketing by late participation at low prices in established markets.

4. Avoid direct competition with major competitors by careful selection of market segments and channels of distribution.

---

to modify the physical properties and handling characteristics of the products, and a need for significant change in the marketing communication patterns. Access to those new market opportunities, however, would be eased considerably if Gilbert can either maintain or perhaps enlarge his position in market A, where the major customers in market A are developing strength in their new markets.

Some of the above mentioned changes have already been initiated. However, the effort seems to be moving much slower than necessary. Gilbert is concerned that the opportunity could fade before D/M gets "its act together." The big obstacle, Gilbert thinks, seems to be with the process research and facilities planning people who seem to be "dragging their feet" on the project. John Gilbert is not really clear as to why such things happen in these projects, but it certainly is posing considerable problems for him, Maxine Watkins, and other marketing people.

Market A is dominated by other producers (described in Exhibit 35–4) who are going through a major transition in their own technology and market orientation. D/M once held 40 percent of sales in market A, but this figure has fallen significantly based upon the results reflected in the current year-to-date sales figures. Volume figures for D/M are somewhat incomplete except for the past 6 months when they began to be kept on a reliable basis. Since there have also been several waves of price changes over the past year, this, too, has clouded the share-of-market figures.

Customer and Supplier Activity

According to call reports from a few of D/M's sales regions and reports from technical service personnel over the past year, several break-throughs have been made in manufacturing processes by some of Gilbert's key customers who process basic chemicals into compounds. These reports, however, are sketchy and incomplete. Also, there are rumors within market A that a few of Gilbert's major customers have uncovered some significant new applications for their products. There is a possibility that some of these applications could have a major influence on purchase specifications for their raw materials and ultimately could affect their demand for Gilbert's products. Marketing research has provided only limited information on how extensively Gilbert's customers' products have permeated the new markets. All that is definitely known is that several industrial users of D/M's market A customers discussed the new developments at a cocktail party sponsored by the trade association.

Other changes also are beginning to occur in relationships with some of Gilbert's key customers. Maxine tracked the buying patterns for key accounts and noticed that five accounts have substantially reduced purchase commitments for the next quarter. Rumor has it that a couple of the key accounts have attempted to purchase manufacturing rights from Macronite. In spite of the fact that D/M has a contractual pricing arrangement with these firms, Gilbert is beginning to wonder if the arrangements will hold, and how he should approach the firms about the rumors.

Another event stimulated some interest and concern. Over the past couple of months, several well-known distributors had made inquiries about contracting for larger volumes of Gilbert's products at lower prices. This had never occurred before and D/M is not yet prepared to deal with the subject.

A few of D/M's raw materials suppliers have increased their prices substantially over the past six months. They informed D/M that their higher energy costs will be passed along to D/M through a quarterly price adjustment. Such increases are causing D/M and Gilbert to reflect on their own pricing policies.

Recently, another disturbing piece of news was received from a supplier of one of the principal raw materials for Gilbert's products. The supplier announced that, over the next eighteen months, it planned to phase out this material. The D/M purchasing people are aware of alternative sources of supply, but in the past they have not been satisfied with product quality consistency from other suppliers. Since this particular material is crucial to D/M's finished product quality, the principal supplier has practically been the "exclusive" supplier.

The EPA Makes a Visit

To further complicate matters, the EPA has made several visits to D/M's manufacturing facilities in the past year. On the most recent visit, preliminary findings indicated that effluent* from the plant making Gilbert's products exhibited properties far in excess of standards established for the process and the technology. The normal course with the EPA is to present a report of its findings about 2 months after a visit and threaten action if operations are not modified to compliance levels within a prespecified period, normally about one year. D/M was aware of the compliance problem potential well before the EPA visit but had elected to hold expenditures until the next fiscal year, since the expenditures would be substantial and market conditions appeared to be changing and not well understood. Furthermore, D/M management hoped that the process research being conducted within D/M would provide a lower cost solution to the effluent problem. As mentioned previously, however, there had been some delays introducing new production processes developed by the process research group into the manufacturing area. In addition, a few of Gilbert's customers reported they were experiencing some disposal problems with D/M's products, as well as those of Minitrol. Technical personnel for D/M have been asked to investigate, but their reports have not been completed.

The D/M—Noxxe Organization and Planning System

John Gilbert, since he is relatively new to the assignment, has not developed the close working relationships he would have liked with either the regional sales organizations or the technical service group. He does, however, chair monthly meetings at which selected representatives of technical service, sales, production, advertising, and distribution are present. Occasionally, as the need arises, members of other support groups are asked to participate. The purpose of these meetings is to help all concerned keep abreast of new developments in the product/market area and to provide an opportunity to coordinate activities within the team. Gilbert faithfully and actively participates in these meetings, but frequently walks away from them feeling frustrated and confused. The frustration arises from feelings of personal ineffectiveness in being unable to convert commitments made in the meetings into actions. Confusion arises from the conflicting comments he has heard about the reasons given for delays in the product development program and in achieving sales objectives. Although John Gilbert does not know it, other participants in the meetings often leave with the same feelings.

---

* An effluent is the waste material from processing often dumped into rivers and streams.

Although formal marketing planning is a way of life in D/M, the plan Gilbert inherited is, in fact, a program covering a one-year timeframe. Because of its short-term orientation, the document does not provide the continuity and direction that Gilbert feels his industry groups need. As a result, Gilbert is faced with having to develop both a program for the next year, as well as a plan covering several programming periods.

Financial Considerations

Another development of note was highlighted in a report Gilbert received recently from the business analyst tracking expenses and sales for Gilbert's industry group. The report indicated that, because of rising costs and shifts in markets and distribution (as indicated by marginal income deviations), the profit contribution for Gilbert's industry group had begun to slide. The divisional ground rules, in effect for all industry groups, called for marketing efforts to restore contribution levels without sacrificing market share. In light of these constraints, it is apparent that Gilbert has to take action or prepare a defense for his floundering market position.

Capital investment for the facilities producing Gilbert's products had been recouped long ago. However, to accomplish the multiple tasks of contribution recapture, market penetration, and market development, it appears to Gilbert that substantial new investment in plant and equipment will likely be required in addition to realignment of the marketing efforts previously discussed.

Watkins and Gilbert Go to a Marketing Seminar

It is with this state of affairs that John and Maxine leave to attend one of the programs the company has developed on the topic of marketing management and planning. As they board the train to travel to the program location, Maxine remarks, "Here we are with all these situations to deal with at the office, and we have to go to this darned marketing seminar." John continues, lamenting their woes,

> Every time we turn around or go off to another conference, the market or the company changes something which just confuses matters more. I sure hope we have a little time to think about the real issues and to discuss them with some of the other marketing people at the session. The one thing I don't want is to be lectured to about a bunch of theories and company policies that only make our job more complicated.

Minicase 1—Market Research

"There is no question that our markets, especially market A, are in a state of flux . . . and we are not really prepared to react effectively!" Maxine Watkins commented to Gilbert as they were taking the airport limosine to their Chicago hotel and the annual industry exposition. "The channel of distribution is behaving in an unusual fashion, and frankly, I'm afraid we have been pushing service when the market really isn't willing to pay the price."

Gilbert: "Max, I share your concerns but with the sketchy and dated infor-
               mation we have, I really don't know the actual conditions in the
               marketplace and find it tough to make general statements about
               our product life cycle position. Field sales reports rarely seem to
               give the detail or precision needed and by the time market research
               gets a report together the market is likely to have changed several
               times."

Watkins: "Well, we might try to grab Fred (Fred Nutley, manager of market
               research, appointed 18 months ago) and try to get him involved
               in this problem. He seems like a good guy, and from what I've
               heard, he is willing to tackle some difficult problems. He's a tough-
               minded, no "b.s." guy and won't be too interested in getting in-
               volved without a clear definition of the issues."

Gilbert: "Sounds like a great idea! Let's try to meet with him at 3:30
               tomorrow afternoon. If we have to, we can work right up until the
               cocktail-reception at 6:00. In the meantime I'll call Fred and
               tell him what we want to do. And then—let's you and I spend some
               time this afternoon in pulling together our thoughts. Okay with
               you?"

Watkins: "Fine, John, I think we can get our act together pretty well—
               especially given my experience in the marketing research area. Let's

catch lunch and get to work. Incidentally, it's a good thing I brought along the market A and competitor profiles."

Gilbert: "I'll call Fred right now."

Nutley: "Sure, John, I can spring loose for a couple of hours. I've been meaning to talk with you about your market research requirements for some time. This is a perfect opportunity to talk about your general needs and our capabilities as well as the specific problem at hand. In the meantime, I'll give some thought to the subject and to what my group might be able to do for you.

Discussion Question

Assume you are either Gilbert or Watkins.

1. Prepare a list of the major areas of concern to present to Nutley.
2. Describe what kinds of information you will need.
3. Describe how the information you seek will be used in your decision making.

Minicase 2—Pricing

Over the years the Noxxe Division has been able to price above the market 5–10 percent of average price, largely because it offered a quality product and technical service support. However, as the market growth rate slowed and competition increased, the pressures to meet competitive prices grew to the point that Noxxe began to "fall in line." By meeting competition, the contribution margin in market A has fallen below planned levels—as was made perfectly clear to Gilbert by the business analyst. In addition, the general erosion of price levels, as shown in Exhibit 35–3, has been at a faster rate than the rate of cost decreases along D/M's experience curve, and while there is still a profit margin, the trend toward convergence of price and cost curves is discomforting.

Furthermore, although the information is very tentative, it appears that because of the growth of substitute products available in market A, the demand is moving from an inelastic to an elastic condition.

With these facts in mind, Gilbert and Watkins are faced with a decision to respond to a 15 percent price cut on key products announced by Minitrol.

Discussion Questions

Prepare a brief report responding to the following:

1. What are the major considerations you would make?
2. What information would you seek, from whom, and how would you use it?

D/M Inc.

Minicase 3—Marketing Communications

In reviewing the files of the previous industry manager and from interviewing advertising and field sales representatives, Gilbert and Watkins find that little has been done to develop sales and promotional objectives for market A. As this situation became evident, Gilbert called Ms. Watkins into his office and the following dialogue occurred.

Watkins: "Well, John, it looks as if we'll have to really start from scratch in developing a promotional and selling plan for next year. I can't find much of anything, in writing, which pinpoints the advertising and trade show commitments in market A. There is only passing mention made of the objectives in a memo to advertising—something about maintaining a position as a quality supplier."

Gilbert: "Yeah, the budget for this year is $70,000 for shows and advertising, and so far we've either spent or committed $40,000. I really question whether there is any merit in committing the rest until we have a fix on what we want to do and what the impact of the expenditures has been to date. Listen, Maxine, I'd like you to look into this further and to report back to me next week with some recommendations for evaluating the program to date, as well as for continuing the program for the remainder of the year. While you're at it, I'd like you to start preparing a total communications plan for next year as well—you know, objectives, markets to cover, coordination with field sales, and so on."

Watkins: "Okay, I'll do what I can—but you must understand that with the limited information available, I'm going to be doing a lot of groping in the dark."

Gilbert: "I understand—just make sure you come up with something that we can think about in a more structured manner."

Discussion Question

You are Maxine Watkins. Prepare an outline of the actions you will take in responding to Gilbert's assignment.

Chautauqua Lakeside Estates*

Terence A. Shimp, University of South Carolina
Richard W. Skinner, Kent State University

The past decade has observed the growth of condominiums as a major housing alternative for American families. The condominium concept combines features of renting and traditional home ownership. The condominium unit is purchased, as with traditional home ownership, but the owner is relieved from performing various aspects of maintenance inherent in traditional home ownership. In effect, the condominium concept has combined the positive features of renting and traditional home ownership and reduced the negative aspects of each. The resultant effect has been a very attractive and marketable housing package.

Chautauqua Lake is situated in the extreme western country of New York state bordering Pennsylvania. The lake provides a beautiful natural setting and an all-seasons recreational center. Chautauqua Lake, which is approximately 20 miles long and ranges from 1–3 miles wide, is surrounded by a large number of cottages and year-round homes. In 1969, one of the cottages was purchased by Don Hunter who had camped in the area for years. In 1971 a beautiful 20-acre parcel of land directly across the lake from his cottage became available for purchase. This represented a "chance of a lifetime" for Hunter, who for years had wanted to construct a condominium resort. He related: "It's been my dream, but I never thought I would be so fortunate as to build it in a place like Chautauqua." Recognizing the tremendous capital necessary to support such a large project, Hunter contacted the Pioneer County Savings and Loan Company of Pioneer, Ohio. Emerging from this contact was a joint venture partnership between Hunter Development, Inc. (owned by Don Hunter) and Chautauqua Lakeside Estates, Inc. (a wholly-owned subsidiary of Pioneer County Savings and Loan). According to Hunter, "This partnership has enabled us to expedite the construction of the units and, since construction costs are going up at approximately 1 percent per month, the sooner the condominium units are finished, the less we will have to charge for them."

---

* Some names have been changed to provide anonymity to persons involved in the study.

The sponsors of Chautauqua Lake Estates believed they were offering future condominium purchasers with more than attractive, well-built second homes. Lake Chautauqua offers an excellent recreational center for outdoor enthusiasts. In the summer, boating, fishing, sailing, and water skiing are extremely popular on the lake. In addition, a beautiful golf course is adjacent to Chautauqua Lakeside Estates. Winter sporting enthusiasts are offered over 400 miles of snowmobile trails, and seven major ski areas are available within a one-hour drive of the development. An extra attraction is the Chautauqua Institution located almost directly across the lake from Chautauqua Lakeside Estates. This institution has fostered religious, intellectual, and social pursuits for 100 years and has attracted world-wide support and participation. There is an influx during the summer months of 8,000 to 10,000 people per week at the Institute.

Financial and architectural planning were done, and construction of the condominium project began in the spring of 1972. 13 buildings, containing a total of 147 one-to-four bedroom units, were planned on the 20-acre parcel of land.

Marketing Strategy

Developers of Chautauqua Lakeside Estates felt that a major marketing research project was unnecessary prior to the construction of the condominium units. Instead, it was believed that the lake's tremendous beauty and recreational opportunities offered, in effect, an "automatic" market. Moreover, four metropolitan centers from which to attract purchasers were located within three hours driving time of Lake Chautauqua: Pittsburgh, Pennsylvania; Cleveland, Ohio; Buffalo, New York; and Erie, Pennsylvania. The developers were of the opinion that the major market for the condominiums would consist of middle-aged individuals in the upper income categories. Since the units were to be primarily marketed as second homes, the developers deemed it advisable to construct luxury units compatible with resort living—but at reasonable prices.

Due to financial arrangements, it was necesary to coordinate construction with sales. Originally, three buildings containing 39 of the intended 147 units were constructed. The New York bank through which financing was obtained stipulated that no additional funds would be supplied until 11 units were sold. With the sale of each 11 units, funding would be supplied for one more building. The fact that funding could be obtained only after a prescribed number of units were sold imposed on the developers the necessity of immediately marketing the already constructed units. Model condominiums were placed on display shortly after the first building was under roof (before landscaping, driveways, walks, etc. were installed).

Promotional Efforts

Since the developers believed the area would sell itself, initial promotional efforts were minimal. An advisory board of successful businessmen encouraged the developers of Chautauqua Lakeside Estates to market the resort condominiums to professional people. Accepting this suggestion, the developers formulated a direct mail program whereby the names of doctors, lawyers, and other profesionals were selected from telephone directories in Cleveland, Pittsburgh, Erie, and Buffalo. Direct mail pieces were sent to the selected people requesting they return the card if interested in additional information concerning Chautauqua Lakeside Estates. These efforts generated very little response. Consequently, follow-up plans were arranged and efforts were initiated to personally contact the professional prospects. These efforts, however, also received resistance since the doctors and lawyers were unable or unwilling to release time from their busy schedules. In addition, mail and telephone follow-up of those who looked at models was actively pursued.

Efforts to sell the completed units failed to fulfill the developers' expectations. Therefore, near the end of the first full year of marketing efforts, the developers evaluated the possibility of employing an advertising agency to perform the promotional task. Several agencies, including real estate sales companies, were contacted and requested to review the situation and prepare a proposal. One such proposal from an advertising agency offered the following major recommendations:

(a) Saturate, "blitz," the Cleveland, Buffalo, Pittsburgh, and Erie markets with a 3-week advertising campaign.

(b) The basic media thrust would be in two areas: radio and newspaper. At the time of year that this campaign will begin (spring), the target audience will be mobile. Saturation of the two media is recommended for the first week with sustained coverage throughout the campaign.

(c) Because of the heavy investment in radio time, it is recommended that the very best talent available be used for development and production of spots. Highly selective choice of stations is desirable.

(d) Newspaper ads will be of one format to develop instant familiarity with the condominium project. They should be no less than 1,000 lines in order to avoid being lost on a page. Exclusive use of major metropolitan dailies and Sunday papers is recommended. Ads are to be placed in sports, finance, and travel sections as well as real estate sections.

(e) Although the basic thrust will be in these two media, secondary consideration should be given to outdoor advertising in key locations, ads in programs at Chautauqua Institutions, and ads in programs in selected music and art centers and summer theaters.

A summary of the proposed media budget to support these recommendations is provided in Exhibit 36–1.

This budget and others were rejected as too costly.

Pricing Strategy

Although the Chautauqua Lake condominium units were well-built and offered all the amenities of gracious resort living, the developers desired to price the units at a "reasonable" level, since marketing efforts were directed primarily to the second-home market. However, as a result of the very stringent condominium

Exhibit 36-1
Proposed Media Budget

Market	Radio & Newspaper Budget
Cleveland	$28,634
Pittsburgh	22,912
Buffalo	14,322
Erie	4,410
Total	$70,278

laws of New York state and environmental concerns for the lake with respect to sewage treatment facilities, construction costs and legal fees were considerably higher than originally anticipated. Also, land preparation costs and water treatment facility costs exceeded expectations. It was necessary to price the units several thousand dollars in excess of what was planned. Exhibit 36–2 presents pertinent information concerning illustrative pricing of the 1–4 bedroom condominium units.

Current Status of Project

It is now 30 months since the construction of the Chautauqua condominium project began and a total of 59 of the proposed 147 units have been constructed. Thirty-seven units have been sold and occupied, but the developers still are seeking buyers for the remaining 22 units. (The problem is compounded by a tight money situation.) They have decided not to construct any additional buildings until the remaining 22 units are purchased and, hopefully, 75 percent of the units in the next building (to be constructed) are presold. Needless to say, the developers are perplexed as to what they should have done differently and, more importantly, what they should do now to market the remaining units so they can complete the planned 147-unit project. Sales must pick up or cash flow problems will place the total development in jeopardy.

Don Hunter and his associates in the project agreed that a meeting with the advisory board was imperative to discuss what efforts could be undertaken to expedite successful completion of the project. A meeting date was set for the following week. Hunter realized that the decisions emanating from the meeting would be crucial in determining the future direction and success of the product. After devoting considerable thought to the meeting, Hunter prepared and mailed an agenda to each member of the advisory board. Four items were included in the agenda; the issues accompanying each item were detailed by Hunter to bring each member up to date on the project and provide a common base for discussion at the upcoming meeting. The agenda items with Hunter's remarks appear in Exhibit 36–3.

Exhibit 36-2

**Illustrative Pricing Information on
1-4 Bedroom Units**

Description	Sales Price	Minimum Down-Payment	Estimated Monthly Mortgage Charges 20 Yrs.*	Estimated Monthly Common Charges **	Estimated Monthly Real Estate Taxes	Estimated Total Monthly Payments
4 Bedrooms, 2½ Baths, Balcony	$54,900	$11,000	$381.05	$94.62	$102.98	$578.65
3 Bedrooms, 2½ Baths, Balcony	47,900	9,600	332.44	83.51	89.94	505.89
2 Bedrooms, 2 Baths	44,900	9,000	311.61	80.86	84.25	476.72
1 Bedroom, 1 Bath	28,900	5,800	200.61	41.92	54.29	296.72

* Based on 8.5 percent interest; 20-year mortgage.
** Common charges are assessed condominium owners for the maintenance of "common" facilities used by all occupants of the units, including swimming pool, tennis courts, sewage-water treatment facilities, etc.

667

Exhibit 36-3
Advisory Board Meeting Agenda

Item #1: Toward what market segment(s) should future efforts be directed?

At present, the buyers of the 37 units constitute a diversified group. Past purchasers have run the gamut of demographic/socioeconomic characteristics. The condominium units have been sold to singles and to married couples of various age groups. The only commonality among the purchasers is that the majority are from Ohio and many are friends (or friends of friends) of the developers. We are uncertain as to what market(s) future efforts should be directed. One alternative is to direct efforts to the young adult market, singles and married couples who are socially mobile and outdoor recreation enthusiasts. Another alternative is to devote efforts to the market of older well-to-do families who desire a weekend and vacation retreat all family members will enjoy. A third alternative is to emphasize the retired or near-retired market of older couples who have accumulated the financial wherewithal to purchase a condominium. Although these alternatives do not exhaust the potential market segments, we are very interested in selecting the right market(s) since all future marketing efforts will be influenced by the choice of market(s).

Item #2: What future promotional methods should be utilized?

We have continued to employ a direct mail campaign since construction began. Other promotional efforts have relied largely upon our professional contacts and favorable word-of-mouth generated by purchasers. Interested prospects are invited to visit Lake Chautauqua and receive a guided tour of the facilities by hostesses employed from the surrounding community. We are dissatisfied with current promotional efforts and are contemplating employment of a professional marketing agency to be responsible for developing a coordinated marketing plan. However, we have not been overly impressed with such agencies as no one has experience marketing a resort condominium in the northeastern United States.

Item #3: What is the potential of marketing the condominiums as investments?

There is some indication that many of our current owners are using their condominiums for investment purposes. During the 10-week period in which Chautauqua Institute is open, many of the owners have rented their units to families for summer vacations. The going rental rate has been approximately $225 per week for 1-bedroom units, $300 for 2 bedrooms, and $350 for 3-bedroom units. Moreover, there appears to be a viable rental market during the snow skiing season. However, we are not permitted by the Securities Exchange Commission Act to market the rental aspects of condominium purchase. It is feasible, however, to register with the SEC, thereby enabling us to market the condominiums for rental and other investment purposes. Registration would require an expenditure of approximately $50,000 and would take six months or longer. We are uncertain whether to pursue this channel.

Item #4: Should buildings to be constructed in the future contain 3 and 4-bedroom units or be restricted to 1 and 2-bedroom units?

Buildings constructed to date have included 3 and 4-bedroom units as well as the less expensive 1 and 2-bedroom units. Although there has been some success in selling the expensive 3 and 4-bedroom units, we are uncertain whether future construction of the larger, more expensive units is warranted. There seems to be a great deal of appeal for the 1 and 2-bedroom units, and we have considered the efficacy of limiting all future construction to buildings containing only these units. The ultimate decision will depend upon what market segment(s) is(are) selected to direct future efforts toward and whether or not it is decided to market the condominiums for investment purposes.

TransAirways, Incorporated:
A Marketing Strategy for Air Freight

Edwin C. Hackleman and Subhash C. Jain
The University of Connecticut

Bill Brown turned from his desk and looked out the window of his twenty-third floor office in the TransAmerica Building and saw a tri-jet 727 climb steeply out of San Francisco International and back away toward the East Coast. It was Wednesday afternoon, and the vice-president in charge of freight operations at TransAirways knew he should begin to organize his thoughts for next year's freight marketing plan. He had scheduled a meeting for Friday morning with his staff of planners and had invited the financial people from TransAirways to attend. Next Monday afternoon he and Bob Pursell, the marketing administration director at TA, would present the freight marketing plan for 1975 to Mr. George B. Johnson, who was TransAirways senior vice-president for planning and marketing. Although freight sales had been increasing steadily for the last several years, TransAirways had shown no improvement in market share in its air cargo operations and would, it appeared, show a significant operating loss in its freight operations for the current year. To make matters worse, a decision was due in six weeks on the initial financial commitment necessary to begin production of new aircraft scheduled for delivery in 1978, according to TransAirways' present forecast. Bill knew that whatever plan he brought to the meeting Monday had better provide the answers to put the freight operations back on course.

William C. Brown graduated *cum laude* from Columbia University in 1952 and had worked in marketing and market analysis positions at two other airlines before coming to TransAirways in 1961. In his nine years with the company, he had worked exclusively in the area of air cargo, responsible for eastern operations from 1965 to 1970 (which included the New York JFK, Chicago ORD, and Dallas DAL freight operations), and accepting responsibility for the entire company freight operation in 1971, nearly six years ago.

TransAirways: History and Status

TransAirways, Inc. was started in 1930 by Bradley J. Barkley and T. Phillip Kruger, two ex-World War I fighter aces who had amassed a small fortune in an expanding air mail service in the early 1930s. With the passage of the Air Commerce Act of 1926, air transportation was made a reality, and TransAirways began a domestic passenger service along the West Coast with three airplanes. Although the largest portion of their traffic was among the cities of Seattle, San Francisco, and Los Angeles, their route structure in the mid-1930s included seven cities. Air traffic grew at enormous rates between 1934 and 1937 and, by the end of 1937, TransAirways had accumulated a total of 25 aircraft and was beginning to offer a promising service in air cargo transport aboard its passenger airliners. Managing to retain nominal growth rates over the war years, TransAirways enjoyed substantial growth in the late 1940s because of early investments in the longer range and more comfortable Douglas DC–6 and DC–7 and the Lockheed Constellation. This period represented substantial growth and increased earnings which allowed for more financing through equity funding. With the introduction of jets in 1958, heavy financial commitments and traffic declines led to five years of poor performance, with the company seeing its first year of net loss in 1960. But as traffic revived in the mid-1960s, TransAirways again shared good growth and profits, with revenue passenger miles (RPM) increasing by an average of 11 percent per year and revenue ton miles (RTM) of cargo increasing an average of 14 percent per year. In 1968, TA decided to complement its passenger-cargo service with all-cargo freighter service using Boeing 707 and Douglas DC–8 stretched aircraft. Still, increasing demand for air freight service continued through the late 1960s along with strong demand for passenger service. In the first quarter of 1971, TransAirways accepted delivery of its first wide-bodied jet, a Boeing 747. By January of 1976, TA expected to have a total of 20 wide-bodied aircraft (B747 and DC–10) scheduled and operational. 1975 represented a year of unpredictable changes in the availability and cost of fuel as well as a year of serious decline in pasenger traffic that coincided with the depressed United States and world economies. Although freight sales managed to increase substantially over this period, freight operations produced net losses. Expectations for the future were uncertain, although the general trend of optimism over an improved economy seemed to indicate that the airline industry also might recover. In terms of future commitments, TA was to take delivery of ten new aircraft in 1976, most of which were to replace aging smaller aircraft. It also had orders for aircraft to be delivered in 1977 and 1978. Initial payments for the aircraft to be delivered in 1977 already had been made, and a financial commitment for the 1978 aircraft would have to be made in a month and a half. The '78 orders included options toward purchase of a 747F aircraft, a wide-bodied freighter developed specifically for all air cargo transportation.

The Air Freight Industry

As early as the late 1960s, U. S. scheduled air cargo traffic represented well over a billion dollars in gross revenues to scheduled airlines. But, despite substantial growth in recent years, the air cargo business remains a secondary, though quite significant, segment of the entire domestic air transport operation. Worldwide, air cargo traffic for the ICAO carriers (International Commercial Airline Operators) represents over 15 percent of their total revenues. Air freight is carried both in the belly pits of passenger planes (called combination service) and in freighter planes which carry only air cargo and no passengers. The "combination carriers" operate both freighter and combination planes (for example, TransAirways), but the all-cargo carriers operate only freighter aircraft. Although other categories represent significant portions of the total traffic, the most important area appears to be in scheduled combination domestic passenger-cargo freight operations. Growth patterns for both combination carriers and the all-cargo carriers are averaging around 20 percent for the past several years, although dropping off most recently into the mid-teens.

The air freight industry consists of more than just aircraft and airlines, however. Since the objective of all air cargo traffic is to move goods quickly and efficiently, the coordination of surface and air systems is vital to profitable operations. Air carriers are subject to many restrictions within the framework of the air freight industry. Virtually every air freight shipment requires surface transportation at two or more points in its distribution cycle. Government regulation at the federal level through the Civil Aeronautics Board (CAB) controls the structure of routes and fares as well as provides for safety and operating restrictions. And local governments, through airports and municipal authorities, impose restrictions on environmental qualities, including arrival and departure times, thus providing even less flexibility in the carrier's ability to control industry functions.

Air cargo and air freight growth rates appear to be most closely related to real GNP, the price of air freight, and a service index representing the level of service quality. One model predicts that a one percent change in GNP will result in a 2.8 percent increase in air freight traffic, and that a one percent decline in air freight prices will increase traffic by 1.5 percent.[1] Thus, air freight traffic appears to be both income and price elastic.

Three classifications of goods have been used to describe products that travel by air: emergency traffic, routine perishable, and routine surface divertible. *Emergency traffic* is time essential, unplanned in advance, and the price is of little importance, whereas the penalty for failure to deliver may be significant. Such items as emergency medical shipments of vaccine and antivenom and repair parts of critical machinery would fall into this category. *Routine perishable* is still time essential, but is planned in advance. Examples of this category might include cut flowers, fresh fruit, and, perhaps, some magazines. *Routine surface divertible* products are planned for shipment ahead of time, but speed and time are somewhat less

---

[1] Irving Saginor and David B. Richards, *Forecast of Scheduled Domestic Air Cargo for the 50 States, 1971–1975,* CAB, Washington, 1971.

important and cost factors (rather than demand factors) are significantly more important. This system usually competes through cost with a combination surface transportation field-warehouse system for items with low density and high value per pound. Items that would be described as routine surface divertible include precious metals, expensive machine parts, clothing, and furs.

Although the classifications seem quite distinct theoretically, airlines have had much difficulty determining what percentages of goods that pass through their freight system fall into the various categories, much less give much thought to forecasting future estimates. Yet it is obviously imperative that a marketing strategy for a given carrier rest fundamentally upon which of these three areas (or which combination of areas) is to receive attention.

The areas of flight equipment (aircraft), containerization, and terminal technology should not be underestimated in developing freight system forecasts. But each area represents a wide range of variability in terms of possible costs and returns. Most airline industry experts believe that the success or failure of an airline in the air cargo industry will depend, not so much on the selection of optimal technologies, but rather on the implementation of perceptive management strategy.

Market and Market Position

In 1974, TransAirways was the fourth largest domestic trunk air carrier in the United States in terms of total revenues. TA was third nationally in terms of air freight revenues behind Skyway and U.S. Air Lines. Comparison of financial statistics for TransAirways and its closest competitors for 1976 is presented in Exhibit 37–1. Of the three carriers, TransAirways was the only one estimated to project a loss for the year, although Skyway and U.S.'s profit levels are quite meager.

TransAirways served 21 major U.S. cities, including Chicago and New York in the eastern portion of the country, but maintained the major concentration of their services along routes linking the Southwest and the West. The company's base of operations and headquarters is in San Francisco and their maintenance

Exhibit 37-1
Financial Statistics: Passenger Plus Cargo
1976 Estimated (in millions)

Airline (Carrier)	Operating Revenue	Operating Expense	Operating Profit	Net Profit
Skyway	1,200	$1,100	$100	$30
U. S.	1,100	1,050	50	10
TransAir	1,000	990	10	(1)

Exhibit 37-2
1975 Capacity and Competitive Positions – Transairways' Seven Major City Pairs

Routes	Skyway				U. S.				TransAir			
	Flts.		ATM		Flts.		ATM		Flts.		ATM	
	#	%	#	%	#	%	#	%	#	%	#	%
LAX-SFO	42	40	4575	40	33	21	2396	21	30	19	1832	16
LAX-JFK	22	31	2290	32	22	31	2289	32	12	17	1249	18
SFO-ORD	16	26	1263	28	NR				24	39	1416	32
LAX-DAL	NR				5	24	551	23	5	24	683	28
SEA-SFO	11	26	976	28	NR				21	49	1394	40
SFO-DAL	12	27	889	28	11	24	815	25	17	38	1055	33
LAX-DEN	NR				10	21	205	23	11	23	1007	53

Key: Flts.: Flights
ATM: Available Ton Miles
NR: No Route Between City Pair

LAX: Los Angeles
JFK: New York
DAL: Dallas
DEN: Denver
SFO: San Francisco
ORD: Chicago
SEA: Seattle

and overhaul facility and engine repair center is adjacent to Los Angeles International Airport (LAX). The airline offered freight and passenger service between all of its regular terminal points, although the majority of its freight operations occurred between points of the seven major and largest cities on its route. Although studies in 1971 had shown no significant difference among the costs or revenues of either the seven major city routes or the smaller routes, profitability of the large city routes proved to be about 2 percent higher than that of the smaller city routes. Yet analysis of market potential for the cities on TransAirways' system indicated that the large city routes were relatively saturated and could improve profits only through improved market share capture, while the smaller city routes offered a better potential for an expanding market. The most recently available competitive comparison among TA and its prime competitors is presented in Exhibit 37–2.

TransAirways' position in terms of general market share also seemed to be deteriorating. Exhibit 37–3 shows the recent trends of market share development for each of the three large air freight handlers in their own respective markets. (It should be noted that since the airline industry is highly regulated by the CAB, information dealing with all aspects of a carrier's status must be filed with this authority on a regular basis for all carriers. Thus, financial and operating statistics for each airline are consistently drawn and available from the public record.)

Advertising

Since Jim Evans had taken over control of freight operations, a major effort had been launched to emphasize advertising as a means of increasing market share. At a cost of $15,000, a market research program was conducted in 1974 in the four largest volume city pairs. The study indicated that 80 percent of the goods shipped by air in these markets fell into the routine perishable category. The value of freight shipment for the remaining 20 percent of goods in the surveyed markets was not established. Other city pairs were not surveyed. Based upon the study, an advertising campaign was developed using the following themes: fast system of delivery, door-to-door service, high quality control. This campaign has been used for the past two years.

In 1976, an advertising campaign had been outlined that was to attempt market

Exhibit 37-3
Market Shares of Airlines in
Total Respective Air Freight Markets

Airline	1970	1971	1972	1973	1974	1975	1976
Skyway	28%	27%	29%	31%	31%	32%	32%
U. S.	28	26	28	27	27	28	28
TransAir	25	27	24	21	21	21	20

penetration into the surface divertible market that probably comprised a good portion of the remaining 20 percent of air shipped goods. The theme of this program was to focus on a comparison between the costs and advantages of air freight shipment and those of the ground transportation-based distribution and remote warehouse complex. But funds for the new promotion were curtailed after profits turned to losses in the third quarter of 1976.

Developing a Strategy

After reviewing company statistics, it was obvious to Bill Brown that the company's freight operations were not suffering from a lack of capacity but rather from a loss in market share and increased operating expenses. Freight load factors for all aircraft were much lower than expected, and this fact was especially true for the wide-bodied jets whose performance did not seem to exhibit expected economies of scale. Additionally, the wide-bodied jets had greater-than-anticipated introduction costs.

Brown felt that some revision of his freight marketing plan could possibly improve market share and load factors. With a better freight marketing plan and a generally expected overall improvement in the national economy, TransAirways might again become profitable, possibly to the point of justifying extensions of orders for more, new narrow and wide-bodied freighter aircraft for the late 1970s. Brown wondered how he should proceed.

Mirco Games

Lonnie Ostrum, Arizona State University
William E. Reif, Arizona State University
Robert B. Kaiser, Former Director of Marketing, Mirco Games

Mirco Games, a division of Mirco, Inc., designs, develops, and markets table soccer, electronic video, and pinball games for the coin-operated and home entertainment industries. Located in Phoenix, Arizona, the firm has experienced rapid growth in sales. Although Mirco Games was enjoying an increase in demand for its product lines, John Walsh, chairman of the board, was concerned about what strategies the Games division should employ over the next few years.

History of Mirco, Inc.

Mirco was incorporated in Arizona on November 11, 1971, to succeed and acquire the assets of a partnership known as John L. Walsh & Associates, composed of Messrs. John L. Walsh, Bruce E. Kinkner, and Robert M. Kessler, founders. As of January 1, 1976, the company consisted of the parent company, Mirco, Inc., and five divisions: (1) Mirco Electronics Distributors, (2) Mirco Systems, (3) Mirco Games, (4) Mirco Games Australia Pty., Ltd., and (5) Mirco Games of Europe.

At its founding, the company's business was to design, develop, and market computer software for automatic testing systems used in high volume production maintenance, depot, and field testing facilities for electronic equipment. The Mirco Electronic Distributors division was established on December 15, 1972, to engage in business as a distributor of component parts to electronic equipment manufacturers. On December 18, 1973, another division, Mirco Systems, was formed to carry on the electronic test business through continued design and marketing of the company's software and to design and market test equipment. On December 26, 1973, the company acquired the assets and business of Arizona Automation, Inc., which was merged into another division called Mirco Games.

The business of Mirco Games is to design, manufacture, and market table soccer, pinball, and electronic video games.

Generally, the parent company provides planning, accounting, legal, and financial services to each of the divisions. As of March 1976, corporate headquarters had 35 employees: The chairman of the board, president, vice-president/operations, vice-president/controller, an accountant, an office manager, 4 bookkeepers, 2 secretaries, 1 personnel specialist, and 22 purchasing, maintenance, quality control, and warehouse personnel.

In fiscal year 1976 (ending January 31, 1976), the company achieved sales of more than $9 million, an outstanding growth record. Exhibit 38–1 contains consolidated income statements for the years 1973–76, and Exhibit 38–2 presents consolidated balance sheets for 1975 and 1976.

The Distribution Business

Mirco Electronic Distributors supplies component parts, such as semi-conductors, capacitors, connectors, and resistors to (1) manufacturers of electronic equipment, and (2) users of the equipment for modification, replacement, or spare parts. This division performs an economic role by purchasing components from manufacturers (and sometimes from other distributors), maintaining an inventory, filling orders on demand, and providing quick delivery. In addition, it complements the other Mirco divisions by providing accurate information about the status of parts and equipment in the industry and supplying component parts and equipment at reduced cost.

The distribution business is highly competitive. To meet competition, one must obtain different components lines, anticipate customers' future needs, and maintain inventories. If Mirco Electronic Distributors stocked components for which demand failed to develop, working capital would be tied up in unprofitable inventories that would have to be disposed of at or below cost.

Mirco Electronic Distributors is regional. Its market area includes Arizona; the Albuquerque, Las Cruces, and Roswell areas of New Mexico; the Denver and Henderson areas of Colorado; Los Angeles, California; Las Vegas, Nevada; and Salt Lake City, Utah.

The Test Business

Mirco Systems designs, develops, manufactures, and markets hardware and computer software for the automatic testing of commercial and military digital electronic equipment. "Software" is a term generally used to describe computer programs; that is, a set of instructions which cause a computer to perform desired operations. The term "hardware" is used to describe the actual equipment.

Electronic equipment generally consists of numerous integrated circuit boards, each containing approximately 10 to 300 components. These boards are tested for defects by the manufacturer at the completion of the manufacturing and assembly process. Boards also are tested after the equipment has been put into use as part of a preventive or remedial maintenance program.

Recent advances in technology have led to the development of computer systems that perform such testing automatically. These automatic test systems determine and identify faulty components in circuit boards. Automatic test systems are used primarily in high volume production and maintenance testing facilities. The users of such systems are equipment manufacturers and owners who use semi-

Exhibit 38-1
Consolidated Statement of Income
For the Years Ended January 31, 1976-75-74-73

	1976	1975	1974	1973 (Unaudited)
Net Sales	$9,394,397	$5,033,717	$2,078,266	$1,156,319
Cost of Sales	6,045,170	3,286,400	1,383,670	601,782
Gross Profit	$3,349,227	$1,747,317	$ 694,596	$ 554,537
Operating Expenses				
Engineering	$ 897,407	$ 268,207	$ 255,130	$ 85,924
Selling	1,218,905	775,188	164,411	54,934
General and administrative	891,822	525,256	327,723	293,988
	$3,008,134	$1,568,651	$ 747,264	$ 434,846
Income from operations	$ 341,093	$ 178,666	$(52,668)	$ 119,691
Interest Expense	84,995	68,390	17,648	4,168
Income before Income taxes and Extraordinary Item	$ 256,098	$ 110,276	$(70,316)	$ 115,523
Provision for income taxes	123,000	48,625	31,048	55,145
Income before Extraordinary Item	$ 133,098	$ 61,651	$(101,364)	$ 60,378
Extraordinary Item— Income tax reduction resulting from loss carry-forward benefits	—	48,625	—	15,708
Net Income	$ 133,098	$ 110,276	$(101,364)	$ 76,086
Income Per Capital and Equivalent Share				
Before extraordinary item	$ .08	$ .04	$(.08)	$ .05
Extraordinary item	—	.04	—	.02
	$ .08	$ .04	$(.08)	$ .07
Average Number of Capital and Equivalent Shares Outstanding During the Year	$1,575,939	$1,450,112	$1,232,623	$1,114,173

Exhibit 38-2
Consolidated Balance Sheet
For the Years Ended January 31, 1976 and 1975

Assets	1976	1975
Current Assets:		
Cash and certificates of deposit	$ 129,556	$ 17,700
Accounts receivable, less allowance of $45,000 at January 31, 1976, and $181,500 at January 31, 1975, for doubtful accounts	839,730	813,473
Account receivable from Membrain Inc. (a stockholder)	27,148	—
Notes receivable	14,586	—
Inventories	1,573,684	1,223,169
Prepaid expenses and other assets	27,497	5,986
Leasehold Improvements and Equipment, at Cost:		
Leasehold improvements	$ 47,812	$ 38,117
Machinery and equipment	300,197	178,902
Automobiles	13,028	14,324
Furniture and fixtures	56,627	26,579
	$ 417,664	$ 257,922
Less Accumulated Depreciation	112,782	53,603
	$ 304,882	$ 204,319
	$2,917,083	$2,264,647

Liabilities and Shockholders' Investment	1976	1975
Current Liabilities:		
Notes payable	$ 610,000	$ 445,503
Current portion of long-term debt	15,213	12,923
Accounts payable	709,032	713,102
Accrued payroll	37,570	6,221
Accrued interest	6,702	8,727
Other accrued expenses	73,113	23,790
Income taxes currently payable	104,000	—
Total Current Liabilities	$1,555,630	$1,210,266
Long-Term Debt, Less Current Portion	$ 33,838	$ 49,051
Stockholders' Investment:		
Capital stock; no par value; 5,000,000 shares authorized; 1,607,423 shares outstanding at January 31, 1976, and 1,391,880 shares outstanding at January 31, 1975	$1,270,037	$ 947,863
Note receivable taken as consideration on sale of capital stock	(132,987)	—
Retained earnings	190,565	57,467
	$1,327,615	$1,005,330
	$2,917,083	$2,264,647

conductor components. It is possible to test circuit boards manually, but it is becoming increasingly difficult and costly to do so because of advanced technology and the time required to test the more complex boards.

At present, Mirco Systems markets its proprietary Fault Logic and Simulation Hybrid (FLASH) program. The FLASH program aids in the development of software for logic card testers, including simulation of complex test patterns and generation of a fault directory for logic components on printed circuit boards. It also is used to develop testing programs for specific circuit boards.

Mirco Systems also manufactures and markets automatic test equipment (hardware). In addition, it purchases test equipment from Membrain Limited, a United Kingdom corporation, for sale in the United States. Such equipment usually is sold in conjunction with the sale of software products generated by Mirco Systems. Although FLASH is considered a proprietary product, in reality the program has little protection from competition. Because there is a constant risk of obsolescence in the test business, the firm's long-run success may depend ultimately upon the success of its research and development program.

Test Programming Services is a group that creates software and specific test programs. It functions primarily in support of hardware sales. This capability is considered to be critical to the test business as it enables Mirco Systems to offer complete test systems. Mirco Systems has had no difficulty in recruiting suitable people to write test programs and expects to have no difficulty in the future.

Management believes that competition in the test business is based on quality, product performance, price, and postdelivery support. There are several other companies in the business, most of whom are larger, well-financed, diversified electronics firms. Each competitor has their own system.

The Games Business

On December 26, 1973 Mirco, Inc. acquired the business of Arizona Automation, Inc. founded in 1970. The company issued 174,000 shares of its capital stock, without par value, to Richard N. and Virginia A. Raymond, who were the sole shareholders. The shares were valued for the purposes of that transaction, at $3.50 per share. Arizona Automation was merged into Mirco, Inc. and became Mirco Games. Of the 174,000 shares, 30,000 shares were escrowed for a period of one year. The escrowed shares were to be available to Mirco in case any claims arose against the former shareholders in Arizona Automation for any breach of warranty made in connection with the transaction. The purpose of the acquisition was to acquire an existing marketing organization for the distribution of electronic games and to acquire Mr. Raymond's "know-how" in the games business.

Of approximately 150 employees in Mirco, Inc., about half are in the Games division. The company has two main product lines: (1) table soccer, marketed under the name "Champion Soccer," which comes in a variety of models, and (2) video games, consisting of two versions of electronic ping-pong and which come in either an upright cabinet or a cocktail table cabinet. Exhibit 38–3 provides a display of the basic models offered by Mirco Games.

Of the $9.4 million sales in fiscal year 1976, about $7.3 million were from the

Exhibit 38-3

Reliability • Playability • Durability

Games division. Of the $7.3 million Games sales, $1.2 million were from table soccer and $6.1 million from video games. Broken down geographically, $6.5 million were in U.S. game sales, $200,000 in German game sales, and $600,000 in Australian game sales. This compares with games sales of just under $1 million both in fiscal 1973 and fiscal 1974.

The company believes that competition in the games business is based upon playability, price, and quality. Unlike soccer games, which have been marketed in Europe for over 50 years and have a more recently established strong market in the United States, it is difficult to predict whether electronic games will continue over time to have consumer appeal.

Mirco Games has several competitors in soccer and video games. The major soccer competitors are Dynamo, Tournament Soccer, Garlando, and Deutsch Meister; in video games they are Atari and Ramtek. There is also a risk that a major, well-financed firm will enter the market in which case the industry would be faced with much stiffer competition.

Australia and Europe were perceived to be good potential markets for video games. In order to avoid high import duties, Mirco began to assemble the video games in Australia in April 1975, and in Germany in September 1975.

Amusement Games Industry

The term "coin industry" often is applied to manufacturers and distributors of coin-operated equipment for consumer use. The two main segments of this industry are vending machines (food, drink, cigarettes) and amusement machines.

Amusement machines consist of coin-operated phonographs (juke boxes) and amusement games, such as pool tables, pinball machines, table soccer, and video games. The principal manufacturers of pinball machines are Gottlieb, Balley, Chicago Coin, and Williams. Coin-operated phonographs are manufactured by Seeburg, Rock-ola, and Rowe. The newest development, video games, were spawned by new companies outside of the traditional industry network.

Sales are seasonal. New products are introduced in the fall and generally are available in the following first quarter (February, March, and April). New product introductions are geared to the Music Operators of America trade show held annually in late October or early November.

The present structure of the amusement games industry was developed in the 1930s. At that time, the need for distributors arose because of the introduction of coin-operated phonograph and pinball machines. The primary purpose of the distributor was to provide electrical and mechanical servicing. Distributors either were owned by the manufacturers or were independent. They, in turn, helped set up the operator who was responsible for locating the game equipment and sharing revenues with the location owner. This distribution network remains virtually intact today.

The operator is the owner of the equipment. In addition to seeking out new locations, the operator is responsible for routine servicing and, typically, has a route to maintain, making periodic collections from the cash boxes attached to the equipment and dividing the earnings with the location owner (typically 50–50). The specific functions associated with each member of the conventional channel are identified in Figure 38–1.

Table Soccer

Table soccer appears to have originated in Germany in the late 1920s or early 1930s. Soccer is known as football in many European countries, and the German word for football, fussball, is the alternative name used for table soccer in the United States (under a variety of spellings). Presently, European versions of the game are manufactured in West Germany, France, and Italy.

The first soccer games exported to the United States in the mid-1950s were not readily accepted. In 1962, L. T. Patterson Distributors of Cincinnati made the first major commitment to distribute a German-produced table called "Foosball." Because it was a relatively unknown sport in America and required a high skill level, acceptance was slow, and it was not until the late 1960s that table soccer became a significant factor in the games industry. One of the factors contributing to its growth in popularity in the United States was the demand created by military personnel who had been introduced to the game while stationed in Europe.

In 1967, Dick Raymond and John Walsh, while working for General Electric in Germany, became interested in table soccer. Soccer tables were found in many of the bars and taverns of France, Germany, and Italy and were avidly played by

Figure   38–1
Distribution Channels for the
Amusement Games Industry

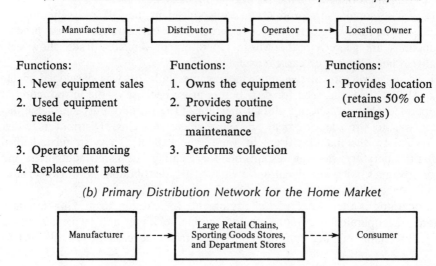

(a) Conventional Distribution Network for Coin-Operated Equipment

| Manufacturer | Distributor | Operator | Location Owner |

Functions:

1. New equipment sales
2. Used equipment resale
3. Operator financing
4. Replacement parts

Functions:

1. Owns the equipment
2. Provides routine servicing and maintenance
3. Performs collection

Functions:

1. Provides location (retains 50% of earnings)

(b) Primary Distribution Network for the Home Market

| Manufacturer | Large Retail Chains, Sporting Goods Stores, and Department Stores | Consumer |

Europeans as well as American military personnel and business associates. Raymond and Walsh saw the potential for such a game and made plans to export tables to the United States.

When Raymond and Walsh returned to Phoenix in 1970, they formed Arizona Automation. Within a year of incorporation, Raymond purchased Walsh's share and became sole owner. In 1971, Arizona Automation began building a soccer table known as Champion Soccer. In four years, annual sales climbed from $15,000 to approximately $1 million.

Manufacturing

The component parts for Champion Soccer are purchased from outside vendors and the game is assembled by Mirco Games. There presently are alternate sources for all of the components except the figurines. Should that source fail, it is estimated that production would be delayed for approximately two months while a new source was found.

Patents, Trademarks and Licensing

The company has registered Champion Soccer as a trademark in the United States and Canada. An application for trademark registration has been filed with respect to the design of figurines for the soccer game, and a patent has been granted for the "two point ball control" figurine. There are no other patents or other protection for table soccer products.

Competition

Due to the high quality of its soccer tables, Mirco has been a dominant force in the United States market with about $1.2 million in sales out of an industry total of $12 million. Recently, however, Mirco has experienced increased competition from a number of firms, especially Dynamo and Tournament Soccer. In order to maintain its leadership role in the market, Mirco was forced to significantly redesign its tables to improve their appearance, playability, and durability. Dynamo's approach is similar to Mirco's in that they cultivate a high quality image and have introduced several technical innovations, among them the textured tempered glass playfield, the massive table to prevent table movement during play, the balanced figurine, and precision ground steel rods. Mirco subsequently incorporated some of these innovations to maintain their market position. Tournament Soccer pursued the market through an active and expensive program using table soccer tournaments throughout the United States. Their current tournament program offers prize money in excess of $250,000 per year.

Marketing

Mirco markets its coin-operated soccer games through approximately 50 distributors located for the most part in the United States and Canada (see Figure 38–1). As is typical of the industry, there are no binding contractual arrangements with any of these distributors. They are free to deal in competitive products or to discontinue distribution of Mirco's products at any time. Home table soccer games are distributed through major retail chains, sporting goods and department stores, and the American Express catalog. In addition, a small amount of government business is handled via the Government Services Administration.

Pricing
Pricing is consistent with Mirco's image as a quality producer of soccer games. There is only one distributor price regardless of quantity. A typical selling price to the operator for a high quality, coin-operated table soccer game is around $675. The channel markup is approximately 35 percent.

Promotion
Mirco Games advertises in the coin-operated equipment trade journals, such as Cashbox, Playmeter, Replay, and sporting goods magazines. It also promotes its products at trade shows like the National Sporting Goods Association and the Music Operators of America. Bob Seagren, Olympic gold medal winner, is used extensively in advertisements and trade show displays.

Mirco also has engaged in a series of promotional events, mainly in the form of statewide tournaments in key metropolitan cities. In 1973 and 1974, they sponsored the Louisiana State Soccer Tournaments, both of which were $2,000 events. In 1975, Mirco tournaments were held in Detroit, Minneapolis, Omaha, and Kansas City, with total prize money exceeding $16,000. The 1976 schedule includes St. Louis, Rochester, and Detroit.

Market Research
Market information is obtained from three principal sources: distributors, operators, and location owners. At times, games are "test marketed" by placing them in selected locations and analyzing them in terms of their earning power over a given period of time.

Electronic (Video and Pinball) Games

Atari was the first company to successfully market a video game. It was called "Pong" and was a two-player tennis-type game operated with electronic paddles and a ball. Acceptance of this product was phenomenal, and before long, more than 30 producers of video games were in the market, from the large established companies to the newly-formed "garage-type," operations. Although it is relatively easy for a new company to enter the video games market, the failure rate for new entrants is extremely high, due primarily to a lack of adequate testing capability, poor service, high operating costs, limited financing, and little marketing expertise. According to one financial analyst who observed 24 games companies during 1974, 20 went out of business, 2 were marginal, and the remaining 2 were Mirco and Atari.

Mirco Games entered the market in 1973 with its two-player video game, Champion Ping Pong. At the same time its competitors were introducing a great variety of more sophisticated games. It was felt that the company's expertise in the area of electronic testing equipment could provide them with two immediate advantages over their major competitors: quick turnaround in servicing (24 hours) and a more reliable product. Unfortunately, these advantages were not sufficient to offset Champion Ping Pong's lack of playability, which is the primary competitive factor in video games. The urgent need to develop new products was recognized by Mirco at that time; however, an extremely tight cash-flow position position prevented major R&D expenditures for video games. In 1973, the Mirco Systems division had invested heavily in R&D to develop its computer-controlled test equipment, which was not yet ready for production, a project which had severely drained the company's finances.

In March 1974, Mirco Games introduced the Challenge upright four-player video game which featured one free game in the event that one or two players beat the machine in the player versus machine mode. Unfortunatly, this innovative feature was not sufficient to offset the fact that competition had introduced four-player games twelve months earlier and the market was now saturated. In July 1974, the "Challenge" cocktail table version was introduced. The major advantage of this game was its appeal to sophisitcated locations, such as Holiday Inns, Playboy Clubs, and country clubs which previously had not been a viable market for video games. Unfortunately, the conventional distribution network was ill-equipped to implement a marketing strategy to take advantage of this new and rapidly expanding market.

Distribution
In order to exploit this new market for cocktail table models, Bob Kaiser, marketing manager, decided to set up an entirely new distribution channel known as the nonconventional distribution network (see Figure 38–2). He sought out individual entrepreneurs, such as real estate people and sales representatives for stocks and bonds, who, due to the recession, were without a product to market but had sufficient capital to invest in a new venture. This strategy proved very successful and, in fact, helped stimulate sales of the table top video games through conventional distributors and operators. One major advantage of the nonconventional channel is that terms are cash, whereas in the conventional channel they are net 30 days and the manufacturer frequently is forced to extend credit for 60 to 90 days.

Innovation
Innovation is a survival requirement in the industry. Mirco's achievements in this area have not been spectacular. However, a micro-processor pinball machine, which was a first in the industry, was introduced in late 1975. Management felt that this product would successfully lead Mirco into a new segment of the coin-operated market.

Pricing
Two pricing constraints are active in the marketplace. In the segment of the market dominated by innovative games, particularly video, pricing is determined primarily by the earning power of the machine; that is, its ability to sit in a location and, without being promoted, attract players. (The location life of a

Figure   38–2
Nonconventional Distribution Network for Video Games

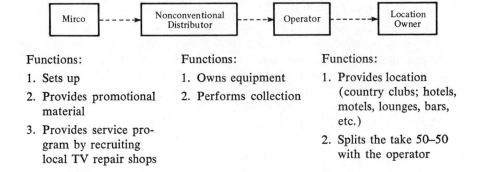

Functions:

1. Sets up
2. Provides promotional material
3. Provides service program by recruiting local TV repair shops

Functions:

1. Owns equipment
2. Performs collection

Functions:

1. Provides location (country clubs; hotels, motels, lounges, bars, etc.)
2. Splits the take 50–50 with the operator

video game is less than 90 days as a rule.) In that segment of the market where the products are stable and have a long life in a specific location, such as pool tables and table soccer, pricing is solely a function of competition.

Manufacturing

With respect to electronic games, Mirco purchases all components, such as television monitors and sub-assemblies from outside vendors and assembles the games itself. At present, the sole source for television monitors is Motorola. Although no difficulties are anticipated in obtaining sufficient quantities from Motorola, significant production delays and expenses probably would be encountered in changing to another vendor.

Home Video Games Market

Along with coin-operated electronic games, video and pinball games for the home promise to have a great future: projections go as high as $1 billion by 1980. In 1972, Magnavox brought out the first home video game "Odyssey" for a price of over $100. Several new entrants now are active in this area, including Atari which introduced their home model version of "Pong" in 1975. One of the obstacles in this new market is that FCC approval is required for any games that hook up to a TV antenna.

Brisk sales were reported by both Magnavox and Atari during the 1975 Christmas season. Atari's version of "Pong" was sold by Sears who stated that it could sell all it could get. Magnavox, which had introduced an improved version of Odyssey a few months earlier, marketed its products through its vast network of approximately 2,500 dealers throughout the United States.

It is anticipated that home video games soon will be available for $30 to $40 retail. Most products will include multiple games, color, sound, and remote controls. On-screen score display and variable difficulty are possible features.

In January 1976, Mirco entered into an agreement with Fairchild Camera and Instrument to jointly develop and produce home video games. Christmas 1976 is targeted for a major promotional effort for creating a new consumer mass market.

Computerized Pinball

In 1975, Mirco was the first on the market with a micro-computer pinball machine in which one printed circuit board handles all electronic functions. The game featured an electronic semiconductor memory, LED (digital display) read-outs, and a self-diagnostic capability for quick troubleshooting. Although it was the hit of the annual Music Operators of America trade show, it is too early to tell what impact it will have on the traditional coin-operated pinball market. One concern is that because of Mirco's lack of expertise in backglass and playfield design (both strong competitive features in pinball machines because of their association with playability in the minds of players), it may not be able to take full advantage of being first in the micro-computer pinball market.

The Future of the Games Business

In 1976, the electronic games market was still in its infancy. Atari was the leader in video sales, with about $18 million in 1975, and "close to $30 million" projected for 1976. Although sales information is difficult to obtain about other firms in this industry, it was believed that Mirco Games was number two. Whereas Atari produces many different types of video games, Mirco has concentrated its efforts on producing a few models of one basic game. During the same period that Mirco successfully marketed the "Challenge" table top video game, Atari introduced 50 new game designs.

It is expected that semiconductor companies will play a major role in the games business. In early 1976, research was underway at General Instrument, Texas Instruments, and National Semiconductor to develop video products. With the possibility of many companies invading the territory of the traditional manufacturer of coin-operated games, the long-run outcome is somewhat uncertain. Traditional companies are likely to react strongly to protect their markets.

Table soccer appears to have a good 15 to 20 percent per year growth potential. In contrast to the video market, this market appears to be extremely stable.

Another uncertainty is the extent to which the expanding home game market will affect the sales of coin-operated games. The traditional companies feel that home games will stimulate rather than take away from their businesses, and they predict steady growth in the next few years.

Home Games Market

Strategies in the home games market are difficult to determine because of rapid technological changes. Games with their own video displays are likely to evolve and may be tied in with the computer terminal that one day will be installed in most homes. One definite advantage for new companies entering this market is that because home electronic games (video and pinball) are so new, there is no strong brand loyalty.

United States Instrument Rental*

Barton Weitz, U.C.L.A.

In October 1977, Mr. Tony Schiavo, the marketing vice-president of United States Instrument Rental (USIR), was reexamining his marketing strategy in light of a survey just completed by a group of MBA students. USIR had gone through a period of rapid growth in sales. Mr. Schiavo's efforts had been directed toward establishing a national sales force using advertising to make customers aware of USIR as a potential source for renting electronic instruments. Recently, Mr. Schiavo had shifted his advertising toward developing new customers for the rental service.

The Electronic Test Equipment Industry

The term "electronic test equipment" refers to a broad range of standard measurement and display instruments. Some specific types of instruments are oscilloscopes, multimeters, recorders, and signal generators. The instruments are widely used throughout the communications, aerospace, automotive, computer, and electronic industries. The instruments have a wide variety of applications within a company. Research engineers use instruments to design electrical and electronic products. Electronic instruments are used by production technicians to verify product performance during the production process. Field service technicians use test equipment to install, maintain, and repair products.

In 1976, sales of electronic test equipment exceeded $900 million worldwide (excluding communist countries). Domestic sales were estimated at $600 million. There are approximately 45,000 companies in the United States in which instru-

---

* This case was prepared as a basis for class discussion rather than to illustrate either effective or ineffective handling of marketing problems. The names and data in the case have been disguised to protect proprietary information.

ments are used. The annual growth is about 9 percent per year, and most industry observers believe this growth rate will be maintained over the next 10 years. Approximately 800 companies manufacture test equipment. Two companies, Hewlett-Packard and Tektronix, account for approximately 60 percent of the total sales volume. Five other companies have annual sales between $20 and $50 million, and the remaining companies are below $20 million.

Electronic instruments range in price from $200 to $20,000. Since the instruments are generally purchased as capital equipment, several people in a company are usually involved in recommending, evaluating, and approving purchases. Since there are significant performance differences between the same type of instruments produced by different manufacturers, the end user of the instrument (either research and development, production, or field service engineers) has the most influence over which manufacturer is selected. However, approval is often required by purchasing agents, various levels of management, and people responsible for maintaining instruments.

The business of renting electronic instruments is relatively young. Spawned by the aerospace-defense boom of the mid-1960s, its real growth began during the collapse of the aerospace industry in 1970. Instrument users were faced with severe capital constraints, and, with vivid memories of canceled contracts, were reluctant to purchase new equipment. Instrument manufacturers responded to this situation by cutting back on production, and by responding slowly to increase production as economic conditions improved in 1971 and 1972. Delivery times lengthened as demand increased. These were fertile times in which to create awareness of the availability and value of the rental service. During this period, 4 firms were engaged on a nationwide basis in the instrument rental business: Electro Rents, Rental Electronics, General Electric, and Leasemetrics.

The Instrument Rental Service

The service offered by instrument rental companies is a simple one. The rental companies maintain an inventory containing a broad range of instruments and accessories. Customers who would like to rent an instrument contact a rental company. If the rental company has the instrument in its inventory and offers satisfactory terms, the customer places an order and typically receives delivery within 48 hours. Occasionally, rental company personnel assist customers in selecting the instrument most appropriate for the customer's applications.

The monthly charge for renting instruments ranges from 7 to 10 percent of the instrument's sale price. Thus, the typical instrument that sells for $2,000 rents for $140 to $200 per month. The monthly rental charge, however, is quite flexible. It varies with the length of the rental period and the size of the order. Companies contracting for longer rental periods or for large quantities of instruments pay a lower monthly rental charge. The average monthly rental charge on an order is $300 and the the average rental time period is four months. Thus, the average order size is $1,200.

Rental customers are billed each month for instruments rented. Frequently, customers do not return instruments when the contracted rental period expires. When this occurs, the rental companies continue to bill the users at the contracted monthly rental charge until the instrument is returned.

There are a number of instances where instrument rental is attractive. When the application is novel or the adequacy of an instrument is uncertain, rental is a means of "trying before buying." In military contract work, the cost of renting equipment is an allowable expense, although depreciation of purchased equipment under current Armed Services Procurement Regulations might not provide the contractor with an adequate recovery of equipment costs. Finally, poor planning coupled with long manufacturer delivery schedules makes instrument rental the only means by which a user can satisfy immediate equipment needs.

The Competitive Environment

USIR has four major competitors in the instrument rental market: Electro-Rent (ER), General Electric (GE), Leasemetrics, and Rental Electronics (RE). Estimated sales volumes over the last five years for those companies, plus USIR, are shown in Table 39–1. All of these companies operate nationwide, stock a broad range of instruments, and operate service centers to repair and calibrate their instruments.

General Electric

GE's rental inventory consists of general purpose test equipment with a specialization in instruments used in industrial applications. These industrial-oriented instruments are used to measure pollution, environmental quality, mechanical properties of materials, and operating characteristics of motors. The rental service is provided as an adjunct to GE's service business. GE provides on-site repair and maintenance from 40 service centers nationwide. Many industrial companies and manufacturers of industrial capital equipment contract with GE to maintain

Table   39–1
Five Year Sales History of Rental Companies ($M)

	1972	1973	1974	1975	1976	1977
USIR	0	0	.6	4.5	6.5	9.1
Rental Electronics	3.4	4.2	5.9	5.9	6.3	7.2
Electro-Rent	1.2	2.7	4.1	4.8	6.1	6.5
Leasemetrics	.5	3.1	4.3	5.3	7.2	8.7
General Electric	2.8	2.9	3.1	4.1	4.6	5.4
Others	5.2	4.7	4.2	3.5	3.1	3.1
Totals	13.2	17.6	21.2	28.1	33.8	39.6

their equipment. The rental and maintenance services are sold by over 100 GE sales representatives. They maintain a standard pricing policy at medium to high levels, offering few discounts.

Leasemetrics

Leasemetrics, like the major rental companies other than GE, maintains an inventory of "state-of-the-art," sophisticated, electronic instruments used in high technology industries. Although Leasemetrics aggressively pursues all rental business, the company is particularly successful in renting equipment to the telecommunications industry. Due to this success, Leasemetrics' inventory contains some special purpose instruments not readily available from other rental companies. Distribution is handled by 13 regional inventory centers.

Although Leasemetrics' catalog rental prices are high, the firm maintains a flexible pricing policy. The rental service is sold through 20 direct sales representatives. Most of Leasemetrics' promotional efforts are through an extensive direct-mail program.

Electro-Rent

In 1965, ER was formed as a tax shelter for wealthy investors. Initially, activities were concentrated in California, but eventually a nationwide organization of manufacturer representatives was established. The firm was virtually bankrupt in 1970 when new management was hired to salvage the company. In 1973, the company became a wholly-owned subsidiary of Telecor, Inc. Telecor is a NYSE-listed company that acts as a western United States distributor for Panasonic electronic home appliances and entertainment products.

Electro-Rent maintains 10 regional warehouses from which rental instruments are distributed. The rental service is sold through 13 independent manufacturer representative organizations. Each organization has an exclusive geographical territory and is paid 12 percent commission on all rental income generated in their territory. In addition to Electro-Rent, the representatives represent between 10 and 20 noncompetitive, small manufacturers of electronic test equipment. The number of sales representatives in each organization varies from 2 in the Pacific Northwest to 15 in California. Electro-Rent's promotional efforts are similar to those used by other rental companies. They place periodic advertisements in trade journals and do some direct mailings (a catalog) describing the instruments in their inventory. Catalog rental prices are moderate and are frequently discounted below catalog prices.

Rental Electronics

Rental Electronics (RE) was started as a venture capital project in 1966. In 1967, the firm was acquired by Pepsico and folded into Pepsico's leasing division. Until recently, RE was the largest company in the business. During the previous two years, the firm had been losing market share because of an uncertain relationship between the company and its parent company. Pepsico, a major soft drink manufacturer, had been gradually divesting itself of business units in its leasing division. In 1975, RE was purchased by a group of investors headed by a former president of Electro-Rent.

Due to its substantial experience in the rental business, RE is adept at purchasing appropriate instruments for their rental inventory. It obtains substantial discounts from instrument manufacturers by purchasing in large quantities.

RE has been successful in securing large rental contracts from the largest rental customers—companies in the aerospace industry. These contracts are obtained by offering low rental prices. The firm maintains 10 inventory centers nationwide, and sells its services through a network of representatives. Although the RE's representative network is similar to Electro-Rent's organization, the two companies do not have any common representatives. Promotion is done through catalogs, direct mailing, and substantial journal advertising.

USIR's History in the Rental Business

United States Leasing established USIR in 1973 because it felt that the instrument rental business had significant growth potential and that the companies in the business lacked management sophistication. The management team established at USIR had extensive experience in the leasing and the instrument business. Gary Stern, the president, and Tony Schiavo, the marketing vice-president, were Harvard MBAs. Gary Stern had been employed previously by US Leasing, and Tony Schiavo had been the marketing manager for a fast-growing instrument manufacturer. Ernie Matlock, the vice-president for inventory management, had been in charge of repair and maintenance for HP, the largest instrument manufacturer.

With substantial financial backing, USIR acquired a large inventory of instruments and established warehouses in New York, Chicago, Dallas, and San Francisco. A sophisticated, computer-based inventory control system was established. Monthly reports were generated to indicate the utilization rate (percentage of time an instrument was on a rental contract) and repair cost for each instrument in USIR's inventory. This information was used in making decisions about what instruments should be purchased in the future.

Interactive computer terminals located in each sales office provided real-time access to the availability and location of all instruments in USIR's inventory. The ability to locate instruments quickly allowed USIR to get maximum utilization of their inventory. USIR's utilization rate was 60 to 70 percent although the industry average was only 45 to 55 percent. By using air freight to ship instruments, USIR was able to provide the same 24 to 48 hour delivery service provided by its competitors, even though USIR had fewer regional inventory centers.

Initially, USIR's personal selling effort was through independent manufacturer representatives. Due to United States Leasing's financial commitment and Mr.

Schiavo's experience in the instrument business, USIR was able to convince a number of representatives for competitive rental companies to terminate their relationships with the competitive companies and represent USIR.

In addition to establishing a strong representative organization, USIR made a heavy investment in advertising. Advertising was done exclusively in trade publications read by engineering management and engineers in the electronics industry. The advertising informed customers that the instrument rental service was now available from a new company.

As USIR's sales grew, it became apparent that the representatives were not aggressively pursuing rental customers. Although coverage of large rental customers was good, few new customers for the rental service were uncovered. Gradually, the representative organization was replaced by a direct sales force. In 1976, all territories were covered by a direct sales force of 25 salespeople.

The income statement for USIR in fiscal 1976 (ending in September 1976) is shown in Table 39–2, and the organization chart is shown in Figure 39–1. In Table 39–3, the sales volume and estimated potential for each sales territory are shown.

In the summer of 1976, Mr. Schiavo mailed 1000 questionnaires to customers who had rented instruments over the past three years. The name of a fictitious market research company was used to disguise the true source of the questionnaire. The response rate was 21 percent. A summary of the results of the questionnaire is shown in the appendix.

Table 39–2
Income Statement—Fiscal 1976*
(in $000s)

Rental Income			$9,150
Expenses:			
Corporate Asset Charge (interest as assets)	$1,170		
Depreciation	3,860	$5,030	
Overhead—Management	$ 260		
Communications/Computer	520		
Salespeople—Salaries and Expenses	1,050		
Sales Office Expenses	350		
Maintenance personnel/equipment	820		
Advertising	230		
Other	70	3,300	8,430
Profit Before Taxes			$ 820

* Financial data has been disguised. It does not represent the actual income of this division of U. S. Leasing.

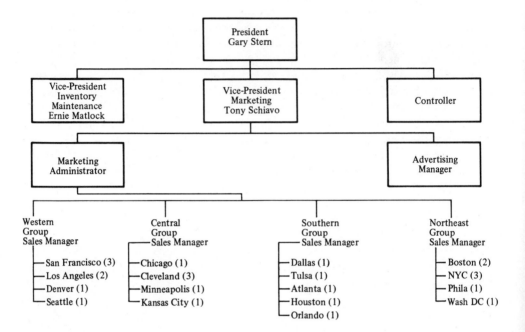

Figure   39–1
Organization Chart of USIR
Marketing Department

USIR's Marketing Efforts

Ben Bossin, the advertising manager of USIR, describes USIR's advertising program:

> You know, there really isn't a lot of difference among the rental companies. Except for GE, we all have the same instruments to rent. Prices and delivery are about the same. Our computerized inventory systems offer some advantages to our customers as well as improving our internal control system. We stress these advantages in our advertising. We developed the acronym "IDIOM" for Inventory and Delivery Information in One Minute for our interactive system. This gives the customer something to differentiate us from other rental companies. A customer in need of an instrument can call a sales office and find out in a minute if we have the instrument available. We can quote availability and delivery time during one phone conversation. There is no need for our salespeople to take the customer's requirements, check around to see if the instrument is available at an inventory center, and then call the customer back. This instant availability information saves the purchasing agent a lot of time.
>
> In addition, our advertising has stressed a recall reminder service. With the computerized inventory control system, we can notify customers when their contracted rental period has expired. This can save customers a lot of money. Fre-

Table 39–3
USIR Sales by Territory

Territory	Salespeople	estimated percentage of national rental sales in territory	1977 Sales ($000)
Washington, Oregon	1	2%	190
Northern California	4	9	1370
Southern California	3	13	1075
Rocky Mountain States	1	5	205
Minnesota	1	3	290
Plains States	1	2	235
Illinois, Wisconsin, Indiana	1	5	390
Ohio, Western Pa.	3	7	1035
Oklahoma	1	1	160
Texas	3	8	895
Ga., Miss., Ala., Tenn., N.C., S.C.	1	4	300
Florida	1	4	325
New England	2	8	740
New York, Northern NJ	3	15	1170
Eastern Pa.	1	6	305
Washington DC, Virginia, Md.	1	8	415
	28	100%	9100

quently, they forget to return an instrument and continue to pay the rental charge even though they no longer need the instrument. (Two ads focusing on IDIOM are shown in Figures 39–2 and 39–3.)

In the last six months, we shifted our advertising theme to convincing customers that they should rent rather than buy instruments (see Figure 39–4). We are trying to get this message to as many potential customers as possible. We are using twenty different publications. Many of these are vertical publications aimed at special segments, like the telephone companies, railroads, utilities, and the communications industry. We need to spend more money on advertising. I think we are reaching only 50 percent of the potential customers with our present level of expenditures.

We just completed a 24-page high quality brochure that explains why renting is more advantageous than purchasing in some situations. There is a detailed description with examples illustrating the tradeoff between rental cost, ownership cost, and utilization. Using graphs provided, the customer can determine when it is more economical for him to rent. We are doing a lot of direct mail distribution of this brochure. (An example of one of the charts in the brochure is shown in Figure 39–5.)

Christa Mathews is a salesperson in the San Francisco office. She is 29 years old and has been a USIR salesperson for two years, although she has neither a

Figure   39–2

**Send for your IDIOM button today!
Wear it proudly!**

**But read this first and
see what you're getting into.**

IDIOM stands for Inventory and Delivery Information in One Minute. It is the rental industry's first and only nationwide real time computer system. What does it do for you? Just dial our number and tell us your rental requirements. Instantly, the computer queries all warehouses and gives you a firm commitment on availability, delivery and rental rate. No more runaround, delays or broken promises. Just a quick, accurate response.

IDIOM is a service of U.S. Instrument Rentals, Inc., a brand new company that was born well established, thanks to the resources of one of the country's leading financial institutions and the experience of the world's oldest and largest leasing organization, United States Leasing International.

We offer the largest on-the-shelf inventory of new, up-to-date instruments in the industry. And **IDIOM** and inventory are just the beginning. USIR has developed a number of unique programs tailored specifically with your needs in mind. Things like our *automatic return reminders*, to help you save money by terminating the rental when the job is over.

...our *New Product Evaluation Program*, under which you can get your hands on selected newly introduced instruments at greatly reduced rental rates.

...the industry's only *service claims with teeth*: a money penalty if a unit fails in operation and we don't turn it around or ship a suitable replacement within 48 hours.

In all there are eight sound reasons why it makes more sense to rent from us than from someone else. There are also ten excellent reasons why you should consider renting in the first place. Not as an expedient, but as a prudent money management tool.

If you use (note: we didn't say "own") electronic instruments, send us this coupon or the reply card in the back and we will send you 1) your **IDIOM** button and 2) our catalog (including the rest of USIR's new rental ideas).

U.S. Instrument Rentals, Inc.
951 Industrial Road, San Carlos, CA 94070

Please send my button and your catalog.

Name_____

Title_____

Company_____

Address_____

City_____State (Zip)_____

**US
INSTRUMENT RENTALS, INC.**

☎ (415) 592-9230   ☎ (213) 849-5861   ☎ (201) 381-3500

Figure 39–3

KIND HEARTS, BUT NO CORNETS.

No tubas, no trombones, no clarinets, no oboes, or flutes, no drums, no bass fiddles, or bassoons, nor guitars, nor pianos, nor anything on John Philip Sousa's list.

We haven't a thing that makes music. Unless you count ticking, buzzing and whirring...the sounds of science! We are U. S. Instrument Rentals... ...that's oscilloscopes, counters, analyzers, amplifiers, recorders, meters, and state of the art test instrumentation, you name it.

What is special about us is not so much kind hearts, but a commitment to tune out some of the sour notes of renting.

Sour Note Ever forget to return a piece of equipment and then get stuck for the payments?

Sweet Note Only we send you an automatic reminder when the rental period is up.

Sour Note Ever get the telephone runaround when you're trying to locate equipment?

Sweet Note Only we have IDIOM, a real time computer capability for instant inventory commitment.

Sour Note Ever have service turnaround problems?

Sweet Note Only we will pay you a 25% penalty in dollars if we can't speed a replacement to you within 48 hours.

With US, service is an essential refrain.

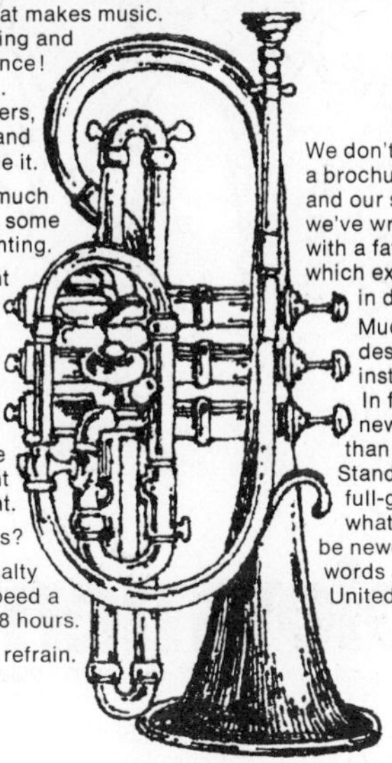

We don't have room to write a brochure about ourselves and our services here. Besides, we've written one already... with a fat catalog included which explains the foregoing in detail and much more. Much more includes a full description of the rental instruments we have. In fact, we probably have more new equipment on the shelf than any other rental company. Stands to reason: We were born full-grown just months ago—what you get from US is bound to be newer! And now, our catalog, words and music by United States Instrument Rentals

US INSTRUMENT RENTALS, INC.

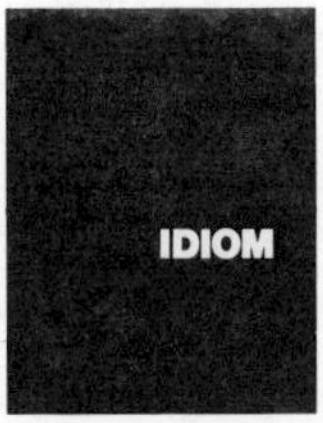

Gentlemen:

I understand you have the only Instrument Rental Catalog in the world that doesn't read like a telephone directory. Please

☐ Send it to me without cost or obligation.

☐ Just send me a copy of pages 6 & 7 which chart the breakeven relationship between rental cost, ownership cost and utilization.

NAME ______

COMPANY ______

ADDRESS ______

CITY ______ ZIP ______

PHONE ______

951 Industrial Road, San Carlos, CA 94070

IDIOM Inventory and Delivery Information in One Minute

(213) 849-5861 (301) 340-1353 (214) 234-3392
(415) 592-9230 (201) 381-3500 (713) 462-6803

Reprinted from Electronic News and Electronics magazine.

Figure   39–4

From the people who brought you IDIOM *
United States Instrument Rentals introduces…

*Inventory Delivery Information in One Minute.

Unemployment Insurance
(FOR TEST INSTRUMENTS)

Does it break your heart to see your test instruments just standing around idle while you're kept busy paying for them? Look around on your shelves . . . Are your test instruments not working to their full capacity because you don't need them all the time?

Well, U.S. Instrument Rentals believes that you shouldn't have to worry about paying *or* caring for instruments that are not working for you all the time. USIR feels that your valuable capital should be spent for equipment that can be employed all the time.

So, U.S. Instrument Rentals offers you Unemployment Insurance.

Unemployment Insurance means that by renting your test instruments from USIR only when you need them, you're protected against paying for idle equipment. You pay for our instruments *only* when they are working full-time for you. And when the job is finished, you simply return the equipment to USIR until you need it again.

In addition, by renting from USIR, you're protected against those expensive calibration, maintenance and repair cost worries. We take care of all our instruments' needs.

And to insure that you get the equipment you need, USIR has thousands and thousands of instruments that are seeking gainful employment, giving you a better chance of finding the instrument that is just right for your needs.

So for a list of instruments you might like to employ and suggestions for solving your test equipment unemployment problems, send for our Unemployment Insurance Booklet . . . The USIR Rental Catalog. It's your best guide to full employment for test instruments.

Headquarters   951 Industrial Road   San Carlos, CA 94070   (415) 592-9225

Figure 39–5

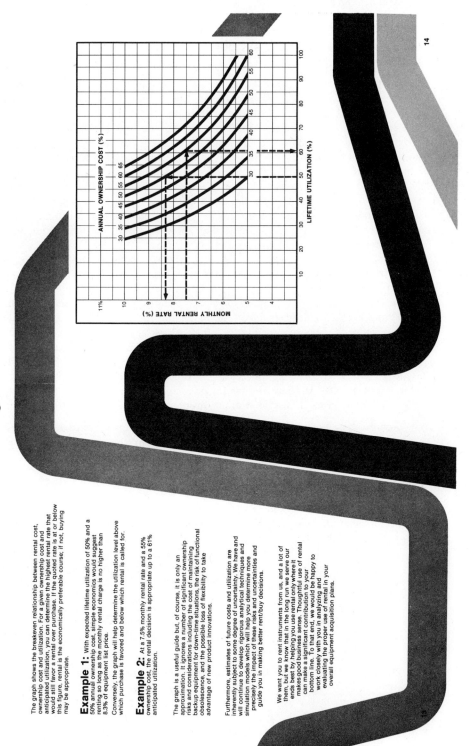

The graph shows the breakeven relationship between rental cost, ownership cost and utilization. For a given ownership cost and anticipated utilization, you can determine the highest rental rate that would still favor a rental over purchase. If the quoted rate is at or below this figure, rental is the economically preferable course; if not, buying may be appropriate.

Example 1: With expected lifetime utilization of 50% and a 50% annual ownership cost, simple economics would suggest renting so long as the monthly rental charge is no higher than 8.3% of equipment list price.

Conversely, the graph will help determine the utilization level above which purchase is favored and below which rental is called for.

Example 2: At a 7.5% monthly rental rate and a 55% ownership cost, the rental decision is appropriate up to a 61% anticipated utilization.

The graph is a useful guide but, of course, it is only an approximation. It ignores a number of significant ownership risks and considerations including the cost of maintaining backup equipment for down-time situations, the risk of functional obsolescence, and the possible loss of flexibility to take advantage of new product innovations.

Furthermore, estimates of future costs and utilization are inherently subject to some degree of uncertainty. We have and will continue to develop rigorous analytical techniques and simulation models which will help you determine more precisely the impact of these risks and uncertainties and guide you in making better rent/buy decisions.

We want you to rent instruments from us, and a lot of them, but we know that in the long run we serve our ends best by helping you use rental only where it makes good business sense. Thoughtful use of rental can make a significant contribution to your bottom line. To that end, we would be happy to work closely with you in analyzing and evaluating the proper use of rental in your overall equipment acquisition plans.

701

technical background nor prior experience in the instrumentation business. She had been in sales for a drug company prior to joining USIR. Christa describes her sales activities as follows:

I make ten to twelve calls a day. About 60 percent of my calls are prospecting for new customers. In the Bay Area, there are a lot of small electronics companies that are not even aware of the instrument rental service. I usually contact the purchasing agent first, but he is often not the key person. In many companies, each engineer can decide to rent an instrument. He contacts rental companies, locates one with the instrument he needs, and then gives this information to the purchasing agent. Usually, the purchasing agent places the order with the company suggested by the engineer. If the order size is large, the purchasing agent might check around for a good price. In some companies, one person is in charge of maintaining their instruments. Purchase requests for instruments are funneled through him. He can suggest that some of these requests be filled by renting rather than purchasing instruments.

The rest of my time is spent servicing our present customers and trying to get business from companies renting from our competitors. I regularly stop by and chat with the key people at our present customers. They really get upset when a rental instrument stops working. Instruments usually are rented for a specific test or project. When the instrument isn't working, the project is at a standstill. When this happens, I try to expedite the repair or get a replacement unit shipped.

I have some companies in my territory that rent a lot of equipment. I try to get them to place more business with USIR but it's tough. I stress the benefits offered by IDIOM. Most of the purchasing agents won't admit that they lose track of rental instruments. The recall reminder does not turn them on. The only thing they talk about is price. If we want more business, we have got to cut our prices.

Tom George has been working for USIR in Southern California for three years. He previously worked for Rental Electronics in the same area. He gives the following opinion on increasing business:

I spend most of my time calling on the big aerospace companies. They rent a lot of equipment each year. Seventy percent of their rental requirements are procured through competitive bidding. They make up a list of instruments they will need for the next three months and ask all the rental companies to bid on the package. They really like our service and would like to give us more business. We have not done too well on the big contracts. We just aren't aggressive enough in our pricing. I just lost another large contract yesterday. We bid 5.5 percent and weren't even close. If we could cut our prices more, we could get the business we want.

Al Kest has been promoted recently to western group sales manager. He has been with USIR for four years. Prior to USIR, he had extensive experience selling instruments. He commented recently:

Since I became a group manager, I spend most of my time working on some big companies that do very little renting. During the last month, I have discussed the benefits of renting versus purchasing with all the engineering section managers and the purchasing agent in charge of capital equipment procurements at Western Telecommunications. I have shown them how a lot of their instruments are only used part time for short-term projects or as a backup reserve in case an operating unit malfunctions. When you own the unit, you are paying for it even when it is on the shelf. If you rent the instrument, you only pay for it when you use it.

I have had pretty receptive audiences. It makes sense to them. The problem is that the managers have fairly big capital equipment budgets for buying instruments. They don't have large enough budgets for expenses to cover the monthly rental charges. I think they are going to do more renting soon. We really have the inside track since I have been working so closely with them.

Tony Schiavo summarizes his thoughts about USIR's present position and future marketing strategy by saying:

We have grown rapidly and probably are the industry leader in sales volume. It's going to be hard to maintain this growth rate. IDIOM has done something to differentiate us from our competitors. The recall is really a great benefit we offer, but the salespeople have not pushed it enough.

At this point, we ought to build more awareness of the instrument rental concept. Even though I am wary about over-interpreting the results of the survey because of the low response rate and the biased sample, the survey shows that rental only accounted for 3 percent of the instrument requirements. More than 10 percent of the instrument requirements must be for short-term projects. Rental is ideally suited for these situations.

We have had 1700 customers over the last four years. Only 600 rented from us during the last 12 months. There are a lot of companies that should be renting but don't. I am having our group sales managers concentrating on selling the rental concept to some big potential customers.

I'm not sure about whether we should emphasize advertising more or hire more salespeople. Advertising is really economical for informing customers about the advantages of instrument rentals. On the other hand, people we have added in the last few years have done great. The man we had in Oklahoma seven months ago has exceeded our expectations. I never thought the territory could support a salesperson.

appendix

Summary of Mail Survey

Sample: 1000 individuals at companies who have rented from USIR

Response Rate: 21%

1.   What is the principal business of your company?

aerospace	26%
communications	16
industrial	17
electrical/electronic components	10
electrical/electronic instrumentation	13
computer/computer peripheral	8
other	10
	100%

2.   What is your function in your company?

purchasing	29%
engineering	34
maintenance, calibration	19
manufacturing	15
field service	2
other	1

When evaluating a rental company to contact for renting electronic instruments, rate the importance of each factor on an 11-point scale (0 to 10):

	mean responses
3. *price*—rental cost as a % of equipment cost per month	6.6
4. *delivery time*	8.9
5. *availability*—likelihood an instrument you need will be available for rental	8.7

6. *repair/replacement time*—time required to service or replace
    a rental unit that is not functioning properly   9.5

7. *availability status response*—time required to indicate if an
    instrument is available for rental   7.7

8. *instrument performance on arrival*—likelihood an instrument
    will be operating properly when it arrives   9.2

9. *recall reminder*—notice sent when contracted rental period
    expires   3.6

10. *application assistance*—help in selecting the best instrument
    for application   3.6

11. Please check with which rental companies and rental company
    sales agents you are familiar

	familiar with company	familiar with sales reps
Rental Electronics	61%	37%
US Instrument Rental	83%	79%
Electro-Rent	59%	38%
Leasemetrics	65%	36%

For each of the factors below indicate how you think each rental company with
which you are familiar performs:

	RE	*USIR*	*ER*	*Lease*	
12. Price (in % of equipment cost per month)	8.4	8.5	8.4	8.8%	
13. Average Delivery Time (in days)	2.8	2.8	2.9	3.0	days
14. Typical Availability (% of time company will have an instrument you need)	80	83	83	79%	
15. Typical Repair/Replacement time (in days)	3.3	3.1	3.1	3.9	days
16. Typical Availability Response Time (hours to indicate whether an instrument is available)	3.4	3.0	3.0	4.1	hours
17. Percent of a Rental Instrument working on Arrival	92	94	92	91%	

18. Does Rental Company Offer a
    Recall Reminder (% re-
    sponding yes)   15   36   15   19

19. Application Assistance offered
    (rating on a 0 to 10 scale) 5.2   6.2   5.5   5.7   rating

20. What is the percentage of times
    you contact each company
    first when a rental re-
    quirement develops?   22%   38%   21%   14% other = 5%

21. Do you have a strong preference in selecting a rental firm?
    Yes   41%
    No   59%

22. For your future equipment needs, which method do you prefer?
    Single Sourcing   30%
    Multiple Sourcing   70%

23. How did you originally hear of the rental firms?
    Word-of-Mouth   38%
    Advertising   27%
      (Trade Journals)
    Direct Mail   25%
    Sales Representatives   18%
    Yellow Pages   17%

24. What type of request do you make when renting?
    Specific instrument   68%
    Specific need   32%

25. What portion of your instrument requirements are met by:
    Purchasing   96%
    Renting   3
    Leasing   1
                  ‾‾‾‾
                  100%

26. Who in your firm makes the decision to rent instead of buy?
    Management   69%
    Engineers   29%
    Purchasing   2%

27. Given the decision to rent, who chooses the firm to be used?
    Engineers   38%
    Purchasing   30%
    Management   24%
    Other   7%

28. What general problems do you have in renting electronic test equipment?

Availability	43%
Reliability	32%
Delivery Time	13%
Lack of Knowledge	12%
Price	4%
Other	6%

Affiliated Bankshares of Colorado, Inc.

Rex O. Bennett, University of Colorado

John Quinlan, vice-president of administration of Affiliated Bankshares of Colorado, Inc., was discussing with Wendy Wimbush, director of marketing, the corporation's possible strategies in response to the new law about to be passed by the Colorado legislature. The new law would enable commercial banks, savings and loans, and other financial institutions in Colorado to establish off-site electronic banking terminals. These terminals would greatly enhance the bank's ability to provide locational and time convenience for present and potential customers.

Legal Situation

Colorado is a unit banking state, that is, commercial banks are restricted by law to one main location plus an additional facility that can be no more than 3,000 feet from the main office. These restrictions apply to both state and federally chartered banks and are similar to laws in force in Illinois and Texas.

Other states, such as California and New York, allow statewide branching. That is, one commercial bank can establish and operate offices (branches) anywhere in the state (subject to appropriate regulatory approval). The effect of the unit banking law has been widely debated for a number of years. Relatively large financial institutions argue that the law tends to stifle competition. The law essentially grants exclusive distribution territories and prevents banks from aggressively competing for new customers by serving the market's need for geographical convenience.[1] Smaller banks, on the other hand, argue that branching would adversely

---

[1] Numerous studies by different researchers employing differing techniques have determined that the most significant factor in an individual's selection of a commercial bank is *convenience of location*. Many consumers apparently feel that "a bank is a bank is a bank" and that because services are very similar, convenience is the discriminating factor. Checking accounts particularly seem to be viewed as convenience goods.

affect their operations and would result in the consumer having less choice (because of consolidations and mergers). They argue that it would eventually lead to less personalized service and less ability on the part of the banking industry to design and tailor services to the specific needs of areas, communities, and individual people. Because of their numbers and political influence, the smaller banks have usually been successful in thwarting efforts to ease branching restrictions.

Electronic Funds Transfer Systems (EFTS)

During the late 1960s and 1970s, the commercial banking industry became extremely concerned about the amount of checks being handled. The cost of handling and processing a check was estimated to be between $.15 and $.20 per item. This estimate did not include checks or deposits handled by tellers at the financial institution. In addition to the $.15 to $.20 per item, teller salaries, supervision expense, equipment depreciation, building depreciation, and utilities had to be considered. Because these expenses varied widely, the estimated cost for a teller to cash a check and to have it processed also varied significantly. The low figure probably was $.50 to a high of $1.25 or more. These costs were expected to rise substantially in the future because of increased salaries, personnel benefits, and other expenses.

Response to this dilemma of rising costs was essentially production oriented. The banking industry conceived of transferring funds electronically instead of using either the paper-based system or live tellers. Point-of-sale terminals (POS) and automated teller machines (ATM) formed the basis of the system. Access to the system would be provided by a plastic card (similar to a credit card) with a magnetically encoded stripe on the back. The magnetic stripe would contain the customer's account numbers and a secret code that the customer would use to verify that he/she was the authorized holder of that card.

In the case of POSs, the customer would insert the card into a terminal at a retail location and key in the secret code. The retail clerk would enter the amount of the transaction and the funds would be transferred electronically and instantaneously from the customer's account to the store's account.

Automated teller machines were designed to perform 3 basic categories of financial transactions: (1) cash withdrawals, (2) acceptance of deposits, and (3) transfers between accounts. The customer would insert the access card, key in the secret code, and follow the instructions that appear on either a rotating drum or a cathode ray tube. The ATM provided a significant increase in time convenience for the customer. Transactions could be conducted 24 hours a day, 7 days a week, 365 days per year.

There are two operational modes for ATMs: off-line and on-line. In the off-line mode the ATM is not tied directly into the bank's main-host computer. The number of times the card could be used per day and the maximum amount of withdrawal were coded on the magnetic stripe. The customer's account balance was not updated instantly; a computer tape was created by the ATM, and the account was updated daily. In the on-line mode, deposits to or withdrawals from the account were credited or debited instantly. This allowed the customer to inquire about the balance in the account and to receive an accurate amount excluding uncleared checks. And, generally, higher withdrawal limits were allowed.

Consumer Perceptions of Automated Equipment

One significant factor that would influence decisions about ATMs was consumers' perceptions and attitudes. The Bank Marketing Association conducted a survey of consumers to determine their reactions to automated machines early in 1972.[2] The results of this basically exploratory research are not conclusive, but they do indicate possible hypotheses about consumer perceptions.

Most individuals in the survey accept the idea of automated equipment and see it as a logical and, in many cases, progressive extension of retail banking. Perhaps important in individuals' acceptance of the concept is the widely held view that increased automation is inevitable. Such attitudes range from resignation ("What can you do—it's coming") to positive support based on expected benefits.

The most resistant groups have several possible sources of objections: (1) conservatism in wanting to continue present ways, (2) difficulty in learning new methods, (3) the "artificialty" of new ways, (4) the dangers involved with new ventures, and (5) loss of human skills, among others. Many of these objections are most threatening to older and more mature people; thus, this group tends to be most opposed.

On the other hand, there are positive outlooks supporting the automated machine concept, such as (1) automated equipment is necessary for survival, (2) automation is progress, (3) automation is efficient in time, cost, capacity, and accuracy, and (4) automation contributes to a higher quality of life. The younger people (21–35) predominate in this category. People who feel they are busy and stress competence are the most positive about the automated equipment.

It is important to note that these conflicting attitudes are not unique to automated banking equipment. They are, in fact, consistent with the experience encountered in the introduction of almost any new and different product or concept. Products that fit into this category are *not* adopted by all types of people at the same time. This concept indicating the adoption pattern for new products is called *diffusion of innovation.*

Current favorable attitudes toward automated equipment are probably held by people in the innovator and early adopter categories; the extremely negative attitudes probably are held by those in the late majority and laggard categories. It is interesting to note that adoption of bank credit cards followed this diffusion of innovation process.

Further information on consumer attitudes was generated in a Unidex study on automatic teller equipment conducted between February 25 and March 11, 1974.[3]

---

[2] Sidney J. Levy and Shirley Greene, *Man's Interface With the Money Machine* (Chicago: Bank Marketing Association, 1972).

[3] "Reception to Automatic Teller Equipment," *Unidex Quarterly Customer Motivation Series* (Bloomington, Ind.: Unidex Corporation, May 1974).

A total of 304 respondents were surveyed in 20 locations across the nation. A portion of the study dealt with a comparative analysis of the perceived advantages and disadvantages of automated equipment. The respondents were read six advantages, to be ranked in order. The overall rankings were as follows:

1. Open after banking hours, 24-hour service.
2. Available on weekends when banks and savings institutions are closed.
3. Machine locations are convenient.
4. Shorter transaction time; finish transactions quickly.
5. Like impersonal nature of machines, privacy.
6. Enjoy operating machines, fun to use.

Although the categories are *not* precisely the same as those in the BMA study, the results are consistent. Convenience in terms of hours and time appears to be the primary perceived benefit of automated banking equipment.

In summary, consumers have conflicting perceptions concerning the benefits and drawbacks of automated banking equipment. This type of reaction is consistent with the attitudes toward most major innovations. In order to diffuse the innovations, the individual bank should concentrate on emphasizing positive attributes and minimizing or overcoming negative perceptions and attitudes.

Characteristics of Current Users

To evaluate the feasibility and desirability of automated equipment as a service, either to retain present customers or to attract new ones, it is necessary to determine the characteristics of the users. A number of research studies and reports will be reviewed to provide a current perspective and frame of reference.

A study sponsored by the DEFT (Direct Electronic Funds Transfer) Committee of the BMA contained an analysis of the demographic characteristics of nonusers, infrequent users, and frequent users of automated equipment.[4] A summary of these characteristics is shown in Table 40–1. Since the sample size of this survey was small, the results should be viewed only as indicators, not definitive and conclusive findings.

When the characteristics of the frequent users were compared to those of the total sample, few definitive differences appeared, although there were some trends. Generally, the frequent users were younger, of a higher social class, somewhat better educated, and had higher incomes than the nonusers or of the total sample. This description is consistent with the general characteristics of innovators and early adopters and the patterns followed in the diffusion of innovation.

Although the frequent user tended to have the characteristics noted above, there were also frequent users who were older, of a lower class, with less education, and with lower incomes. In fact, the proportion of frequent users with these characteristics was only slightly smaller than the proportion of the entire sample with the characteristics.

---

[4] Levy, *op. cit.,* pp. 54–56.

Table   40–1
Demographic Characteristics of Users and
Nonusers of Automated Equipment

Demographic Characteristic	Nonuser	Infrequent User	Frequent User	Total
Sex				
Male	53.9%	64.0%	64.9%	59.1%
Female	46.1	36.0	35.1	40.9
Age				
21–34	36.8	49.3	54.5	43.4
35–49	47.4	44.0	39.0	43.4
50 and over	15.8	6.7	6.5	13.1
Social Class				
Upper Middle	27.6	14.7	33.8	23.7
Lower Middle	38.2	53.3	39.0	45.6
Upper Lower	34.2	32.0	27.3	30.7
Marital Status				
Married	86.8	85.3	87.0	86.9
Single	7.9	10.7	9.1	8.4
Widowed, Divorced	5.3	4.0	3.9	4.7
Education				
Postgraduate	13.2	13.3	14.3	12.8
College Graduate	23.7	32.0	29.9	27.7
Some College	28.9	32.0	28.6	30.3
Sub-Total	65.8	77.3	72.8	70.8
High School Graduate	25.0	17.3	19.5	22.6
Some High School	6.6	5.3	6.5	5.5
Eighth grade or less	2.6	—	1.3	1.1
Income				
Under $5,000	2.6	4.0	2.6	2.9
5,000– 7,999	3.9	6.7	2.6	5.1
8,000–10,999	21.1	22.7	10.4	17.2
11,000–13,999	19.7	24.0	15.6	20.1
14,000–17,999	13.2	10.7	18.2	16.1
18,000 and over	34.2	22.7	44.2	32.8
Refused	5.3	9.3	6.5	5.8

Another survey, conducted by the Unidex Corporation, attempted to measure the likelihood of respondents using automated teller equipment. The responses were categorized by age, income, and sex.[5] The data are summarized in Table 40–2.

---

[5] "Use of and Preference for Automatic Teller Equipment/Drive-Up Window Facilities in the Handling of Financial Tranactions," *Unidex Report* (Bloomington, Ind.: Unidex Corporation, 1974).

Table 40–2
Likelihood of Using Automated Teller Equipment

Characteristic	Very Likely	Somewhat Likely	Somewhat Unlikely	Very Unlikely	Total Very plus Somewhat Likely
Age					
18–34	34.1%	21.7%	11.2%	29.2%	55.8%
35–49	33.2	18.6	11.3	33.2	51.8
50–64	19.8	12.5	14.7	49.6	32.3
65 and over	10.9	7.8	14.7	51.9	18.7
Income					
Under $7,500	15.2	11.0	11.0	51.7	26.2
10,000–15,000	25.8	20.8	11.9	37.7	46.6
7,500–10,000	34.8	17.4	12.1	32.6	52.2
15,000–20,000	34.1	20.3	14.8	26.8	54.4
Over 20,000	28.9	12.3	15.8	41.2	41.2
Sex					
Male	26.8	16.7	15.0	37.0	43.5
Female	28.0	16.2	10.5	40.0	44.2

Although these data are based on anticipated rather than actual usage, they do reveal 3 findings: (1) anticipated usage is not dependent upon sex (male and female are about equal); (2) younger age groups (18–34 and 35–49) indicate a much higher anticipated usage than older groups, but there is little difference between the 18–34 and 35–49 groups (about one-half indicate likely usage); (3) the $10,000–$20,000 income group anticipates the highest amount of likely usage; this group is followed by $7,500–10,000, over $20,000, and, finally, under $7,500.

Another Unidex report asked respondents to indicate whether the advantages with automated teller equipment outweigh the disadvantages.[6] The responses, categorized by occupation, age, and income, indicated the results shown in Table 40–3.

These data basically are consistent with the Unidex study on the likelihood of usage. White collar workers, younger age groups, and middle-income households perceive the most advantages versus disadvantages. The data are even more revealing when an analysis is made of the characteristics of those believing that disadvantages outweigh advantages. Specifically, a large proportion of blue collar workers (about 62 percent), lower income (about 63 percent), and older people (about 67 percent) say that the disadvantages are greater than the advantages. This would indicate that it would be much more difficult to generate usage among these groups than among those groups with a more favorable attitude toward the

---

[6] "Reception to Automatic Teller Equipment," *op. cit.*

Table   40–3
Advantages Versus Disadvantages of
Automated Teller Equipment

Characteristic	Advantages Outweigh	About Equal	Disadvantages Outweigh	Advantages Outweigh plus Equal
Occupation				
White Collar	31.6%	38.6%	29.8%	70.2%
Blue Collar	25.4	12.8	61.7	38.3
Professional	12.9	45.2	42.0	58.0
Housewife	23.6	31.1	45.3	54.7
Retired	23.5	5.9	70.6	29.4
Other	41.2	35.3	23.5	76.5
Age				
18–23	40.0	40.0	20.0	80.0
24–34	27.5	25.8	46.7	56.3
35–44	16.7	33.3	50.0	50.0
45–55	20.3	29.7	50.0	50.0
56–64	16.7	16.7	66.7	33.3
65 and over	33.4	13.3	53.4	46.6
Income				
Under $5,000	12.5	25.0	62.5	37.5
5,000–10,000	32.6	30.2	37.3	62.7
10,000–15,000	38.2	21.8	40.0	60.0
15,000–20,000	25.0	36.5	38.5	61.5
Over 20,000	29.2	33.3	37.5	62.5
Refused	17.1	31.4	51.4	48.6

automated equipment. However, these groups should not be excluded as a whole from consideration because each group has significant numbers of people with favorable attitudes.

Automated Teller Machine Systems in Colorado

A large number of commercial banks in Colorado operate ATMs. The 3 largest systems are: (1) United Banks of Colorado, (2) Affiliated Bankshares of Colorado, and (3) First National Bank of Colorado.[7]

1. United Banks of Colorado is a $1.5 billion-asset, statewide holding company. United calls their ATMs "Mini-Banks," and in the fall of 1977 had 13 Docutel Corporation machines in 12 on-site locations. United currently

---

[7] Much of the data in this section is from an article published in the *American Banker*.

has issued about 140,000 cards that access the system. The holding company has invested about $400,000 in media and direct-mail support of the system in the past year.

Direct-mail teasers, information, directories, and follow-up material was the backbone of the campaign to familiarize customers with the machinery. Demonstrators stayed with the machines for 6 weeks.

The result of the campaign, which has not ended, according to Ms. Haddon, vice-president and director of marketing, is the largest ATM system in Colorado. During June, she said, 93,873 transactions were conducted on the machines, an average of 7,013 transactions per machine per month.

She also said that nationwide, only 18 percent of transactions are handled on machines during working hours. United Mini-banks handled 45 percent of their transactions during working hours.

One reason for the success of ATMs in Colorado, she continued, is the nonbranching law. It makes regular banking less convenient and gives the machines an advantage in convenience, Mrs. Haddon explained.

The holding company's objectives by the end of the year are a 5 percent gain per month to 121,000 transactions in December; a customer base of 29,000 as opposed to the current 23,000; and handling 60 percent of the machine transactions during business hours.

She said that 16 percent of the card-carrying customers now are using the machines and the goal is 70 percent in 3 years.

2. First National Bank of Denver started its automated teller program in November, 1976.

The bank leases ATMs from International Business Machines Corp. and subleases them to affiliates and correspondent banks at the same price.

First National Bank of Denver probably relied most heavily on the successful program at the $1 billion deposit First American National Bank of Tennessee.

That bank, according to Mr. Lucey, senior vice-president and director of marketing, averaged about 15,000 transactions per machine per month, including balance inquiries, for its 10 machines by the end of the first year of operation. The national average, he added, is about 1,300 transactions a month for a machine, and the Colorado average is between 4,000 and 5,000 transactions a month per machine.

The bank, with 5 affiliates and one correspondent bank, issued 150,000 transaction cards, including 40,000 check guarantee cards to customers along with mailers explaining the system and its uses.

At the same time, First National Bank of Denver started an employee incentive program, as did First American in Nashville, and a $120,000 advertising campaign.

Two weeks before the system went on line, the machines were available in bank locations for testing by customers.

Bank employees who traditionally met customers were given 25 cents each for the first 25 persons they steered to the terminals for a supervised test, and they were given 50 cents for each additional customer.

Those bank employees who did not traditionally meet customers received 50 cents for the first 25 customers and $1 each after that.

And, the customers also received an incentive. For each use of the machine, they received a gift. The gift was a certificate for a free single scoop of "transmint" ice cream from Baskin-Robbins Ice Cream, Inc. The ice cream parlor chain donated the ice cream and changed the name of its chocolate mint flavor. The bank program helped draw customers to the ice cream stores as well.

The bank does not yet have a full month of figures from which to work, but picking a one-day segment from its survey of its 7 machines, Lucey said 1,927 transactions were completed in one day, the day before the Independence Day holiday weekend.

3. Affiliated Bankshares of Colorado (ABC) is one of the pioneers in Colorado in the use of ATMs. It started its network in 1972, and in the fall of 1977, had 13 machines in 9 locations. ABC named its ATM program "PocketTeller" and has about 60,000 cards in the hands of its customers. The annual advertising and promotion budget has been about $150,000.

The company's marketing program primarily was personal contact with individual bank customers, and the degree of acceptance by those customers was dependent upon each bank's enthusiasm and dedication to the use of the machines.

The current average is 4,500 transactions per machine a month, according to Ms. Wendy Wimbush, director of marketing; although as yet, the system does not have a balance inquiry function which should increase transaction volume as much as 20 to 25 percent.

The system's volume is up about 65 percent from a year ago, she added, and 70 percent of the holding company's cardholders have used the cards.

One bank in the Affiliated Bankshares System, the $69 million-deposit University National Bank, Denver, which is near a large shopping mall, has the most active location in the state. The two ATMs on-site at the bank do an average combined volume of 8,500 transactions a month, according to Ms. Wimbush.

The New Law

On May 20, 1977, the Colorado legislature passed a bill allowing commercial banks to establish off-site electronic terminals (ATMs and POSs) effective January 1, 1978. The key provisions of the law are:

1. Terminals on the premises of a Colorado bank or its detached facility not be shared, but off-site terminals must be made available to any other Colorado bank requesting the use of such a machine.

2. Any Colorado bank desiring to use another bank's terminal must meet reasonable technical standards and pay charges for the use of the machines.

3. Charges must be fair, equitable, and nondiscriminatory and shall not exceed an equitable proportion of both the cost of establishing the communications facility (including provision for amortization of development cost and capital expenditures over a reasonable period of time) and the costs of operation and maintenance of the machine, plus a reasonable return on such costs.

4. Each bank using such a communications facility must be given equal prominence in visual or oral data in public view at the electronic terminal facility, and no advertising regarding the facility may suggest or claim exclusive control or use of the facility by any one bank.

5. Off-site electronic terminals may not be operated by an employee or agent of the bank, and no bank employee may be permanently located at the electronic terminal. Employees may be temporarily stationed at a terminal only for the purpose of instructing customers in the use of the machine or for servicing or observing the operation of the terminal.

The new law gave ABC the opportunity to greatly expand the geographical and time convenience it could provide its present and potential customers. However, the provision that made sharing of off-site ATMs mandatory, that required equal prominence in visual or oral display at the site, and that prohibited the location of bank employees at the site (thus, severely restricting the bank's ability to open new accounts) made the establishment of off-site ATMs financially risky.

Because of the strategic importance of the decision, a management team was formed to enumerate possible EFT strategies and to evaluate their implications for Affiliated Bankshares of Colorado. The team was comprised of the director of marketing, the new product development manager, a financial executive, executives from ABC's computer and operations center and Mastercharge Center, and an outside consultant.

In examining secondary data on the subject, the group discovered that commercial banks have installed automated teller equipment for a variety of reasons. Among them were:

- Increase customer service and convenience;
- Enhance image;
- Gain experience with Electronic Funds Transfer Systems (EFTS);
- Use as a marketing tool;
- Gain competitive advantage (gain new accounts);
- Meet competitive need (retain present accounts);
- Offer Saturday or extended hours by an alternative to traditional means;
- Generate growth in deposits and profitability.

Economic Justification Factors

Economic justification involves an examination of 4 different yet interrelated factors which could either individually or, more likely, collectively offset the costs incurred in installing, maintaining, and promoting automated teller equipment. These factors are:

(1) *Personnel Cost Reduction.* The primary areas of possible cost reduction is in the present number of human tellers employed (probably unlikely in the short run) or a reduction in the number of new additional tellers needed to serve increased activity and business. Obviously, transactions through automated equipment result in fewer activities that have to be performed by human tellers. John F. Ingram, Jr., senior vice-president, Citizens and Southern National Bank in Atlanta, stated,

> One of our banks was competing with Saturday openings, and the management felt that by going to an automated teller machine that they could delay the Saturday openings. And they were able to do so successfully. Now this is quite a savings.[8]

Calculation of possible cost reduction involves developing a forecast of automated teller machine activity, and then comparing the costs of a human teller for the same volume of transactions with the cost of the automated equipment to determine the amount of cost reduction or added expense for the automated equipment.

(2) *Higher Retention of Present Customers.* One benefit often cited relative to the installation of automated equipment is that it reduces customer loss compared to the amount of customer loss without the equipment. It is assumed that this is achieved through better customer service, increased convenience, increases in the number of services used, and by either matching or exceeding competitive services. Garry Meiser of Seattle-First indicated that, "for the most part, our growth (from automated tellers) comes from the reduction in lost accounts." [9]

Although it is extremely difficult to forecast this factor as a separate and distinct entity, it does represent a positive contribution to profits (assuming the accounts are profitable); thus, its effect should be included in the cost/benefit analysis.

(3) *Generation of New Accounts and Customers.* The generation of profitable new accounts by automated teller equipment is a factor that offsets the costs associated with the machines. The following examples provide evidence of the new account generation hypothesis.

In the 1975 *Cash Dispensers and Automated Tellers* status report, 41.2 percent of automated teller institutions indicated that they could attribute new credit card accounts to automated tellers, 56.2 percent indicated new checking accounts were generated, and 34.7 percent indicated new savings accounts were generated.[10] Marine Midland, Buffalo, reported that 10 percent of the consumers who applied to use the machine were not previously doing business with the bank.[11]

(4) *Fees From Transactions.* Direct revenue is generated if a fee is charged for each transaction.

All of the secondary data that could be uncovered dealt with on-site (at

---

[8] "Correspondents Examine Economics of EFTS," *Banking*, November 1975, p. 88.
[9] Ibid., p. 80.
[10] *Cash Dispensers and Automated Tellers* (Park Ridge, IL: Linda Fenner Zimmer, 1975), p. 104.
[11] "Automated Tellers," Revolving Credit Letter, April 11, 1974.

Figure 40-1

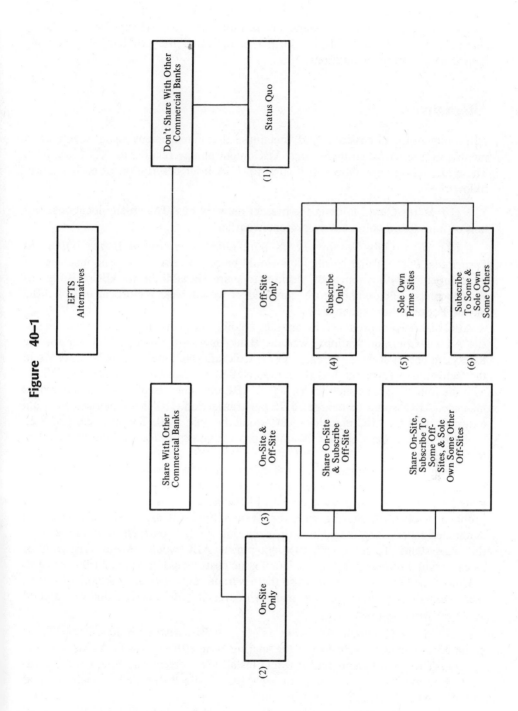

main office or branch) ATM locations. There was little, if any, hard data on transaction volumes and economic justification for off-site locations. Mandatory sharing and equal visual display further complicated the problem of generating data from any other institutions.

Alternatives

After numerous discussions and meetings, the management team identified a number of alternative strategies that ABC might pursue relative to ATM locations. These alternatives are shown in Figure 40–1. A brief description of each strategy follows:

(1) *Status Quo.* Maintain the present network of ATM on-site locations. Details of transaction volume were presented earlier.

(2) *Share Only On-Site ATMs With Other Commercial Banks Willing to Participate.* PocketTeller cardholders would be able to use the on-site machines of the competitor with whom ABC decided to share (in addition to ABC existing on-site Docutels). The competitor's cardholders would have reciprocal use of ABC on-site PocketTeller machines.

ABC had been approached by another holding company in the state to share on-site ATMs. Colorado National was the BankAmericard processing center for the Rocky Mountain Region. In early 1977, Colorado National had only 3 ATMs in the Denver area (ABC had 8). Colorado National proposed sharing on-site ATMs with the following fee structure: (a) if an ABC customer used a Colorado National machine, ABC would be charged $.75 per transaction, (b) if a Colorado National customer used an ABC machine, ABC would be paid $.50. The difference of $.25 would be paid to the Colorado National processing center for performing the electronic switch.

Sharing with the United Mini-bank system or First National's Transaction system also was theoretically possible, although ABC would have to rename its program "TransAction" to participate with First National. Also, there was a technical problem involved in sharing with the TransAction system: IBM versus Docutel automated tellers. The magnetic stripes and information on them was different for the two systems. To share with IBM equipment, ABC would have to reissue all of its cards with both types of stripes. Total issue costs would be about $1.00 per card.

United used Docutel equipment so there were fewer technical problems; however, their willingness to share on-site machines (even if ABC decided this was a good strategy) was unknown.

(3) *Share On-Site and Off-Site ATMs with Participating Banks.* PocketTeller cardholders would be able to use the sharing competitor's on-site ATMs and any off-site ATMs that the competitor would install. Conversely, the competitor's card-holding customers would be able to use ABC on-site PocketTeller machines, and any off-site machines ABC might install.

The same technical and cost situation discussed for alternative (3) would exist for this alternative.

(4) *Subscribe to Others' Off-Site ATMs.* Under this alternative, PocketTeller cardholders could use selected ATMs installed in off-site locations by a competitor, and ABC would pay fees for this usage. ABC customers would continue to have the use of ABC on-site Docutel machines also. The competitor's customers would be able to use both the competitor's on-site and off-site ATMs, but would not have access to ABC on-site Docutel machines.

(5) *ABC Own Prime Off-Site Locations.* PocketTeller cardholders would be able to use both ABC on-site Docutel machines and off-site machines which ABC would own and install. Customers of other banks would be granted access to the off-site machines under Colorado law if their own bank chose to subscribe and could meet technical requirements.

The cost per location varied depending upon such factors as land costs. It was estimated that the capital expenditure per site would be between $90,000 and $130,000. Annual operating expenses (including capitalized costs) would be between $35,000 and $45,000 per machine location. These expenses do not include marketing costs (mass media advertising, direct mail, personal demonstrations of the machines). A tentative budget of about $150,000 was thought to be needed in the first year if this alternative was selected.

(6) *Sole-Own Some Off-Site ATMs and Subscribe to Others.* This is a combination of alternatives (4) and (5).

Other Significant Data

PocketTeller versus Live Teller Costs

ABC does not have a sophisticated standard costing system. Based on a limited survey and cost compilation, it was estimated that the costs of a PocketTeller transaction and a live teller transaction were approximately equal. Thus, at present transaction volumes, no savings in costs accrue from shifting transactions from live tellers to the ATMs.

Transaction Fees

None of the ATM systems in Colorado charge a fee for transactions conducted through either ATMs or live tellers. The most common checking account fee structure is 1–2–3. That is, if the minimum balance in an account falls in the $200 to $299 range, a fee of $1.00 per month is charged; between $100 and $199, $2.00; and below $100, $3.00. If the minimum balance is above $300, there is no charge for the account.

Federal Reserve Bank functional cost analysis shows that it costs a bank about $45 to $50 a year to service each checking account. Without any fee charges, it would require an average balance of about $1,100 or $1,300 for a bank to break even on an account.

One method of offsetting the costs associated with the ATMs would be to charge a fee per transaction. (Seattle-First charges $.20 per transaction. The fee was dropped for a 6-month period; after it was reinstated, transaction volume declined only slightly.)

Alternatives available to ABC are (1) no charge for transactions—thus matching competition, (2) a fee for off-site machines only (if the decision is made to proceed with these), and (3) charge a fee for all ATM transactions including on-site locations; however, no charge would be made for live teller transactions at the same site.

Market Share

Increased market share through acquisition of new customers or a higher retention rate of older customers could offset the cost of ATMs. The ability to achieve increased market share depends on the service area of a bank and increased penetration in that area or using off-site ATMs to expand that service area.

Service areas are the geographic distribution of customers around a bank. Service areas vary from bank to bank, but generally are related to a certain area of "convenience" within which people are willing to travel to conduct banking business.

For downtown banks, the residential addresses of customers are scattered throughout the community, reflecting commuting and work patterns.

For suburban banks, residential addresses of customers are located within more concentrated areas around the banks. These areas reflect (a) convenience to home, (b) travel patterns for other convenience services, (c) travel to work, and (d) location of competitors.

The likelihood of attracting new customers is affected by both (1) location of the bank where accounts must be opened, and (2) the location of the ATM where banking services will be carried out once the account has been opened. In other words, the farther away a remote ATM is from the bank's service area, the less likely new customer prospects would be to travel to the bank to open accounts. The law restricts the ability of a bank to open accounts at an off-site ATM location.

A detailed examination of the Denver metropolitan area revealed over 30 high potential locations for off-site ATMs. About 20 of these were fairly distant from ABC banks; for example, large shopping malls and complexes. Justification for machines in these locations would depend upon signing other banks as subscribers, and charging the other banks (not their customers—that would remain their decision) a fee for each transaction. Significant volume would have to be generated for the ATM to be profitable. If sufficient subscriber transaction volume were not generated, market share shifts would be needed to offset the cost.

About 10 locations were identified adjacent to the primary service areas of existing ABC banks. The management team believes that market share shifts might be more feasible in these areas because their proximity makes the opening of accounts at an ABC office relatively convenient. Sample data on five of these areas are shown in Table 40–4.

Although specific data were not available, the profit associated with capturing the accounts of a household (including mortgage loans) was estimated to be about $70.

Table 40–4
Sample Data on Areas Adjacent to
Primary Service Areas of Existing ABC Banks

Area 1

1. Total Households   6,910
2. Checking Accounts/Household

Income	% in Range
Less than $9,000	.049
$9,000 to $19,999	.140
$20,000 to $49,000	.541
More than $50,000	.269

3. ABC Market Share   about 15%

Area 2

1. Total Households   35,845
2. Checking Accounts/Household

Income	% in Range
Less than $9,000	.110
$9,000 to $19,999	.252
$20,000 to $49,000	.516
More than $50,000	.122

3. ABC Market Share   about 10%

Area 3

1. Total Households   16,826
2. Checking Accounts/Household

Income	% in Range
Less than $9,000	.115
$9,000 to $19,999	.231
$20,000 to $49,999	.458
More than $50,000	.198

3. ABC Market Share   about 9%

Area 4

1. Total Households   12,963
2. Checking Accounts/Household

Income	% in Range
Less than $9,000	.074
$9,000 to $19,999	.209
$20,000 to $49,999	.550
More than $50,000	.167

3. ABC Market Share   about 3%

Area 5

1. Total Households   15,293

2. Checking Accounts/Household

Income	% in Range
Less than $9,000	.151
$9,000 to $19,999	.260
$20,000 to $49,999	.420
More than $50,000	.165

3. ABC Market Share   about 16%

Discussion Question

Prepare a presentation for the board of directors of Affiliated Bankshares of Colorado. Detail the advantages and disadvantages of each strategy and make a specific recommendation including pricing strategy, advertising strategy, and promotion strategy. Justify your recommendations.

Chapter 10

Extending Marketing to Contemporary and Nonprofit Settings

Traditionally, marketing has been viewed as an activity conducted by profit-oriented firms. That is, it has been described in terms of the exchange process among businesses, such as manufacturers, wholesalers, retailers, and other profit-making institutions. Contemporary marketing scholars and practitioners, however, have broadened the concept and application of marketing to encompass non-business organizations engaged in social, government, and other nontraditional marketing. Examples are the application of marketing concepts to social problems such as family planning, safe driving, and immunization against disease. Other applications include marketing political candidates, the metric system, the armed forces, and religion.

Proponents of broadening the marketing concept explain how market segmentation and product, price, promotion and channel/distribution decisions can apply to the exchange processes in nontraditional marketing settings.

Kotler and Levy pioneered the idea of a broadened marketing concept by describing how traditional marketing principles have been and can be applied to any nonbusiness organization serving a consuming public. They proposed that nonbusiness organizations actually "perform classic business functions." [1] Libraries offer educational and entertaining products to the general public; police and fire departments provide protection as a product offering, religious organizations offer ultimate truth and a relationship with a supreme being to church members; and college fraternities offer close friendship and brotherhood to students. See Table C—10–1.

However, a broadened marketing concept is not without its critics. David Luck voices his concern that extending the concept of marketing to hospital services, education, labor unions, and welfare agencies broadens the concept too far. [2]

---

[1] Philip Kotler and Sidney J. Levy, "Broadening the Concept of Marketing," *Journal of Marketing,* **33** (July, 1969), p. 11. Published by the American Marketing Association.

[2] David J. Luck, "Broadening the Concept of Marketing—Too Far," *Journal of Marketing,* **33** (July 1969), pp. 53–55. Published by the American Marketing Association.

Table   C—10–1
**Illustrations of Some Organizations,
Their Products, and Customer Groups**

Organization	Product	Customer Group
Library	Education and Entertainment	General Public
Police and Fire Departments	Protection	General Public
Religion	Ultimate Truth, Relationship with Supreme Being	Religious Followers, Church Members
College Fraternities	Friendship, Brotherhood.	College Students
United Nations	Peace	World-Wide Countries and Territories
Alcoholics Anonymous	Physical and Mental Health	Problem Drinkers

Luck believes that marketers are attempting to extend the marketing concept to include social goals in order to salve their conscience for being profiteers. Further, Luck believes that broadening the concept to the extreme expounded by its proponents is to provide limitless boundaries to the definition of marketing, since it would include any task performed by anybody anywhere. In short, Luck defends the traditional view that marketing should be restricted to the ultimate purchase and sale of goods and services.

Kotler, on the other hand, feels that the earlier "broadening" of the concept did not go far enough. Instead, he proposes a *generic concept of marketing* which includes any transaction involving the creation and offer of values between social units for the purpose of achieving a desired response. Kotler presents his argument for a generic concept of marketing by examining the shift in the focus of marketing in a historical perspective. Marketing focused initially on commodities (such as agricultural products); then, marketing institutions (wholesalers, retailers); next, marketing functions (buying, storage, transportation); later, on managerial decision making (planning, organizing, control); and still later on social problems (market efficiency, social impact).[3]

Kotler believes that each time marketing has developed a new focus it has emerged "with a refreshed and expanded self concept."[4] Kotler distinguishes among three levels of consciousness concerning the boundaries of the marketing discipline and its application to human activities.

---

[3] Philip Kotler, "A Generic Concept of Marketing," *Journal of Marketing,* **36** (April 1972), p. 46. Published by the American Marketing Association.
[4] Ibid.

Consciousness one is the traditional view that marketing involves transactions between buyers and sellers of "economic" products and services. *Consciousness two* broadens the core concept of market transactions to include organization-client transactions. That is, consciousness two is concerned with situations in which an organization, client group, and broadly-defined products can be identified.[5] Consciousness two is the level earlier identified by Kotler and Levy. However, Kotler now feels that he and Levy had not broadened the concept far enough. As a result, he has introduced an expanded focus referred to as consciousness three.

Consciousness three expands the boundaries to include any "organization's attempt to relate to all of its publics, not just its consuming public." [6] Figure C—10–1 provides a picture of nine various publics with which an organization deals. "A public is any organization with potential interest and impact on an organization." [7] Three of the publics shown in Figure C—10–1 are referred to as *input* publics. They are supporters (such as stockholders and directors), employees, and suppliers. There also are two *output* publics. They are agents and consumers. And, finally, an organization has four sanctioning publics—government, competitors, special publics, and general public.[8] "All of these publics are targets for organizational marketing activity because of their potential impact on the resource

[5] Ibid., p. 47–48.
[6] Ibid., p. 48.
[7] Ibid., p. 51.
[8] Ibid.

Figure   C—10–1
An Organization's Publics

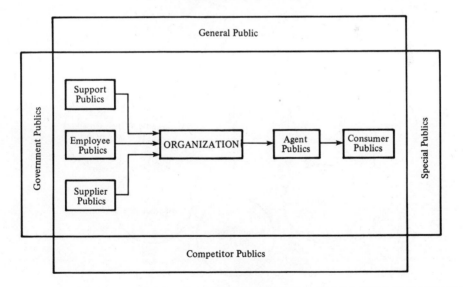

Source: Philip Kotler, "A Generic Concept of Marketing," *Journal of Marketing,* **36** (April 1972), p. 51. Published by the American Marketing Association.

Figure   C—10–2
The University and Its Publics

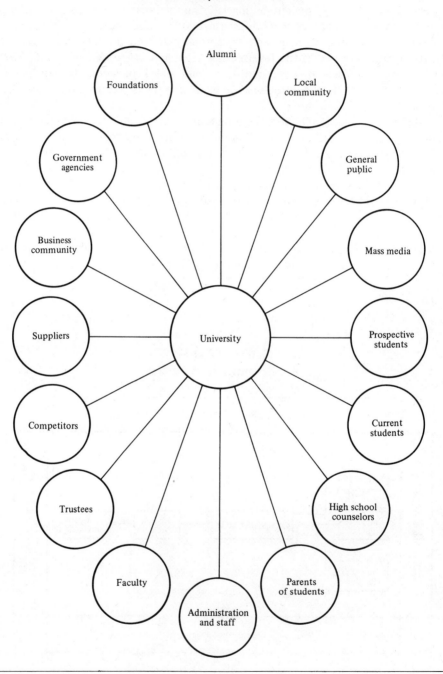

Source: Philip Kotler, *Marketing for Nonprofit Organizations* (Englewood Cliffs, NJ: Prentice-Hall, Inc., 1975), p. 18.

converting efficiency of the organization. Therefore, a target-market classification of marketing activity consists of supporter-directed marketing, employee-directed marketing, supplier-directed marketing, agent-directed marketing, consumer-directed marketing, general public-directed marketing, special public-directed marketing, government-directed marketing, and competitor-directed marketing." [9] An example of a university and its various publics is shown in Figure C—10–2.

The generic concept of marketing holds that marketing principles apply to any organization involved in any transaction with any group (or public) which impacts upon that organization, and where the creation and offering of value is directed at publics to elicit a desired response. Thus, corporate advertising can promote goodwill, favoritism, and loyalty from employees, suppliers, lending institutions, stockholders, state, local, and federal governments, consumers, etc. Kotler's conclusion is that basic marketing principles and concepts can be applied and adapted to all of these nine major publics. These applications are discussed in the following sections.

Market Segmentation and Contemporary Marketing Problems

Market segmentation is a concept which can be applied to any field of human endeavor where a transaction between two organizations might transpire. Market segmentation is a subset of or at least overlaps with opportunity analysis. The general of an army analyzes opportunities of an opposing force. In a sense, a general segments the opposing force into smaller elements, determining which areas to attack. In the same sense, market segmentation and opportunity analyses can be applied to any business and nonbusiness organization. Candidates for political office conduct research studies to determine the characteristics, profiles, and sentiments of their voting constituency—those who are supportive, those who are in support of the opposition, and those who are undecided. Strong supporters of candidates represent segments whose minds are highly unlikely to change, and therefore, voters to which few resources should be committed. The important segment upon which to concentrate is the uncommitted or undecided voter. Understanding their opinions, life styles, and other socioeconomic and demographic profiles are of utmost importance to a political candidate. This segment represents the most fertile area in which to concentrate resources and to develop political appeals. This segment generally represents the margin of victory or defeat for a political candidate.

Universities have realized a "crunch" in student enrollments over the past decade. Potential markets include more than 18-year old, high school graduates. Today, university officials are looking to new market segments from which to recruit students. In particular, market segments for universities have been identified as business managers, executives, and personnel for retraining, advanced educa-

---

[9] Ibid.

tion, and continuing education (updating) in their particular fields; military personnel either returning to college or those who are high school dropouts; housewives bored with their daily routines; blacks and other minorities, underprivileged and poor, handicapped students; and local police departments, government agencies, and special interest groups for whom universities often set up special educational programs and seminars.[10]

Market segmentation also has been applied to public transportation. Lovelock describes how multidimensional segmentation can be applied to the choice behavior of particular groups for various transportation modes.[11] Although Lovelock's focus was on public transportation, he concludes that the concept of market segmentation is equally applicable to toll-road pricing, ramp metering, preferential freeway lanes, parking supply management, and highway safety campaigns, because of the common behavioral patterns of the transportation public.

Another example of the use of market segmentation in a nonbusiness setting is Julian Simon's description of how segmentation of the "fertility" market can aid in promoting family planning.[12] Simon contends that social planners can induce more people to practice contraception through sound campaign planning aimed at particular market segments.

Simon identifies five basic market segments for contraception. The "modern methods" segment is characterized as users of modern, artificial contraceptives, with a low birth rate, concentrated usually in Sweden and the urban United States. The "folk methods" segment's approach to contraception is withdrawal and abstinence. Areas of the world with "heavy" users of this approach are Jamaica, and Taiwan. The "want to regulate" segment does not currently contracept but would like to do so. This segment has more children than they want but are otherwise similar to the "folk methods" segment.

The "suited for regulation" segment currently is not ready to contracept but may change their attitudes if presented with appropriate, additional information. Mexico and urban Brazil are illustrative of areas heavily composed of this segment. Finally, the "not ready for regulation" segment does not want to contracept and will not alter their attitudes easily. This segment belongs to a population where death rates are high and the economy is weak. For each segment he identifies, Simon suggests market approaches and themes to elicit the desired response for contraceptive measures.

As these examples have shown, the concept of market segmentation can be useful in nonbusiness programs. Market segmentation has been practiced through the ages. An early axiom among generals, "divide and conquer," illustrates that the concept has been around for a long time and applied to many situations. We have only recently rediscovered its usefulness.

---

[10] See Robert L. Stahr, "In a Bear Market, Everyone's a Hunter," *College and University Business* (June 1974), pp. 21–31.

[11] Christopher H. Lovelock, "A Market Segmentation Approach to Transit Planning, Modeling, and Management," *Proceedings,* Sixteenth Annual Meeting, The Transportation Research Forum, **16,** No. 1, 1975.

[12] Julian L. Simon, "Market Segmentation in Promoting Contraception," *Studies in Family Planning* (March 1974), pp. 90–97.

Developing Marketing Mixes
For Contemporary Marketing Problems

The previous sections described how the concept of marketing and market segmentation can be used in nonbusiness settings. This section focuses on how the
four major marketing mix variables—product, promotion, channels/distribution,
and price have been and can be used in nonbusiness organizations.

Product Decisions

Product decisions, which include service decisions, are becoming increasingly
important to nonprofit and nonbusiness organizations. Museums, for example,
are beginning to show interest in applying marketing principles by using differentiated shows and exhibits (products) to appeal to different market segments.
They also have increased their use of promotion and merchandising techniques
and, as a result, have attracted more people to their museums. And, they have
gained greater philanthropic and government support.[13]

Whereas libraries used to be little more than storehouses of books, now they
offer records, art pieces, and playthings to children.[14] Libraries now are loaning
practically any items that will attract adults and children to their "place of nonbusiness."

The federal government also is getting into the act. It is marketing postal
service as a product, census data, and other government publications (they set up
their "products" at national and regional associations), military hardware to
foreign countries, and savings bonds. Currently, the federal government is using
the most modern marketing techniques to market its products.[15]

Promotion Decisions

Promotion is a form of communications that can be used equally as effectively
by business, nonprofit organizations, government agencies, and others to inform
and to persuade their various publics. Branches of the armed forces use advertising on television, billboards, student newspapers, and other media vehicles;
they use personal selling through recruiters on university campuses and recruiting
stations; they use sales promotion in the form of air shows, demonstrations, "point-
of-purchase" materials; and they use public relations activities.

Many university administrators, realizing the tremendous fixed costs associated
with running a college campus, have begun to push summer school recruitment.
University promotional efforts have included advertising on billboards, television,
radio, and newspapers, colorful posters with catchy slogans, news releases, theme
songs, classified ads, sales promotional items (such as frisbees stamped with a
summer school slogan), in-house publications (such as weekly college announce-

---

[13] *Wall Street Journal,* August 14, 1975.
[14] *Wall Street Journal,* May 7, 1975.
[15] *MSU Business Topics,* Summer, 1973.

ments on bulletin boards and in student newspapers), and personal selling effort by faculty, staff, and administrators.[16]

Special interest groups such as Common Cause, "Nader's Raiders," NOW (National Organization of Women), and ERA (Equal Rights Amendment) supporters also have recognized the importance of promotion, particularly advertising, in advancing their causes. Recently ERA proponents have been preparing to use a "pull" strategy by using an advertising blitz aimed at citizens to call or write their legislators to vote for passage of the ERA in their states. The recommended media in order of importance is suggested as (1) radio, due to high frequency/ low cost, geographic flexibility and audience targeting (i.e., distinct audience groups listen to particular radio station formats); (2) newspapers, because of its advantage of high readership among upper educational and high income groups and its geographic targeting capability; and (3) television, (assuming available funding) due to its high overall reach. However, television is rated a third choice because of its high absolute cost, its time limitation of 30-second commercials to tell a complex story, and the low need for visualization of the issue.[17]

Other organizations becoming more heavily involved in promotion are state and local governments. In 1972 approximately $80 million was spent by state and city governments for industrial development campaigns, travel and tourism promotions, and consumer education programs.[18]

The Advertising Council has spent billions of dollars over more than three decades on such issues of national concern as anti-litter, anti-pollution, energy conservation, forest fire prevention, rehabilitation of handicapped people, and nutrition and health. Promotion has been and continues to be used by many nonbusiness organizations.

Distribution Decisions

Although the use of advertising and other promotional tools by the nonbusiness sector is rather apparent, distribution decisions among nonbusiness organizations are not. Recycling solid wastes, for example, may be considered as a channels-of-distribution problem. Zikmund and Stanton examined this problem by viewing recycling as a "reverse" distribution process which uses a "backward" channel. Reverse distribution views consumers in the role of having a product to sell *back* to a manufacturer. Since consumers do not consider themselves as producers of waste materials, the manufacturer must assume the role of developing the marketing strategy for reverse distribution and the responsibility for setting up the backward channel.[19]

A major problem in reverse distribution is how to overcome the resistance of "backward" channel members to participate. Soft drink bottlers is a familiar

[16] Patricia Reinfeld, "The Selling of the Summer School," *College Management* (March, 1974).

[17] Ibid.

[18] "States, Cities Spend $80,000,000 for Their Advertising," *Advertising Age* (November 21, 1973).

[19] William G. Zikmund and William J. Stanton, "Recycling Solid Wastes: A Channels of Distribution Problem," *Journal of Marketing,* 35 (July 1970), p. 35. Published by the American Marketing Association.

example of producers who have used reverse distribution to lower production costs. This backward channel was successful for many years, but over the last two decades, supermarkets and grocers have resisted the reverse distribution process since it ties up storage space, creates handling problems, and takes up employee time. Resistance among grocers has increased to the point where bottlers are being forced to use no deposit/no return bottles. Because of the environmentalists' concerns, bottles are being developed which also are biodegradable.

Because of ever-increasing scarce resources, recycling and reclamation are becoming increasingly important. Thus, the concept of reverse distribution takes on greater emphasis among many U.S. producers.

Pricing Decisions

Price also is an important marketing variable for nonbusiness organizations. Prices for the products and services produced by profit organizations are familiar to everyone. The prices for nonbusiness organizations are less apparent. These "prices" are referred to by a variety of names, such as fees, fares, contributions, honoraria, tolls, assessments, tuitions, and dues. A country club charges dues, a college charges tuition, a bridge owner charges a toll, a charity charges a contribution, a church asks for gifts, and labor unions charge assessments. Pricing is an inherent part of all these organizations. However, how well do these organizations understand the nature of their pricing decisions and the marketing principles which apply to their pricing strategies?

Price can be defined as the amount of money (or anything else of perceived value) given in exchange for something valued by the purchaser. The "something" valued by the purchaser can be either a physical product, a service, or an intangible "piece" of satisfaction. A gift of $100 to a Boys' Home is the price a person might pay for the satisfaction (or peace of mind) that he has done something for a fellow human being. Tax is the price people pay for national defense, police protection, clean city streets, highways, parks and recreation centers, schools, and welfare, among other services.

The price consumers pay for either a product or service can either encourage or discourage consumption. Public mass transit companies have used price (fares) to both encourage and discourage "product" usage. During rush hours, higher fares have been used to discourage the use of certain bridges and roads, for example. On the other hand, lower prices for subways and other mass transit vehicles have been used to encourage their use and reduce the use of automobiles. "No-fare" transit is an example of pricing used successfully in a number of large cities. The benefits include reduced pollution, reduced fuel usage, and less traffic congestion. Of course, the "price" of no-fare transit is paid by the citizens in taxes to gain the benefits cited above.[20]

To combat the ever-growing increase in consumer shopping at suburban shopping centers, some cities have helped in-town retailers by employing "free" parking meters. The meters are set to provide "free" parking for 30 minutes be-

---

[20] Jon Twichell and Christopher H. Lovelock, "No Fare Public Transit: Seattle's $64,000 Question," *Metropolitan* (January/February 1974), pp. 19–32.

fore the driver must insert coins to have the car remain parked. Merchants became enthusiastic about this new program and demanded the continuation and addition of the "free" meters.[21]

For several years, United Way has provided suggested gift guidelines (prices) to contributors. An effective gift is one hour's pay per month or one percent of annual income if the individual's income is over $10,000 per year. This price has been packaged around the theme, "Your Fair Share." In fact, pricing tables have been given to employers and employees alike as to the amount they *should* give according to their incomes. Some companies have made the contribution virtually mandatory as a part of the person's employment, although this requirement is illegal. Nevertheless, these voluntary contributions provide charitable satisfaction to some and employment and job security to others.

Applying Marketing Principles To Nontraditional Settings [22]

The previous sections examined briefly the usefulness of marketing concepts in developing programs for nonbusiness organizations in general. This section presents conceptual frameworks to be used in creating specific marketing programs in the areas of social marketing, health services marketing, public services marketing, and political candidate marketing.

Social Marketing

Marketing principles are increasingly being applied in programs designed to gain acceptance of a social idea or practice, such as brotherhood, safe driving, and family planning.[23] Farley and Leavitt examine the world population problem and the role marketing can play in alleviating the rapidly expanding worldwide population.[24] Although a market opportunity appears to exist for birth control services and devices, little effort has been exerted to stimulate market development, with the possible exception of Population Services, Inc. based in New York. The key marketing variables to solve this problem are distribution (to provide the delivery system of birth control services and devices) and promotion (to communicate availability and effective use of prophylactic devices and techniques).

Another illustration of the role of marketing in gaining and increasing the acceptability of a social idea or practice is in the area of safe driving. The National Safety Council provides drivers with a defensive driving course. "Its staff includes an advertising manager, a sales promotion manager, an Advertising

[21] *The American City* (January 1974), p. 16.

[22] This section is based largely upon the organization of Philip Kotler, *Marketing for Nonprofit Organizations* (Englewood Cliffs, NJ: Prentice-Hall, Inc., 1975), pp. 281–388.

[23] Philip Kotler and Gerald Zaltman, "Social Marketing: An Approach to Planned Social Change," *Journal of Marketing,* **35** (July 1971), pp. 3–12. Published by the American Marketing Association.

[24] John U. Farley and Harold J. Leavitt, "Marketing and Population Problems," *Journal of Marketing,* **35** (July 1971), pp. 28–33. Published by the American Marketing Association.

Council of America coordinator, a research director, and a program director . . . (who reach) . . . potential prospects through business firms, service organizations, schools, and the police and court system.[25] Their objective is to communicate safe driving methods to reduce highway accidents and fatalities. The National Safety Council and other social agencies are increasing their effectiveness through the development of full-time marketing organizations.

Within the context of the social marketing planning process, an integrated administrative framework, such as the one shown in Figure C—10–3, can be used. Regardless of the social issue, one or more agencies will be responsible for planning, organizing, staffing, directing, and controlling the activities involved in developing an integrated program to achieve a social aim. As shown in Figure C—10–3, the change agency operates within economic, political, technological, cultural, and competitive environments. To be responsive, the change agency must continuously monitor changes in these environments through the collection of information. To effect programs to meet the needs of society, the change agency can use the collected information to develop a product, promotion, place, and price mix to create desired changes in its publics. The total product package is delivered through channels which include mass and specialized media, paid agents, and voluntary groups and organizations. All of these efforts are directed at particular target markets (or publics) to elicit a socially desirable response. Publics of government include special consumer groups, business, minority groups, and labor union groups.

Through marketing, social programs can be created which will deliver a safer, healthier, more enjoyable way of life for a state or nation's citizens. Problems in pollution control, drug abuse, and mass transit, are in need of public attention and support and can be aided by sound programs using marketing principles.

Health Services Marketing

Health services marketing represents another nonprofit organization with important social concern. Figure C—10–4 shows the most important elements in a health care program.

The health care industry can be characterized in terms of health industry facilitators, such as medical societies, insurance carriers, and local, state, and federal departments and agencies. These facilitators provide assistance and in many instances the catalytic forces to energize the entire health care system. Health-care suppliers include pharmaceutical companies, medical supply companies, medical equipment manufacturers, and medical furnishings companies. These suppliers provide the equipment and medical provisions to operate health-care providers. Health-care providers include private physicians, hospitals, medical laboratories, nursing homes, pharmacies, and clinics which administer services to health-care patients. Finally, health-care consumers are those who are served by the previously-named organizations to satisfy health problems and illnesses.

In Figure C—10–4, all organizations are dependent upon the others for the entire process to function. Thus, it is necessary that each separate organization

---

[25] Kotler and Zaltman, *op. cit.,* p. 11.

Figure C—10–3
Social Marketing Planning System

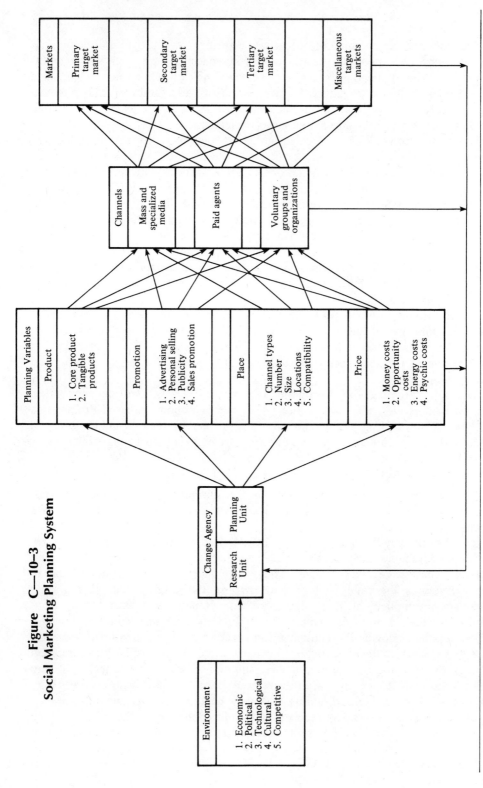

Source: Philip Kotler, *Marketing for Nonprofit Organizations* (Englewood Cliffs, NJ: Prentice-Hall, Inc., 1975), p. 297.

Figure   C—10–4
The Health Care Industry

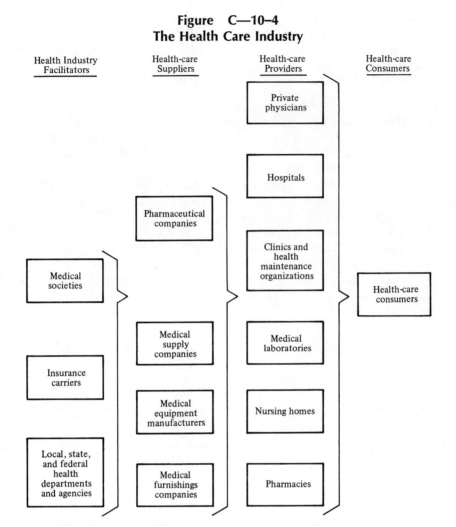

Source: Philip Kotler, *Marketing for Nonprofit Organizations* (Englewood Cliffs, NJ: Prentice-Hall, Inc., 1975), p. 305.

understand its publics in order to operate efficiently and to serve the needs of others in the system.

The delivery of health care requires understanding of various needs of the consuming publics. For example, hospitals depend very much upon donors of eyes, blood, and other vital organs and physical materials for an on-going operation. The price donors pay is the organ, blood, etc., they supply, while the product they receive is human satisfaction, and social responsibility. To sell these "product" benefits requires a marketing effort.

A marketing analysis must be conducted to determine who the recipients of health care are. Areas high in heart disease require proficient cardiac units. Areas requiring medical attention to the aged (e.g., Florida) require special equipment and physicians for that purpose. As one can see, a different marketing strategy is required for each of these different "market segments."

Public Services Marketing

Public services marketing represents another form of marketing application to a special segment. Government agencies, like other organizations, have special publics they must serve. Government agencies now are beginning to realize the benefits of marketing principles in their operations.

Four types of government agencies are shown in Table C—10–2. Government agencies are divided into these four types because each requires a different form of marketing activity.

"A business-type government agency, also called a public enterprise, is one that produces goods and services for sale." [26] The business-type government agency can use similar marketing management and strategies as profit-oriented business firms. They identify market segments, analyze consumer needs, and develop tra-

---

[26] Ibid., p. 331.

Table   C—10–2
Four Types of Government Agencies

Type	Function	Examples
Business-type government agency	Produces goods and services for sale	Postal service, toll roads, nationalized industries
Service-type government agency	Produces and disseminates services at no charge to the users	Public schools, public libraries, police and fire department, park districts, public hospitals, highway commissions, government tourist bureaus
Transfer-type government	Effects unilateral transfers of money	Social Security Administration, city and state welfare departments, Internal Revenue Service
Intervention-type government agency	Exists to regulate the freedom of some group for the sake of promoting the public interest	Penitentiaries, courts, Federal Trade Commission, Federal Food and Drug Commission

Source: Philip Kotler, *Marketing for Nonprofit Organizations* (Englewood Cliffs, NJ: Prentice-Hall, Inc., 1975), p. 331.

ditional marketing mixes to meet their consumers' needs. However, two major differences distinguish the public enterprise from the profit-oriented firm. First, public enterprises are not profit-oriented, rather they provide for some public need. Secondly, public enterprises usually are not in competition with other organizations since most are state monopolies.[27]

A second kind of government agency is service agencies, such as police departments, libraries, and public schools. Service agencies have specific client groups toward whom they direct their services. Public libraries serve the reading public, police and fire departments provide protection to citizens, and park centers offer recreation.[28] These service agencies are faced with product, place, promotion, and sometimes price decisions. For a park, the product configuration might include swings, sliding boards, park benches, fountains, and monkey bars. Place decisions would include analysis of geographic locations in which people would use park facilities. Promotion could include a park sign, publicity through news releases, and radio advertising. Although pricing may not be a decision faced by a park's service agency, some museums and zoos do have to make pricing decisions.

A third set of government agencies are transfer-type agencies. These include welfare agencies, the U.S. Custom Service, and the Internal Revenue Service. Although transfer agencies do not produce goods and services in a traditional sense, they do need to perform certain marketing activities, such as identifying client groups and their needs, developing communications programs to inform their clients of what they provide and where, and providing channels for supplying their services. However, they are rarely involved in product development and pricing.[29]

The last set of government agencies are intervention-type agencies, which include regulatory bodies, such as the Federal Trade Commission, and courts. Kotler illustrates how intervention-type government agencies, such as penitentiaries, do in reality need and to some extent use marketing concepts. Rather than viewing any one group as consumers of penitentiary services, it is better to look at the various publics with which penitentiaries interact. Prisoners are one public. In a sense they are consumers, but not purchasers. A prison attempts to sell prisoners a better life through rehabilitation. The product package includes teaching job skills and proper attitudes to succeed in society.

Another public includes society who are the purchasers of a prison's services of protection and rehabilitation. A third public includes legislators who provide the budget to operate a prison system. And, finally, the business community is a public with which prisons interact. Prisons attempt to sell rehabilitated, ex-convicts to business as "potentially good employees." [30] As we can see, marketing management is and can be useful for a variety of government agencies.

Political Candidate Marketing

Even before *The Making of the President 1960* and *The Selling of The President 1968,* political candidates have understood the need for good personal selling and

---

[27] Ibid., p. 332.
[28] Ibid.
[29] Ibid., p. 333.
[30] Ibid., p. 334.

advertising. Only in recent years, however, have political candidates begun to *market* themselves in a professional marketing sense. In addition to political advertising and personal selling with a handshake and a smile, political candidates are using marketing research (opinion polling) to identify various market (voter) segments, their needs, and attitudes. In addition, they now conduct "sales" analyses (computer analysis of voter patterns) and have created marketing organizations to implement a well-conceived marketing strategy.[31]

Figure C—10-5 shows a comprehensive political marketing map of a candidate's marketing problem. At the far left of the figure is the environment within which political issues and opportunities are defined. The sellers are "the candidates, their parties, and their interest group alliances." [32] The candidates' products include their political philosophies, stances on issues, personal styles, and qualifications for the office. Their communication and distribution channels are mass and selective media, personal appearances, and volunteer and party workers. And, finally, their market consists of various voter segments toward whom various marketing approaches are used to gain their support.

The political candidate's marketing strategy is much more complex than just winning the support of the voting public. As Figure C—10-6 shows, a political candidate must include in his or her grand marketing strategy functional strategies to gain support from the party, contributors, and interest groups.

It should be evident that making or selling a political candidate is a sophisticated marketing management operation, involving market research and analysis, product concept development, advertising, personal selling, sales promotion decisions, public relations, and distribution/logistical strategy.

Summary

The purpose of this chapter has been to demonstrate how marketing principles can apply to any nonbusiness organization. As Kotler points out, an organization should apply marketing principles and strategies to *all* publics with which the organization interacts, not just its consuming public. Marketing concepts can be applied successfully in any situation where any transaction occurs, because the purpose of a transaction is to elicit a desired response on the part of the other party. This chapter does *not* support the notion that marketing (its concepts and principles) has been expanded, but that its role and responsibility in society have been expanded.

Discussion Questions

1. The federal government attempted to market the $2 bill during the bicentenial year, 1976. The Treasury Department announced on November 3, 1975, that it would reissue the $2 bill first authorized during the Civil War and discontinued

---

[31] Ibid., p. 366.
[32] Ibid., p. 368.

Figure C—10—5
A Comprehensive Political Marketing Map

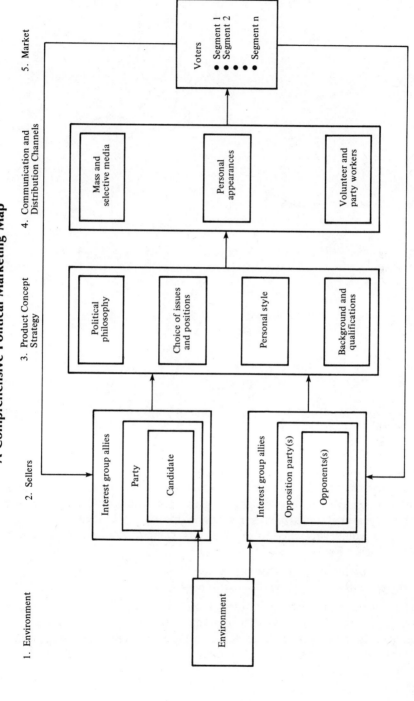

1. Environment 2. Sellers 3. Product Concept Strategy 4. Communication and Distribution Channels 5. Market

Source: Philip Kotler, *Marketing for Nonprofit Organizations* (Englewood Cliffs, NJ: Prentice-Hall, Inc., 1975), p. 369.

Figure   C—10–6
Four Markets Faced by the Candidate

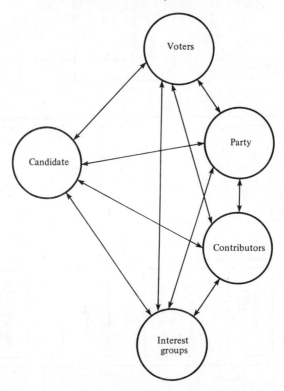

Source: Philip Kotler, *Marketing for Nonprofit Organizations* (Englewood Cliffs, NJ: Prentice-Hall, Inc., 1975), p. 370.

in 1966. The Treasury Department's approach to "market" the $2 bill in 1976 was to elicit the support of banks and retailers to substitute the $2 bill for $1 bills when possible. However, so far the program has been a failure. Why do you feel that the Treasury Department's marketing of the $2 bill was a failure? What suggestions would you make to the Treasury Department for successfully marketing the $2 bill? Explain.

2. Do you feel that Kotler's generic concept of marketing is broadening the concept of marketing too far? Why or why not?

3. The United States has committed itself to converting to the metric system. What suggestions do you have for marketing the metric system in this country? Develop a framework similar to the ones shown in the several figures in this chapter to show the various publics with which the U.S. Metric Board must interact. How would the marketing strategy vary toward each of the publics you have identified? Explain.

4. New York City is undergoing a serious financial crisis. What mistakes from a marketing point of view has New York City made over the past several years? How might competent marketing help NYC to return to a solvent, thriving status? Explain.

5. The United States postal system has come under severe criticism in recent years. Describe the postal system's publics and suggest how it might alter its marketing mix (price, product, promotion, and channel/distribution) to better meet the needs of its publics on a profitable basis.

6. Consider the state in which you live, and describe the various publics with which the state's tourism interacts. Suggest how the tourism agency can market its tourist attractions. In answering this question, consider the state's tourist resources, market segments, etc.

New York City

William L. Shanklin, Kent State University

It is August 1975 and New York City (NYC) is teetering on the brink of bankruptcy. In the opinion of many, the question is not "if" NYC will succumb, but rather "when" the inevitable financial collapse will occur. Later this month the city is scheduled to meet a $255 million bi-monthly payroll and $741 million in notes—on top of a seemingly insurmountable volume of other debts. New York State is not in much of a position to assist the city, as the state itself is in severe financial straits.

NYC already has appealed to Washington for federal guarantees or insurance for NYC bonds. But U.S. Treasury Secretary William Simon and Federal Reserve Chairman Arthur Burns have turned down the plea on the grounds that federal help (1) would require congressional approval which appears doubtful, (2) would set a dangerous precedent which might lead to the federal government bailing out debt-ridden local governments across the nation, and (3) would leave NYC's fundamental problems unresolved. Ostensibly, Secretary Simon and Chairman Burns are reflecting popular opinion in the United States. For instance, a Wall Street analyst, who has been testing sentiment toward the city's bonds, recently commented that, "The country has long seen NYC as arrogant." The prevailing attitude is "So now you're in trouble, then help yourself, Big Mouth!" [1]

The City [2]

NYC has a population of 7,646,818 with the metro area approaching 10 million people. The city covers 320 square miles. It is one of the world's 3 largest cities, the

---

[1] Background information and data for this case are drawn largely from: "New York's Last Gasp," *Newsweek* (August 4, 1975), pp. 18–27; and "Why New York City Won't Make It Financially," *Business Week* (August 18, 1975), pp. 94–97.

[2] The source of most of the information and statistics in this section is *The CBS News Almanac 1977* (Maplewood, NJ: Hammond Almanac, Inc., 1976), pp. 451–452.

financial hub of the globe, a sports and cultural capital, and the richest port in the United States. NYC is a national leader in business, finance, manufacturing, communications, service industries, and fashion, being the home office of many of the *Fortune* 500 corporations and the location of the New York and American Stock Exchanges.

The city is served by 7 daily newspapers, 15 AM radio stations, and 6 commercial television broadcasters. It has numerous institutions of higher learning and professional academies. Popular attractions include Central Park, the Bronx Zoo and Botanical Gardens, Hayden Planetarium, the Fifth Avenue shops, the Broadway theatrical district, the United Nations headquarters, Radio City Music Hall, the Statue of Liberty, Rockefeller and Lincoln Centers, Madison Square Garden, Yankee and Shea Stadiums, the Metropolitan Museum of Art, and the World Trade Center.

The city's citizens elect a mayor every 4 years. The present mayor is Abraham Beame who is an accountant by education and training and a former city budget director and controller. The city is governed by the mayor and elected city council. NYC has a vast bureaucracy encompassing, for example, over 26,000 police force members and more than 11,000 fire fighters.

The Financial Tangle

NYC's financial dilemma did not happen all at once. It has been building up over the last decade or so. As shown in Exhibit 41–1, the city's budget has increased from $3.4 billion in 1964–65 to $11.1 billion in 1974–75, for an increase of 231 percent. Welfare alone accounted for a 482 percent increase in the 10-year period. Most important, however, is the city's payroll which amounts to half of the total budget. NYC's work force grew from 163,270 in the early 1960s to 295,902 in the early 1970s, and stands today at some 320,000 city employees. The city has one civil servant for every 24 citizens, in contrast to Los Angeles and Chicago where the comparable ratios are one to 55 and one to 73, respectively. In 1977, NYC will spend $1 billion on workers' pensions that provide half-pay after 20 years for police and fire fighters, even though retirees are free to obtain new jobs.

New York State's Municipal Assistance Corporation (MAC) was formed in June of 1975 when NYC was unable to sell its own securities. MAC's finance chairman, Felix Rohatyn, is a highly respected investment banker and former chairman of the New York Stock Exchange's "crisis committee." In the latter role, he is credited with keeping numerous brokerage firms from financial collapse in 1970. Mr. Rohatyn has been called, admiringly, the Henry Kissinger of the financial world.

MAC's major function is to raise funds for NYC so that the city will be able to meet its burgeoning debts. A concomitant function is to oversee NYC's financial practices, a function that Mayor Beame currently is resisting.

Although MAC raised $1 billion for NYC in July 1975, it now is unable to sell much more. This situation is a particularly critical turn of events because, as shown in Exhibit 41–2, the city's short-term debt repayment schedule is both large and imminent.

Exhibit 41-1
New York City's Budget
1964-65 vs. 1974-75

| | Millions of Dollars | | Percent |
	1964–65	1974–75	Increase
Welfare	$ 416	$ 2,421	482%
Education	675	1,912	183
Debt Service*	470	1,435	205
Pensions	326	791	143
Police	236	734	211
Environment	144	330	129
Fire	120	307	156
Other	675	2,147	218
Total	$3,355	$11,104	231%

* Includes interest of $144.3 million in 1964–65 and $646.6 million in 1974–75.
Source: Citizens Budget Commission.

Exhibit 41-2
New York City's Short-Term Debt

Notes Due on	Amount (Millions of Dollars)
August 22, 1975	$ 741
September 11	46
September 15	400
October 17	420
November 10	250
December 11	400
January 12, 1976	620
January 13	200
February 13	290
March 12	341
June 11	280
Total	$3,988

Source: Office of the Comptroller, New York City.

MAC's problems stem from several interrelated factors. First, New York State's governor, Hugh Carey, has yet to reassure prospective buyers that MAC bonds are a moral obligation that the state will stand behind. Second, investors fear NYC accounting practices. For instance, one banker says that "The city doesn't have good accounting information. How can you base decisions when you know your information isn't accurate?" Another banker asserts that NYC has an accounting error of $250 million "every now and then." Moreover, NYC has a sordid history of financial gimmickry. When Mayor Beame was budget director and controller, he formulated a system whereby notes were sold on the strength of vast amounts of state and federal funding that would eventually be received for city programs. Often, these revenues were purposely overestimated to balance the budget. Traditionally, the last wage period of one fiscal year has been charged to the next year's budget (when checks were actually distributed), which has led to a $2 million hidden deficit. The city long has practiced the procedure of "rolling over" notes and bonds for new issues, and now the city debt exceeds $12 billion. In pensions, projections of city costs were lowered by figuring on a 1914 actuarial base. The Citizens Budget Commission states that the budget is so confused that it is impossible to determine the total cost. Third, MAC has become identified with NYC and, accordingly, suffers from a huge credibility problem.

Service Offerings and Pricing

NYC historically has put great emphasis on the mentality or psychology of "service to NYC citizens." Consequently, it is not surprising that the city offers a wide array of services. A previous mayor of the city even went so far once as to state, rather condescendingly, that he did not intend NYC to be constrained in service delivery by mere financial considerations. Another erstwhile mayor demonstrated a marked propensity to "cave-in" to municipal worker demands for increased wages and fringe benefits, rather than risk the temporary disruptions in city services which would be caused by work stoppages.

Any city service has a price. A service can be paid for wholly through taxes levied on citizens; prominent examples includes taxes for elementary and secondary schools, roads, libraries, and police and fire protection. Alternatively, a service can be supported by directly charging users of the service, such as charging users of public transportation, water, sewer and sanitation, and the city zoo. Finally, the costs of a city service can be recovered partially through taxes and, in part, via direct charges to users. The salient point is that all city services have prices; there is no free service in the true sense.

NYC provides numerous so-called free services and below-cost subsidized services to its residents. For example, the city maintains a heavily subsidized $.35 subway fare, a $.05 Staten Island Ferry fare (apparently unchanged since 1898), city-owned radio and television stations, 6-day-a-week garbage removal, a tuitionless City University of New York, and literally countless social services. The inordinate per capita costs of various city services in NYC, compared with 5 other major metropolitan areas in the United States, are shown in Exhibit 41-3.

Exhibit 41-3
City Service Costs
NYC vs. Selected Metropolitan Areas

				Per Capita Spending				
	Police and Fire	Health and Hospitals	Education	Public Welfare	Debt Interest	Pension Fund	Other	Total
New York City	$100	$151	$295	$316	$66	$88	$430	$1,466
Atlanta	41	68	245	10	34	12	252	650
Chicago	69	30	260	21	24	14	297	715
Detroit	70	60	241	26	25	5	266	693
Los Angeles	75	51	260	144	15	21	309	875
Philadelphia	91	48	217	18	41	22	294	731

Source: U.S. Department of Commerce, Bureau of Census.

NYC's high service costs stem mainly from the city's philosophy of service to its citizens, inexorable union pressures, and the giant bureaucracy formed to satisfy both. However, there are other exacerbating factors, mostly unique to NYC. For instance, NYC pays over $200 million a year for its courts and prisons. New York State carries this burden for every municipality in the state except NYC. Chicago, the nation's second largest city, has a school board with its own $1 billion budget, an independent transit authority, and large state contributions in the fields of health, education, and welfare. NYC has none of these benefits. It pays far more than a normal share of welfare costs—and the city has one million people on welfare.

The price (taxes) of residing in NYC is extreme for middle income people and businesses. This fact, along with the deteriorating quality of general living and working conditions in the city, has caused residents to flee in significant numbers. The exodus has devastated the city's economic base. At the same time, poor people increasingly have been moving into the city, and these people require more services than any other group.

The City's Response

Frantic actions are being take to save NYC from financial disaster. MAC officials are trying to sell more securities to the New York State pension fund. Mayor Beame already has fired 20,000 to 40,000 city workers and is contemplating releasing 10 percent more of the city's remaining 300,000 workers. Nevertheless, he intends to hire them back gradually by imposing new taxes and redeploying federal job training funds. In reality nobody knows for sure how many employees are on the city payroll nor how many have left it. MAC directors want to hire a public accounting firm to audit layoffs, but the city has refused to cooperate. The mayor is considering instituting a wage freeze, cutting the pay of higher-paid city workers, mandating payless furloughs, enforcing a job freeze, and reforming city work rules to increase productivity.

Some of the city's municipal unions reluctantly are accepting the inevitability of layoffs and a wage freeze. But the police and fire fighters unions are belligerently opposed and the 60,000 plus members of the United Federation of Teachers plan to strike at the expiration of their current contract. The municipal unions want other groups, particularly bankers, to make sacrifices, but the New York banks hold so much NYC paper that buying any more could endanger their stability. Additionally, the banks already have sacrificed some interest income—a tack that the unions have denounced as a public relations facade.

The mayor intends to institute reforms in the budget-making process to rid it of gimmicks. He wants to increase subway fares from $.35 to $.50, although that will not be enough to end the system's deficit. Also under study is the possibility of reducing the city's $32 million subsidy for the City University, even though this might not require the end of free tuition. Critics, however, are demanding the termination of free tuition for those students financially able to pay their way. City services are being cut drastically; for example, some streets smell of garbage as

Sanitation Department layoffs have slowed pickups. Some observers say that private carriers could perform the sanitation job better for a lot less money.

Tax reform is another major area under examination. Analysts point out that there are gaping holes in property tax exemptions that could be closed. Approximately 36 percent of all real property in the city, assessed at $22 billion, currently is tax exempt. To cite one prominent example, it is estimated that if the World Trade Center paid normal taxes, it would owe the city $40 million a year. Critics also want to end rent controls which, they say, would curb the abandonment of tax-producing apartments.

Irrespective of all the actions being considered or taken by MAC, Mayor Beame and the City Council, and Governor Carey, many experts believe that the only feasible solutions are either bankruptcy or a federal government bail-out of some sort. This muddled state of affairs is the scenario in NYC in August 1975.

The Consultants [3]

You are a marketing specialist with the renowned international management consulting firm of SOLVE, Inc. Your firm has been retained by Governor Carey to advise the Emergency Financial Control Board (EFCB) that will be formed shortly to supervise NYC operations. SOLVE staff is to have an initial meeting with EFCB officials one week from today. The staff that SOLVE has assembled contains one expert each in accounting and finance, labor relations, organizational analysis, and marketing. Each staff member will concentrate primarily on his or her area of expertise. You, the marketing counsel, have been included on the team because SOLVE's chief executive feels that a city serving its diverse public is highly similar to a private sector firm serving multifarious customer groups. In addition, the city has obvious needs in the area of promotional programs.

At the first meeting with EFCB officials, you are to discuss how NYC management's adoption of marketing philosophy and strategies may be able to help it to weather the present crisis and circumvent future problems. As you sit in your office contemplating the upcoming meeting, a number of possible approaches to your marketing presentation are running through your mind.

First, you recall reading an article by 2 marketing professors on how marketing thinking and techniques can be useful to public sector and other nonprofit organizations, as well as to commercial enterprises. You decide to read the article again to refresh your memory. (See Philip Kotler and Sidney J. Levy, "Broadening the Concept of Marketing," *Journal of Marketing,* January 1969, pp. 10–15.)

Second, you have before you a paradigm called a "marketing matrix" (see Exhibit 41–4). It was devised by a Harvard Business School professor to assist managers to both understand the marketing concept and to approximate the extent to which their respective organizations actually are implementing it, that is, fulfilling consumer needs and wants in order to achieve organizational objectives. You also have devised a "Typology of Municipal Services" which classifies city services into the categories of essential and nonessential, compensatory and noncompensatory,

---

[3] At this point in the case, actual facts end and a hypothetical situation is delineated.

and differentiated and undifferentiated categories (See Exhibit 41–5 for the typology and explanation.)

As you view the marketing matrix and typology of municipal services, a number of questions are suggested:

(1) In the marketing matrix, what vertical cell should be assigned to NYC government? Why?

(2) In the marketing matrix, what horizontal cell(s) should be assigned to high, middle, and low income segments of the city's population? Why? What about corporate citizens?

(3) Is "service orientation" synonymous with "marketing orientation"?

(4) If profitability is the organizational objective of commercial firms in marketing products and services, what is the organizational objective of a city government in providing services to its citizens? Does the or-

Exhibit 41-4
Marketing Matrix*

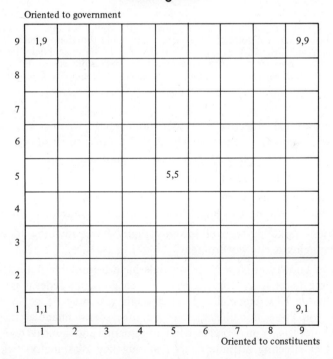

* The horizontal axis depicts the degree to which government's actions are oriented toward satisfying constituents' needs. The vertical axis shows the extent to which government's initiatives are in its own best interests. On both scales, 1 is the lowest (worst) and 9 is the highest (best) rating.

Source: The Marketing Matrix (adapted from T. Levitt, *The Marketing Mode: Pathways to Corporate Growth* (New York: McGraw-Hill, 1969), p. 220.

Exhibit 41-5
A Typology of Municipal Services*

	Essential		Nonessential	
	Compensatory	Noncompensatory	Compensatory	Noncompensatory
Undifferentiated:	Subways Buses Water Sewer Sanitation	Fire Police Courts	Zoo	Parks Libraries Radio-TV Stations
Differentiated:	Low-income Housing	Welfare Medical Care Primary Schools Secondary Schools	Museums Universities Swimming Pools Skating Rinks	

* Essential services are services without which a city could not long survive. Nonessential services are those which, if absolutely necessary, a city could function without. Undifferentiated services are those which the vast majority of the city population uses; differentiated services are utilized selectively. Compensatory services generate revenues sufficient to defray all or part of their costs of operation whereas noncompensatory services are supported entirely by taxes.

ganizational objective vary, depending upon whether the city service is compensatory (revenue-producing) or noncompensatory?

(5) How should a city go about determining what city services, especially nonessential ones, to offer its citizens?

(6) What happens when the taxes needed to support a plethora of city services become too high? What can city management do about it?

(7) Does marketing-type philosophy really have anything to contribute to managing a city government?

Finally, you know that New York officials have formidable public relations and personal selling tasks to perform if they are to convince federal government officials to help the city financially. Even though you may be personally opposed to such aid, you know nonetheless that seeking federal financial help is in your client's best interests. You wonder what arguments and appeals would have the best chances of effecting attitude change among key Washington figures.

You know that you will come under tough questioning at the EFCB meeting, no matter what you say. Many of the officials in attendance will not have much knowledge of marketing. Some individuals may fail to see its relevancy to managing a city and, consequently, could be hostile. There is only one week until your presentation and you have a lot of work to do to get ready.

Developing a Religious Program

Denis F. Healy, University of Delaware
M. Wayne DeLozier, University of South Carolina

Robert Murray was contemplating the problems facing his church. The General Council of the Methodist Church was in its quadrennial meeting and as president of the conference, Bob Murray was faced with a burdensome responsibility. Membership and attendance were declining. He faced a decision between the practical and the ideal which he learned from the seminary. Specifically, the practical problem was to reverse declining membership in the United Methodist Church. Ideally, his basic commitment was to convert people throughout the world to Christianity. His personal goal had always been to bring people to know Christ and not to "play the numbers game" of increasing enrollments in the Methodist Church.

Over the past several years, Bob had taken a number of courses at the university for self-edification. Both the Church and his personal beliefs were instrumental in his seeking a continuing education in the arts, psychology, history, and business. Bob believed that to be a good minister it was important that he learn about and keep current in a wide array of subjects. Several psychology courses had proven useful to Bob in marriage counseling, human relations, and developing sermons. In the past two years, Bob had taken several courses in business administration. His finance and accounting courses helped him to develop a church budget and to obtain financing for new building projects. Recently, he took an MBA course in marketing management and began to feel that churches and other nonprofit organizations could benefit from an understanding and use of marketing concepts.

During his marketing management course, Bob wondered how he might apply the marketing concepts he was learning to his church. Although a church is not "out to make a *financial* profit," it is out to win souls for Christ, which, he felt, could be analagous in a sense to a business profit.

At first, these notions seemed crass, almost sacrilegious. But the more Bob thought about it, the more he felt that he should reverently consider the application of marketing and business principles to his church. During the course he elected to do a research project on the application of marketing perspectives to the religious institution. His research provided him with several revelations. The following is a copy of Bob's research paper.

The Application of Marketing
Perspectives to the Religious Institution
by
Robert N. Murray

One might ask when viewing the religious waters
of today, "Is the pond deep?" to which I would
reply, "No, it's only muddy."

Rev. R. H. Hayden

In its report, "Religion in America: 1976," the *Gallup Opinion Index* indicates that organized religion appears to be holding its own after a period of sharp decline in the 1960s. On the other hand, the study shows that there is considerable belief that organized religion has "failed to meet the needs of the people." This indictment is lodged chiefly by those in the younger age groups.[1]

Like all social institutions, the religious institution functions in a dynamic environment. Changes in life-styles, family structures, and socal attitudes have a major impact on religious practices and organizations. To survive and be of value to society and to the individual, the various organized forms of religion must become more aware of the changing social fabric and must develop better ways of accomplishing their mission.[2]

Various approaches used to improve the relationship of the institution with its public, range from tactical changes in the organization or its services to strategic changes, such as actions taken as a result of Vatican II. Frequently, the methods employed depend heavily on persuasive communications or ceremonies, events or atmospherics to entice wayward believers and nonbelievers to the institution and to solidify other existing relationships.

Where the orthodox religions have faltered or responded inappropriately, new religious movements have filled the gap. Such movements result from the mutual interaction of four important variables, the intersection of the established social order and innovative individuals, institutions supportive of particularistic needs, the American tradition of self-help, and the stress resulting from rapid social change.[3]

The religious bodies that are flourishing are those that have identified, clarified, and satisfied the basic needs of individuals to find the ultimate truth and to have

---

[1] Tom Reinken (editor), *Religion in America: 1976* (Princeton, NJ: The Gallup Opinion Index, 1976), Report No. 130.

[2] Gibson Winter, *The New Creation as Metropolis* (New York: Macmillan, 1963); Gerald Heard, *The Human Venture* (New York: Harper, 1955); Irving I. Zaretsky and Mark P. Leone, *Religious Movements in Contemporary America* (Princeton: Princeton University Press, 1974); Martin E. Marty and Dean G. Peerman (editors), *New Theology No. 8: On the Cultural Revolution* (New York: Macmillan, 1971).

[3] Zaretsky and Leone (editors), *op. cit.*, p. 11.

a personal relationship with a supreme being. The success of these religious groups can be attributed to their theological foundations, their resource gathering capabilities, and their skill in applying marketing concepts and principles to the accomplishment of their mission.

Trends in the Religious Institution

Changing life-styles, attitudes towards religion, and the influence of other institutions present opportunities and threats to the survival and vitality of the religious institution. The Gallup organization conducts extensive, periodic surveys of religious beliefs and practices in America and throughout the world, thereby making it possible to see the development of trends in such areas as membership, attendance, attitudes towards various belief systems, and the perceived influence of religion on life-styles. Selected findings from the fifth study in the Gallup series (*Religion in America: 1976*) are presented below to document the nature and direction of change in the institution.[4]

First Gallup found that of the industrial nations, the United States led the list in terms of the importance given to religious belief (56 percent—very important; 34 percent—important). Of all the major areas studied, the African (73 percent; 13 percent) and Far Eastern (71 percent; 16 percent) nations were leaders and Western European (27 percent; 32 percent) nations were last in terms of importance ascribed to religious beliefs. In addition, there appears to be widespread belief in a universal spirit or the existence of God. The extremes are Africa (96 percent expressed belief) to Western Europe (78 percent expressed belief). And in terms of immortality, in the African nations studied, 69 percent of the respondents indicated belief, although in Western Europe, only 44 percent reported belief in life after death. In virtually every category of the study, the United States was at or near the top of the list of nations expressing strong religious belief, and positive attitudes and behaviors toward religious expression and practice.

Contrary to popular opinion, the Gallup study also found that religious belief and practice in America has remained relatively stable over the past 25 years. The findings do suggest, however, that a "collapse of faith" may be occurring in certain European nations and other scattered areas of the world.

Religious preference in the United States has also been tracked over the past decade by Gallup. Tables 42–1 and 42–2 show the pattern and trend of religious preferences in the United States since the mid-1960s. There have been marked shifts in preference with a decline of seven percentage points (10.3 percent for Protestantism and a gain of four percentage points [200 percent]) for those indicating no religious preference.

As shown in Table 42–3, the sharpest decline in denominational preference for the period 1964 to 1974 has been among Methodists. Other sources indicate that the number of Methodists has dropped by one million between 1966 and 1976 and that unless something happens to reverse the trend, another one million will be lost by 1985.

---

[4] Virtually all of the information presented in this section has been obtained from Reninken, Ed., *Religion in America, 1976.*

Table   42–1
Religious Preferences in the United States

	Protestant	Roman Catholic	Jews	All Others	No Religious Preference
LATEST	61%	27%	2%	4%	6%
1974	60	27	2	5	6
1971	65	26	3	2	4
1966	68	25	3	2	2

Table   42–2
Protestant Preferences
(As a percent of total U.S. population)

	1975	1974	1969	1967
Baptist	20%	21%	21%	21%
Methodist	11	14	14	14
Lutheran	7	7	7	7
Presbyterian	5	6	6	6
Episcopalian	3	3	3	3

The growth of the Southern Baptist Convention has been the greatest, for the period 1964–1974 nearly 1.9 million new members. The increase of 700,000 new members over the 1971–1974 period is dramatic, particularly in light of the record of the other denominations listed.

During the 1960s, many young people became disenchanted with formal religious belief and practice. Declines in regular attendance at church services, particularly of those under 30 years of age, dropped steadily from about 40 percent attendance in the 1960s to 30 percent at the beginning of the 1970s. The figure has held firm since then. Today about 40 percent of the total population attends church or synagogue service weekly and about 20 percent take part in other religious programs and events during a typical week.

Table 42–4 shows a comparison of attendance trends between Catholics and Protestants for various age groups. Note the dramatic drop in Catholic attendance during the decade. Attendance at synagogue services among Jews has remained stable, according to Gallup, with about 20 percent attending services during a typical week. Other factors affecting attendance at religious services, other than age and denomination, are education, sex, marital status, and regional location. Table 42–5 summarizes these relationships.

Table   42–3
Membership in Major U.S. Religious Bodies
1964–1974

Religious Body	Membership (millions of persons)			
	1974	1971	1966	1964
The Roman Catholic Church	48.7	48.4	46.8	45.6
The Southern Baptist Convention	12.5	11.8	10.9	10.6
United Methodist	10.1	10.5	10.3	10.3
Jewish Congregations	n/a	5.9	5.7	5.6
The Lutheran Church in America	3.0	3.1	3.1	3.1
The Episcopal Church	2.9	3.2	3.4	3.3
The Lutheran Church—Missouri Synod	2.8	2.8	2.7	2.7
The United Presbyterian Church in the United States of America	2.7	3.0	3.3	3.3
The American Lutheran Church	2.5 [2]	2.5	n/a	2.6
The Greek Orthodox Archdiocese of North and South America	2.0 [1]	2.0	n/a	1.7
The United Church of Christ	1.8	1.9	2.1	2.1
The National Primitive Baptist Convention	n/a	1.6	1.2	n/a
American Baptist Churches in the United States of America	1.6	1.6	1.6	1.6
American Baptist Association	1.1 [1]	0.8	0.7	0.7
The Presbyterian Church in the United States	0.9	0.9	0.9	0.9

[1] 1975 data
[2] 1973 data
Source: Yearbook of American and Canadian Churches, Office of Research, Evaluation and Planning of the National Council of the Churches of Christ in the USA, 1965–1976.

Finally, and importantly, the Gallup survey has regularly asked, "At the present time, do you think religion as a whole is increasing its influence in American life or losing its influence?" The results, presented in Table 42–6, show a dramatic and encouraging reversal in the downward movement of the past several years. Nevertheless, over 50 percent of the respondents indicated that religion is losing influence.

The trends discussed above suggest that the religious institution and its component bodies are participants in and agents of change. There are a multitude of complex forces acting on the institution and society that, over time, must be identified and responded to if the institution, and particularly the mainline religious bodies, is to survive. Harvey Cox, in viewing the contemporary religious scene, believes that:

Table 42–4
Attended Church in a Typical Week

	Catholics	Protestants
Adults under 30 years old		
1975	39%	31%
1974	41	30
1973	38	29
1972	45	29
1966	55	31
30–49 years old		
1975	56%	38%
1974	57	36
1973	56	37
1972	56	37
1966	71	38
50 years and older		
1975	64%	42%
1974	66	42
1973	68	42
1972	69	39
1966	76	41

Table 42–5
Other Factors Associated with
Attendance at Church Services

	Likelihood of Attendance	
Factor	Relatively Low	Relatively High
Marital Status	Single	Married
Regional Location	East, West	Midwest, South
Sex	Men	Women
Education	Noncollege	College

Table 42–6
Influence of Religion

Question: "At the present time, do you think religion as a whole is increasing its influence on American life or losing its influence?"

	Increasing	Losing
LATEST	39%	51%
1974	31	56
1970	14	75
1969	14	70
1968	18	67
1967	23	57
1965	33	45
1962	45	31
1957	69	14

Some form of institutionalized religious expression is going to survive. Man is not only a religious being but a social one as well. He's not going to accept a completely do-it-yourself approach on anything this central to survival. Oh, the denominational type of Christianity headquartered in skyscrapers with branch officers in the suburbs is fated for rapid extinction, and it can't disappear too quickly for me. Yet, some form will rise out of the present resurgence of spiritual concern.[5]

Environmental Pressures on the Religious Institution

Religion is under great pressure because the traditional organizations have failed either to recognize the need to adapt or have been unable to respond effectively. This situation has caused Martin Marty to write:

The massive silhouette the churches create on the American skyline is that of a self-preservative institutionalism . . . The clergyman exists as a promoter of the organization . . . Since the institutional self-interest preoccupies the churches and does not directly serve the community it seems to incarnate irrelevance.[6]

There are a host of factors which present opportunities and threats to the religious institution. Although it is impossible to present an exhaustive listing of even the major areas of change, several important factors are listed below:

1. The changing character and role of the family unit.

2. The shifting demographic patterns of the population, especially the growth of the 25 to 44 year-old age group.

---

[5] T. George Harris, "Religion in the Age of Aquarius: A Conversation with Harvey Cox and T. George Harris," *Psychology Today*, April 1970.

[6] Martin E. Marty, *Second Chance for American Protestants* (New York: Harper, 1963), p. 65.

3. The continuing controversy over the degradation of the physical environment.

4. The growing impact of technology in such areas as the life sciences, nuclear physics, neurology.

5. The shifting character and role of the educational and governmental institutions.

6. The growing use of and addiction to artificial stimulants.

7. The increasing challenge to the quality of human relationships as evidenced by crime levels, poverty, human rights, and hunger.

8. The decreasing adherence to the Protestant work ethic.

9. The expanding allegiance to the need for instant gratification.

10. The declining confidence in business and political leaders as a result of numerous "Watergates."

11. The increasing secularization of society and the growing role of non-religious institutions in the solution of human problems.

12. The growing importance of empiricism.

13. The changing attitudes and life-styles of all age groups.[7]

Some of these factors may be the result rather than the cause of pressure on the religious institution, but there is no question that all are affecting and will continue to affect the nature and extent of religious belief and practice.

The challenge to the institution is clear, according to O'Dea:

> . . . to be relevant today, religion must support those human aspirations that cry for fulfillment in terms of the modern technological capacity. It must become relevant to the effort toward a more abundant life for man. It must teach not only the appropriateness of justice, wisdom, fortitude, and courage, but it must also bear witness to a faith, hope, and charity rendered relevant to the new world man has made and the new man whose promise it contains.[8]

Engel and Blackwell indicate that changing social values, such as the growing need for "immediate gratification," may be a factor bringing about a growing allegiance to movements which deal directly with leading a better life today or which deal with improving interpersonal as well as intrapersonal relationships. They point out that ". . . many within the organized church seem to be oblivious to

---

[7] These observations are based in part on the work of Margaret Mead, *Twentieth Century Faith* (New York: Harper, 1972), pp. 88–112; Merton P. Strommen (editor), *Research on Religious Development* (New York: Hawthorne, 1972); Allan W. Eister, *Changing Perspectives in the Scientific Study of Religion* (New York: John Wiley and Sons, 1974); Louis Schneider, *Sociological Approach to Religion* (New York: John Wiley and Sons, 1970); Martin E. Marty and Dean G. Peerman (editors), *New Theology No. 10: The Ethical and Theological Issues Raised by Recent Developments in the Life Sciences* (New York: Macmillan, 1973).

[8] Thomas F. O'Dea, "The Crisis of Contemporary Religious Consciousness," *Daedalus,* winter, 1967.

these changes." [9] Even the most cursory examination of traditional methods used to disseminate religious truth would lead one to conclude that preachers and churches have confused, ritualized, used elaborate rhetoric, and buried the message they seek to communicate. Furthermore, according to Margaret Mead:

> Christian institutions continue to follow an inappropriate, inadequate and no longer relevant style of individual Christian charity. In doing so, they surrender to the secular world . . . the wider goals of feeding the hungry, caring for the sick, and protecting the poor. [10]

Those religious bodies which have grown, on the other hand, have several attributes in common. They tend to be readily distinguishable from other bodies. They have precise and easily understood requirements for membership. And they tend to have well-organized and highly effective promotional units dedicated to increasing membership and to reinforcing the values and belief systems of members.

In an era where reverence for pragmatism, materialism, and empiricism appears to be the norm, there is rapidly growing interest in the transcendental. [11] Although many would have thought that the emergence of a technological culture would mark the downfall of transcendence, further reflection indicates that:

> . . . just as the disappearance of transcendence was enforced by the dominance of technology, the reaction against technological control induces a search to escape its electronic confines. [12]

Harvey Cox, in examining the reasons why individuals (especially the young) are gravitating by the millions to the mystical, neo-Oriental systems, identified four basic objectives being satisfied by the movements:

1. Friendship—seeking of warmth, affection, close ties of feeling, a sense of belonging.
2. Immediacy—direct encounter with God, life, nature, other people—absence of complexity of ideas, ritual, concepts.
3. Authority—need to overcome uncertainty, doubt, confusion—reduce "over-choice"—simplify.
4. Natural—need for purity, freshness, rejection of traditionalism and the effete nature of organized religion. [13]

The long-term impact of these environmental changes on the moral, ethical, and intellectual character of society must be of concern to all institutions, especially

---

[9] James F. Engel and Roger D. Blackwell, "Communicating Religious Truth in a Changing World," paper presented at the American Marketing Association Educators' Conference, Boston, MA, 1970.

[10] Margaret Mead in Hugh C. White, Jr. (editor), *Christians in a Technological Era* (New York: Seabury, 1964), p. 17.

[11] Martin E. Marty and Dean G. Peerman (editors), *New Theology No. 7: The Recovery of Transcendence* (New York: Macmillan, 1970).

[12] Frederick Sontag and John K. Roth, *The American Religious Experience: The Roots, Trends and Future of American Theology* (New York: Harper, 1972), p. 298.

[13] Harvey Cox, "Why Young Americans Are Buying Oriental Religions," *Psychology Today*, July 1977, pp. 36–42.

the religious institution. Gerald Heard, in observing the response of society to increasing complexity and technological sophistication commented:

> . . . every time man has made a new physical invention giving him more control over his outer world, he has had to make a corresponding psychological invention to hold himself together.[14]

A Model of the Religious System

By definition, a system consists of a set of organized units and the interactions between the units. For the purposes of this paper, the only interactions to be discussed are between the religious institution, the believer/nonbeliever publics, and the system of beliefs. The composition of the subsystems and the generic nature of transactions between subsystems are described in this section.

The religious institution operates in a complex environment in which it must be both formative and adaptive. The institution, when placed in an environmental context, may be viewed as a system in which various bodies or organizations interact to accomplish mutual objectives. The religious system, as diagrammed in Figure 42–1, includes the religious institution, the major constituencies of the institution, the system of beliefs, and the environment. These major system components (subsystems) interact in a variety of ways, and thereby shape the mission and practices of all religious bodies.

The religious institution plays a change-agent role in bridging the gap between the public and the system of beliefs. The institution is a mechanism for assisting individuals to seek ultimate truth, profess their faith, and obtain religious experiences. As a result, one of the institution's principal tasks is to facilitate the communication of religious truth. As indicated in Figure 42–1, the institution can be circumvented and the system of beliefs can be pursued individually and directly. Survival and growth of the institution is dictated by how well it can articulate a set of programs which aid the laity in achieving its objectives.

The Religious Institution

This subsystem contains the numerous religious bodies which have been designed to advocate and communicate a particular system of beliefs. In addition to the major bodies of Catholicism, Judaism, and Protestantism, there are other bodies such as Islam, Buddhism, and the neo-Oriental groups. There are approximately 221 organized religious groups with over 300,000 churches and over 130 million active members in the United States.[15]

The religious institution contains groups that are highly organized and managed, such as those listed in Table 42–3, as well as newer and less structured groups about which little is known. When viewed from an institutional life cycle perspective, some of these bodies are in the growth state, others are mature, and still others may be in the decline phase.[16]

---

[14] Gerald Heard, *The Human Venture* (New York: Harper 1955), p. x.

[15] This information is a result of a compilation of the National Council of the Churches of Christ, *Yearbook of American and Canadian Churches,* 1976. The data are based on information reported by the various churches, each with its own set of membership requirements.

[16] Zaretsky and Leone, *op. cit.,* p. 768.

Figure   42–1
A Model of the Religions System

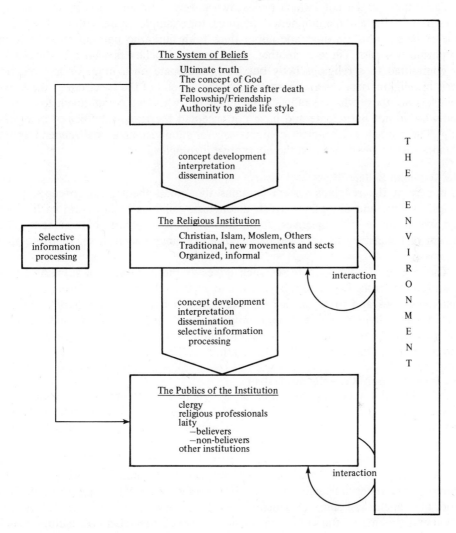

The System of Beliefs

Ultimate truth
The concept of God
The concept of life after death
Fellowship/Friendship
Authority to guide life style

concept development
interpretation
dissemination

The Religious Institution

Christian, Islam, Moslem, Others
Traditional, new movements and sects
Organized, informal

interaction

Selective
information
processing

concept development
interpretation
dissemination
selective information
processing

The Publics of the Institution

clergy
religious professionals
laity
    —believers
    —non-believers
other institutions

interaction

THE ENVIRONMENT

The Major Publics of the Institution

There are two basic ways to view the publics of the religious institution. From an ideological standpoint, there are those who have allied themselves to a particular system of beliefs ("the Believers") and those who have not ("the non-Believers"). From a societal perspective, the publics are represented by those who play major roles in the total institutional structure. By this definition, the publics would include those in government, education, and business, as well as those associated directly with the religious institution. Considering the specific membership of the "Believer" public one can identify a wide range of commitments expressed by individuals. For instance, there are the levels of clergy, next are the nonordained religious professionals, such as nuns, lay ministers, and educators.

Then, there is the laity which on its own covers a broad spectrum in terms of strength of belief and commitment. One finds, for example, those with total belief—true believers who are dogmatic about their faith and who participate actively in corporate worship. There is another large group of believers who are less active or committed to a religious body but who participate on a more or less regular basis in religious services and programs. At the far end of the spectrum of the laity-believers are those who are officially members but who lack commitment to a body and who do not participate and have not accepted the responsibilities of membership. The nonbeliever segment contains several subdivisions as well depending on the intensity of resistance and the alternative ideologies held.[17]

The System of Beliefs

This part of the religious system contains the broad theological concepts, principles, canons, and disciplines which distinguish religious bodies from each other and which shape the objectives, faith, and religious practices of members. The system of beliefs, by its very nature, tends to be anchored in a set of irrefutable axioms.

The system of beliefs addresses such issues as the concept of a supreme being and ultimate truth. It provides a visible and focused means for believers to attain their objectives and to organize their lives. In this context, the system of beliefs provides an individual with an opportunity to achieve higher levels of understanding and fellowship, to identify with an authoritative force for guilding life direction, and to reinforce the belief in life after death.[18]

The Environment of the Religious System

Surrounding the religious institution is a dynamic environment which contains all the other institutional structures and systems of society. At any particular point in time, these other institutions and systems impose pressures on the religious sector as described earlier. For instance, in some Communist countries the government exerts debilitating force on the religious institution. In the United States, some have accused the business institution of secularizing society by marketing products giving temporal and material benefits and thus drawing people away from products offering more permanent and spiritual benefits.

Other segments of the environment also influence the religious institution and practice. The family and the educational system, in particular, are major transmitters of values and knowledge. The changing objectives and behaviors of these sectors influence the religious institution by shaping the values, beliefs, and life styles of the members of society.

---

[17] For a particularly stimulating and philosophical treatment of the concept of faith and belief refer to Paul Tillich, *The Courage To Be* (New Haven: Yale University Press, 1952) and Paul Tillich, *Dynamics of Faith* (New York: Harper, 1957).

[18] The issues in this section are theological in nature and beyond the scope of this paper. The topic is covered in the following works: Elton Trueblood, *A Place to Stand* (New York: Harper, 1969); Goodenough, *The Psychology of Religious Experiences;* Cox, *The Seduction of the Spirit* (New York: Simon and Schuster, 1973); O'Dea, *op. cit.;* Marty and Peerman, *op. cit.;* Heard, *op. cit.*

Interactions Within the System

Although numerous flows within the system will be considered in the context of marketing activity, the principal flow of concern here relates to information creation and transfer. As noted previously, the religious institution is a change agent in the process. The principal activity of the institution, relative to the system of beliefs, involves the interpretation of religious principles, the development of religious concepts, and the dissemination of such knowledge throughout the institution, namely to the clergy and religious professionals.

The interaction between the institution and the laity involves a host of transactions which, in the broadest sense, involve marketing communication activities designed to bring the message closer to the psyche of the laity and to bring the laity closer to the system of beliefs. The response to communication attempts is highly selective and frequently many attempts must be made before awareness is achieved. For the information dissemination process to reach high levels of effectiveness, the laity must not only become aware of, but also must comprehend, retain, and be influenced by the communication.[19]

The success or failure of a particular religious body, as well as the religious institution as a whole, is directly affected by how effectively it engages in these transactions. The most visible measure of performance is in terms of the membership and participation levels. A less visible and more profound index of institutional effectiveness is the level and trend of religious fervor of faith exhibited by the laity. Table 42–7 presents a brief descriptive listing of the main methods of interaction with the religious institution and the system of beliefs.

Identifying the Marketing Issues Confronting the Religious Institution

It is evident from the previous analysis that the system is in a state of flux. Moreover, it is apparent that the institution survives and grows by how effectively and

---

[19] Everett M. Rogers and F. Floyd Shoemaker, *Communication of Innovations* (New York: Free Press, 1971) and James F. Engel, David T. Kollat, and Roger D. Blackwell, *Consumer Behavior*, 2nd ed. (New York: Holt, Rinehart and Winston, 1973).

Table   42–7
Methods of Interaction with the Institution and
The System of Beliefs

Worship —	a prayer, service, or other rite showing reverence for a deity
Evangelism —	a preaching of, or zealous effort to spread the gospel, as in a revival meeting
Catechize —	to teach by the method of question and answer
Stewardship—	the giving of one's time and energies to support the organization
Liturgy —	prescribed forms or ritual for public worship in any of various Christian churches

efficiently it communicates information about the system of beliefs and how well it provides religious experiences.

The marketing perspective and the use of marketing management approaches can help the institution and its various bodies understand the forces on the system and can aid in the development of religious programs. The use of the marketing approach should assist religious leaders in making decisions about such issues as:

1. Are there identifiable segments of the laity that would selectively respond to one approach versus another?

2. What organizational structures and objectives are appropriate to the accomplishment of the religious objectives and programs?

3. What kinds of information are needed to better understand the behaviors and expectations of the laity?

4. What can be done to expand interest and participation in religious vocations?

5. Is it possible to design religious communications and experiences for various segments?

6. Is there any way to explain and emulate the dramatic impact of the neo-Oriental approaches on wide segments of the population?

These questions and others of a similar nature can be addressed by the application of marketing concepts and techniques, such as marketing research, market segmentation, marketing auditing and planning, and consumer behavior.

Marketing Program Development

A basic marketing program development model provides a useful marketing perspective for planning religious programs.[20] The flow of this model moves from consideration of market opportunities and a definition of the generic product of the organization, to marketing segmentation (target market selection), to the development, implementation, and control of programs for each target market. The Enis model has been adapted to the religious institution and is presented in Figure 42–2.

The basic product of the institution is providing religious experiences. This is accomplished through the dissemination of information about the system of beliefs and involvement of the laity in religious services and other programs. Once the generic product has been clearly defined, there is a need to examine the characteristics of various segments of the laity. In addition, as shown in Figure 42–2, organizational and operating characteristics of the religious body must be considered. For instance, in some bodies, the hierarchical structure is so inflexible that developing effective religious programs for some market segments may be impossible. By reconciling the characteristics of various segments of the laity with the strengths and weaknesses of the particular body, a series of viable target markets should become identifiable. Several possible segments are shown in Figure 42–2. As

---

[20] Ben M. Enis, *Marketing Principles: The Management Process* (Pacific Palisades, CA: Goodyear, 1974).

Figure   42–2
Framework for Marketing Program Development in the Religious Institution

Generic Product/Service

The dissemination of:
• the ultimate truth
• a system of beliefs

Segment Characteristics

• Believers/Nonbelievers
• Demographic/attitudinal
  characteristics
• Laity, Clergy
• Other publics

Organizational Characteristics

• Organizational flexibility/rigidity
• Financial flows and structure
• Receptivity to management principles, organizational
  development or marketing activity
• Clergy and religious professional strengths and
  weaknesses

Target Market Selection

• Receptive believers
• Youth
• Other special interest groups
• Nonbelievers

Selection of Specific Product/Service Elements

• Worship services
• Social action projects
• Educational programs
• Religious events

Formulation of the Marketing Program

• Configuration (product) considerations
• Valuation (price) considerations
• Symbolization (promotion) considerations
• Facilitation (place) considerations

Implementation of the Marketing Program

• Clergy and religious professional responsibilities
• The location, timing, and frequency of the offering
• The ritual/ceremonial approach

Control and Evaluation of the Program

• Attendance levels at worship services, education programs, etc.
• Survey and informal feedback
• Duration of membership
• Revenues
• Conversions
• Stewardship reports

important as delineating viable target markets is the identification of areas which cannot be effectively reached under present conditions. This is not to suggest that nonviable segments be abandoned. Rather, the purpose is to point out that certain segments can be reached only by alteration of either the organizational structure or conduct of the religious body.

For each target market there is likely to be a unique, total religious offering which will be perceived as having high potential value by members of the segment. For example, those with a strong orientation toward the philosophical and theological aspects of religion would be most interested in programs involving worship, scripture reading, seminars, and events with high symbolic content. For those seeking social involvement, participation would most likely be highest in social action programs, service activities, and fellowship events.

The total religious offering is the end result of marketing programming activity. Marketing programming involves the creation and augmentation of the basic product offering by the commitment to and coordination of activities in each of the marketing decision variables (the marketing mix elements). Combining elements of one area with those of other areas results in the creation of unique total product offerings tailored to the needs of the target market segments. These programs may be altered as conditions change.

In summary, this paper has attempted to demonstrate the applicability of marketing concepts to the forces acting on and within the religious institution. Through the use of current marketing principles, religious institutions should be able to carry out their missions more effectively.

The Current Situation

Bob was delighted to receive an "A" on his research project, but was wondering what all of this means to him and to his work for God. His paper was written in an "objective" sense as a student in a marketing course, but did it have relevance for him? Did he do the paper for a grade? Did he sacrifice his religious beliefs and training? Or did he take a close look at what his faith was trying to accomplish?

Bob wondered if the marketing ideas he had learned were really applicable to his mission. If so, how could he translate these concepts into a religious, and particularly a Methodist, framework? He also wondered how he could make "managerial use" of his research to better the Methodist church and his conviction in Christ. Furthermore, how could he present these ideas to the General Conference?

Discussion Questions

1. As with any organization, churches have missions, goals, and objectives. State what you feel are several goals of the religious institutions (clergy and religious professionals). What do you feel are the objectives of the laity?

2. From a marketing perspective, what are the "products" (product mix) offered by a religious institution? Describe the "pricing" element, the "promotion" element, and the "place" element in the religious institution's "marketing mix."

3. What marketing management principles would you recommend that Bob Murray use to attain the objectives you stated in your answers to question 1? How would you use them?

4. If you were Bob Murray, how would you present ("sell") your ideas on applying marketing principles to the Methodist Church to the General Conference?

5. Are marketing principles new to religious institutions or have they been using them for thousands of years without labeling them as such?

6. What are your feelings about applying marketing principles to religious institutions?

Marketing a Nontraditional Product: College Sports Programs

Philip E. Downs, Sarah Bane, and William D. Binion
The College of William and Mary

In September 1977, the College of William and Mary's football team was expected to have its most successful season in 6 years. Sportswriters of state newspapers predicted a 9–2 record. Sam Baker, director of promotions for the Athletic Department, was optimistic that season ticket sales would reach the highest point ever. Since his hiring just 6 months earlier, he had worked hard to promote the revenue-producing sports program at William and Marry and to increase the season ticket sales for both football and basketball. His hard work was paying off. It had to, because the program had depended on student athletic fees to meet expenses but had to be totally self-sufficient by 1979.

Background

The second oldest institution of higher learning in the United States, the College of William and Mary was founded in 1693. A state-supported, coeducational university, the college had an enrollment of 5,280 students in 1976. A highly selective admissions program has worked to keep academic requirements stringent for prospective students. The mean college score for 1036 freshmen in the 1976 class was 1220. Because the College of William and Mary is a state-supported institution, 70 percent of the freshmen were Virginia residents.

From its beginning, the orientation of the college has been strongly academic. Phi Beta Kappa was founded at William and Mary in 1776, and the first Honor System was begun there in 1779. Thomas Jefferson as well as many other famous Americans were graduates.

Located in historic Williamsburg, Virginia, the campus covers more than 1200 acres. The Sir Christopher Wren Building, the oldest academic building in continuous use in the United States, is located at one end of the famous Duke of Gloucester Street and houses the College's English Department. Thus, the college campus is part of the historic area (colonial Williamsburg), visited by 1.25 million tourists during 1976.

Thomas Graves, president, has stated that the goals of the institution are to remain a small coeducational university with primary emphasis on the development of the whole individual through a liberal arts education.

Priority of Athletics at William and Mary

The battle of athletics versus academics has been fought at the college for many years. In a 1974 decision, the board of visitors, the governing body at the college, established a policy to upgrade the entire sports program at William and Mary. This decision set the course for the future of the Athletic Department. The student newspaper, *The Flat Hat,* reported the final proposal to be a compromise among those who wanted a strong sports program, those who didn't, those who wanted parity for women's sports, and students who wanted to stop paying the $64 per semester fee to subsidize the athletic program. The final approved proposal permitted upgrading football and basketball, but also required that these sports become self-sufficient by 1979. At that time, the college would stop subsidizing the revenue sports but continue its support of the 13 nonrevenue producing sports for both men and women. This program, it was felt, would allow William and Mary to develop an athletic program which would grow and complement the academic orientation of the college.

Sources of Revenue for Football and Basketball Programs

One of the provisions of the 1974 decision was just beginning to receive publicity in March 1977. In 1979, student monies would not be available for athletic scholarships. The student fee would continue to pay for operating expenses of nonrevenue sports, but no scholarship money would be available. Presently, the college provides $44,000 for nonrevenue sports scholarships. In 1979, these programs must find a way to generate the funds or do without.

Ben Carnevale, athletic director at William and Mary, believes that 2 sources of funds, gate receipts and private contributions, must be further utilized to meet expenses as of 1979. Currently, these sources fund between 60 and 70 percent of the entire athletic budget. In 1976–1977, gate receipts totalled $350,000 while the Athletic Educational Foundation (AEF) fund drive netted $261,000. The 1977–78 Athletic Department budget is presented in Table 43–1.

Past Promotional Policies
(up to 1977)

The William and Mary Athletic Department has never had anyone formally in charge of ticket promotion until Sam Baker was appointed in April 1977. Past efforts focused on trying to resell season tickets to those who previously had shown

Table   43–1
Athletic Department Budget
1977–78*

Revenues			
Gate Receipts			
Football		$275,000	
Basketball		75,000	
AEF Contribution		250,000	
Student Fees		675,840	$1,275,840
Expenses			
Revenue Sports:			
Football	$580,000		
Basketball	133,000	$713,000	
Nonrevenue Sports		143,000	
Other:			
Administrative	164,250		
Medical	40,250		
Publicity	40,000		
Contingencies	10,000	254,500	$1,110,500

* Estimated by authors.

an interest in William and Mary sports. Typically, someone in the Athletic Department would be given responsibility for assuring that past season ticketholders were contacted by letter, requesting that they resubscribe.

Therefore, Sam Baker was faced with some rather serious problems. Since no previous work had been conducted, he would have to build a promotional program in one year to support both the football and basketball programs. There also was the possibility that if the revenue sports were profitable enough, funds could be diverted to the other nonrevenue sports to partially meet their needs.

Because there was neither a set plan nor followup in the past, ticket sales for football and basketball games had been erratic, at best. Sales and football and basketball team records for the past five years are shown in Table 43–2. A breakdown of 1976–77 season ticket sales by various ticket and spectator classifications is shown in Table 43–3.

Various ticket prices are available and are dependent upon "placement" (end zone, 50-yard line, etc.) and whether a special discount is justified. For example, a military rate is available to qualified personnel. It is reasoned that certain incentives

Table   43–2
Sales and Team Records for
Football and Basketball, 1972–77

Year	Football		Basketball	
	Season Tickets Sold	Team Record	Season Tickets Sold	Team Record
1976–77	1,464	7–4	998	16–14
1975–76	1,551	2–9	928	15–13
1974–75	1,689	4–7	1,645	16–12
1973–74	1,749	6–5	1,741	8–18
1972–73	1,536	5–6	765	10–17

Table   43–3
Season Ticket Sales, 1976–77

	Football		Basketball	
	Number of Tickets	$ Price Per Season Ticket*	Number of Tickets	$ Price Per Season Ticket
Military	36	20 and 12	0	n/a
End Zone	131	16	n/a	n/a
Regular	1,029	28, 20, 16	846	$35
Faculty	204	20 and 12	152	$28
Total	1,400		998	
Revenue: Football	$46,037			
Basketball	$33,866			

* Four home games.

are necessary to make season tickets "desirable" to various classes of people. Included in this special class are ministers, faculty, and military. Community groups also can get discounts if they order a minimum of 25 tickets for a single athletic contest. To date, no one has taken advantage of the group rate.

With the new policy implementation nearing, Sam Baker had already taken steps, before his appointment in April 1977, to generate a promotional plan to sell season tickets. The problem, as he saw it, was not only to generate the funds necessary for revenue sports, but also to establish a policy for the Athletic Department to follow in the future to sustain season and general admission ticket sales.

Changes in Promotional Policies—1977

A recent recipient of his master's in sports communication, Sam Baker, an energetic and enthusiastic individual, received his undergraduate degree from James

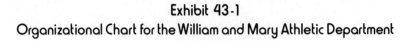

Exhibit 43-1

Organizational Chart for the William and Mary Athletic Department

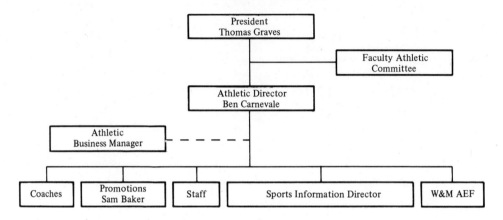

Madison University (Harrisonburg, Virginia) and his master's from Ohio University. The job that faced him now would require use of his Virginia background and his knowledge of Virginia sports. His job as director of promotions was newly created. The organizational chart for the Athletic Department, as shown in Exhibit 43-1, placed Mr. Baker directly under the Athletic Director.

Mr. Baker felt that his primary responsibility was to increase season ticket sales within the immediate area. The target market for sales would be Williamsburg and the surrounding metropolitan areas of Richmond, Hampton, and Newport News, Virginia. "In the past, we have had the reputation of being cliquish and selling only to alumni of the college. I want to change this and make the William and Mary sports program one where all the families of the area can enjoy good college sports," Mr. Baker commented.

To increase season ticket sales, Mr. Baker began asking for money to develop and implement a promotional campaign. In the past, season ticket sales were haphazardly approached with no monies allocated from the already tight Athletic Department's budget. With the following memo to the Athletic Director, Sam Baker began his work to develop a marketing plan for the revenue sports. (See Exhibit 43-2.)

Up until the summer of 1977, the Athletic Department had never promoted the sports program through paid advertising. Local radio stations publicized sports programs through public service announcements, promoted upcoming games, and broadcast most of the games to the Williamsburg audience. WTAR-TV in Norfolk, Virginia televises the Big Five Game of the Week (Big Five stands for the 5 major colleges in Virginia which have football programs), and William and Mary was televised several times in 1976.

Mr. Baker believed that William and Mary's sports audience includes all areas within an hour's driving distance of Williamsburg. This area includes Richmond, Norfolk, Newport News, and Hampton as well as the surrounding heavily populated

Exhibit 43 - 2
Memo to Ben Carnavale from Sam Baker

April 1, 1977

Memo to: Ben Carnavale

From: Sam Baker

Re: Promotional Budget

Since being named director of promotions, I have been looking over the budgeting needs necessary to do an adequate promotional job on football and basketball. I realize that the money available is limited, but I feel that $5,000 is necessary to begin our efforts. I have broken down the budget needs into the following areas:

Postage		
Football	$ 500	
Basketball	300	$ 800
Advertising		
Football	$2,300	
Basketball	1,500	3,800
Miscellaneous		400
TOTAL		$5,000

It will be necessary also to have the ability to use tickets for promotional giveaways and also for trade outs. I have plans to do some extensive radio and newspaper advertising during the months of July and August. In making preparations for this, I have talked with sales managers of many radio stations who are willing to take payment in tickets.

Tidewater area. All are within 60 miles of the campus, but each exhibits different characteristics so far as supporting William and Mary sports. Norfolk, with no major football teams, is expected to be a prime target for football. However, Mr. Baker did not expect Norfolk to have many potential basketball fans since the city's Old Dominion University (ODU) has been the NCAA Division II college basketball champion in recent years. ODU enjoyed a strong basketball following in the Norfolk area. Mr. Baker believed that only William and Mary alumni could be expected to support William and Mary basketball from the Norfolk area.

The Richmond area, approximately 50 miles away, has several colleges with basketball and football programs. Despite direct competition in the surrounding metropolitan areas, Richmond, Newport News, and Hampton all are considered to be prime target areas for ticket sales. Tables 43–4 and 43–5 and Exhibit 43–3 present income, population, and other data along with pertinent information for Williamsburg and the surrounding metropolitan areas.

Table   43–4
Annual Income*

	Norfolk/ Newport News	Richmond/ Tri-Cities
Households	332,700	283,865
Effective Buying Power (EBP)	$4,449,401,000	$3,508,855,000
EBP Per Household Income Distribution by Household:	$13,373	$12,361
Under $3,000	11.4%	8.3%
$ 3,000 to $ 4,999	7.8	9.5
$ 5,000 to $ 7,999	13.7	19.1
$ 8,000 to $ 9,999	10.5	14.1
$10,000 to $14,000	25.9	28.5
$15,000 and over	31.6	20.0
Total	100.0%	100.0%

* Figures for SMSAs were used.
Sources: 1975 Sales Management "Survey of Buying Power," *Characteristics of Population: Virginia,* Department of Commerce; WRVQ Research Department.

Table   43–5
Metro Population

	Miles from Williamsburg	1960	1970	Growth
Norfolk	46	304,869	307,951	1.0%
Portsmouth	49	114,773	110,963	−3.3
Chesapeake	62	73,647	89,580	21.6
Virginia Beach	58	85,200	172,106	102.0
Newport News	29	113,662	138,177	21.6
Hampton	25	89,258	120,779	35.3
Williamsburg	0	6,832	9,069	32.7
York County	(adjacent to Williamsburg)	21,558	33,203	53.8
Richmond	49	219,958	249,430	13.4
Hopewell	41	17,895	23,471	31.1
Colonial Heights	51	9,587	15,097	57.5
Petersburg	49	36,765	36,103	−1.8

Sources: U. S. Census—1960 and 1970.

Exhibit 43 - 3
The Primary Market Area

	Number of Alumni
Northern Virginia	2,418
Norfolk, Portsmouth, Chesapeake	3,420
Richmond	300
Williamsburg	1,652
TOTAL	8,000

The Athletic Educational Foundation

A second source of funding for basketball and football is the Athletic Educational Foundation (AEF). AEF-generated funds will become increasingly important by 1979 since athletic scholarships must be funded by the AEF beginning in that year. Contributions made to the AEF can be either earmarked for specific sports or put into the general fund. A designated gift is placed into an escrow account of the AEF and is used for scholarships in a given sport.

Recently, there has been growing concern for the success of the designated gift policy. Executive director of AEF, Barry Fratkin, refuses to make a special appeal for the nonrevenue sports and will not release the foundation's mailing list to coaches of nonrevenue sports. His reasoning is that such a tactic could jeopardize his own fund-raising efforts. Mr. Fratkin also has raised doubts about the foundation's ability to sustain contributions at a level that would continue to provide the necessary scholarship funds for the football and basketball teams.

Over the years, some of the coaches have developed their own sources of funds, which they combine with the student fee to meet their individual scholarship needs. For 1976–77, this amount totalled $15,000 and had to be directed through the AEF for legal reasons. NCAA rules restrict coaches from starting their own separate fund-raising "organizations," stating that each school can have only one source of contributions. Therefore, the coaches are forced to work through the AEF.

The AEF has traditionally reached or surpassed its fund-raising goal. AEF performance in previous years is presented in Table 43–6.

Scheduling Policy

In 1976, William and Mary decided to drop out of the Southern Conference because it was no longer economically feasible to remain in the conference and run a profitable sports program. Since William and Mary did not typically draw big crowds for out-of-state schools, the Athletic Department's scheduling policy was to play as many state schools as possible, filling in the remainder of the schedule with known schools within a reasonable distance from Williamsburg (300 miles). Also because of the size of William and Mary's football stadium (15,000), Sam Baker felt that the most profitable combination was to play state schools at Williamsburg

Table   43–6
Athletic Educational Foundation Information
Facts of the 1976 Drive

Area	Number of Donors	Amount Raised
Williamsburg	426	$ 63,579.72
Richmond	362	44,058.93
Hampton, Newport News	302	35,172.00
Norfolk, Chesapeake, Portsmouth	321	31,347.00
Northern Virginia	271	23,067.00
Western Virginia	108	12,620.99
Petersburg, Hopewell	61	9,873.00
Other Virginia Cities	50	4,220.00
Other States	325	32,962.50
Miscellaneous		4,407.72
TOTAL		$261,308.24
Goal		$250,000.00

Table   43–7
Total Number of Donors and
Amounts Raised 1967–1975

Year	Number of Donors	Amount Raised
1975	1,662	$201,372.97
1974	1,204	113,311.00
1973	1,118	94,470.50
1972	1,150	67,189.54
1971	1,178	59,000.85
1970	1,251	70,417.58
1969	1,178	63,402.33
1968	1,179	79,055.64
1967	1,129	46,461.17

Exhibit 43 - 4
William and Mary Football and Basketball
Schedules for 1977-78

Date	Opponent	Time	Where Played*
September 3	Norfolk State	1:30	H
September 10	VMI	1:30	A
September 17	Pittsburgh	1:30	A
September 24	Louisville	8:00	A
October 1	Villanova	1:30	H
October 8	Virginia Tech (Tobacco Bowl)	1:30	A
October 15	Open		
October 22	Navy	1:30	A
October 29	Rutgers (homecoming)	2:00	H
November 5	The Citadel	1:30	A
November 12	East Carolina (Oyster Bowl)	1:30	A
November 19	Richmond	1:30	H
	Basketball		
November 25–26	Richmond Invitational Tournament		
	W&M vs. Virginia Commonwealth Univ.		A
November 28	Christopher Newport College	8:00	H
November 30	West Virginia University	8:00	H
December 3	Radford College	8:00	H
December 7	North Carolina	8:00	H
December 9–10	Brigham Young Classic; Provo, Utah		A
December 28–29	Tangerine Bowl		A
January 7	East Carolina	2:00	H
January 10	Rutgers		A
January 14	Richmond	8:00	H
January 17	East Carolina		A
January 21	American	8:00	H
January 25	Davidson		A
January 28	Old Dominion		A
February 1	Virginia Commonwealth University	8:00	H
February 4	George Mason	8:00	H
February 7	Navy		A
February 11	Madison	8:00	H
February 15	V.M.I.		A
February 18	Richmond		A
February 20	Virginia	8:00	H
February 22	South Carolina		A
February 25	Old Dominion	8:00	H
March 1	E.C.A.C. Tournament		

* H refers to home games; A refers to away games.

(Cary Field) and other schools away. His reasoning was that state schools would draw bigger crowds in Williamsburg. Also, it would be difficult to schedule "big name" schools at home because both William and Mary and the "big name" competitor could make more money by not playing in Williamsburg. The 1977–78 football and basketball schedules are presented in Exhibit 43–4.

One of the long-term goals of the Athletic Department is to establish a state conference for football and basketball. It was felt that such an arrangement would establish various rivalries and provide the spectator with quality sports entertainment. A state conference would also help cut costs and therefore be more profitable for William and Mary.

Discussion Question

Develop a marketing program directed at making the football and basketball programs at William and Mary self-sufficient.

The Tulsa Philharmonic

Louis E. Boone, University of Tulsa

The city of Tulsa traces its origins to 1836 when a band of Creek Indians, the Lochapokas, chose a settlement site along a bend of the Arkansas River. Tulsey, later changed to Tulsa, began as the center of governmental and religious functions for the Creek nation. But its history took a drastic change when on April 15, 1897, oil was discovered north of the city. Another oil discovery was made 4 years later just west of the city, and the richest small oil field in the world was discovered in 1905 with the nearby Glenn Pool discovery.

Within 2 years, 500 wells were pumping black crude and Tulsa had become the oil capital of the world. The Glenn Pool discovery brought the oil men, Getty, Sinclair, Skelly, and Phillips. It also brought thousands of workers, and the bedroom community of Tulsa had grown in population to 7,298 by the statehood year of 1907.

Among the newcomers moving to Tulsa during the early years of the oil boom were persons interested in developing good musical performances and assuring the availability of good theatre and opera. A small group of musicians played overtures and *entr'acte* music in the Little Theater. Starlight Concerts sponsored by The University of Tulsa were held each summer in Skelly Stadium on the university campus. An orchestra, the Civic Symphony, was formed.

But the orchestra moved to Oklahoma City during the Great Depression, returning occasionally to Tulsa to play winter concerts. Nearly 2 decades passed and the determination to have a permanent orchestra in Tulsa grew. The belief that a full-time symphony orchestra is a civic as well as a cultural asset prompted the chamber of commerce to appoint a committee to determine ways and means of accomplishing this goal. In 1948 the Tulsa Philharmonic Society was formed. The Society had the responsibility for the development, well-being, management, and support of the Tulsa Philharmonic Orchestra. On November 1, 1948, the orchestra held the opening concert of its first season with H. Arthur Brown, formerly of El Paso, as conductor.

Growth of the Philharmonic

Brown served as conductor until 1957 when he left Tulsa to become conductor of the Los Angeles Symphony and the Hollywood Bowl Orchestra. The late Vladimir Golschmann succeeded him and continued with the orchestra for 4 years. The 1961–62 season saw Franco Autori take command of the musical direction of the orchestra. Skitch Henderson served as director until his resignation in 1974, at which time Thomas Lewis was named music director and conductor. Concerts were held in the 2,737-seat Tulsa Municipal Theater. Table 44–1 shows the annual season ticket sales and number of concerts for the years 1954 to 1975.

Specific programs were selected by the conductor and aimed primarily at a classical music audience. Table 44–1 indicates there appears to be a 1,700-person base of classical support. Fluctuations in season ticket sales are affected by such variables as reputation of conductor, program content, and guest appearances. For instance, the increased attendance in 1966 was attributed to a guest appearance by Van Cliburn.

Table   44–1
Season Ticket Sales and Number of Concerts by Year

Year	Season Ticket Sales	Number of Concerts
1954	1738	12
1955	1649	12
1956	2096	10
1957	1742	10
1958	**	1
1959	2557	10
1960	2166	10
1961	2434	10
1962	2451	10
1963	2394	10
1964	2204	10
1965	2163	10
1966	2330	10
1967	2133	10
1968	1974	10
1969	1769	10
1970	1693	10
1971	2737*	10
1972	2737*	10
1973	1794	10
1974	1893	10
1975	1969	10

* sellouts
** no season tickets offered in 1958

The Philharmonic also devoted some of its efforts to the young people in the Tulsa area. Each spring it presented a Lollipop Concert to introduce young children to the arts. Ten Young People's Concerts were conducted annually for fifth and sixth grade students in both the public and private schools. An additional 60 in-school concerts were performed by various Philharmonic ensembles.

The arrival of Skitch Henderson in 1971 resulted in sellouts for his first two years. His attempts to mix classical and pop music, coupled with heavy advertisements as classical concerts, resulted in disaster the third year. The classical audience was upset at concerts advertised as classical yet containing pop music; those who preferred popular music were unhappy with the classical arrangements. Season ticket sales for 1973 dropped 34 percent below those of the previous year.

A New Business Manager

In 1975, Ken Hertz joined the staff as assistant business manager. Hertz, age 26, received his undergraduate degree in music from State University of New York and had previously served as manager of the Cape Cod Symphony. At SUNY, he had taken an elective course in principles of marketing.

Hertz was one of the growing ranks of persons who recognized that business expertise was a crucial, though often nonexistent, requirement for a successful philharmonic. Table 44–2 shows the 1975 budget for the Philharmonic.

By 1977 Hertz felt that the budget would approximate $500,000. Cash flows were a continuous problem since season ticket renewals were made in January and February, but cash was not received until September.

Also, there was a question of what target audience the Philharmonic was attempting to satisfy. One faction simply felt that "good" music should be the objective; the right audience would appear. Others felt strongly that musical education should be an important role. Still others felt that a blend of pop and classical music would allow the Philharmonic to best serve the community.

Another question concerned whether Monday night was the most appropriate week night for Philharmonic performances. The Philharmonic had already decided to move into the new $15-million Tulsa Performing Arts Center when it was

Table   44–2
1975 Budget of the Tulsa Philharmonic

Receipts		Disbursements
Sales	58,000	
Contributions	100,000	
Endowment	60,000	
Other	74,000	
Total	$292,000	$292,000

completed in early 1977. The new Center would have a seating capacity of 2,364, almost 300 less than the Municipal Theater. The reduced capacity and increased rental fees would further affect revenues and expenses. Hertz wondered what effect a price increase would have on attendance. He also was studying a new report from the Ford Foundation.

The Ford Foundation Study [1]

In 1974, the Ford Foundation sponsored a study of the audience for 4 performing arts—ballet, opera, symphony, and theater—in 12 cities. Three cities were chosen from each of the 4 geographic regions of the country: New York, Philadelphia, and Boston (East); Washington, Atlanta, and Houston (South); Chicago, Cincinnati, and Minneapolis (Midwest); and Los Angeles, San Francisco, and Seattle (West).
The study had 3 objectives:

(1) To measure the size and the characteristics of the audience for the 4 performing arts to answer the question: How many people attend what? How often? Under what circumstances?

(2) To measure the attitudes and motivations of attenders and prospective attenders to answer the question: What satisfactions do they believe the performing arts provide?

(3) To identify opportunities for the performing arts; to assess what might be done by performing arts organizations or by others to attract more people to performances and to induce those who now attend occasionally to attend more frequently.

The sample size was 6,000: 500 persons in each city contacted by telephone after being randomly selected from telephone directories. Once the interviews were completed, the sample was weighted in order to conform to the sex, age, and education distribution of the population of the 12 cities as reported by the 1970 census.

Findings of the Ford Study

Tables 44–3 through 44–8 summarize key findings of the Ford Foundation audience study.

The Tulsa Study

Hertz recognized a number of questions concerning the Tulsa Philharmonic that needed answers if he was to be successful in increasing attendance, providing maximum audience satisfaction, and increasing revenues. Concerning current season ticketholders, he sought out methods for increasing the number of times they ac-

---

[1] The information in this section is based upon *The Finances of the Performing Arts—Vol. II. A Survey of the Characteristics and Attitudes of Audiences for Theatre, Opera, Symphony and Ballet in 12 U.S. Cities.* Ford Foundation, 1974.

Table   44–3
Percentage of Respondents Attending a Live Professional
Symphony Concert in the Past Year

Method	Percent Exposed During Past Year:
On Television	30
On Radio	28
On Records/Tape	25
Live Amateur	6
Live Professional	10
Any Form	51

Source: Ford Foundation Study, p. 6.

Table   44–4
Exposure to Live Professional
Performances of the Four Arts

Among Those Who Attended	Percent Who Also Attended:				Percent Attending No Other Arts
	Theater	Opera	Symphony	Ballet	
Symphony	45	27	—	27	36
Theater	—	13	31	19	63
Opera	50	—	75	25	25
Ballet	60	20	60	—	20

Source: Ford Foundation Study, p. 11.

Table   44–5
Exposure to Live Professional Symphony
During Past Year by Age

Age	Total Percent Exposed
Under 20	13
20–29	11
30–39	10
40–49	9
50 and Over	7

Source: Ford Foundation Study, p. 17.

Table   44–6
**Income Composition of Audiences to Live Professional
Symphony During Past Year**

Income	Total Percent Exposed
Up to $7,500	12
$7,500 to $15,000	37
$15,000 to $25,000	34
$25,000 and over	19

Source: Ford Foundation Study, p. 13.

Table   44–7
**Educational Composition of Audience of Live Professional
Symphony During Past Year**

Education	Percent
Some High School	21
High School Graduate	18
Some College	24
College Graduate	37

Source: Ford Foundation Study, p. 14.

Table   44–8
**Total Percent Exposed to Live Professional Symphony
Last Year, by Occupation**

Occupation	Percent
Executive-Managerial	14
Professional	18
Teaching	27
Student	15
Homemaker	7
White Collar	11
Blue Collar	4
Retired	7

Source: Ford Foundation Study, p. 13.

tually attended each season. He wondered if potential audiences could be converted into ticket purchasers if he changed such variables as time, concert location, concert night, ticket prices, parking and transportation, guest artists, different types of music, advertising, image.

After reading the Ford Foundation report, he wondered whether the national characteristics truly reflected the Tulsa audience. What types of people actually attended the concerts and why? Where did they obtain information about the concerts?

He simultaneously recognized a danger of alienating present concert goers if he made the wrong decisions in his attempts to increase attendance. The Philharmonic could not be "all things to all people" and any changes must take into consideration the reactions of the core market of season ticketholders.

Hertz decided to contact a local university professor and discuss the need for a profile of current concert goers and a determination of the best methods of satisfying present and potential market targets.

Development of Hypotheses

The Tulsa Philharmonic needed greater attendance at its concerts, but lacked pertinent information to stimulate increases. The research focused on 8 hypotheses:

(1) The typical Tulsa concert goer is demographically similar to concert goers in other cities.

(2) The image of the Tulsa Philharmonic curtails the desire of people to attend.

(3) More people will attend concerts if a greater variety of music is performed.

(4) Concert time and night do not meet consumer desires.

(5) Attendance will increase if information pertaining to concerts (subject, date, and time) is widely publicized.

(6) Current promotional activities do not reach the market target.

(7) People who attend Tulsa Philharmonic also attend other cultural events in Tulsa (opera, ballet, theater).

(8) Newspaper advertising will better reach the market target.

Methodology

Two separate surveys were conducted to test the hypotheses: one survey focused on persons who attend Tulsa Philharmonic concerts, and the second study was designed to obtain information from potential concert goers. The universe for the first survey was defined as all individuals living within the Tulsa SMSA who hold season tickets; the universe for the second survey was defined as the entire population within the city of Tulsa.

A systematic sample of 331 persons holding season tickets was selected from a list of subscribers. A questionnaire then was mailed to each household (see appendix a). The expected response rate was high because of the interest of season ticket holders in the future of the Philharmonic.

For the survey of the general public, a stratified probability sample of 236 residence telephones was selected. All residence telephones in Tulsa were divided according to telephone exchange (geographical area), and the number of respondents selected for the sample in each area corresponded to the size of that area in relation to the other exchanges. For those exchanges with more than one telephone prefix, the number of calls to be made within that exchange was divided equally among each prefix. The 4-digit numbers required to complete each telephone number were chosen at random from a table of random pairs.

Telephone interviews were used to obtain information from the general public. The questionnaire was divided into 2 parts—one for persons who were aware of the existence of the Tulsa Philharmonic, and one for those who were not. The telephone questionnaire is shown in appendix b.

Findings

The results of the surveys are shown on the two questionnaires in appendix a and appendix b.

Discussion Questions

1. Compare the findings with the hypotheses established for the survey. In what ways are Tulsa residents similar to concert goers in other cities? What are the major differences?

2. Should Hertz use these findings to develop a marketing strategy for the Tulsa Philharmonic? Explain.

3. What steps would you recommend that he take in developing plans for the future?

Mail Survey of Season Ticketholders
And Responses to Each Question

Cover Letter for Mail Questionnaire

Dear Tulsa Philharmonic Subscriber:

We need your help! You can help us by completing the enclosed questionnaire.

Your answers will provide us with some much needed information regarding the interests and characteristics of current Tulsa Philharmonic subscribers. This information will help the Tulsa Philharmonic better serve you and other subscribers.

I am currently a marketing student at the University in charge of coordinating thirty-five students working on this project. We need your help in order for this study to be successful. Your help will make a major contribution to our education.

Since this is a statistical study, you represent many subscribers. Won't you please answer the questions and return them to me *within the next few days* in the stamped envelope provided.

We are counting on your help.

Thank you very much,

Diane J. Jackson

Diane J. Jackson

Mail Questionnaire
Percent Responding in Each Category

Please check the appropriate answer

1a.   How many times did you attend Tulsa Philharmonic concerts last season?

____15.5____ none of the concerts
____9.8____ 1–4 concerts
____41.8____ 5–9 concerts
____33.0____ every concert

1b.   If 4 or less concerts attended, please indicate the principal reasons why?

____9.3____ conflicts with other activities
____2.6____ inadequate parking facilities
____4.1____ location of concerts
____2.6____ inconvenient night and time
____.5____ transportation
____2.1____ didn't enjoy the music
_____ others (please specify) _____

2.   Which night of the week is most convenient for you to attend the concerts?

__75.8__ Mon   __13.9__ Tues   __9.8__ Wed   __7.7__ Thurs
__10.3__ Fri   __6.7__ Sat   __2.6__ Sun

3.   What concert starting time would be most convenient for you?

__1.0__ 7:00 p.m.   __14.9__ 7:30   __73.8__ 8:00   __8.2__ 8:30
__2.6__ No response

4.   Do you think the current ticket price is:

__6.3__ too high   __3.7__ too low   __87.3__ just right
__2.7__ No response

5.   Where have you seen/heard advertisements for the Tulsa Philharmonic?

__63.4__ Newspaper   __24.7__ TV
__39.2__ Radio   __11.3__ Magazines
__64.9__ Mail Brochure   __13.9__ None/Do Not Remember

6. What radio station do you listen to most often?

    __31.4__ KWEN   __9.3__ KVOO   __4.1__ KXXO
    __32.5__ KRAV   __3.1__ KELI   __13.4__ KWGS
    __3.6__ KAKC   __38.1__ KRMG   __10.3__ Other/None

    Most frequent time of listening?

    __45.9__ 7:00 am–12 noon   __24.7__ 4:00 pm–6:00 pm
    __16.0__ 12 noon–4:00 pm   __43.3__ After 6:00 pm

7. Which type(s) of music would you prefer to hear at the Tulsa Philharmonic?

    __5.7__ Jazz   __0.0__ Rock
    __93.3__ Classical   __8.2__ Popular
    __38.1__ Modern Classical   _____ Other (please specify _____
    __0.0__ Country & Western   _____

8. In your opinion, is the Tulsa Philharmonic:

    __42.8__ Good family entertainment
    __41.8__ Good for an evening with friends
    __78.9__ Cultural experience
    _____ Other (please specify) _____

9. Please check events attended in the last year.

    __7.7__ Ballet   __17.0__ Opera and Theater
    __6.2__ Opera   __27.8__ All three
    __19.6__ Theater   __11.3__ None
    __4.1__ Ballet and Opera   __2.6__ No response
    __3.6__ Ballet and Theater

    Though it is not necessary to identify yourself in any way, would you please answer the following questions for statistical tabulation purposes only.

10. A. Age:

    __1.5__ 18–24   __6.7__ 25–34   __24.2__ 35–49   __39.2__ 50–64
    __27.3__ 65+   __1.0__ No response

    B. Head of household education:

    __.5__ Some high school   __68.0__ College graduate
    __5.7__ High school graduate   __2.1__ No response
    __23.7__ Some college

C. Family Income:

_5.2_ under $7,500	_20.6_ $25,000–$50,000
_7.7_ $ 7,500–$10,000	_17.0_ $50,000+
_14.4_ $10,000–$15,000	_11.3_ No response
_23.7_ $15,000–$25,000	

D. Occupation of household head:

_5.7_ teaching	_23.6_ homemaker
_21.3_ professional	_12.7_ retired
_1.0_ student	_1.3_ blue collar
_13.3_ executive/managerial	_4.0_ other
_8.6_ white collar	

Thank you very much for your cooperation.

Telephone Survey of Tulsa Residents And Responses to Each Question

Telephone Survey for General Public

Hello. This is _____ from the Marketing Department at the University of Tulsa. We are interested in your opinion of the Tulsa Philharmonic Orchestra and would like to ask you a few questions. This is in no way a solicitation of business and will take only a small amount of your time.

1. Did you know that Tulsa has a Philharmonic Orchestra?

    _____80%_____ Yes _____20%_____ No

    (check one of the following if respondent volunteers additional information)

    ___12.7___ Have heard of it, but know little about it.
    ___3.5___ Am quite familiar with the orchestra.
    ___3.5___ Attend the concerts.
    ___0.0___ Am a season ticketholder
    ___0.0___ Have never heard of it.
    ___0.0___ Not familiar with it.
    _____ Other _____

If the Respondent Answers "Yes" to Question No. 1

2. Have you ever attended a Tulsa Philharmonic concert(s)?

    (Don't ask if answered above) ___39.3___ Yes ___60.7___ No

    If yes: Approximately how many concerts did you attend last season?

    ___1.7___ All ___20.8___ 1–4
    ___17.9___ 5–9 ___59.5___ None

3. Would you attend more concerts if they were more widely publicized?

    ___46.2___ Yes ___53.8___ No

3a. If yes, what would be the best way to inform you about the concerts?

21.4	Newspaper	4.6	Brochure
22.5	Radio		Other
23.7	Television		No opinion
.6	Magazine		

3b. What radio stations do you listen to most often?

8.7	KWEN	7.5	KELI
4.6	KRAV	11.6	KRMG
12.1	KAKC	6.9	KXXO
8.1	KVOO	8.1	None

What is the most frequent time of listening?

21.4	7:00 am–12 noon	11.6	4:00 pm–6:00 pm
6.4	12 noon–4:00 pm	23.1	After 6:00 pm

4. Which type(s) of music would you prefer to hear at the Tulsa Philharmonic?

19.1	Jazz	15.6	Rock
50.3	Classical	22.5	Popular
22.0	Modern Classical		Other
20.8	Country and Western		

5. In your opinion, is the Tulsa Philharmonic:

38.7	Good family entertainment
41.6	Good for an evening with friends
52.0	Cultural experience
	Other (please specify) _____

6. Have you attended the ballet, opera or theater in the last year?

9.2	Ballet	0.0	Opera and Theater
2.9	Opera	2.9	No response
11.6	Theater	4.0	All three
2.3	Ballet and Opera	65.9	None
1.2	Ballet and Theater		

7. Would you be interested in attending concerts in the future?

    63.0 ___ Yes   37.0 ___ No

If yes: a. Which night of the week is most convenient for you to attend the concerts?

9.2 Sun	19.1 Mon	16.2 Tues	
12.7 Wed	12.1 Thurs	32.9 Fri	38.7 Sat

b. What concert starting time would be most convenient for you?

(Give choices)

___7.57___ 7:00 pm ___21.47___ 7:30 ___32.9___ 8:00
___1.7___ 8:30 ___36.4___ No response

c. What do you think is a reasonable ticket price per concert?

___4.0___ Less than $2.00 ___21.4___ 2–3.99 ___23.1___ 4–6.00
___4.0___ Above $6.00

Though it is not necessary to identify yourself in any way, would you please answer the following questions for statistical tabulations purposes only?

8. A. Age:

___19.7___ 18–24 ___28.9___ 25–34 ___24.9___ 35–49
___19.1___ 50–64 ___2.9___ 65+ ___4.7___ No response

Thank you very much for your cooperation.

If the Respondent Answers "No" to Question No. 1

2. In your opinion, do you think it is desirable for Tulsa to have a Philharmonic?

___90.7___ Yes ___9.3___ No

3. What is your favorite type of music?

___9.3___ Jazz ___25.6___ Rock
___20.9___ Classical ___25.6___ Popular
___9.3___ Modern Classical _____ Other
___37.2___ Country and Western (please specify)

4. Have you attended the ballet, opera, or theater in the last year?

___7.0___ Ballet ___2.3___ Ballet and Theater
___2.3___ Opera ___88.4___ None
___0.0___ Theater

5. Would you attend more concerts if they were more widely publicized?

___37.2___ Yes ___62.8___ No

If yes: a. What would be the best way to inform you about concerts?

___14.0___ Newspaper ___4.7___ Brochure
___11.6___ Radio _____ Other
___20.9___ Television _____ No Opinion
___2.3___ Magazine

b. What radio station do you listen to most often?

4.7	KWEN	7.0	KRMG
4.7	KRAV	0.0	KXXO
11.6	KAKC	29.3	Other/None
7.0	KVOO		

What is the most frequent time of listening?

20.9	7:00 am–12 noon	9.3	4:00 pm–6:00 pm
2.3	12 noon–4:00 pm	9.3	6:00 pm–7:00 am

Though it is not necessary to identify yourself in any way, would you please answer the following questions for statistical tabulation purposes only?

6. Age:

27.9	18–24	16.3	25–34	18.6	35–49
18.6	50–64	16.3	65+	2.3	No response

7. In your opinion, are symphony concerts:

32.6	Good family entertainment
18.6	Good for an evening with friends
20.9	Cultural experience
	Other (please specify) _____

Thank you very much for your cooperation.

Marketing Program for a University Center

Louise Luchsinger, Texas Tech University

The University Center (UC), located in the center of the campus of Midlands University (MU), serves a current enrollment of over 22,000 students and, according to the *1975 U.C. Operational Handbook,* is the:
- hub of MU out-of-class activities
- place to spend one's leisure hours
- popular place to eat, drink, and meet friends
- sponsor of a well-rounded activity program
- place where students can better themselves by participating in UC activities.

University Center first opened its doors in the spring of 1953. The original building consisted mainly of the current snack bar, color television lounge, and the Coronado Room upstairs. In 1962 the first addition opened, consisting of the ballroom, cafeteria, faculty club, game rooms, and additional lounges and meeting rooms. The latest addition opened in mid-1976 and approximately doubled the size of the previous building. It features a 1,000-seat auditorium-theater, 600-seat recital hall, expanded snack bar and games area, new offices, and a large sky-lighted lounge. The new facility connects to the Music Building with which University Center will share some meeting rooms and 2 auditoriums.

Priority for use of each of the two auditoriums is determined by the University's Board of Regents. The theater is used mainly by University Center, whereas the recital hall is used mainly by the Music Department.

University Center offers students a variety of services at little or no charge. Free services include check cashing, meeting rooms for official campus organizations, "for sale" board, television, and magazines. A minimal amount is charged for table games, mimeographing, poster printing, and typing.

University Center's operation can be divided into two major categories: building operations (food service, operations, and theater and building services), and activities (cultural events and programs). The functions of the different areas of building operations is apparent in the UC organizational chart (see Figure 45–1).

Figure 45–1
University Center Organization Chart

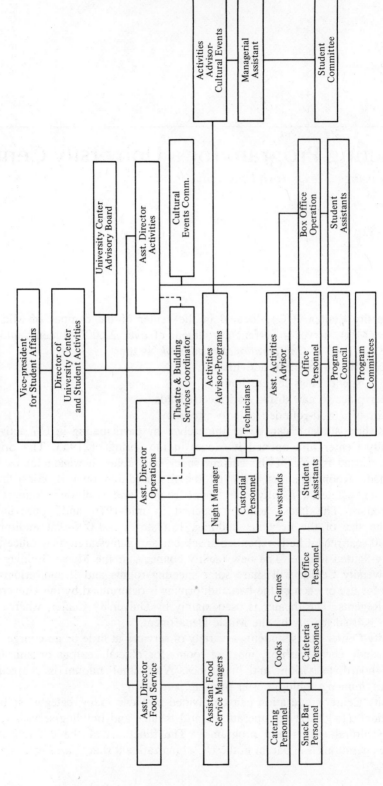

The difference between cultural events and UC programs is that the former receives financing from student services fees while the latter gets its funds from the UC fee. Since cultural events receive funding from student services fees, regulations restrict its using that money for only programs that have "cultural" value, whereas UC programs are not so restricted and can offer a much greater variety of events. It was not until recently that cultural events came under control of UC management. Previously, the only connection University Center had with cultural events was providing office space in the building for them.

The programs' prominent feature is that all events are planned and run primarily by volunteer student committees. There are currently nine committees whose functions are as follows:

The *Entertainment Committee* sponsors pop concerts on campus, including the Lone Star Muzik Festival, big-name concerts, miniconcerts, and dances. It is primarily a money-making committee.

The *Films Committee* attracts students of all types through varied visual media programs. This year the Cinematheque Film Society is part of this committee, bringing classical films of all types. Along with the regularly scheduled feature film program, videotapes and educational films also play an important part of this committee's work. It, too, is primarily a money-making committee.

Fine Arts Committee specializes in visual arts, although music and dance are becoming a big part of its responsibilities. Members plan exhibits and displays for University Center, bring in artists to share their talents with the community, and sponsor an annual 2-day art show and sale.

Free University is probably the one committee that reaches the most people in the university community and in Midland City on a long-term basis. It strives to supplement students' and community residents' education by providing slates of free courses in subjects usually not found in a regular university curriculum.

Ideas and Issues Committee attempts to challenge the members of the university community in their thinking and in their way of life. It attracts students aware of current issues and interested in raising the level of awareness on campus through programming knowledgeable speakers, panel discussions, and films.

International Interest seeks to familiarize the community with foreign peoples and cultures. Committee members work toward furthering interaction and understanding between American and foreign students, sponsoring foreign language films, displays of other cultures, and foreign nation seminars.

Leadership Board calls upon its members to have leadership skills and the interest to share, as well as to develop, those skills. Its goal is to promote better campus communication by planning and leading retreats and informal get-togethers for interested campus groups. This committee seeks to help other people to learn leadership and membership skills.

Recreation Committee involves students in various outdoor/indoor activities. It offers a wide area of programming including road rallies, sport demonstrations, tournaments, and daytime events in the University Center which draw students together between classes.

Task Force is an organization which transcends the boundaries between committees. It is composed of students who work with all the committees on projects of their choosing and who further intercommittee communications.

Building and Surveys is a special committee comprised of interested members of other committees who study both the operations and programs of University Center and suggest improvements. This committee also obtains feedback from the student body.

Regulations governing University Center are outlined in Exhibit 45–1. The top management position within the University Center is the director of the University Center and Activities, whose duties also are outlined in Exhibit 45–1. This position is currently held by Mary Stoudlemeir. Mary became director in 1956 after serving as assistant director for approximately one year. She received a bachelor's degree in sociology and a master's degree in counseling and guidance from Andover State University.

Exhibit 45-1
Regulations Governing The University Center

Article I: University Center Activities Advisory Board

The Advisory Board, as the governing body of the University Center, shall have jurisdiction over any and all areas of operations and activities within the University Center. The decisions and actions of the Advisory Board shall be subject to review at the request of the Vice-president for Student Affairs.

Section A: Membership

1. The University Center Advisory Board shall consist of:
   a. The Director of the University Center
   b. Assistant Director—Activities
   c. Activities Advisor—Cultural Events
   d. Assistant Dean of Students
   e. Chairman of the Department of Music
   f. Faculty Representative-at-Large
   g. President of the Student Association
   h. Coordinator of the University Center Program Council
   i. Two Student Representatives-at-Large
   j. Student member of the University Artists and Speakers Series Committee
   k. Editor of the Campus Newspaper

2. The faculty representative (at large) shall be recommended to the Vice-president for Student Affairs by the Advisory Board and shall be appointed for a period of 2 years.

3. The chairman of the Advisory Board shall be the Director of the University Center who shall vote only in case of a tie.

4. The Program Council Assistant Coordinator shall serve as the secretary to the Advisory Board and shall vote only in the absence of the Program Council Coordinator.

5. The 2 student representatives shall be jointly recommended by the President of the Student Association and the Coordinator of Program Council with one representative being appointed each year for a 2-year term.

6. Various committees and subcommittees may be established at the discretion of the Chairman and/or Advisory Board in order to carry out the Advisory Board's objectives.

Section B: Powers of the Advisory Board

1. All trips made with University Center funds shall be subject to approval of the Advisory Board.

2. Any special uses of the University Center, other than those covered in succeeding sections and articles of these regulations, are subject to the approval or rejection of the Advisory Board.

3. The use of the University Center Building or Center facilities by any group or department of the campus for academic activities shall be subject to approval of the Director and/or the Advisory Board.

4. All requests for commercial use of the University Center shall be subject to the approval of the Director and/or the Advisory Board.

5. Recommendations for normal operating hours and for closing times and dates for the University Center for repairs, maintenance, holidays, and other special reasons shall be made by the Director, and shall be subject to the approval of the Advisory Board.

6. The University Center Advisory Board shall maintain the right to review expenditures of the University Center.

7. The Advisory Board shall have the right to review all gift offers to the University Center.

8. The Advisory Board has the right to approve or disapprove the sale and/or distribution of any and all publications within the University Center.

9. All requests for the use of the University Center by groups other than registered student organizations and/or campus sponsored activities shall be subject to approval of the Advisory Board.

10. The Advisory Board shall have the right to interview and recommend in the selection of all major administrative staff personnel.

11. The Advisory Board shall maintain the right of recommending policy for the University Center operation.

12. The Advisory Board has jurisdiction over any and all policies concerning University Center Activities (Program).

13. The Director of the University Center in conjunction with the Advisory Board shall formulate and recommend the fiscal year operating budget for the University Center in the spring semester of each year.

14. The Constitution of the University Center Program Council shall be subject to review and comment by the Advisory Board.

Article II: The University Center's Director

Section A: The Director of the University Center shall be the administrator of the University Center, answerable to the Advisory Board under the provisions of Article I of the regulations governing the University Center. The director's duties shall include carrying out the policies of the University Center as determined by the University Center Advisory Board, although many of the Advisory Board's policies may come as a result of the Director's recommendations.

Section B: While in the University Center, students are expected to abide by the Code of Student Affairs. Individual and group offenses shall be referred for disposition to the office of the Assistant Dean of Students for Administration.

Section C: The Director and any representative the Director may designate may cash student checks to and including $20.00 only after proper identification is presented and during times approved by the University Center Director.

Section D: The Director shall bring a copy of these regulations to the attention of the Advisory Board for consideration of necessary revisions at the first regular meeting of each school year.

Section E: The Director may, in an emergency, make decisions affecting these regulations after polling available members of the Advisory Board.

Section F: The Director shall submit a monthly financial report to the Board outlining expenditures and income for the total University Center operation.

Article III: University Center Reservation Procedures

Section A: Reservations for the University Center facilities will be made on a priority basis: (1) University Center activities, (2) student functions, all campus, (3) student functions, closed, (4) Midlands University faculty and staff organizations, (5) state, regional, and national conferences or groups of which a Midlands University organization is a member, and (6) all others shall be considered on an individual basis by the Director and/or the Advisory Board.

Section B:

1. Fees for the use of the University Center facilities by registered student organizations for (admission-free) social functions and for business meetings and conferences shall be as follows:
    a. For admission-free, social functions:
        (1) Ballroom, all—$50
        (2) Ballroom, large section—$30
        (3) Ballroom, small section—$25
        (4) Coronado Room—$30
        (5) Meeting rooms, with special equipment or arrangements—$2.50
    b. Business meetings and conferences:
        (1) Ballroom, all, 8 hours—$25
        (2) Ballroom, all, 4 hours—$20
        (3) Ballroom, large section, 8 hours—$20
        (4) Ballroom, large section, 4 hours—$15
        (5) Ballroom, small section, 8 hours—$15
        (6) Ballroom, small section, 4 hours—$15
        (7) Coronado Room, 8 hours—$15
        (8) Coronado Room, 4 hours—$10
        (9) Meeting rooms, 4 or 8 hours—$2.50
2. Fees for the use of the University Center facilities for social functions and for conferences and business meeting use that charge an admission shall be as follows:
    a. Social functions for registered student organizations:
        (1) Ballroom, all—$70
        (2) Ballroom, large section—$50

      (3) Ballroom, small section—$40
      (4) Coronado Room—$40
      (5) Meeting rooms—$3.50
   b. Conferences and business meetings for registered student organizations:
      (1) Ballroom, all, 8 hours—$40
      (2) Ballroom, all, 4 hours—$30
      (3) Ballroom, large section, 8 hours—$30
      (4) Ballroom, large section, 4 hours—$25
      (5) Ballroom, small section, 8 hours—$25
      (6) Ballroom, small section, 4 hours—$20
      (7) Coronado Room, 8 hours—$25
      (8) Coronado Room, 4 hours—$20
      (9) All meeting rooms, 4 or 8 hours—$3.50
     No room charge for luncheons or dinners if they do not exceed 2 hours. A $2.50 charge may be added to any of the above charges when exceptional equipment or arrangements are requested.
   c. Midlands University faculty and staff organizations and departments: The above fees apply to MU faculty and staff organizations.
   d. Groups sponsored by the University: The above fees apply to groups sponsored by the University.

Section C:

1. Registered campus organizations requesting the use of the meeting rooms for business meetings will not be charged unless there is a request for additional chairs, tables, or other special equipment. There will be $2.50 fee for all such requests.

2. The Director may waive fees for the use of University Center facilities for institutional offices or agencies.

Section D: All requests for the use of University Center facilities shall be made and scheduled through the office of the Director and will be handled on "first come, first served" basis.

Section E:

1. Meeting rooms will not be scheduled by any one organization for more than one meeting at one time.

2. Requests for the University Center facilities other than in a current semester must be made in writing. Included in the request should be: date, hours of function, type of function, and organization or group making the request.

Section F: Solicitations and/or use of University Center facilities not otherwise covered in these regulations are prohibited except upon special approval of the Director and/or the Advisory Board.

Article IV: General University Center Regulations

Section A:

1. All posters and/or decorations for functions held in/or advertised in the University Center must have the approval of the Director.

2. All decorations used in the University Center must be fire proof.

Section B:

Smoking is not permitted in the Coronado Room during social functions.

Section C:

1. No student advertising will be allowed in the University Center except on designated bulletin boards.

2. Posting of student election campaign material will not be allowed in or on the University Center.

Section D:

No equipment belonging to the University Center shall be allowed outside the building without the approval of the Director or the Assistant Director-Operations.

Section E:

The University Center observes a rigid "no tipping" rule.

Section F:

Groups which have reserved facilities in the University Center will be held liable for the behavior or actions of any individuals attending their events. Such groups also shall be responsible for the condition of any equipment used at such events.

Article V: Activation

These regulations shall automatically be in effect at such times as they are approved by a majority of a quorum of the University Center Advisory Board.

Article VI: Meetings

Regular meetings shall be called at a minimum of once every month. Special meetings shall be called as needed by the Chairman or at the request of two or more members of the Advisory Board.

Article VII: Quorum

A quorum shall consist of two-thirds of the voting membership of the Advisory Board.
The Advisory Board shall decide, at its last spring meeting, the number of members for quorum during summer school.

Article VIII: Amendments

These regulations may be amended by a majority vote of a quorum of the University Center Advisory Board. Such amendments shall be in effect when such a vote is recorded.

Article IX: Availability

Copies of these regulations will be filed and made available for inspection in the office of the Director and the office of the Vice-president for Student Affairs.

Financial Information

Financially, University Center is not considered part of Midland University and, thus, is not eligible for state funds. Rather, it gets its income from 2 main sources: one-third from a separate University Center fee paid each semester by students (currently $5 for each regular semester and $2.50 for each summer session) and two-thirds from revenue generated through building operations and programs.

In the past few years, University Center has run into serious financial trouble. The current fee of $5 has been in effect for over 20 years; but, although the number of students paying the fee has increased, this added revenue has not kept up with inflation. In the past few years University Center personnel have seen huge increases in the costs of utilities, food, and, particularly, labor. Two legislated pay increases last year hit the budget especially hard. For the fiscal year ending September 1, 1977, the UC payroll rose an average of 20 percent. Payroll now accounts for nearly one-third of total expenses. However, even with such tremendous cost increases, University Center ended the past year with a very slight profit.

To deal with rising costs, management has had to raise prices on many food items, services, and programs. Also, many programs once free to MU students now charge admission. In addition, management has put off maintenance expenditures, such as replacing worn-out furniture, so that the building and its furnishings have become quite run down.

In an effort to ease the financial strain, management sought to have the current UC fee doubled to $10 (and $5 per summer session). To do so, MU students first had to approve the increase before the Board of Regents could approve it. Therefore, a referendum was set for students to vote on the fee increase.

One week prior to the referendum, University Center launched an intensive campaign to promote passage of the increase. Promotional articles appeared in the MU newspaper, and UC committee members and KTXT, the University radio station, campaigned for the increase.

During the campaign, management promised that a number of improvements would take place if the fee were raised. They promised an immediate price cut on some food items, particularly on drinks, and that many other prices would be held steady. Admission prices on some events would be lowered and a greater number of programs would be offered free to MU students. Renovation of the existing building also could begin. This would entail relocating and enlarging the newsstands and automated post office, enlarging the cafeteria, refurnishing the lounges, and generally upgrading the overall appearance of the building.

When the final vote was tallied, the fee referendum passed by a landslide with a vote of 2,908 for and 779 against, thereby assuring approval by the Board of Regents. The new fee would go into effect the next semester—just in time, too, because the budget for the upcoming fiscal year would be over $1 million. Without the increase, University Center would have been in the red by $195,000 if it continued to operate at its current level.

Additional Information

UC's potential market consists primarily of MU students, faculty, and staff. However, many major events are open to the public. University Center programs offer a wide variety of events that cater to the varied tastes and interests of the MU community. Although it is not important to go into detail, U.C. committees do operate on a fixed budget. Therefore, it is necessary for some programs to show a profit to make up for losses incurred by other programs with limited or specialized appeal.

However, even events with broad appeal seldom attract more than 5 percent of the student population (Exhibit 45–2). Feature films generally are the only programs that consistently show a profit; however, fewer and fewer movies broke even during the current semester. Programming personnel believe that attendance at many programs, particularly movies, will rise when the new building opens because of the better facilities. Overall, programs showed a loss last year, but not as great a loss as in previous years because of the increased admission prices.

Exhibit 45-2
U C Programs Events 1974-1975

Date	Name of the Event	Attendance	Expense	Income
Sept. 6 & 7	**What's Up Doc?**	535	$ 380.50	$ 534.75
Sept. 9	Free Ice Cream-All UC	1,000	—	—
Sept. 9 & 10	Buzz Brothers-Concert	135	—	—
Sept. 9, 11, 13	Red Raider Movie	50	—	—
Sept. 9–18	**Nashville Sound,** Video Tape	500	50.00	—
Sept. 10 & 12	Pottery Demonstration	200	—	—
Sept. 10	Coffee & Doughnuts	83	—	—
Sept. 11	Ranch Tour	10	—	—
"	Western Dance	60	—	—
"	Cheeseburger & Coke	379	—	—
Sept. 12	Billiards & Pool	41	—	—
Sept. 13	Free Bar-B-Q	1,800	—	—
Sept. 13 & 15	**Life & Times of Judge Roy Bean**	832	265.50	77.74
Sept. 13	Street Dance	500	515.93	—
"	Tobacco Spitting Contest	20	—	—
"	Penny Candy	120	—	—
Sept. 20 & 22	**The Godfather**	1,000	650.00	995.00
Sept. 22	Free-for-all	150	78.43	—
Sept. 27 & 29	**Class of 44**	325	234.20	325.00
Oct. 4 & 6	**Executive Action**	565	304.50	565.00
Oct. 7	Roten Gallery	250	—	—
"	Jackson Brown Concert	1,600	8,910.00	6,496.00
Oct. 8	Donald Freed, Speaker	225	935.00	168.00
Oct. 12 & 13	**Save the Tiger**	455	295.75	455.05
Oct. 14	**Reefer Madness,** Video Tape	7,000	141.00	—
Oct. 18	Starving Artist Show	150	—	—
Oct. 19 & 20	**Up the Sandbox**	57	306.50	57.00
Oct. 23–25	Free U. Registration	2,492	—	—
Oct. 24	International Fair	300	8.50	—
Oct. 25	Poster Sale	1,000	—	175.00
Oct. 25 & 26	**Skin Game**	70	81.00	69.00
Oct. 29	Amnesty Program/Kerry Gershowitz	50	351.00	12.80

Oct. 30–Nov. 1	Film Festival	103	459.00	25.75
Oct. 31	Halloween Carnival	300	33.00	5.27
Nov. 2 & 3	**Butch Cassidy & the Sundance Kid**	380	250.00	350.00
Nov. 2	Retreat	40	—	—
Nov. 3	International Dinner	450	157.14	268.00
Nov. 4	Bubble Gum Blowing Contest	55	—	—
Nov. 5	Jump Rope Contest	30	—	—
Nov. 7	Phone Booth Stuffing Contest	107	—	—
"	Fiesta Folklorico	987	1,076.46	711.60
Nov. 8	Goldfish Swallowing Contest	312	9.49	—
Nov. 8 & 10	**Blume in Love**	229	166.30	229.00
Nov. 11–15	**Solzhenitsyn,** Video Tape	700	83.00	—
Nov. 15 & 17	**O Lucky Man**	279	201.30	279.00
Nov. 19	**Acapulco Gold**	589	383.51	589.00
Nov. 22	50's Dance	175	9.35	—
Nov. 20	Dr. McCary, speaker	477	645.55	477.00
Nov. 23 & 24	**Dirty Harry**	669	474.30	668.00
Dec. 2–6	**Heavyweight Championship Fights,** Video Tape	850	141.00	—
Dec. 7 & 8	**The Way We Were**	492	525.00	492.00
Dec. 9	Jack White-Billiards Demo.	950	252.07	—
Dec. 9	Christmas Tea	427	85.03	85.51
Dec. 12	Linda Ronstadt Concert	2,209	8,104.65	10,527.00
Dec. 13 & 15	**Paper Moon**	292	250.00	292.00
Jan. 15–17	Free Coffee Coupons	86	—	—
Jan. 17–22	Hallmark Card Exhibit	865	126.06	—
Jan. 24 & 26	**French Connection**	624	439.40	679.00
Jan. 25	Concert—BABY	763	74.82	298.50
Jan. 17–19	Leadership Retreat	114	5,691.58	6,075.00
Jan. 27–31	**Twilight Cheat,** Video Tape	1,000	96.00	—
Jan. 31–Feb. 2	**McCabe & Mrs. Miller**	279	201.30	279.00
Feb. 1	Casino Party	250	18.00	175.70
Feb. 7 & 9	**The Emigrants**	301	216.70	301.00
Feb. 8	Gene Cotton Concert	125	541.99	151.00
Feb. 10	Basketball Flick	6	—	—
Feb. 11 & 12	Scarborough Faire	1,550	628.63	224.86
Feb. 12	**Camelot**	413	306.00	412.95
Feb. 14 & 16	**The Ruling Class**	377	303.75	377.00
Feb. 15	Edmunds & Curley-Comedy Team	40	856.07	54.65
Feb. 19	Basketball Flick	2	—	—
Feb. 21 & 23	**Clockwork Orange**	1,036	606.00	1,038.00
Feb. 26	Basketball Flick	175	—	—
Feb. 26–28	Free U. Registration	1,599	—	—
Feb. 27	Jerry Rothman-Artist	116	485.25	58.00
Feb. 28– Mar. 2	**Scarecrow**	350	251.00	350.00
Mar. 1	Cartoon Film Festival	321	78.50	159.00

Date	Name of the Event	Attendance	Expense	Income
Mar. 3–7	Poster Print Sale	1,150	—	—
Mar. 3	Z, Film, WAC	113	327.31	112.00
Mar. 4	Reading of "Antigone" WAC	60	16.30	—
"	Coffee, WAC	40	16.30	—
"	Lecture "Greece: A Land for All Seasons" WAC	30	16.30	—
Mar. 5	Lecture: The Greece I Love	30	16.30	—
Mar. 6	Greek Folk Dance Workshop	75	173.03	—
Mar. 6	Panel Discussion, WAC	35	16.30	—
Mar. 7	Greek Olympics, WAC	50	27.50	—
Mar. 7	Greek Banquet, WAC	96	509.67	262.00
Mar. 7 & 9	**Love & Pain**	92	229.50	92.00
Mar. 10–14	**TV Madness,** Video Tape	825	141.00	—
Mar. 10	Frederic Storaska, speaker	465	1,097.00	382.50
Mar. 14 & 16	**Jeremiah Johnson**	679	481.30	679.00
Mar. 15	Car Rally	188	152.14	282.00
Apr. 1–4	**Stevie Wonder,** Video Tape	400	155.00	—
Apr. 1	**Comeback Africa**	40	120.00	22.00
Apr. 3	Goldsby/Shockley Debate	923	2,042.45	746.25
Apr. 4 & 6	**Deliverance**	502	366.75	502.00
Apr. 7–10	**Lenny Bruce,** Video Tape		117.00	—
Apr. 7–10	Student Art Show	400	—	—
Apr. 8	Macrame Demonstration	150	—	—
"	Karate Lecture & Demonstration	40	—	—
Apr. 9–10	Painting Workshop	70	—	—
Apr. 9	**Inherit the Wind**	46	104.75	100.00
Apr. 10	Creativity Lecture	150	—	—
Apr. 11 & 13	Double Feature Movie	128	—	115.75
Apr. 16	Victor Marchetti-CIA	400	1,114.75	611.00*
Apr. 18 & 20	**Magical Mystery Tour**	483	430.07	483.00
Apr. 19	Golf Tournament	55	230.63	275.00
Apr. 21–25	**High on the Range,** Video Tape	1,800	105.00	—
Apr. 25	**American Graffitti**	570	423.90	569.25
Apr. 26	Lone Star Muzik Festival	6,000	3,090.31	367.65
May 3	Flea Market	100	12.00	—
May 4	Free-For-All	30	16.50	—
June 5	**Paint Your Wagon**	36	54.50	27.00
June 11	**Klute**	83	53.00	62.75
June 16	Roten Gallery	150	—	—
June 1–28	Coaches All-American Games, Film	30	5.99	—
June 18	**His Girl Friday**	36	—	27.00
June 25	Cartoon Film Festival	121	71.25	90.75
June 26	Street Dance***	150	616.10	250.00**
June 27–July 1	Dinner Theatre	1,128	2,089.80	3,550.20

July 9	**Woman under the Influence**	139	188.78	209.75
July 16	**Friends**	65	79.50	48.75
July 22	**Civilisation,** Video Tape	60	—	—
July 23	**On the Waterfront**	58	25.11	43.50
July 30	**The Graduate**	130	68.00	96.50
July 31	**Endless Summer**	21	43.00	15.74
Aug. 6	**Giant**	54	53.00	40.50
Aug. 9	Road Rally	22	95.95	63.00
Aug. 13	**Love Machine**	32	53.00	24.00
Aug. 14	Mini Concert****	400	444.35	200.00
	TOTALS	56,978	$53,216.91	$45,914.87

* Includes $503.00 from Cultural Events for their share of expenses.
** From RHA for their share of expenses.
*** Wild Bill and Buffalo Yankees.
**** Man Mountain and Green Slime Boys.

Food service (snack bar, cafeteria, and catering) and the game room are the most profitable areas (Exhibit 45–3). The game room cleared $15,000 last year while food service made $9,000. In contrast, the 2 newsstands barely broke even.

The bulk of the business in the building occurs between 10:00 am and 2:00 pm weekdays. The snack bar, cafeteria, and game room generally are filled to near capacity between these times. Evenings and weekends, the snack bar and game room show quite a large drop in the number of customers. The cafeteria is open only on weekdays during lunch hours.

University Center programs spend approximately $400 to $500 per month on advertising, the bulk of the money going for ads in the MU newspaper. A lesser amount is spent on posters and on radio spots for major events. Approximately $1,000 is spent each semester for calendars, brochures, and other promotional handouts. Two hundred dollars is spent annually for "Dial-an-Event", a telephone recording advertising upcoming events. University Center programs also tries to get as much free publicity as possible, such as public service announcements on radio programs.

In the past, there has been little effort toward controlling and coordinating the advertising purchased by the various committees. As a result, there has been much waste and some overlapping advertising. However, there has been greater co-ordination between the programming committees and cultural events in this area during the current semester.

Other than advertising for events, very little is done to promote UC's operations. Most of this type of promotion occurs during the first week of school with "All-UC Week," featuring free events, half-priced games, and a free barbeque. Seventeen hundred dollars was budgeted for All-UC Week this year. In addition, $2,200 has been budgeted for the grand opening of the new building.

Each summer the different areas of operation of the University Center file an

Exhibit 45-3
Daily U C Customer Counts – September 1975

Date	Snack Bar	Cafeteria	Newsstand A	Newsstand B	Game Room*
2	3,834	932	1,110	412	648
3	4,431	1,073	1,338	530	514
4	3,383	865	1,128	436	540
5	3,297	897	1,027	422	508
6	490	—	180	—	318
7	447	—	254	—	332
8	3,445	898	1,190	534	536
9	3,209	801	1,080	398	444
10	3,807	947	1,293	505	672
11	3,298	760	1,175	371	492
12	2,591	930	1,103	470	632
13	499	—	470	—	348
14	425	—	334	—	284
15	3,248	850	1,286	500	470
16	3,096	720	1,122	431	462
17	3,774	951	1,331	525	552
18	3,501	834	1,229	433	334
19	2,661	850	1,119	438	488
20	535	—	422	—	424
21	499	—	367	—	252
22	3,058	864	1,279	545	510
23	3,954	775	1,164	440	458
24	3,358	898	1,311	518	448
25	2,621	771	1,151	379	382
26	2,204	764	901	436	476
27	487	—	320	—	168
28	393	—	322	—	282
29	2,923	790	1,269	525	402
30	3,012	805	1,141	424	388

* Does not include electronic games.

Receipts for September

U.C. Machines	$ 3,555
Lovell's Machines	15,846
Snack Bar	38,480
Cafeteria	14,800
Newsstand A	8,988
Newsstand B	2,685
Games Room	3,040
Room Rentals	77
Mimeo and Line-o	400
Amount of Checks Cashed	134,468

annual report for the fiscal year ending August 31, citing major accomplishments and problems of the past year and major goals for the upcoming year.

Statement of Problem

Investigation of the facts and figures about University Center reveals a number of problem areas. However, many of these problems have been recognized in the annual reports and are in the process of being solved or have already been solved. Problem areas are increased costs, quality and innovativeness of food service, turnover, hot check collection, and problems arising from joint usage of the new Music-University Center addition. Although specific problems disclosed in the annual reports should be of concern, in most cases they are managerial rather than the much larger marketing problem with which this study will deal.

After weeks of data-gathering and talking to management and personnel in various areas of University Center, a major concern surfaced: for a school the size of MU, relatively few students take advantage of the variety of services and programs offered by the University Center. The extreme difference between the amount of customer traffic on weekdays and at night and on weekends tends to suggest that students merely use the center as a place to hang out between classes. Poor attendance at UC-sponsored events cannot always be blamed on the quality of the speaker or musical group. Favorable reviews and comments by newspaper critics and those in attendance confirm that many of the programs are of the highest quality.

Rather, there seems to be a general misconception among the student body that the center is not capable of being much more than a lounge or a check-cashing center. Despite the fact that University Center soon will be housed in a multi-million dollar facility and, as of next year, will have a budget of over $1 million, it does not project the image of being a well-run, dynamic enterprise.

Much of this image is a direct result of the bad publicity about the University Center which has appeared in the MU newspaper in the past few years. Editorials and stories are run at least several times a year relating the UC's financial problems. When a major concert bombs out or is cancelled due to poor ticket sales, there is almost sure to be a related article in the next day's paper. This has created a negative attitude in the minds of students toward all UC-sponsored events. Some students have quit buying concert tickets altogether for fear that they may be cancelled. (See Exhibit 45–4.)

More recently, financial problems have caused cutbacks in operations and maintenance. As a result, the quality of service and the appearance of the building have suffered.

Program committee members also have contributed to UC's poor image through their haphazard planning and execution of many programs, especially those of the "low cost/no cost" variety. If any program is executed poorly, no matter how well the artist performs, those in attendance generalize that all UC-sponsored events

Exhibit 45-4
Article in Midlands University Campus Newspaper

Free Concert Hurts UC Entertainment Future
by Jane Leander, Fine Arts Editor

We bring a high quality act to the campus for a low price, and we're not getting any response. We're starting to think that if it's not a big name, perhaps we should just forget it (sponsoring a concert). And we're wondering if concert entertainment is fading away and going to the bars. We can't serve beer. But it seems that if you can pop-a-top, you can draw a crowd.

This thought was one of many aired by University Center committee member Barbara Ross in an interview concerning the poor ticket sales which forced the University Center to offer last Thursday's concert by The Wright Brothers Overland Stage Company as a free show.

Her viewpoints were shared by activities advisor, Ray Faircloth, entertainment committee member George Barton, and external coordinator Leslie Hampton. None of the four could understand why only 25 tickets had been sold for a concert in the 3,000 seat Municipal Auditorium, and all agreed that being forced to "give the concert away" (an estimated 900 finally attended) would have serious repercussions regarding future University Center programs.

The University Center spent $2,500 as initial payment to the musical group. They had planned to pay the symphony orchestra (who also performed at the concert) $600 toward a scholarship fund. With the cost of the rental of the hall and publicity, it was a $4,000 concert.

Faircloth added, "We still have some funds. But we can't keep on programming events and having people not come."

Hampton elaborated on the publicity given the concert, saying "we used all the media: newspapers, radio, and TV. The band visited dorm cafeterias. We had banners on trucks, outdoor advertising, and posters in toilet stalls. Skywriting's about the only thing we haven't hit yet."

It was suggested that MU students will only attend big-name concerts "like Elton John or something." But Faircloth said, "They (students) can't expect us to book a super-top act if we can't rely on the public to show up. A couple years ago we asked the students who they wanted to see, and the top choice of practically everyone was Loggins and Messina. We brought them and nobody showed up."

"Promoters have an advantage since they have more funds to work with. But we're concerned with the reputation of the University Center. We're not going to bring people like Jerry Jeff Walker because he's unreliable. We want concerts to be quality shows. That's why we've brought people in the past like Linda Ronstadt and Jackson Brown and Bonnie Raitt."

As for the effects of providing the concert without charge, Barton said, "Financially, it's going to kill us. We're going to have to be more specific about where we dish out dollar bills . . . We can't afford to take any gambles, but the group that goes for the money we can afford is just not going to be known all over."

Barton expressed a desire for students to have an "entertainment fee" added to their fee statement at the beginning of the fall semester. He said the fee is successful at nearby Carlton University, and would give the University Center more money to work with and an assured crowd (those who paid the fee could attend University concerts at no charge).

Asked if he thought such a fee had a chance of being instated here, Barton said, "It's something to look into. We've got to do something. This campus is just not interested in experiencing anything new. Here we're handing it (The Wright Brothers) to them on a silver platter—a two and one half hour show with no crummy front acts—and there's still not much in the way of response."

---

are run in the same manner. In addition, there is very little in the way of a continuous promotional campaign to either counteract bad publicity or to highlight the positive aspects of the University Center.

Since passage of the fee referendum, lack of money is not as great a problem as it has been in the past. The student body has been promised improvements in operations and certainly will expect to see visible signs of this in the near future. Certainly, with the overwhelming margin by which the referendum passed, management has been given a mandate to make these improvements. If it fails to do so, not only will UC retain its image of being a poorly-run enterprise, but it will also have to deal with the added problem of credibility with the student body. The best time for UC management to change its image is now.

As a member of the UC managing board, suggest what steps University Center can take through building operations, planning and execution of events, and promotion to project the image of being an efficient, dynamic enterprise and a place where students will want to spend their time.

Not-For-Profit Marketing Management: Tallahassee, Florida

John R. Kerr and James M. Stearns
The Florida State University

Mr. Dan Kleman, city manager of Tallahassee, Florida, was pondering an upcoming meeting with the city commissioners. Mr. Kleman had been appointed by the commissioners in 1974; and as the city's chief administrator he was charged, among other responsibilities, with overseeing and making recommendations for funding, type, and level of services provided by the city. As city manager, Mr. Kleman felt a strong responsibility to be sensitive to his client publics as well as to the general public. Because of this responsibility, he believed that sound marketing principles were just as applicable in his situation as they would be for a profit-seeking enterprise.

The agenda of the meeting called for discussion of a recent resident survey that Mr. Kleman had received which he hoped would provide insight into the feelings of Tallahassee residents. The survey, completed in June 1977, focused on residents' views of the effectiveness of services provided or performed by the city, as well as residents' use of these services. The 1977 survey was designed to complement one that had been completed in June, 1976 which identified and measured residents' attitudes toward how the city spent its funds for various services and their perceptions of the major problems facing Tallahassee.

As Mr. Kleman reviewed the 1977 survey and looked back at the results of the 1976 study, he knew that the commissioners would want recommendations concerning courses of action for the future. He felt the two surveys provided him with some information about his various client groups, but also was aware of the problem of trying to satisfy as many of them as possible. He realized that available resources were limited and that allocating them in the most efficient and effective manner would be difficult. Certainly, he wanted to upgrade as many services as possible, but only after considering user attitudes and preferences and using sufficient foresight to anticipate any change in those attitudes and preferences, due to changes in the composition of the residents. In making recommendations to the commissioners, he would also have to consider costs, since it was obvious to him that upgrading some programs or services would be much more expensive than others.

The City Manager

The organization chart of the city of Tallahassee is presented in Exhibit 46–1. The city manager is appointed by the city commissioners and is responsible for managing the city's business and executory policies set by the commissioners.

Mr. Kleman also is the major liaison between the city departments and the policy-making city commissioners. He works closely with Dean Block, director of the Office of Management and Budget for Tallahassee, in order to carry out this liaison function.

Exhibit 46-1
Organizational Chart of
The City of Tallahassee

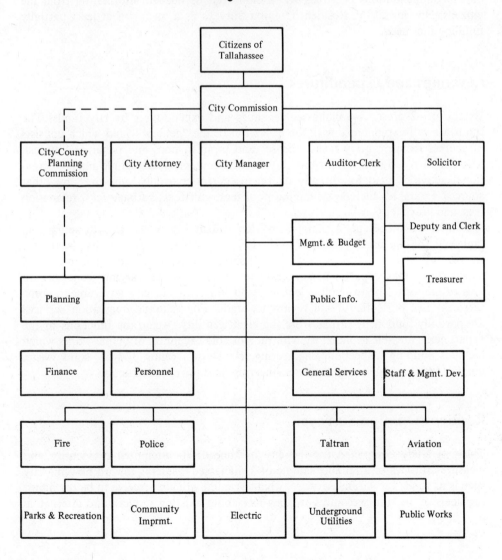

One of the most important duties of the city manager is submission of a budget to be approved by the city commissioners. Mr. Kleman viewed the budget as more than just a painful necessary duty. To him the budget was:

> . . . a management planning tool, a vehicle for apprising the public of city activities, and providing information for commission policy discussion. More importantly, the budget also ultimately reflects the philosophy of the elected officials of a community and the community itself. Why this department gets so much and that department gets so much in the way of personnel, materials, and equipment is the result of the interplay of a complex set of variables, finally resulting in decisions which must be in consonance with the goals and needs of the community.

Mr. Kleman also felt the budget should be used as a "change" vehicle, reflecting a changing community. He believed his budgets fulfilled these criteria in the past and he wished to have them continue to do so in the future. In order to make the best recommendations possible, Mr. Kleman felt he needed information from the citizens. He viewed the Resident Opinion Surveys as a means of at least partially fulfilling that need.

Revenues and Expenditures

Exhibit 46–2 presents Tallahassee revenues and expenditures by city funds. The funds are self-explanatory with the exception of the "general" fund which consists of sources from property taxes, licenses and permits, fines and penalties, interest, leases, and revenue from current services. Current services include many recreational activities paid for directly by the users and partially subsidized by other sources. Examples include swimming pool fees, golf fees, garbage fees, recreation fees, and grave fees.

Exhibit 46–3 presents a summary of department expenditures, both actual and budgeted for the fiscal years 1974–75, 1975–76, 1976–77. (The city fiscal year runs from October 1 to September 30.) It should be remembered when evaluating expenditures that departments generate levels of revenues varying from zero to tens of millions (for example, electric), and inherently in city government, some services "live off" others with regard to funds. For example, recreation services are partially funded by profits from the electric utility. Again the functions of the departments are self-explanatory with the possible exception of public works which includes building inspection, engineering, cemeteries, rights of way, solid waste, landfill, street maintenance, traffic engineering, and sewer construction.

Resident Opinion Surveys

The first study completed for the city in June 1976 attempted to identify and measure attitudes of a reliable sample of Tallahassee residents toward how the city spends its funds for various services, what these individuals perceive to be the major problems of Tallahassee, and how they feel about existing services and alternative

Exhibit 46-2
City of Tallahassee
Comparison of Revenues and Expenditures
All Appropriated Funds*
(In thousands)

Description	Actual FY 74–75	Original Budget FY 75–76	Revised Budget FY 75–76	Budget FY 76–77
General Fund				
Revenue	$13,104	$14,277	$14,216	$15,484
Expenditures	15,011	17,569	17,035	19,796
Surplus/(Deficit)	(1,906)	(3,292)	(2,819)	(4,310)
Airport Fund				
Revenue	1,052	1,154	1,278	1,473
Expenditures	895	1,202	1,238	1,456
Surplus/(Deficit)	156	(48)	39	17
TALTRAN Fund				
Revenue	459	519	507	617
Expenditures	516	663	631	778
Surplus/(Deficit)	(57)	(143)	(124)	(160)
Electric Fund				
Revenue	30,833	38,125	38,327	44,390
Expenditures	28,877	34,919	34,593	41,271
Surplus/(Deficit)	1,955	3,205	3,733	3,118
Gas Fund				
Revenue	2,494	2,742	3,149	3,939
Expenditures	2,247	2,502	2,632	3,353
Surplus/(Deficit)	247	239	517	585
Water Fund				
Revenue	2,034	2,314	2,135	3,121
Expenditures	1,896	2,283	2,130	2,382
Surplus/(Deficit)	137	30	5	739
Sewer Fund				
Revenue	2,846	3,790	3,493	4,242
Expenditures	3,088	3,780	3,878	4,233
Surplus/(Deficit)	(242)	10	(385)	10
All Funds				
Revenue	52,825	62,922	63,108	73,271
Expenditures	52,534	62,922	62,141	73,271
Surplus/(Deficit)	$ 291	$ 0	$ 967	$ 0

* Slight errors in totals are due to rounding.

Exhibit 46 - 3
City of Tallahassee
Summary of Expenditures
All Departments**
(In thousands)

Department	Actual 74–75	Original Budget 75–76	Revised* Budget 75–76	Budget 76–77
City Commission	$ 55	$ 104	$ 70	$ 64
Legal	90	118	115	117
City Auditor-Clerk	1,805	2,327	2,333	1,022
Executive	280	304	296	944
Finance	0	0	0	1,422
Personnel & Training	114	175	180	248
Fire	1,677	1,971	1,952	2,254
Police	2,717	3,325	3,237	3,441
Public Works	3,920	4,901	4,797	4,921
Parks & Recreation	1,262	1,539	1,492	1,745
General Services	1,073	1,193	1,181	3,871
Planning	210	375	365	719
Housing & Community Development	31	125	119	919
Special Appropriations and Contingency	0	434	190	4,534
Aviation	895	987	1,025	1,232
TalTran	516	663	631	778
Electric	29,142	35,248	34,922	41,602
Internal Auditor	0	0	25	0
Underground Utilities	7,232	8,409	8,484	9,969
Subtotal	$54,755	$65,352	$64,586	$79,812
Less Working Capital	2,220	2,430	2,445	6,056
Less Other	0	0	0	483
TOTAL	$52,534	$62,922	$62,141	$73,271

* Not Adjusted for July/October Reorganization
** Slight errors in totals are due to rounding

uses of funds. The following year a similar undertaking focused on residents' views of the effectiveness of services provided or performed by the city, as well as their use of these services.

Procedures used for the surveys were similar for both years. An interval sampling technique of every fifth residential utility customer was used to approximate a stratified random sample. A mail survey yielded 1454 usable questionnaires in 1976 and 1369 in 1977. The mail portion of the samples was augmented by 101 and 300 personal interviews in 1976 and 1977 respectively.

Mr. Kleman thought it would be useful to review the major findings and conclusions of both studies as well as some of the more pertinent data, so that he could formulate suggestions for the commissioners as well as answer any questions they might have.

The 1976 Survey

Mr. Kleman found that the 1976 Resident Opinion Survey results were segmented into three categories: resident attitudes pertaining to the funding processes of the city, resident rankings of their perceptions of the three most important problems facing Tallahassee, and resident opinions toward existing services and alternative uses of funds by the city. Mr. Kleman felt the most significant findings of the 1976 data were:

1. *The relationship between funding attitudes and perceived problems facing Tallahassee generally match.* Only in the instance regarding attracting new industry was there a gap in the relationship between problem and funding. Traffic congestion and inadequate street maintenance were stipulated as the most important and second most important perceived problems. Both were singled out as areas that should receive additional funding in 1977. (See Exhibits 46–4 and 46–5.) However, attracting new industry was the third most important problem and should have received more support for additional funding. Less than two of ten respondents wanted more funding for the chamber of commerce. Since the support of noncity organizations included social service organizations as well as the chamber of commerce, it is possible that respondents were reluctant to answer for more funding.

2. *There was more support for certain alternative uses of funds for bus service, recreation programs, the downtown area, social service programs, and widening of some roads than was anticipated.* (For a summary of attitudes toward services see Exhibit 46–6, and for funding priorities see Exhibit 46–7.) Between four and six of every ten respondents indicated favorable attitudes toward these services. In addition, the proposed tradeoff between a reduction of electric utility rates and a corresponding increase in property taxes drew a favorable response, particularly from renters and those who have recently moved in Tallahassee.

3. *Cross classification of respondents' personal characteristics with funding priorities, perceived problems, and alternative uses of funds for city services provided needed insights into differences in attitudes.* It was evident that maintaining and improving streets and traffic control were the two most important problems perceived by respondents. Those who saw traffic congestion as an important problem were generally in the 18 to 54 age group, long-time (greater than 10 years) residents, home owners, both males and females, and in the over $10,000 income range. For the "inadequate street maintenance" problem area, residents tended to be overrepresented in the 18 to 24 and 25 to 44 age groups, had varying lengths of residence, were male renters, and had incomes either $6,000 to $15,000 or $20,000 to $40,000.

1977 Resident Opinion Survey

In general, Tallahassee residents who responded to the 1977 Survey gave their opinions regarding the effectiveness of city services and their use of these services. The responses obtained in the personal interviews closely corresponded with the responses obtained by the mail questionnaires. There were, however, proportionately more females who were interviewed than males, although the reverse was true for the mail questionnaire.

Mr. Kleman believed, as a result of analyzing the survey, several findings could impact on his recommendations concerning city services:

Exhibit 46 - 4
1976 Resident Opinion Survey
Residents' Funding Attitudes

More Funding	About the Same Funding	Less Funding
1. Maintaining and improving Streets (71.1%)	1. Fire Department (73.2%)	1. Support of noncity organizations (38.8%)
2. Traffic control (47.5%)	2. Street lighting (61.9%)	2. Low income housing (27.5%)
3. Storm drainage (44.2%)	3. Police department (59.5%)	3. Building new streets (27.0%)
4. Recreation and parks (40.4%)	4. Recreation and parks (50.0%)	4. Parking (20.0%)
5. Bus service (37.4%)	5. Sidewalks (47.7%)	5. Bus service (15.8%)
6. Sidewalks (36.1%)	6. Bus service (44.1%)	6. Sidewalks (12.3%)
7. Parking (35.9%)	7. Storm drainage (44.0%)	7. Police department (9.6%)
8. Low income housing (35.9%)	8. Traffic control (42.6%)	8. Street lighting (9.0%)
9. Building new streets (30.1%)	9. Parking (40.7%)	9. Traffic control (7.3%)
10. Police department (27.8%)	10. Building new streets (39.3%)	10. Recreations and parks parks (6.5%)
11. Street lighting (26.4%)	11. Support of noncity organizations (39.2%)	11. Storm drainage (5.1%)
12. Fire department (18.2%)	12. Low income housing (33.1%)	12. Fire department (5.0%)
13. Support of noncity organizations (17.2%)	13. Maintaining and improving streets (24.6%)	13. Maintaining and improving streets (2.2%)

Exhibit 46-5
1976 Resident Opinion Survey
Perceived Problems Facing Tallahassee

Most Important Problems	Second Most Impotant Problem	Third Most Important Problem
1. Traffic congestion (21.4%)	1. Traffic congestion (16.4%)	1. Inadequate street maintenance (10.0%)
2. Inadequate street maintenance (10.0%)	2. Inadequate street maintenance (13.6%)	2. Not enough downtown parking (8.8%)
3. Attracting new industry (8.9%)	3. Attracting new industry (8.9%)	3. Traffic congestion (7.5%)
4. Inadequate bus service (8.0%)	4. Inadequate bus service (7.6%)	4. Attracting new industry (7.0%)
5. Low income housing (4.2%)	5. Inadequate drainage ditches (5.9%)	5. Inadequate bus service (6.8%)
6. Inadequate environmental protection (4.2%)	6. Low income housing (5.9%)	6. Inadequate drainage ditches (6.2%)
7. Inadequate downtown parking (3.4%)	7. Inadequate downtown parking (5.8%)	7. Inadequate environmental protection (5.7%)
8. Not enough police patrols (3.3%)	8. Inadequate environmental protection (4.4%)	8. Not enough bike trails (5.0%)

1. *Tallahassee residents are generally favorably impressed with the services performed or provided by the city* (see Exhibit 46–8). Over half of the residents indicated either excellent or good ratings for 10 of the 15 services. One-fourth of the residents rated 10 of 15 services as either fair or poor, while approximately 20 percent responded they did not know enough about the services to rate them. Many of the "don't know" responses were from people who either do not use the specific services or are relatively new to the community. Traffic control and street maintenance continue to be major sources of dissatisfaction, which substantiates the major finding of the 1976 Survey.

2. *Nearly 3 out of every 4 residents make use of recreational programs and parks in Tallahassee.* These residents tend to have stronger favorable opinions regarding parks than they do recreational programs. The major reason cited for not using these programs and parks was that the residents were busy with other activities.

3. *Over 20 percent of the residents surveyed make use of TALTRAN (city bus service) and most of these residents rated bus service as either excellent or good.*

4. *Resident attitudes toward services involving transportation were not unexpected. Over 80 percent of the residents feel their neighborhood streets need minor*

Exhibit 46-6
1976 Resident Opinion Survey
Resident Attitudes Toward Services

1. "Better bus service is more important than building new or widening existing streets."

Attitude	% Response
Strongly disagree	21.0
Disagree	25.7
Neutral	11.3
Agree	18.5
Strongly agree	21.2

2. "The City of Tallahassee has about all the recreation programs it needs."

Strongly disagree	11.5
Disagree	27.8
Neutral	22.2
Agree	28.2
Strongly agree	8.0

3. "Electric rates should be reduced even if it means an increase in property taxes."

Strongly disagree	18.9
Disagree	23.5
Neutral	15.6
Agree	19.2
Strongly agree	19.7

4. "Police protection in the City is about as good as it should be."

Strongly disagree	6.4
Disagree	24.8
Neutral	22.7
Agree	38.5
Strongly agree	5.3

5. "Enhancing and preserving the downtown area should be a high priority item for the City."

Strongly disagree	7.7
Disagree	16.8
Neutral	17.4
Agree	34.5
Strongly agree	21.5

6. "Overall, I think the level of municipal services is about where it ought to be."

Strongly disagree	6.1
Disagree	24.1
Neutral	26.2
Agree	37.7
Strongly agree	3.0

7. "The City should fund social service programs for the low income and the elderly."

Strongly disagree	11.9
Disagree	16.2
Neutral	17.5
Agree	33.6
Strongly agree	18.6

8. "Some roads should be widened in order to ease traffic congestion even if it means a change in the natural environment."

Strongly disagree	20.7
Disagree	19.1
Neutral	8.0
Agree	26.0
Strongly agree	23.3

---

or major repair. Although generally satisfied with street lighting, residents find traffic signs and street name signs either sometimes or often hard to see and to understand. Nearly half felt this way about traffic signs, and nearly three-fourths about street name signs. Six of every 10 residents have little or no difficulty getting places easily in Tallahassee, although 4 of 10 have either some or great difficulty.

5. *For other city services resident attitudes were mixed.* Although residents generally had favorable opinions of street cleanliness and garbage and trash collection, they were concerned about police protection, particularly walking in their neighborhoods at night. The Tallahassee police generally received favorable ratings in their handling of people, in responding to calls quickly, and overall courtesy. Many residents did not have contact with the police and, therefore, were unable to express an opinion.

6. *Most residents neither sought information nor complained to city officials during the past year.* Of those who did, the majority said that city officials always or usually responded satisfactorily to these requests and complaints.

7. *The personal characteristics of Tallahassee residents were essentially the same as those surveyed in 1976* (see Exhibit 46–9).

8. *When cross classifying resident ratings, usage, and attitudes with resident characteristics, a number of interesting observations can be made:*

Generally as the age of respondents increased, the ratings of city services and attitudes became more favorable. However, this relationship was not true for use of recreational programs and parks.

The longer respondents live in Tallahassee, the more opinionated they become. Those who have been here less than one year tend to give more favorable attitudes than residents who have been here longer. These new residents also are more likely not to express an opinion. The opinions of the older residents vary by specific services.

Owners are more opinionated than renters, and owners have more favorable ratings, use, and attitudes than renters.

Exhibit 46-7
1976 Resident Opinion Survey
Resident Funding Priorities

City Service	About the Same Level	Less Funding	More Funding	No Response	Total
Recreation and Parks	50.0%	6.5%	40.4%	3.1%	100.0%
Street Lighting	61.9	9.0	26.4	2.7	100.0
Traffic Control	42.6	7.3	47.5	2.6	100.0
Building New Streets	39.3	27.0	30.1	3.6	100.0
Maintaining and Improving Streets	24.6	2.2	71.1	2.1	100.0
Police Department	59.5	9.6	27.8	3.1	100.0
Bus Service	44.1	15.8	37.4	2.7	100.0
Parking	40.7	20.0	35.9	3.3	100.0
Low Income Housing	33.1	27.5	35.9	3.5	100.0
Fire Department	73.2	5.0	18.2	3.6	100.0
Sidewalks	47.7	12.3	36.1	3.9	100.0
Support of Noncity Groups	39.2	38.8	17.2	4.8	100.0
Storm Drainage	44.0	5.1	44.2	6.7	100.0

Exhibit 46-8
1977 Resident Opinion Survey
Resident Ratings of City Services

Service	Excellent/Good	Service	Fair/Poor	Service	Don't Know
Water Service	72%	Street Conditions	86%	Gas Service	46%
Garbage Collection	66	Traffic Control	72	Bus Service	42
Parks	59	Street Cleanliness	45	Fire Services	37
Police Services	59	Street Lighting	39	Handling Services/	
Electric Service	58	Electric Service	37	Information Requests	34
Recreation Programs	57	Handling Service/		Recreation Programs	23
Street Lighting	57	Information Requests	32	Sewer Service	17
Sewer Service	55	Garbage Collection	28	Parks	14
Fire Services	54	Bus Service	26	Police Services	14
Street Cleanliness	53	Parks	25	Water Service	9
Gas Service	35	Sewer Service	25	Street Conditions	7
Handling Service/Information		Police Services	24	Garbage Collection	4
Requests	31	Recreation Programs	18	Traffic Control	2
Bus Service	30	Water Service	17	Street Lighting	2
Traffic Control	23	Gas Service	14	Electric Service	2
Street Conditions	11	Fire Services	6	Street Cleanliness	0

825

Exhibit 46-9
1977 Resident Opinion Survey
Respondent Characteristics

Age of Resident Respondents	1977	1976
18–24	23.9%	24.5%
25–34	30.7	29.1
35–44	12.7	13.4
45–54	11.4	12.7
55–64	10.7	10.2
65+	8.1	8.4
No Response	2.6	1.7
	100.0%	100.0%

Number in Household	1977	1976
1	19.1%	17.6%
2	38.5	40.9
3–4	31.6	30.8
5–6	6.4	7.2
7+	2.3	1.2
No Response	2.1	2.3
	100.0%	100.0%

Length of Residence in Tallahassee	1977	1976
Less Than 3 Months	1.6%	1.7%
3–12 Months	10.7	9.5
1–5 Years	31.1	32.5
5–10 Years	. 16.6	16.7
10+ Years	37.7	37.1
No Response	2.3	2.5
	100.0%	100.0%

Rent or Own	1976	1977
Rent	46.4%	47.1%
Own	51.0	50.5
No Response	2.6	2.4
	100.0%	100.0%

Sex of Resident Respondents	1977	1976
Male	52.1%	66.4%
Female	44.8	30.0
No Response	3.1	3.6
	100.0%	100.0%

Income Before Taxes	1977	1976
Under $6,000	24.5%	22.9%
$6,000–$9,999	16.0	16.5

$10,000–$14,999	15.2	17.2
$15,000–$19,999	14.2	15.0
$20,000–$29,999	15.4	15.2
$30,000–$39,999	5.0	5.3
$40,000+	2.8	3.0
No Response	6.8	4.9
	100.0%	100.0%

Educational Level	1977	1976
Eighth Grade or Less	2.8%	2.6%
Attended or Completed High School	14.9	9.2
Attended or Completed Technical or Vocational School	5.4	5.4
Attended or Completed College	45.1	48.8
Attended or Completed Graduate School	29.6	31.4
No Response	2.2	2.7
	100.0%	100.0%

The sex of residents, with the exception of neighborhood safety, does not appear to affect ratings, use, and attitudes.

As incomes increase, the excellent and good ratings and attitudes generally increase. The middle-income groups generally use the recreational programs and parks more often than low and high income groups.

Generally, residents with high school, technical, and vocational education backgrounds have more favorable ratings and attitudes than those with college and graduate education backgrounds.

Residents in the northwest, northeast, and southeast quadrants of the city tend to have more favorable attitudes and use recreation programs and parks more often than residents in the inner city and in the southwest quadrant.

Tallahassee and Leon County

Tallahassee, the capital of Florida and county seat of Leon County, is located in north central Florida. The community is rich with the heritage of the old South and was founded as the site for Florida's capital in 1823. The city is quite different from its central and south Florida neighbors. Although most large cities in central and south Florida rely on agriculture and tourism as an economic base, Tallahassee is the state center for government activity as well as the location of two state universities. The city of Tallahassee dominates Leon County, comprising more than 64 percent of its population in 1975 (see Exhibit 46–10). Most Leon County households outside city boundaries either have members who are employed in the city or make use of the many city services.

Tallahassee, like much of Florida, experienced explosive growth during the 50s, 60s, and early 70s (see Exhibit 46–10). Migration to Tallahassee has been responsible for most of the city's growth in the past 20 years. Between 1960 and 1970, migration accounted for 60 percent of the population increase and has been esti-

Exhibit 46-10
Historical and Projected Population Growth
1930-1990

Year	Tallahassee		Leon County	
	Population	Percent Change	Population	Percent Change
1930	10,700	—	23,476	—
1940	16,240	51.8%	31,646	34.8%
1950	27,237	67.7	51,590	63.0
1960	48,174	76.9	74,225	43.9
1970	72,586	50.7	103,047	38.8
1975	86,404	19.0	133,204	29.3
1980	100,099	15.8	142,999	7.3
1990	134,488	34.4	192,125	34.4

Source: Tallahassee Chamber of Commerce

mated to be as high as 75 percent in recent years. Many of the migrants since 1970 are intrastate movers, leaving their south Florida homes to move northward to Tallahassee. These individuals often complain that south Florida has become what they attempted to move away from in the North. Northern-like cost of living, traffic congestion, and crime have forced these individuals to seek an area in Florida without these problems.

Population characteristics of the area generally reflect the influence of the two major employers, state government and the two state universities. Low median age (23.5 years as compared with the 1975 national average of 27.9) and high educational achievement (one out of every four is a college graduate) are dominant characteristics of the area (see Exhibit 46–11). This can be attributed not only to the presence of the institutions of higher learning and the relatively skilled employment required by the government sector, but also to the lack of heavy manufacturing which might attract large numbers of semi-skilled workers.

Employment in the city has been both stable and growing (84.1 percent growth in the last decade). State government is the prime generator of Tallahassee's economic base, employing nearly 12,000 and occupying 2.5 million square feet of space. Florida State University, Florida A&M University, and Tallahassee Community College have a total enrollment in excess of 30,000 students, and some 8,000 faculty, staff, and part-time employees. This fact, combined with county and city workers, is credited with keeping Tallahassee unemployment between 4 and 5 percent although the statewide average currently is close to 9 percent and the national average approximately 7 percent.

Growth at area universities and schools, proposed new shopping centers, a new $27 million civic center, new office buildings, and other businesses attracted to the "sun" belt, along with state government's predicted 4 percent increase in employees from 1975 to 1985 are all good signs for Tallahassee employment.

Due to the nature of employment, the city and county have large numbers of professional and white collar employees. This fact, coupled with an incidence of

Exhibit 46 - 11
Characteristics of the Population
By Census Tracts Leon County
1970

Census Tract	Total Population	Age Median	Persons Per Household	Median Years School Completed
1	1,077	24.6	2.01	12.5
2	4,106	28.6	2.13	13.1
3	3,946	30.4	3.07	13.1
4	3,373	20.1	2.36	13.8
5	3,371	21.5	1.96	13.0
6	4,304	23.2	2.90	9.1
7	2,388	27.5	2.48	12.2
8	2,387	33.0	2.66	13.3
9	5,249	26.1	3.29	12.8
10	3,912	24.4	3.27	12.3
11	4,626	20.6	3.60	11.2
12	1,982	24.0	3.11	8.4
13	4,308	19.7	1.72	17.0
14	4,380	21.9	3.25	11.5
15	3,301	26.2	3.51	13.8
16	3,034	26.8	3.64	13.4
17	4,057	31.4	3.57	16.0
18	3,625	24.3	3.32	11.1
19	6,557	22.8	2.92	12.6
20	7,921	23.4	2.79	13.0
21	3,835	25.8	3.19	14.3
22	4,278	23.9	3.15	12.6

Source: Tallahassee Chamber of Commerce

working wives (50 percent of all women between 19 and 64 are employed), yields one of the highest average household incomes in Florida. Household income in Leon County in 1976 was $14,304 compared with the state's average of $12,858 and the national average of $14,797. Tallahassee ranks fourth in the state, after West Palm Beach which has an average income of $15,482. The Miami area's average income is $14,900, and Fort Lauderdale is $14,500 in household income.

Income distribution varies significantly throughout Tallahassee. Exhibit 46–12 indicates that north, northeast, and southeast areas have much greater household income than the university areas (central) and the lower income areas (central and southwest). Some variation is, of course, always expected. But the presence and domination of the universities in the central and to some extent in the southwest region magnifies the income anomaly in Tallahassee.

The future of Tallahassee is extremely bright. The city is becoming the hub of a vast and growing trade area including north Florida, southwest Georgia, and

Exhibit 46-12
Census Tracts in the Tallahassee, Florida SMSA
Average Household Incomes
(1974)

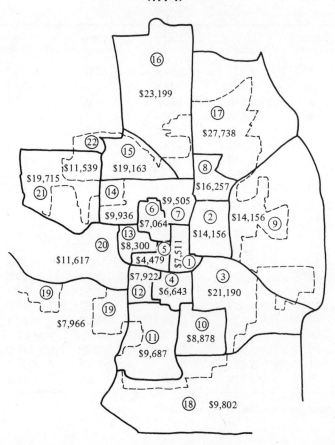

southeast Alabama. Tallahassee is aggressively seeking industry to complement the city's large public sector. Its central location and excellent transportation base provide tremendous potential for the city to benefit from the national trends of business relocation. Tallahassee already is the financial center for the area and should have little trouble attracting new businesses considering its cost of living, tax structure, and climate.

Surveying the Situation

As Mr. Kleman reviewed his situation, he found that he had a wealth of information. He realized Tallahassee residents have definite opinions, use certain services, and expect the city government to be responsive to their needs.

Mr. Kleman believes in the marketing concept and sees the public as his market. Based on the information he has and considering probable cost/benefit inquiries by the commissioners, he feels he must first evaluate his marketing strategy to date and then prepare the best marketing approach for the city's immediate future. He believes that residents have indicated some areas of concern, and he has to make some hard decisions with regard to changes in emphasis for the proposed 1977–78 budget.

Index

NAMES